Beswick and Wine:
Buying and Selling Private Companies and Businesses

Beswick and Wine:
Buying and Selling Private Companies and Businesses

Tenth edition

Susan Singleton
Solicitor

Bloomsbury Professional

Bloomsbury Professional

An imprint of Bloomsbury Publishing Plc

Bloomsbury Professional Ltd	Bloomsbury Publishing Plc
41–43 Boltro Road	50 Bedford Square
Haywards Heath	London
RH16 1BJ	WC1B 3DP
UK	UK

www.bloomsbury.com

BLOOMSBURY and the Diana logo are trademarks of

Bloomsbury Publishing Plc

© Bloomsbury Professional Ltd 2018

The editor, Elizabeth Susan Singleton, asserts her right to be identified as the author.

British Library Cataloguing-in-Publication Data

A catalogue record for this book is available from the British Library.

ISBN:	PB:	978 1 78451 700 7
	Epdf:	978 1 78451 699 4
	Epub:	978 1 78451 702 1

Typeset by Phoenix Photosetting, Chatham, Kent
Printed and bound by CPI Group (UK) Ltd, Croydon, CRO 4YY

To find out more about our authors and books visit www.bloomsburyprofessional.com. Here you will find extracts, author information, details of forthcoming events and the option to sign up for our newsletters

Contents

Contents

Downloadable precedents

In previous editions of *Beswick and Wine: Buying and Selling Private Companies and Businesses*, the precedents have been available separately on a CD-ROM.

For the new 10th edition, the precedents are available to download electronically from www.bloomsburylawonline.com/beswick10.

They are password-protected and the password is xC4Rk9Zd.

They can be downloaded individually or in totality.

If you have any problems downloading the precedents or have any questions, please contact Bloomsbury Professional customer services on 01444 416119 or by email at customerservices@bloomsburyprofessional.com.

For a Licence agreement relating to the use of this Data, please see overleaf at p x.

Licence agreement

The Data on www.bloomsburylawonline.com/beswick10 is © Bloomsbury Professional 2017.

Bloomsbury Professional ('the Publishers') grant you a non-exclusive and non-transferable licence to use the Data from www.bloomsburylawonline.com/beswick10.

You may download, copy or print the Data from www.bloomsburylawonline.com/beswick10 for private use or use in the ordinary course of your business but you may not make any profit from the use of the Data other than would ordinarily be made in the course of your business. You may not sell the Data under any circumstances or make or sell any copy or reproduction of it. You may not copy or print out any part of the Software for any purpose or make any modifications to the Software.

If you have any queries about the use of the Data from www.bloomsburylawonline.com/beswick10, please contact customer services at Bloomsbury Professional: customerservices@bloomsburyprofessional.com.

Preface

This book is primarily designed for solicitors, accountants and corporate financiers involved in private company mergers and acquisitions. It seeks to provide a step-by-step guide to the sale and purchase process and the key commercial, tax and legal issues arising from it.

This edition is, and earlier editions were, written by practitioners actively engaged in private company merger and acquisition transactions. It is structured to reflect the buying and selling process in practice and considers the issues arising from both the seller's and the purchaser's perspective. The sale and purchase process varies depending upon the identity of the party initiating it. Accordingly, in Part I, the book covers the sale process from the seller's perspective and, in Part II, the acquisition process from the purchaser's perspective.

The book covers most of the issues which the seller or purchaser (and their advisers) are likely to encounter. Due to the way this book is structured, issues of particular significance to the sale and purchase process are not addressed as separate topics in the conventional manner. Instead they are addressed in the context in which they would usually appear in the transaction.

This tenth edition, the fourth for which the current author has been responsible, reflects the impact of a number of significant changes to the law and applicable regulations since the last edition. In particular it has been revised to include:

- Finance Acts 2015–2017 which reflect changes to tax law;
- changes to corporation tax and stamp duty;
- Brexit where relevant and competition law changes.

A full range of useful precedents is provided.

The companies expressed to be bought or sold in this book are: (i) unquoted; and (ii) limited by shares and incorporated under the Companies Acts; and (iii) private. Although some acquisitions are of public companies and indeed when I worked at Slaughter and May that would frequently be the case, most acquisitions in the UK are not of public companies and my practice since has largely been private sales. This is the market addressed by this book. Readers should be aware there are important additional rules applicable to sales of public companies which are not addressed in this book.

In the case of a sale of shares, this book assumes that, unless specific reference to a corporate seller is made, the seller is an individual. In the case of a business transfer, the seller is assumed to be a corporate seller. This book also assumes that the purchaser is a single, corporate purchaser. The company or the business to be sold and purchased is subsequently referred to as the 'target'.

This work was originally conceived by Humphrey Winc (hence 'Beswick & Wine') and the early editions were written solely by him. The fourth to sixth editions were edited by Simon Beswick (now International CEO of solicitors Osborne Clarke) to whom we owe the present useful structure. I, Susan Singleton, Singletons, Solicitors am the editor/writer of the seventh, eighth, ninth and tenth editions.

For this edition I would like to thank my various clients involved in buying or selling a business. As I write I have just completed three business sales, all, by chance, in the property sector and settled one corporate dispute. It has been a busy period for my corporate work. Every transaction is different and lawyers learn from them all. This edition has had a thorough update following a year with not one, but two, Finance Acts due to the 2017 general election. Although the important fundamental clauses and the law applicable to them in areas such as warranties and indemnities has not changed of late, the constant tinkering (particularly with tax legislation) by the Government never seems to stop. Whether 2019 Brexit will mean continued 'alignment' with EU company law or ultimately some divergence remains to be seen. However it is in my practice as a competition lawyer particularly advising on the single market, exhaustion of intellectual property rights and parallel imports throughout the EEA, where a bigger Brexit impact is likely than in the business sales field where the most significant change is likely to be in relation to the very few mergers which will need, or be advised to have, both EU and UK competition law clearance after the UK leaves the EU.

The law is as stated at 1 February 2018.

Any errors and omissions are my own.

Susan Singleton
Pinner Hill
1 February 2018

For comments and suggestions for inclusion in a later edition, and legal advice on sales and acquisitions and the intellectual property and competition law aspects of such transactions, contact:

Susan Singleton
Singletons, Solicitors *www.singlelaw.com*

The Ridge
South View Road
Pinner
HA5 3YD
Tel: 020 8866 1934
Email: susan@singlelaw.com

Dedication

To my solicitor daughters, Rachel (at Macfarlanes) and Rebecca (at M&C Saatchi). May you continue to have as much fun in the law as I have had.

To my sons Ben, Joe and Sam who teach me much more than I teach them.

To my two grandchildren Rose and Frederick. It is all before you.

To my late parents Dr Peter and Anne Morgan.

About the author

Susan Singleton

Susan Singleton is a solicitor with her own London firm of solicitors, Singletons (www.singlelaw.com) which specialises in commercial law, sales and acquisitions, competition law, intellectual property law and IT/ecommerce. Trained at Nabarro, she joined Slaughter and May's EC/Competition Law Department on qualifying and then moved to Bristows where she remained until founding her own firm in 1994. Since then she has advised nearly 1,000 clients from all over the world. She acted for the claimant in the first damages action for breach of the EU competition rules to come before the English courts, *Arkin v Borchard Lines and Others*. On the corporate side in 2017/18 she has advised on a wide range of sales and purchases and MBOs in sectors as various as property, toys and recruitment. In May 2014 one of her merger cases was cleared by the then new Competition and Markets Authority and she has advised on corporate litigation matters such as fraud on the minority actions. She regularly advises on company law disputes, shareholder disagreements and litigates those cases where necessary. In 2017 she won a trade marks case and settled several commercial agency compensation matters. In 2015/17 she advised the tipping paper claimants in High Court, Court of Appeal and CJEU proceedings relating to EU and UK law in the tobacco sector.

She is the author of over 30 law books on topics such as internet and ecommerce law, competition law, commercial agency law, data protection legislation and intellectual property. She is co-author of *Buying and Selling Insolvent Companies and Businesses*, also published by Bloomsbury Professional. She is author of Bloomsbury's *Joint Ventures and Shareholders' Agreements* (5th edn, 2017) and edits the three volume looseleaf *Comparative Law of Monopolies* (Kluwer). She is author and editor of the looseleaf books *EContracts* and *Business the Internet and the Law* and is contributing author to *Company Secretary's Factbook*. Some of her clients are law firms who do not have in-house intellectual property and competition law expertise for whom she advises on those aspects of sales and purchases. She is a frequent speaker in the intellectual property, competition and commercial law fields, both in the UK and abroad speaking at about 20 events a year including in recent years in Iran, Dubai, Nigeria, Switzerland, France and Belgium. She is a member of the Licensing Executives Society (EC/ Laws Committee) and until 2017 was Vice Chairman of the Competition Law Association. From September 2005–September 2010 she sat as an independent member on the Direct Marketing Authority. She publishes ten subscription newsletters acquired from Informa plc – IT Law Today, Corporate Briefing, Finance & Credit Law, International Trade Finance, Pensions Today, Food and Drink Law Monthly, Housing Law Monitor, Education Law Monitor, Environmental Law Monthly and Farm Law.

She has five children and two grandchildren. She lives in London. Her hobbies include choral singing, skiing, reading and bikram yoga.

Contact:
Email: susan@singlelaw.com
Singletons, Solicitors, The Ridge, South View Road, Pinner HA53YD
Tel: 020 8866 1934
www.singlelaw.com
Twitter: @singlelaw

About Singletons, Solicitors

London commercial law solicitor's firm Singletons provides advice to clients from all over the UK and abroad from large plcs to small start-up business in the area covered by this book as well as the following:

- Buying and selling private companies and businesses;
- Joint venture and partnership agreements;
- Commercial litigation/disputes;
- Competition law – advisory and guidance, litigation CMA, EU;
- Intellectual property;
- IT/e-commerce law particularly data protection law and the General Data Protection Regulation;
- Commercial agency regulations and claims;
- Commercial contracts.

Abbreviations

The following abbreviations are used in this book:

CA 1985	Companies Act 1985
CA 2005	Companies Act 2005
CA 2006	Companies Act 2006
CRA 2015	Consumer Rights Act 2015
CTA 2009	Corporation Tax Act 2009
CTA 2010	Corporation Tax Act 2010
FSA 1986	Financial Services Act 1986
FSMA 2000	Financial Services and Markets Act 2000
IA 1986	Insolvency Act 1986
ICTA 1970	Income and Corporation Taxes Act 1970
ICTA 1988	Income and Corporation Taxes Act 1988
ITA 2007	Income Tax Act 2007
TCGA 1992	Taxation of Chargeable Gains Act 1992
TUPE 1981	Transfer of Undertakings (Protection of Employment) Regulations 1981
TUPE 2006	Transfer of Undertakings (Protection of Employment) Regulations 2006

Table of Statutes

References in *italics* refer to the Precedents

Table of Statutory Instruments

References in *italics* refer to the Precedents

Table of EC Material

References in *italics* refer to the Precedents

Table of Cases

Part I
The Seller's Perspective

Chapter 1

An overview of the sale process

1.1 THE SALE PROCESS

1.2 RATIONALE FOR SELLING
    1.2.1 Non-commercial motivations
    1.2.2 Financial reasons
    1.2.3 Commercial factors

1.1 THE SALE PROCESS

The sale process should always be planned with care. It can be broadly broken down into the following five steps:

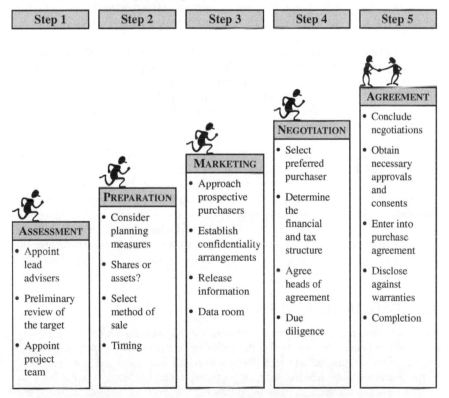

Step 1	Step 2	Step 3	Step 4	Step 5
ASSESSMENT	**PREPARATION**	**MARKETING**	**NEGOTIATION**	**AGREEMENT**
• Appoint lead advisers	• Consider planning measures	• Approach prospective purchasers	• Select preferred purchaser	• Conclude negotiations
• Preliminary review of the target	• Shares or assets?	• Establish confidentiality arrangements	• Determine the financial and tax structure	• Obtain necessary approvals and consents
• Appoint project team	• Select method of sale	• Release information	• Agree heads of agreement	• Enter into purchase agreement
	• Timing	• Data room	• Due diligence	• Disclose against warranties
				• Completion

Each step is detailed and discussed within the chapters that form Part I of this book. In discussing steps 1, 2 and 3 it is assumed that the seller will have initiated the sale with no particular purchaser in mind.

Chapter 2 covers the first stage (step 1) of the process: the appointment of advisers to help with the sale and a review of the target to assess whether a sale is feasible. In the case of most individual sellers, who will be inexperienced in the complexities of the sale process, the appointment of a lead adviser, who will act as project manager, for the transaction will be their starting point. If the outcome is favourable, the seller can then start the sale process in earnest by establishing the full team necessary to implement the disposal.

Having decided the objectives of the sale, obtained an independent opinion that a sale is likely at a price satisfactory to the seller and established a team to advise on and throughout the disposal, the next step (step 2) in the process is the formulation of a sale strategy, which is discussed in Chapter 3 together with pre-sale planning measures. The key elements of the sale strategy are the method of sale (whether by auction or individual negotiation), the structure of the sale (for example shares or assets) and the timing of the sale.

Chapter 4 deals with the marketing aspects of the sale (step 3) and covers the preparation of the sales literature (which normally comprises one principal document, the information memorandum), the approach to potential purchasers, the establishment of confidentiality arrangements with interested purchasers, the release of information to those purchasers and the solicitation of offers from them.

The next step (step 4) in the sale process – negotiation – is discussed in Chapter 5. Having received various indicative offers, the seller (often through the lead adviser) will negotiate with the prospective purchasers to obtain the preferred offer. Chapter 5 covers the selection of the preferred purchaser(s), negotiations with them, striking the deal in principle, the need for heads of agreement and the seller's response to the purchaser's due diligence investigations.

The concluding steps in the process, entering into the acquisition agreement and completion of it (step 5), are discussed in Part III.

The time interval between having made the decision in principle to sell and completion will vary enormously depending on the particular circumstances of each sale. It is unlikely that this process would take less than six months and, in the absence of radical planning measures such as becoming non-resident, would normally be expected to take in the region of 12 months for a sale by way of auction.

1.2 RATIONALE FOR SELLING

Some advisers are fortunate to be involved in the selling process at an early stage, either instructed directly by the seller or instructed for a specific purpose by the seller's financial advisers. Others are less fortunate and are instructed at the eleventh hour, leaving little opportunity to add value to their advice or otherwise act in a proactive manner. Whatever the case, an understanding of the reasons for sale and how the terms agreed with the purchaser, or sought by the seller, have been arrived at is of paramount importance in order to provide the best possible advice. Without this understanding and knowledge, advisers are ill-equipped to identify the key commercial objectives of the transaction, and accordingly to advise and document the transaction effectively and efficiently.

The reasons for selling a business are usually numerous and varied and will differ depending upon whether the seller is a corporate group, an individual or a group of individuals. They can, however, be broadly categorised as being for financial, commercial or non-commercial reasons. Perhaps surprisingly, it is extremely unlikely that anyone sale is motivated by purely financial or commercial reasons. If the negotiation is to result in terms acceptable to both the seller and purchaser, then both parties need to understand each other's motivation for entering into the transaction. For example, if one of the seller's main reasons for selling his business is the pressure and burden of managing it, he is unlikely to proceed with, or even attract in the first instance, a corporate purchaser, unless that purchaser has sufficient management resources of its own to support the target after the acquisition.

1.2.1 Non-commercial motivations

Non-commercial factors frequently provide the motivation for the sale. Examples include:

- the need for a corporate group to refocus on core activities;
- the illness, poor health or forthcoming retirement of the proprietor;
- the lack of management succession (this is quite common in small family companies);
- the burden of managing the business;
- matrimonial reasons (to finance a 'clean break');
- the limited scope for career development;
- the lack of interest in carrying on the business (for example, in the case of a business transferred to children or inherited on the death of the original proprietor).

1.2.2 Financial reasons

The main financial reasons for selling usually revolve, in one way or another, around the desire to convert paper into cash for a variety of personal reasons.

Other financial reasons for sale include:

(A) Diversification of investments

The seller may have decided that all his assets are tied up in the business and a sale of that business would allow him to minimise his financial risk by investing the proceeds of the sale across a wide range of investments.

(B) A means of raising finance

Having exhausted other sources, sellers sometimes resort to selling a business as the only means of financing the next stage in its development. This is common in the case of start-ups where a new product has been developed but finance from the usual sources to fund the marketing of it is unavailable or in fast changing industries, such as the TMT sector (technology, media and telecomms).

(C) To avoid failure

A further financial reason for sale is the need to avoid failure, in the form of receivership or liquidation or closure of the business concerned.

(D) The unsolicited offer

Sometimes the only factor is the unsolicited offer at a price which the seller finds irresistible; the offer is simply too good to refuse.

1.2.3 Commercial factors

By their very nature, commercial factors are more relevant in the decision to sell a poorly performing business or a business which has ignored the need to develop its products or the next generation of products. Commercial reasons include the need for new technology, new product development (especially where the product is at the end of its lifecycle) or the need to protect the business from new or stronger competition; in each case these new developments may be beyond the financial resources of the business.

Chapter 2

Assessment of marketability

2.1 APPOINTMENT OF A LEAD ADVISOR

2.2 PRELIMINARY REVIEW OF THE TARGET

2.3 APPOINTMENT OF THE PROJECT TEAM

2.1 APPOINTMENT OF A LEAD ADVISOR

Once the decision to sell has been made in principle, what should a seller do next? For the inexperienced individual seller, the starting point is the appointment of advisors to help the seller achieve his objective, and, for the corporate seller, it is the appointment of a project team to handle the sale. In either case the appointment of a lead advisor or team leader to project manage the process and to lead and guide the internal team and external advisors is key to the success of the sale.

The role of lead advisor is vital. The lead advisor needs to be experienced in the disposal of companies, have an understanding of all aspects of the transaction and hold the respect of the seller and fellow advisors. The role is frequently carried out by one of the target's professional advisors, or, if they do not possess the necessary experience, by specialists experienced in private company sales and acquisitions or, occasionally, when the projected sale price justifies the fees, a merchant bank experienced in this area.

Project management is not just about drawing up a timetable, a list of parties and a list of documents and leaving everybody to get on with it. The lead advisor should be given the authority to assist the seller through each stage of the sale process, to instruct other advisors as and when required, to consider appropriate planning measures, advise on the timing, marketing, method and structure of the disposal, co-ordinate and disseminate instructions and information, insist on compliance with the timetable and review and negotiate sale terms with prospective purchasers.

At this initial stage, it is important to the success of the sale for the seller to impart to the lead advisor, and for the lead advisor to understand, the seller's rationale for wishing to sell the target and the seller's objectives for the sale. It may well be that all the seller wants to achieve is a partial realisation of value, for example to finance the purchase of a new house. If this is the case then an outright sale may not be the only option available. The seller could achieve his ambition of realising value and at the same time retain control of the company by the company purchasing its own shares (CA 2006, s 690).

2.2 PRELIMINARY REVIEW OF THE TARGET

Having understood the seller's rationale for wishing to sell the target and identified the seller's objectives, the next step is to review the target and its business from the viewpoint of a prospective purchaser. The overriding objective of this review is to establish the marketability of the target and the likely sale price. A secondary, but important, objective of the review is to highlight areas of the business which may prevent a sale or prove to be unattractive to a purchaser. Remedial action can then be taken to ensure that the target is marketed for sale in its most attractive form or, alternatively, the unattractive feature can be presented as an opportunity. For example, if the business is solely dependent upon the owner to manage it and the recruitment of supporting managers is not possible in the timescale, this requirement for a broader based, and possibly younger, management may be attractive to a large conglomerate with ranks of young managers seeking opportunities to prove themselves.

In assessing the likely sale price of the target, the lead advisor will usually base the price on a multiple of the target's earnings or net asset. He will then use his experience and knowledge of the market to adjust the base price, upwards or downwards, to reflect various matters from potential cost savings for prospective purchasers to the benefits available to prospective purchasers through market customer synergies. A more detailed discussion of the methods of valuing a business is set out in Part II (see Chapter 8).

2.3 APPOINTMENT OF THE PROJECT TEAM

Assuming the preliminary review is favourable and the assessment of the likely sale price falls within a range of prices acceptable to the seller, the next stage is the establishment of the full team to deal with the disposal. The make-up of the team will depend largely upon the seller's circumstances.

Individual sellers, for example, often have limited resources and prefer to shelter the business from the stresses of the sale process while preserving their negotiating position. As a result, the team usually comprises professional advisors in the form of lawyers, accountants, valuation experts and, where appropriate, separate tax and pension advisors.

Depending on their size and corporate structure, corporate sellers are more likely to use greater internal resource and less external professional advice. The team will often comprise the principal manager responsible for the business being sold, and members of the in-house legal, accounting and tax departments. In certain situations, members of the project team may lose their jobs on achievement of the sale. In these situations the managers affected are often incentivised by the seller, usually in the form of an 'exit bonus' payable on achievement of the sale.

Although more expensive in the short term, the involvement of the full team at this early stage should produce benefits and cost savings over the period of the whole transaction, for example it should avoid a structure or method of sale being adopted, and the incurrence of expenses relating to its adoption, which is later jettisoned at the detailed planning stage.

Whichever sale structure is chosen, effective management of the sale process is the key to success. All members of the project team must be kept aware of developments at all times and sufficient project team meetings should be built into the timetable to enable effective communication across the team.

Chapter 3

Preparing for the sale

3.1 PLANNING THE SALE

CHECKLIST:

- Sale of shares or assets
- Tax issues
- Best structure
- Sale by auction or private treaty?
- When will the sale take place?

The key to a successful sale is planning. Voluntary disposals initiated by the sellers obviously provide the maximum opportunity to plan ahead. In such cases, the seller is in control of the sale process and should be encouraged to consider planning measures early in the process. A carefully planned disposal strategy should maximise the seller's return from the sale, both gross and net of tax, and minimise the risks associated with the sale.

The objectives of any planning measures need to be defined at the outset and, at the very least, prior to devising and agreeing with the purchaser the structure of the transaction. From a seller's perspective the objective of any particular planning measure should be to:

- increase the attractiveness of the target;
- maximise the net sale proceeds; or
- minimise the tax payable as a result of the sale.

Save for packaging the business for sale, the overwhelming majority of commercial and financial planning measures will only become apparent from a thorough and detailed business review of the target and its business. Accordingly, it is not proposed to provide an analysis of these measures. However, it is important that the seller and lead adviser are mindful of this when conducting the preliminary business review.

In the case of corporate sellers, if the target business forms part of a larger business or is one of a number of divisions of the seller, it may need to be placed on a stand alone footing prior to, or co-terminus with, the sale. In these situations a number of issues will need to be considered, including:

- Are there any shared contracts between the target, other parts of the seller's group, and third parties that need to be separated out? Can this realistically be achieved before the sale is announced? (Confidentiality and commercial sensitivities may prevent this happening at least until the sale is substantially agreed.)
- Should the target businesses be 'hived' down into separate companies newly formed for this purpose so that shares rather than assets are sold? This may make the sale structure simpler.
- Are there any shared assets, and if so, which business will they be sold with or does the seller need to retain them for use in the remainder of the group?
- Are there any services provided by the seller's group, including the use of computer systems, accounting, and head office functions, or the occupation of any property owned by the seller, which the businesses will need to continue to use for a period after the sale?
- Are there any employees who work for more than one business, and if so, which business should they transfer with?
- Are there separate records for each business? If not, what will the purchaser expect to see and who needs to be involved in this? For example, the seller may need to extract pro-forma financial information from the latest statutory accounts if it is selling a business which is one of several owned by the company preparing statutory accounts.
- Are there any shared intellectual property rights which will require assignment and/or a licence?
- Are there any tax-planning or pension issues which may require action before the sale occurs, such as the transfer of assets to other parts of the seller's group? In 2011 entrepreneur's relief from capital gains tax was doubled to a lifetime allowance of £10m taxed at only 10% (rather than the 20% higher rate capital gains tax for higher rate tax payers for sale of

shares (and 28% for sales of real property)) and each family member who owns shares has the benefit of the lifetime's £10m allowance – see HMRC Helpsheethttps://www.gov.uk/government/publications/entrepreneurs-relief-hs275-self-assessment-helpsheet. Ensuring shares are issued to take advantage of this in advance can save large amounts of capital gains tax. Pension issues will include the need to ascertain if the seller's existing scheme is being transferred or if employees will be required to stop participating. Many sales founder because pension liabilities are too high.

- Would a purchaser be concerned about any items within the business which are not absolutely required, such as unwanted leaseholder premises which the seller is currently sub-letting? If so, can these be transferred to elsewhere in the seller's group? A purchaser may still seek an indemnity from the seller for any contingent property liabilities which remain, but at least the problem is one step removed from the buyer.

Some of these issues are looked at later in this chapter.

The extent to which issues such as these can be addressed before the sale is completed depends on the timetable 'drivers' and the extent to which the purchaser's likely requirements can be identified at the planning stage. Their effect on the price if not resolved must also be taken into consideration. The seller may also be reluctant to commit itself to wholesale restructuring in the absence of concluding a deal with a purchaser. However, some measures, such as tax planning, may be more difficult to implement successfully at a late stage.

3.2   SHARES OR ASSETS?

There are two methods of selling a commercial enterprise. The first is to sell the assets (and possibly certain agreed liabilities) which make up that enterprise. The second, which applies only if the business is being conducted by a company, is to sell the shares owned by the company in relation to the business in question.

These two methods are fundamentally different in their legal effect, even if the commercial effect may prove similar. Often businesses do not realise how different these are and have not decided early enough which route they will take. In the case of the sale of a business, the purchaser acquires a collection of tangibles and intangibles which will be incorporated directly into the purchaser's balance sheet. Where, however, a company is sold, the company remains largely unaffected by the acquisition; its underlying assets and liabilities will continue to belong to the company and the only items appearing in the purchaser's balance sheet will be the shares in the company at their acquisition cost. All the rights of and against the company being acquired will continue to be enforceable by or against that company with no direct effect on the purchaser, except on the value of its investment. The agreements are totally different and it is vital that the client is clear as to whether for tax or other reasons it needs an asset or share sale as it is very expensive to start with new contracts later having already drafted an agreement on the alternative basis.

Sometimes there is no choice in the method to be used for selling the assets of the business since the circumstances dictate that the only feasible option is the sale of the business itself rather than the company in which it is being carried on. This is most common when:

- the seller is an administrator or receiver – usually a receiver is only appointed over the assets of a company, thereby limiting the choices to a sale of assets only. Even where an administrator/receiver is appointed over the assets of the target's holding company, given receivers' overriding desire to sell free from contingent liabilities (ie warranties), purchasers are unlikely to acquire shares due to the lack of protection against unknown liabilities;

- the business being disposed of forms a division of the seller company – where the business being sold forms a division of the seller company rather than a separate subsidiary, the purchaser will have no choice but to acquire the relevant assets direct or, if it wishes to preserve the benefits of a share purchase, to acquire a new subsidiary of the seller into which the relevant assets are transferred immediately prior to the sale to the purchaser;

- there are dissentient minority shareholders – where some of the target's shareholders are opposed to the sale the only practicable solution, if the consenting shareholders control the board of the target, is to structure the sale as a sale of assets. Even then, either through restrictions contained in the target's articles of association, or a shareholders' agreement, the sale may be prohibited without the consent of the dissenting shareholders or may be blocked by the courts pursuant to the minority protection provisions under CA 2006, s 994.

Under s 994, a shareholder of the target may apply to the court for an order that the sale of the target's assets is unfairly prejudicial to the interests of its members generally or to some part of its members. Accordingly, where there are dissentient minority shareholders, the seller shareholders who are also directors will need to consider their fiduciary duties to the target, and they should also take into account the minority protection provisions available to dissenting minorities under s 994. Whether a sale of a target's assets would be unfairly prejudicial in that way would depend on the circumstances of the transaction and whether or not its terms conferred additional benefits on some of the shareholders as compared with others. For example, a court is likely to look more sympathetically at a petition where the favoured majority shareholder was offered a lucrative consultancy agreement with the purchaser when a similar offer was not available to a minority shareholder who previously held an executive position within the target.

Whether it is the shares or the assets of the target that will be sold is a matter for negotiation. Depending upon the relative negotiating position of the seller and the purchaser, the seller's preference is likely to prevail because, after all, the seller is the party to the transaction who will have the immediate tax liability. However, the assessment of whether one party will prefer an asset sale or a share sale can only be done after a full examination of the implications of each, having regard to the particular circumstances of each party. Because the circumstances of one seller will nearly always differ from those of another, they will need to be considered afresh in every case, and this book can give only general guidance. Most buyers require a board minute approving the sale although that is still not guarantee a minority shareholder has not been prejudiced by the sale.

3.2.1 Tax considerations

To determine whether a share sale or a sale of assets is most tax effective, it is necessary to look at the whole situation, including the seller's aspirations and the nature and destination of the consideration. The tax implications, including the schemes and exemptions available under the alternative routes, must be carefully considered to determine how the deal should be structured. Even if the choice between assets and shares has already been determined, the schemes and exemptions available should be identified so that the seller can structure the deal to the best effect.

On the sale of shares, tax (capital gains tax in the case of individuals and trustees, corporation tax in the case of companies) will normally be payable on any chargeable gain made by the seller. The chargeable gain is basically the difference between the proceeds of disposal and the allowable expenditure. The allowable expenditure is the aggregate of the cost to the seller, plus enhancement expenditure and incidental costs, calculated under the rules contained in TCGA 1992, s 38. This is known as the base cost. In the past, assets held on 31 March 1982 could be rebased (ie the base cost uplifted) to market value on that date (TCGA 1992, s 35). The base cost was then increased by the rise in the retail prices index from the date of acquisition (or if rebasing, from 1 April 1982) to April 1998 with taper relief applying from April 1998 (this relief is outlined further in section 3.3.1). However, for disposals of assets by an individual, trustees or personal representatives on or after 6 April 2008 there is no longer any taper relief. Instead, a flat capital gains tax (CGT) (20% for higher rate tax payers) now applies to all disposals made on or before 22 June 2010. However in many cases the 10% rate is applied, as from 6 April 2011 individuals have a lifetime CGT allowance for business sales called 'entrepreneurs' relief' of £10m (previously £5m) taxed at only 10% for CGT purposes. Gains after 22 June 2010 are charged at the then relevant prevailing rates for individuals depending on the total amount of taxable income, 20% for 2017/18 sale for trustees or personal representatives of a deceased person and 10% for gains qualifying for entrepreneurs' relief discussed below. The 'indexation allowance', which was given to counter the effects of inflation between 31 March 1982 and 6 April 1998 is now abolished and those who had accumulated any allowance during that period on assets which are still owned at 6 April 2008 lost that allowance. This is only of historical relevance now as it only affected assets acquired before 6 April 1998. At the same time the so-called 'kink test' was abolished so now all assets held on 31 March 1982 are deemed to have had a cost equivalent to their market value on that date.

Entrepreneurs' relief was introduced in the tax year 2008/09 to replace taper relief for the disposal of a business. Unlike taper relief it does not always apply to the disposal of single assets. The rules are complex and legal advice should be sought. It results in a CGT rate when the conditions are met of only 10% but individuals have a £10m lifetime allowance so some people, by the time the sale being considered occurs, may already have used up their allowance or part of it. Thus had they sold a business the year before for £10m and used the allowance, when they sell the next one their gains will be likely to be taxed at the higher 20% CGT rate , not 10%. If they had sold one business the year before for £5m, and another the next for £10m, the first sale is taxed at 10% and the second as to half of the gain at 10% and the balance likely to be taxed at 20%. If instead the shares are divided between family members who each have a £10m annual lifetime allowance all the gains may be taxed only at 10% although advice should be taken to ensure any restructuring of shares does not fall foul of tax legislation and that every family member shareholder meets the conditions for eligibility for entrepreneurs' relief. The types of disposal which attract relief are:

- the sale by a sole trader of his or her business as a going concern (including incorporating it);
- the sale of chargeable assets which were used by a sole trader in his or her business, which has ceased trading within the last three years;
- the disposal by a partner in a partnership of his or her share in the firm, or of part of his or her share; and
- the disposal of shares and securities in a company, to which further conditions apply.

Where the business disposed of is run through a company, the disposer must own at least 5% of the ordinary share capital of the company which must entitle him to 5% of the votes; he must be an officer or employee of the company, and the company must be carrying on trading activities, and to no substantial extent any other activities. For most owner shareholders this requirement is easily met. This will not necessarily be the case for other family member shareholders so it can be important when setting up a business to consider the exit structure and roles given to family members if it is desired that several sellers will each benefit from the relief. There was a similar requirement under taper relief. Any company which qualified for business asset taper relief, will also qualify under these rules. There is also relief available on the proceeds of winding up or dissolving a former trading company, provided this is done within three years of ceasing trading activities.

The £10 million is a 'lifetime limit'. This limit has effect for qualifying disposals on or after 6 April 2011. The lifetime limit was originally £1 million, this was increased to £2 million for qualifying disposals on or after 6 April 2010, and to £5 million for qualifying disposals on or after 23 June 2010. This means each disposal will use up relief which would otherwise be available on subsequent disposals. It can make it wise for the seller, for example, where possible to run his or her businesses through three other family members too so that the family has £40m of lifetime limit relief although tax advice would need to be sought as stated above.

On the sale of assets, a variety of taxes may be payable by the seller. Capital gains tax or corporation tax on chargeable gains may be due on the sale of capital assets whereas income tax or corporation tax may be due on the sale of stock and on assets on which capital allowances have been claimed. Value Added Tax is also an issue.

One important point to note is that a liability to tax arises by reference to the date of the contract, not completion (TCGA 1992, s 28). If the contract is subject to a condition precedent, the disposal occurs when the condition is satisfied.

Pros and cons of assets sales

One major disadvantage of an asset sale by a company is the fact that a further tax charge may arise if the proceeds are to be passed out to shareholders. This makes plenty of small business sellers insist they sell shares not assets, whereas buyers often prefer the cleaner route of picking off those assets they want and leaving behind those they do not, although the downside is that important commercial contracts may not be assignable but were it a share sale would be unaffected (unless they contained change of control clauses). If, having sold the business, the seller has no ongoing need for the company, it may be liquidated to realise its assets. This gives rise to a second potential charge to capital gains tax, because the seller will be treated as disposing of his shares in return for the capital distribution. Depending upon the amount of the target's distributable reserves, that second charge can be reduced by distributing by way of dividend sufficient cash so as to leave in the company an amount equal to the seller's capital gains tax base cost of the shares. In this way the overall charge to tax may be reduced. For an explanation of the rationale of this, see section 3.3.1 (J)(iv).

Either way, the seller will normally pay less tax if the shares had been sold directly to the purchaser.

3.2.2   HMRC worked tax examples 2015

See HMRC Helpsheet 275: https://www.gov.uk/government/publications/entrepreneurs-relief-hs275-self-assessment-helpsheet/hs275-entrepreneurs-relief-2015.

Example 1

You dispose of your manufacturing and retail business which you had owned for the last eight years. You make gains and losses on the business assets as follows:

Factory premises	£1,250,000
Good will	£1,300,000
Retail shop	loss (£500,000)
Shares	£800,000

The gains and losses on the factory premises, the goodwill and the shop are aggregated and will together qualify for entrepreneurs' relief which will be due in respect of the net gain of £2,050,000.

The gain on the shares is not aggregated with the gains or losses on the other business assets. Entrepreneurs' relief may be due in respect of the gain on the shares if the conditions are met for shares to qualify for the relief.

Example 2

You have been a partner with three other persons in a trading business for several years. Each partner had a 25% interest in the partnership's assets. You retire and dispose of your 25% interest in the assets of the business, which continues, to the other partners.

You make gains of £125,000 when you dispose of your 25% share of the business goodwill and premises to an incoming partner who is an individual. All of your gains will qualify for entrepreneurs' relief because you have disposed of the whole of your interest in the assets of the partnership..

Example 3

In September 2014 you dispose of the shares you had owned for the last 20 years in a company of which you were a director. You owned 20% of the shares of the company that entitled you to 20% of the voting rights. You made a gain of £860,000. The company had been a trading company but its trade ceased in August 2012 and the company then ceased to qualify as a trading company. Your gain will still qualify for entrepreneurs' relief because the disposal was made less than three years after the company ceased to qualify as a trading company.

Example 4

On 5 April 2015 you sell the shares in your personal company in which you have been a director and shareholder since 2005. You make gains of £8,000,000 on the sale of your shares. You also personally owned the premises which you purchased on 6 April 2005 and from which date the company trades. The company paid you a full market rent from 6 April 2012 but no rent was paid before this date. You make a gain of £4,500,000 on the disposal of the premises.

This is a gain on the 'associated disposal'. Your gain on the disposal of your shares and your gain on the disposal of the premises qualify for relief. However, because you owned the premises personally and for part of the period a full market rent was paid to you by the company, a proportion of the gain relating to the premises will not attract relief.

Only the period for which rent was paid after 5 April 2008 is taken into account in restricting the amount of the £4,500,000 gain which qualifies for relief. This would be three of the ten years the property was in use for the business. A 'just and reasonable' figure in these circumstances would be:

Total gain on the sale of the premises		£4.5 million
Gain accruing for 3 years of use from 6 April 2005 to 5 April 2008	£4.5 million × $\frac{3}{10}$	£1.35 million
Gain accruing for 4 years of use when no rent paid by company from 6 April 2008 to 5 April 2012	£4.5 million × $\frac{4}{10}$	£1.8 million
Gain accruing for 3 years of use when rent paid by company from 6 April 2012 to 5 April 2015	£4.5 million × $\frac{3}{10}$ not eligible for Entrepreneurs' Relief	
Gain on premises on which Entrepreneurs' Relief may be available		£3.15 million
Plus gain on disposal of shares on which Entrepreneurs' Relief may be available		£8 million
Total gains on which Entrepreneurs' Relief may be available		£11.15 million

If you have not used up any of your lifetime limit on earlier claims, £10,000,000 of the total £11,150,000 gains on your shares and the premises will attract entrepreneurs' relief.

3.2.3 Preferred structure

The preferred structure for a seller will vary depending upon whether the seller is an individual or a company.

(A) Individual seller

An individual seller who actually wishes to get hold of the sale proceeds in cash will usually prefer to structure the transaction as a sale of shares for the following reasons:

- Single charge to tax – the most significant advantage of a share sale is that the purchase price is paid directly to the seller and this will involve only one charge to tax, namely CGT on the gain realised on the sale of the shares. Where assets are sold, the purchase price is received by, and potentially suffers tax in, the company. To obtain access to the purchase price, the net proceeds (ie after tax) need to be distributed to the shareholders and this gives rise to a further potential charge to tax.

- Clean break – a sale of shares enables the seller to disengage totally from the business being sold. More importantly, except in relation to any warranties, indemnities and covenants given on the sale to the purchaser, the seller will have no continuing liability for the debts of the business, all obligations remain with the company and the responsibility for running it falls on the purchaser.

- Simplicity – an asset purchase involves the identification and transfer of each and every asset. For example, movable plant and equipment will need to be transferred by delivery whereas other assets, such as land and contracts, will have to be documented and may be subject to the consent of a third party. By comparison, a share sale involves the transfer of only one asset, namely the shares of the target, which can be transferred by way of stock transfer forms. This may lead to reduced costs and makes the transaction more straightforward.

- Speed – the process of acquiring assets may take longer than an acquisition of shares because it involves the transfer of each and every individual asset of the business. Some of the assets (for example, leasehold property and trading contracts) cannot be transferred without the consent of third parties and, due to the risk of a third party withholding consent or terminating the contract, it carries with it more uncertainty about ongoing trading.

- Less disruption to the target's business – the management and operation of the underlying business are likely to be disrupted less in the sale process. A sale of assets may require discussions with customers, suppliers, landlords and licensing or regulatory authorities relating to obtaining consent to the transfer of the individual assets. Most commercial contracts with suppliers and customers are not terminable where the company suffers a 'change of control' (on sale of shares), but many may not be assigned or transferred to a buyer of assets without permission by the supplier or customer with whom the company contracted. If those contracts are crucial to the buyer and might be in jeopardy on a sale then the buyer may indeed not proceed with the sale.

Notwithstanding the general preference of individual sellers to structure the transaction as a sale of shares, such a structure does have certain disadvantages over a sale of assets, and these should be drawn to the seller's attention. They include:

- Increased costs of marketing – the costs of marketing the target for sale may be increased as a result of the 'investment advertisement'/ 'financial promotion' approval requirements in FSMA 2000. These are discussed in greater detail in Chapter 4 (see section 4.5).

- Greater risk of warranty claims – there is a greater risk of warranty claims since more extensive warranties are usually required to protect the purchaser from hidden liabilities, which are normally excluded in business transfers.

- Less attractive to a purchaser – for the reasons listed in the corresponding section of Part II (Chapter 9, section 9.6), a purchaser may prefer to acquire assets and accordingly structuring the transaction as a share sale may make the business less attractive to potential purchasers.

The advantages and disadvantages to a seller of structuring the transaction as a sale of assets are, in effect, the reverse of the above.

(B) Corporate seller

Because of the double charge to tax referred to in section 3.4, it is unlikely that individuals would form a corporate vehicle to own the target unless that vehicle also owned other companies and they could obtain benefits by organising them as a group of companies. Accordingly, corporate sellers tend to be from groups of companies, which, in turn, often divest businesses for substantially different reasons from individual sellers and may use the sale proceeds for reasons other than distribution to shareholders.

As a result, a corporate seller may be coming from the opposite direction from an individual seller when structuring the sale. If, for example, it is important to obtain roll-over relief (which allows a gain to be deferred where the proceeds are reinvested in new assets), the sale will have to be structured as a sale of assets because roll-over relief may not be available in the case of a sale of shares (discussed in section 3.4.1). Notwithstanding the other April 2008 CGT changes, business asset roll-over relief continues to be available. Roll-over relief enables the CGT payable on the gain on a chargeable asset to be deferred until a point in the future. Plenty of people sell one business and buy another to ensure no tax is payable at the time of first sale.

3.3 TAX PLANNING ON THE SALE OF SHARES

3.3.1 Checklist of principal tax planning opportunities for individuals on the sale of shares

The principal tax saving opportunities available to individual shareholders can be summarised as follows:

(A) Cash and entrepreneurs' relief

The first and most obvious choice for the payment on the sale of any company is cash. Shareholders taking cash will normally pay CGT at 20% (18% for lower rate tax payers).

Each individual taxpayer is entitled to an annual exemption from CGT of £11,300 from 6 April 2017. Trustees have a lower annual tax free band of £5,650 (2017/18). Any gain over the annual exemption is taxed at the 20% rate (or up to 28% for residential property) or 10% for lower rate tax payers. There are special rates for 'carried interest'. For lower rate tax payers only, the CGT rate was 18% on gains made before 6 April 2016 (assuming no entrepreneurs' relief at 10% CGT). For gains made after this the rates for sale of shares and other gains other than on residential property are 10% (for lower rate tax payers) and 18% for resident property gains for such tax payers. As explained above, on sales of a business most individuals now pay only 10% if they are within their lifetime limit of £10m and qualify for entrepreneurs' relief. This encourages individuals to own companies for shorter periods and sell before the limit is reached,

The availability of losses needs to be considered as capital losses may normally be set against capital gains.

(B)   Shares and loan notes

A purchaser may be willing to offer a share or loan note alternative to cash. By exchanging shares in the target for shares or loan notes in the purchaser, the shareholder may be able to defer capital gains tax until such time as the replacement shares or loan notes are sold. Where loan notes are taken, the shareholder should always consider asking for a bank or other guarantee. Loan notes are alternatively referred to as debentures. The type of loan note taken can also be important as this may affect the ability of taper relief to apply to any loan notes received as consideration.

(C)   Pensions

It is always worth reviewing the pension arrangements of a shareholder working in the business. Additional money can be contributed to his/ her pension fund, if appropriate, to upgrade benefits. There may have to be a corresponding reduction in the value of the offer to be made by the purchaser, but overall it may be good tax/financial planning. Additionally, in certain circumstances, it may be beneficial to the shareholder to transfer funds into another pensions vehicle such as a self-invested personal pension (SIPP).

Aside from tax and financial planning reasons, there may also be more practical reasons for shareholders to review their pension arrangements on a share sale, particularly if their pension arrangements are either a small self-administered scheme (SSAS) or an executive pension plan (EPP) which provide benefits solely for the shareholder. The reason for this is that because these arrangements are occupational pension schemes, the target may well have important powers and rights in respect of those arrangements, which the shareholder may not feel comfortable with the purchaser being able to exercise after completion. Appropriate steps can be taken in these circumstances either to transfer those powers to the trustees of the scheme or, alternatively, to replace the target as the sponsoring employer by another employer of the shareholder and the other members.

Many business sales founder because pension liabilities the buyer would have to take over are too large. It is important to take pensions advice early on any potential sale. The Pensions Act 2014 made some changes to pensionable age and the latest position should always be checked, particularly given the Finance Act 2014 changes to rights to take pensions as lump sums (subject to highest rate tax being deducted at source for high earners on 75% of the fund (25% being available tax free) when the whole fund is taken at age 55 or older (this will rise to a minimum age of 57 years) under the 'pensions freedom' rules.

(D)   Termination payments

Certain termination payments on the cessation of employment are tax free up to £30,000 and it may be possible to build such payments into the overall package. However, this does need to be thought through carefully as HM Revenue and Customs (HMRC) is steadily chipping away at the opportunities to use this exemption. Also, there may be financial assistance implications if the payment is in excess of what is contractually due and termination payments linked to the sale of shares are rarely tax deductible for the target.

From 6 April 2011 the rules in this area slightly altered. An 0T tax code is applied to the sum in excess of the tax free £30,000. So if someone were paid £40,000, £30,000 remains tax free (where it meets the conditions of the law for tax free payments and that can depend what is stated in the employment contract) but the £10,000 excess is deemed to be a monthly payment and inflates the individual's earnings. Even though the £30,000 is tax free it is still added to income to work out upper tax bracket so a total redundancy payment of £42,500 may bring the individual into the £150k plus 45% tax bracket and all earnings for the rest of the year may be taxed at the highest rate. Refunds may be possible when a new job is begun, a pension is taken or if someone chooses not to work but claims no taxable social security benefits but only if an application is made for this.

The Finance (No 2) Act 2017 (which made changes to foreign payments and termination) and proposed legislation in 2018 will result in changes in this area. In particular it is likely that all pay in lieu of notice (PILON) payment will be fully taxed even if under the £30,000 limit, but that damages under the limit will remain tax free. Reference should be made to the new legislation once it is promulgated. Employer national insurance contributions (currently 13.8%) will be payable for payments over £30,000 from April 2019.

(E)   Gifts to family members

A gift of shares to another member of the family, perhaps the shareholder's spouse, is often tax effective. The recipient of the gift will thereby realise the gain and make use of his/her capital gains tax exemption and lower rate tax bands. This can be more beneficial if the spouse or other relative also has capital losses. There is no capital transfer tax on gifts under current UK tax law, although if the giver dies within seven years inheritance tax at 40% may become due so timing is crucial in tax planning of gifts.

(F)   Pre-sale dividends

Pre-sale dividends and their tax consideration has been subject to recent change to make dividend payments less attractive from a tax avoidance standpoint. The government's dividend summary is below:

Dividend Taxation after 2016 (https://www.gov.uk/tax-on-dividends)

The government's summary is below:

Tax on dividends

You may receive a dividend payment if you own shares in a company.

You don't pay tax on the first £5,000 [*planned to be reduced to £2000*] of dividends you receive in the tax year (from 6 April to 5 April the following year).

Above this allowance the tax you pay depends on which income tax band you're in. Add your income from dividends to your other taxable income when working this out. You may pay tax at more than one rate.

The rules are different for dividends from tax years before April 2016.

Tax band	Tax rate on dividends over £5,000 [*planned to reduce to £2000*]
Basic rate	7.5%
Higher rate	32.5%
Additional rate	38.1%

HM Revenue and Customs (HMRC) has examples of how your tax is worked out if you're over the dividend allowance.

You don't pay tax on dividends from shares in an ISA.

Dividends that fall within your Personal Allowance do not count towards the £5,000 dividend allowance.

The Finance (No 2) Act 2017 with effect from 6 April 2018 reduces the £5,000 to £2000 which will affect the examples below.

'Examples

1. The way the allowance will work in different situations is demonstrated in the examples below.

Where appropriate to the calculations, the examples use the limits that will apply from April 2016:
- Personal Allowance: £11,000
- Basic Rate Limit: £32,000
- Higher Rate Threshold: £43,000

2.1 Example 1

"I receive less than £5,000 per year in dividends"

From April 2016 you won't have to pay tax on your dividend income as it is within your new Dividend Allowance.

2.2 Example 2

"I receive dividends of £600 from shares invested in an ISA"

As is the case now, no tax is due on dividend income within an ISA, whatever rate of tax you pay.

2.3 Example 3

"I have a non-dividend income of £6,500, and a dividend income of £12,000 from shares outside of an ISA"

With a Personal Allowance of £11,000, £4,500 of the dividends are under the threshold for tax. A further £5,000 comes within the Dividend Allowance, leaving tax to pay at Basic Rate (7.5%) on £2,500.

2.4 Example 4

"I have a non-dividend income of £20,000, and receive dividends of £6,000 outside of an ISA"

You won't need to pay tax on the first £5,000 of dividends due to the Dividend Allowance, but will pay tax on £1,000 of dividends at 7.5%.

2.5 Example 5

"I have a non-dividend income of £18,000, and receive dividends of £22,000 outside of an ISA"

Of the £18,000 non-dividend income:
- £11,000 is covered by the Personal Allowance
- the remaining £7,000 to be taxed at Basic Rate

Of the £22,000 dividend income:
- the Dividend Allowance covers the first £5,000
- the remaining £17,000 of dividends to be taxed at the Basic Rate (7.5%)

2.6 Example 6

"I have a non-dividend income of £40,000, and receive dividends of £9,000 outside of an ISA"

Of the £40,000 non-dividend income, £11,000 is covered by the Personal Allowance, leaving £29,000 to be taxed at basic rate.

This leaves £3,000 of income that can be earned within the basic rate limit before the higher rate threshold is crossed. The Dividend Allowance covers this £3,000 first, leaving £2,000 of Allowance to use in the higher rate band. All of this £5,000 dividend income is therefore covered by the Allowance and is not subject to tax.

The remaining £4,000 of dividends are all taxed at higher rate (32.5%).'

The Finance (No 2) Act 2017, s 8 reduces the £5000 dividend allowance to £2000. From 6 April 2018 individuals who have a single person's income tax allowance ('SPA') are able to earn up to £13,850 in dividends (being the £2,000 dividend allowance plus £11,850 personal allowance) and pay no tax (and £2,000 for those tax payers with no SPA).

Those earning dividend income in the higher tax band (over £45,000 for 2017/18), will pay 32.5% dividend tax, or 38.1% where the dividend income falls into the additional rate band (ie over £150,000).

(G)   Stock dividends

There will be a limit on the amount which can be paid by way of dividend, which is fixed primarily by the level of distributable reserves in the target. It is possible to do a share reconstruction prior to the sale which would allow shareholders to imitate the effect of receiving a cash dividend. This is achieved by allowing shareholders to take a 'stock dividend'. There is some risk in this scheme, in that ideally the stock dividend is declared a day or so before contracts are exchanged, at which point an income tax charge arises. That income tax charge remains if the deal subsequently fails to materialise.

(H)   Use of trusts

By establishing an 'interest in possession' trust, typically for children, the capital gains tax rate may be less than would otherwise be the case. However, since 22 March 2006, such trusts have been subject to periodic and exit charges. Changes to trusts and inheritance tax limits in 2014 have made these less popular for inheritance tax planning purposes.

(I)   Offshore arrangements

Although the anti-avoidance rules have changed in recent years, UK tax can be avoided by the shareholder moving abroad before the shares are sold in certain circumstances. The General Anti-Abuse Rule (GAAR) came into force on 17 July 2013 and advice should always be sought on this too (see https://www.gov.uk/government/publications/tax-avoidance-general-anti-abuse-rules). Even so there may be some tax saving opportunities available if the shares are transferred to an offshore trust holding structure prior to the sale. Always take tax advice as the rules are subject to current scrutiny and change.

The individual needs to make a clear break with the UK and in recent years HMRC appear to have changed their stance on this and taken a tougher approach in cases such as *Lyle Dicker Grace v HMRC* [2011] UKFTT 36 where a BA pilot worked from Heathrow/Gatwick and retained his house in the UK when he bought a house in South Africa after his divorce which he argued was his principal residence. The High Court held that those already resident in the UK will find it harder to shake off an earlier residence. The residence can be adhesive. His job was based in the UK and he had kept his home here. He would be taxed here.

In *Gaines-Cooper v HMRC* [2011] UKSC 47 the individual did not spend longer than HMRC allowed but had not severed ties sufficiently with the UK even though in 1976 he moved to the Seychelles. The Supreme Court found against him by 4 to 1. Even though he said he had followed HMRC guidance in terms of nights spent in the UK as he had not made a totally 'clean break' he would be pursued for UK taxes from 1992 to 2004. He still had a family house in Henley-on-Thames, a UK-based collection of classic Rolls-Royces and made trips to Ascot. The 90-day residence test applied only to taxpayers who had clearly left the UK, and this did not apply in his case.

See also J(vi) below for the new HMRC statutory residence test (guidance at https://www.gov.uk/government/publications/rdr3-statutory-residence-test-srt) which for periods from 2013 now applies in place of that considered in the case law above.

(J)   EIS reinvestment relief and other investment reliefs

Under this scheme, tax on the capital gain may be deferred by reinvesting that gain into shares in certain unquoted trading companies. Also, a measure of relief similar to reinvestment relief can be obtained by investing sums up to the current cap in a venture capital trust. The benefits may be even greater where the reinvestment is made into certain companies or entities, such as an EIS company, where all future gains are tax-free and there is also some income tax relief on the investment. Income tax liability is reduced for certain sums invested each tax year in VCTs. Income from and capital gains on VCT investments are exempt from tax if the shares are held for five years. For the tax year 2011/12 the rate of income tax relief available under EIS rose from 20% to 30% and the amount of investment per company in any one tax year that can attract upfront tax relief doubles in 2012 from £500,000 to £1m. In addition, it is worth noting that there is an option scheme, the Enterprise Management Incentive Scheme, which encourages investment into small companies and gives certain capital gains benefits. Some of these ideas will now be examined in greater depth:

After 6 April 2014, VCTs are prevented from returning share capital to investors where the return of capital is not paid out from the profits of the VCT. Distributions made to investors from profits were unaffected by this change. Where share capital is returned to investors and not sourced from profits, the VCT status is lost and the relief withdrawn. The government announced in 2014 that it would exclude investments in VCTs which were conditionally linked with share buy backs or investments that have been made within six months of disposal of shares in the same VCT. The purpose of these measures was to encourage well-targeted VCT investments which support the high-growth potential of small and medium sized companies. The measures appeared to be aimed at the more structured and lower risk VCT available to taxpayers. The change then went ahead.

Also announced was the intention to launch a wider consultation focusing on other areas of both EIS and VCT products. The proposals confirm that the consultation will focus on low risk structures that benefit from income guarantees via government subsidies and where VCT investments are in the form of convertible loans. These measures continue the theme set by the government to target EIS and VCT products which are structured to minimise risk to taxpayers as opposed to the more entrepreneurial ventures.

HMRC summarises its tax reliefs in this area as follows:

'HM Revenue and Customs (HMRC) offers tax relief to encourage individuals to invest in companies through a number of venture capital schemes.

You can get tax relief when you invest in small UK companies and social enterprises that qualify for venture capital schemes.

The amount and type of tax relief you can claim depends on what venture capital scheme you use to invest in a company and you meet certain conditions.

You can get tax relief through the following venture capital schemes:

Scheme	annual investment limit you can claim relief on	Income Tax relief	minimum qualifying period for share relief	tax payable on dividends
Enterprise Investment Scheme (EIS)	£1 million	30%	3 years	Yes
Seed Enterprise Investment Scheme (SEIS)	£100,000	50%	3 years	Yes
Social Investment Tax Relief (SITR)	£1 million	30%	3 years	Yes
Venture Capital Trusts (VCT)	£200,000	30%	5 years	No

You can invest in a number of companies during a year and those investments might qualify for the schemes, but you can't claim relief for the same investment. You'll get relief by investing in newly issued shares.

As well as shares, there's also the option to invest through a debt instrument for SITR.

You can claim Income Tax relief based on the amount that you invest in a qualifying company. You can also get Capital Gains Tax relief on any profits you make on your investment.'

See https://www.gov.uk/guidance/venture-capital-schemes-tax-relief-for-investors.

(i) Shares and loan notes

Tax can be deferred if the consideration is satisfied by the issue of shares in the purchaser or loan notes issued by the purchaser. In broad terms, the base cost of the seller's shares in the target is transferred to the shares/loan notes issued by the purchaser in exchange for the target's shares. CGT is then payable when these shares are subsequently disposed of or the loan notes are repaid. This is known as a 'roll-over relief'.

The basic relief is contained in TCGA 1992, s 135 and will apply where a purchaser issues shares or debentures to a seller in exchange for shares in or debentures of the target. Provided certain conditions are satisfied, the exchange is not treated as involving the disposal of the target's shares or the acquisition of the new shares in the purchaser, but the new shares in the purchaser are treated as having been acquired at the same time and for the same consideration as the target's shares. Thus no taxable gain or allowable loss will arise on the exchange of shares, nor on any subsequent exchanges as long as the conditions are satisfied. Tax is therefore deferred until there is an actual disposal. The relief operates in the same way where debentures are issued rather than shares, except where the debentures are qualifying corporate bonds (which are considered later in this section). An exchange of shares for qualifying corporate bonds still gives a tax deferral but it operates differently. The CGT roll-over provisions (in relation to shares for debentures) require that shares be exchanged for 'debentures' in the acquiring company. The term 'debentures' is not defined, so one would simply rely upon the normal usage of that term. Hence, advisers have for many years used long form loan notes as against short form loan agreements. It is important not to tamper with certain essential features of a security or debenture, so that, for example, the loan notes should be transferable by the holder from time to time (although it may be possible to impose some restrictions on transferability).

The essential condition for the relief to apply is that the purchaser must hold, before or in consequence of the exchange, more than one-quarter of the ordinary share capital of the target. Alternatively, the relief is also available where the purchaser issues the shares or debentures in exchange for shares as a result of a general offer made to members of the target, provided that the offer is made in the first instance on condition that the purchaser will control the target.

A further condition is that the exchange must be effected for bona fide commercial reasons and must not form part of a scheme for the avoidance of CGT (TCGA 1992, s 137). This condition does not apply to a shareholder holding 5% or less of, or of any class of, shares or debentures in the target. There is a clearance procedure provided by the TCGA 1992, s 138 and either the purchaser or the target may apply to HMRC for clearance.

A debenture will normally be treated as a qualifying corporate bond within the terms of the TCGA 1992, s 117. A qualifying corporate bond is exempt from capital gains tax, so that neither a gain nor a loss can arise on its disposal. On a share for debenture exchange the debentures are not, as would otherwise have been the case, treated as having been acquired at the same time and for the same consideration as the target's shares. Instead, the capital gain made on the sale of the shares is calculated but held over until the debenture is disposed of. The gain then automatically crystallises on disposal even if the seller is not paid the face value of the debenture (this is known as a 'hold-over relief). Consequently, there is a risk in taking a debenture, which constitutes a qualifying corporate bond, of paying more tax than the cash recovered from the purchaser. However, it is possible to structure the debenture so that it does not constitute a qualifying corporate bond (a 'non-QCB'), so that roll-over relief will apply.

One reason for taking a non-QCB to achieve a roll-over are that the treatment of subsequent losses is accommodated in the case of a roll-over. There are a variety of ways to ensure that a loan note is treated as a non-QCB for the purposes of the tax legislation, and the detail must be left to the tax advisers on the deal.

As noted, as a matter of broad principle, the tax benefits of a roll-over are available to sellers to the extent that purchaser shares or loan stock is received. A key concern for the seller will be the strength of the covenant to pay. For this reason, the seller will often demand that the loan note is secured, either on the assets of the issuer or by a bank. For the same reason, loan notes issued by a company which is not the ultimate parent of the group, should, at the very least, be guaranteed by the parent.

The ability of the issuer of the note to set off warranty claims against the payment of interest or the ultimate redemption of the note should also be considered carefully by the sellers.

(ii)   Entrepreneurs' relief

This lifetime £10m of relief per individual reduces the CGT rate on a sale from 20% to 10%. See section 3.2.1 above for more details. There used to be a relief called taper relief and also indexation allowance but both were abolished on 6 April 2008.

(iii)   Gifts to family members

A gift of shares to another member of the family prior to the sale will often be tax effective as it allows the recipient of the gift to use his/her CGT exemption. The gift must be absolute, so that the cash cannot be repaid after the sale. However, where the gift of shares is to a spouse, the cash can be applied for the joint benefit of both spouses. A gift between spouses who are living together is tax-free. The spouse receiving the gift is deemed to acquire the shares at the same cost as the donor. Hence, the recipient of the gift is deemed to make the ultimate chargeable gain when the shares are sold on to the purchaser.

A gift of shares from a shareholder to someone other than a spouse can benefit from similar tax treatment. This is because of a relief in TCGA 1992, s 165, applying on the gift of certain business assets. This relief is available on a gift of shares or securities of a trading company (or the holding company of a trading group), provided that neither the shares or securities are quoted on the London Stock Exchange or, if they are so quoted the trading company or the holding company is the transferor's personal company (a 'personal company' is one in which the seller exercises at least 5% of the voting rights). Companies listed on the Alternative Investment Market (AIM) are unquoted for these purposes.

The broad effect of this relief is that the base cost is passed over to the recipient, although it is important to understand the technical effect of the section before using it as a detailed planning tool. If a seller is thinking of making a gift out of the proceeds of sale to, say, his/her children, it may be more efficient from a tax point of view to make a gift of shares prior to the sale. A gift of shares between spouses is also exempt from inheritance tax. A similar exemption is not available for other gifts. Inheritance tax will not normally pose insurmountable problems, but its impact needs to be considered. At its most basic, such a gift will normally constitute a potentially exempt transfer, so that inheritance tax will only be payable if the donor dies within seven years. Life insurance should be considered to fund the inheritance tax in the event of death within seven years the proceeds of which can be written in trust again to avoid inheritance tax (IHT).

As with any tax planning concept, regard must be had to the commercial considerations. For example, will it be necessary for the recipient to give warranties and will the recipient co-operate on the sale? It may be possible for the donor to take a power of attorney, but care must be taken. The donor could retain bare legal title. The important thing to note is that for the gift to be effective for tax purposes the recipient must become beneficial owner.

(iv) Pre-sale dividend

For so long as income and chargeable gains were taxed at the same rate, there were significant advantages to the seller in taking a pre-sale dividend. To understand the point here it is necessary to run briefly through some of the basic rules of corporation tax. However, since 6 April 2008, CGT has been 28% (now 20% on disposal of shares and 10% for low earners) (10% with entrepreneurs' relief) and income tax 20% or 40% and now 45%. Therefore it will virtually never be advantageous for an individual seller to take a payment as dividends at tax rates rather than at 20% (or 10%) CGT rates. (Residential property CGT rates are up to 28%.)

Historically, until 2008, there was a period where income and CGT rates were the same (and indeed for CGT was 40% and higher rate income tax 40% for a time) but before that period and post-2008 it should be noted that it was (and now also is) common practice to avoid a pre-sale dividend. The anti-avoidance provisions contained in ITA 2007, s 684 (previously ICTA 1988, s 703, and its predecessor ICTA 1970, s 460) might then have applied, the result of which may have been an income tax liability on the seller. These provisions are now important again.

(v) Trusts

Trusts which confer an interest in possession are liable to CGT. If a shareholder would like to make a gift to someone else (other than to his/her spouse), it is worth considering making the gift initially into a trust. A trust can be drafted in flexible terms, even to the extent that the life interest can be revoked at some stage in the future and replaced with other terms. Shareholders who have children should consider setting up a trust for their benefit, particularly if they are still responsible for maintaining those children.

The money in the trust cannot be used by the shareholder personally. However, if made for children, it can be used to pay school fees and provide for general maintenance and benefit. Even in other cases, a shareholder may simply wish to make a gift of some of the cash proceeds on to his/her children (or to someone else). The full legal and tax implications of this proposal must be explored and explained to the client.

(vi) Non-resident sellers – Statutory Residence Test

A seller who is not resident in the UK at the date of disposal is not normally liable to CGT. Clearly there is no further UK tax planning to be done if the seller is already firmly established in another jurisdiction, although he may be liable to tax in that jurisdiction. However, the most radical approach to tax planning for a seller currently resident in the UK is to delay a sale until after the date on which the seller has become non-resident. Since 6 April 2008, so called 'non-doms' who live in the UK have been liable to an annual tax charge (originally £30,000 and now £50,000) or, if they prefer, to have their foreign income taxed in the UK (with some de minimis exclusions and exclusions for children).

In 2014 HM Treasury announced plans to tighten the rules for 'dual contracts', used to exempt from the UK tax the income some earn abroad. It introduced CGT on property for foreign investors who are not resident in Britain, a group that does not include non-doms although they have been affected by the introduction of an annual charge for properties held in offshore companies. Always tax specialist tax advice in these areas from solicitors expert in this field or accountants.

In 2013 the rules on tax residency changed (for the earlier case law see 3.3.1 (I) above). Connections with the UK must be severed as the *Gaines Cooper* and *Grace* cases (see 3.3.1(I) above) show.

HMRC says (at https://www.gov.uk/tax-foreign-income/residence):

> **'UK residence and tax**
>
> Your UK residence status affects whether you need to pay tax in the UK on your foreign income.
>
> Non-residents only pay tax on their UK income – they don't pay UK tax on their foreign income.
>
> Residents normally pay UK tax on all their income, whether it's from the UK or abroad. But there are special rules for UK residents whose permanent home ('domicile') is abroad.
>
> **Work out your residence status**
>
> Whether you're UK resident usually depends on how many days you spend in the UK in the tax year (6 April to 5 April the following year).

You're automatically resident if either:

- you spent 183 or more days in the UK in the tax year
- your only home was in the UK – you must have owned, rented or lived in it for at least 91 days in total – and you spent at least 30 days there in the tax year

You're automatically non-resident if either:

- you spent fewer than 16 days in the UK (or 46 days if you haven't been classed as UK resident for the 3 previous tax years)
- you work abroad full-time (averaging at least 35 hours a week) and spent fewer than 91 days in the UK, of which no more than 30 were spent working

Get help

If your situation's more complicated or you need to confirm your status, you can:

- use HM Revenue and Customs' (HMRC) Tax Residence Indicator (use the link under 'Information you might need')
- read HMRC's guidance on the Statutory Residence Test
- obtain professional tax help

Your residence status when you move

When you move in or out of the UK, the tax year is usually split into 2 – a non-resident part and a resident part. This means you only pay UK tax on foreign income based on the time you were living here. This is called 'split-year treatment'.

You don't need to claim split-year treatment – it's applied automatically.

You won't get it if you live abroad for less than a full tax year before returning to the UK. You also need to meet other conditions – to find out if you qualify, you can:

- use HMRC's Tax Residence Indicator (use the link under 'I already know my residence status')
- read chapter 5 of HMRC's guidance note on the Statutory Residence Test
- contact HMRC

If your situation changes

Your status can change from one tax year to the next. Check your status if your situation changes, for example:

- you spend more or less time in the UK
- you buy or sell a home in the UK
- you change your job
- your family moves in or out of the UK, or you get married, separate or have children

Residence and capital gains

You work out your residence status for capital gains (for example, when you sell shares or a second home) the same way as you do for income.

UK residents have to pay tax on their UK and foreign gains. Non-residents have to pay tax on income, but only pay Capital Gains Tax either:

- on UK residential property
- if they return to the UK

Residence before April 2013

There were different rules for working out your residence status before 6 April 2013.'

Even under the newer rules it would be possible in an appropriate case for a shareholder to have secured non-resident status by the time that the sale occurs. Typically, this will require the shareholder to leave the UK in the tax year prior to the sale and sever ties, sell properties etc. Clearly, this may not be possible for shareholders in key management positions.

Alternatively, if this is not possible, a shareholder may initially take shares or debentures in exchange (thereby rolling-over the gain) and then arrange to be non-resident at the point in time when the shares are sold or the loan notes redeemed. This sort of arrangement does have certain risks attaching to it and it would need to be planned carefully. In particular, it is not likely to work where the shareholder has a settled intention to move abroad when due exchange occurs, because HMRC would not give the roll-over relief tax clearance (see above).

Whatever the potential tax saving, no one should be encouraged to live abroad unless it would suit their lifestyle and their plans for life. In other words, someone who likes warm beer and is not happy unless he is able to watch the football results as they come in on Saturday afternoon may not be happy sitting on a beach in the Virgin Islands or even in Bulgaria with its flat tax rate of 10% for all. The tax tail should never wag the dog.

Find out more

1   The HMRC guidance on the 2013 Statutory Residence Test (105 pages) is at https://www.gov.uk/government/uploads/system/uploads/attachment_data/file/547118/160803_RDR3_August2016_v2_0final_078500.pdf.

2   *Gaines-Cooper* Supreme Court decision see http://www.taxation.co.uk/taxation/Articles/2011/10/20/30821/gaines-cooper-loses-supreme-court-appeal.

(vii) Offshore trusts

Prior to the Finance Act 1991, offshore trusts were widely used as vehicles to own UK shares. Gains on the sale of shares by offshore trusts were not liable to CGT until the capital proceeds were received by UK beneficiaries. In the meantime the gross sale proceeds were available to generate additional income and capital growth. Hence, offshore trusts offered a good tax deferral mechanism.

In March 1991 (and subsequently), the rules were changed radically. Gains in new offshore trusts where the settlor, his spouse and children can benefit are now taxed on the settler in the normal way. Pre-March 1991 trusts fall within the new regime if property is added to them. Otherwise, pre-March 1991 trusts enjoy the original tax treatment, save that there is a surtax on realised gains if they are not repatriated in a given period.

As a result, there is perhaps a tendency to discount offshore structures in tax planning by UK shareholders. In fact, offshore trusts still offer significant tax planning opportunities as there are still a number of circumstances where they can be used. There are a number of key points to note:

- the anti-avoidance rules do not apply to trusts made by settlers who are non-UK domiciled;
- trusts for certain people, including remote relations and non-family members, are outside the rules; and
- since 1991 a range of more complicated offshore trust and company structures has been developed which seek to retain some of the advantages of using offshore trusts.

In 2014 changes were proposed to trusts and inheritance tax making it less attractive to shelter assets in trusts. In addition there is a new tax charge for property held in offshore trusts. These measures were ultimately included in the Finance (No 2) Act 2017. BDO summarised them at https://www.bdo.co.uk/en-gb/insights/tax/private-client/tax-changes-for-non-uk-domiciliaries as follows:

'As a brief summary, the changes due to be brought in are as follows:
- The introduction of the deemed domicile rule for all tax purposes for those who have lived in the UK for 15 of the last 20 tax years
- The ability to rebase foreign sited assets for capital gains tax purposes for those deemed domiciled individuals
- Specific measures for those born in the UK with a UK domicile of origin to treat them as UK domiciled
- The ability to cleanse mixed funds for all non-doms who have previously claimed the remittance basis of assessment
- Certain protections for offshore trusts as well as tainting provisions
- The introduction of 'look through' Inheritance Tax rules where UK residential property is held within a corporate, partnership or trust structure.'

See also the HMRC guidance for non-resident trusts – https://www.gov.uk/guidance/non-resident-trusts. See also 'Non Resident Trusts and Capital Gains Tax' https://www.gov.uk/government/publications/non-resident-trusts-and-capital-gains-tax-hs299-self-assessment-helpsheet/hs299-non-resident-trusts-and-capital-gains-tax-2015.

(viii)   EIS Reinvestment relief

Broadly, a seller may claim relief from CGT where the proceeds of sale are reinvested in shares in a 'qualifying company'. The gain will be deferred until the seller sells the replacement shares, receives value in respect of those shares, or certain charging provisions are triggered. The replacement shares must be ordinary shares (which do not carry preferential rights) in the qualifying company.

Where the conditions are satisfied, the gain may be rolled over into the acquisition of shares in the qualifying company. The consideration received on the disposal of the assets is treated as reduced by the amount of the gain, and the consideration for the acquisition of the replacement shares is treated as being reduced by the same amount. The acquisition of the replacement shares may be made at any time in the period beginning 12 months before and ending three years after the disposal of the asset.

Essentially, the qualifying company must be an unquoted company carrying on a qualifying trade. Once again, shares in a company listed on the AIM are unquoted for these purposes. Non-trading activities, whether in the company or in a subsidiary, may disqualify the company. A trade will be a qualifying trade provided that it does not consist to a substantial degree of, amongst certain other dealings:

- dealing in land, commodities, futures, shares, securities or other financial instruments;
- dealing in goods otherwise than in the course of an ordinary trade of wholesale or retail distribution;
- banking and other financial trades;
- leasing and similar activities;
- legal or accountancy services; or
- providing services to any of the above.

The relief can be lost in a number of circumstances, notably if within three years of acquiring the shares the company ceases to be a qualifying company or the seller becomes non-resident. There are, additionally, a series of anti-avoidance provisions which need to be watched carefully.

A form of reinvestment relief can also be obtained by investing in a venture capital trust. A venture capital trust is rather like an investment trust, save that it invests in unquoted companies. Again, shares on the AIM are unquoted. Venture capital trusts have a number of significant tax advantages. Benefits are available to the extent that shares acquired in each tax year do not exceed set limits in value:

- a form of reinvestment relief from capital gains tax will be available when an individual subscribes for new shares in the venture capital trust. The scheme here is similar to the reinvestment relief scheme, although there are some important differences;
- tax relief is available on the amount subscribed for new shares in the venture capital trust;

- there is an exemption from capital gains tax on disposals of shares in a venture capital trust;
- dividends on shares in a venture capital trust will be exempt from income tax.

The tax reliefs on offer are therefore generous under both headings, but shareholders will need to give careful thought before making an investment. The investment must be right from a commercial point of view, so tax should not be the sole motivating factor.

For the tax year 2011/12 the rate of income tax relief available under EIS rose from 20% to 30% and the amount of investment per company in any one tax year that can attract upfront tax relief doubles in 2012 from £500,000 to £1m. See more at https.//www.gov.uk/guidance/venture-capital-schemes-apply-for-the-enterprise-investment-scheme.

HMRC state in their Guidance at https://www.gov.uk/government/publications/enterprise-investment-scheme-income-tax-relief-hs341-self-assessment-helpsheet/hs341-enterprise-investment-scheme-income-tax-relief-2017:

> 'Subject to what follows, you can get relief at the rate of 30% on the aggregate of the amounts claimed for shares issued to you in tax year 2016 to 2017 (after taking account of any claims to treat shares as issued in the year prior to their actual issue).
>
> However, you can't get relief on more than £1 million and if your tax liability isn't high enough to absorb all the relief, you have to forgo the excess. In either of these cases, you can opt for the relief to be attributed to certain shares, or to be attributed proportionately to all the shares. For example, if you had subscribed £250,000 for shares in each of 4 companies, but you're limited to claiming relief on £500,000, you could opt for relief to be given at 30% on the subscriptions for all the shares in 2 of those companies, or you could opt for relief to be given at 15% on all the shares in the 4 companies. You may want to take professional advice on which course to take.
>
> Also, if you have received value from the company, the amount on which you claim relief must be restricted (the company will have stated the amount on form EIS3).
>
> The notes on forms EIS3 and EIS5 explain situations when your relief might be withdrawn or reduced, and in which you would be obliged to make a report to us.'

3.3.2 Checklist of tax planning opportunities for trustees on the sale of shares

Certain of the possibilities for tax saving mentioned in section 3.3.1 in relation to individuals may also be available to trustees. To provide a point of comparison, the principal tax saving opportunities are summarised under the same headings and in the same order as for an individual seller and are as follows:

(A)   Cash

The rate of tax for trustees will vary according to the circumstances but, like individuals, gains will be taxed as though they were income.

(B)   Shares and loan notes

The same considerations apply as for individuals.

(C)   Pre-sale dividends

Dividends can also be appealing to trustees, although they do need to give careful thought to the trust law implications. For example, converting capital into income may mean that part of the proceeds are diverted to the life tenant, whereas the proceeds of sale would not have been so available.

(D)   EIS Reinvestment relief and other investment reliefs

Unfortunately, reinvestment relief and relief for investing in a venture capital trust are only available to individuals.

3.3.3   Checklist of tax planning opportunities for companies on the sale of shares

Many of the tax planning ideas listed in section 3.3.1 for individuals will apply equally to situations where a company is the seller. The principal tax planning opportunities can be summarised as follows.

(A)   Cash

A company is liable to corporation tax on chargeable gains on the disposal of a capital asset. Corporation tax is set at 19% for the year to 31 March 2018 no matter what its profits (with an exception for oil and gas). There are plans to reduce the 19% in 2020.

A company, unlike an individual, does not have an annual exemption for chargeable gains and the thresholds just mentioned are shared on the basis of a straight apportionment where there is a group of associated companies.

(B)   Shares and loan notes

Similar considerations apply as for individuals.

(C)   Reinvestment relief

Reinvestment relief and venture capital trust relief are not available for companies, although corporate venturing relief is available and is similar to EIS and venture capital trust relief but geared towards companies.

(D)   Pre-sale dividends

A pre-sale dividend is more attractive to a company, because a dividend received by one UK company from another UK company is tax free.

(E)   Tax losses

The rules on the utilisation of losses are complex, particularly in the context of groups, but the basic principles can be stated quite simply. Capital losses can be set against chargeable gains for the same period and any surplus capital losses can be carried forward. Trading losses can be utilised against profits of whatever nature (ie income and chargeable gains) for the current year and, in certain circumstances can be carried back for up to three years before the current period when the business ceases (known as terminal loss relief) and previously this was allowed more generally. Any surplus trading losses can then be carried forward but can only be utilised against income from the same trade.

In addition, trading losses can be surrendered from one company in a group to another. Trading losses made by a fellow group member can be surrendered on a current year basis to reduce the chargeable gain made on the sale of shares. Capital losses cannot be surrendered from one company in a group to another. However, the seller can seek to offset the chargeable gain arising on the disposal against capital losses which have arisen in another group company by transferring the target to the company within the group which has capital losses. TCGA 1992, s 171 allows capital assets to be transferred within a group on a no gain no loss basis, so that there is no tax charge when the asset is transferred to the fellow subsidiary, but the chargeable gain arises when the asset is eventually sold to the purchaser.

This whole area has been significantly affected by legislation introduced in the Finance Act 1993. This is now to be found in TCGA 1992, Sch 7A and imposes a restriction on the set off of pre- entry losses. Effectively, this legislation is designed to stop a company buying in to the group a subsidiary with capital losses and then using those losses in this way to shelter a gain. The legislation is complicated and can extend to cases where tax avoidance was not the original motive behind buying in the subsidiary.

Also, whilst the attraction of this tax planning measure is obvious, its dangers are less so. Careful planning is needed to ensure pre-sale, intra-group transfers of assets do not fall into the many traps for the unwary. First, a liability to stamp duty may arise as the relief contained in the Finance Act 1930, s 42 may not be available because of the restrictions contained in the Finance Act 1967, s 27. Second, a number of problems may arise if the shares are sold at an undervalue. In the first instance, the element of undervalue may be treated as a deemed distribution *(Aveling Barford Ltd v Perion Ltd* [1989] 5 BCC 677) and, if the transferor has no distributable reserves, unlawful under CA 2006, s 830 (a distribution can only be made out of profits available for the purpose). Third, if the transferor is insolvent and subsequently enters into insolvent liquidation within two years of the intra-group transfer, the liquidator may require compensation for the element of undervalue or otherwise the return of the asset (IA 1986, s 238). Fourth, the directors of the transferor company may be in breach of their fiduciary duties.

3.3.4 Tax avoidance and GAAR

No commentary on tax planning would be complete without a review of the series of cases which explain the powers of HMRC to ignore transactions which are motivated for tax avoidance. These points apply equally to sections 3.3 and 3.4.

The subject is often addressed by reference to the case of *Furniss v Dawson* [1984] AC 474, [1984] 1 All ER 530, although it was first fully expounded in *Ramsay v IRC* [1982] AC 300, [1981] 1 All ER 865 and was subsequently clarified in *Craven v White* [1989] AC 398, [1988] 3 All ER 495. It is sufficient for the purposes of this book simply to mention the main points, although the principle does need to be thought through rather more carefully and specialist advice taken in cases where more aggressive tax planning techniques are adopted.

The House of Lords in *Craven v White* said that there is no general principle that the court should strike down any step whatsoever which a taxpayer might take with a view to avoidance of tax. The House of Lords decided that a transaction entered into with the sole purpose of mitigating tax could be ignored and regarded as part of a composite transaction if four basic conditions were satisfied. Lord Oliver, who gave the leading judgment, summed up the position as follows:

'As the law currently stands, the essentials emerging from *Furniss v Dawson* appear to me to be four:

(1) that the series of transactions was, at the time when the intermediate transaction was entered into, pre-ordained in order to produce a given result;

(2) that the transaction had no other purpose than tax mitigation;

(3) that there was at that time no practical likelihood that the pre-planned events would not take place in the order ordained, so that the intermediate transaction was not even contemplated practically as having an independent life; and

(4) that the pre-ordained events did in fact take place.

The court can be justified in linking the beginning with the end so as to make a single composite whole to which the fiscal results of the single composite whole are to be applied.'

Even if the court finds that there is a composite transaction, HMRC has to go a stage further. *Craven v White* remains the definitive source of what may constitute a pre-ordained series of transactions. However, developments in recent years have chipped away still further at the Revenue's position. A significant case was that of *Countess Fitzwilliam v IRC* [1993] 3 All ER 184, [1993] 1 WLR 1189. In this case the taxpayers were trying to rely on certain exemptions from capital transfer tax (now inheritance tax) by interposing a series of steps. Lord Keith summed up the second hurdle that the Inland Revenue (now HMRC) had to surmount as follows:

'... the fact of preordainment ... is not sufficient in itself ... to negate the application of an exemption from liability to tax which the series of transactions is intended to create, unless the series is capable of being construed in a manner inconsistent with the application of the exemption.'

Hence, in addition to showing a pre-ordained series of transactions, the Revenue must construe that series of transactions to produce the taxing results which they are arguing for. Significantly, the House of Lords was not prepared to ignore totally steps in the transaction which had enduring effect. Furthermore, in the recent case of *MacNiven (HMIT) v Westmoreland Investments Ltd* [2001] UKHL 6, Lord Hoffmann stated that *Ramsay* did not establish any new legal principle and the paramount issue is always one of giving effect to the statutory language and, even if a statutory expression refers to a business or economic concept, one cannot disregard a transaction which comes within the statutory language, construed in the correct commercial sense, simply on the ground it was entered into solely for tax purposes.

In *PA Holdings v Revenue and Customs Commissioners* [2010] STC 2343 the courts looked at whether the payment of dividends to employees using a tax avoidance structure should be taxed as dividends or employment income and *Ramsey* was applied. The sums were not taxed as employment income, but under ICTA 1988, s 20(2) for the purposes of national insurance, NI as due. The issue was whether the payment was earnings under the Income Tax (Earnings and Pensions) Act 2003. The decision may be applied.

In *Peter Schofield v Revenue and Customs Commissioners* [2010] UKFTT 196 (TC) the parties in the case had formed a complex structure to create an artificial loss on four interlinked transactions which on their own did indeed show a capital loss. The court following *Scottish Provident Institution v Revenue and Customs Commissioners* [2005] STC 15 held that *Ramsey* applied.

Notably, whilst it remains a difficult and important area, the Revenue have not met great success recently in cases based upon *Furniss v Dawson*.

In 2013 the General Anti-Abuse Rule (GAAR) came into force contained in Part 5 and Schedule 43 to Finance Act 2013. It attempts to counter 'abusive' tax arrangements. Other forms of potentially illegal evasion remain also subject to HMRC investigation although often the borderline between illegal evasion and lawful avoidance is hard to draw.

On 30 September 2017 the Criminal Finances Act 2017 came into force. It brought in the following offences:

- failure to prevent the facilitation of tax evasion; and
- failure to prevent the facilitation of foreign tax evasion.

HMRC provide guidance on the Act at https://www.gov.uk/government/uploads/system/uploads/attachment_data/file/642714/Tackling-tax-evasion-corporate-offences.pdf.

See *Corporate Briefing* journal October 2017 issue.

Find out more

There is also a general duty on promoters of lawful tax avoidance schemes to notify them to HMRC. Information on this and the relevant HMRC forms are available at: https://www.gov.uk/guidance/forms-to-disclose-tax-avoidance-schemes.

3.4 TAX PLANNING ON THE SALE OF ASSETS

A sale of assets is very different from a tax point of view as compared with a share sale. A share sale normally involves the sale of one asset, ie the shares. A sale of assets involves the sale of each asset of the business, so it is necessary to calculate the tax charge which will arise on each.

The sale of capital assets (eg goodwill, land and buildings and certain intellectual property rights) may create a chargeable gain whereas any profit on the sale of stock will be brought into account as income. Equally, the sale of assets which have qualified for capital allowances will also constitute income for tax purposes, to the extent that the price exceeds their tax written down value.

The overall price must be apportioned between these assets and this apportionment will often be tax driven. Apportionment issues are dealt within section 13.2.4(B), and the remainder of this chapter will concentrate on tax planning to mitigate the charge to tax. Trustees will rarely hold assets, so discussion is limited to individuals and companies.

3.4.1 Checklist of tax planning opportunities for individuals on the sale of assets

As before, there follows a brief summary of tax saving opportunities available to individuals, on the sale of assets. This needs to be read in conjunction with section 3.3.1.

(A) Cash

The comments referred to in section 3.3.1(A), apply equally, although the income tax considerations on the sale of stock and plant, and on the termination of the business, will need to be considered. Again, the availability of losses must be assessed.

(B)   Shares and loan notes

The section on shares and loan notes in section 3.3.1(B), concentrated on TCGA 1992, s 135. This particular section has no direct application in the case of an asset sale, because it only applies on a share for share or debenture exchange. However, there are two possible avenues of relief available to the seller of assets if he is to take shares and/or debentures from the purchaser.

First, TCGA 1992, s 162 provides a roll-over relief on the transfer of a business. As always, the terms of this section need to be reviewed very carefully. In essence, a roll-over is given where a business is transferred as a going concern, together with the whole of the assets of the business, wholly or partly in exchange for shares. The first point to note is that the roll-over relief is only available to the extent that shares are issued (although this could include preference shares). Cash or loan notes issued by the purchaser will cause a partial chargeable gain to arise. The second point to note is that it is essential that all of the assets of the business are transferred.

It may be that the consideration is to include loan notes. In this case, as a second avenue, it may be possible to incorporate the business relying on the relief in TCGA 1992, s 162 and then to procure an exchange of shares for shares and/or loan notes subsequently, under TCGA 1992, s 135.

There is no clearance mechanism attaching to the TCGA 1992, s 162, but the same comments made in section 3.3.1 apply with regard to clearance for the purposes of the TCGA 1992, s 135.

(C)   Entrepreneurs' relief

The comments in section 3.3.1(C) apply equally. There is a lifetime allowance of £10m per person. For gains of up to £10m CGT is charged at 10%. The usual rate is 20% except for lower rate tax payers making small gains. Even 20% is lower than 45% top tax rate for income tax purposes although for many years CGT and top rate of income tax were both charged at 40% and there was no advantage in taking profits as capital gains rather than income. Now the difference is marked, and with a 10% CGT rate for the first £10m of gains, this relief is very useful indeed.

(D)   Pensions

Once again, it is worth reviewing the pension arrangements. This should be done well in advance of the sale if a tax deduction is to be secured against the profits of the original business. Alternatively, it may be that the seller will continue to work for the business, under the control of the purchaser, in which case future remuneration and pension planning can form part of the sale negotiations.

(E)   Dividends, gifts and trusts

Dividends, gifts and trusts do not sit happily with the sale of assets.

(F)   Offshore arrangements

Moving abroad may be a possibility, although a sale of assets tends to imply that a small business is involved, which may therefore rely upon the presence of the seller to operate it.

Transferring shares to an offshore trust holding structure would really need to be done in conjunction with a prior incorporation.

(G)   EIS reinvestment relief

Reinvestment relief, and the opportunity for tax deferral on investing in a venture capital trust, is available on the disposal of any assets.

(H)   Roll-over relief

The seller may wish to stay in business, in which case roll-over relief offers a valuable tax deferral.

Although substantial changes were made to CGT in 2008, including abolition of earlier indexation and also retirement relief, business asset roll-over relief continues to be available. Roll-over relief enables the CGT payable on the gain on a chargeable asset to be deferred until a point in the future.

There are two concepts which need to be addressed in more detail. First, the use of losses and, second, roll-over relief.

(i)   The use of losses

An individual may have capital losses or trading losses. Capital losses can be used to relieve the chargeable gain arising on the sale of capital assets and trading losses can be used to relieve any charge to income tax, such as on the sale of stock, or on plant and equipment sold in excess of its written down value. In addition, there are some provisions in the Finance Act 1991, s 72 which allow a measure of relief for trading losses against capital gains.

(ii)   Roll-over relief

Where the consideration received on the disposal of chargeable assets used in a trade is applied in the acquisition of other chargeable assets to be used in the same or another trade, the disposal proceeds are deemed to produce neither a gain nor a loss and the acquisition cost of the new assets is treated as reduced by the amount of the gain which would have been chargeable on disposal of the old assets (TCGA 1992, s 152).

The old and new assets must be within certain classes, although it is not necessary that assets in one class be replaced by other assets in the same class. The classes of qualifying assets include any building or land occupied and used for the trade, fixed plant and machinery and goodwill (TCGA 1992, s 155). The acquisition of the new assets must take place, or an unconditional contract for the acquisition entered into, within the period beginning one year before and ending three years after the disposal of the old assets.

There are also some important qualifications to roll-over relief, which distinguish it from reinvestment relief. In particular, there are restrictions on the relief where only part of the consideration from the sale of the old assets is applied in acquiring new assets.

3.4.2   Checklist of tax planning opportunities for companies on the sale of assets

The principal tax planning opportunities on the sale of assets can be summarised as follows:

(A)   Cash

The same comments made in section 3.3.1 (A) apply.

(B)   Shares and loan notes

As in the case of individuals, roll-over relief in relation to shares and loan notes can have no application on the sale of assets. Nonetheless, there are one or two possibilities which may give the same effect. For example, if the business to be sold is one business forming part of a group, then it may be possible to hive-out the assets which are to be retained into another company within the group and then to organise a share sale of the company which will then simply hold the target assets. In this case, it will be essential to use market value, not only for the reasons stated in section 3.3.1(B), but also because of the rules against financial assistance. Surplus value can then be distributed back out again, distributable reserves permitting, as distributions are not restricted by the prohibition on the giving of financial assistance rules.

Equally, it is possible to hive-down the target assets into a new company and then sell the shares in that company. This does bear some risks, which are considered in section 3.4.3 below.

(C)   Pre-sale dividends

Pre-sale dividends have no place in relation to a sale of assets, although they can be used in conjunction with some of the ideas referred to in section 3.4.3 below.

(D)   Tax losses

Once again, the availability of tax losses must be considered.

(E)   Roll-over relief

This is equally available to companies and, where a group is involved, the investment may be in another group company.

3.4.3   Hive-downs

The concept of a 'hive-down' needs further explanation. This involves the sale by the seller of the business, normally to a subsidiary but perhaps to an associated company.

The transfer of capital assets from the seller to another member of the group is treated, for tax purposes, as being for a consideration such that the seller makes neither a gain nor a loss (TCGA 1992, s 171). This will not be the case if an associated company is used instead of a group company. In such a case the transaction is deemed to take place at market value and it will be treated for tax purposes in the same way as a straight assets sale.

Here we shall assume that the new company is a subsidiary. TCGA 1992, s 171 clearly offers useful relief, but there is a sting in the tail. The subsidiary is deemed for capital gains tax purposes to have acquired the assets for the same consideration as the seller company, so that no charge arises when the asset is transferred within the group. However, to stop this relief being used for tax avoidance purposes, a charge to capital gains tax will arise if the acquiring company (ie the subsidiary) leaves the seller's group within a period of six years (TCGA 1992, s 179). In these circumstances, the acquiring company is treated as if, immediately following the transfer within the group, it had sold and immediately acquired the asset at market value. The acquiring company will therefore be liable to pay capital gains tax to the extent that the market value exceeds the inherited base cost.

Each asset must be valued separately. Just because the new company is subsequently sold, say for £1, it does not mean that the assets hived-down had no value. The value of the company may have been depressed by liabilities assumed (eg bank borrowings) and the assets themselves may be relatively valuable. A hive-down should be approached with caution where there is a possibility of this charge arising: one asset to watch out for is goodwill which may well have a value for tax purposes in spite of the fact that it has not been valued by the parties.

A further relief is contained in CTA 2010, Pt 22 (previously ICTA 1988, s 343). This provides that where one company ceases to carry on a trade and another company begins to carry it on, unrelieved trading losses may be taken over by the successor company and deducted from taxable income of the same trade. This is subject to the proviso that on, or at any time within two years after the transfer of the trade, not less than a three-quarter's interest in the trade belongs beneficially to the same persons as it did at some time within the year preceding the transfer and, during that period, the trade is carried on by a company assessable to UK tax. The case of *Leekes Ltd v HMRC* (TC4298) considered these provisions.

Strictly speaking, all that is necessary is for the seller to do the hive-down and to hang on to the subsidiary for a few days whilst it carries on the trade as successor to the seller. In *Barkers of Malton Limited v HMRC* [2008] UKSPC 689 90 minutes was not sufficient and it did not help that the minutes recorded the brevity. It is certainly not necessary for the seller to retain a three-quarter's interest in the subsidiary for two years. However, there are two major stumbling blocks in the application of the CTA 2010, Pt 22 (previously ICTA 1988, s 343), as follows:

- the value of trading losses assumed by the subsidiary is restricted if and to the extent that there are net liabilities left behind in the seller following the transfer of the business (CTA 2010, Pt 22, previously ICTA 1988, s 343(4));
- relief under CTA 20010, Pt 22 (previously s 343) is not available if the hive-down takes place after the seller has agreed to sell the subsidiary. This is because at that stage the seller has lost beneficial ownership in the subsidiary, so the first stage of the condition (three-quarter's interest) is not satisfied. In addition, the subsidiary is required to have commenced the trade whilst it is still beneficially owned by the seller. It is necessary to show that this is factually the case to be sure that the losses are transferred. Hence the subsidiary must be put into the position of being able to trade in its own right and evidence should be preserved for HMRC to prove that it did actually trade in its own right up to the period of its sale.

The losses may still be in jeopardy for the future, even if HMRC accept that they are inherited under Part 22 (previously s 343). First, the losses are only available to set against income of the same trade so that, if the old trade actually ceases, it is not possible to set the losses against the income of a new trade. There are, however, special rules which do help where a part of a trade is transferred. There are a number of old cases dealing with whether a trade has ceased; see generally *Gordon and Blair Ltd v IRC* [1962] 40 TC 358 and, for a case on s 343, *Falmer Jeans Ltd v Rodin* [1990] STC 270.

Second, there are anti-avoidance provisions which deny the use of brought forward trading losses where there is a change of ownership and a change in the nature or conduct of the trade within a three-year period (CTA 2010, s 673, previously ICTA 1988, s 768).

Part 22 additionally provides that the successor will take over the seller's capital allowances position, so that the successor merely claims allowances on the same written down values as the seller had on cessation of its trade.

3.5 METHODS OF SALE

The target or its business would normally be sold by auction or through negotiation with a specific purchaser. Over the last few years it has become commonplace for businesses of substance to be sold by way of auction since the competitive nature of the sales process gives sellers confidence in the price they receive from the sale, and the terms of the sale represent the best deal available in the market.

3.5.1 Sale by auction

In favourable seller market conditions sale by auction is a popular method of sale as it is perceived to maximise the price of the target, and the terms on which the target is sold, by stimulating competition between a number of prospective purchasers. It also enables sellers to control the sales process much more effectively than a sale by private treaty. However, it is an expensive process for the seller and is inappropriate in the author's view in the case of targets with few successful competitors, under-performing targets or targets with serious business issues.

The key feature of the auction process is the delivery to potential purchasers of identical pre-packaged due diligence material and contractual documentation, and the requirement that all bids are submitted on the basis of this information and on the same underlying principles, for example on the assumption that they are acquiring the target 'debt and cash free'. A sale by auction usually involves the production of an information memorandum (alternatively referred to as a sales memorandum), usually by the seller's lead adviser, from information supplied to it by the seller, the preparation of a data room where all material information relating to the target and its business is made available to interested parties and the preparation of a formal sale agreement. Issues relating to the preparation of the information memorandum, the approach to prospective purchasers and the preparation of a data room are covered in Chapter 4.

A typical auction process will involve the following sequence of events:

- *Stage 1*
  — Advertisement of auction in financial and trade press and/or dispatch of auction details to selected potential purchasers.
  — Receipt of notices of interest to participate in sale procedure, including identity of bidder and demonstration of credible interest.
  — Notices of admission or rejection to parties who have filed notices of interest.
  — Receipt of confidentiality agreement duly executed on behalf of the admitted interested parties.
  — Transmission of information memorandum to admitted interested parties having returned the executed confidentiality agreement.
  — Receipt of indicative offers by stated deadline.
  — Notice to interested parties having made an indicative offer whether or not they are selected for further participation in the sale process.
- *Stage 2*
  — Access to data room.
  — Management presentations.
  — Site visits (if appropriate).
  — Receipt or firm offers by selected parties.

- *Stage 3*
    - — Selection of buyer.
    - — Conclusion of acquisition agreement.
    - — Fulfilment of remaining conditions precedent, if any and completion.

3.5.2 Sale by private treaty

In most sales, however, having marketed the business widely the seller will negotiate with only one purchaser. The negotiation process is discussed in Chapter 5.

3.6 TIMING OF SALE

Where the sale process is initiated by the seller, the timing of the sale is an important consideration. The sale can be timed to improve the target's attractiveness. For example, the sale of the target should take place sufficiently long after an acquisition or material capital investment to ensure sales/costs reflect the benefit of the acquisition/investment.

The sale should also be timed to be most convenient and beneficial to the seller. For example, an individual seller seeking non-resident status prior to the sale will want it delayed until after the year of assessment in which he became non-resident.

It is common for the seller's lead adviser to review the state of the market, identify potential bidders and determine other factors which will influence the timing of the sales process. The outline timetable will then be agreed with the seller and the project team.

Chapter 4

Marketing

4.1 GENERAL

When marketing the target to a number of prospective purchasers, the seller will need to provide a certain amount of information regarding the target and its business. The extent and the timing of that information disclosure will depend upon the method of sale and the relative negotiating position of the seller and the prospective purchasers. Whichever method of sale is adopted, before disclosing any information containing confidential business information, the seller should require that prospective purchasers sign a confidentiality undertaking to protect the seller from unauthorised use of the information.

The timing and extent of the information disclosure in individually negotiated sales will vary considerably depending upon the particular circumstances. For example, where sale discussions are initiated by the purchaser, the provision of information will usually follow requests from the purchaser.

In more structured sales, the information will be given in accordance with a predetermined timetable and the extent of the information can be as open or as limited as the seller may require and can be drip fed throughout the process so that the more sensitive information is held back until much later in the process.

Although confidentiality undertakings offer reasonable protection to a seller, breaches are sometimes difficult to police and losses stemming from breaches often prove difficult to quantify. In view of this, control of the information is very important. A seller with a serious concern regarding the use of confidential information by a prospective purchaser should, in theory, never let the confidential information pass to the purchaser until an unconditional exchange of contracts. In practice, however, to achieve the best price for the target it may prove necessary for the seller to impart some, but not all, of the confidential information prior to exchange of contracts. For example, if the seller's concern is the disclosure of his customer list, he may have to disclose a sample of customers prior to exchange, after which full disclosure would be made.

4.2   PREPARATION OF THE INFORMATION MEMORANDUM

When a sale is promoted on an auction basis, to ensure equality of information between competing prospective purchasers, an information memorandum describing the target and its business will be prepared and distributed to the prospective purchasers. As well as being the means of providing information, the information memorandum is usually the principal selling document and, as such, it should identify in a clear and concise manner the characteristics of the business which make it an attractive acquisition. Both the strengths and the weaknesses of the business need to be identified; the strengths used to emphasise the attractiveness of the business and the weaknesses to be presented positively as opportunities, as areas where a buyer can add value.

Although there are no hard and fast rules about the content of the information memorandum, typically it would comprise an executive summary of the market in which the target operates and a description of the target's position and prospects in that market. It would also contain detailed information on the target's:

- history;
- product/services;
- market sectors in which it operates;
- customers;
- suppliers;
- management;
- organisation and employees;
- IT systems;
- financial record;
- current trading; and
- prospects.

The information memorandum would also include, or be accompanied with a note containing, a summary of the sales process itself, including the expected timetable and required format of final bids. This format will be designed to enable competing bids to be compared on a consistent basis.

Notwithstanding that many recipients of a target's information memorandum will be competitors of the target and, as such, knowledgeable about it and the market in which the target operates, the information memorandum may also be read by people who know little about the target and its market, and therefore excessive jargon/ technical details should be avoided.

Utmost care should be taken in the preparation and distribution of the information memorandum for a number of reasons, including:

- purchasers will form their initial views based on this document, in particular with regard to price. Therefore, any misunderstandings as to what the information meant may give the purchaser scope to renegotiate the price at a later stage;
- the purchaser may seek to obtain a warranty in the sale agreement on the accuracy of statements of fact or forecasts in it. This is often successfully resisted by a seller on the basis that the purpose of the information memorandum is to assist a prospective purchaser to decide whether it wishes to proceed with a further investigation of the target. However, such a warranty is occasionally forced through in instances where the prospective purchaser has sufficient leverage in the negotiations;
- any false or misleading statements may, notwithstanding the exclusion of liability normally sought by sellers in the sale agreement, constitute misrepresentation and a criminal offence under the EU Market Abuse Regulation (Regulation 596/2014) ('MAR') which replaced FSMA 2000, s 118; MAR contains duties to report suspicious transactions and other matters (see section 4.5);
- there is potential liability under common law for negligent mistake (*Caparo Industries plc v Dickman* [1989] QB 653, [1989] 1 All ER 798); and
- the information memorandum may constitute a 'financial promotion' under FSMA 2000 and, accordingly, will need to be issued or authorised by 'an authorised person' (see section 4.5); and
- to ensure that it does not create any binding obligations on the seller to sell to the highest bidder or on any specific terms.

Accordingly, the financial information contained in the information memorandum should be reconciled with the target's audited accounts and latest management accounts and otherwise the information should be verified prior to its release. In practice, although care is taken to ensure the information contained in the information memorandum is accurate, formal verification rarely takes place. As a consequence it is not unusual to find that incorrect information in the information memorandum not only diminishes the seller's leverage in the subsequent price renegotiation but also tends to place the prospective purchaser on notice and as a result greater or more in-depth due diligence results.

4.3 APPROACH TO PROSPECTIVE PURCHASERS

The next step is to consider the types of buyers to be targeted and the sources from which these types of buyers may be identified. Direct competitors are easily identifiable and are usually well known to the seller. However, direct competitors will often aim to integrate the target within their existing operation such that it loses its identity. For this reason, some sellers may prefer the buyer to be a customer or a company operating within the same market, but not in direct competition.

The range of buyers has increased enormously in recent times with foreign, and in particular US and European, companies having become more active in acquiring UK private companies and with the emergence of financial institutions as direct purchasers. This makes the task of identifying prospective purchasers much more difficult. The advent of management buy-ins has also added to the complexity of finding a buyer.

In the absence of a readily identifiable buyer from trade contacts, an inexperienced seller is likely to rely on the support of the lead adviser to identify prospective purchasers. As well as searching his own database, the lead adviser will source potential purchasers from trade contacts and business associates of the seller, industry surveys and other industry research, trade directories, other databases and professionals and from advertisements in the trade and financial press.

In finding a buyer a seller must balance his efforts to maximise the price of the target by stimulating competition between a number of buyers with the need to preserve confidentiality. Potentially, the more buyers, the more people that know of the intended disposal and the greater the risk.

4.4   CONFIDENTIALITY

There are a number of matters a seller will typically want to keep confidential, some only during the period leading up to the sale and some at all times, for example:

- the fact that the target is being marketed for sale;
- details of the negotiations;
- details of the agreed deal terms; and
- the target's confidential business information.

Knowledge that the target is up for sale can have an unsettling effect on customers and employees of, and suppliers to, the business. Where more than one party is bidding, leakage of the details of the negotiation with one party may erode the seller's leveraged position in negotiation with the other parties. Whilst publicising the deal terms may only have an embarrassment consequence for the seller, use of confidential business information in competition with the target could have life threatening consequences. To a certain extent the seller can protect himself against breaches of such confidences by taking simple precautions such as conducting the sale through an agent, requiring all information requests to be made via the agent and through the timing and extent of disclosure. These precautions are, however, unlikely to provide absolute protection on their own, especially when some of the parties may be more interested in finding out information about the target business than having a serious intent to buy.

Although there is no statutory framework governing ownership or other rights in confidential information, the principle of 'confidentiality' is well enshrined in common law. However, due to the uncertainties of common law and the need to seek quick enforcement of the seller's rights of confidentiality, it has become common for sellers to protect themselves in contract rather than rely on the common law.

Confidentiality and related undertakings are restrictive in nature and will be construed strictly against the discloser. They should be very carefully worded as every case will be considered on its merits by the courts. The strength of the parties' respective positions will rest on the facts. To prove facts, evidence will be needed based on the discloser's written records and any other reasonable evidence. A signed confidentiality letter will be evidence that the information was imparted in circumstances importing an obligation of confidence. A centralised record system and appropriate evidential 'paper chains' should be established to ensure that the disclosure can demonstrate exactly what information was disclosed, when and to whom. Any confidential information supplied to the recipient should be recorded with dates and times. Letters should always set out the enclosures or they should be separately documented, and the recipient should be asked to acknowledge receipt of all written confidential information.

If they were not required to do so at the outset of negotiations, before any information is made available time wasters need to be managed out of the process and serious buyers should be required to enter into a confidentiality undertaking to protect the seller from unauthorised use of the information and to prevent prospective purchasers from making a public announcement to undermine the seller's negotiating position.

Even where a confidentiality agreement is signed before any disclosure, the discloser must consider whether it is in a position to disclose information. The discloser should check that it is not party to any prior agreements with third parties under which it has undertaken not to disclose the information it now proposes to provide to the recipient. In *Vestergaard Frandsen v Bestnet Europe* [2011] EWCA Civ 424 the Court of Appeal held that breach of confidence does require knowledge of the act. The Court of Appeal judgment was appealed without success to the Supreme Court ([2013] UKSC 31) which held that a party who is the subject of an admitted duty or obligation of confidence must have actual or objective knowledge that the acts complained of constitute a breach of that duty or obligation. An action for breach of confidence is based ultimately on conscience. In order for the conscience of the recipient to be affected, she must have information which she has agreed, or knows, is confidential, or she must be party to some action which she knows involves the misuse of confidential information. The law should not discourage former employees from benefitting society and advancing themselves by imposing unfair potential difficulties on their honest attempts to compete with their former employers. However many restrictive covenants and confidentiality obligations in employment contracts are upheld so ex-employees should always act with caution.

Prior agreements may include technology or similar licensing agreements, joint ventures, distribution agreements or long-term customer supply contracts. To avoid inadvertent disclosure, all confidentiality undertakings given by the target should be centrally recorded and monitored. There may also be legal restrictions on disclosure of information, such as personal data held on computer or information in the financial services or banking sectors.

A precedent confidentiality undertaking is set out in Part VI as Precedent E. When using this or any other precedent it is important to remember that for it to be enforceable against the recipient of the information, the recipient must be a contracting party, so that an agreement with one group company will not cover information supplied to another group company. Accordingly, in group situations, either all group companies should be made a party to the agreement or the ultimate holding company is made the party and undertakes to 'procure' that all group companies comply with the obligations in it.

As well as a clear definition of what constitutes confidential information, the key features of the precedent confidentiality undertaking are an acknowledgement by the purchaser that:

- information is being given to it on a confidential basis and that, unless the transaction proceeds to completion, none of the confidential information will be disclosed to other parties or used by the purchaser;
- it will only use the confidential information for the purpose of assessing the acquisition of the target;
- no disclosure of the negotiations shall be made;
- if the transaction aborts, all documents and other written information of a confidential nature given to the purchaser shall be returned and any copies of such documents destroyed; and
- the seller shall be entitled to injunctive relief for any breach of confidentiality.

Some sellers will require a further level of protection by including an undertaking not to solicit employees of the business and, where the seller is a listed company, an undertaking not to acquire any of its shares whilst the purchaser has the benefit of this inside information.

The undertaking also contains permitted exceptions to allow disclosure as required by law/regulatory authorities and disclosure of information which comes into the public domain, was held before negotiations began or is acquired after negotiations cease.

If a purchaser were to use the confidential information for purposes other than evaluating the target, it is likely that the seller would want to pursue injunctive relief to prevent the use rather than to rely on damages. For this reason, the precedent confidentiality undertaking contains an acknowledgement by the purchaser that the seller shall be entitled to injunctive relief.

These undertakings may need to remain in place not only during the term of the agreement or during the negotiations, but also for a fixed period after the

56

agreement terminates or the negotiations cease. In such circumstances, consider carefully what duration (and geographic area) would be appropriate to ensure that such undertakings are not held to be an unreasonable restraint of trade at common law or otherwise to infringe relevant competition laws.

If the agreement is signed after confidential information has been disclosed, the danger is that even if the agreement expressly covers such information, it may still be unenforceable with regard to that information, on the grounds that only past consideration has been given. This problem can easily be overcome by drafting the agreement to provide for additional consideration, which can be nominal but must be valuable, say £1. Alternatively, the agreement can be executed as a deed.

4.4.1   General Data Protection Regualtion and Data Protection Act

If any of the information is 'personal data' under the General Data Protection Regulation in force from May 2018 (which replaced the Data Protection Act 1998) and needs to be read with the UK Data Protection Bill/Act due to come into force in 2018 then it should not be used other than in accordance with that legislation. Information such as employee home addresses, wages and sickness records should be disclosed only under conditions of confidence and even then the legislation may be breached if the individuals have not given consent such as a general data protection consent to future processing when they joined the company. Wherever possible anonymised and sample employment contracts and details should be supplied with the aim of ensuring that the data is not identifiable as relating to one individual. In 2018 penalties for breach of the legislation rose to up to 4% of worldwide group turnover (breach of which is a crime already under English law). Under the previous Act fines were up to a potential £500,000 although they are very unlikely to be imposed in the context of disclosures on business sales where parties have signed confidentiality undertakings and the normal precautions are taken. The ICO has given the following guidance in relation to employment practices and mergers.

In paragraphs 2.12. The Employment Practices Code provides:

'2.12 Merger, acquisition, and business re-organisation

Business mergers and acquisitions will generally involve the disclosure of information about workers. This may take place during evaluation of assets and liabilities prior to the final merger or acquisition decision. Once a decision has been made disclosure is also likely to take place either in the run-up to or at the time of the actual merger or acquisition. A similar situation arises in business re-organisations that involve the transfer of workers' employment from one legal entity to another. This sub-section of the Code will be relevant to such situations.

2.12.1 Ensure, wherever practicable, that information handed over to another organisation in connection with a prospective acquisition, merger or business re-organisation is anonymised.

Key points and possible actions

- Ensure that in any merger or acquisition situation, those responsible for negotiation are aware of the Code, including its provisions on sensitive data.
- Assess any request for personal information from the other organisation. If at all possible, limit the information given to anonymised details.

2.12.2 Only hand over personal information prior to a final merger or acquisition decision after securing assurances that it will be used solely for the evaluation of assets and liabilities, it will be treated in confidence and will not be disclosed to other parties, and it will be destroyed or returned after use.

Key points and possible actions

- Remind those negotiating that they must receive strict assurances about how personal information will be used and what will happen to it should discussions end.
- Consider setting up a "data room" with accompanying rules of access.

2.12.3 Unless it is impractical to do so, tell workers if their employment records are to be disclosed to another organisation before an acquisition, merger or re-organisation takes place. If the acquisition, merger or re-organisation proceeds make sure workers are aware of the extent to which their records are to be transferred to the new employer.

Key points and possible actions

- In some circumstances "insider trading" or similar restrictions will apply. An example is where providing an explanation to workers would alert them to the possibility of a takeover of which they would otherwise be unaware and could thereby affect the price of a company's shares. The obligation to provide an explanation to workers is lifted in such circumstances.

2.12.4 Where a merger, acquisition or re-organisation involves a transfer of information about a worker to a country outside the European Economic Area (EEA) ensure that there is a proper basis for making the transfer.

Key points and possible actions

- Review the Information Commissioner's guidance at https://ico.org.uk/ if you intend to pass workers' information outside the EEA.
- Check that there is a legal basis for the transfer that you intend to make.

2.12.5 New employers should ensure that the records they hold as a result of a merger, acquisition or re-organisation do not include excessive information, and are accurate and relevant.

Key points and possible actions

- Remember that a new employer's use of workers' information acquired as the result of a merger, acquisition or re-organisation is constrained by the expectations the workers will have from their former employer's use of information.
- When taking over an organisation assess what personal information you now hold as outlined in 0.3 and 0.4 (see page 12 [of the code of practice]).'

The Employment Practices Code supplementary guidance provides:

'2.12 Merger, acquisition and re-organisation

2.12.1 Wherever practicable, information from which individual workers cannot be identified should be used, so details such as names and individual job titles should be omitted. This might be possible where, for example, a company merely wants to know how many workers of a particular type are employed and their average rates of pay. In other cases a company might require detailed information about particular workers in order to appraise a company's human resources assets properly. This might be the case where the expertise or reputation of individual workers has a significant bearing on the value of the company. Similarly where a company has a significant liability, perhaps as the result of a worker's outstanding legal claim, it may have to disclose information identifying the worker with details of the company's liability.

In some cases even the removal of names from the information will not prevent identification, for example where without a name it is still obvious that the information relates to a particular senior manager. Removal of names may nevertheless help protect privacy, even if identification is still possible. Remember that handing over sickness records will entail the processing of sensitive personal data (see page 72 [of the supplementary guidance]).

2.12.2 It is important to gain formal assurances about how the information will be used. Information should be returned or destroyed by the shredding of paper or the expunging of electronic files, should the merger or acquisition not go ahead. The provision of information is sometimes achieved by the use of a "data room" in which information about the business is made available to prospective purchasers. Strict conditions must be accepted by those granted access to the "data room".

2.12.3 Businesses may not always expect to be involved in mergers acquisitions, or reorganisations and may not therefore have told their workers, at the time they were recruited, what would happen to their personal information in such an event. Reasons of commercial confidentiality and legal duties relating to matters such as "insider trading" may make it difficult to be explicit at the time the merger or acquisition is being considered. In some circumstances the corporate finance exemption in the Act may be relevant and may relieve companies of the obligation to inform workers of the disclosure of their information. This could occur, for example, where providing an explanation to workers could affect the price of a company's shares or other financial instruments.

One business may also be under a legal obligation to disclose to another. Where there is a legal obligation to disclose, there is an exemption from some of the provisions of the Act. The employer is relieved of the obligation to inform workers of the disclosure if this would be inconsistent with the disclosure, perhaps because it would breach commercial confidentiality.

The processing of sensitive personal information involved in a disclosure related to an acquisition or merger must satisfy a sensitive data condition. This will not be an obstacle where there is an employment related legal obligation on one business to disclose to another, but may well prevent the disclosure of sensitive personal information in the run up to a merger or acquisition where there is no such obligation and the worker has not been asked for and given explicit consent.

See page 72 [of the supplementary guidance] for conditions to be satisfied.

2.12.4 The Act imposes restrictions on the transfer of personal information to countries outside the EEA. Countries in the EEA are the member states of the European Union together with Iceland, Norway and Liechtenstein. The Information Commissioner provides separate detailed guidance on international transfers. The European Commission provides both a model contract that can be used to legitimise a transfer outside the EEA and a list of countries outside the EEA that are deemed to provide adequate protection by virtue of their data protection law. The European Commission has also entered into a special arrangement with the USA known as "the safe harbor".

[*This is now replaced by the 'Privacy Shield' which in 2017/18 is also subject to legal challenge*]

See the Information Commissioner's website: https://ico.org.uk/ Data Protection: Your Legal Obligations: International Transfers. The European Commission website is at http://ec.europa.eu/internal_market/imi-net/data_protection/index_en.htm

2.12.5 It is the new employer who now has a responsibility for the type and extent of personal information retained and who will have liability for it under the Act. The new employer must not assume that the personal information it receives from the original employer is accurate or relevant and not excessive in relation to its purposes. Within a few months of the merger or takeover it should review the records it has acquired, for example by checking the accuracy of a sample of records with the workers concerned and should make any necessary amendments.'

4.5 DISTRIBUTION OF THE INFORMATION MEMORANDUM

Once prospective purchasers have been identified, they need to be approached. Typically the seller or the lead adviser will contact prospective purchasers either verbally or in writing. If the seller wishes to keep confidential the fact that the target is being marketed for sale, the contact will be made by the lead adviser on a 'no names' basis. However, to interest prospective purchasers a limited amount of information is usually imparted in the form of a one page note (sometimes referred to as 'the flyer'), giving basic details of the market in which the target operates, its position in the market and summary turnover and net profit/EBITDA (Earnings Before Interest, Taxes, Depreciation and Amortization) figures. Having obtained initial interest and secured a confidentiality undertaking from them, the information memorandum would then be dispatched to interested parties.

In the case of a sale of the business and assets of the target, the seller is free to approach prospective purchasers and distribute information to them without restriction. However, in the case of a sale of shares, consideration currently needs to be given to the provisions of FSMA 2000, which potentially makes such an approach to purchasers (or an advertisement inviting offers for the company) an offence unless it was issued or approved by an 'authorised person'. The law governing the issue of information memoranda relating to the sale of shares in a company is contained in FSMA 2000.

Care must also be taken to ensure that it is not widely distributed in a way which may mean that it constitutes a public offering of securities requiring publication of a prospectus. Consideration should be given to the rules on prospectus regulations – Prospectus Regulations 2005 (SI 2005/1433) which replaced the Public Offers of Securities Regulations 1995 (SI 1995/1537) and in due course the new EU Regulation. In particular this contains an exemption from producing a formal prospectus in cases where an offer is made to fewer than 100 persons.

The EU Prospectus Regulation (EU) 2017/1129 was adopted in July 2017 and in most parts will come directly into force across the whole EU from 21 July 2019, other than the following provisions which will apply earlier:

- *from 20 July 2017* – certain exemptions from the obligation to publish a prospectus, such as where an issuer has securities admitted to trading on a regulated market and wishes to admit further securities up to a limit of 20% over 12 months;
- *from 21 July 2018* – the exemption from the scope of the Regulation for offers of securities to the public with a total consideration in the EU of less than €1,000,000 (calculated over a period of 12 months);
- *from 21 July 2018* – the option for member states to exempt offers of securities to the public from the obligation to publish a prospectus where the total consideration of each offer in the EU is less than €8,000,000 (calculated over a period of 12 months) and it is not subject to notification under Art 25.

Solicitors, Norton Rose Fulbright summarise the EU Regulation changes at http://www.nortonrosefulbright.com/knowledge/technical-resources/capital-markets-union/getting-funding/prospectus-directive-proposal/ as follows:

- '• Bonds issued in €100,000 denominations will still be exempt from the "public offer" trigger;
- The wholesale disclosure regime is being retained, along with the €100,000 denomination distinction, and wholesale bond prospectuses will be exempt from the summary requirement;
- The scope of the wholesale disclosure regime will be widened to include issues of debt securities that are admitted to a specific segment of a regulated market where access is limited to qualified investors;
- A potentially less onerous "EU Growth" prospectus will be available for small and medium-sized enterprises (SMEs) and in certain cases non-SMEs for eligible issues up to €20 million;
- Potentially lighter disclosure requirements will apply to secondary issuers where an issuer is already admitted to a regulated market or SME growth market;
- Risk factors will need to be categorised depending on their nature, with the most material risk factors being mentioned first in each category;
- Summaries may pose a challenge, as they will be shortened to seven sides of A4 sized paper and more prescriptive in content and the number of risk factors that can be included in the summary will be capped at 15
- From July 21, 2018 no prospectus will be required for issues below €1 million, which fall outside the scope of the legislation; and
- From July 21, 2018 the threshold beyond which a prospectus is mandatory is increasing from €5 million to €8 million; however, Member States will have the discretion to exempt issues of between €1 million and €8 million or establish other disclosure requirements for issues below €8 million'

4.5.1 Financial promotions

As a general rule, FSMA 2000, s 21, precludes any person other than an authorised person from issuing or causing the issue of a 'financial promotion' under the Act in the UK unless the contents of such financial promotion have been approved by an authorised person. This is a very difficult and technical area and if in doubt expert advice should be taken rather than reassuring a client that a particular form of seeking investment is inside or outside the rules.

FSMA 2000, s 21 states that: 'A person ("A") must not, in the course of business communicate an invitation or inducement to engage in investment activity' unless, (a) 'A is an authorised person' or (b) 'the communication is approved ... by an authorised person'. It goes on further to state:

'(8) "Engaging in investment activity" means—
    (a) entering or offering to enter into an agreement the making or performance of which by either party constitutes a controlled activity; or
    (b) exercising any rights conferred by a controlled investment to acquire, dispose of, underwrite or convert a controlled investment.
(9) An activity is a controlled activity if—
    (a) it is an activity of a specified kind or one which falls within a specified class of activity; and
    (b) it relates to an investment of a specified kind, or to one which falls within a specified class of investment.
(10) An investment is a controlled investment if it is an investment of a specified kind or one which falls within a specified class of investment.'

The sale and purchase of shares will constitute 'engaging in investment activity'.

It should also be noted that FSMA 2000 can potentially cover any form of communication 'whatsoever and wherever made'. Section 21(13) is very wide in that it states that 'communication' includes 'causing a communication to be made'. The intention was to ensure that the restriction was media neutral, in that it was capable of catching any form of communication. Section 21(3) also has the effect of including 'communication[s] originating outside the United Kingdom' within the general restrictions if the 'communication is capable of having an effect in the United Kingdom'.

Section 21 covers 'communication' containing an 'invitation or inducement'. In other words, there would appear to have to be some element of active encouragement of recipients.

In practical terms, s 21 on its face probably catches the individual, informal, private approach.

MiFID 2

From 3 January 2018 MiFID 2 (EU Regulations 2014/65 and 600/2014) apply. The FCA has issued guidance on the financial promotions rules in Art 44 of the Delegated Regulation (Organisational Requirements). Firms must treat professional/institutional) investors like retail investors and communications with professional clients are classed as financial promotions. More clarity on fees (see Art 50 of the Delegated Regulation is required which has an effect on communications and marketing materials not just applicable to sales materials but also other communications with the client. There are extended risk warnings to be given and requirement on font size and lay out. Information on future performance had to become more detailed.

See https://www.fca.org.uk/markets/mifid-ii.

For a comparison between the previous and the 2018 rules see https://www.perivantechnology.co.uk/compliance-blog/the-impact-of-mifid-ii-on-financial-promotions-what-you-need-to-know.

Social Media and 'Promotions'

The FCA has issued guidance on social media and promotions (see https://www.fca.org.uk/publication/finalised-guidance/fg15-04.pdf).

It states at paragraphs 1.4 ff:

'1.4 We remind firms that any form of communication (including through social media) is capable of being a financial promotion, depending on whether it includes an invitation or inducement to engage in financial activity. This could include, for example, "advergames", where promotional messages are placed in entertainment applications. [*The guidance then gives below an example which*] is a non-promotional communication but would constitute a financial promotion if, for example, the second sentence read: "We also invest in our trading technology, to help get you the best returns!"' …

1.5 A financial promotion must also be made "in the course of business" to be within our regime. We have published guidance on this in our Perimeter Guidance manual (PERG). The "in the course of business" test requires a commercial interest on the part of the communicator. It is intended to exclude genuine non-business communications. Social media conversations involving groups and individuals not acting in the course of business are therefore outside our regulation. Where capital is raised for small private companies and the company is already in operation, it will be acting "in the course of business" when seeking to generate additional capital. At the pre-formation stage, however, individuals who are proposing to run the company may approach friends and relatives to see if they are willing to provide start-up capital.

Such individuals will not, in our view, be acting "in the course of business" during this pre-formation stage, and so such communications will fall outside our regime. But this will not be the case if they are forming companies with such regularity that they would be regarded as carrying on the business of forming companies.

In principle, however, there is no reason why an individual, such as a sole trader, cannot act "in the course of business": the key factor is the purpose of the communication rather than who is making it. And as we say in our guidance at PERG 8.5.2G, there has to be a commercial interest on the part of the communicator.

Where a personal social media account (such as a Twitter account) is used by someone associated with a particular business, for example a senior person at the business, that individual and the firm should take care to distinguish clearly personal communications from those that are, or are likely to be understood to be, made in the course of that business (see Figure 9 [*in the guidance*]).

1.6 There is a specific requirement that financial promotions for investment products are identifiable as such. Our view is that – for social media in particular – it is important that, in all cases, it is clear that a promotion is a promotion. This can be by labelling the promotion as such, or it may be clear from the context.'

4.5.2 Exceptions to FSMA

The exemptions to the general prohibition on 'financial promotion' are currently contained in the Financial Services and Markets Act 2000 (Financial Promotion) Order 2005 (SI 2005/1529) (previously the Financial Services and Markets Act 2000 (Financial Promotion) Order 2001 (SI 2001/1335)). The Financial Conduct Authority has a page on financial promotions on its website https://www.fca.org.uk/firms/financial-promotions-adverts. See also January 2018 and later versions of the FCA handbook with latest rules on promotions at https://www.handbook.fca.org.uk/handbook/PERG/8/20.pdf (FCA Perimeter Guidance Manual – 'Chapter 8 – Financial promotion and related activities').

The first thing to note about the exemptions contained in this Order is that a distinction is made between 'non-real time' and 'real time' communications and between solicited and unsolicited real time communications.

'Real time' communications are described as any communications made in the course of a personal visit, telephone conversation or other interactive dialogue. The communication will be considered to be solicited when it is made in response to an express request from the recipient.

Article 7 provides:

'(1) In this Order, references to a real time communication are references to any communication made in the course of a personal visit, telephone conversation or other interactive dialogue.

(2) A non-real time communication is a communication not falling within paragraph (1).

(3) For the purposes of this Order, non-real time communications include communications made by letter or e-mail or contained in a publication.

(4) For the purposes of this Order, the factors in paragraph (5) are to be treated as indications that a communication is a non-real time communication.

(5) The factors are that—

(a) the communication is made to or directed at more than one recipient in identical terms (save for details of the recipient's identity);
(b) the communication is made or directed by way of a system which in the normal course constitutes or creates a record of the communication which is available to the recipient to refer to at a later time;
(c) the communication is made or directed by way of a system which in the normal course does not enable or require the recipient to respond immediately to it.'

A 'non-real time' communication includes letters, emails, paper publications, website and sound and TV broadcasts.

The approach of the Order sets out circumstances in which a communication will fall outside the control created by FSMA 2000, s 21. In each exemption the Order specifies whether it applies to real time communications (solicited or unsolicited) and non-real time communications. Thus, it is important to determine whether the communication is real time or non-real time. Whilst in some cases it will be clear into which category the communication falls, in others it will not. Although the regulations specifically provide that emails are non-real time communications, in practice there presumably comes a point where rapid response emails or customised websites cease to be non-real time communications and start to become real time communications.

Some specific exemptions

The following exemptions in the Order might be of use:

Article 12 contains a useful exemption for those overseas:

'12. Communications to overseas recipients

(1) Subject to paragraphs (2) and (7), the financial promotion restriction does not apply to any communication—
(a) which is made (whether from inside or outside the United Kingdom) to a person who receives the communication outside the United Kingdom; or
(b) which is directed (whether from inside or outside the United Kingdom) only at persons outside the United Kingdom.

(2) Paragraph (1) does not apply to an unsolicited real time communication unless—
(a) it is made from a place outside the United Kingdom; and
(b) it is made for the purposes of a business which is carried on outside the United Kingdom and which is not carried on in the United Kingdom'.

Article 18 exempts 'mere conduits' from s 21 of FSMA 2000. A person acts as a 'mere conduit' if:

- he communicates it in the course of his business, the principal purpose of which is to transmit material provided by others; and
- the content of the communication is devised by others; and
- he does not select or otherwise control the material.

Article 18(2) provides a mere conduit will be where:

'(a) he communicates it [the promotion] in the course of an activity carried on by him, the principal purpose of which is transmitting or receiving material provided to him by others;

(b) the content of the communication is wholly devised by another person; and

(c) the nature of the service provided by him in relation to the communication is such that he does not select, modify or otherwise exercise control over its content prior to its transmission or receipt'.

Article 18A provides:

'18A. Electronic commerce communications: mere conduits, caching and hosting

The financial promotion restriction does not apply to an electronic commerce communication in circumstances where—

(a) the making of the communication constitutes the provision of an information society service of a kind falling within paragraph 1 of Article 12, 13 or 14 of the electronic commerce directive ("mere conduit", "caching" and "hosting"); and

(b) the conditions mentioned in the paragraph in question, to the extent that they are applicable at the time of, or prior to, the making of the communication, are or have been met at that time'.

Thus, internet service providers, telephone companies and the like are likely to be exempt.

Article 28 exempts 'one-off' communications, which are either solicited real time communications or non-real time communications. A 'one-off' communication is a communication:

- which is made to one recipient or group of recipients in the expectation that they will engage in an investment activity; and
- whose subject matter (the service or asset) has been determined with reference to the identity of the recipients; and
- which is not part of a co-ordinated promotional strategy.

In effect, the circulation of a business plan to certain select potential investors would probably be exempt.

Article 19 permits all communications (real time, non-real time, solicited and unsolicited) to be sent to investment professionals.

Article 48 permits certain non-real time communications and solicited real time communications to 'high net worth' individuals and 'sophisticated investors' (article 50). The communication may only relate to shares, debentures or units in a collective investment scheme and the potential exposure of the investor must be limited to the amount he pays for the investment. Thus, derivatives or leverage investments may not be promoted. A 'high net worth' individual is an individual whose accountant has certified that he has had an annual income of at least £100,000 over the previous two years or he has held net assets to the value of not less than £250,000. Additionally, the individual must have certified himself that he is a high net worth individual, that the advertisement is outside the protections afforded by the legislation and that he understands the risks involved. Thus, business plans sent to wealthy individuals are likely to be exempt. However, what is less clear is what the liability of an accountant who wrongly certifies an investor as being of high net worth should be.

Article 49 permits communications to certain larger corporations (high net worth companies) and unincorporated associations. The financial promotion restriction does not apply to any communication which is made only to recipients whom the person making the communication believes on reasonable grounds to be:

- persons to any body corporate which has a called-up share capital or net assets of:
  (i) in the case of a body corporate which has more than 20 members or which is a subsidiary undertaking of a parent undertaking which has more than 20 members, not less than £500,000;
  (ii) in the case of any other body corporate, not less than £5,000,000;
- any unincorporated association or partnership which has net assets of not less than £5,000,000;
- the trustee of a high value trust;
- any person whilst acting in the capacity of director, officer or employee of a person falling within any of the sub-paras alone, being a person whose responsibilities, when acting in that capacity, involve him carrying on controlled activities.

Article 50 permits non-real time communications and solicited real time communications to 'sophisticated investors'. A 'sophisticated investor' is an investor who has been certified as such by an authorised person. Additionally, he will have to state that he is a sophisticated investor and that he understands the risks involved in engaging in investment activity in consequence of an unapproved communication. Again, questions of liability of the authorised person arise in respect of wrongful certifications.

A sophisticated investor under article 50 is someone who meets at least one of the following criteria:

- has been a member of a network or syndicate of business angels for at least the six months preceding the date of the certificate;
- has made more than one investment in an unlisted company in the two years preceding that date;
- has worked, in the two years preceding that date, in a professional capacity in the private equity sector, or in the provision of finance for small and medium enterprises;
- has been, in the two years preceding that date, a director of a company with an annual turnover of at least £1 million.

As with high net worth individuals, a sophisticated investor must have a certificate that they are such in a prescribed format and the promotion (and those for high net worth investors) must include warnings set out by the legislation. The sophisticated investor exemption allows promotions about unlisted companies. If marketing other investments to them then article 48 mentioned above may apply.

Under article 50A sophisticated investors can self certify that they are such.

Article 51 permits any non-real time communication or solicited real time communication which is made to associations of high net worth or sophisticated investors.

Article 62 permits any communication by an individual, a body corporate, a partnership, a group of connected individuals or one or more persons acting as trustees which relates to the acquisition or disposal or shares in a body corporate other than an open-ended investment company and which may reasonably be regarded as having as its object the acquisition or disposal of day-to-day control of the affairs of that body corporate.

- A communication has this object if:
  (i) the shares consist of, or include, 50% or more of the voting shares in the body; or
  (ii) shares, together with any shares already held by the person acquiring them, consist of or include, at least that percentage of such shares;
  and if the acquisition or disposal is, or is to be, between parties each of whom is an individual, a body corporate, a partnership, a group of connected individuals or one or more persons acting as trustees.

Article 64 permits any communication made in connection with a takeover offer for a relevant private company provided the requirements of this section are fulfilled, ie that the communication is accompanied by the material listed in Part II of Sch 4 of the Order and information.

4.5.3 Issuing/approving a financial promotion under FSMA

Authorised persons are outlined in FSMA 2000, Part III, s 31. The legislation provides a uniform and single route to authorisation.

The predominate means of obtaining authorisation is by applying for permission under Part IV. Such permission may be granted to individuals, bodies corporate, partnerships and incorporated associations, provided they meet the threshold conditions as outlined in Sch 6 of the Act.

Authorisation can also be obtained by an 'EEA firm' (European Economic Area firm). An EEA firm should not have its head office in the UK and includes investment firms, credit institutions and financial institutions, all of which should have received authorisation from their home regulator. Consequently, once an EEA firm who is seeking to establish a branch in the UK satisfies the establishment conditions, it qualifies for authorisation.

Schedule 4 also extends the possibility of other 'Treaty firms' obtaining authorisation beyond those covered by single market directories provided they satisfy the conditions set out in the Prospectus Regulations 2005 (previously FSMA 2000, Sch 8, para 3(1)).

It should also be noted that the Society of Lloyd's is deemed to be an authorised person under s 315.

4.5.4 Consequences of a breach of 'financial promotion' legislation under FSMA

Breach of the financial promotion prohibition attracts the same sanctions as those for breach of the general prohibition.

Section 25 provides that anyone who is guilty of such an offence will be liable to six months' imprisonment or a fine, or if a conviction or an indictment, imprisonment for a period of two years, a fine or both.

However, a defence is available if it can be shown that the offeror believed:

- on reasonable grounds that the communication was approved by an authorised person; and
- that he took all reasonable precautions and exercised all due diligence to avoid committing the offence.

FSMA 2000, s 400(1) provides that if an offence is committed by a company, its directors can also be held to be liable, if it can be shown that the offence has been 'committed with the consent or connivance' of the director or if it is 'attributable to any neglect on his part'. Section 400 was amended by Sch 9 to the Financial Services Act 2012 to include offences relating to financial services in Pt 7 of the Financial Services Act 2012.

FMSA 2000 contains provisions in respect of innocent persons recovering money/property transferred and to claim compensation for loss.

4.5.5 Other relevant legislation

The Financial Services Act 2012 (FSA 2012), Pt 7 from 1 April 2013 contains important provisions relating to misleading information which replaced s 397 of FSMA 2000. Section 89 of FSA 2012 created a criminal offence relating to the making of a statement which the person making it knows to be false or misleading in a material respect or is reckless as to whether it is false or misleading or the dishonest concealment of any material fact. A person commits an offence if the person makes the statement or conceals the facts with the intention of inducing, or is reckless as to whether they will induce, another person to engage in, or refrain from engaging in, market activity in relation to a relevant agreement or relevant investment (defined under s 93). This largely restated the effect of s 397(2) of FSMA 2000 – the previous legislation.

Section 90 created a criminal offence relating to doing any act or engaging in a course of conduct which creates a false or misleading impression as to the market in or price or value of any relevant investment (defined in s 93) where the person doing the act or engaging in the conduct intends to create the impression. If the person intends to induce another person to deal or refrain from dealing in the investment, the person commits an offence. Alternatively, if the person knows or is reckless as to whether the impression is false or misleading and intends by creating the impression that a gain may be made or a loss avoided, the person commits an offence. This provision replicated and extended the effect of s 397(3) of FSMA 2000.

Section 91 created a new offence in 2013 relating to the making of a false or misleading statement, or the creation of a false or misleading impression, in connection with the setting of a relevant benchmark (defined under s 93). The person making the statement or creating the impression must know or be reckless as to whether the statement or impression is false or misleading. It is immaterial for this offence what the motive of the person is (for example, there is no requirement that the person be acting with the intention of inducing a person to engage in market activity or with the intention of making a gain or avoiding a loss).

Section 92 sets out the penalties which apply to Pt 7 of FSA 2012. A person found guilty of an offence is liable to a maximum term of imprisonment of seven years or to a fine, or to both.

There are various defences. It is important to note that dishonesty is not a prerequisite for prosecution under these sections. Recklessness is all that is required. This makes it all the more important for statements made in the information memorandum to be verified in advance in order to establish that there are facts to support them. It should also be noted that if a statement is made to one person which induces another to act, then a prosecution could still be brought.

For misleading statements s 89(3) provides for a defence:

'(3) In proceedings for an offence under subsection (2) brought against a person to whom that subsection applies as a result of paragraph (a) of subsection (1), it is a defence for the person charged ("D") to show that the statement was made in conformity with—
(a)   price stabilising rules,
(b)   control of information rules, or
(c)   the relevant provisions relating to the (exemption for buy-back programmes and stabilisation) of the market abuse regulation (see Financial Services and Markets Act 2000 (Market Abuse) Regulations 2016, SI 2016/680, Pt 3(1), reg 15(2) which amended the previous rules).'

In general market manipulation is prohibited. Given the essentially illiquid nature of shares in private companies, it might be expected that this offence would be largely irrelevant to any sale and purchase of shares in such a company. It is, however, so wide-ranging as to merit consideration. Essentially, any person who does any act or engages in any course of conduct which creates a false or misleading impression as to the market in or the price or value of shares is guilty of an offence if he does such act or engages in such course of conduct for the purpose of creating such an impression and thereby inducing another person to buy or sell shares or refrain from doing so. A seller who deliberately spreads a rumour that another party is interested in acquiring his shares would, therefore, be liable under this section unless he could show that he reasonably believed that by doing so he would not create a false or misleading impression in the mind of the prospective purchaser.

4.5.6   Other offences

(A)   Section 398 of the FSMA 2000 – misleading the Authority

FSMA 2000 also contains offences in s 398 (as amended by the Financial Services Act 2012) for misleading the regulator (FCA or PRA, previously 'the Authority'). A person who 'knowingly or recklessly' gives 'the regulator information which is fake or misleading in a material particular is guilty of an offence'.

A person guilty of such an offence is liable to a fine.

(B) Section 399 of the FSMA 2000 – misleading the Competition and Markets Authority (ex Office of Fair Trading)

Section 399 of FSMA 2000 also states that the offences connected with the provision of fake or misleading information also apply in relation to any function of the Competition and Markets Authority (ex Office of Fair Trading).

4.6 DATA ROOMS (OFF OR ONLINE)

Where the target has been marketed to a number of prospective purchasers, the seller and his advisers will invite initial indications of interest and indicative offers based on the information memorandum, and from those indicative offers a short list of prospective purchasers will be drawn up.

Depending upon the number of indicative offers which meet the seller's objectives, the sale process can proceed into stage two in one of two ways. If only one offer meets those criteria then the seller will enter into negotiations with that party with a view to striking terms in principle. Having done so, the prospective purchaser will want to carry out due diligence on the target before entering into a formal sale and purchase agreement. These investigations will usually include an accountant's report and an investigation by the purchaser's lawyers based around a request for information (sometimes known as pre-contract enquiries).

When a number of prospective purchasers have given indicative offers which fall within the seller's objectives, the seller will use the indicative offers to reduce the number of prospective purchasers to serious contenders (ie those who have submitted offers falling within the required price range and who have the means to finance the acquisition). Having selected prospective purchasers to enter stage two of the auction process, the next step in the process is to put the information which the seller and its advisers believe the bidders will need to see in order to finalise bids into a data room. The process of preparing a data room can be time consuming for the seller, diverting resources away from running the business of the target at a time when business interruption is least welcome. The best way to mitigate against this is to be organised from the start; time spent planning a focused approach to the process will invariably be time well spent.

The main issues are:

- making decisions on what to leave out;
- taking account of timing and resources;
- preparing a good index; and
- one room or two?

Once the data room has been organised, each bidder is then allowed access to the data room at the allotted time with its various advisers and very frequently the documents are uploaded such as to an online but secure 'drop box' instead. The preferred purchasers are then invited to submit final offers in the form of sealed bids by a set deadline and from those sealed bids the seller chooses the most attractive offer. In theory, the seller should then be in a position to enter into the sale agreement, but in practice some negotiation on the terms of the sale agreement will then follow.

As an alternative to the data room approach, the lead adviser may invite preferred purchasers to forward requests for information, which are then responded to, or send a pack of detailed information (replicating the information found in the data room) to the preferred purchasers. Whichever method is chosen, to avoid duplication, confusion or misunderstanding at a later stage it is important for one person, preferably the lead adviser, to deal with all these requests and for that person to keep a careful record of the information provided.

One of the advantages of inviting bids on the basis of information contained in the information memorandum and the data room and on the basis of a standard acquisition agreement is the ability to do so without advertising to the company's workforce, customers or suppliers that the business is for sale. This is certainly the case if the information memorandum is prepared by the seller's advisers, the data room is located at one of the adviser's offices and the information obtained from the seller is channelled through one person and coincides with an event in the calendar of the seller (for example, year end) when such information would normally be requested. Other advantages include the physical retention of the due diligence documents within the control of the seller and the consistency of information available to each bidder.

Whether preparing the data room, replies to the purchaser's request for information or a pack of information for distribution to the preferred purchasers, it is important to avoid making false or misleading statements as these may amount to a misrepresentation, and they may also constitute a criminal offence under s 89 (and Pt 7 ff) of Financial Services Act 2012 (previously FMSA 2000, s 397) (see section 4.5.5).

4.6.1   Preparing the data room

The seller's approach to preparing and compiling the data room may also be influenced by the following although increasingly the 'data room' is an online access:

(A)   The timetable for the transaction

Although a short timetable for completion of the transaction may be unavoidable, to proceed on the basis of a poorly prepared data room may be a false economy of time if the bidders are unable to progress their due diligence to the point where they feel equipped to make their offer for the target.

(B)   The resources available to the seller

If knowledge of the proposed transaction is to be restricted to the seller's most senior executives only, it may be difficult for them to access a significant amount of information in the target without jeopardising the confidentiality of the proposed sale.

(C)   The nature of the transaction

If, for example, the target comprises a business and assets rather than shares in a company and the seller is prepared to indemnify the buyer for the liabilities of the business prior to completion, that will limit the level of historic information required in the data room.

(D)   Indexing

The effort spent in compiling information, will only bear fruit if the data room itself is well organised. From the perspective of the competing bidders a disorganised data room will, at best, give rise to complaints and an increased number of further enquiries and, at worst, may antagonise bidders to the point where it affects the progress of the transaction. The key to data room organisation is a clear and accurate index of the documents which correspond to clearly numbered and labelled files.

Categorising the information in this way will enable the representatives of the competing bidders who access the data room to focus their review on the aspects of the data room which interest them the most. If new documents are added to the data room they must also be added to the appropriate category of the index, making sure that they are easily identifiable as new documents (possibly by underlining the document description or by adding a reference to the date on which they were added). The index numbering should not be changed overall; this can be achieved by using different levels of numbering or lettering for new documents. Bidders should be given an opportunity to review any material documents which are added after their allotted time for visiting the data room.

(E)   Location

It is generally sufficient to have only one data room in operation. In a particularly large transaction, however, an auction with a considerable number of bidders or a transaction where there is a particularly tight timetable, it may be appropriate to set up a duplicate data room. If so, best practice is to ensure that it is hosted at a different site (for example, one data room at the offices of the seller's lawyers and the other at its financial adviser's offices). This makes it easier to operate the two rooms without the possibility of an inadvertent meeting of two teams of competing bidders. It will be important for the two hosts of the data rooms to co-ordinate the addition of any new material to ensure complete duplication.

Some deals involve virtual data rooms with information uploaded and held online.

4.6.2 Data room rules

Whenever a data room is to take place the seller's advisers normally produce data room rules limiting the number of people who may attend on behalf of a bidder, the hours and days that the data room is open, and whether documents can be copied (and, if so, limits on the number of copies that may be made). The rules will generally cover the following:

(A) Opening times

These are generally usual business hours, but will vary depending on the timetable for the transaction.

(B) Instructions for making appointments

The bidders are generally required to provide details of those attending to the contact at the seller's lawyers or financial advisers.

(C) Registration requirements

Visitors to the data room will probably be asked to sign a register in order to maintain a record of exactly who has had access to the data room. It is essential that a different register is maintained for each bidder or a speed read of the previous attendees could reveal the names of the competitors.

(D) Capacity

The rules will probably specify the maximum number of visitors who may attend the data room at one time.

(E) Supervision

The rules will generally provide that the data room is to be supervised by a representative of the seller (often a junior member of the legal team) who will most likely be available to deal with questions regarding the whereabouts of documents.

(F) Equipment

It is becoming increasingly unusual to prohibit the use of laptop computers and dictaphones in a data room. To do so is unlikely to be well received by the bidders, particularly as they are subject to a confidentiality undertaking and their time in the data room is often fairly limited.

(G) Copying

The bidders will almost inevitably request copies of certain documents for further review and the seller should discuss its preferred approach to the copying of documents before the data room is opened. A blanket restriction on copying is not unjustifiable given that the main purpose of the data room is to provide information to a number of interested parties without the need for copying information to each of them. The seller, however, may feel that it is appropriate to be more flexible in relation to non-sensitive documents (particularly if they are long or complex) in order to encourage the smooth running of the transaction. The rules may provide that the visitor must make a written note of the documents that it wishes to copy (generally on a form provided) at the end of each day in the data room for consideration by the seller overnight.

4.6.3 Scope of data room information

The seller and its advisers will prepare an index of core information to be included in the data room, and determine the location and number of data rooms required. The data room enables the seller to control the information supplied to bidders, saves the expense of copying and distributing information, and reduces the risk that sensitive information could potentially be used by an unsuccessful bidder (in breach of the confidentiality agreement) after completion of the sales process.

The information which would typically be included in the data room is the same or substantially similar information to that which a purchaser would obtain through its accountant's and lawyer's usual investigations.

To avoid subsequent 'fishing expedition' information requests, the data room index should specify if there is no relevant information in relation to a specific question, such as, for example, the absence of any litigation affecting the business. The index may also indicate if further information is being withheld, which will be disclosed to the preferred bidder(s).

Bidders will justifiably expect the data room, which replaces conventional due diligence, to contain all relevant information, and care needs to be taken to ensure that the data room is as complete as possible. This is also important as the data room is normally disclosed to the ultimate buyer to qualify the seller's liability under the warranties. Failure to disclose significant contingent liabilities in the data room may cause bidders to withdraw at a later stage when they become known.

However, the seller may legitimately balance the buyer's expectation of full disclosure with its (and the eventual purchaser's) requirement to maintain the confidentiality of commercially sensitive information from the data room until the number of bidders has been narrowed down following the submission of definitive or second round bids or even until the successful bidder has been selected.

If any information is to be withheld until the second round or later, it is essential that the bidders are informed that this will be the case and given an indication of the nature and content of the documents to be withheld. The benefits of restricting the availability of confidential or commercially sensitive information until the seller is almost certain that the sale will go through, however, may be outweighed by the effect the eventual release of the information may have on the bidders' views of the business and on the amount they are prepared to pay. In addition, the seller should appreciate that where documents have been withheld from the data room, the bidder will need a reasonable period of time to absorb their contents when they are released. Excluding information may also give rise to issues of possible misrepresentation, fraud or even liability for concealing material facts (which in some jurisdictions, such as the UK, could be a criminal offence). All such issues should be carefully considered in the jurisdiction(s) concerned.

There is no need to include in the data room documents which are in the public domain and readily available to the bidders; for example, each bidder can reasonably be expected to carry out its own company, trademark and patents searches and the usual searches on any properties to be sold. Sellers should resist any temptation to 'throw in the kitchen sink': there is no standard size for a data room. The nature of the target will dictate the number of documents required to give a proper picture of the business.

In setting up the data room the seller may be able to capitalise on other elements of the auction process in order to save time and resources. For example, information which was compiled for financial advisers prior to their appointment to act for the seller in relation to the auction or compiled in relation to the preparation of the information memorandum which was sent to bidders earlier on in the controlled auction process may be a useful starting point.

Although, on balance, it is generally preferable to include rather than exclude information from the data room, the seller will not be thanked for including files which contain random invoices, copy correspondence containing elliptical references to ongoing matters and incomplete documents. Putting such items in the data room without explanation will only prompt enquiries from bidders' lawyers.

Where the target is a listed company or where its shares are traded on a regulated market and it is subject to any insider dealing or similar provisions, it is important to consider whether any of the information which the seller proposes to add to the data room will render the bidders 'insiders'. If the data room is likely to contain such inside information, the seller may wish to make the bidders aware of this fact (either in the text of the confidentiality letter or the data room rules) and remind them of the relevant restrictions.

Bidders may, having had time to consider the information contained in the data room, request additional information. The seller should resist requests to answer the bidder's standard form information requests – as the seller has done its share of the work, the bidder should invest a day or so in the data room, seeing what information is actually there. Specific requests for additional information should be directed to the lead adviser, who will manage the preparation of responses.

A record of additional queries (and answers) should be maintained to keep a consistent approach between all members of the seller's team and also between one bidder and another. The lead adviser should ensure that additional information provided to one bidder is also provided to others. This avoids the risk of the seller and its advisers becoming confused as to which bidder knows what and also reduces the risk of offending a bidder's sense of 'fair play' – an offence which may cause them to withdraw from the process.

The seller must also avoid misleading bidders about the extent of interest in the target in an attempt to increase the bids, as it runs the risk of liability for fraudulent misrepresentation or potential liability under Financial Services Act 2012, s 89 (previously FSMA 2000, s 397). See, for example, *Smith New Court Securities Ltd v Scrimgeour Vickers (Asset Management) Ltd* [1992] BCLC 1104. In this case, the claimant bought shares in a public company following false representations by the second defendant, who was acting as a broker for the first defendant. The Court of Appeal found that the broker had on separate occasions fraudulently misled the claimant into believing that it was in competition with other bidders, that two other sealed bids had been received by it, and that another bidder had made a bid at a stated price per share, when no such bid had been made either at that price or at all. It is not possible to exclude liability in English law by any contract term for fraud or fraudulent misrepresentation. In *BSkyB v HP (previously EDS)* [2010] EWHC 86 (TCC) the court overturned an exclusion clause capping liability at £40m where fraud was found and the parties settled the claim at about £300m, it being a claim for allegedly defective IT systems.

The remedies for fraudulent misrepresentation are rescission and damages. In the *Smith New Court* case, the claimant had already sold the shares and rescission was not possible. Accordingly, the claimant was only able to recover damages. The measure of damages was the amount necessary to restore the claimant to the position that it would have been in if the representation had not been made. The court found that the claimant would have paid a lower price for the shares, and the damages finally confirmed by the Court of Appeal were the difference between what the claimant had paid and what the claimant would have been paid if the misrepresentations had not been made.

Chapter 5

Negotiation process

5.1 SELECTION OF THE PREFERRED PURCHASER

In a sale by auction, the shortlisted prospective purchasers will submit final offers on the basis of the investigations they have made, the information memorandum and (if applicable) a standard form sale agreement. These offers will usually contain details of the price that the offeror is prepared to pay, a set of conditions which must be fulfilled prior to entering into formal contracts, the other principal sale terms and a list of 'non-compliant' issues relating to the sale agreement. From these offers the seller, aided and assisted by his lead adviser, will choose the preferred prospective purchaser. In choosing the preferred purchaser the price offered naturally tends to have a significant influence. In certain situations, however, other matters may be of similar significance. For example, a potential purchaser may bring merger control issues and if there is more than one potential purchaser this may affect whether that purchaser is likely to be chosen as the preferred purchaser.

It is often best to get the seller's team and all advisers together in one location to facilitate speedy communication of key points arising out of the bids, and to enable meetings to be convened at short notice to assess strategy in the light of the bids received.

Once an overall view has been formed of the value of each bid, the seller or its advisers may need to negotiate points of significance with competing bidders, to try to increase the bid price or remove unfavourable terms. The bidder should anticipate these negotiations and ensure that its key negotiators and board members are accessible to the seller's team on a 24-hour basis during the bid review process.

Negotiations will take place to convert the offer into heads of agreement (for a discussion on the merits of having heads of agreement please refer to section 5.4), or into the formal sale agreement.

5.2 NEGOTIATION PROCESS

Although the negotiation process will undoubtedly vary depending upon the various different methods of sale used and the particular circumstances of the parties at the time, typically the seller will receive an offer from the purchaser and will use those terms as the basis of negotiation.

The terms of the offer will usually include the proposed purchase price, the assets to be acquired and the liabilities to be assumed, the method and timing of payment and other principal terms. For a discussion on the methods of valuing the target from a purchaser's perspective, please refer to Chapter 9 (section 9.2).

From the terms contained in the offer, the seller and the purchaser will usually meet on a number of occasions to negotiate on the individual terms to suit their particular requirements and this process will usually involve a number of revised offers before finally reaching agreement in principle.

5.3 RESPONSE TO THE PURCHASER'S PROPOSALS

Difficult tax issues can arise where the consideration is payable by instalments, whether it be certain or contingent (ie on an earn-out).

5.3.1 Deferred consideration

Deferred consideration raises two significant issues for the seller:

- security for the deferred payment;
- tax treatment of the deferred payment.

(A) Security

Whether security is necessary depends upon the creditworthiness of the purchaser. In the first instance, the seller should obtain information as to the purchaser's creditworthiness and this could be obtained from one of the number of credit agency companies who are set up for that sole purpose. If there is any doubt as to the purchaser's creditworthiness resulting from that search and, sometimes even where it gives rise to no doubt, a cautious seller will, especially in the light of some of the spectacular collapses of the late 1980s, seek security for the deferred element of the consideration. In its simplest form, the purchaser could obtain a guarantee from its ultimate holding company or its bankers in favour of the seller. Alternatively, the purchaser could charge the assets of the company or business it is purchasing in favour of the seller. In such a case, the financial assistance provisions referred to in section 9.5.1 (A)(ii) will need to be considered in detail.

(B)   Tax treatment

The major issue for the seller is a potential cash flow problem due to the tax treatment of the deferred element of the purchase price. Here, we are looking at a situation where the amount of the consideration has been ascertained, but payment is deferred. As the liability to tax itself is fixed by reference to the disposal, not by reference to the date on which the proceeds are received, the seller may become liable to pay tax on the deferred consideration before it is received. TCGA 1992, s 48 provides that the gain must be calculated without any discount because the right to receive the consideration is deferred and without regard to a risk of any part of the consideration being irrecoverable or to the right to receive any part of the consideration being contingent. The whole gain is brought into account, but will be recomputed, and the tax liability discharged or repaid, if the seller does not in fact receive the full amount of the deferred consideration. Hence, a seller who agrees to take £10,000 up front with a further £200,000 in two years' time, may be in real trouble. Assume that the gain he makes is £100,000. Tax on this (up to £40,000) will be due in January following the year of assessment in which the disposal is made, but he realised only £10,000 in cash and therefore needs to find the balance from other sources.

Where the whole or part of the consideration is payable by instalments over a period exceeding 18 months from the date of disposal, TCGA 1992, s 280 gives the Inspector the discretion to allow tax to be paid by instalments. The taxpayer must satisfy HM Revenue and Customs (HMRC) that he would otherwise suffer undue hardship. Interest will not generally be payable until an instalment falls due.

5.3.2   Earn-outs

Although an earn-out involves the deferral of consideration, the 'deferred' element of consideration on an earn-out will be incapable of calculation on completion as it depends upon future performance. Hence, the amount of the consideration is unascertained.

By comparison to the typical deferred consideration pricing format (a specified sum payable at a predetermined future date) which, save for cash flow considerations is broadly neutral, the tax treatment of an earn-out is potentially penal; as well as incurring a liability to pay tax on the fixed element of the purchase price, the seller is faced with:

- a tax liability in respect of the right (albeit contingent) to receive the 'earn-out' consideration;
- the potential loss of retirement relief in respect of the 'earn-out' consideration;
- the possible loss of roll-over relief on the issue of shares by the purchaser in payment of the 'earn-out' consideration; and
- the risk that the 'earn-out' consideration will be treated as income not capital.

(A)   Tax on the right to receive the earn-out consideration

In *Marren v Ingles* [1980] 3 All ER 95, [1980] 1 WLR 983 it was decided that TCGA 1992, s 48 did not apply where the deferred element was 'of a wholly uncertain and unascertainable amount'. The House of Lords established that in such circumstances the seller will be treated as having disposed of his shares on completion and will become liable to pay tax both on the cash received on completion (if any) and the market value of the right to receive the earn-out consideration.

In *Marren v Ingles*, the taxpayers agreed to sell shares in their company for £750 each, plus half the profit when the company was floated. It was accepted by the taxpayer and the Inland Revenue (now HMRC) that there was a disposal for capital gains tax purposes when the agreement was struck and that the value of the consideration for capital gains tax purposes was the aggregate of the cash received plus the market value then of the right to receive the further consideration.

The point at issue was whether there was a further tax liability when the deferred consideration was actually paid. The court decided that the right to receive the further consideration was a chose in action, and therefore that it was an asset for capital gains tax purposes, and this asset was disposed of when the further consideration was paid.

Assume, for example, that Mr B has agreed to sell his company for £100,000 payable immediately and a further sum calculated by reference to 25% of the net profit before tax over each of the next three years. It is agreed that his base cost for capital gains tax purposes (including indexation) is £50,000 and that the right to receive the further consideration is at the date of disposal worth £200,000. The capital gain for the year of disposal will be £250,000, ie the aggregate of £100,000 and £200,000, less £50,000.

Assume that the deferred consideration is paid three years later and he in fact receives £500,000. His liability when the deferred consideration is finally ascertained, is based on the disposal of an asset (the chose in action) for £500,000 and his base cost is £200,000. Assuming a rise in RPI of 10% over the three years, his further gain is £280,000, and he has further tax to pay by reference to this.

This does not appear too unreasonable. The difficulty arises in cases where the deferred consideration comes out lower than expected. Assume that the deferred consideration payable is in fact only £100,000. In this case Mr B will make a capital loss of £120,000 when the deferred consideration is ascertained, because he disposes for £100,000 of an asset which he acquired for £200,000 (increased to £220,000 by indexation). Capital losses cannot be carried back, so he gets no relief and ends up paying tax on a higher gain than he actually received.

The capital loss can be carried forward for use in future years but this will only be of benefit if he actually makes gains in the future. Relief is not available under

TCGA 1992, s 48 because the loss was made on the disposal of the new asset, not on any contingent consideration payable for the disposal of the shares.

Consideration which is wholly unascertainable will therefore fall under the *Marren v Ingles* principle. Valuing the right to receive it is often very difficult in practice. It may be that there is a strong factual argument that the right to receive the future consideration is worthless. For example, where deferred consideration is payable by reference to profits, HMRC may accept a low value because there is no certainty of the profits figure being reached. On the other hand, if the profits figure looks easy, particularly by reference to the target company's past performance, then HMRC may argue that the right is worth something.

TCGA 1992, s 48 will apply, and not *Marren v Ingles* – where the consideration is ascertainable, but its payment is simply contingent. It is possible, therefore, to some extent to choose which provision the deferred consideration will fall under by carefully constructing the deferred consideration rights. Merely putting a cap (or a long-stop) on an otherwise unascertainable consideration is probably not sufficient to bring in s 48 in place of *Marren v Ingles*. Fixing the consideration at a sum certain, with adjustments depending on performance, may well achieve this, although the parties must give careful thought to the commercial considerations here and should only change the deal if they have fully thought through all of the ramifications.

Why would one wish to adjust things in this way? At first sight it looks as though the operation of the *Marren v Ingles* principle may be beneficial provided that a low valuation of the chose in action can be agreed. After all, if s 48 applies, all the tax is payable upfront, subject to the possibility of claiming relief by instalments.

The answer is that each case turns on its own facts. There are two particular examples of cases where a seller would prefer to fall under s 48 rather than under the *Marren v Ingles* principle:

- an individual who is eligible to claim retirement relief (before it is phased out) may not be liable to pay tax even on the maximum gain if s 48 applies. However, if the deal is structured in such a way that the principle in *Marren v Ingles* applies, then strictly speaking the retirement relief is only available on the first disposal (in the example above a gain of £250,000), not on the second disposal (an additional gain of £280,000) because the second disposal is the disposal of a chose in action, not of shares in a company;
- alternatively, the seller may be a company with significant current year trading losses making a gain on the sale of a part of its business. Let us assume that the losses are sufficient to shelter the full gain made if s 48 applies, so once again the taxpayer does not in fact have a tax liability up front. If *Marren v Ingles* applies, part of the gain will be made in a subsequent year of assessment and brought forward trading losses can only be used against trading profits, not against chargeable gains.

In *HMRC v Collins* [2009] EWHC 284 part of the payment for the purchase was payment of a pension contribution and this also fell within the *Marren v Ingles* principle. This followed *Spectros International Plc v Madden* [1997] STC 11.

Consequently, it is very important to look at the facts of each case carefully to determine how deferred consideration should be structured.

There are a number of situations where a share for share exchange can be used to mitigate the harsher effects of the receipt of deferred consideration. For example, if the sellers have agreed the consideration for the sale of shares at £100,000 per annum over five years, why not persuade the purchaser to pay an initial instalment of cash of £100,000 and then issue a medium-term debenture for the balance of £400,000? Subject to clearance under s 138, the tax will be deferred until the debenture is redeemed.

Issuing shares or debentures can also alleviate the effects of deferred and contingent consideration, whether it falls under TCGA 1992, s 48 or *Marren v Ingles*. The commercial considerations are again important. For example, if a specified but contingent consideration has been agreed and the full value of the consideration is paid in the form of shares, does the purchaser issue all the shares and make the seller pass cash back if the contingency is not satisfied or does it hold some shares back? The logical answer is to issue an initial tranche of shares and issue the rest when the contingency has been ascertained. The tax consequences of this are not as straightforward as they might appear. For example, deferred consideration on the *Marren v Ingles* principle which is itself satisfied by the issue of shares does not strictly fall within the terms of TCGA 1992, s 135 because the new shares or debentures when issued, say, three years after the sale of shares are not issued in exchange for shares in the target company, but in exchange for the chose in action which was created on the sale. However, under TCGA 1992, s 138A the chose in action is treated as a security so that roll-over relief can be obtained. The terms of s 138A must be read carefully as, amongst other things, the quantity of shares or debentures to be issued must be unascertainable when the right is conferred.

HMRC summarise the two cases above in their guidance CG14990 – Deferred consideration: unascertainable: tax cases, as follows:

> 'The capital gains treatment of unascertainable future consideration was established in two important tax cases, *Marson v Marriage* (54TC59) and *Marren v Ingles* (54TC76). Both cases concerned agreements for the sale of assets in which the vendor received a quantified amount of money plus a conditional and unquantifiable further amount payable at an unascertained future date. The point in dispute in both cases was whether any chargeable gain arose when the further amounts were received.

> In *Marson v Marriage*, Justice Fox held that TCGA92/S48 applies when the sum to be brought into account represents ascertainable consideration even when the right to it is contingent. It does not apply when the amount is unascertainable.

Several principles were established in *Marren v Ingles*:

- the right to receive future unascertainable payments is a "chose in action". This is an incorporeal asset which is a chargeable asset for Capital Gains Tax purposes,
- when the future amounts are ascertained and received they are "capital sums derived from assets" within TCGA92/S22,
- when the future amounts are ascertained and received they are "capital sums derived from assets" within TCGA92/S22,the future sums received are not payments in satisfaction of a debt within the terms of TCGA92/S251.'

(B)   Income not capital

There is a risk that the consideration calculated by reference to future profits may be treated as income and not capital where the seller remains an employee of the target or the new group. This risk is more acute when the seller is an employee and is entitled to more by way of consideration than the other sellers and/or where payment of the earn-out consideration is to be terminated on ceasing to be employed. In these cases HMRC may seek to argue that the earn-out will be treated as referable to the seller's future services and not to his shares in the target.

5.4   HEADS OF AGREEMENT AND EXCLUSIVITY

5.4.1   Heads of agreement

Having reached agreement in principle and before the expensive programme of due diligence and drafting documents commences, it is a matter of judgement for the parties to the sale to record the principal terms of the transaction in writing. This is referred to either as heads of agreement or heads of terms, a memorandum of understanding or a letter of intent.

Heads of agreement can vary in form from scribbling on the back of an envelope to carefully drafted, word-processed documents prepared by lawyers. Whatever their form, their usual purpose is to provide a brief, non-legally binding record of the terms of a transaction as agreed by the parties to the transaction at a particular stage in the negotiation process.

Whether heads of agreement are a useful tool in the negotiation process is a matter for much debate. The process of producing heads of agreement is a fine balance between having all the terms of the transaction discussed, agreed and recorded in writing and spending too much time and effort discussing details of the transaction which should be dealt with at a later stage.

Reasons for the seller to use heads of agreement include:

- if there is a danger of a misunderstanding between the parties developing, which is more likely in complicated transactions, then they may provide

> a useful mechanism for disclosing the misunderstanding at a stage in the negotiation process when the issue can be addressed;

- they can provide a means of identifying difficult issues early on and avoid a waste of time and costs if the deadlock cannot be broken at this stage;

- they can form a convenient and sometimes helpful basis of instruction to professional advisers;

- they can also be of help in providing a means of verification of the terms of the transaction; and

- most importantly, the seller will be negotiating the heads from a position of strength given that, at this stage, the seller will know far more about the business than the purchaser and, accordingly, the seller may be able to persuade the purchaser to agree to issues which the purchaser might not have accepted at a later stage.

Although they create a moral commitment, because heads of agreement tend to be non-legally binding, they cannot stop either party from seeking to renegotiate some of the terms. Accordingly, sellers sometimes consider them to be a waste of time, or where they become too detailed, sellers often regret the loss of time and effort which could have been spent more productively in addressing the draft acquisition agreement.

If the heads are intended to be non-binding then, at the very least, the magical words 'subject to contract' should be inserted. There is much case law regarding the use of the term 'subject to contract' and whether or not it protects the document to which it relates from becoming legally binding. In order to avoid any uncertainty, in addition to the words 'subject to contract' it should be expressly stated that the parties do not intend for the provisions of the heads of agreement to become legally binding and that the terms as finally agreed between the parties will be embodied in a detailed acquisition agreement to be drafted at a later stage.

If part or parts of the heads of agreement are to be legally binding and others not, again this must be expressly stated and, in relation to those parts which are to be binding, the legal requirement for the creation of a valid contract must be satisfied. For example, if the heads of agreement are to incorporate a confidentiality undertaking (see section 4.4) and/or exclusivity provisions which are intended to be legally binding, those provisions in the heads need to be capable of forming a contract in their own right. Accordingly, the heads must clearly state that they are to be legally binding, the commitments on both parties need to be clear and definite, and consideration must flow from the obligee to the obligor.

When preparing heads of agreement the following points should be taken into account:

- to avoid points of discussion which should be reserved for the formal documentation, it is important that the heads should cover important commercial points, not routine or legal ones. To specify that the heads are not exhaustive may help focus the parties on the key points;

- unless a particular issue is unduly complicated or unusual, the heads should state the principle and leave the detail for the formal contract;
- conditions should identify clearly what needs to be done or fulfilled. For example, a condition that updated financial information is required leaves plenty of scope to disagree whereas a condition to forward management accounts for company X for specific months is more helpful;
- if determined by a formula, the use of a worked example may help explain how the purchase price is to be calculated;
- defining the circumstances when an obligation to pay costs arises in the event that the transaction never proceeds to completion can be extremely difficult, especially if it only arises due to the paying party's fault; and
- usually a confidentiality undertaking will be in place before the parties are able to agree the heads. In such circumstances, the heads need only confirm or acknowledge the application of the existing confidential undertaking.

5.4.2 Exclusivity

It is common for a purchaser to seek an undertaking from the seller not to negotiate or solicit other offers during an agreed period, so as to give the purchaser a period of exclusivity in which to complete the proposed transaction.

The necessity for, and form of, exclusivity undertakings are discussed in Part II (Chapter 9, section 9.8.2). A precedent form of exclusivity undertaking is contained in Part VI. Whether the seller agrees to exclusivity depends upon the seller's negotiating position. Because of their very nature, a seller's opening position will be to reject the idea. Exclusivity undertakings are therefore more common in sales initiated by the purchaser. In sales initiated by the seller they tend to be forced upon the seller where the prospective purchaser seeking the exclusivity is the sole bidder, the preferred bidder in an auction process or a management buy-out team with little or no resources to fund the due diligence exercise.

Although the enforceability of some exclusivity provisions is questionable (see Chapter 9, section 9.8.2) in giving such an undertaking, the seller must assume that it is enforceable and consider the inclusion of provisions:

- bringing the period of exclusivity to an end on the earlier of the discussions terminating for whatever reason or in a number of more subjective circumstances designed to ensure that the purchaser is genuinely progressing the transaction with a view to completion within the timescale set by the seller. For example, if the purchaser is relying on third party finance the seller may require sight of an offer letter to the purchaser from a reputable financial institution at some stage during the exclusivity period; and
- ensuring the scope and limit of the seller's cost undertaking is clearly defined.

5.5   RESPONSE TO DUE DILIGENCE ENQUIRIES

In the case of a sale by auction, the need for due diligence on the part of the purchaser may have been pre-empted by the seller through the provision of information or in the variations on that theme discussed in Chapter 4, section 4.6.

In other cases, it is likely that the agreement in principle will have been struck between the seller and the purchaser without the purchaser having the benefit of material amounts of 'inside' information relating to the target. In these circumstances, it is unlikely that the purchaser will proceed up to formal contracts without conducting due diligence on the target. Whatever methods are chosen, they are likely to involve requests for the supply of information in supporting documents from the seller. It is important that the seller is aware of the importance of this exercise to the purchaser and that the purchaser will place reliance on the information supplied to it, using the form of warranties in the sale agreement, and of the fact that in the case of a sale of shares any false or misleading statements may constitute misrepresentation and a criminal offence under FSA 2012, s 89 (previously FSMA 2000, s 397).

To avoid disruption to the business, it is usually preferable for the due diligence enquiries to be channelled through the lead adviser. Where the source of information cannot be obtained easily by the seller without the assistance of others within the target's business, consideration needs to be given as to the reasons why this information is being requested to avoid undue speculation.

Part II

The Purchaser's Perspective

Chapter 6

An overview of the acquisition process

Achieving a successful acquisition is a complex and demanding exercise with many pitfalls. Getting it wrong may not only jeopardise the acquired business but also the acquirer itself. As the late Lord White (of Hanson Plc) once said: 'I never ask myself how much can we make out of this. I ask what can we lose.'

Studies suggest that the financial and commercial success of an acquisition is far more likely when that acquisition has been clearly planned to meet the business objectives of the purchaser. A carefully prepared and designed acquisition strategy is even more important when the purchaser envisages a series of acquisitions.

In the case of a planned acquisition initiated by the purchaser, the key steps to acquiring the target are as follows:

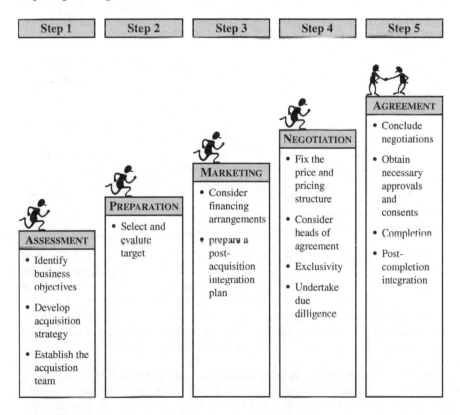

Step 1	Step 2	Step 3	Step 4	Step 5
ASSESSMENT • Identify business objectives • Develop acquisition strategy • Establish the acquistion team	**PREPARATION** • Select and evalute target	**MARKETING** • Consider financing arrangements • prepare a post-acquisition integration plan	**NEGOTIATION** • Fix the price and pricing structure • Consider heads of agreement • Exclusivity • Undertake due dilligence	**AGREEMENT** • Conclude negotiations • Obtain necessary approvals and consents • Completion • Post-completion integration

The growth and development of the business requires the formation of a business strategy and plan to implement that strategy (usually referred to as a business plan) which is regularly updated to meet the changing needs of the business. The very first stage in the acquisition process is the preparation or review of the business plan and the identification of a need to grow or develop the business by way of acquisition. Whatever the need for the acquisition, the purchaser should develop an acquisition strategy covering not only why the acquisition is necessary but also how the target should be identified and the key criteria for the target to meet. In tandem with this, the purchaser needs to identify an acquisition team to implement the acquisition strategy. All this is referred to in step 1, and it is discussed in more detail in Chapter 7.

Once the acquisition strategy has been formulated and the team established, the next step, step 2, is the search process, and this is discussed in Chapter 8. In the first instance, potential targets need to be identified, and as much information as possible regarding these targets needs to be collated. From this information those potential targets which fall within the purchaser's acquisition criteria should be selected and a careful evaluation of each of them carried out to ascertain those which seem more attractive. Having reduced the search process down to a manageable number (usually between three and five) the purchaser will need to approach the owners of potential targets to ascertain whether they are interested in selling and, if so, on what terms.

If, after the initial exploratory discussions, the purchaser finds a target which, with the benefit of information gleaned from those discussions, continues to match the purchaser's acquisition criteria and the owners are willing to consider a sale, the purchaser will have to negotiate terms with the owners. This will inevitably revolve around the price payable, the timing and method of payment of the purchase price and the structure of the transaction. Having agreed these terms in principle, the purchaser has to judge whether it should record those terms in heads of agreement and/or require a period of exclusivity from the seller to enable it to carry out its investigations and to come to a formal agreement with the seller without fear that the seller will walk away or will only be using the purchaser as a stalking horse for a higher offer. These issues are discussed in Chapter 9.

It is often tempting for the purchaser to look upon having reached heads of agreement as being the end of his involvement in the process, as the rest will be sorted out by the lawyers. In practice, there ought to be nothing further from the truth. At this stage, the purchaser and the acquisition team should be clearly focused on investigating the target and examining the results of those investigations. This process, often referred to as due diligence, and the various investigations that can be carried out are discussed in Chapter 10.

Once the initial results of the due diligence are available and if, after having considered then, the purchaser wishes to continue with the acquisition, the next step in the process is the preparation and negotiation of the sale agreement. If the due diligence investigations were to reveal issues or liabilities not apparent or disclosed to the purchaser earlier in the process, especially where the purchaser has already agreed to pay a fixed price, the preparation of the sale agreement will usually be preceded by a renegotiation of the principal sale terms.

The general principles relevant to the purchaser in preparing agreements to record the terms of a share purchase or business transfer and specific issues relevant to each type of transaction are dealt with in Part III. In parallel with the drafting of the agreement, the purchaser and its lawyers will be considering what approvals it and the seller require to authorise the transaction, and if any of those are required prior to entering into the contract, the timetable will need to make provision for this. Part III details the principal consents, approvals and clearances normally required.

Occasionally events (for example, the receivership of a competitor) present themselves in such a way that the acquisition process is condensed into a much shorter timescale, but nevertheless the process will probably still involve steps 3, 4 and 5.

As the process is linked to the business objectives of the purchaser, there is no standard timescale for an acquisition. With the exception of administration purchases or other such opportunistic acquisitions, there is likely to be at least a six to nine month time period between making the decision to acquire the business and completion of the acquisition.

Chapter 7

Acquisition strategy

7.1   BUSINESS OBJECTIVES

7.2   ACQUISITION STRATEGY

7.3   THE ACQUISITION TEAM

7.1   BUSINESS OBJECTIVES

The first step of the process is the development, or review and update, of the prospective purchaser's own business plan which may identify the need to expand, diversify or move into new markets by way of acquisition. The most common business objectives often include:

- to increase market share, when this cannot be achieved through organic growth, in the hope that the increased market share will lead to increased margins through greater efficiency, economies of scale and cross-fertilisation of ideas;
- to widen the purchaser's product range in existing markets;
- to enter into new markets quickly;
- to acquire new technology;
- the need to diversify out of products and services which are vulnerable to change or are in recession or decline;
- to secure sources of supply or the design or manufacture of such supply or outlets for the sale of its goods or services;
- to obtain assets which are undervalued in the expectation that these assets may be worth more to the purchaser, or to a third party the purchaser has in mind, because it believes it can make more efficient use of them than the current owners; and
- to acquire resources in which the purchaser is perceived to be weak. For example, the manufacturer of a retail product sold through independent retailers throughout the country may, if it feels that its distribution of those products is poor, devise an acquisition strategy to enable it to purchase a distribution company with the geographical coverage it requires.

Whatever the strategy, the purchaser should consider potential target companies in the light of that strategy and not abandon its carefully prepared and designed policy when presented with target companies.

Before looking at potential targets, the purchaser should calculate the maximum amount which it can afford to pay and should avoid investigating target companies with an asking price well beyond the resources available to it.

95

7.2 ACQUISITION STRATEGY

Having identified the business objective(s) to be satisfied by way of acquisition, the next step should be the development of an acquisition strategy to achieve these objectives. The acquisition strategy should define the criteria against which potential acquisition targets are to be evaluated. Typically the criteria would include objective criteria, for example:

- type of business to be acquired;
- market sectors to be covered by target;
- range of products/services manufactured/supplied by target;
- preferred size of target in terms of manufacturing capacity/number of employees/market share/turnover/profitability;
- location of target;
- how much the purchaser can afford to pay;
- rate of return required; and
- subjective criteria such as the quality of the management, the culture of the target, the quality of the target's products or services and growth potential.

Once the acquisition criteria have been finalised, the search process can begin. To avoid unnecessary waste of time and expense, as with any search process, it is important to ensure the search is tailored to locate potential targets fitting the predetermined acquisition criteria.

7.3 THE ACQUISITION TEAM

Once the acquisition strategy has been established and approved internally, the next phase is to appoint the acquisition team. The extent of the purchaser's internal resources usually determines the need to enlist the help of professional advisers. The acquisition team should include employees and/or professional advisers with the necessary expertise to cover the wide range of issues likely to be confronted. Usually this will mean having expertise in:

- accountancy;
- tax law;
- employment law,
- environmental law;
- finance;
- pensions;
- intellectual property,
- commercial property; and
- many other specialist areas will be required.

Larger companies frequently involved in the acquisition and disposal of companies may be able to staff the entire team with in-house employees, or largely with in-house employees, supplemented by professional advisers where necessary. Companies not experienced in the acquisition process are unlikely to have the in-house resources and will tend to rely on professional advisers.

The key appointment is that of the lead adviser who will usually also act as the project manager. The role of the lead adviser is vital and is discussed in Part I (see Chapter 2, section 2.1).

Chapter 8

The search process

8.1 IDENTIFYING POTENTIAL TARGETS

Having established an acquisition strategy, the search process may begin. Whether the research is carried out by the purchaser itself or by external advisers will depend upon the internal resources of the purchaser and the choice of external advisers.

The external advisers who offer the service of identifying potential targets include:

- business brokers;
- merchant bankers;
- stockbrokers;
- management consultants;
- corporate finance boutiques/venture capital firms; and
- the corporate finance arms of accountancy firms.

Most of these advisers will have businesses on their books which are available for purchase, they will have access to relevant business directories, merger and acquisition and business databases, and financial information, and they will have established networks to otherwise locate potential targets. Some of these external advisers now operate online search facilities.

To identify potential targets, these various sources should be explored as well as the trade contacts and business associates of the purchaser and its employees. In addition, advertisements in the trade and financial press can also be used.

8.2 SELECTING AND EVALUATING POTENTIAL TARGETS

There is a considerable amount of information which the purchaser can obtain about potential targets without alerting those targets to the impending approach. In the first instance, the purchaser can, via a company search agent or its own professional advisers, obtain a search on the target company which reveals all the information registered with the Registrar of Companies, including memorandum and articles of association, share capital, directors, secretary and registered office. In particular it will reveal:

- the names of the directors, so that the purchaser can check that the directors purporting to act on behalf of the company are, in fact, the directors of the company as registered at the Companies Registry, and therefore have power to act;

- whether there are any charges over the assets of the company, thereby raising the question of whether or not these charges should be discharged on completion;

- in the case of an asset sale, whether the directors have power under the memorandum and articles of association of the company to sell the assets concerned;

- whether the articles contain any restrictions on the transferability of shares and, if so, what consents have to be obtained. Most articles of unquoted companies contain restrictions on the transfer of shares, the general effect of which is to forbid the transfer of any share by a member of the company to an outsider if any other member of the company is willing to purchase at a stated price. This is sometimes referred to as a right of pre-emption. Such a right normally contains a notice procedure, which must be complied with by any intending seller of shares and it often contains a provision that the restriction will not apply to any transfer to which all the members of the company have consented in writing. A purchaser must satisfy himself that either the notice procedure has been complied with or the consents obtained, not only in respect of the proposed transfer to himself but also in respect of transfers by previous owners of the shares in question.

Unfortunately, by the very nature of the returns required to be made, a lot of the information on a company's file is out of date. For example, only shareholders at the date on which the company's last annual return is made are shown, unless there has been a subsequent allotment of shares, when the return of the allotments will show to whom they were made. In addition, charges registered against the company will be shown, but since a secured creditor has 21 days in which to register a charge in order to obtain priority against the company's other creditors, there can be no guarantee that there are no recently made charges about to be registered.

There will also have to be filed with the company's last annual return a set of audited accounts which, read together with the audited accounts of earlier accounting periods, may yield historical information. It is stressed that these accounts will only yield historical information. The period allowed for presenting and delivering accounts or reports for private companies is nine months after the end of the relevant accounting reference period (CA 2006, s 442(2)). As a result, accounts revealed by a company search may be up to 21 months old.

A company search will also reveal whether the company is in liquidation or receivership.

Undoubtedly quite some time will normally be taken up with sifting and evaluating prospects to ensure that they fall within the purchaser's predetermined acquisition criteria including, in particular, how much the purchaser can afford. Whether relying on external advice or not, the purchaser should always contact its own business contacts for an independent opinion.

At the end of this stage the purchaser should have identified no more than five, and no fewer than three, potential targets which match the purchaser's acquisition criteria. Any more would suggest that the acquisition criteria needs defining more clearly, and any fewer would obviously limit the choice.

8.3   APPROACHING POTENTIAL TARGETS

8.3.1   The approach

The owners of potential targets can either be approached directly by the purchaser or by an intermediary acting on behalf of the purchaser. The approach can be in writing, by telephone or during a carefully planned 'impromptu ' crossing of paths. Whichever method is chosen, it should be discreet and tailored to the particular circumstances of the sellers. For example, if the target is a subsidiary of a large group which regularly buys and sells businesses, an approach to the acquisitions/business development director of the parent company is more likely to succeed than an approach to the board of directors of the target, who may consider their jobs to be at risk.

In the case of private companies not forming part of a larger group, the majority shareholder is the obvious person to approach. Before the approach is made, consideration needs to be given as to who will make the approach, in what context it will be made and whether the identity of the prospective purchaser will be revealed. Experience suggests that, save in the case of approaches to shareholders or decision-makers detached from the target business, the approach is best made in an indirect way, such as 'with a view to the mutual development of our presence in the market'. Experience also suggests that the identity of the prospective purchaser needs to be revealed if the target is to take the approach seriously and that the approach should be made by one of the directors of the prospective purchaser personally and, if necessary, with the assistance of a professional adviser. The initial approach to the sellers of a number of potential targets will usually result in a mixture of responses, from rebuttal to mild interest and the occasional green light. Provided the approach was made to the most appropriate person (in most cases the founder/majority shareholder) there is little point in the purchaser spending time trying to persuade reluctant sellers. However, if the initial approach is successful, the purchaser should arrange a meeting between directors of the purchaser (with or without advisers) and the seller (with or without advisers) to establish whether there is any interest on the seller's part to take the process forward to the next stage, to gauge the expectations of the seller and, at the same time, to obtain as much information as possible regarding the target which has proved unavailable to the purchaser through its initial searches.

8.3.2 Confidentiality

To make those discussions meaningful the purchaser will usually require the seller to release information regarding the target. To protect the seller from use of that information for purposes other than evaluating the target, the seller will normally seek a confidentiality undertaking. The seller's requirement for a confidentiality undertaking and its terms are discussed in greater detail in Part I (see Chapter 4, section 4.4). Typically, the confidentiality agreement will be prepared by the seller's lawyers and will contain several potentially onerous provisions so far as the purchaser is concerned.

At this point in the process, where the purchaser is trying to build a rapport with the seller, the purchaser may not want to take issue with the form of the confidentiality agreement since to do so may give the seller the wrong impression as to why the purchaser requires the information, especially if the purchaser is a trade competitor.

Despite these concerns, the purchaser should pay due consideration to the obligations being imposed on it to ensure that, in the particular circumstances of the proposed acquisition:

- the obligations are reasonably necessary for the protection of the target's business;
- in practice, the purchaser can comply with them;
- where obligations extend to third parties, the purchaser can control their actions;
- the obligations do not relate to information in the public domain, information the purchaser already has, information subsequently coming into the public domain, information given to the purchaser through no fault on the part of the purchaser, and information the purchaser is obliged to disclose (eg pursuant to a court order or the rules of the Stock Exchange); and
- the obligations cease on completion of the proposed transaction or, if the transaction does not proceed, on a predetermined date.

At this stage the purchaser may also require the seller to sign a confidentiality undertaking if, for example, it was proposed that the acquisition proceeds by way of share for share exchange and as a result the purchaser was likely to impart confidential information relating to it and to its business.

In addition, the purchaser may wish to consider obtaining a period of exclusivity from the seller to avoid becoming involved in an auction process. At this early stage in the process (ie before a deal in principle has been agreed) the seller is unlikely to agree to such a request. Nevertheless, the issue is worth consideration on the part of the purchaser and can be revisited if and when negotiations result in heads of agreement or otherwise an agreement in principle being reached.

Chapter 9

Negotiation

9.1   THE NEGOTIATION PROCESS

When a seller and purchaser sit down to negotiate a sale they will normally complete two tasks. First they will identify their relative attractiveness, and secondly they will assign an economic value limit to that attractiveness. A seller views his economic limit as the least amount he would be willing to accept, and a purchaser as the most he would be willing to pay. Each does this from their own unique perspective. If the alternative investment value to a purchaser is greater than the expected benefit of incremental profit, there is no objective profit motive to proceed and, in the absence of subjective motivation, a seller would seem better off to accept, say, income from the investment value of the required capital and forego expansion.

9.2   VALUATION

Agreeing the price is normally the most complex part of negotiating the deal, as the value of the target to a purchaser is unlikely to be the same as the value of the target to the seller. For example, one of the reasons stated earlier for acquiring a business is the desire to obtain assets which are undervalued in the eyes of the purchaser because it believes it can use them more efficiently than the original owners. In such instances, the purchaser may be prepared to pay more for the target than the value placed on it by the seller.

Given that the purchaser will be approaching the sellers of the potential targets with a view to persuading them to sell, the purchaser will need to carry out an initial valuation of a target to identify a range of prices it is prepared to offer. Establishing this price range is complicated by the fact that there is no standard means of valuing a business. Typically a purchaser will arrive at a range of prices by applying one of a number of formulae to the basic financial information available to it and adjusting the resultant figure to reflect additional benefits, savings or costs to the purchaser from the acquisition.

The objective and subjective elements of the typical valuation method are discussed in sections 9.2.1 below and 9.2.2, respectively.

9.2.1   The objective element

The scientific element of the valuation process is to apply various financial formulae to the available financial information on the target. The three most well-known financial formulae applied are; (a) price earnings; (b) net assets plus; and (c) discounted cash-flow.

(A)   Price earnings

A price earnings valuation is arrived at by multiplying the target's current or historic or averaged pre- or post-tax earnings by a gross or net price earnings (P/E) ratio.

The price earnings ratio of a listed company can be found on a daily basis in the financial pages of many national newspapers and is calculated by dividing the company's share price by its earnings per share. As a private company or business will not have a published p/e ratio, its p/e ratio is usually calculated by taking the average P/E ratio of comparable listed companies in the relevant business sector, adjusting it to reflect the performance of the target against the average and discounting the adjusted p/e multiple by anything up to one third.

When calculating a price earnings valuation, the earnings should not be taken as read but should be carefully considered to identify distortions in the profit figures (management charges, directors' drawings, depreciation charges, etc) and adjustments to the earnings should be made accordingly. Adjustments are sometimes made to the earnings to take into account future earnings if they will, for one reason or another (for example, the loss of a key proprietor), be materially different from historic earnings.

(B)   Net assets plus

The net assets plus means of valuation consists of two elements: a present day value of the net assets of target, and a value to reflect the earnings potential to the purchaser.

The first element is calculated by adjusting the target's balance sheet value of net assets to reflect their market value and to include any hidden liabilities. Examples of market value adjustments include:

- unless purchased or revalued recently, freehold land and buildings may be over- or undervalued;
- leasehold property may be overvalued because inadequate provision is included for depreciation, or undervalued if the target enjoys a fixed rent below market value;
- exclusion of any value attributed to goodwill (goodwill reflects the surplus over market or book value of the price paid on acquisition), and
- stocks may be overvalued due to obsolete or non-selling items not being recognised as such.

Examples of hidden liabilities include:

- costs of clean-up measures required to meet environmental regulations;
- contingent liabilities for claims not known or established at the balance sheet date;
- costs associated with the termination of leases, employment, property, etc if rationalisation is necessary.

Calculation of the second element, the value of the future earnings potential to the purchaser, is much more of an art than a science. It needs to take into account forecast profitability, cost savings and other synergistic benefits and a degree of realism.

(C)   Discounted cashflow

Discounted cashflow techniques are more common in the appraisal of major capital projects than in the valuation of acquisition targets. When applied to the acquisition of a company or business, these techniques place a net present value on that company or business equivalent to the sum of its expected free cashflows stemming from ownership (dividends, proceeds of sale, etc) to a horizon discounted by its cost of capital plus the forecasted value of the business at the horizon, also discounted back to present value. To arrive at such a valuation, an estimate must be made of the amount and timing of all cashflows during the estimated period of ownership and to this estimated figure a discount rate (also referred to as the cost of capital or required rate of return) is applied to convert future cashflows into a present value. The attractiveness of the discounted cashflow method of valuation reduces considerably if less than 100% of the company or business is acquired, because the purchaser will not have absolute control over the target's cash.

9.2.2 The subjective element

The adjustments mentioned above to the net asset value and earnings fall into the subjective category as they are, by necessity, subjective in nature. The valuation attributed to the target solely by use of financial formulae will not, of itself, reflect the value of the target to the purchaser. The valuation will need adjustment to take into account any benefits, savings or costs occurring to the purchaser as a result of the acquisition. Benefits may include the synergistic benefits arising as a result of cost savings and future trade between the target and other members of the purchaser's group and the intangible benefits to a purchaser. For example, a purchaser may be prepared to pay more for a business than is justifiable to prevent a competitor from acquiring the same business or to diversify out of a market in recession. Savings, for example, may include research and development costs scheduled to be incurred elsewhere in the purchaser's group but no longer necessary due to technology owned by the target. Costs may vary from those directly relating to the acquisition, for example the financing costs of the purchase price, to the costs of implementing a post-completion rationalisation plan.

9.3 PRICE

Taking into account the value placed on the business by using one of the methods outlined in section 9.2.1, and other relevant information obtained during discussions with the seller, the purchaser will need to formulate the terms of its opening offer to the seller. In doing so, the price offered will be of fundamental importance to the seller, as will the terms and method of payment. In formulating the terms of its opening offer the purchaser should bear in mind the following:

- the price it can afford to pay;
- the comparative cost of the alternative ways (if any) of achieving its business objective; and
- whether the anticipated returns from the target meet the required rate of return on the aggregate capital employment in the investment. In the case of a sale by tender or auction bid, the purchaser will also need to take into account the price likely to be tendered by competing bidders.

Where the acquisition has been initiated by the purchaser, the negotiation process will begin with the purchaser putting forward an offer, usually on terms it can improve if pushed by the seller. In putting forward the offer, if the purchaser wishes to avoid creating a binding offer, it must ensure that the offer is made on a subject to contract basis. The merits of using these magic words are discussed in Part I (Chapter 5, section 5.4).

However careful a purchaser may have been in formulating the terms of its offer, it is extremely unlikely that those terms will be acceptable to the seller without some negotiation. Typically the process would involve a number of offers, rejections and counter-offers. Ultimately the price is that which the purchaser is willing to pay and which the seller is prepared to accept. Earn-outs, where the seller remains in the business after it is acquired and part of the consideration for the sale of the target will depend upon the future results of the target, can often be used in negotiations to bridge the gap between the expectations of the seller and the purchaser.

9.4 PRICING STRUCTURES

In determining the terms of its offer to the seller and, in particular, the price, the purchaser will need to consider the various pricing structures available to it and the attractiveness of those structures to both the seller and it. The various structures range from the most straightforward, fixed consideration payable in cash on completion, through to more complex structures such as a price based wholly or partly on future performance. These various different structures are discussed below.

9.4.1 Fixed cash price

Fixed consideration payable in cash on completion is the most typical pricing format. It has the benefit of clarity and simplicity and avoids the potential for post-completion wrangles which might be encountered in other formats. A fixed price will often be the result of negotiation between the parties of a price originally based on a price earnings/net asset formula applied to historic financial information as adjusted to take into account benefits, savings and costs to the purchaser.

There are, however, occasions when the fixed price format may not be acceptable. For example, the purchaser may be unwilling to pay cash on completion for a business valued on a multiple of forecast earnings rather than actual figures, whilst the seller may be unwilling to sell on a value based on historic earnings because that valuation will not take into account what they may see as a certain future growth in earnings. In such cases, the parties may reach a compromise where an initial payment in cash on completion is made based on historic earnings and further consideration is payable dependent upon future profits of the business.

9.4.2 Formula cash price

Where the price for the target is struck by reference to a formula, such as a multiple of earnings or net assets, the parties have the choice of applying that formula to historic, actual or future financial performance. Applying the formula to future financial performance will only be acceptable if the seller is to continue to work in the business after the sale, otherwise the key determinant of price will be beyond the seller's control. Accordingly, in a majority of cases the parties' choice is, in practice, limited to historic or actual financial information. Where the historic and actual figures are unlikely to differ significantly the parties may, for reasons of simplicity, prefer to apply the formula to the historic information so that a price can be agreed and paid on completion. On the other hand, where the figures are likely to differ significantly the parties may agree to apply the formula to the financial position on completion. To do so it will be necessary to draw up an account of the business as at completion so that the earnings or net assets of the target can be calculated at that date. That account is commonly referred to as 'completion accounts'.

Unless the target is an extremely small business, it will usually take the parties some time to prepare and agree the completion accounts. To avoid the seller being out of pocket whilst the completion accounts are being prepared, the seller will commonly require payment on completion of a sum on account of the purchase price and for a final instalment to be paid immediately after the purchase price has been determined.

In practice, the use of completion accounts can lead to difficulties and disagreements if they are not used carefully. By and large the difficulties result from the fact that the purchase price is determined post-completion when the goodwill generated between the parties in the negotiation process has begun to dissipate, and from poor drafting of the appropriate provisions in the sale and purchase agreement. A more detailed discussion of completion accounts can be found in Part III (Chapter 12, section 12.2.6).

Where the price results from the application of a formula, as an alternative to applying the formula to the financial position on completion the acquisition could be structured as a fixed price payable in cash on completion (the fixed price reflecting the parties' view of the actual financial position) with the purchaser obtaining protection against the actual figures turning out to be materially different to those anticipated by the use of warranties or an indemnity (see Part III, Chapter 12, section 12.2.9, for a discussion of the differences between a warranty and an indemnity). In such cases, it will also be necessary to calculate the value of net assets on completion, and to do so completion accounts will be required. From the purchaser's point of view, it is preferable to structure the transaction on the basis of a formula rather than at a fixed price subject to warranty protection. This is because the formula will adjust the purchase price to reflect the underlying financial information (earnings or net assets) whereas a claim for breach of warranty (see Chapter 12, section 12.2.8) may not give rise to such a loss.

9.4.3 Deferred consideration

Deferring payment of part of the consideration until agreed future performance targets are met has obvious attractions to a purchaser. However, given that the attractions of deferred consideration to the purchaser will have the opposite effect on the seller, the use of deferred consideration is often limited to the following set of circumstances:

- to bridge the gap between the expectations of the seller and the purchaser; price negotiations frequently run into difficulties where the target is being sold on the basis of future potential value rather than past results. In such circumstances, the purchaser would be unwise to pay in full for the 'hope' value and the seller would be unwilling to sell unless the future potential was recognised in the price; and
- to motivate the seller in circumstances where the seller is required to manage the target after completion.

Sellers are usually most reluctant to accept a proposal to leave part of the purchase price outstanding on a deferred basis unless there is absolutely no alternative, although in practice it is not uncommon. Where they do, sellers will usually seek security for the part of the purchase price outstanding in the form of:

- retaining title to the assets until the consideration is paid in full;
- taking a charge over the assets of the business being sold (subject to financial assistance limitations – see section 9.5.1 (A)(ii)); or
- a parent company or bank guarantee of the purchaser's obligations.

As a purchaser does not offer such security, of course and many a seller 'has' to sell because of a need for the capital sum or financial problems some sellers will accept deferred consideration without such security. Note that any clause in a contract which specifies what will occur if the buyer goes out of business before the deferred consideration is paid may be subject to challenge under insolvency legislation – the right to set aside onerous contracts.

The most common form of deferred consideration is known as an 'earn out', where the seller is to continue to manage the target in the purchaser's ownership after completion, and is based wholly or partially on the level of future profits of the target. Earn-outs were common in the acquisition of service businesses as a means of providing the seller with an incentive to perform post-completion. A typical proposal might include an initial payment for the target shares to be made in cash on completion, followed by two or three annual instalments of additional consideration calculated by reference to the profits of the target in each of the two or three accounting periods after completion.

Whilst the concept of an earn-out is quite simple and its attractions in the above circumstances are quite obvious, earn-outs present certain practical and technical complications (for example, tax) and conflicts which have made them less popular. From the purchaser's point of view the major limitation on the use of earn-outs is the conflict between the seller's obvious desire to maximise profits in the short term and the purchaser's wish to retain the right (if necessary) to take steps during the earn out period which, although they may be in the long term interest of the target, potentially reduce profitability during the earn out period. The two interests may prove difficult to reconcile.

Calculations of earn-outs, although similar to completion accounts, give rise to additional problems since they are usually calculated over a period of a number of years and the business will then be controlled by the purchaser.

There are substantial taxation issues for the seller to consider if the price is deferred. In formulating a proposal based on a deferred consideration the purchaser will need to be aware of those issues, which are discussed in Part I (Chapter 5, section 5.3.2).

9.4.4   Fixed or formula price payable in shares

The purchaser can preserve its cash resources or avoid the raising of debt to finance the acquisition by satisfying the consideration payable by the issue of its shares to the seller or the placing of its shares to finance the purchase.

Depending upon the seller's personal circumstances and his need to have cash on completion, the issue of shares direct to the seller in whole or partial satisfaction of the consideration has the advantage of enabling the seller to postpone his capital gains tax liability until the consideration shares are sold. This is discussed in more detail in Part I (Chapter 3, section 3.2.1). Against this tax benefit, the seller will normally consider the commercial risk that the value of his consideration shares may go down as well as up, the price at which the consideration shares are to be valued for the purpose of calculating the number to be issued in satisfaction of the purchase price and the marketability of the consideration shares. Given that most private companies do not have a market in their shares this pricing structure is more likely to be applicable if the purchaser is listed on a recognised stock market.

9.5   FINANCING THE ACQUISITION

Whilst most sellers require the purchase price to be paid in cash on completion some will prefer to receive shares or loan notes in the capital of the purchaser because, amongst other things, it allows them to defer payment of tax arising from the sale.

Purchasers have three means of financing the purchase:

- cash;
- issue of shares;
- issue of loan capital.

The choice of financing the acquisition from borrowings or by the issue of shares depends upon a number of factors. For a listed public company purchaser, the effect of the acquisition on its own earnings per share will be a key factor in determining whether to issue shares since it could obtain an immediate improvement to its earnings per share by acquiring a company which is less highly rated in terms of its price earnings ratio. In addition, listed public companies usually prefer to issue shares in consideration for the acquisition if the acquisition would otherwise include a substantial goodwill write-off. Unless the purchaser is able to use merger accounting and/or merger relief (see paragraph 6 of section 9.6.3), which are only available in the context of a share for share exchange, the goodwill arising on the acquisition (being an amount equal to the purchase consideration less the value of the assets acquired) will be written off either against reserves or the purchaser's profit and loss account, in both cases having a depressive impact on future earnings.

From a seller's perspective, the immediate need for cash and his tax position will have a bearing on the method of funding.

9.5.1   Cash

Although the most frequent form of consideration, given that the purchaser is unlikely to have unallocated cash reserves waiting to be utilised in this way, the cash required to finance the purchase is often raised through borrowings or the issue of shares.

(A)   Borrowings

Two key considerations for the purchaser when the consideration is borrowed are usually whether:

- the borrowings attract tax relief; and
- the assets of the target can be used to secure the borrowings.

(i)   Tax relief

Relief is presently available to individuals on borrowings provided they are incurred for the purpose of investing in a close company (ITA 2007, ss 383, 392 – previously ICTA 1988, s 360) or purchasing an interest in an employee controlled company. The interest must be on a loan specifically taken out to make the investment (as opposed to overdraft interest) and the loan would normally be with a UK bank, although other loans may also qualify.

A close company is one controlled by five or fewer persons (or by its directors, however many). The company must meet certain qualifying conditions, but a trading company or a trading group would normally qualify and the individual must either have a material interest in the company (basically an interest of more than 5% of the ordinary share capital) or must work for the greater part of his time in the management or conduct of the company. An employee works for the greater part of his time for the company if he works for more than half of the normal working day (or half the normal working week, as the case may be). A person will only be treated as working in the actual management or conduct of the company if he is a director or has significant managerial responsibilities.

Relief for interest may be withdrawn at some stage in the future. For example, relief would be withdrawn (either in whole or in part, as the case maybe) if the employee sells or gives away shares, receives or is treated as receiving any payment of capital from the company, fails to retain a material interest in the company or fails to satisfy the necessary working requirement. However, interest does not cease to qualify for relief solely by reason of the fact that the company ceases to be a close company, although it is important that the company is close for a meaningful period after the time the investment is made. Timing issues can be important here, especially on management buy-outs.

The position should be straightforward for a corporate purchaser as a result of the Finance Act 1996. Essentially, wherever a loan relationship exists, a company will normally account for payments and receipts on an accruals basis. Hence, broadly, the tax treatment of interest should follow the accounting treatment. This is because, subject to certain exclusions, the legislation covers all profits and gains arising to a company within the charge to corporation tax on its loan relationships. The 1996 legislation moved away from a rigid income/capital divide in the way which taxation is applied to profits and losses for corporate debt and now follows accountancy practice quite closely.

In general, all profits and gains arising to a company from its loan relationships are treated as taxable income in the company's hands so that all profits, gains and losses arising from loan relationships (whether of an income or a capital nature) are to be charged or relieved as income consistently with the way they are recognised in the company's accounts. A loan relationship is defined as covering all loans to which a company is party, whether as a debtor or creditor, although trade debtors and creditors are outside the new regime. The definition of a loan relationship does not, however, extend to shares.

The old rules relating to the tax treatment of loans used to make the distinction between 'yearly interest' and 'short interest' important, but now this is only relevant for withholding purposes and tax is withheld on yearly interest at the lower rate of 20%.

As a rule of thumb, it is generally accepted that yearly interest is interest on a loan which is capable of exceeding one year (which would include a bank overdraft even though this could be called at any time), so that short interest is interest payable under an obligation which cannot exceed a year. This is something of an over-simplification and it is well worth reading the authorities, in particular *Minsham Properties v Price* [1990] STC 718.

Accordingly, where any yearly interest is paid to a company, or by any person to another person whose usual place of abode is outside the UK, the payer has an obligation to withhold tax from the payment of interest at the rate referred to in section 9.5.1 (A)(i). There are various exemptions, including that a company does not need to withhold tax on making any payment of interest to a bank which brings the interest into charge in the UK, or where a double tax treaty applies to reduce the withholding, or, most recently, a payment to another UK company.

The use of a holding company, set up by the individual purchaser or purchasers to buy the target company, will facilitate the financing, both from a commercial point of view and from a tax point of view. The tax issues can be best illustrated with an example. Assume that four individuals propose to buy a target company for £200,000. They have a total of £50,000 (ie £12,500 each) to invest by way of equity and will raise the remaining £150,000 by loan from the bank, on terms that the principal be repaid by equal instalments over ten years.

112

The individuals could buy the target company direct and borrow the money from the bank to finance this acquisition. They would then be entitled to claim tax relief on the interest. In principle they could fund the interest payment out of salary, bonuses or dividends so that their net income tax position would be neutral. In other words, they would have taxable income but also a matching tax relief. Repayment of capital, however, would be out of taxed income.

By comparison, repayment of capital by using a holding company was sometimes more tax efficient. The holding company would borrow money secured on the target company's assets (subject to the rules against financial assistance (now abolished for private companies) which are covered in detail later in this chapter). Relief from corporation tax is still available for the interest charge. However, as the taxable profits arise in the target company (which is now a subsidiary) it will need to pay a dividend to the parent to fund the interest expense arising in the holding company. This will satisfy the cashflow requirements of the parent company, and previously involved no additional costs when a dividend received by one UK company from another is tax free (this was in ICTA 1988, s 208). However s 208 was replaced with CTA 2009, s 1285 which itself was replaced by the Finance Act 2009 by way of amendment now in CTA 2009, Pt 9A and Finance (No 3) Act 2010). Interest is therefore paid out of the parent, and provided that the expenses are surrendered down to the subsidiary by way of group relief the cash and the interest expense end up in the correct company. Hence, the interest expense incurred by the new holding company can be used by the target company to reduce its taxable profits. The position on interest is therefore the same as with personal borrowings.

The advantage of using a holding company is in the repayment of capital. Rates of corporation tax presently (2014/15) vary from 20% (up to £300,000) to 21% (over £1,500,000), compared with the rates of income tax which vary, essentially between 20% and 45%. The new group will still have to repay the principal out of taxed profits but the profits used to repay principal will have borne a lower rate of tax than if they are first paid to the employee.

The rules are complex and as can be seen above have changed over the years so specialist tax advice should be sought. HMRC summarise their position on borrowing to fund purchase of shares in a close company as follows:

'SAIM10210 – Relief for interest paid: interest in a close company

Loan to buy interest in a close company

ITA07/S392 gives relief for interest paid on a loan applied:

- in acquiring any part of the ordinary share capital of a close company (see CTM60000 onwards and SAIM10220) including shares acquired before a material interest is obtained (see SAIM10240),
- in lending money to a company, which is used wholly and exclusively for the purposes of its business or that of any associated close company qualifying under ITA07/S393 (see SAIM10220). "Associated company" has the same meaning as in ICTA88/S416 (1) (see (g) of CTM60310). Lending to a close company would include using a loan to acquire

convertible loan stock in the company, provided the other conditions for relief are satisfied, or

- in paying off another loan if interest on that loan would have been eligible for relief if it had continued. ITA07/S408 provides that in such a case, the loans are, for the purpose of the rules in ITA07/S392, to be treated as if they were one loan.

Cases where relief is not due

Relief is not due where the individual who acquires the shares, or his or her spouse or civil partner, makes a claim for relief under the Enterprise Investment Scheme under Part 5 of ITA07 or under Schedule 5B TCGA92.'

From: http://www.hmrc.gov.uk/manuals/saimmanual/saim10210.htm.

'SAIM10220 – Relief for interest paid: interest in a close company: "eligibility requirements"

Eligibility for interest relief on loans to buy interest in a close company

ITA07/S393 sets out the following two conditions for relief:

- when the interest is paid the company must not be a close investment holding company, and
- both the "capital recovery condition" (SAIM10250) and either the "full time working condition" (SAIM10230) or the "material interest condition" (SAIM10240) must be met.

The company must therefore have been a close company for tax purposes throughout the period beginning immediately after the application of the money and ending with the payment of interest giving rise to the claim for relief.

SP3/78 provides that relief should not be refused in a case where, after the application of any loan, the company ceases to be close, provided that all the other conditions for relief, including those referred to in SAIM10250, are satisfied.

Close investment holding companies

CTM60700 onwards has guidance on close investment holding companies.

No relief under ITA07/S392 is due unless at the time the ordinary share capital is acquired and when the interest is paid the company exists wholly or mainly for one of the purposes listed at (a) – (f) of CTM60710. A company will exist wholly or mainly for a particular purpose if at the requisite time that "purpose" is the end or ultimate object of the company (see the case of Lord v Tustain (65TC761)). As regards companies which commence liquidation, see CTM60780.'

From: http://www.hmrc.gov.uk/manuals/saimmanual/saim10220.htm.

The HMRC page on relief for interest payments in general to which the above pages link is at http://www.hmrc.gov.uk/manuals/saimmanual/saim10010.htm.

A further HMRC summary is below:

'Qualifying loans and alternative finance arrangements

Tax relief is available for interest on loans where the borrowed money is used for certain specific purposes.

You can also claim relief for alternative finance payments paid on a qualifying alternative finance arrangement on the same basis as someone claiming relief for interest paid on a loan.

You may be able to claim relief for interest paid or for alternative finance payments where the loan or alternative finance arrangement is used to:

- buy ordinary shares in, or lend money to, a close company in which you own more than 5% of the ordinary share capital on your own or with associates
- buy ordinary shares in, or lend money to, a close company in which you own any part of the share capital and work for the greater part of your time in the management and conduct of the company's business, or that of an associated company
- acquire ordinary share capital in an employee controlled company if you are a full-time employee – we regard you as a full-time employee if you work for the greater part of your time as a director or employee of the company or of a subsidiary in which the company has an interest of 51% or more
- acquire a share or shares in, or to lend money to, a co-operative which is used wholly and exclusively for the purposes of its business
- acquire an interest in a trading or professional partnership (including a Limited Liability Partnership (LLP) constituted under the LLP Act 2000, other than an investment LLP)
- to provide a partnership, including an LLP with funds by way of capital or premium or in advancing money, where the money contributed or advanced is used wholly for the partnership's business
- buy equipment or machinery for use in your work for your employer, or by a partnership (unless you have already deducted the interest as a business expense) – relief is only available if you, or the partnership, were entitled to claim capital allowances on the item(s) in question – if the equipment or machinery was used only partly for your employment, or only partly for the partnership business, only the business proportion of the loan interest or alternative finance payments qualifies for relief)

You should enter interest on loans and alternative finance payments, under an alternative finance arrangement to buy or improve rental properties, on the UK property pages.

You cannot claim relief for interest on overdrafts or credit cards.

If you are not sure whether you can claim relief for any interest paid or alternative finance payments, ask HM Revenue and Customs (HMRC) or your tax adviser.

Limit on Income Tax reliefs

The limit on Income Tax reliefs restricts the total amount of qualifying loan interest relief and certain other reliefs in each year to the greater of £50,000 and 25% of "adjusted total income".

For more information about the limit on Income Tax reliefs, go to Helpsheet 204 Limit on Income Tax reliefs.'

(See HMRC Guidance (updated May 2017) *HS340 Interest and alternative finance payments eligible for relief on qualifying loans and alternative finance arrangements* at https://www.gov.uk/government/publications/interest-and-alternative-finance-payments-eligible-for-relief-on-qualifying-loans-and-alternative-finance-arrangements-hs340-self-assessment-help-shee/hs340-interest-and-alternative-finance-payments-eligible-for-relief-on-qualifying-loans-and-alternative-finance-arrangements-2015#qualifying-loans-and-alternative-finance-arrangements.)

(ii)   Security for borrowings

Where the consideration is borrowed, the lender will usually require the purchaser to provide a means of securing the repayment of those borrowings. In a typical case where the purchaser has already fully charged its assets to secure its existing borrowings, the only means of providing security is to charge the newly acquired assets of the target.

Where the purchaser is purchasing the shares of the target, it cannot secure the borrowings on the assets of target without considering the financial assistance provisions of CA 2006. Earlier restrictions on 'financial assistance' as they applied to **private** companies were abolished with effect from 1 October 2008. They are therefore not addressed below. However, it is vital to be aware that there are important provisions relating to public companies prohibiting financial assistance which are still relevant. This book considers private company acquisitions only, not public acquisitions and therefore they are not described below. Even the old provisions of CA 1985 only related to the acquisition of shares and had no relevance whatsoever to business transfers.

The relevant provisions concerning financial assistance were contained in CA 1985, ss 151–168 (now abolished by CA 2006, ss 678–680). Subject to an important exception for private companies, CA 1985, s 151(1) made it unlawful, where a person was acquiring or proposing to acquire shares in a company, for the company or any of its subsidiaries to give financial assistance directly or indirectly for the purpose of that acquisition either before or at the same time as the acquisition takes place. Section 151(2) provided that where a person has acquired shares in a company and any liability has been incurred (by that or any other person) for the purpose of that acquisition, it is not lawful for the company or any of its subsidiaries to give financial assistance directly or indirectly for the purpose of reducing or discharging the liability so incurred. There were various exemptions too under the old law.

The prohibition on financial assistance by private companies (including the so-called 'white wash procedure') was repealed from 1 October 2008. CA 2006 provisions relating to financial assistance for purchase of own shares are in force. The Companies House summary below provides a useful indication of the practical issues arising under the rules:

Are private companies prohibited from giving financial assistance for the acquisition of their own shares under the Companies Act 2006?

The Companies Act 2006 does not prohibit a private company from giving financial assistance for the acquisition of its own shares (although if it has a subsidiary which is a public company, the public company may not assist the acquisition of shares in the private holding company). The Companies Act 1985 prohibits private companies from giving financial assistance for the acquisition of their own shares unless certain conditions are satisfied. The prohibition will be repealed in October 2008: until then, the prohibition remains in place.

When did the rules change that govern the giving of financial assistance by private and public companies for acquisition of shares in themselves or their holding companies?

The rules changed for private companies on 1 October 2008. The rules did not change for public companies.

Why did the changes to the financial assistance provisions not come into force with the rest of the share capital provisions in October 2009?

Although financial assistance is part of the share capital provisions of the Act it is a simple matter to abolish the prohibition for private companies, and 'whitewash', separately from those provisions.

How have the changes to the rules that govern financial assistance for acquisition of shares, brought in by Companies Act 2006, affected private and public companies?

The Companies Act 1985 prohibited a company from granting financial assistance (for example by means of a non-commercial loan) for the acquisition of shares in itself or its holding company: but one exception was that private companies may grant such assistance by going through a complex and expensive procedure, often referred to as 'whitewash'.

Under the Companies Act 2006, the prohibition on granting financial assistance has been wholly lifted for private companies but has remained in place for public companies.

What is the effect of the lifting of the prohibition against financial assistance by private companies on transactions of a type previously

---

117

covered by both the prohibition and court rulings that they were unlawful for other reasons?

It has been agreed with stakeholders the terms of a 'saving' in the Commencement Order, and an explanatory passage in the accompanying Explanatory Memorandum, which makes clear that a transaction will be lawful if the only reason for it previously being unlawful was the prohibition in section 151 of the 1985 Act on financial assistance for the acquisition of shares; it remains unlawful under Companies Act 2006 if there was some other reason for it previously being unlawful.

The 'saving' will force directors to assess lawfulness according to common-law rules. How will they know 'where to draw the line'?

'Where to draw the line' is a matter of which directors already needed to be aware under the provisions of the Companies Act 1985; if they are not, they are at risk of causing their companies to enter unlawful transactions. A purported whitewash of something otherwise unlawful at common law would be ineffective, so directors and companies already have to satisfy themselves before applying whitewash that the proposed transaction is not one that would be unlawful at common law.

Do these implementations have any effect on Companies House forms?

Yes, these changes have involved the withdrawal of the following Companies House forms:

155(6a) – Declaration in relation to assistance for the acquisition of shares

155(6b) – Declaration by directors of a holding company in relation to assistance for the acquisition of shares.

(Companies House Summary)

(iii) Financial assistance whitewash – abolished October 2008

The requirement for what was known as 'whitewash' for private companies was abolished from 1 October 2008. This was an important exception limited to private companies. The section below is therefore no longer relevant but is likely to remain of some historical interest and readers may read about 'whitewash' and wish to know what it was. It is therefore retained below. CA 1985, s 155 permitted a private company to give financial assistance for the acquisition of its shares (or those of its holding company being a private company with no intermediate public company) if the provisions of that section and ss 156–158 of CA 1985 were complied with. Such assistance may, however, only be given if the company has net assets which are not thereby reduced, or, to the extent that those assets are thereby reduced, if the financial assistance is provided out of distributable profits. In order to take advantage of s 155 a company must comply with a number of formalities. These include:

- the making of a statutory declaration by the company's directors in Form No 155(6)(a) as prescribed by the Companies (Forms) Regulations 1985 (SI 1985/854) (or Form No 155(6)(b) where the financial assistance is for the acquisition of shares in the company's holding company). Among the matters to be sworn by the directors is a statement that the company 'will be able to pay its debts as they fall due during the year immediately following the date on which the financial assistance is proposed to be given'. Where the financial assistance is being given by a target company, its directors prior to change of control will not wish to swear such a statement except in the (unlikely) event of their retaining control for the year following the assistance being given. For similar reasons auditors appointed by the old regime will be unwilling to give a report as next mentioned;

- there must be attached to the statutory declaration a report by the company's auditors in accordance with CA 1985, s 156(4);

- the provision of financial assistance must be approved by a special resolution of the company in general meeting, unless it is a wholly-owned subsidiary. Where the provision of assistance is for shares in a holding company, the holding company and any intermediate holding company, must also approve the provision of financial assistance by special resolution; and

- the financial assistance must be given within the time limits provided in CA 1985, s 158, and may not be given where an application for the cancellation of any such special resolution is made under s 158(3) before the final determination of the application, unless the court otherwise orders. Such an application may be made by the holders of not less than 10% in aggregate in nominal value of the company's issued share capital or any class thereof, or if the company is not limited by shares, by not less than 10% of the company's members.

It should be noted that whether the company giving financial assistance is public or private, it will, in addition to fulfilling the statutory conditions, need to alter its articles if these incorporate reg 10 of Table A of CA 1948, which regulation repeats the prohibitions on a company providing financial assistance for the purchase of its shares formerly contained in s 54 of that Act.

Consequences of a breach of the financial assistance provisions of CA 1985 included civil actions by the company in breach against its own directors for misfeasance or breach of fiduciary duties and/or duties of fidelity, to recover the loss to the company, which will normally be a sum equal to the extent of the financial assistance provided. Civil consequences may also include an action against the recipient of the financial assistance if it can be proved that the recipient actually or constructively knew that the directors were acting in breach of their fiduciary duties. In addition to the civil liabilities, officers of the company in breach may face criminal penalties (CA 1985, s 151(3)).

As stated above, since 1 October 2008 the financial assistance provisions do not apply to private companies so any need to "whitewash" in this way has been removed. This change was a very useful simplification for companies. Public companies are still caught and should take legal advice. They are not covered in this book which concentrates on private acquisitions.

(B)   Shares

As an alternative to borrowing money to finance a cash consideration, the purchaser may wish to consider the prior issue of shares to fund the acquisition. The financing of an acquisition by the issue of equity is more common in the case of listed companies due to the marketability of listed shares, but nevertheless the prior issue of equity to raise finance for the purchase is available to private companies, especially in these days of venture capitalists actively seeking development capital opportunities.

The issue of shares commonly takes the form of a rights issue, an open offer or a placing. A rights issue broadly means a share offer to shareholders pro rata to their existing holdings, whereas a placing means the sale of new shares to selected persons. An open offer is similar to a rights issue in that it is a share offer to shareholders pro rata to their existing holdings. It differs, however, in that shareholders are given an opportunity to take up excess shares if and to the extent that other shareholders do not take up their entitlement. Because of this, open offers do not include any arrangements to sell any shares not taken up for the benefit of shareholders. If excess applications cannot be met in full, applications for the excess are usually scaled down.

Purchasers proposing to raise cash to fund an acquisition by way of a rights issue, placing, seller placing, open offer or other form of share issue should give consideration to the following points.

(i)   Does the purchaser have sufficient unissued authorised share capital?

If the purchaser does not have sufficient authorised but unissued share capital, a general meeting of its shareholders will need to be called to pass a resolution authorising an increase to enable the consideration shares to be issued. If so authorised by its articles, CA 1985, s 121 allows a company to increase its share capital by new shares in such amounts as it thinks expedient. Generally, articles of association provide for the authorised share capital to be increased by ordinary resolution. The CA 2006, s 617 made changes to s 121. CA 2006 abolished the concept of authorised share capital entirely. However many many companies still have authorised capital so it is not correct to assume this issue will never now arise. Companies set up before 1 October 2009 will have an authorised share capital unless later they have changed their memorandum of association. That company can then only issue shares up to the amount specified in its articles of association as its authorised capital. Under CA 2006 shares can simply be created and allotted by Board resolution, subject to the necessary shareholder authorisation. The requirement to state a company's share capital at the outset is abolished for new companies. The memorandum and articles, and amendments to them, should always be checked in every case.

(ii) CA 2006, s 549 et seq (ex CA 1985, s 80) – authority to allot

Since 1 October 2009, for most private companies there is no need for authority to allot shares so the paragraphs below are simply of historical relevance. Some companies however may have enshrined such provisions in their Articles. The position should always be checked. CA 1985, s 80 until 1 October 2009 prohibited the directors of a company from allotting 'relevant securities' (which includes ordinary shares) unless authorised by an ordinary resolution of the company in general meeting or by the company's articles. Usual practice was for the authority to be given by an ordinary resolution. It had to state the maximum amount of relevant securities that may be allotted and the date on which the authority will expire, which must not be more than five years from the date on which it is given.

A private company normally gave a five-year authority over all of its authorised but unissued capital, whereas a listed public company will wish to comply with the guidelines of the Investor Protection Committees (IPCs). These are committees through which the large institutional shareholders such as the insurance companies and pension funds co ordinate their policies. They comprise the Association of British Insurers (ABI) and the National Association of Pension Funds (NAPF). The IPCs have no statutory or other legal standing, but since they represent the owners of the majority of shares in UK listed companies their 'guidelines' are as effective as if they had been enacted.

The directors' power to issue shares should, therefore, be checked by looking at the purchaser's articles and its latest s 80 authority, which is likely to have been obtained at a recent extraordinary or annual general meeting. If the directors do not have sufficient authority then a general meeting of the purchaser will be necessary to give such approval by way of ordinary resolution.

(iii) CA 2006, s 561 – pre-emption rights

Since 1 October 2009, CA 2006, s 561 applies. This provides:

's 561 Existing shareholders' right of pre-emption

(1) A company must not allot equity securities to a person on any terms unless—
   (a) it has made an offer to each person who holds ordinary shares in the company to allot to him on the same or more favourable terms a proportion of those securities that is as nearly as practicable equal to the proportion in nominal value held by him of the ordinary share capital of the company, and
   (b) the period during which any such offer may be accepted has expired or the company has received notice of the acceptance or refusal of every offer so made.

(2) Securities that a company has offered to allot to a holder of ordinary shares may be allotted to him, or anyone in whose favour he has renounced his right to their allotment, without contravening subsection (1)(b).

(3) ... [Repealed by SI 2009/2561]

(4) Shares held by the company as treasury shares are disregarded for the purposes of this section, so that—

    (a) the company is not treated as a person who holds ordinary shares, and

    (b) the shares are not treated as forming part of the ordinary share capital of the company.

(5) This section is subject to—

    (a) sections 564 to 566 (exceptions to pre-emption right),

    (b) sections 567 and 568 (exclusion of rights of pre-emption),

    (c) sections 569 to 573 (disapplication of pre-emption rights), and

    (d) section 576 (saving for certain older pre-emption procedures).'

As can be seen this is very similar to s 85 of CA 1985 below, including the provisions in CA 2006, ss 569–573 disapplying pre-emption rights.

By virtue of CA 2006, s 569 ('Disapplication of pre-emption rights: private company with only one class of shares'), since 1 October 2009, the directors of a private company that has only one class of shares may be given power by the articles, or by a special resolution of the company, to allot equity securities of that class as if s 561 (existing shareholders' right of pre-emption) (a) did not apply to the allotment, or (b) applied to the allotment with such modifications as the directors may determine.

In addition to the statutory pre-emption rights, listed public companies are also subject to the IPCs' guidelines and the pre-emption rules contained in the Listing Rules (paras 9.3.11 and 9.3.12). These are similar to the statutory pre-emption rights but more flexible in a number of areas.

The current IPCs' guidelines relating to rights issues state that the IPCs will advise their members to approve a s 95 resolution for an annual disapplication of s 89 provided it is restricted to 5% of the issued ordinary share capital (or 7.5% in any rolling three-year period) and that any discount on issue shall be restricted to a maximum of 5% of the middle of the best bid and offer prices immediately prior to the announcement of the issue or proposed issue.

In the context of vendor placings, it is a requirement of the IPCs that where an issue amounts to more than 10% of the existing issued equity capital of the issuer or where the consideration shares are to be placed at a discount to market value in excess of 5%, then the consideration shares should be offered in the first instance to the shareholders of the issuer. This process is known as 'clawback'. A shareholder clawback may be achieved by a vendor placing with an 'open offer' to shareholders or a rights issue. In both cases, the purchaser's merchant bank or stockbroker will agree with the sellers to purchase or procure purchasers for the consideration shares and then to offer them on a pro-rata basis to the company's shareholders.

Because the conditions which have to be satisfied in order to comply with s 89 are strict, if the circumstances of a proposed rights issue make compliance with these conditions impossible, consideration has to be given to the disapplication of s 89 pursuant to the CA 1985, s 95. (See below for the equivalent provision from 1 October 2009 under CA 2006, s 569.)

In such cases, disapplication has the following advantages:

Duration of the offer

The 21-day period during which the offer has to be open to shareholders under CA 1985, s 90(6) only starts to run once the offer is made. If sent by post, the offer is deemed to be made at the time when the letter would be delivered in the ordinary course of business. This makes the offer period longer than the straightforward 21-day period required by the UK Listing Authority for acceptance of a rights issue.

Fractional entitlements

Section 89(1)(a) requires an offer to be made to each person holding relevant securities of a proportion 'which is as nearly as practicable equal to the proportion in nominal value held by him of the aggregate of the relevant shares'. The view generally taken by practitioners is that fractions of a share arising on a rights issue should be rounded up or down to the nearest whole number in order to comply with s 89. This means that it is practically impossible for the company to raise a round sum, and results in the company losing the benefits that it would otherwise have had from the sale of fractions. If s 89 is disapplied, provision can be made for fractions to be sold for the company's benefit.

Overseas shareholders

Probably the most important reason for having a s 95 disapplication is with regard to the problem of overseas shareholders. In certain cases it may be preferable not to offer shares to overseas shareholders to avoid breach of the local securities laws (especially if the shareholder is based in the United States), but instead to give those holders the money's worth of those rights.

The statutory pre-emption procedures require that the offer is made to all shareholders (including overseas shareholders), although it allows the offer to be made to them by way of a notice in the London Gazette. Section 90 of CA 1985 provides for two alternative forms of publication in the London Gazette, either to advertise the offer itself or to insert a notice specifying where a copy of the offer can be obtained. The publication of the notice in the London Gazette coupled with the distribution of a circular letter to overseas shareholders will almost certainly breach the local securities laws in a number of countries including, in particular, the United States in cases where the number of shares held by US or Canadian shareholders exceeds 1.5% of the offeror's issued share capital.

If overseas shareholders are a concern, it is preferable to disapply the statutory pre-emption rights so that the offer is not made to them, with arrangements being made for their entitlements to be aggregated and sold in the market with the net proceeds being remitted to them.

Prior to 1 October 2009, s 89(1) of CA 1985 provided that, except in certain circumstances, shares shall not be issued to any person unless an offer is made to each shareholder to allot to him on the same or more favourable terms a proportion of the shares to be issued which is equal to the proportion held by him of the aggregate issued share capital. Section 89(1) did not, however, apply to an allotment of shares wholly or partially paid up otherwise than in cash (s 89(4)). This means that an issue of shares in consideration for the acquisition of the target company or business can be made without having first to offer the consideration shares to existing shareholders. Although the statutory pre-emption right contained in s 89 is not a concern in this context, the purchaser's articles may (although it would be unusual) contain additional pre-emption rights and, as such, they should always be checked.

(iv)   Listing particulars

If the shares to be issued in connection with an acquisition increase the shares of a class already issued by 10% or more and a listing is sought for the acquisition shares issued by the purchaser, Listing Particulars will be necessary containing the information required by Chapter 5 of the Listing Rules. In addition to the specific information required to be included by Chapter 5, the general duty of disclosure imposed by FSMA 2000, s 80 must be satisfied.

The requirement for the purchaser to publish Listing Particulars is in addition to the requirement, in the case of Class 1 and related party transactions, to publish a circular to its shareholders pursuant to Chapters 10 and 11 of the Listing Rules.

9.5.2   Issue of shares

As an alternative to raising cash to pay the seller through an issue of shares, the purchaser may prefer to issue shares direct to the seller in satisfaction of the whole or part of the purchase consideration. A seller may be persuaded to accept the issue of shares rather than the receipt of cash if it allows him to defer the capital gains tax payable and the shares in question are both readily marketable and of stable value or if the purchaser is the only choice and has no other means of financing the purchase. The marketability requirement usually rules out the issue of shares by unlisted companies and the stability issue rules out many of the listed companies!

Where the purchaser would prefer to issue shares but the seller requires cash, the conflicting objectives of each party may be realised by a seller placing. A seller placing involves the issue of new shares by the purchaser to the seller (thereby satisfying the merger relief/accounting requirements) and the placing of the new shares by the purchaser's merchant bank or stockbroker on behalf of the seller to provide the seller with an immediate cash consideration. Where it is agreed that the seller shall receive shares in consideration of the target it must be made clear whether those shares in the purchaser rank for the current dividend or not.

From the purchaser's perspective, the advantage of the issue of shares is the potential availability of merger accounting or merger relief (see section 9.5.3). The other points purchasers need to consider when issuing shares are:

- where a public company purchaser is proposing to issue shares on the acquisition of certain assets rather than all the assets and liabilities or the shares of the target, it may be required to have the target's assets valued. CA 2006, s 593 prohibits a public company from issuing shares otherwise than for cash unless the consideration for the allotment has been valued, a report of its value has been made to the company during the six months prior to the allotment and a copy of the report has been sent to the proposed allottee. Under s 594(1) the general prohibition from issuing shares otherwise than for cash does not apply to shares allotted in consideration of the transfer of shares and, under s 595(1) (s 595(2) was repealed by SI 2009/2561), to the allotment of shares in consideration of the acquisition of all the assets and liabilities of a company,
- where the shares issued to the seller represent a material proportion of the purchaser's shares, a listed purchaser or a purchaser whose shares are traded on a recognised exchange may wish to impose restrictions on the sale of the consideration shares to avoid them being 'dumped' on the market with a corresponding impact on the purchaser's share price.

9.5.3 Issue of loan capital

When the seller is willing to take part or all of the consideration in a form other than cash in order to defer the capital gains tax payable as a result of the sale, as an alternative to shares the purchaser may prefer to issue, and the seller accept, a loan note or series of loan notes. A loan note is usually a fairly straightforward document recording the grantor's indebtedness to the holder, the interest payable and the terms of repayment. A loan note may or may not be secured and obviously from the seller's perspective the attraction of a loan note will partly depend upon the credit-worthiness of the purchaser and/or the security being offered by the purchaser and partly on the interest rate payable.

From the seller's point of view the attraction of loan notes and shares is the ability to spread the cash realisation over a number of years, allowing him to spread the period for reinvestment and roll-over the tax charge into a number of tax years thereby taking advantage of his annual exemptions.

However, loan notes may be preferred to shares where the purchaser is a private company, given that the loan notes will rank ahead of shares if the worst were to happen and the purchaser were to be liquidated.

From the purchaser's point of view, the issue of loan notes would be preferable if they are unsecured and carry a rate of interest less than that at which it could borrow a corresponding amount.

Loan notes are sometimes requested by sellers to spread the capital gain on the sale of the target over a number of tax years, thereby giving them the benefit of their annual exemption. In addition, from the seller's point of view they also have the attraction of spreading the period for reinvestment and give the seller more time for a considered investment strategy to be developed. However, unless the loan notes are guaranteed by the purchaser's bankers or in some other way secured on the assets of the purchaser, by accepting a loan note the seller is accepting a huge credit risk and the financial covenant of the purchaser should be considered before doing so.

9.6   SHARES OR ASSETS?

9.6.1   Preferred choice

Where a purchaser has the choice of structuring the purchase as a share purchase or a purchase of assets, subject to circumstances particular to the proposed transaction or that purchaser, in many cases the purchaser will opt for a purchase of assets for the following reasons:

9.6.2   Advantages of a purchase of assets

The principal reasons for choosing to purchase assets rather than shares are as follows.

(A)   Ability to avoid unknown liabilities

In buying the target itself, the purchaser takes on all liabilities of that company and its business, even those it does not know about or want. The purchaser will have the opportunity to protect itself against actual, contingent or unknown liabilities at the time of purchase, either by means of warranties or indemnities or a retention of part of the purchase price, but this is often unsatisfactory. Warranties and indemnities are usually subject to limitations, they are difficult to enforce when the seller is retained in the business and, in practice, their enforceability is subject to the seller having the means to meet the claim. A retention, on the other hand, only really protects the purchaser from known or contingent liabilities.

(B)   Opportunity to select assets and liabilities to be acquired

An asset purchase is the purchase of a bundle of identifiable assets and liabilities. With a few exceptions, the purchaser can therefore select those assets and liabilities which it wishes to take on and, by excluding them from the purchase, the purchaser can avoid the risks associated with unknown contracts or liabilities it cannot quantify. The few exceptions include employee liabilities and environmental liabilities (see Chapter 10, section 10.2.5).

(C)   Ability to charge target's assets

If the purchaser requires debt finance to pay for the acquisition, the purchase of assets has the great advantage of enabling the purchaser to charge the assets being purchased as security for the sums borrowed. By contrast, the granting by a target of a charge over its own assets to secure borrowings incurred by a purchaser for the purpose of acquiring its shares is, for public companies but not private companies (see above on financial assistance), prohibited by CA 2006, s 678. Public companies are prohibited, and since 1 October 2009 there is criminal liability for this both on the part of the company and every officer.

(D)   Apportionment advantages

The cost of trading stock is normally deductible for tax purposes. The purchaser can thereby gain an advantage by arguing for a relatively high apportionment of the purchase price to trading stock (as against something like goodwill which does not qualify for deduction). This is considered in more detail in the section on apportionment in Part III (see Chapter 13, section 13.2.4 (B)).

The cost of acquiring certain assets (plant and machinery, certain intellectual property rights and industrial buildings) will qualify for a deduction against income as a capital allowance, and provided these assets continue to be held by the purchaser, the purchase price is effectively reduced by the capital allowances received. At present, the purchaser can claim no deduction for tax purposes for the cost of acquiring shares in the target (except for capital gains tax purposes as and when the shares are subsequently disposed of), although this may be under review. The benefits to the purchaser through the availability of capital allowances must be weighed against the risk for the seller of balancing charges if the assets are sold for more than their written down value.

(E)   Availability of roll-over relief

The attraction of roll-over relief to certain sellers has already been noted in Part I. It may be that the investment being made by the purchaser qualifies as a reinvestment of the proceeds of a previous sale of qualifying assets for roll-over relief purposes. New assets must generally be purchased within three years of the sale of the old assets, and it may be that the purchase of a business (with its goodwill, land and buildings, etc) is crucial so far as the purchaser is concerned to ensure that the gain made on the disposal of the old assets is deferred.

The HMRC summary below helps explain roll over relief:

Business Asset Roll-Over Relief

This applies when you dispose of some types of business asset, which you intend to replace. You may be able to 'roll-over' or postpone the payment of any Capital Gains Tax that would normally be due.

Who qualifies?

You can claim the relief if you're trading and you use both the assets sold or disposed of and the new assets in your trade. For example, you may be able to get relief if you sell your butcher's shop and buy a new one.

Conditions you must meet

You must buy the new asset between 1 year before and 3 years after the date you disposed of the old asset.

HM Revenue & Customs (HMRC) may extend this time limit in exceptional circumstances.

There are different additional conditions for different types of disposal. For example, land and buildings must be occupied as well as used for your trade.

See the helpsheet below for more on the qualifying conditions and time limits.

See the latest helpsheet on Business Asset Roll-Over Relief – Helpsheet 290 (at https://www.gov.uk/government/publications/business-asset-roll-over-relief-hs290-self-assessment-helpsheet which is regularly updated by HMRC).

How the relief works

If you've reinvested all of the proceeds from the sale or disposal in new business assets, you can 'roll-over' (or postpone) all the gain. There'll be no tax to pay at that time.

You may still be able to postpone part of the gain if either of the following applies:

- you only reinvested part of the proceeds
- your old asset has only partly been used for your business, for example, you rented out a property for a time and then started using it in your trade

You only work out the tax due when you sell or dispose of the new asset. You then work out the tax due by reducing the cost of the new asset by the amount of the postponed gain.

Example

You sell your shop for £75,000 and buy a new shop costing £90,000. If you claim relief you'll not pay tax on the gains made on the sale of the old shop until you sell the new one.

Example

You bought a freehold office for £45,000 and sell it for £75,000.

You make a gain of £30,000.

You reinvest all of the proceeds in new freehold business premises costing £90,000.

You can postpone the whole of the £30,000 gain made on the sale of the old office, as you have reinvested all of the proceeds.

When you sell the new business premises and work out your Capital Gains Tax bill, you'll treat the cost of the new premises as £60,000 (£90,000 less the £30,000 gain).

Example – proceeds partly reinvested

You bought a freehold office for £50,000 and sold it for £100,000.

You made a gain of £50,000

The new business premises cost £80,000.

The office was disposed of for £100,000 and you reinvested £80,000. The amount not reinvested is £100,000 − £80,000 = £20,000.

The amount of the gain that you can postpone is restricted.

You deduct the amount not reinvested (£20,000) from the gain (£50,000). You can postpone the difference of £30,000 (£50,000 − £20,000 = £30,000).

When you sell the new office and work out your Capital Gains Tax bill, you'll treat the cost of the new business premises as £50,000 (£80,000 less the £30,000 gain postponed).

Example – assets used partly for business

You bought a freehold shop for £80,000 and sell it for £100,000, reinvesting all of the proceeds in a new asset.

You make a gain of £20,000.

But you've only used the shop in your trade for 5 years out of the 10 years you've owned it. Therefore it only qualifies as a business asset for 50% of the time.

You can only postpone 50% of the gain, so the postponed gain is £10,000 (50% of the £20,000 gain).

You'll need to work out the Capital Gains Tax due on £10,000 (the remaining 50% of the gain).

Depreciating assets

If you reinvest in a 'depreciating asset', the rules are slightly different. You may need to work out the tax due before you sell or dispose of the new asset.

A depreciating asset is one of the following:

- fixed plant or machinery, not forming part of a building
- an asset that will have a life of 60 years or less from the time you acquire it (for example a short term lease)

You can still postpone the gain but not always for as long – just until the earliest of the following dates:

- 10 years from when you bought or acquired the new asset
- the date you stop using the new asset in your trade
- the date you sell or dispose of the new asset

Example

You sold your shop for £125,000 and spent £135,000 on a 30 year lease on 1 August 2013.

You made a gain of £20,000 on the sale of the shop and postponed all of the gain.

You use the leased premises in your trade and sell the lease on 1 July 2025.

You can only postpone the original gain until the earlier of:

- 31 July 2023 (10 years from the date the lease was acquired)
- 1 July 2025 (the date you stop using the lease)
- 1 July 2025 (the date of sale)

So the gain is postponed until 31 July 2023 (the earliest date). You'll include the gain when working out the Capital Gains Tax due for the 2023–24 tax year.

How to claim the relief

To make a claim, use the link to the helpsheet below. You'll find a claim form on the last page.

There's a time limit for making a claim.

To work this out you take the later of the following 2 dates:

- the date the old asset was disposed of
- the date the new asset was acquired

You then work out when the end of the tax year is that follows this date and add 4 years on.

Example

You sold an asset on 12 May 2013 and bought a new asset on 14 June 2014, so the later date is 14 June 2014.

The end of the tax year in which 14 June 2014 falls is 5 April 2015.

You must make the claim by 5 April 2019, which is 4 years later.

Download the latest helpsheet on Business Asset Roll-Over Relief – Helpsheet 290.

The HMRC downloads mentioned above are accessible at http://www.hmrc.gov.uk/cgt/businesses/reliefs.htm#2 and https://www.gov.uk/government/publications/business-asset-roll-over-relief-hs290-self-assessment-helpsheet.

(F) Increased CGT base cost

A purchaser of assets will clearly acquire those assets at market value, at least where the parties are dealing at arm's length, in the same way as a purchaser of shares would acquire those shares at market value. However, in the latter case, the company itself will hold its operating assets, which after all is what the purchaser wishes to get its hands on, at historic cost for capital gains tax purposes. A purchaser intending to rationalise and break up a business may therefore prefer to buy assets so that a gain is not made (or is at least minimised) on break-up, although there may be other ways around the problem if the purchaser is forced into buying shares by the seller.

(G) Quicker and cheaper due diligence and warranty negotiation

Because of the ability to select assets and liabilities and avoid unknown liabilities, the purchaser's due diligence enquiries can be specific to those assets and liabilities agreed to be acquired. In the case of a company acquisition those enquiries need to be more extensive to protect the purchaser from unknown liabilities. Similarly, the warranties necessary to protect the purchaser are likely to be fewer and more specific and accordingly cheaper and quicker to negotiate.

9.6.3 Advantages of a share purchase

Share purchases are not all bad news for the purchaser. By comparison with an assets purchase, they do offer some advantages.

(A) No change to the underlying business

In acquiring the shares of the target the purchaser acquires the complete company as a going concern leaving the business carried on by the target largely unaffected by the acquisition. Where necessary, this can be used to lessen the impact of the business having new owners since they can distance themselves from the target, whose own identity remains preserved as far as all those with whom it does business are concerned. In the absence of change of control termination provisions, all-important trading contracts of the business will remain with the business, without any need for them to be novated to the purchaser. In addition, because the underlying assets and liabilities of the target continue to belong to it, an acquisition of shares avoids the risk of an important asset of the business being inadvertently omitted from the acquisition.

(B) Availability of reinvestment relief and EIS relief

A purchaser who is an individual may be able to claim reinvestment relief on buying shares. The Enterprise Investment Scheme (EIS) is the successor to the Business Expansion Scheme (BES). It may certainly bring advantages to a passive investor and its rules on paid directors, etc are less onerous than the old BES. At first sight the availability of these reliefs would appear to favour a share deal, but there is no reason in principle why the purchaser could not set up a new company, subscribe for shares and purchase assets. In the Finance Act 2011 the tax advantages of such schemes were improved further.

(C)   Simplicity

An asset purchase involves the identification and transfer in its own way of each and every asset. For example, moveable plant and equipment will need to be transferred by delivery whereas other assets, such as land and contracts, will have to be documented and may be subject to the concerns of a third party. By comparison, a share sale involves the transfer of only one asset, namely the shares of the target, which can be transferred by way of stock transfer forms. This may lead to reduced costs and makes the transaction more straightforward.

(D)   Speed

The process of acquiring a business may take longer than an acquisition of shares because it involves the transfer of each and every individual asset of the business. Some of the assets (for example, leasehold property and trading contracts) cannot be transferred without the consent of third parties such as landlords, customers and suppliers and, due to the risk of the third party withholding consent or terminating the contract, it carries with it more uncertainty about ongoing trading.

(E)   Stamp duty and Stamp Duty Land Tax (SDLT)

There used to be a significant stamp duty disadvantage to a purchaser of an assets deal is the fact that stamp duty is calculated at up to 5% (for non-residential commercial real property) (as at 6 April 2017), rather than 0.5%. The value of the consideration for stamp duty purposes included liabilities assumed, although duty was not liable on certain items, such as goods, wares and merchandise, which are transferred by delivery. Stamp duty on the sale of shares should be on the net amount actually paid for the shares (with no regard to the underlying liabilities within the company).

Stamp duty on the acquisition of assets (with the exception of shares and marketable securities) was abolished by the Finance Act 2003. Therefore, depending on the nature of the assets of the target company, there may be no stamp duty payable by the buyer. There is, however, SDLT levied on UK land and buildings, up to a maximum of 5%.

HMRC summarise this by way of an example:

'If you buy a freehold commercial property for £275,000, the SDLT you owe is calculated as follows:

- 0% on the first £150,000 = £0
- 2% on the next £100,000 = £2,000
- 5% on the final £25,000 = £1,250
- Total SDLT = £3,250.'

For residential property (which is unlikely to be owned by most trading companies) the rates are as follows:

Residential Property or lease premium or transfer value	SDLT rate
Up to £125,000	Zero
The next £125,000 (the portion from £125,001 to £250,000)	2%
The next £675,000 (the portion from £250,001 to £925,000)	5%
The next £575,000 (the portion from £925,001 to £1.5 million)	10%
The remaining amount (the portion above £1.5 million)	12%

Different rules apply for those buying a first home for up to £500,000. There is no SDLT on first homes up to £300,000 and for first home buyers they pay 5% on the portion from £300,001 to £500,000. If the home costs over £500,000 they do not benefit from the concession and instead pay the rates on the table above from 0–12% within the relevant bands above for residential property purchases.

Scotland   Land and Buildings Transaction Tax

The above are the UK rules other than of Scotland and Wales (Wales having a new Land Transaction Tax in force 1 April 2018). Scotland now has its own land tax regime. It can therefore be important to ascertain which tax jurisdiction applies to the individual concerned in a transaction. HMRC in 2018 were endeavouring to ascertain more detail about who lives in Scotland for tax purposes as income tax rates now also differ. As for real property/land the place within the UK where it is situated determines the tax rate applied. In Scotland SDLT is called Land and Buildings Transaction Tax (LBTT).

The Scottish Government summaries the position as follows:

'Non-residential property transactions – LBTT rates and bands

For non-residential property transactions, the rate of tax is determined in the same manner as for residential property transactions but by reference to different rates and bands:

Purchase price	LBTT rate
Up to £150,000	0%
Above £150,000 to £350,000	3%
Above £350,000	4.5%

LBTT(S)A 2013 section 24 provides for the calculation and section 59(2) sets out what counts as non-residential property. Where a non-residential transaction involves any element of residential property LBTT(S)A 2013 section 24(4) provides that the transaction will still be as a non-residential property transaction.

If the value is above the payment threshold, LBTT is charged at the appropriate rate on the amount of the chargeable consideration within that band. For example, an office bought for £465,000 is charged at:

- 0% for the first £150,000
- 3% for the next £200,000 and
- then 4.5% for the remaining £115,000
- so £11,175 must be paid in LBTT

LBTT(S)A 2013 schedule 2 sets out how chargeable consideration is to be determined and amongst other things non-monetary consideration is chargeable consideration.

These rates and bands should also be used to determine the tax due on any premium paid for the assignation of a lease (other than those treated as the grant of a new lease).'

See https://www.revenue.scot/land-buildings-transaction-tax/guidance/ calculating-tax-rates-and-bands.

England, Wales, NI: Higher rate for corporate bodies – residential dwellings only

From 20 March 2014 SDLT is charged at 15% on interests in **residential** dwellings costing more than £500,000 purchased by certain non-natural persons. 'Non-natural persons' include companies, partnerships including a company and collective investment schemes. There are exclusions for trustees of a settlement, property rental businesses, property developers and traders, properties made available to the public, financial institutions acquiring dwellings in the course of lending, dwellings occupied by employees and farmhouses. Annual Tax on Enveloped Dwellings is a tax payable by companies on high value residential property (a dwelling) and came into effect on 1 April 2013 and is payable each year. See further at https://www.gov.uk/guidance/annual-tax-on-enveloped-dwellings-the-basics.

The Budget 2014 announced a reduction in the threshold from £2 million to £500,000 introduced over two years. From 1 April 2015 a new band came into effect for properties with a value greater than £1 million but not more than £2 million with an annual charge of £7,000. From 1 April 2016 a further new band came into effect for properties with a value greater than £500,000 but not more than £1 million with an annual charge of £3,500. For future years these charges were indexed in line with the previous September CPI. Always check the HMRC webpages for updates as taxes on property have been a very political issue recently.

Chargeable amounts for chargeable period 1 April 2014 to 31 March 2015 (Residential Property)

Property value	Annual charge 2017/18
More than £500,000 but not more than £1 million	£3,500
More than £1 million but not more than £2 million	£7,050
More than £2 million but not more than £5 million	£23,550
More than £5 million but not more than £10 million	£54,950
More than £10 million but not more than £20 million	£110,100
More than £20 million	£220,350

Some companies own residential property including accommodation for staff and the like. Legal advice should be sought from tax solicitors or accountants if there is any doubt as to whether these taxes on residential dwellings apply or not. Most private companies however will have no residential dwellings and their highest SDLT therefore will be 5%, not 15%, for commercial properties.

See https://www.gov.uk/guidance/annual-tax-on-enveloped-dwellings-the-basics and https://www.gov.uk/government/publications/annual-tax-on-enveloped-dwellings-annual-chargeable-amounts-for-2018-to-2019:

'**Meaning of "dwelling"**

Your property will be a dwelling if all or part of it is used, or could be used as a residence, for example a house or flat. It includes any gardens, grounds and buildings within them.

Find out about valuing different types of properties for example mixed use, more than one dwelling and multiple interest properties.

Some properties are not classed as dwellings. These include:

- hotels
- guest houses
- boarding school accommodation
- hospitals
- student halls of residence
- military accommodation
- care homes
- prisons

Section 19 of the ATED technical guidance (at https://www.gov.uk/government/publications/annual-tax-on-enveloped-dwellings-technical-guidance) explains more about the meaning of "dwelling".'

ATED applies throughout the UK including Scotland. Those owning enveloped dwellings which are caught by ATED must submit an annual return and the property will need to be revalued every five years.

The buyer needs to consider this when considering the structure of the acquisition, as there is only a 0.5% stamp duty cost on the purchase of shares.

(F)   Availability of tax losses

It is possible that the purchaser may be influenced by tax considerations in buying the target company rather than the business, perhaps because the target company has significant brought forward tax losses or surplus advance corporation tax. There are rules which may deny the benefit of these to the purchaser if there is a major change in the nature or conduct of the business, but the purchaser may consider it a risk worth taking.

(G)   Benefits of merger accounting and merger relief

(i)   Merger accounting

In an acquisition of shares the target becomes a subsidiary of the purchaser and the purchaser will be required to consolidate the results of the target with its results. On a group basis, a purchase of assets has a similar result.

The presentation of the profits and assets of the target will, however, vary according to whether acquisition or merger accounting is adopted and it is in this context that a purchase of shares can be distinguished from a purchase of assets. A purchase of assets precludes altogether the use of merger accounting and of certain methods of eliminating goodwill under acquisition accounting.

Accounting for acquisitions is governed by the Financial Reporting Standards (FRS). FRS 2 is a standard which deals with group accounts. FRS 7 should also be considered as should FRS 10 (which was precluded by FRS 22) which deals with goodwill. Another relevant standard is FRS 102 on 'accounting for acquisitions and mergers' which replaced FRS 6 from January 2015.

FRS 102 defines a 'merger' as:

> 'An entity combination that results in the creation of a new reporting entity formed from the combining parties, in which the controlling parties of the combining entities come together in a partnership for the mutual sharing of risks and benefits of the newly formed entity and in which no party to the combination in substance obtains control over any other, or is otherwise seen to be dominant. All of the following criteria must be met for an entity combination to meet the definition of a merger:
> (a) no party to the combination is portrayed as either acquirer or acquiree, either by its own board or management or by that of another party to the combination;
> (b) there is no significant change to the classes of beneficiaries of the combining entities or the purpose of the benefits provided as a result of the combination; and

136

(c) all parties to the combination, as represented by the members of the board, participate in establishing the management structure of the combined entity and in selecting the management personnel, and such decisions are made on the basis of a consensus between the parties to the combination rather than purely by exercise of voting rights.'

It defines 'business combination' as:

'19.3 A business combination is the bringing together of separate entities or businesses into one reporting entity. The result of nearly all business combinations is that one entity, the acquirer, obtains control of one or more other businesses, the acquiree. The acquisition date is the date on which the acquirer obtains control of the acquiree.

19.4 A business combination may be structured in a variety of ways for legal, taxation or other reasons. It may involve the purchase by an entity of the equity of another entity, the purchase of all the net assets of another entity, the assumption of the liabilities of another entity, or the purchase of some of the net assets of another entity that together form one or more businesses.

19.5 A business combination may be effected by the issue of equity instruments, the transfer of cash, cash equivalents or other assets, or a mixture of these. The transaction may be between the shareholders of the combining entities or between one entity and the shareholders of another entity. It may involve the establishment of a new entity to control the combining entities or net assets transferred, or the restructuring of one or more of the combining entities.'

Section 19.3 above defines a business. Under FRS 6 this was not defined. The result of 19.3 is that there now needs to be greater scrutiny to ascertain if a business or purely assets are transferred. On balance this has not resulted in any major changes.

The now replaced FRS 6 paragraphs 6–11 set out five criteria, all of which had to be satisfied for a merger to exist, producing a much stricter test than under the SSAP which it in its turn had replaced. The five criteria were:

- no party to the combination is portrayed as either acquirer or acquired, either by its own board or management or by that of another party to the combination;
- all parties to the combination, as represented by the boards of directors or their appointees, participate in establishing the management structure for the combined entity and in selecting the management personnel, and such decisions are made on the basis of a consensus between the parties to the combination rather than purely by exercise of voting rights;
- the relative sizes of the combining entities are not so disparate that one party dominates the combined entity by virtue of its relative size;
- under the terms of the combination or related arrangements, the consideration received by equity shareholders of each party to the combination, in relation to their equity shareholding, comprises primarily equity shares in the combined entity; and any non-equity consideration,

or equity shares carrying substantial reduced voting or distribution rights, represents an immaterial proportion of the fair value of the consideration received by the equity shareholders of that party; and

- no equity shareholders of any of the combining entities retain any material interest in the future performance of only part of the combined entity.

In merger accounting, even though the target becomes a subsidiary of the purchaser there is an assumption that there has been no transfer of control and neither party is viewed as being the acquirer – the FRS describes the parties to a merger as 'combining parties' rather than purchaser and seller. The two entities are treated as though they have been put together for the whole of the current and preceding years. This means that results of the target are included in full in the results of the purchaser in the year of acquisition. Merger accounting allows for the balance sheets of the target and the purchaser to be aggregated without establishing new asset values, but some changes may be necessary to achieve uniformity of accounting policies. In addition, shares issued in consideration of the acquisition of the target are recorded at their nominal value, avoiding the creation of a share premium account or other reserve.

Acquisition accounting is based on the concept of 'fair value'. The rules require the purchaser to attribute fair values to the individual assets and liabilities acquired. In doing so, the purchaser should allocate the purchase consideration between the underlying net tangible and intangible assets (other than goodwill) on the basis of their fair value to the purchaser on the completion date.

The fair value of the consideration received must then be ascertained (fair value being on the basis of an arm's length transaction between informed and willing parties) and the difference between the fair value of the consideration received and the fair value of the net assets acquired is deemed to represent goodwill and will appear as such in the purchaser's consolidated balance sheet.

Goodwill arising under the acquisition method of accounting for the purchase has to be eliminated either by a write-off to reserves immediately on acquisition or by amortising it on a systematic basis over its useful economic life (see discussion of FRS 102 on goodwill below). This write-off can be a severe penalty, and for the acquisition of certain types of businesses, such as service companies, can lead to a situation where the acquiring company does not have sufficient retained reserves against which to charge the write-off. In such cases, the purchaser will need to amortise the write-off over a number of years but this has the disadvantage that such goodwill amortisation must be charged to the profit and loss account.

The other major disadvantage of the acquisition method of accounting is that the results of the target can only be brought into the group accounts from the date of acquisition. In comparison, merger accounting assumes that the two entities have always been combined. As a result, under acquisition accounting the purchaser is unable to distribute out of pre-acquisition reserves of the target. Any dividend declared to the purchaser by the target which is out of pre-acquisition reserves must be written-off by the purchaser against its costs of investment and not taken through as profit. Under the merger accounting method, however, all the reserves of the target are available for distribution and can be presented as a profit in the group accounts.

FRS 10 and now FRS 102 confirmed that inherent goodwill should not be capitalised. Where goodwill is purchased the standard goes for capitalisation, with amortisation over the useful economic life of the goodwill and other intangible assets are treated the same.

Amortisation must be on a systematic basis. There is a rebuttable presumption that useful life will not exceed 20 years. No residual value may be attached to goodwill, and the straight line method of amortisation is usually utilised.

The 20-year rule may be ignored, but only if there is strong argument in favour of a longer life, and the goodwill will be capable of continuous measurement. 'Impairment reviews' are required after the first full financial year following acquisition, and also after that if circumstances suggest a review is needed. If goodwill is amortised over more than 20 years, impairment reviews are required at the end of every reporting period. Negative goodwill has to be shown separately on the balance sheet Accountants must show their valuation methods and amortisation methods and periods must be disclosed, along with any changes in those methods. Movements in cost/valuation and accumulated amortisation must be reconciled.

Since it came into force, FRS 10 had been useful and has ensured consistency of treatment between goodwill and other intangible assets and it reduced the scope for creative accounting. The impairment review procedure can be expensive and subjective. The choice between amortisation and impairment review may hinder comparability. The treatment of negative goodwill creates a "dangling credit" and may prove difficult in terms of its amortisation. It is now subsumed into FRS 102 which deals with goodwill as follows:

FRS 102 – Goodwill

'Goodwill

19.22 The acquirer shall, at the acquisition date:

(a) recognise goodwill acquired in a business combination as an asset; and

(b) initially measure that goodwill at its cost, being the excess of the cost of the business combination over the acquirer's interest in the net amount of the identifiable assets, liabilities and contingent liabilities recognised and measured in accordance with paragraphs 19.15, 19.15A to 19.15C.

19.23 After initial recognition, the acquirer shall measure goodwill acquired in a business combination at cost less accumulated amortisation and accumulated impairment losses:

(a) An entity shall follow the principles in paragraphs 18.19 to 18.24 for amortisation of goodwill. Goodwill shall be considered to have a finite useful life, and shall be amortised on a systematic basis over its life. If, in exceptional cases, an entity is unable to make a reliable estimate of the useful life of goodwill, the life shall not exceed 10 years.

(b) An entity shall follow Section 27 Impairment of Assets for recognising and measuring the impairment of goodwill.

Excess over cost of acquirer's interest in the net fair value of acquiree's identifiable assets, liabilities and contingent liabilities

19.24 If the acquirer's interest in the net amount of the identifiable assets, liabilities and provisions for contingent liabilities recognised in accordance with paragraph 19.14 exceeds the cost of the business combination (also referred to as 'negative goodwill') , the acquirer shall:

(a) Reassess the identification and measurement of the acquiree's assets, liabilities and provisions for contingent liabilities and the measurement of the cost of the combination

(b) Recognise and separately disclose the resulting excess on the face of the statement of financial position on the acquisition date, immediately below goodwill, and followed by a subtotal of the net amount of goodwill and the excess

(c) Recognise subsequently the excess up to the fair value of non-monetary assets acquired in profit or loss in the periods in which the non-monetary assets are recovered. Any excess exceeding the fair value of non-monetary assets acquired shall be recognised in profit or loss in the periods expected to be benefited'.

FRS 102 is at http://www.frc.org.uk/getattachment/e1d6b167-6cdb-4550-bde3-f94484226fbd/FRS-102-WEB-Ready-2015.pdf.

It can therefore be seen that merger accounting has two principal advantages: it avoids the problem of goodwill and the results of the target are included for the whole of the financial year in which the acquisition is made.

A comparison between the newer FRS 102 rules and the earlier replaced rules is at http://frs102.com/blog/2015/12/17/frs-102-summary-section-19-business-combinations-and-goodwill/. Recognition of contingent assets is not allowed under FRS 102 but had been under FRS 7.

(ii) Merger relief

CA 2006, s 610, provides that where a company issues shares at a premium to nominal value, whether for cash or otherwise, a sum equal to the aggregate of the premiums on those shares must be transferred to a share premium account. A share premium account cannot be used except for making capitalisation issues and paying certain expenses and cannot be reduced without the consent of the court.

CA 2006, s 612, excludes the application of s 610 and avoids the transfer to share premium account of any premium on the consideration shares where the purchaser, by issuing the consideration securities:

'... has secured at least a 90 per cent equity holding in another company in pursuance of an arrangement providing for the allotment of equity shares in the issuing company on terms that the consideration for the shares allotted is to be provided –

(a) by the issue or transfer to the issuing company of equity shares in the other company, or

(b) by the cancellation of any such shares not held by the issuing company.'

The company issuing the consideration shares must be the company to which the company's shares are transferred. The relief will not be available if the shares are transferred by the sellers directly to a subsidiary of the company issuing the shares, although ownership by a subsidiary can be achieved by an intra-group transfer following the acquisition by the parent company. Merger relief is only available if the consideration comprises or includes 'equity shares' (see CA 2006, s 616(1)). Loan stock (whether convertible or not) and conventional preference shares do not qualify.

9.7 TAX ISSUES FOR THE PURCHASER

The purchaser should look critically at the seller's tax saving proposals and ensure that there is no downside for the future. Although the purchaser can be indemnified against any adverse consequences, in some cases the purchaser should consider taking some form of security, or perhaps even a reduction in the purchase price, to ensure it is fully protected. A few examples by reference to typical proposals follow.

9.7.1 Deferred consideration

The purchaser should not be adversely affected by the seller's requirements on deferred consideration, but it is important to work through the commercial ramifications. The purchaser could also consider putting part of the deferred consideration into the seller's remuneration package if the seller is remaining an employee, as this may have tax advantages for the purchaser.

A performance related bonus if reasonable, justifiable and structured carefully should qualify for a tax deduction in the target's hands. Although a bonus will give rise to an additional national insurance charge the target will receive an overall saving. The seller would currently be charged to tax at the same rate, whether it is income or capital, but runs the risk of income tax rates moving ahead of the rate of capital gains tax for the future.

9.7.2 Non-deductibility of expenses

All expenses paid out as part of the seller's package should be reviewed carefully by the purchaser. The purchaser should not automatically accept that costs paid by the company, whether bonuses, pension contributions or compensation payments, are tax deductible. For example, compensation for loss of office is normally non-deductible in these circumstances, and large one-off pension contributions are spread over a few years, rather than taken as a deduction in the year of payment.

9.7.3 Subsequent reorganisations

The purchaser should always consider carefully the ultimate destination of the business which is to be bought. Whilst it is generally possible to transfer the shares around the group at will, the purchaser should also consider carefully the tax planning steps proposed by the seller in the context of the purchaser's plans. For example, the seller may have organised assets to be transferred around a target corporate group at any time before acquisition which would be done on a no gain, no loss basis for tax purposes if done within a tax group. If the purchaser intends to sell any of the target group on in the foreseeable future after the acquisition, this may trigger a tax charge if one of the companies to be sold has had assets transferred to it by one of the other group companies.

9.7.4 Stamp duty

Stamp duty is payable at 0.5% on a share purchase and up to 5% (April 2017 rates – non residential property) for land only (SDLT) on an asset purchase as seen at section 9.6.3 (E) above in more detail including for the different regime in Scotland and Wales. For assets other than land, stamp duty was abolished by the Finance Act 2003.

Once upon a time there was a device known as 'the pref trick' which allowed duty on a share sale to be avoided. It involved creating a bonus issue of shares on renounceable letters of allotment and converting the existing shares into deferred shares. All the value therefore passed with renounceable letters and these could be transferred by delivery without stamp duty. The loophole was blocked in 1986, followed by a subsequent variant which has also been blocked. Avoiding stamp duty on share sales is still possible but no longer simple. See also Part IV (Chapter 16, section 16.3) along with other stamp duty planning considerations.

9.8 HEADS OF AGREEMENT AND EXCLUSIVITY

9.8.1 Heads of agreement

Having struck a deal in principle with the seller, the purchaser will wish to carry out a detailed investigation of the target prior to committing itself legally to the purchase. Depending upon the extent of the proposed due diligence, it may involve the considerable expense and effort of engaging professional advisers. To avoid a waste of that effort and cost by the seller subsequently deciding not to proceed any further or to proceed with another interested party, the purchaser may wish to consider whether to sign heads of agreement before proceeding to the next stage. The form of heads of agreement, their legal effect and the typical content of them are discussed in Part I (Chapter 5, section 5.4). Whether heads of agreement are a useful tool for the purchaser is of much debate. The advantages of them to a purchaser over and above the advantages referred to in Part I are:

- by setting down the main terms, the purchaser can proceed with a detailed and expensive investigation of the target with a reasonable degree of confidence that the purchase is achievable;
- by including a 'lock-out' and a costs undertaking the purchaser can proceed with a much greater degree of confidence that if the sellers withdraw, its costs will be underwritten (as long as the heads are drawn up to be legally binding in that regard); and
- this may prove advantageous to a purchaser seeking third party finance to enable the transaction to proceed.

Even where not legally binding, a purchaser will find that the heads give rise to a moral commitment and tend to limit its ability to renegotiate the principal terms even though the outcome of its due diligence investigations may suggest otherwise. For this reason and the fact that the lock-out and costs undertakings can be negotiated as a separate document, a purchaser should seriously consider whether the benefits of heads outweigh the disadvantages.

There will be occasions (for example, a sale initiated by the seller where the purchaser is one of a number submitting bids) when the purchaser has decided that heads of agreement should be avoided for the reasons stated above but the seller is insistent and the purchaser is forced into signing them. In such cases the purchaser would be well advised to incorporate into the heads a list of the key assumptions upon which the price and other main terms have been derived together with a provision allowing for re-negotiation if the due diligence reveals inconsistencies with those assumptions.

9.8.2   Exclusivity

By comparison to heads of agreement, from the purchaser's perspective the case for exclusivity (sometimes referred to as 'lock-outs') is overwhelming. Exclusivity is obviously one-sided in favour of the purchaser but is nevertheless something the seller may have to accept if the approach has been made by the purchaser or, where the approach is made by the seller, the purchaser is the sole or preferred bidder.

Exclusivity is usually achieved by the seller undertaking in favour of the prospective purchaser that the purchaser will have the exclusive opportunity to negotiate with him and that he will not negotiate with a third party to sell or otherwise deal with the relevant assets for a period of time. It is crucial to ensure this is contained in a legally binding document. A mere letter of intent or document market 'subject to contract' or 'this document is not legally binding' would not do.

This prevents the seller from using the purchaser's offer to seek higher bids and allows a prospective purchaser an interval to conduct due diligence and carry out negotiations without the constraints and pressure imposed by competitive bidding. It is also important in limiting the down side costs of due diligence (legal and accountancy fees) in the event that the seller breaks off negotiations and sells to somebody else, because the lock-out restricts the seller's ability to market the target, and it is frequently limited in time to an agreed period which the seller considers is reasonable to complete the transaction.

Until the Court of Appeal decision in *Walford v Miles* (1991) 62 P & CR 410 lock-out clauses were commonplace in negotiations for the purchase of companies and businesses. In this case, the Court of Appeal threw into question this widely used type of provision when it decided that such clauses constituted an agreement to agree and, as such, were void and unenforceable because the parties had not agreed to anything at all. In coming to their decision, the Court of Appeal relied upon the principle laid down by Lord Denning MR in *Courtney & Fairbairn Ltd v Tolaini Brothers (Hotels) Ltd* [1975] 1 All ER 716, [1975] 1 WLR 297 that the law cannot recognise a contract to negotiate. In laying down this principle, Lord Denning MR extended the principle that a contract to enter into a contract, where there is a fundamental term to be agreed, is unenforceable.

The case was heard on appeal by the House of Lords ([1992] 2 AC 128, [1992] 1 All ER 453), where the Court of Appeal decision on the facts was unanimously endorsed. However, the House of Lords has now clarified the position to a certain extent by distinguishing between the two elements of a typical lock-out provision. Lord Ackner observed that there is no reason in English contract law why one party, for good consideration, should not achieve an enforceable agreement with another party binding that party not to negotiate with anyone else for a specified period. In doing so, he particularly emphasised that the requirement for certainty is crucial for the lock-out to be enforceable and it was the absence of this requirement (in the form of no fixed period for the lock-out to last) which was the critical factor in the *Walford* case. In his judgment, Lord Ackner drew a distinction between 'lock-in' agreements and 'lock-out' agreements. An agreement which purports to commit the parties to negotiate with each other is unenforceable on the established grounds that it is an agreement to agree. Parties cannot be 'locked-in' to negotiations in this manner because true negotiations must involve the ability to threaten to withdraw, or withdraw in fact, in the hope of securing improved terms. This would involve so much uncertainty in principle that it is impossible for the courts to police such agreements effectively.

This House of Lords decision is to be welcomed and draws English law closer in line with laws in most other European jurisdictions where the validity and enforceability of lock-out clauses are unquestioned. It is clear from this case that to be enforceable a lock-out requires careful drafting. It is important that:

- the period of exclusivity is clearly defined;
- the consideration passing from the purchaser for the lock-out is identified; and
- the extent of the costs undertaking is clearly defined to identify whose costs are covered, for what period and on what basis they are calculated.

There are many enforceable option agreements drawn up regularly in all kinds of business areas such as options to make a film from a book and as long as there is good consideration and certainty they will be enforceable. The same principles apply here. The consideration passing from the purchaser is often drafted as the occurrence of fees relating to the due diligence investigations of the target. In these cases it is important to note that the undertaking will be unenforceable until such time as the purchaser incurs these fees. If, therefore, the seller withdrew after signing the undertaking but before the due diligence investigations to which the lock-out refers began, the purchaser would be unprotected.

In *Petromec v Petroleo* ([2006] 1 Lloyds Report 121) the Court of Appeal looked at the issue of whether an express obligation in an agreement between the parties to negotiate in good faith was enforceable. In *Cable & Wireless plc v IBM United Kingdom Ltd* ([2002] EWHC 2059) a contract included a provision that the parties should 'attempt in good faith' to resolve disputes arising between them 'through an alternative dispute resolution ('ADR') procedure as recommended to the parties by the Centre for Dispute Resolution'. The court said this was an enforceable obligation because it gave enough detail. So it seems clear that where a clause gives much detail on the negotiations to be undertaken it may be enforceable but not otherwise.

Chapter 10

Due diligence

10.1　INTRODUCTION

Due diligence is the term used to describe the investigation of the target and its business by the purchaser and its advisers before entering into the purchase agreement. Due diligence is an essential part of the acquisition process; if carried out carefully, it should not only help the purchaser's understanding of the target's business, but also identify potential risks.

The common law rule of caveat emptor (buyer beware) applies to the acquisition of a UK business or company. Accordingly, a purchaser cannot rely on the law to imply terms to ensure that the target it acquires is the target described to it during the negotiations and that the key assumptions relied on by the purchaser in striking the deal in principle are correct.

Given the absence of statutory protection, it has become common practice for purchasers to seek protection in the form of contractual warranties about the business of the target. Unless the seller has an incredibly strong negotiating position or is an administrator or administrative receiver, or the purchaser is a management buy out team, most purchasers will acquire the target with the benefit of some warranties. However, although warranties give the purchaser the right to sue the seller after completion, in practice they can sometimes prove to be limited or impracticable to enforce (for example, if, post-completion, the seller is employed in a key position by the target or the purchaser), or unsuitable as a remedy (for example if the seller has spent the consideration). For this reason, a prudent purchaser will prefer (and the only option available to a purchaser from an administrator or administrative receiver is) to learn as much as possible about the target business as early as possible in the negotiating process prior to committing itself to terms it may not otherwise have done had it had a full understanding of the target or the underlying business and assets to be purchased.

Due diligence will usually consist of a combination of reports on the business or specific parts of it by professional advisers (including accountants, lawyers, environmental consultants, surveyors, pension advisers and insurance brokers) and searches of publicly available information, enquiries of the seller and a physical inspection of tangible assets. Despite the increasing willingness of professional advisers to accept contingency fees, due diligence can be an expensive exercise and one a purchaser is unlikely to sanction unless it believes that the seller is committed to the sale. As a result a purchaser will usually wait until it has reached agreement in principle with the seller (ie heads of agreement have been signed) before instructing professionals to carry out any due diligence investigations.

The objective of a typical due diligence exercise is to provide the purchaser with the maximum amount of independently verified information regarding the target as soon as possible so as to enable the purchaser to make an informed investment decision and to assess whether the assumptions and basis upon which it agreed in principle to purchase the target at the agreed purchase price are correct. If the due diligence exercise reveals unknown liabilities, problems or other information not known when striking the deal in principle it provides the purchaser with an opportunity to renegotiate terms.

The extent of the due diligence exercise is usually determined by the purchaser in the light of whether the purchaser is acquiring shares or assets, the importance of the transaction to the purchaser, the time available to the purchaser to carry out investigations, and the access to information allowed to it by the seller. When a purchaser has limited resources (whether financial or in terms of manpower) or is under severe time pressure, it should carefully consider the investigations which are feasible within the timescale or within its resources and the relevance of those investigations to the target company or the assets and liabilities being acquired.

In determining the extent and nature of the due diligence exercise, the purchaser should be aware that enquiries of third party sources are, in general terms, inconclusive in that they offer no formal protection if the information provided as a result of the enquiry proves to be inaccurate. They do, however, provide the purchaser with comfort and are a means of verifying the information given to it by the seller.

Where a purchaser is acquiring assets and liabilities rather than the target company itself, the investigations tend to be less burdensome as they need only relate to the specific assets and liabilities to be taken over. Unless specifically excluded, in the acquisition of shares all the assets and liabilities of the company, including unknown or contingent liabilities, are taken over. This means that the investigation needs to be that much more thorough.

10.2 MATTERS REQUIRING INVESTIGATION

The list of matters requiring investigation will to some extent depend upon whether the purchaser is purchasing shares or assets and, in the case of assets, the identity of those assets. Accordingly, at the outset of the due diligence exercise the purchaser should take time to consider which matters require investigation in the light of the structure of the transaction, the nature of the target's business, the relative importance of the target's various assets and the basis upon which price has been determined.

Assumptions relied upon by the purchaser in striking the purchase price probably merit the most keen investigation by the purchaser. For example, if the purchase price has been agreed to reflect a multiple of the previous year's earnings, the purchaser will want to ensure that those earnings have not been distorted in any way, whether by overstating sales, understating costs or otherwise.

The main areas for investigation by the purchaser's solicitors are listed below and are reflected in the precedent forms of due diligence requests contained in Part V. These due diligence checklists should always be tailored to the business by being reviewed and the due diligence investigations should be carried out by other advisers.

10.2.1 Title to the target's shares

A due diligence review relating to a proposed acquisition of shares should establish whether the seller has good title to the target company.

The starting place is a review of the target's statutory register of members since a person does not become a member (shareholder) until his name has been entered into the register of members. Although this review will reveal legal ownership of the target's shares, it will not disclose beneficial ownership (if different). Without notice of beneficial ownership being transferred to another party, the members entitled to legal ownership will be those entitled to sell the target. Where beneficial ownership is held by somebody else and the purchaser is aware of this, that party should be included as a party to the acquisition agreement but only for the purposes of transferring beneficial ownership.

Having checked that the seller is the registered owner of the target's shares, the purchaser will want to investigate the seller's title to those shares. That is to say, the purchaser must investigate the transfer to the seller of the shares

149

in question and each preceding transfer as far back as the original allotment of the shares by the target company. If on any such occasion the transfer or allotment required, for example, some resolution of the directors, the purchaser must satisfy himself that the persons who purported to pass the necessary resolutions were indeed the properly appointed directors of the target company at the relevant time.

The Old s 80 – Allotment: Purchasers used to have to consider CA 1985, ss 80 and 89 replaced by CA 2006, s 549 from 1 October 2009 (but with changes – see below) which applied to any allotment of shares which took place after 21 December 1980 but before CA 2006 came into force. Section 80 provided that directors of a company might not allot shares or convertible stock unless authorised by the company in general meeting or by the company's articles. Any such authority had to state the maximum amount of security to which it applied and the date of expiry of the authority. The maximum period for an authority was five years, but it could be renewed by the company in general meeting for further periods, up to a maximum of five years, *ad infinitum*.

Section 89(1) of CA 1985 (now also superseded) provided that a company could not allot any 'equity securities' unless it first offered to allot the same amongst existing holders of relevant shares pro rata to their existing holdings and on the same or more favourable terms. Offerees had to be given at least 21 days' notice before the offer can be withdrawn. A private company could, however, exclude the operation of s 89(1) by a provision in its memorandum or articles that that section would not in any event apply to a particular allotment of equity securities which are to be wholly or partly paid up otherwise than in cash. Furthermore, s 89(1) was permitted to be made inapplicable or modified by the articles or by special resolution so long as the directors had an authority for the purposes of s 80.

With the above points in mind, the purchaser used to have to seek at least a title to the shares in question which can be clearly traced by entries in the register of allotments and/or transfers and in the register of members together with either the original registration application forms, where shares had been allotted, or duly stamped share transfer forms, where transfers had been transferred, together with the share certificates relating to the shares to be sold. Where share certificates were unavailable because they have been lost or mislaid, the purchaser should ensure that the target company held a suitable indemnity so as to enable it to issue a replacement certificate.

Current Law – Allotment: From 1 October 2009, however, s 550 of CA 2006 ('Power of directors to allot shares etc: private company with only one class of shares') provides that where a private company has only one class of shares, the directors may exercise any power of the company: (a) to allot shares of that class; or (b) to grant rights to subscribe for or to convert any security into such shares, except to the extent that they are prohibited from doing so by the company's articles. However it is necessary still to check the articles for any restrictions and s 551 for public companies and private companies not within s 550 still need authorisation.

10.2.2   Title to the target's assets

When acquiring a company the purchaser will assume and expect the target to own or hold a valid lease of or licence to use the underlying assets so that the business of the target can be operated from completion without interruption. When acquiring a business the same considerations will apply.

As part of the purchaser's due diligence review, it is important to ensure that title to the key assets used in the business is held by the target or seller (as the case may be) free from encumbrances. It is quite possible, for example, that another group company owns certain assets used in the target's business.

Except for certain property and intellectual property assets, title to business assets cannot be established conclusively by, for example, reference to a register. Accordingly, due diligence investigations can only aim to establish whether the target acquired (or received a licence to use) the assets in question, the nature of the interest acquired that no competing claims to title have been made and that the assets haven't been sold, charged, leased or otherwise disposed of.

The following paragraphs consider in more detail the establishment of title to property and intellectual property rights, which can be established conclusively.

(A)   Property

It is difficult to envisage a transaction that does not require at least some investigation of the property assets. The type and extent of investigations will depend upon the type of property asset and whether the transaction is a share or asset purchase. The importance of the property to the business will be a key factor on approach: if the location of the property is fundamental to the business a claim in damages for breach of warranty will never be sufficient to remedy the situation. It must always be remembered that where shares are to be acquired the ownership of the property remains the same, whereas when assets are acquired the ownership of the property changes and transfer documentation will be needed to effect this.

Either the purchaser's solicitor can carry out an investigation of title (which may be full, or more limited, dependent upon the circumstances of the deal) or the seller's solicitors can provide the purchaser with a certificate of title.

In choosing its method of investigation, a purchaser should consider the following factors:

- costs – rather than carrying out an investigation of title it may be more cost-effective to accept a basic certificate of title when considering the value of the transaction; it is also usually considered that certificates are a less expensive route for a purchaser, if the process is run efficiently;
- the timing and convenience of each method if there is a tight timescale: investigation by the purchaser's solicitors is usually a more effective route to meeting a short deadline, as less liaison is required and the

> purchaser's solicitors have greater control over the receipt of title and search information;

- the relative bargaining power of the seller and the purchaser; and
- the purchaser's existing knowledge of the property: if the vendor has recently purchased the property, its solicitors will usually provide a certificate;
- the relative remedies and protection each method provides;
- the volume and the respective importance of the properties in the portfolio;
- whether the transfer of any property is unregistered and its transfer will trigger first registration: in these circumstances the title will need to be reviewed for submission for first registration to HM Land Registry so it is more cost-effective for the purchaser's solicitor to investigate the title as a pre-test to submitting the first registration;
- the identity of the firm of solicitors acting for the seller giving the certificates; both the type of firm and the level of its personal injury cover will be relevant.

(i) Investigation

Investigation of title will involve a review of the target's title to the property and the carrying out of all the usual conveyancing searches, preliminary enquiries and other enquiries of the seller and third parties as if the transaction were a normal conveyancing matter. Investigation of title may not, however, be practicable in the timescale allowed. In such a case warranty cover will be the only feasible route.

Title to the property assets should be deduced by the seller's solicitors in the usual way depending on whether it has registered or unregistered title. In the case of registered titles, office copy entries and filed documents (if any) will be obtained from the Land Registry. In the case of registered leasehold property, an office copy or a certified copy of the lease should be inspected. In the case of unregistered land, certified copies of the title deeds should be reviewed. As in most transactions where exchange of contracts and completion occur simultaneously, all usual pre-contract and pre-completion searches should be carried out. These will include searches of the relevant local authority, the Land Charges Registry, the Local Land Charges Registry and the Land Registry and/or Companies Registry. Depending upon the location of the property, additional searches (for example, Commons Registry, Coal Mining, Brine or Clay) may be necessary.

An often forgotten enquiry is whether the property requires, and if so, whether it has, a fire certificate. Factory, office and shop premises require such a certificate where more than 20 persons are at work at any one time or more than ten persons are at work at any one time elsewhere than on the ground floor of the building, or if a building contains two or more sets of premises where the aggregate of persons at work at any one time in both or all premises exceeds these same totals. A certificate is also required where explosive or highly flammable materials are stored or used regardless of the number of people at work. Briefly, the consequence of the absence of a fire certificate or any breach of its requirements can result in the user of the property being unlawful, and may lead to substantial expenditure to alter or reinstate the property so that it complies with the certificate, the imposition of penalties by the fire authority and the invalidating of fire insurance against the property.

Additional enquiries will be needed for particular categories of properties, for example licensing for leisure property.

(ii) Certificate of title

A certificate of title should be the easiest and least time-consuming method of investigation, especially if the seller's solicitors have recently acquired the property. The form of certificate, however, can give rise to lengthy negotiations as solicitors acting for sellers rarely provide certificates of title in the form required by the purchasers' solicitors. This means that on occasion, the factual element of the certificate is not provided to the purchaser's solicitors until later in the transaction, which can be problematic where title defects are revealed.

(iii) Preferred choice

In general, purchasers tend to investigate title rather than rely on certificates of title, as they are often qualified. When opting to investigate title a purchaser should take care to ensure that its investigation and the seller's disclosure against warranties does not cancel out the effectiveness of the warranties, although the level of warranty cover will automatically reduce where the purchaser undertakes title investigation.

Even where the purchaser undertakes full due diligence on title, some warranty cover will always be required, whether the acquisition is a share or an asset purchase. In the case of an asset purchase, at the very least, replies to enquiries provided by the sellers should be warranted. Additional warranty cover may be sought where replies to enquiries provided by the vendor prove inadequate.

In the case of a share acquisition, the same level of warranty cover as required for an asset purchase is needed, but in addition details of the properties owned/occupied must be warranted as being all of the property liabilities affecting the company. Additionally, warranty cover to deal with contingent liabilities, usually arising from assets previously owned, or properties in respect of which guarantees have been given will be needed.

As the level of due diligence undertaken diminishes, a greater level of warranty cover will be sought, unless the company's interest in the relevant property and the liability relating to it are viewed as negligible.

(B) Intellectual property rights

Intellectual property rights exist in every business. However, depending upon the nature of the business, intellectual property rights may or may not be a key asset. There are four main categories of intellectual property rights: copyright, designs (registered and unregistered – unregistered designs being called 'design right'), patents and trademarks. Of these, registered designs, patents and trademarks are registered rights and title to them is determined conclusively by the state of the register kept by the appropriate body. A search of the appropriate registers at the Intellectual Property Office (https://www.gov.uk/government/organisations/ intellectual-property-office) will reveal UK rights. Some companies possess valuable know-how too, although this is not strictly in law a property right.

Although there are no registers of copyright, unregistered design right and know-how, enquiry can be made of the management of the target to establish what unregistered intellectual property rights exist and whether they have been challenged or enforced in the past.

Always ask who wrote the unregistered works and if they have the original drawings or designs and if they are dated. Also check if that person were an employee at the time of creation. If not, for copyright, the ownership may remain with the consultant or other author and an assignment where possible may be necessary at the time of the acquisition. Ask what licences have been granted to third parties of the rights and check their terms. If revenue is paid under those licences check if they may be terminated by the licensee in the event of a change of control or sale of the intellectual property right, where an asset sale and if the licence is assignable.

10.2.3 Capacity of the seller

Having identified the seller(s) with the power to sell, the purchaser will then need to ascertain whether the seller is prohibited or restricted in any way from selling the target/assets.

(A) Individual sellers

In the case of individuals, the individual's right to sell can be a matter of concern if that individual is a minor, a bankrupt or a receiver.

(i) Minor

Contracts made by minors (ie persons under 18) are governed by the rules of common law as altered by the Minors' Contracts Act 1987. The general common law was that a contract made by an infant was voidable at his option. The general rule and the exceptions to it are reasonably complex and beyond the scope of this book. For a detailed summary, see *Cheshire, Fifoot & Furmston's Law of Contract* (17th edn, 2017).

(ii) Bankrupt/trustee in bankruptcy

A bankruptcy search in the Land Charges Registry against individual sellers should always be carried out immediately prior to the exchange of contracts to ensure that, as opposed to his trustee in bankruptcy, the seller has title to pass to the purchaser. If the search reveals a bankruptcy order or a bankruptcy petition, the consent of the bankrupt's trustee in bankruptcy (in the case of a bankruptcy order) or the court (in the case of a bankruptcy petition where a bankruptcy order is subsequently made) will be required. Where appropriate, certified copies of the bankruptcy order and trustee in bankruptcy's certificate of appointment should be obtained.

(iii)   Receivers

Receivers can sometimes be appointed over assets owned by individuals, and the considerations in section 10.2.3 (B)(i) apply.

(B)   Corporate sellers

In the case of a corporate seller, its memorandum and articles of association will need to be considered to check who has the power to sell its investment (usually the board of directors) and whether there are any restrictions on that power of sale. If it is the board of directors that has power then the purchaser will be concerned to ensure that a board meeting is convened in accordance with the company's articles of association, that a requisite quorum is present, that any directors interested in the sale declare their interest, that the sale is approved and one or more directors are empowered to execute the agreement on behalf of the corporate seller (CA 2006, s 40).

In addition, the purchaser will need to check that the corporate seller is not in receivership, administration or liquidation. Different considerations apply depending on the insolvency regime concerned.

(i)   Receivers

Administrative receivers

Administrative receivers are appointed under a power in debentures, which usually grant fixed charges over most known assets and a floating charge over the remainder. Such a receiver has all the powers within the debenture and Sch 1 of IA 1986. These powers include the power to sell (IA 1986, Sch 1, para 2). It will, however, be necessary, as with all non-court appointed receivers, to check whether there is any security which has priority over the appointor's security or inter-creditor agreements which alter the usual rules of priority. In addition, it will need to be examined to see whether the appointment of the receiver was performed in accordance with the provisions of the debenture and that the debenture itself is valid. Section 232 of IA 1986 provides that the acts of an administrative receiver (and administrator, liquidator or provisional liquidator) but not any other sort of receiver 'are valid notwithstanding any defect in his appointment, nomination or qualifications'. However, this would not operate to protect acts done where there is no power to appoint at all. With the appointment of a receiver, whether pursuant to a court order or otherwise, this must be notified to the Registrar of Companies within seven days of the appointment under s 859K of Companies Act 2006 on form RM01. It is important to note that with a debenture created after 4 February 1991 any defects in the target company's constitutional documents will not affect the validity of the security as, provided it acted in good faith, the charge holder will be protected by the provisions of CA 2006, s 40.

Fixed charge Law of Property Act receivers

Receivers are also appointed under fixed charges which usually also grant powers under the Law of Property Act 1925. Special care needs to be taken where powers under the Law of Property Act 1925 are not included within the charge because the power to appoint under s 101 only arises in limited circumstances (subject to s 21 of the Commonhold and Leasehold Reform Act 2002 (no disposition of part-units)). It is also necessary to check that the receiver was appointed in accordance with the charge and that the charge itself is valid. In addition, it is necessary for the purchaser to verify whether the assets subject to the sale are included within the security documentation, such as goodwill.

Court appointed receivers

Section 37 of the Senior Courts Act 1981 provides for the appointment of receivers where it is 'just and convenient'. This sort of appointment is rare and usually arises where there is either a deadlock in management, no power of appointment elsewhere or in circumstances where assets of a company are in jeopardy. The powers of a court appointed receiver are contained in the court order which often are restricted to safeguarding assets of the target company rather than realising them. If the order is limited, it will be necessary for the receiver to seek a further order from the court permitting a sale of company assets. The purchaser should seek a sealed or certified copy of the relevant court order.

(ii) Administrators

Administration is a process which involves the appointment of an administrator following the making of an administration order. This used to have to be by court order, but from15 September 2003 this requirement was removed by the Enterprise Act 2002.

Administration – grounds

The Enterprise Act 2002 replaced the previous four statutory purposes of administration with a single purpose made up of three objectives, which the administrator should consider in turn. The administrator must perform his/her functions with the objective of:

(1) rescuing the company as a going concern, which should be taken to mean retaining as much as possible of its business;

(2) achieving a better result for the creditors as a whole than would be likely in an immediate winding-up, for example by sale of the business(es)

or its assets. This objective can only be pursued where rescue is not reasonably practicable, or where it would give a better outcome for creditors than objective 1;

(3) realising the company's property so as to make a distribution to one or more secured or preferential creditors. This objective can only be pursued where it is not reasonably practicable to achieve either of objectives 1 or 2.

Administration is not an alternative to liquidation in cases where properly the affairs of the company should simply be wound up and there is no benefit to the creditors from trading on under the protection of the administration moratorium.

For further information about the administration process, see: https://www.gov.uk/government/organisations/insolvency-service.In order to obtain an order the target company must be insolvent and have shown to the satisfaction of the court that it has a reasonable prospect of achieving the single purpose mentioned above made up of the three objectives

The application for an administration order is made following the presentation of an administration petition either by the company, the directors, or by a creditor(s) where the court route is used. Following the making of an administration order (and also the presentation of an administration petition), a moratorium freezing action from most creditors applies (see ss 10 and 11 of IA 1986, as amended, and the Enterprise Act 2002).

Administrators have the same powers as an administrative receiver under Sch 1, which include the power of sale, but there are also requirements that an administrator's proposals should be approved by creditors. This can lead to difficulties where there is a possible early sale of the target company before a meeting of creditors under s 23 of IA 1986. The recent authority, *Re T&D Industries plc* [2000] 1 BCLC 471, held that leave of the court is not required for an administrator to sell. Specific advice on this issue should be obtained by the purchaser where appropriate.

(iii) Liquidators

Liquidators have the power to sell any of the company's property without sanction (see Sch 4, Part III, para 6 of IA 1986).

There are two types of insolvent liquidation, compulsory (instituted usually by a creditor through the courts) and creditors voluntary liquidation (CVL), which is instituted by the company itself and does not involve the court.

A purchaser should be aware that after a winding-up petition is presented against a company, dispositions of a company's property and shares are void unless the court orders otherwise. There is a similar restriction in a CVL on the transfer of shares (see ss 127 and 88 of IA 1986).

In a CVL, the winding-up resolution passed by members must be filed with the Registrar of Companies within 15 days, and care needs to be taken as this may be inadequate for a purchaser to receive notice of the same. In relation to compulsory winding-up petitions, a register of pending petitions (liquidation and administration) is maintained at the Royal Courts of Justice in the Strand who can be contacted by telephone to check whether there are any relevant pending winding up or administration petitions. In order to minimise the risks of the target company/assets being in liquidation, company searches should therefore be carried out on a regular basis and prior to completion to check if any notices of resolutions or appointments are shown at the Register of Companies.

The old s 320 of CA 1985 could have applied to the sale of assets by a receiver and possibly an administrator, but not a liquidation following the decision in *Demite Ltd v Protec Health Ltd* [1998] BCC 638. CA 2006, s 190 made some changes to s 320. Under s 190 'Substantial property transactions: requirement of members' approval' a company may not enter into an arrangement under which:

(a) a director of the company or of its holding company, or a person connected with such a director, acquires or is to acquire from the company (directly or indirectly) a substantial non-cash asset; or

(b) the company acquires or is to acquire a substantial non-cash asset (directly or indirectly) from such a director or a person so connected,

unless the arrangement has been approved by a resolution of the members of the company or is conditional on such approval being obtained.

If the director or connected person is a director of the company's holding company or a person connected with such a director, the arrangement must also have been approved by a resolution of the members of the holding company or be conditional on such approval being obtained. A company shall not be subject to any liability by reason of a failure to obtain approval required by the section. No approval is required under this section on the part of the members of a body corporate that:

(a) is not a UK-registered company, or

(b) is a wholly-owned subsidiary of another body corporate.

An arrangement involving more than one non-cash asset, or an arrangement that is one of a series involving non-cash assets, is treated as if they involved a non-cash asset of a value equal to the aggregate value of all the non-cash assets involved in the arrangement or, as the case may be, the series. Section 190 does not apply to a transaction so far as it relates to:

(a) anything to which a director of a company is entitled under his service contract; or

(b) payment for loss of office as defined in s 215 (payments requiring members' approval).

Section 191 defines substantial non-cash asset:

'(2) An asset is a substantial asset in relation to a company if its value –
    (a) exceeds 10% of the company's asset value and is more than £5,000, or
    (b) exceeds £100,000.
(3) For this purpose a company's "asset value" at any time is –
    (a) the value of the company's net assets determined by reference to its most recent statutory accounts, or
    (b) if no statutory accounts have been prepared, the amount of the company's called-up share capital.
(4) A company's "statutory accounts" means its annual accounts prepared in accordance with Part 15, and its "most recent" statutory accounts means those in relation to which the time for sending them out to members (see section 424) is most recent.
(5) Whether an asset is a substantial asset shall be determined as at the time the arrangement is entered into.'

If the target is a business, in addition to the investigations referred to in section 10.2, the purchaser will need to establish who has the right to sell each individual asset used in the business. With a few exceptions (for example, patents and other forms of intellectual property) there is no statutory register of ownership of the various assets comprised in the business. As a result, however detailed the purchaser's due diligence investigations are, they will not be able to establish an absolute right to ownership and the purchaser will need to rely on warranties for that protection, but such warranties are generally unavailable when purchasing a business from an insolvency office-holder.

10.2.4 Consents/approvals required

The due diligence review should establish whether the seller and/or the target require any consents or approvals to enable the proposed acquisition to proceed. At the same time the purchaser will also need to give consideration to the consents and approvals it may require to approve the acquisition and to authorise it to enter into the acquisition agreement. Where an approval and/or consent is required it is usual practice for the approval/consent to be obtained between the exchange of contracts and completion and for completion to be conditional upon such approval/consent being obtained.

The consents and approvals required will differ depending upon whether the sale is structured as a sale of shares or assets and the identity of the seller(s). The following is an outline of those most commonly required.

(A) Shareholders

The approval of the seller's shareholders may be necessary where:

- the seller is a listed public company and the sale represents a significant disposal;

- within the previous ten years the target's shares have been listed or advertised on a regular basis or the target has issued a prospectus;
- the seller's articles of association and any agreements between the shareholders (commonly called a shareholders' agreement) relating to the conduct and management of the target require; and
- one or more of the directors of the seller are connected with the purchaser.

(i) Listed company sellers

If the seller is listed on the official list of the UK Listing Authority, it will be subject to various continuing obligations under the Listing Rules published by the Financial Conduct Authority. They are available on the FCA website: www.fca.org.uk. The Listing Rules contain special provisions to deal with transactions, principally acquisitions and disposals, by a listed company. The Listing Rules describe how transactions are classified and what the requirements are for announcements, and whether either a circular and/or shareholder approval is required. The Listing Rules also deal with transactions with so-called 'related parties'.

The term 'transaction' is widely drawn and includes transactions by subsidiary undertakings, but excludes a transaction of a revenue nature in the ordinary course of business. If considering a transaction the company must, at an early stage, consider the classification of the transaction by assessing the size of the transaction relative to that of the company. The comparison of size is made by the use of percentage ratios, being the figure, expressed as a percentage, resulting from comparing each of the following:

- assets – the gross assets the subject of the transaction divided by the gross assets of the listed company;
- profits – the profits attributable to the assets the subject matter of the transaction divided by the profits of the listed company;
- turnover – the turnover attributable to the assets the subject of the transaction divided by the turnover of the listed company;
- consideration to market capitalisation – the consideration divided by the aggregate market value of all the ordinary shares of the listed company; and
- gross capital – the gross capital of the company or business being acquired divided by the gross capital of the listed company (this percentage ratio is only to be applied in the case of an acquisition of a company or business).

In addition, where relevant, industry specific tests may be submitted by, or on behalf of, the listed company to support the standard calculations set out above.

In circumstances where any of the above calculations produce an anomalous result or where the calculations are inappropriate to the sphere of activity of the listed company, the UK Listing Authority may disregard the calculation and may substitute other relevant indicators of size, including industry specific tests.

The different classifications are:

- Class 1 – a transaction where any percentage ratio is 25% or more;
- Class 2 – a transaction where any percentage ratio is 5% or more but each is less than 25%;
- Class 3 – a transaction where all percentage ratios are less than 5%; and
- Reverse takeover – an acquisition by a listed company of a business, an unlisted company or assets where any percentage ratio is 100% or more or which would result in a fundamental change in the business or in a change in board or voting control of the listed company.

The Listing Rules set out further detailed provisions as to how each of these calculations is to be made and each of these class tests is to be applied.

Class 1 transactions

In the case of a Class 1 transaction:

- an explanatory circular must be despatched to the company's shareholders;
- the company must obtain the prior approval of its shareholders in general meeting to the transaction; and
- any agreement effecting the transaction must be conditional upon shareholder approval being obtained.

A Class 1 circular is a detailed document which must comply with various information requirements set out in the Listing Rules.

Details of the transaction must be notified to the Regulatory Information Service without delay after the terms of the Class 1 transaction are agreed. From 15 April 2008, a new mechanism for disseminating regulatory information became effective. Listed companies choose which Regulatory Information Service they wish to use to make their regulatory information available to the market. There are currently seven services that act as Regulatory Information Service providers.

Class 2 transactions

There is no requirement for a circular to be prepared in connection with a Class 2 transaction or for shareholder approval to be obtained. However, the company must notify the CAO without delay after the terms of the Class 2 transaction have been agreed and the notification must include various details as to the transaction terms as set out in the Listing Rules.

Class 3 transactions

Again, there is no requirement for a circular or shareholder approval to be prepared in connection with a Class 3 transaction.

In the case of a Class 3 transaction which is an acquisition in respect of which the consideration includes the issue of shares for which listing will be sought, the company must notify the CAO without delay after the terms of the acquisition are agreed. The Listing Rules specify the information to be included.

In the case of other Class 3 transactions, if the company releases any details to the public they must also be notified to the CAO.

Reverse takeovers

Upon the announcement of a reverse take-over, the UK Listing Authority will suspend listing of the company's shares. The company must prepare a Class 1 circular and Listing Particulars, in broad terms, as though the company were a new applicant and obtain the prior approval of the shareholders to the transaction.

If shareholder approval is given and the transaction is completed, the existing listing will be cancelled and, if the company wishes to become listed again, it will be treated as a new applicant.

Transactions with related parties

The Listing Rules provide certain safeguards against current or recent directors of the company or of any of its subsidiary undertakings, or substantial shareholders (or associates of either), taking advantage of their position.

Where any transaction is proposed between the company (or any of its subsidiary undertakings) and a related party, a circular and the prior approval of the company in general meeting will generally be required although these are assumptions for small transactions. The related party will not be permitted to vote at the meeting.

Any circular sent to shareholders in connection with a transaction with a related party must provide sufficient information to enable any recipient of the circular to evaluate the effects of the transaction on the company.

The expression 'related party' is defined widely, as is the expression 'transaction with a related party', although the latter definition does not include a transaction of a revenue nature in the ordinary course of business.

If the company (or any of its subsidiary undertakings) proposes to enter into a transaction which could be a transaction with a related party, and if there is any doubt as to whether or to what extent the provisions of the Listing Rules apply, the company must consult the UK Listing Authority at an early stage. The relevant draft contract must be supplied to the UK Listing Authority, if requested.

The Listing Rules prescribe the information which should generally be included in related party circulars. The rules also contain detailed exceptions to the usual requirements, which include arrangements involving employees' share schemes, long-term incentive schemes, and also small transactions.

Listing Particulars

In addition to the above requirements, if the transaction involves the issue of shares by the listed company which would increase the shares of a class already listed by 10% or more, Listing Particulars will be required. Listing Particulars have to comply with Chapters 5 and 6 of the Listing Rules and must be approved by the UK Listing Authority in advance.

AIM companies

If the seller is listed but its shares are traded on the Alternative Investment Market (AIM) of the London Stock Exchange as opposed to the official list of the UK Listing Authority, it will be subject to similar approvals and disclosure requirements, albeit less onerous. Those rules so far as they relate to AIM companies are contained in the Prospectus Regulations 2005 (SI 2005/1433) which implement EU Directive 2003/71/EC on the prospectus to be published when securities are offered to the public or admitted to trading on a regulated market (known as 'the Prospectus Directive'). See also regulations made implementing changes to Directive 2003/71/EC in Prospectus Regulations 2012 (SI 2012/1538) and FSA Prospectus Amending Directive Instrument 2012 which amended the FSA Handbook – ie Prospectus Rules, Listing Rules and Disclosure and Transparency Rules.

Section 85 states the general rule that a person may not make an offer of securities to the public in the UK, or seek admission to trading on a regulated market in the UK, unless a prospectus approved by the FCA has been published. Under the AIM rules all companies admitted to AIM must have a nominated adviser ('NOMAD') who must work closely with the company and advise it on its obligations as a company whose shares are traded on the AIM market.

(ii)   City Code on Takeovers and Mergers

Where the target is resident in the UK, the Channel Islands or the Isle of Man and:

- its equity share capital has been listed on the Official List of the UK Listing Authority, the AIM or the London Stock Exchange or Nex Exchange (which in 2017 changed its name from *ICAP Securities and Derivatives Exchange* (ISDX)) (earlier rebranded in 2012 from Plus Markets and previously from 'OFEX' – see: http://www.nexexchange. com/) at any time during the ten years prior to the acquisition; or
- dealings and/or prices in the target's equity share capital have been published (whether via newspaper, electronic price quotation system or otherwise) on a regular basis for a continuous period of at least six months during such ten years; or
- their equity share capital has been subject to a marketing arrangement as described in CA 2006, s 693(3) at any time during such term; and
- the target has filed a prospectus for the issue of equity share capital at the Companies Registry at any time during such ten years;

the purchase of shares in the target will be subject to the City Code on Takeovers and Mergers produced by the Panel on Takeovers and Mergers. A copy of the City code is available at: http://www.thetakeoverpanel.org.uk. However, where a public company has 12 or fewer shareholders and they all consent in writing, the Panel may be approached for its agreement that the City Code should not apply.

Although a discussion on the terms of the Takeover Code is outside the scope of this book, it is important to ensure that a purchaser considering the acquisition of shares in a private company caught by the Takeover Codes Rules should be au fait with those rules before making any share purchases, otherwise a costly mistake may be made.

(iii) Shareholders' agreement/articles of association

The provisions of the target's articles of association, or any shareholders' agreement regulating the conduct and management of the target, may contain restrictions (for example, on the transfer of the shares in the target without first offering the shares proposed to be transferred to existing shareholders on a pro rata basis) or require prior approval to certain transactions (for example, class consent rights in the articles or institutional/minority shareholder protection provisions in a shareholders' agreement). Although this is more likely to be the case with a management buy-out vehicle, joint venture company, a company owned by a large number of shareholders or a company financed partly by venture capital, the articles of association and, where relevant, shareholders' agreement of all target companies should be checked to ensure no such restrictions apply.

(iv) Transactions involving directors

If the purchaser is a director of the seller (or its holding company) or a person connected with such a director then, depending upon the value of the transaction, the sale may require shareholder approval pursuant to CA 2006, s 190 (see discussion of s 190 above). It is important to note that s 190 prohibits a company from entering into 'an arrangement' unless 'the arrangement is first approved' by the company in general meeting. Therefore, it seems that conditional contracts are of no help and the resolution should be passed before the contract is entered into. 'Connected persons' are defined in CA 2006, s 252:

> '(a) members of the director's family (see section 253);
> (b) a body corporate with which the director is connected (as defined in section 254);
> (c) a person acting in his capacity as trustee of a trust—
>> (i) the beneficiaries of which include the director or a person who by virtue of paragraph (a) or (b) is connected with him, or
>> (ii) the terms of which confer a power on the trustees that may be exercised for the benefit of the director or any such person,
>
> other than a trust for the purposes of an employees' share scheme or a pension scheme;
> (d) a person acting in his capacity as partner—
>> (i) of the director, or

    (ii) of a person who, by virtue of paragraph (a), (b) or (c), is connected with that director;

  (e) a firm that is a legal person under the law by which it is governed and in which—

    (i) the director is a partner,

    (ii) a partner is a person who, by virtue of paragraph (a), (b) or (c) is connected with the director, or

    (iii) a partner is a firm in which the director is a partner or in which there is a partner who, by virtue of paragraph (a), (b) or (c), is connected with the director.'

References to a person connected with a director of a company do not include a person who is himself a director of the company.

(B) Board

In the case of a share purchase, it will be necessary to investigate the share transfer provisions of the target's articles of association to ascertain the share transfer process, which may either require shareholder or board approval. The purchase of assets, on the other hand, will almost invariably require approval by the target's board of directors. This will involve the convening of a board meeting to approve the proposed transaction, where practicable the prior circulation of a copy of the proposed sale agreements, and a vote of the directors to approve the sale in principle and to authorise any one or more of the directors to sign the sale contract on behalf of the seller company.

In deciding whether to approve the proposed transaction, each director must act in good faith in what he considers to be the best interests of the company of which he is a director. If any director is personally interested in the proposed transaction (for example, because he is a director of the purchaser), under CA 2006, s 182, he is required to declare his interest at the meeting of the board to discuss the transaction. In addition, the seller's articles will need to be further checked to ascertain whether, having declared his interest, the interested director can vote or be counted in the quorum.

Section 182 'Declaration of interest in existing transaction or arrangement' provides that where a director of a company is in any way, 'directly or indirectly, interested in a transaction or arrangement that has been entered into by the company, he must declare the nature and extent of the interest to the other directors in accordance with this section. This section does not apply if or to the extent that the interest has been declared under section 177 (duty to declare interest in proposed transaction or arrangement).'

The declaration must be made:

  (a) at a meeting of the directors, or

  (b) by notice in writing (see section 184); or

  (c) by general notice (see section 185).

A director need not declare an interest:

(a)   if it cannot reasonably be regarded as likely to give rise to a conflict of interest;

(b)   if, or to the extent that, the other directors are already aware of it (and for this purpose the other directors are treated as aware of anything of which they ought reasonably to be aware); or

(c)   if, or to the extent that, it concerns terms of his service contract that have been or are to be considered:

(i)   by a meeting of the directors; or

(ii)   by a committee of the directors appointed for the purpose under the company's constitution.

(C)   Landlord

Most commercial leases have provisions for the landlord's consent to be obtained for any assignment of the lease. Some leases may have an absolute prohibition against assignment. It is also worth noting that some leases include the acquisition of shares in their definition of an assignment. Accordingly, both share and asset purchasers should be aware of the need to check whether landlord's consent is needed, and be aware that the process can often lead to delay as the landlord and its advisers consider the seller's application for consent. The advent of the Landlord and Tenant (Covenants) Act 1995 has meant that consent will usually be harder to obtain for leases granted after 1 January 1996, as leases are now being drafted with more stringent criteria for an assignee. In addition, a landlord may (where specified in the lease) as a condition for granting consent to assignment require the rectification of any subsisting breaches of lease covenants, for example the payment of all outstanding rent or the rectifying of dilapidations.

Where a landlord's consent is required, the consent is not to be unreasonably withheld (even if the lease does not specifically say so: Landlord and Tenant Act 1927, s 19(1)). More importantly, since the introduction of the Landlord and Tenant Act 1988, there has been a statutory duty on a landlord to consider an application for consent 'within a reasonable time'. As a result, since 1 January 1996, there have been more leases with an absolute prohibition against assignment to which s 19(1) will not apply.

(D)   Customer/supplier

The purchase of assets will involve the transfer of customer and supplier arrangements to the purchaser. Unless the existing arrangement with the target contains a free right of assignment the transfer of the arrangement will require the approval of the relevant customer or supplier. This is discussed in more detail in section 10.2.4 (E).

Although the purchase of shares will not involve the transfer of the target's underlying contracts, some of the target's customer and supplier arrangements may be specific to the target whilst in the ownership of the seller and contain termination provisions on the change of control of the target.

For the reasons stated in section 10.2.4 (D), the key supplier and customer arrangements should be investigated to ascertain those which cannot pass to the purchaser (or the target in the purchaser's ownership) without the consent of the other contracting party. Ministry of Defence contracts, for example, would prohibit either the sale and purchase of the target or its business without the Ministry's prior approval.

(E) Trade/industry and consumer credit FSMA 2000, s 178 notices

To carry on business in certain market sectors requires a licence from the governing body. Accordingly, a target engaged in any of the following businesses should be investigated to ascertain whether any prior consents are necessary and the industry requirements relating to the transfer of their operating licence:

- banking and building societies;
- insurance;
- Ministry of Defence contractors;
- newspapers;
- restaurants, bars and other establishments selling liquor; and
- telecommunications.

If the target company offers consumer credit to customers of its business there may need to be a prior clearance of the purchaser by the Financial Conduct Authority. This can significantly delay the transaction and specialist legal advice should be sought. Previously notification was only necessary to the FCA. The FCA has strict rules on changes of control of an entity such that, even if only the shares of a business involved in the consumer credit field are sold, prior clearance is needed. Readers should be aware that it is a criminal offence not to obtain control in advance. The FCA gives the following summary:

'Change in control

Individuals or companies that wish to acquire or increase control in a firm that we regulate must seek our prior approval.

Regulated firms are also obliged to notify us of proposed or actual changes in control (see SUP 11.4 in the Handbook for further information).

Dual-regulated firms (banks, building societies, credit unions etc) need to obtain approval from the Prudential Regulation Authority.

A change in control can also take place when an existing controller of a firm decreases its control. See FSMA section 191D or SUP 11 in the Handbook for full details of the thresholds and requirements.

It is a criminal offence under FSMA section 191F to:

- acquire or increase control without notifying us first
- fail to obtain prior approval in such circumstances

You may also be liable on indictment to a fine that exceeds the statutory minimum.

Read our quick reference guide (PDF) which gives a definition of controllers, the various control bands and an example structure chart.

Section 178

Notifications for changes in control are known as Section 178 notices – you should send us a notification as soon as you have made a decision to acquire a control in an authorised firm. Making a decision to acquire could for example include circumstances where a proposed controller decides not to take any action to prevent or reduce its increase in control to below the relevant threshold.

We have 60 working days (excluding any interruption period) to assess a change of control case. This period begins on the day we acknowledge receipt of a complete Section 178 notice.

What you should send us

These documents can be sent to us either by the controller(s) or jointly by the controller(s) and the target FCA authorised firm:

Notification forms

These are required from all controllers (Section 422 of FSMA).

Name of form	Who should use it
Corporate controllers form	A firm that is either a limited company or a limited liability partnership
Partnership controllers form	A firm that is a partnership
Individual controllers form	An individual
Trust controllers form	A trustee, settler or beneficiary of a trust
Fund manager form	An FCA-authorised fund manager (subject to satisfying the four conditions set out in SUP 11.3.5B)
Intragroup transactions form	A firm undertaking an internal reorganisation

Supporting documents

These will include, but may not be limited to:

- post-transaction structure charts
- CVs for individual controllers and directors/members of corporate controllers
- proof and source of funding
- accounts for corporate controllers
- comprehensive business plan
- negative disclosure supporting information/documents

Find out how to disclose an individual's criminal convictions.

Additional requirements

This is where the target firm(s) is relationship-managed by us. For all changes in control where we relationship-manage the target firm(s), we may have additional requirements to those published. The target firm should contact its FCA relationship manager to discuss any proposed changes in control and whether a pre-notification meeting is required.

If you are a proposed controller and do not want to submit a joint notification with such a target firm, please email cic-notifications@fca.org.uk or write to: Change in Control team, Financial Conduct Authority, 25 The North Colonnade, London E14 5HS.'

See further at https://www.fca.org.uk/firms/change-control.

These are substantial requirements and the forms are detailed and may be required to be completed for several entities and persons. Ensure the buyer is aware very early on in the transactions that such prior clearance will be required so this can be included in the timescales given to the parties.

(F)   Bank/finance

Almost all purchasers will require the target's assets to be transferred to it free from any encumbrances and will have agreed to purchase the target on that basis. Where, therefore, the target's assets are charged to its bankers as security for outstanding indebtedness, the consent of the target's bankers will be required to ensure the charges are released on completion. This can, however, result in timing problems because the bank will be reluctant to release the charges until its debt is repaid and, typically, the seller/target will not be in a position to repay the debt until the sale proceeds are received. This impasse can normally be resolved in one of two ways: either by the bank's solicitors undertaking to discharge the charges upon receipt of the outstanding indebtedness together with a mechanism for paying the outstanding amount direct to the bank, or by the bank supplying a release of the charges to the target's lawyers on an undertaking to the bank only to supply the release when funds sufficient to repay the indebtedness are released to them.

Further consent/approval may be required under the terms of any loan or other finance agreements and, accordingly, such terms should be investigated.

(G)   Competition regulations

When reviewing a potential acquisition it is important to consider whether the transaction could be delayed or even thwarted by competition regulators. They are the European Commission, the Competition and Markets Authority in the UK and national competition authorities in the other countries in which the target operates all have power to block mergers which fall within their jurisdiction and which they consider might have serious anti-competitive effects.

Due diligence

A merger will not be considered by the EC and UK competition authorities at the same time. If the EC has jurisdiction, the UK Competition and Markets Authority will not until 2019 Brexit, and the position after that at the date of writing is unclear, although it is likely some mergers may be sent both to the EU and UK competition authorities. For either authority to have jurisdiction the transaction must exceed certain thresholds and so many smaller, private company/business mergers and acquisitions escape scrutiny altogether.

(i)   EC merger control

The European Commission has jurisdiction over any concentration which has a Community dimension (and after Brexit the Competition and Markets Authority is likely to have jurisdiction as well).

Transactions which satisfy these tests must be notified to the European Commission, whether or not there is a substantive competition issue raised by the transaction. The concentration is appraised by the Merger Task Force at the Directorate General Competition of the European Commission under Council Regulation 139/2004 on the control of concentrations between undertakings.

There is no need to notify national competition authorities of the EC Member States of transactions which are notified under the EC merger control rules.

A concentration occurs where there is either:

- an acquisition of control or the ability to exercise decisive influence over a target;
- a merger; or
- a concentrative joint venture is established.

Control can be acquired on a legal basis by the acquisition of 50%+ of the voting rights in a target company. Control can also be acquired on a de facto basis where only a minority interest is acquired where a party has rights which give it the possibility of exercising decisive influence over the commercial strategy of the target company. Such rights are rights which are more than standard minority protection rights. Examples include (but are not limited to) a right of approval or veto over the target's business plan, budget or appointment of senior management. 'Control' is a flexible concept and must be considered in the light of all the relevant circumstances – it could be conferred, for instance, by structural links between the target and a third party with which the target has an important long-term supply agreement.

A party which acquires control of a target is an undertaking concerned and so is the target company.

A Community dimension exists where either of the following tests is satisfied:

Test 1
- the combined aggregate worldwide turnover of all the undertakings concerned must be more than €5,000m; and

170

- the aggregate Community wide turnover of at least two of the undertakings concerned must be more than €250m;

unless each of the undertakings concerned achieves more than two-thirds of its aggregate Community-wide turnover within one and the same EU Member State.

Test 2
- the combined aggregate worldwide turnover of all the undertakings concerned is more than €2,500m;
- in each of at least three Member States the combined aggregate turnover of all the undertakings concerned is more than €100m;
- in at least three Member States included above, the aggregate turnover of at least two of the undertakings concerned is more than €25m; and
- the aggregate Community wide turnover of at least two of the undertakings concerned is more than €100m;

unless each of the undertakings concerned achieves more than two-thirds of its aggregate Community-wide turnover in one and the same EU Member State.

In applying these thresholds the turnover to be taken into account must include turnover of all companies within the same group of companies as the undertakings concerned in the transaction. The exception to these rules is that if the concentration consists of the acquisition of part of a business (whether or not constituted as a separate legal entity) the turnover of the target consists only of the turnover relating to the business acquired.

The turnover thresholds for calculation of Community dimension are reasonably high and therefore the EC Merger Regulation will not always be relevant to UK private company/business acquisitions. However, notification may be necessary where, for example, a joint venture is established involving two private companies which are each part of much larger groups or where an investor which acquires control is part of a larger group, and therefore the aggregate turnover could reach the Community dimension thresholds.

If the concentration does not have a Community dimension it therefore falls to be assessed, if at all, by the relevant national competition authorities and not by the Commission.

The 2004 Regulation made changes to the previous regime to resolve the problem of multiple filings for mergers in several Member States. Companies now may ask to benefit from a 'one-stop shop' if they have to notify in three or more Member States. Where none of the competent Member States object to the referral within 15 working days of receiving the submission, the merger benefits from the one-stop shop and is examined by the Commission.

The EC Merger Regulation contains the following procedure for the notification of concentrations falling within the Regulation and the time periods within which decisions must be taken by the Commission. The 2004 Regulation materially altered the previous rules from 1 May 2005:

First phase of examination of merger

- 25 working days starting the day which follows the receipt of notification to determine if it falls within the scope of the regulation, whether it will be cleared or whether to start formal proceedings.

(Extended to 35 working days if undertakings are offered or a referral request is received.)

Second phase

- 90 working days from the day that follows the decision to carry out an in-depth inquiry.

(+ 20 working days if requested by the notifying parties or by the Commission with the agreement of the notifying parties.)

(+ 15 working days if companies offered remedies after the 54th working day that followed the initiation of the in-depth inquiry.)

The concentration cannot be put into effect either before its notification or until it has been cleared by the Commission. Where a case notified to the Commission only affects a local or regional market within an EC Member State, the case may be 'referred back' to the relevant national competition authorities.

The test the Commission uses to assess the merger was revised in the 2004 Regulation. It introduced a 'substantive test' which the Commission sees as 'the "carbon test", the raison d'être of the Merger Regulation'. The previous Merger Regulation was based on the concept of dominance: a merger would have been blocked if it created a dominant position and therefore would likely result in higher prices, less choice and innovation. This concept had been interpreted by the Commission and the European courts as applying also to situations of 'joint dominance' or duopolies (Kali und Salz/MdK and Gencor/ Lonrho) as well as to situations of 'collective dominance' or oligopolies (Airtours/First Choice).

The test in the 2004 Regulation was adapted to make clear that all anti-competitive mergers resulting in higher prices, less choice or innovation are covered. This is achieved by the new test, which states that a merger must be blocked if it would 'significantly impede effective competition'. Dominance, in its different forms, remains the main issue. However, the test now clearly encompasses anti-competitive effects in oligopolistic markets where the merged company would not be strictly dominant in the usual sense of the word (ie much bigger than the rest). The central question is whether sufficient competition remains after the merger to provide consumers with sufficient choice.

In addition to these formal requirements, the European Commission encourages parties to discuss proposed notifications informally and in strict confidence before notification and can give informal guidance. This is an essential part of the notification process, particularly where a transaction raises substantive competition issues and the time and resource needed to collate detailed market information to support a notification to the Commission should not be underestimated.

The Commission published a Notice on a Simplified Procedure for treatment of certain concentrations under Council Regulation (EC) No 139/2004 which sets out a simplified procedure for treatment of certain transactions which fall within the EC Merger Rules but which do not raise competition concerns. The conditions under which the simplified procedure will be applied are as follows:

(a) two or more undertakings acquire joint control of a joint venture, provided that the joint venture has no, or negligible, actual or foreseen activities within the territory of the European Economic Area (EEA). Such cases occur where:
   (i) in the case of a joint acquisition of a target company, the turnover to be taken into account is the turnover of this target (the joint venture);
   (ii) in the case of the creation of a joint venture to which the parent companies contribute their activities, the turnover to be taken into account is that of the contributed activities;
   (iii) in the case of entry of a new controlling party into an existing joint venture, the turnover of the joint venture and the turnover of the activities contributed by the new parent company (if any) must be taken into account;
   is less than €100 million in the EEA territory; and the total value of assets transferred to the joint venture is less than €100 million in the EEA territory;

(b) two or more undertakings merge, or one or more undertakings acquire sole or joint control of another undertaking, provided that none of the parties to the concentration are engaged in business activities in the same product and geographical market, or in a product market which is upstream or downstream of a product market in which any other party to the concentration is engaged;

(c) two or more undertakings merge, or one or more undertakings acquire sole or joint control of another undertaking and:
   (i) two or more of the parties to the concentration are engaged in business activities in the same product and geographical market (horizontal relationships) provided that their combined market share is less than 15% (from 2014 raised to 20% – see below); or
   (ii) one or more of the parties to the concentration are engaged in business activities in a product market which is upstream or downstream of a product market in which any other party to the concentration is engaged (vertical relationships), provided that none of their individual or combined market shares is at either level 25% (now 30%) or more;

173

(d) a party is to acquire sole control of an undertaking over which it already has joint control.

When all the necessary conditions are met, and provided that there are no special circumstances, the Commission will adopt a short form clearance decision within one month from the date of notification. Pre-notification contact between the notifying parties and the Commission in such cases is essential. Where it considers it appropriate the Commission may launch a full investigation within the longer time limits set out above. See further at: http://ec.europa.eu/comm/competition/mergers/legislation/simplified_procedure.html.

In December 2013 the simplified procedure above was slightly amended:

(i) for markets in which two merging companies compete ('horizontal overlap markets'), the threshold was raised from 15% to 20%;

(ii) for markets where one of the merging companies sells an input to a market where the other company is active ('vertically related markets', for instance where a manufacturer of cars acquires a manufacturer of car parts), the threshold was raised from 25% to 30%;

(ii) mergers can also qualify for a simplified review when the companies' combined market shares are between 20% and 50%, but when the increase in market share after the combination of their activities is limited. These are cases where the merger's change to the level of concentration in the market (the so-called HHI delta) is less than 150.

The 2014 changes ensured that 60–70% of all notified mergers qualify for the simplified merger review, about 10% more than under the previous legislation.

See http://europa.eu/rapid/press-release_MEMO-13-1098_en.htm.

(ii) UK merger control

If the EC Merger Regulation does not apply and either the target or a purchaser/investor who acquires control of the target carries on business in the UK or under the control of a company incorporated in the UK and either:

- the turnover of the target taken over is £70m or more (previously there was an assets test); or
- the purchaser/investor and the target are competitors in the UK and together their UK (or a substantial part thereof) market share is 25% or more,

the Competition and Markets Authority (CMA) will have jurisdiction to investigate the transaction under the Enterprise Act 2002 (formerly mergers were assessed under the Fair Trading Act 1973) for up to four months after the transaction takes place. Where within those criteria above, the CMA must refer any merger which it believes has resulted, or may be expected to result, in a substantial lessening of competition (SLC) in a UK market for a Phase 2 investigation. Although notification of a merger falling within the tests set out in the legislation is not mandatory, even after the Enterprise and Regulatory Reform Act 2013, it may nevertheless be advisable to do so in certain circumstances. Contrast this with EU merger law where notification is mandatory.

As in the case of the EC merger rules, 'control' is not limited to the acquisition of outright voting control but can be simply an ability materially to influence the policy of target. Such influence is usually conferred by the acquisition of 25% shareholding, but occasionally shareholdings of less than 15% can attract scrutiny given the particular circumstances.

Some transactions may give rise to concerns about loss of competition because of an overlap which creates a significant market share but involves only part of the activities of the merged company. In that case binding undertakings may be accepted for the divestment of part of the merged company's business as an alternative to a reference. There are also powers to accept behavioural undertakings regarding the future conduct of the merged entity in relation to any adverse effects on competition of the merged enterprise.

If the transaction is referred further through to Phase 2 and the CMA decides that there is a SLC found it may recommend remedies to counter the concerns that it has identified. The CMA may then order a transaction to be blocked, require parties to divest shares or limit voting powers, order the break-up of a company or control the conduct of the merged entity by, for example, regulating the new company's prices. Any transaction which is investigated by the CMA and in respect of which a decision is made whether or not to refer the matter for further CMA investigation attracts a fee (even if ultimately it is concluded that the transaction does not operate against the public interest).

It used to be possible to apply for informal guidance confidentially before a merger but this possibility was removed from 1 April 2014.

Current (2018) fees are set out below. However companies with a low turnover may be exempt from the fee by virtue of reg 7 as amended of Enterprise Act 2002 (Merger Fees and Determination of Turnover) Order 2003 (SI 2003/1370) see chart below. The fees are set by Enterprise Act 2002 (Merger Fees and Determination of Turnover) Order 2003 as amended by the Enterprise Act 2002 (Merger Fees and Determination of Turnover) (Amendment) Order 2014 (SI 2014/534). Acquirers who are individuals pay no fee by virtue of the 2014 regulations.

Merger fees

Most mergers which are investigated by the CMA and those which qualify for a reference to Phase 2 are subject to a fee, irrespective of whether a reference is made.

Fees vary according to the value of the UK turnover of the business being acquired.

Fee	Charge Band
£40,000	Value of the UK turnover of the enterprises being acquired is £20 million or less
£80,000	Value of the UK turnover of the enterprises being acquired is over £20 million but not over £70 million
£120,000	Value of the UK turnover of the enterprises being acquired exceeds £70 million, but does not exceed £120 million
£160,000	Value of the UK turnover of the enterprises being acquired exceeds £120 million

The fee is payable when the CMA makes its Phase I merger decision. Information on how to pay for your merger can be found in the CMA's *Mergers fee payment document*. There is no fee if informal advice is sought.

No fees are levied for financial years beginning on or after 1 January 2016 and, if the directors of the acquirer so decided, financial years beginning on or after 1 January 2015, the acquirer qualifies as small or medium-sized if it, or the group of which it is a member (as defined in s 474 of the Companies Act 2006), satisfies at least two of the following three criteria in its most recent financial year:

	Turnover	Balance Sheet Total (aggregate amount of assets)	Number of employees
Small company	£10.2m	£5.1m	50
Small group	£10.2m net (or £12.2m gross)	£5.1m net (or £6.1m gross)	50
Medium-sized company	£36m	£18m	250
Medium-sized group	£36m net (or £43.2m gross)	£18m net (or £21.6m gross)	250

The above requirements are as out in ss 382(3)–(6), 383(4)–(7), 465(3) and 466(4) of the Companies Act 2006, as amended by regs 4 and 9 of the Companies, Partnerships and Groups (Accounts and Reports) Regulations 2015 (SI 2015/980). These Regulations apply in respect of financial years beginning on or after 1 January 2016, but the directors of a company may instead decide to apply this aspect of the amended law to the company's financial year beginning on or after 1 January 2015 (but before 1 January 2016) (reg 2).

(See https://www.gov.uk/government/uploads/system/uploads/attachment_data/file/492426/Merger_fees_information_January_2016.pdf.)

For example a company with £2m turnover and ten staff is clearly exempt from the fees (it meets two of the three criteria across one line for 'small company' on the table above no matter how valuable its assets.

A merger fee is not payable if the merger involves the acquisition of an interest that is less than a controlling interest and the CMA investigated the acquisition on its own initiative – see art 4(1) and (3) of the Merger Fees Order. This exception does not apply if the merger parties notified such an acquisition by submitting a merger notice.

Merger Assessment Guidelines

The CMA Merger Assessment Guidance sets out how mergers are treated – https://www.gov.uk/government/publications/merger-assessment-guidelines.

They describe when a merger may be investigated and what is a 'substantial lessening of competition'.

Separate guidance relevant to mergers is published by the CMA from time to time. Such guidance available or under preparation at the date of writing includes:

CMA mergers guidance documents (as at January 2018)

1   Mergers – the CMA's jurisdiction and procedure: CMA2
2   Merger assessment guidelines: CC2/OFT1254
3   Quick guide to UK merger assessment: CMA18
4   Water and sewerage mergers: CMA49
5   Disclosure of information in CMA work: CC7
6   Merger remedies: CC8
7   Variation and termination of undertakings and orders: CMA11
8   Mergers exceptions to the duty to refer and undertakings in lieu: OFT1122 and CMA64
9   Mergers consumer survey evidence design and presentation: CC2com1/ OFT1230
10   Retail mergers commentary: CMA62
11   CMA's mergers intelligence function: CMA56
12   Review of NHS mergers: CMA29
13   Economic analysis submissions best practice: CC2com3
14   Government in markets: OFT1113

See also:

(a)   Mergers orders and undertakings register
(b)   Merger inquiry outcome statistics
(c)   Review of use of the CMA's merger notice and initial enforcement orders
(d)   Understanding past merger remedies

The CMA regularly updates its list of guidance – see current list at https://www.gov.uk/topic/competition/mergers.

De minimis – Exceptions to Duty to Refer

The guidance on 'Exceptions to the Duty to Refer in lieu of reference guidance': OFT 1122 (see https://www.gov.uk/government/publications/mergers-exceptions-to-the-duty-to-refer-and-undertakings-in-lieu) superseded 'Exception to the duty to refer: markets of insufficient importance (OFT516b)', commonly known as the 'de minimis' guidance and should be read in conjunction with 'Mergers: Exception to the duty to refer in markets of insufficient importance', Ref CMA64 (updated June 2017).

The latest guidance documents cover two distinct issues. The first is the discretionary ability not to move the merger to Phase 2 notwithstanding that the duty to refer is met, on the basis of one of the available exceptions to the duty to refer. The second is the CMA's ability to accept remedies in the form of undertakings in lieu of a reference on to Phase 2.

The three exceptions to the duty to refer are: (a) the market concerned is not, or the markets concerned are not, of sufficient importance to justify the making of a reference on to Phase 2 (the 'de minimis' exception); (b) the arrangements concerned are not sufficiently far advanced, or are not sufficiently likely to proceed, to justify the taking to Phase 2; and (c) any relevant customer benefits in relation to the creation of the relevant merger situation concerned outweigh the substantial lessening of competition concerned and any adverse effects of the substantial lessening of competition concerned.

Undertakings in lieu: the Enterprise Act 2002 provides that the CMA (previously OFT) may, instead of taking a merger on to Phase 2 and for the purpose of remedying, mitigating or preventing the substantial lessening of competition concerned or any adverse effect which has or may have resulted from it or may be expected to result from it, accept from such of the parties concerned as it considers appropriate, undertakings to take such action as it considers appropriate.

De Minimis limits: The guidance on de minimis below summarises the CMA's current thinking on de minimis as follows:

'1.The CMA may decide not to refer a merger for an in-depth "phase 2" investigation if it believes that the market(s) to which the duty to refer applies is/are not of sufficient importance to justify a reference.

2. The CMA considers that the market(s) concerned will generally be of sufficient importance to justify a reference (such that the exception will not be applied) where its/their annual value in the UK, in aggregate, is more than £15 million. By contrast, where the annual value in the UK of the market(s) concerned is, in aggregate, less than £5 million, the CMA will generally not consider a reference justified unless a clear-cut undertaking in lieu of reference is in principle available.

3. Where the annual value in the UK, in aggregate, of the market(s) concerned is between £5 million and £15 million, the CMA will consider whether the

expected customer harm resulting from the merger is materially greater than the average public cost of a phase 2 reference (currently around £400,000). The CMA will base its assessment of expected customer harm on: the size of the market concerned; its view of the likelihood that a substantial lessening of competition will occur; its assessment of the magnitude of any competition that would be lost; and its expectation of the duration of that substantial lessening of competition.

4. The CMA will also take account of the wider implications of its decisions in this area, and will be less likely to exercise its discretion, and therefore more likely to refer, where the merger is one of a potentially large number of similar mergers that could be replicated across the sector in question.'

Guidance updated 2017 at https://www.gov.uk/government/uploads/system/uploads/attachment_data/file/619734/CMA64-mergers-de-minimis-guidance.pdf.

Jurisdictional and Procedural Guidance: Reference should be made to the Mergers jurisdictional and procedural guidance – see https://www.gov.uk/government/uploads/system/uploads/attachment_data/file/384055/CMA2__Mergers__Guidance.pdf.

This guidance should be read alongside the CMA publications *Administrative Penalties: Statement of Policy on the CMA's Approach* (CMA4) and *Transparency and Disclosure: Statement of the CMA's Policy and Approach* (CMA6), as well as the documents listed in Annexe D of the jurisdictional guidance, which were first published by the Office of Fair Trading (OFT) and Competition Commission (CC), and have been adopted by the CMA. This guidance incorporates the CMA's guidance on the exercise of its power under s 73A(4) of the Act to extend for special reasons the period during which it must decide whether to accept undertakings in lieu of reference, which the CMA is required to publish by s 73A(5) of the Act. It supersedes the OFT's *Mergers: Jurisdictional and Procedural Guidance* (OFT 527), the CC's *Merger Procedural Guidelines* (CC18) and Appendix A to the CC's *Merger Remedies: Competition Commission Guidelines* (CC8).

Practical guidance

Most small mergers fall outside the £70m turnover/25% market share test so merger control law is not an issue on an acquisition. It is the buyer who is concerned about these issues because the buyer may be required after a sale to sell off the assets if the merger is referred. Therefore it would normally be a buyer which makes the sale agreement subject to a condition of prior clearance under the formal merger notice procedure under the legislation. Where the assets are under £70m but the market share is high there is always an issue as to whether to apply for what used to be called 'confidential guidance' and now 'interim guidance' and/or formal clearance through the merger notice route. Most small value mergers are not examined and many will pass unnoticed by competition authorities. However, even in very small markets after a sale there is a risk a competitor or customer might object and an ex post facto reference could be made under current law. An example of a very small merger where the then OFT's view was that the relevant market for funeral services was a very small geographical area was the writer's case *Lodge Brothers* (ME/4245/09 17 December 2009) although the OFT decided not to refer it to the then Competition Commission and *Micronclean Ltd* ME/6353/13 (*CMA Phase 1 clearance May 2014* – another of the writer's merger cases).

Until 1 April 2014 an informal procedure for notification was possible but this has been abolished. What remains is the voluntary formal notice procedure with, in most cases, substantial fees to pay to the CMA.

10.2.5   Unknown or understated liabilities

Whether liabilities are of concern to the purchaser will depend upon how the acquisition is structured. In the case of a business transfer, pre-contract liabilities will usually remain with the seller, thereby reducing the need to investigate them.

There are four main areas of investigation together with tax. The financial advisers often take responsibility for the tax review (and, for this reason, tax is not covered below) but this should be clearly ascertained by the legal advisers at the outset to ensure the relevant advisers cover all relevant tax due diligence.

(A)   Property

In terms of concealing unknown or understated liabilities, property assets should be of most concern. Typically a purchaser could be faced with three problem areas:

* liability for properties previously occupied by the target company;
* contaminated land; and
* continuing liability for previous breaches of covenant.

(i)   Liability for properties previously occupied

Until recently an original tenant of every lease remained liable for breaches of the lease occurring after it had disposed of its interest. This particularly harsh principle of land law was much used during the recession of the early 1990s by landlords whose tenants had become insolvent. After much political lobbying the Landlord and Tenant (Covenants) Act 1995 was introduced to protect businesses from the uncertainty resulting from the previous practice and specifically provides that in a new tenancy (principally leases granted on or after 1 January 1996 other than pursuant to arrangements prior to that date) a tenant is liable under his covenants only while the lease is vested in him. There are two exceptions to this: the first is where an assignment is made in breach of covenant or by operation of law then the outgoing tenant retains liability until the next assignment of the property not so in breach. The second, which is expected to apply in most cases, is where the tenant is required by the landlord to guarantee the obligations of his immediate successor by an Authorised Guarantee Agreement.

In all leases, whether granted before or after 1 January 1996, a landlord who does not notify former tenants and their guarantors within six months of any default by a current tenant in relation to payment of ascertained sums of money will be unable to pursue those former tenants and guarantors for those sums. In addition, the former tenant, or guarantor of a former tenant, who is required to make good and does make good a current tenant's default, is entitled to call for an intervening lease to be granted to him, interposed between the landlord and the current tenant to enable the former tenant (or the guarantor) to establish a direct landlord/tenant relationship with the defaulting tenant. That new landlord will then have available to it the usual landlord's remedies, including forfeiture of the current tenant's lease, and will thereby regain possession of the premises.

Although the liability of a tenant for payment of rent and performance of covenants years after the tenant has vacated the property and assigned the lease has been alleviated in respect of new leases granted on or after 1 January 1996 to which the Landlord and Tenant (Covenants) Act 1995 applies, the target could still have a liability in respect of leases granted prior to 1 January 1996, whether actual or contingent. The existence, term and current liabilities of such leases should be established, or adequate warranty cover obtained.

(ii)   Contaminated land

The Environment Act 1995 contains a number of provisions which may be relevant in the context of a share or business acquisition (see section 10.2.5 (B)). Other problems arise from the use of hazardous or noxious building materials such as asbestos, or from smells, dust, dirt or noise. Allied to these is the health and safety of the target's employees.

(iii)   Continuing liabilities for previous lease breaches

If leasehold premises are being acquired (whether by an asset or share purchase) the purchaser will take over continuing as well as future liabilities for breaches of the lease covenants. Accordingly, investigation should be made to ensure, at least, that the landlord has not commenced forfeiture proceedings; that there is no outstanding liability for dilapidation as a result of a breach of the repairing covenants, and that there are no rent/service charge arrears. This is an area where there may be substantial hidden liabilities for an unwary purchaser.

(B)   Environmental

Environmental law has grown very significantly in recent years. This has resulted in the imposition of new liabilities making due diligence investigations into this aspect of a target company's affairs increasingly important. Almost every aspect of a company's activities will have some impact on the environment. The environmental due diligence process should therefore seek to identify those aspects of the target company's business where significant liabilities could arise. This will usually involve three broad categories of investigation:

- contaminated land;

- authorisations, licences and consents; and
- compliance with environmental legislation.

(i) Contaminated land

With the passing of the Environment Act 1995, there is now a legislative framework under which owners of land can potentially be liable for cleaning it up if it is contaminated, even though they are innocent of causing the contamination. Whether any such liability will actually arise will largely depend on the nature of the contamination and its potential impact on the environment. The Environment Act 1995 defines contaminated land as being:

'... land which appears to the local authority in whose area it is situated to be in such a condition, by reason of substances in, on or under the land, that:
(a) significant harm is being caused or there is a significant possibility of such harm being caused; or
(b) pollution of controlled waters is being or is likely to be caused.'

The primary responsibility for assessing whether or not land is contaminated lies with local authorities who will be under a duty to have regard to statutory guidance. For especially contaminated or 'special' sites the enforcing authority will be the Environment Agency (the EA, or, in Scotland, SEPA).

Where contaminated land has been identified, the relevant authority is under a duty to consult with those who may be liable and, if no voluntary clean up is offered, to prepare a 'remediation notice' setting out what action must be taken in order to clean up the land. The remediation notice will be served on the 'appropriate person'. This will usually be the person who caused or knowingly permitted the substances which have resulted in the contamination being in, on or under the land. However, where the original polluter cannot be 'found', the owner or occupier (which could be a tenant) for the time being of that land may incur liability for clean-up. The polluter may also, in certain circumstances, transfer his liability to the owner, for example by selling a site with information about the extent of contamination. There is therefore the potential in any transaction involving the acquisition of land that environmental liabilities may be assumed.

The type of environmental investigation required will very much depend upon the specific circumstances of the case. The type of operation carried on at the company's premises may be of a potentially polluting nature and, accordingly, the purchaser will be put on notice of possible land contamination issues. Preliminary enquiries should also be tailored to address environmental matters and replies scrutinised carefully for clues suggesting possible areas of environmental concern.

The next stage should be to consider whether it is appropriate for the purchaser to undertake more detailed investigations. In many cases additional useful information can be obtained from a desktop or 'phase one' survey study. This will involve an historical survey of documents relating to the site and will often provide useful information relating to matters such as previous uses of the site, proximity to waste management sites, groundwater sources and other controlled waters, etc. A desktop study may be supplemented by a walkover of the site by a qualified environmental consultant. The results of such investigations may prompt a 'phase two' study involving, amongst other things, drilling boreholes and taking soil samples for laboratory analysis. The precise nature of the investigations which are to be undertaken will very much depend upon the particular circumstances of the case.

It is important to note that, particularly where phase two investigations are involved, it may take some days or even weeks before results are generated. It is therefore essential that environmental issues are addressed as early on in the acquisition process as possible in order to give plenty of time for such tests and investigations to be undertaken and their results interpreted.

The discovery of contamination may lead to a re-negotiation of the purchase price or the drafting of a detailed environmental indemnity. Much will, of course, depend upon the relative bargaining positions of the purchaser and seller and, accordingly, who should therefore assume the risk. The results of environmental due diligence investigations will also play an important part in determining the nature and extent of environmental warranties.

See also the Contaminated Land (England) Regulations 2006 (SI 2006/1380) which apply to England only and set out provisions relating to the identification and remediation of contaminated land under Part IIA of the Environmental Protection Act 1990. They make provision for an additional description of contaminated land that is required to be designated as a special site (see reg 2 of the regulations): that is, land which is contaminated land as a result of radioactive substances in, on or under that land.

(ii)   Authorisations, licences and consents

Another important area of environmental liability relates to whether the target company has in place all appropriate environmental authorisations, licences and consents. If the target company carries on a 'prescribed process' under Part I of the Environmental Protection Act 1990 (as replaced by the Pollution Prevention and Control Act 1999) then it will require an authorisation for this purpose either from the local authority or EA, depending on the problem. Copies of all appropriate authorisations should be obtained and careful consideration given to the conditions attaching to any such authorisations. Care should be taken to ensure that any target company which claims that it does not require any such authorisation is not actually carrying on a prescribed process without proper authorisation. Not only is this a criminal offence, but it can result in the business being shut down.

An authorisation may well set out as part of the conditions attaching to such an authorisation that upgrading of equipment be put into effect within a specified period of time. Such contingent liabilities are frequently not provided for in company accounts and accordingly it is important to assess whether the target has a potentially significant liability in this respect.

Under the Environmental Protection Act 1990, s 33 it is an offence to treat, keep or dispose of controlled waste except in accordance with a waste management licence. Controlled waste is widely defined and will generally include any matter which the holder intends to throw away. Enquiries should therefore be made as to whether the target company has obtained a waste management licence or exemption and, if not, whether one should have been obtained for the carrying on of the target company's operations.

The temporary storage of small quantities of waste pending its disposal elsewhere by a third party should not of itself require a waste management licence. However, in such circumstances the company will need to ensure that it has complied with the 'duty of care' provisions introduced by the Environmental Protection Act 1990, s 34. Any person who 'imports, produces, carries, keeps, treats or disposes' of controlled waste is under a duty to ensure that all reasonable steps are taken to ensure that such waste is disposed of properly. This duty extends to ensuring that on the transfer of any waste, such waste is transferred only to a person who is duly authorised to transport or dispose of that waste and that there is provided to the waste contractor a proper written description of the waste. It should therefore be determined whether the company disposes of its waste to a reputable waste carrier and whether waste consignment notes have been completed. Under the Producer Responsibility (Packaging Waste) Regulations 1997 (SI 1997/648), businesses with a turnover of more than £2m and which handle more than 50 tonnes of packaging each year are required to provide certain information to the EA and to procure that set proportions of packaging materials are recovered and recycled. These obligations can affect a wide range of businesses.

The disposal of trade effluent does not require a waste management licence as this is dealt with under a separate regulatory framework. A company will normally require a discharge consent from a sewerage undertaker for the purpose of discharging trade effluent into the public sewer and a consent granted for discharge directly into surface waters. Given that it is illegal to discharge trade effluent without any formal consent or agreement from the relevant regulatory authority, appropriate steps should be taken to ensure that all such consents have been obtained and that their conditions have been complied with.

The removal of water from surface waters or boreholes requires an Abstraction Licence from the EA. Full details of all environmental authorisations should normally be available on request from the target company. However, in circumstances where a direct approach is not practicable, such information can usually be obtained from an inspection of the various public registers (see Chapter 10, section 10.3.3), although in certain circumstances specific details relating to the operation of plant may not be available from public sources, ie where the target company has made a successful application for certain information not to be placed on the register on the grounds of commercial confidentiality.

Reference should also be made to the Restriction of the Use of Certain Hazardous Substances in Electrical and Electronic Equipment Regulations 2012 (RoHS) (SI 2012/3032), as amended; Waste Electrical and Electronic

Equipment Regulations 2013 (SI 2013/3113) and Government guidance on the legislation at https://www.gov.uk/government/collections/producer-responsibility-regulations#waste-electrical-and-electronic-equipment-weee.

Since 6 April 2008, waste management licensing legislation has been replaced (for England and Wales) by environmental permitting legislation.

(iii) Compliance with environmental legislation

A company's environmental track record is likely to be of importance in two respects. First, a history of prosecutions may indicate underlying deficiencies in the company's equipment or working practices thus pointing to the need for further investment in terms of new plant and machinery or training. Allied to this is the fact that a history of prosecutions can significantly damage a company's goodwill. Secondly, where shares in the company are being purchased as opposed to assets, the company's prosecution history will be retained. This could result in the company receiving a very heavy fine for a relatively minor offence because of the company's previous prosecution record. Details of any prosecutions (including any threatened or pending) should therefore be requested from the target company.

Enquiries should also be made as to whether there have been any complaints (whether in writing or otherwise) as these will often be the first indication that there has been a failure to comply with environmental legislation. Where the target company is either unwilling or unable to provide relevant information relating to the commission of environmental offences, further information may be obtained from the various environmental registers (see section 10.3.3) held by regulatory authorities. The threat of potential nuisance actions should not be underestimated and may be costly in terms of compensation, wasted management time and bad publicity. These issues are addressed in detail in the monthly legal journal Environmental Law Monthly.

(C) Employees

Where the purchaser is acquiring the target by means of share purchase, all that will change is the ownership of the target company. So far as the employees are concerned, their contracts with the target company remain unaltered as a consequence of the sale, notwithstanding the change in ownership and the fact that the character and aims of the new controlling shareholder may be radically different to those of the old. No question of redundancy or dismissal will automatically arise on the sale of the target company's shares, and the mutual obligations of the company and the employee continue. Of course, once the sale is concluded, then the requirements of the new controlling shareholder may give rise to changes within the workforce.

In the case of a business transfer, the Transfer of Undertakings (Protection of Employment) Regulations 2006 (replacing TUPE 1981) will almost certainly apply. TUPE 2006 operates to transfer the employees of the business automatically to the purchaser, so that on completion the contracts of employment take effect as if they had originally been made between the employee and the purchaser. Therefore, where there has been a business transfer the identity of the employer changes. However, the purchaser, being the new employer, inherits virtually all rights, duties, powers and liabilities in respect of this new workforce (there are certain exceptions, the most important of which is pensions).

While the acquisition of the target's business involves a change in the employer's identity, the share acquisition of the target does not, the status quo essentially continuing. However, in both scenarios the purchaser needs to know what it is taking on. Therefore the purpose of investigating the target's employees will involve broadly the same objectives whether there is share acquisition or a business transfer. This is to identify their contractual terms of employment, any outstanding contractual liabilities such as accrued holiday or sick pay and statutory employment rights such as maternity pay, equal pay or compensation for sex or race discrimination.

Therefore, prior to the acquisition the purchaser will be concerned to have full details of the target's workforce and their terms of employment. The seller should be asked to provide a copy of all standard terms of employment and state to which employees such terms apply. These details can be incorporated into the acquisition agreement by the seller warranting a schedule of employees containing relevant information, which will include their names, dates of birth, dates of commencement of continuous employment, job tide, duties, remuneration, proposed increments and review dates, frequency of payment and place of work. Where the employees have individual service contracts, copies of these may be annexed to the agreement. Details of any trade union recognition agreement will also be required.

The purchaser should obtain information from the seller concerning any outstanding claims that have been, or may be, made by former employees who have been dismissed. They should also discover if any decisions have been taken or implemented which may result in a claim; for example, an employee may have been given notice of dismissal which will not take place until after completion; or an employee could be in dispute in circumstances which could give rise to a claim after completion, perhaps of sexual or racial discrimination, or a resignation which could be constructive dismissal.

Where there has been a share transfer, the mere fact of a change in the target company's ownership will not affect its liability to meet such claims. Similarly, where the purchaser has become the employer following a business transfer, even though it was not involved in these events it will frequently have to face the consequences of such disputes. It may even inherit liability in situations where the seller has dismissed employees prior to completion. The purchaser should therefore seek the appropriate warranty, indemnity or a reduction in the purchase price, depending upon the possible value of such claims.

All this information will enable the purchaser to assess the full extent of employee liabilities of the target company or its business, and, perhaps more importantly, any possible difficulties or liabilities it may encounter should it have plans to change the workforce post- completion. Whenever a company or business is acquired, a key consideration for the purchaser will be to establish what are its rights and liabilities in relation to the existing employees of that company or business. In certain circumstances this may not present a problem. If the purchaser is acquiring a successful company or business, it may wish to retain the existing board, management and workforce and continue 'business as normal'. However, it is frequently the case that following the acquisition of a company or business, the purchaser may wish to make certain changes in the workforce and/or implement a programme of redundancies from the target's workforce, and possibly of its own.

The identity of the workforce is one important piece of information which the purchaser should check. Where the target or its business forms part of a larger group, its day-to-day operation may involve, or even be dependent upon, individuals who work for the target (either exclusively or in part), but whose contracts are with, for example, its holding company. Because a share sale will have no effect on any contract of employment, the purchaser may suddenly find that it lacks key employees required to run the business. If they do not work for the company it has acquired they will be left behind. Similar problems might arise where employees are working in the business to be transferred, but the seller of that business is not their employer or, if it is, the individuals are not allocated to the business or are ones the seller wishes to retain. In such circumstances appropriate arrangements may have to be negotiated with the seller to secure their future services.

Changes in TUPE 2006

The TUPE 2006 regulations made the following changes to the earlier 1981 regulations:

(1)   A new requirement that the transferor provides the transferee with 'employee liability information'. This has to include details of all the rights, powers, duties and liabilities in connection with the contracts of employment of transferring employees.
(2)   A very limited new right was given to change terms and conditions of employment after a transfer where there is an economic, technical or organisational reason ('an ETO') entailing changes in the workforce. This right is not as far-reaching as it may at first appear, because case law has held that an ETO will only entail changes in the workforce where there is a change in the number or functions of the workforce. The ability to change terms and conditions is therefore still restricted to a limited number of very specific situations. The basic rule remains that in most cases no changes are allowed.
(3)   The transferor and transferee share liability for failure to consult with employees in advance.

In relation to all TUPE transfers note that special rules apply where a public sector body is involved.

(D) Pensions

As the UK state pension scheme does not provide a generous level of benefits, most employers with a substantial staff of stable employees operate a pension scheme providing retirement benefits. In addition any employer with five or more employees had to offer a Stakeholder Pension to employees unless the company offered its own pension scheme which anyone could join after one year of service, although the employer was not obliged to contribute to it and the employee did not have to join. This has been replaced with the 'auto enrolment'/'NEST' pension under which initially employees may contribute 1% of salary and their employer 1% (this will eventually increase to 3% employer contribution and 5% employee – total 8%). Employees but not employers may opt out. See www.nestpensions.org.uk. With the introduction of automatic enrolment, the requirement for an employer to provide access for staff to a stakeholder pension scheme has been removed. See http://www.thepensionsregulator.gov.uk/employers/stakeholder-pensions.aspx. Some employers with fewer than 50 staff can put off their 'staging date' (date they have to offer auto enrolment) to 2017 or 2018.

Accordingly, the acquisition of a company or a business frequently involves the transfer of pension assets and liabilities. In some cases the value of the assets required to meet the pension liabilities being transferred will be greater than the purchase price for the company or business. If a purchaser fails to pay proper regard to pension issues, he may be faced in due course with a choice between making provision for pensions at an unacceptable cost or facing the employee relation problems which arise if employees' pension rights and expectations are adversely affected by the sale. A purchaser should be concerned to ensure not only that he can afford continuity of pension provision at existing levels for future service but also that the full cost of providing pensions for past service is met by the seller directly or indirectly. The seller for his part will be anxious to contain within acceptable limits the cost of providing past service benefits and to avoid any continuing liability.

Many pension funds have been found to be underfunded in recent years and a key cause of many acquisitions not proceeding has been because of the under funding and the risk the buyers may have to make good any deficit in due course. Details of the role of the Pensions Regulator and the Minimum Funding Requirement are given below.

(i) Preliminary steps

When undertaking pensions due diligence for a purchaser, one of the first issues to consider is whether you are acting on a share purchase or a business acquisition, and what form any 'deal' on pensions may take. The approach may differ considerably depending on the type of acquisition and the form of deal.

That said, it will always be necessary to establish what pensions arrangements currently exist in relation to the target business or company. On a share purchase, it may also be necessary to establish what schemes were formerly operated by the target company.

The purchaser will need to know whether any of the target's employees are entitled to pension benefits and, if so, what is the nature of the vendor's present pension arrangements for the employees of the company or business being sold? Is it final salary or money purchase, insured or self-administered? Does auto-enrolment yet apply? The purchaser will also need to know the levels of benefits provided and the ongoing costs. They need to know if it is under funded and may need to approach the Pensions Regulator (see below). To this end the purchaser should seek, and the seller should supply, up-to-date copies of all the arrangements governing documentation (including, where relevant, the latest trust deed and rules and all amending deeds, documents and resolutions), a copy of the latest actuarial valuation of any final salary scheme, a list of the scheme's existing members and those who are likely to become members during the course of the next few months on completing service or age qualifications, a copy of the latest scheme booklet, copies of any deeds of appointment of trustees, any deed of adherence by which the company to be sold adhered to the scheme, evidence of the scheme's exempt approved tax status and, if appropriate, a copy of the contracting-out certificate covering the employer. The Pensions Act 2014 (which brought forward a 67 years state pension age) and Finance Act 2014 make important changes to UK pensions law not least improved rights to take funds as a lump sum, but subject to highest rates of taxation, in lieu of buying an annuity or drawdown. However, this does not affect acquisitions directly and therefore is not addressed here.

(ii) Business acquisition or share purchase – why is this important?

If the purchaser is purchasing shares in the target company, the employees will be employees of the target both before and after completion. If the target operates its own stand-alone pension arrangements, the purchaser will effectively be taking over the target's responsibility for and its liabilities under those arrangements, whatever they may be. Where the target company participates in a group scheme, it is unlikely that the target will be allowed to continue to participate in that group scheme post-completion other than on a temporary transitional basis and the purchaser or the target will have to establish its own pension arrangements. In that case the purchaser may wish to negotiate the payment of a bulk transfer by the seller's scheme to his own arrangement to ensure continuity of pension provision for employees who wish to transfer their accrued rights to the purchaser's arrangement.

Merger Pensions issue – the BT Case 2014

In July 2014 the court upheld a guarantee the state had given British Telecommunications (BT) when it was privatised decades before that it would stand behind the BT pension fund in *Secretary of State for Culture, Media and Sport v BT Pension Scheme Trustees Ltd and British Telecommunications Plc* [2014] EWCA Civ 958. This decision of the Court of Appeal on 16 July 2014 illustrates the importance of considering pensions issues on share transfers. BT said in a press statement at the time:

> 'The Court of Appeal has upheld the High Court's decision that the Crown Guarantee covers BT's funding obligation in relation to all members of the Scheme regardless of whether they joined pre or post privatisation (subject to exceptions). In addition, the Court decided that the funding obligation to which the Crown Guarantee relates is not measured with reference to the cost of buying out all the benefits with an insurance company, but instead by reference to BT's continuing obligation to pay deficit contributions under the Rules of the Scheme.'

If BT were to go out of business, which is very unlikely, the taxpayer guarantee could cost the state/taxpayers up to £24 billion.

In any event, any liabilities incurred by the target company prior to completion in relation to the group scheme will remain liabilities of the target company after completion even after it has ceased to participate in that scheme. In a share purchase, details of any closed or discontinued arrangements operated for the benefit of former employees under which the target company has any residual liability will also be relevant since the liability will pass with the target company. This is the effect of s 75 of the Pensions Act 1995 and the Occupational Pension Schemes (Deficiency on Winding Up etc) Regulations 1996 (SI 1996/3128) which broadly provide that in certain circumstances (such as the winding up of a scheme or the insolvency of an employer), employers can become liable to the trustees of the scheme for a proportion of any deficit in that scheme. The amount, if any, of any deficit is calculated on a prescribed basis.

On a business sale, however, the obligations of the employer under the contracts of employment will normally transfer to the purchaser under TUPE 2006. TUPE 2006 excludes from this transfer:

- that part of the contract of employment (or collective agreement) which relates to an occupational pension scheme; and
- any rights, powers, duties or liabilities under or in connection with any such contract or subsisting by virtue of any such agreement and relating to such a scheme or otherwise arising in connection with the person's employment and relating to such a scheme.

The validity of reg 7 under the older TUPE 1981 regulations has in the past been challenged on the grounds that it is not consistent with the EC Directive which TUPE 1981 was adopted to comply with. Although these challenges had some success, it does now appear safe to assume that because of reg 7, the purchaser will be under no legal obligation (in the absence of any requirement in the business sale agreement) to make any pension provision for the transferring employees after completion or assume any liability for pensions rights accrued prior to completion. It is therefore open for the purchaser to decide what pension arrangements post-completion are appropriate to its circumstances and whether it wishes to negotiate any special transfer terms from the seller's scheme for employees who wish to transfer the value of accrued rights to the purchaser's new arrangements.

It should be noted that the exclusion in reg 7 only applied to occupational pension schemes. Therefore, any obligation of the seller to pay contributions to a personal pension plan of an employee (or to a group personal pension plan) will transfer to the purchaser on completion.

TUPE 2006 excludes most pension rights as long as those rights do not transfer (although sometimes courts have held that early retirement benefits will transfer). Under the Pensions Act 2004, buyers are obliged to provide specified pension arrangements for transferring employees who were, prior to the transfer, members of, or eligible to be members of, an occupational pension scheme to which the seller made contributions. There is a requirement that the buyer must make matching contributions of up to at least 6% of salary to the pension arrangements provided for eligible transferring employees. The Pensions Act 2004 gave occupational pension scheme members rights to pension benefits after TUPE transfers for the first time.

The TUPE 2006 regulations were amended by the Collective Redundancies and Transfer of Undertakings (Protection of Employment) (Amendment) Regulations 2014 (SI 2014/16). The BIS guidance (Employment Rights on the Transfer of An Undertaking – January 2014) with the 2014 Regulations includes the following helpful summary:

'Pension Rights following a TUPE transfer

Occupational pension rights earned up to the time of the transfer are protected by social security legislation and pension trust arrangements.

An employee's pension position following a TUPE transfer depends not just upon TUPE, but may depend upon other legislation and policy. This section deals with the main matters affecting the position.

Rights which transfer under the TUPE Regulations

Under the TUPE regulations, an employee's rights related to an occupational pension scheme which relate to benefits for old age, invalidity, or survivors do not transfer. This exclusion from transfer is construed narrowly. As a result, rights relating to redundancy and early retirement benefits that are linked to an occupational pension scheme are likely to transfer under the TUPE Regulations to the new employer. The new employer may need to ask the previous employer for information about such entitlements under an occupational transfer scheme before the transfer to seek to identify what aspects of such a scheme might transfer to it.

Obligations on the new employer to provide pension arrangements

However, the new employer that has taken over responsibility for the transferred employees must provide employees with a new pension scheme in some circumstances.

What the new pension scheme must provide

Under the Pensions Act 2004 and the Transfer of Employment (Pension Protection) Regulations 2005 the new employer must provide a new pension scheme when certain employees are transferred. Employees that are eligible for a pension on transfer are those that are:

(a) already in an occupational pension scheme with their current employer;

(b) not in an occupational pension scheme but could join one with their current employer; or

(c) not in an occupational pension scheme but could join one after they had worked for their current employer for a longer period.

The new employer will need to ask the previous employer for this information before the transfer to identify which employees fall within the criteria a–c above and should be offered the right to join a new pension scheme after the transfer.

The two most common types of work place pension are: a defined contribution scheme (also know as money purchase schemes) or a defined benefit scheme (also known as final salary or salary-related scheme). The new employer may also choose to use a stakeholder pension scheme.

If the employer provides a defined benefit scheme it must comply with one of the following requirements. It must:

– satisfy a test (known as the Reference Scheme Test), which ensures that schemes which are contracted out of the State Second Pension meet specified minimum standards; or

– provide benefits the value of which at least equals 6% of the employee's pensionable pay for each year of employment in addition to any employee contributions; or

– provide employer contributions of up to 6% of the employee's basic pay, provided the employee also contributes.

If the employer provides a money purchase or stakeholder scheme it must provide employer contributions of up to 6% of basic pay, provided the employee also contributes.

Auto enrolment

A new duty on employers automatically to enrol their eligible workers into a workplace pension scheme was introduced in October 2012. Implementation started with the largest employers and will apply to all employers from 1 February 2018. Where the employer uses a money purchase scheme, the incentive for the worker to save is reinforced by a mandatory minimum employer contribution. Minimum contributions are required on a band of earnings, currently 1% employer and 1% worker (including tax relief), rising gradually to 3% employer and 5% worker from October 2018. Automatic enrolment does not affect the TUPE rules. However, where a receiving employer is already subject to the duty to automatically enrol, they will have to automatically enrol all eligible transferring workers.

Public Sector Transfers (Fair Deal for staff pensions: staff transfer from central government)

Arrangements for staff who are members of, or who are eligible to be members of a public service pension scheme who are compulsorily transferred from the public sector are covered in the HMT guidance: 'Fair Deal for staff pensions: staff transfer from central government' (2013). This policy also covers staff who are members of a public service pension scheme, excluding Local Authority Pension Schemes, who are compulsorily transferred to a public service mutual or to other new models of public service delivery.

Staff who are members of a public service pension scheme, excluding Local Authority Pension Schemes, and who are compulsorily transferred out of the public sector will normally retain the right to participate in the relevant public service pension scheme in their new employment for so long as they continue to provide the outsourced services or function. Eligibility will depend on the pension scheme rules. Also in a retender situation where services were originally compulsorily transferred out under Fair Deal (1999 or 2004) if any remaining eligible employees exist, bidders will usually be required to provide them with access to the appropriate public sector scheme. They will continue to (be eligible to) accrue further pension benefits in that scheme in respect of their new employment and their pensionable service will be treated as though it were continuous.

Both employees and employers will be required to pay contributions to the pension scheme. Employees will be required to pay employee contributions in line with those paid by members of the scheme working in the public sector. These will be determined under the scheme regulations and may change following an actuarial valuation of the scheme. Employer contributions will usually be set at the same level as the employer contribution rate paid by all other employers in the scheme.

Further information for employers taking on staff transferred from central Government can be found in HMT guidance note: www.gov.uk/government/publications/fair-deal-guidance.'

(iii)   What are the most common types of pension arrangements?

The most common types of arrangements are occupational final salary (or defined benefit) schemes, occupational money purchase (or defined contribution) schemes and group personal pension plans (which operate on a money purchase basis). Most of the difficult pensions problems arising in the context of acquisitions and disposals relate to final salary rather than money purchase schemes. It is therefore vital that the distinction between the two types of scheme is understood.

Money purchase schemes

Money purchase schemes are schemes under which the rate of employer and employee contributions are fixed and no particular level of benefit is guaranteed. A member's benefits at retirement depend on what the money in his individual account in the scheme will buy by way of retirement benefits in the market at that time. Money purchase schemes have become more popular with employers and particularly with smaller employers in recent years as the open-ended commitment of a final salary scheme has become less acceptable and the need to limit the level of the employers' liability for pension contributions has become more pressing. This trend continued as the major changes introduced by the Pensions Act 1995 continued to impose additional financial and compliance burdens on final salary schemes and their sponsoring employers.

In the context of acquisitions, money purchase schemes give rise to fewer problems than final salary schemes since, owing to their very nature, there are no funding surpluses or deficits to be negotiated and no transfer values to be calculated. Whether the target company has its own scheme or participates in a seller's group scheme, its employees are still entitled to the individual cash funds which they have accumulated in that scheme.

Final salary schemes

In a final salary scheme, the benefits provided are broadly a multiple of a given fraction of the member's final salary and his years of pensionable service. These are becoming more and more of a rarity however, as they have been expensive to run. The employer's contribution to a defined benefit scheme is normally determined on a balance of cost basis (ie the employer meets the balance of the cost of providing the benefits promised over and above members' contributions and investment returns) and will vary depending on the state of funding of the scheme from time to time. The open-ended nature of the employer's liability under a defined benefit scheme is in contrast to the fixed level of employer contribution to a money purchase type arrangement. In spite of the trend towards money purchase schemes for smaller employers, final salary schemes continue to be the more common type of occupational pension scheme for larger employers. It is the need to fund in advance the benefits promised under a final salary scheme and the funding surplus or deficit which may exist under the scheme at any point in time which are the cause of most pensions problems which arise in the context of acquisitions and disposals.

The ability of a final salary scheme to pay pensions calculated on the basis of members' salaries when they retire depends on the scheme having built up and maintained sufficient resources to meet the benefit demand at all relevant times. A scheme's assets and liabilities are in a constant state of flux dependent on the interplay of a number of variable factors such as the rate of salary inflation, the extent of members' real increases in salary due to promotion, etc, the yields on the scheme's investments, the number and age profile of the membership and the number of members leaving service or dying before reaching normal retirement age. It is the role of the scheme's actuary to attempt to balance expected liabilities of the scheme with anticipated resources. Since most employers now contribute to their final salary schemes on a balance of cost basis, one of the actuary's major concerns is to fix the level of the employers' annual contribution needed to maintain that balance. He does this by valuing the scheme periodically on the basis of certain assumptions about the future behaviour of all the relevant variable factors; these assumptions are known as 'actuarial assumptions'.

Actuarial valuation is not an exact science – two actuaries given the same data will rarely produce the same answer, and the experience of a pension scheme over a period will seldom, if ever, match exactly the actuarial assumptions on which contributions during that period have been predicted. As a result, the employer's contributions to the scheme may subsequently be shown to have been either more or less than what was actually required to fund the balance of cost of providing the scheme benefits, and a funding surplus or deficit will be found to have arisen.

In view of concerns about pension scheme solvency that followed in the wake of the Maxwell affair, the Pensions Law Review Committee considered the issue of funding and concluded that some form of statutory funding requirement was desirable. As a result, the Pensions Act 1995 introduced a requirement that the value of the assets of the scheme should not, when calculated on a prescribed basis, be less than the amount of the liabilities of the scheme. This statutory funding requirement is referred to as the Minimum Funding Requirement (MFR). Broadly, the MFR applies to occupational final salary schemes and is a process which involves obtaining valuations, setting contribution schedules and an annual certification that the contributions are adequate for the purpose of securing that the MFR will be met or will continue to be met throughout the schedule period. MFR valuations must be obtained every three years and must be signed within 12 months of the effective date of the valuation. Details of the assets and liabilities need to be taken into account and the way in which the amount and value are to be determined, calculated and verified is set out in regulations and a professional guidance note issued by the Institute of Actuaries and the Faculty of Actuaries.

Since many schemes conducted a valuation immediately before the Pensions Act 1995 came into force (April 1997), the first MFR valuation for many schemes was conducted in the year 2000. The MFR has been subject to considerable criticism since ostensibly healthy pension schemes have had to accept substantial contribution rate rises in order for the actuary to be able to certify that the contribution rates set out in the schedule of contributions are adequate for the purpose of securing the MFR will be met, or will continue to be met throughout the scheduled period or, alternatively, if the scheme has an MFR deficit, would be met by the end of certain prescribed periods. Although the MFR is currently subject to review and may be replaced by a long-term funding standard specific to each scheme and a regime by transparency and disclosure, until it is replaced it is likely that the emergence of MFR deficits will continue to be one of the main pensions issues arising in the context of acquisitions and disposals.

Part 3 of the Pensions Act 2004 replaced the MFR for defined benefit occupational schemes with scheme-specific funding requirements allowing schemes greater flexibility in developing funding strategies appropriate to their circumstances.

In sharp contrast to the current issues surrounding meeting the MFR, the economic and employment conditions of the early 1980s led to the emergence of substantial scheme surpluses and it was this that raised the profile of pensions in the field of company acquisitions. Sellers were reluctant to hand over any part of a scheme surplus to a purchaser, and purchasers were intent on securing for themselves a share of any surplus available in a seller's scheme. Although scheme surpluses are less common than they were in the 1980s, it is worth noting that the problems of ownership of surplus and rights in relation to that surplus in takeover situations have more than any other factor fuelled the growth of pensions litigation. Consideration of the complex issues involved in ownership of surplus is beyond the scope of this chapter, though two of the most important cases on the subject, *Re Imperial Foods Ltd's Pension Scheme* [1986] 2 All ER 802, [1986] 1 WLR 717 and *Re Courage Group's Pension Schemes* [1987] 1 All ER 528, [1987] 1 WLR 495, are referred to in Part III (see Chapter 12, section 12.2.13).

Given the complexities of valuing a final salary scheme's assets and liabilities, where the transaction involves the transfer or assumption of pension liabilities under such a scheme, actuaries should be instructed to advise on the funding and financial implications for the parties and their pension schemes of the assumption or transfer of the pension rights involved in the transaction. For example, the consequences of failing to establish the present state of funding of a final salary scheme may be serious for the seller or the purchaser since the existence of a surplus or deficit may require re-assessment of the purchase price. Where practicable, therefore, actuarial advice should be sought at an early stage in the negotiations so that any funding or other actuarial issues relating to pensions can be taken into account before the basic commercial terms of the deal are struck.

Small Self Administered Scheme/Funded Unapproved Retirement Benefit Scheme

An occupational pension scheme may take the particular form of a Small Self Administered Scheme (SSAS) or a Funded Unapproved Retirement Benefit Scheme (FURBS). Such schemes are usually established on a money purchase basis but occasionally on a final salary basis. They are subject to special HM Revenue and Customs (HMRC) rules of approval and raise additional issues for those undertaking due diligence for a purchaser.

Group personal pension plan

A group personal pension plan (GPP) is not an occupational pension scheme, but is a series of individual personal pension policies arranged by the employer on a group basis. The only employer responsibilities are to pay any contributions which it has agreed to pay under the employees' contracts of employment and possibly to meet any additional administrative expenses. Employers are required to pay to the GPP provider contributions deducted from employee's salaries within 19 days of the end of the month within which those contributions were deducted from the employees' salary.

Ex-gratia pensions

Pensions may also be provided for particular employees on a purely ex-gratia basis.

Auto-Enrolment and Stakeholder Pensions

Gradually to 2017 all employers will be obliged to auto-enrol employees in a pension scheme in a process known as auto-enrolment. The Pensions Regulator summarises who is caught as follows:

'Auto-enrolment – which staff are included?

You must automatically enrol all staff who are:

- aged 22 to state pension age
- working in the UK
- earning over £10,000 a year.

Some staff who don't meet the criteria above are able to opt in to the pension scheme you're using for automatic enrolment. You must put them in if they ask.

You'll have to pay a minimum employer contribution for all staff you put into this scheme.

Certain other staff can ask to join a pension scheme. You must put these staff in a scheme, but the rules are different and there's no requirement for you to pay an employer contribution.

It's the age and earnings of a member of staff that determines what "type" of worker they are and therefore what duties you'll have for them.'

Companies have a 'staging date' based on their size as to when they are forced to come within the scheme. Employees may opt out. Contributions start at 1% employer and 1% employee and will rise to 3% employer and 5% employee (total 8%). Always check a business being bought has complied with pensions obligations and ask about their preparations for auto-enrolment as the rules are complex.

This replaces the previous 'stakeholder' pensions where companies with more five or more employees and no pension fund open to those with one year's service had to offer employees a Stakeholder Pension although the employer was not obliged to contribute to it.

In relation to state pensions the contributory state pension continues. There has been a two tier contributory state pension based on national insurance contributions – SERPS and then SP2. In the Pensions Act 2014 provision is made to merge the two state pensions into one to simplify matters. The Government stated (in its announcement of the then Pensions Bill at https://www.gov.uk/government/collections/pensions-bill):

'The single-tier pension will replace the current basic State Pension and additional State Pension with a flat-rate pension that is set above the basic level of means-tested support for people who reach State Pension age on or after 6 April 2016.'

This applies to those with 35 years of national insurance contributions which may include 10 years caring for young children at home and is likely to be about £150 per person per week.

Role of Pensions Regulator

The Pensions Regulator was created by the Pensions Act 2004 and replaced the previous body known as OPRA. The regulator is the regulator of work-based pension schemes in the UK, with objectives to protect members' benefits, promote good administration and reduce the risk of calls on the Pension Protection Fund. It has the ability to:

- collect information about pension schemes, through scheme returns, under the scheme funding regime and as well as statutory (including whistleblowing) reports;
- issue notices requiring actions to tackle non-compliance, prohibit trustees who are judged not fit and proper to carry out their duties or appoint independent trustees;
- direct pension schemes as to how to calculate their liabilities and the contributions required;
- issue a contribution notice where there is a deliberate attempt to avoid liabilities, or a financial support direction where the employer is a service company or insufficiently resourced.

Clearance

'Clearance' is the term used to describe the voluntary process of obtaining a clearance statement from the Pensions Regulator. A clearance statement gives assurance that, based on the information provided, the regulator will not use its anti-avoidance powers to issue, to the applicants for clearance, either contribution notices or financial support directions in relation to a defined benefit occupational pension scheme and a particular event. Events include transactions, agreements, decisions, other acts and failures to act.

Contribution notices from Pensions regulator

A contribution notice requires payment of a specified sum to be paid into a defined benefit scheme. A financial support direction requires financial support to be put in place for the scheme. These powers have been in place since April 2005.

The Pensions Regulator Determinations Panel

This panel is the decision making body of the Pensions Regulator. Where the regulator wishes to exercise its powers it is required to provide a submission to the panel. A decision is made by the panel as to whether the use of the power is appropriate and a determination notice is used setting out the reasons for the decision. The regulator website provides more information on the panel and the determinations process.

(iv)   What to look out for when doing pensions due diligence

The depth to which the purchaser will need to investigate a seller's or the target's occupational pension scheme will depend on whether the purchaser intends to acquire that scheme as part of the deal or wants to negotiate the payment of a bulk transfer payment from the seller's scheme to his own new or existing arrangements.

If the purchaser is acquiring the seller's or the target's occupational scheme, the purchaser will need to:

- check whether the scheme is established under interim or definitive documentation. If a scheme is established only under interim documentation, it will still be operating under interim approval from HMRC and definitive documentation will have to be executed in due course;
- check it is sufficiently funded and in some cases obtain prior clearance from the Pensions Regulator;
- check that it has received copies of all subsequent deeds of amendment, amending resolutions, announcements to members and booklets together with copies of the latest scheme accounts and actuarial valuations or reports;
- ascertain whether the scheme is an exempt approved scheme approved by HMRC or, if not, whether an application for approval is pending. This is important to ensure that the scheme is obtaining the full benefit of the tax advantages available to approved pension schemes. Obtain a copy of the letter of approval or application for approval;
- establish whether the scheme was contracted in or out of SERPS (which until 2002 was a second state pension now replaced by the State Second Pension (SP2) which itself is being replaced by one single tier state pension as set out in the Pensions Act 2014);
- establish whether the scheme is a final salary scheme or a money purchase scheme;
- establish the benefits provided to members/categories of members;
- establish the current level of employer and employee contributions and the recommended rates if different, and confirm that all contributions due have been paid;
- establish whether lump sum benefits payable on death are insured and, if so, on what terms and at what cost. The purchaser should establish whether these costs are in addition to the disclosed employer's contribution rate or included within that rate;
- confirm that all expenses of the scheme incurred prior to completion have been or will be paid prior to completion;
- check that men and women are treated equally both in respect of the benefits provided and in relation to access to the scheme or arrangement.

The existence of unequalised benefits or benefits that have not been properly equalised could result in claims being made against the scheme. If the scheme is a final salary scheme that contains guaranteed minimum pensions (GMPs), it should be borne in mind that these are unlikely to have been equalised due to the complexity of the calculations required to do so. Notwithstanding this, it is our view that GMP equalisation is something that is likely to have to be done at some point in the future. In reality, however, the cost of equalising GMPs is unlikely to be substantial for most schemes and is likely to be outweighed in any event by the administration costs of making the changes. NAPF (now PLSA) said in its statement on GMP Equalisation at http://www.plsa.co.uk/Policy-and-Research/Defined-Benefit/GMPs:

'GMPs are inherently unequal, but the way that they are paid is set in law. Therefore, equalising GMPs is an impossible task. Depending on when a member leaves service and when he or she begins to draw benefits, he or she may be better or worse off than the opposite sex. Who is better off will vary from year to year. The DWP has suggested that schemes measure the benefits in payment each year and pay each member the better of the benefits due the member as a man or as a woman. This would be cumbersome and expensive and result in a windfall for members. NAPF is working with the Government to come up with legislation that will make it easier to convert GMPs to scheme benefits, which can then be equalised more easily.';

- ensure the scheme provides access to part-timers. This is particularly important if the target company has employed a considerable number of part-timers in the past, the majority of whom are of one particular sex, since a member may argue that exclusion of part-timers amounts to indirect sex discrimination. Successful claims could, if brought within the relevant time periods, lead to claims for retrospective membership of the pension scheme as far back as April 1976. For further details on the part-timer issue, see Chapter 12;
- check whether any augmentations/increases in benefits have been granted which have not been specifically funded;
- check that no discrepancy exists between the scheme rules and any scheme booklet or announcement to members which could result in the scheme booklet being relied on by members as providing more generous (and therefore more expensive) benefits;
- ascertain whether any litigation or Pensions Ombudsman claims relating to the scheme have been instigated or are being considered which may result in the liabilities of the scheme increasing;
- check that the scheme has not accepted any transfer values from schemes whose benefits were not equalised as between men and women since the liability to equalise will have passed to the receiving scheme. It is advisable to seek confirmation that transfers made into the scheme since 16 May 1990 have been from schemes that were at the relevant time properly equalised;
- check if there was a Stakeholder Pension where there ought to have been one before the rules were changed and that their replacement – the auto

enrolment pensions – are in force where the employers staging date has yet been reached (some are not until 2017);

- check that there are no outstanding transfer values due to be paid to or by the scheme.

Occupational pension schemes are subject to and must comply with the requirements of pensions legislation, although there are specific exemptions from some requirements for particular types of schemes (eg SSASs). It is therefore important to ensure that any occupational scheme is Pensions Act compliant. The main items to consider are:

- Have member nominated trustees/directors been appointed? If not, is a valid employer opt-out in place? What are the terms of the opt-out? Obtain copies of the relevant notices.
- Has a statement of investment principles been adopted? If so, obtain a copy.
- Is a schedule of contributions (final salary scheme) or a payment schedule (money purchase scheme) in place? If so, obtain a copy.
- Have professional advisers (ie auditors, actuary and fund managers) been appointed in accordance with s 47 of the Pensions Act 1995? If so, obtain copies of letters of appointment.
- Have audited accounts been produced within seven months of the end of each scheme year?
- Have payments to trustees been made by the target in accordance with the prescribed time limits? Perhaps most importantly, have deductions made from members' pay been paid to the trustees of the scheme within 19 days of the end of the month in which the deductions were made?
- Have the relevant aspects of the disclosure regulations been complied with, ie providing members with basic scheme information?
- Has an internal disputes resolution procedure been established? If so, obtain a copy.
- Have breaches of the Pensions Act 1995 (as amended by Pensions Act 2004) been reported to the Pensions Regulator (which replaced the OPRA). Ask for details of any reports that have been made to the Regulator or OPRA and any correspondence with the Regulator/OPRA and any adviser.
- Have all amendments to the scheme since 5 April 1997 been made in accordance with s 67 of the Pensions Act 1995?
- Establish how the assets of the scheme are invested. Obtain copies of any relevant investment management and custody agreements. Confirm that any self-investment does not exceed permitted levels.
- Establish the identities of the trustees and administrator and check that they have been properly appointed.
- Establish whether the power to amend the scheme is exercisable by the employer or the trustees and whether the consents of any other party is required.

Additional matters to look out for in relation to final salary schemes

Where the seller's scheme is a final salary scheme the purchaser will also need:

- to check whether the scheme is funded or unfunded. If the scheme is unfunded, this means that liabilities have been accruing without any assets being put aside to meet those liabilities in due course. This could have serious implications for a purchaser who takes on the obligation to meet those liabilities;
- if the scheme is funded, to establish the latest funding position and whether the current funding is adequate to meet the liabilities on an ongoing and MFR basis. Obtain the most recent funding information available on the scheme (such as the last actuarial valuation or report). This is particularly important if the scheme operates on a balance of cost basis. If the scheme's liabilities exceeded the value of its assets on an MFR basis, this could result in the purchaser having to make up the deficiency;
- to consider getting an actuary to check that the assumptions on which the most recent valuation was based are realistic and that the funding position is not materially worse (or better) than is represented in that valuation; and
- if a transfer value from the seller's scheme is contemplated, to check that there is an appropriate bulk transfer out clause in the relevant scheme documents and whether any basis of calculation is specified. Given the complexities of valuing a pension fund's assets and liabilities where the transaction involves the transfer or assumption of pension liabilities, actuaries should be instructed to advise on the funding and financial implications for the parties and their pension schemes of the transfer of pension rights involved in the transaction.

Additional matters to look out for in relation to money purchase schemes

When the seller's scheme is a money purchase scheme, the purchaser will also need:

- to ensure the contributions payable by employees and employers have been made and have been made on time and that all expenses of the scheme incurred prior to completion will be paid before completion; and
- to ascertain whether there is any guarantee or targeting of the level of benefits to be provided by the member's account. If there is, establish the likelihood of this guarantee requiring the target company to inject additional sums into the scheme in the future.

Additional matters to look out for in relation to group personal pension arrangements/personal pension plan arrangements

It is important to establish that any employers' contributions due and payable have been paid and are up to date. In addition, from 1 April 2001, the purchaser should check whether contributions deducted from employees' pay have been paid over to the relevant provider within 19 days of the end of the month within which they were deducted from those employees' pay.

When the purchaser is not acquiring an existing scheme but wishes to negotiate the payment of a bulk transfer and special terms payment from a seller's group scheme, the purchaser will still need to investigate most of the matters listed in section 10.2.5 (D)(iv), but paying special attention to the nature of the seller's scheme and confirming its tax and contracted out status, its compliance with equalisation and part timer requirements and its ability to pay a bulk transfer payment.

Where the transaction is a share purchase, the purchaser will also need to check the existence of any residual liability of the target company under the seller's scheme or any previous schemes of the target.

(v)   Stakeholder Pensions (being phased out)

Stakeholder pensions have been replaced with auto-enrolment pensions (see above) but it should be remembered that existing employees may be in stakeholder schemes so they remain relevant.

How does stakeholder impact upon the buying and selling of private companies and businesses?

The section below has been retained despite new auto-enrolment pensions as some companies still have stakeholder schemes and some of the issues listed may also be relevant in relation to other kinds of pensions.

When doing due diligence on the target, it is important for the purchaser to consider whether the target is exempt from stakeholder requirements and, if not, whether the stakeholder requirements are being complied with. This is more of an issue on a share acquisition where the purchaser will effectively be taking over the target's responsibilities and liabilities. However, even in relation to business purchases, it is relevant for the purchaser to know whether the employees of the business have access to Stakeholder Pensions, as the purchaser may wish to replicate such an arrangement after completion.

The first question for a purchaser is whether the target employs 'relevant employees' to whom the stakeholder requirements apply. 'Relevant employees' in this context means all employees save for:

- employees whose employment qualifies them for membership of an occupational pension scheme of the employer even if there is a waiting period of up to 12 months;
- employees who refused to join the employer's occupational scheme when first eligible to do so;
- employees whose earnings were below the lower earnings limit in any week within the last three months;
- employees who would be eligible to join their employer's occupational pension scheme if they were over 18 or more than five years below the scheme's normal pension age;
- employees who have been employed for less than three months; and
- employees who are ineligible by virtue of any requirements of the HMRC to make contributions to a Stakeholder Pension scheme.

If an employer employs any 'relevant employees' then unless the employer falls within one of the specified exemptions it will have to comply with stakeholder access requirements. These exemptions include:

- where the employer offers an occupational pension scheme which allows employees to join within 12 months of commencing employment;
- where the employer has an obligation in respect of every employee over the age of 18 to contribute at least 3% of pay (which excludes bonuses, commission, overtime) to a personal pension scheme which does not impose any penalty if the employee transfers money out of the scheme or ceases to contribute to the scheme. The employer's contributions may be subject to a condition that the employee makes contributions less than or equal to those of the employer or, if the condition is imposed after 8 October 2001, the employee makes contributions at a rate not exceeding 3% of pay; and
- where an employer employs fewer than five people. Employers should also be aware that as soon as its workforce exceeds four, it will have three months in which to comply with the employer access requirement.

In the light of the above, when carrying out due diligence, the purchaser should consider the following issues that arise out of the Stakeholder Pensions legislation:

- whether the target company employs 'relevant employees'; if the target company does employ 'relevant employees', whether any of the exemptions to the stakeholder access requirements apply to the target company. If not, the purchaser should ascertain what steps have been taken by the target to comply with the stakeholder access requirements. If no such steps have been taken, the purchaser may wish to consider seeking an indemnity from the seller in respect of any fines that may be imposed in relation to such non-compliance;
- if the existing arrangements operated by the target company could, with minor adjustments (such as to waiting periods), be brought within one of the exemptions (thereby avoiding the need to comply with the stakeholder access requirements), the purchaser may wish to consider making such an alteration in due course.

Regular updating on pensions law is contained in the monthly Pensions Today journal.

10.2.6   Bribery Act 2010

Companies are advised to have a bribery policy under the Bribery Act 2010. In undertaking due diligence the buyer should check if such a policy has been put in place. Companies who have such a policy will find it easier to prove they have taken 'adequate measures' to prevent bribery which can excuse the company from the corporate bribery offence under English law.

The due diligence invesetigations shall also include a check that there are no bribery cases or allegations or investigations either going on at the time of the acquisitions or in the past in relation to the company.

10.2.7   Gender pay gap reporting

From 6 April 2017 there has been an obligation for larger companies (those with more than 250 employees and more) to report each year on their gender pay gap. The buyer's solicitor as part of legal due diligence should check the target company has been making the necessary reports and indeed whether it has otherwise complied with this and other kinds of discrimination legislation.

In late 2017 several companies were found to have published incorrect statements having shown no gender pay gap when there was one, or supposedly inadvertently having left out senior (and overwhelmingly male) staff in the comparison and just compared low paid staff where there was no gender pay gap. This led to adverse publicity.

ACAS has a guide to gender pay gap reporting – see http://www.acas.org.uk/ index.aspx?articleid=5768 which also gives access to an ACAS model form for this purpose.

10.2.8   Modern Slavery Act 2015

For larger companies there is an obligation to check the company, and further up its supply chain, that its suppliers are not involved in any slavery in the UK or abroad and statements must be published annually. Reference should be made to the Modern Slavery Act 2015 and Modern Slavery Act 2015 (Transparency in Supply Chains) Regulations 2015. The Act has applied since October 2015 and applies to companies with a group turnover of £36m which either trade in the UK or are incorporated in the UK.

The UK has an Anti-Slavery Commissioner whose website is at https://www. gov.uk/government/organisations/independent-anti-slavery-commissioner.

Companies with slave labour in clothing factories abroad or workers in the UK working as contractors in a bonded unpaid fashion are all possibilities and it is therefore important to check in relation to acquisitions. In 2017 prosecutions for modern slavery quadrupled in the UK. Even if there is no slavery failure to post the statutory statement can lead to adverse publicity – see https://www.cips. org/supply-management/news/2017/february/-major-uk-brands-miss-modern-slavery-act-statement-deadline/.

10.2.9   Arrangements infringing competition law

As well as investigating whether the proposed transaction requires notification to UK or EC merger control regulators, the purchaser will need to investigate whether the target is party to arrangements that infringe UK or EC competition law regulations otherwise it may find itself liable to fines of up to 10% of turnover and damages actions from the victims of such practices. This may be so even if all infringements took place prior to the acquisition and have been terminated.

Provisions in contracts that infringe competition rules will also be void and unenforceable and third parties who suffer loss as a result of the infringement may be in a position to bring proceedings for an injunction or damages. In order to protect itself against such risk, the purchaser should review the main agreements and arrangements to which the target is party to ensure that they do not infringe competition rules.

As both UK and EC competition rules apply to informal arrangements as well as formal agreements, the purchaser should also investigate any 'understandings' the target may have which may give rise to competition law concerns.

It is likely that after 2019 Brexit that many UK arrangements will still affect trade in the other EU member states so the EU competition rules will continue to apply in the UK.

(A) EC and UK competition regulation of agreements between undertakings

(i) Article 101 of the Treaty on Functioning of the EU ('TFEU') (the Treaty of Rome 1957 'EC Treaty' has been recently amended by the Treaty of Lisbon and has been renamed the TFEU and what is now Article 101 was previously called Article 81 and before that Article 85). and;

(ii) Chapter I of the Competition Act 1998 provide that agreements, decisions or practices that may affect trade between Member States or within the UK respectively and have the object or effect of preventing, restricting or distorting competition in the common market within the UK respectively are prohibited and automatically void unless granted an exemption by the relevant competition authorities.

Restrictions which need to be considered under art 101 of the TFEU and/or Chapter I of the Competition Act 1998 can fall into two categories:

- vertical restrictions, which are restrictions agreed between parties operating at different levels of the market; and
- horizontal restrictions, which are restrictions agreed between parties operating at the same level of trade.

Horizontal restrictions between competitors or potential competitors are usually likely to affect the structure of the market and to be anti-competitive. (There may in some cases, however, be objective justifications for the restrictions which mean that the ultimate benefit to be derived from a course of conduct outweighs the disadvantages and therefore the agreement might be capable of exemption from the art 101 or Chapter I prohibition.) Examples of horizontal restrictions include non-compete clauses, agreements to share customers or territories and agreements as to trading conditions (including prices) on which to deal with customers. In January 2011 updated guidance on Horizontal Agreements under the EU competition rules was issued.

Examples of vertical restrictions include selective or exclusive distribution, tie-in sales or bundling of products or services, minimum purchase obligations and non-volume related discounts. Vertical restrictions which are highly likely to fall foul of art 101 of the TFEU and/or Chapter I of the Competition Act 1998 include agreements which restrict a buyer's ability to determine its resale prices, the restriction of the territory into which or of the customers to whom a buyer may sell contract goods or services (although there are a limited number of exceptions), the restriction of sales to end users by members of a selective distribution system operating at a retail level of trade, the restriction of cross-supplies between distributors within a selective distribution system and the restriction on the sale of spare pans in certain circumstances. In 2010 the EU issued updated guidance on Vertical Agreements (and a new block exemption Regulation 330/2010 on vertical agreements).

There are a number of block exemptions that exempt specific categories of agreement such as vertical (2010), research and development (2010) and technology transfer agreements (Commission Regulation (EU) No 316/2014 in force 1 May 2014 with accompanying Intellectual Property Guidelines) provided that the agreement falls within the provisions of the relevant block exemption Regulation. In other cases individual exemption should be obtained.

If the target is party to an agreement that may infringe the art 101 or Chapter I prohibition, unless there is a relevant block exemption or an individual exemption has been obtained, there is then a risk of an investigation by the relevant competition authority followed by fines if in fact an infringement is found to have occurred. Immunity from fines can be obtained if full details of the agreement are notified to the competition authorities with an application for exemption under a system known as leniency and plenty of arrangements are disclosed to competition authorities where they are uncovered as part of due diligence on an acquisition. In the UK since 2008 the then OFT (now Competition and Markets Authority since 1 April 2014 when the OFT and Competition Commission merged to create the new body following the Enterprise and Regulatory Reform Act 2013) has offered rewards of up to £100,000 to individuals who disclose illegal arrangements under the legislation which leads to successful prosecutions. Since the Enterprise Act 2002 came into force, it has also been a criminal offence in the UK to engage in dishonest horizontal price fixing and bid rigging. Extradition to the US where jail sentences of 10 years are common is also possible if a parallel offence has been committed in the UK (see *Norris v Government of the United States of America* [2008] UKHL 16 – Mr Norris was extradited and in March 2011 lost an appeal against a US jail sentence – however he was only convicted on one count in the US (of conspiracy to obstruct justice, not price fixing) and jailed for 18 months with a $25,000 fine in addition). In 2008, the first individuals were jailed for breach of the UK competition rules in a case concerning a marine hose cartel following a plea bargain in the US and their subsequent return to the UK.

If there are concerns that a target may have indulged in anti-competitive practices, a purchaser may wish to seek an indemnity from the seller in respect of fines that may be levied on the purchaser arising out of the target's activities prior to the notification as liability for breach of the EC competition rules will remain attached to it.

It used to be essential to check that that target had registered under the Restrictive Trade Practices Act 1976 anti-competitive agreements most of which then went on a public register. The Competition Act 1998 abolished this register after a long transitional period. However in looking at historic agreements which are still in force corporate lawyers may need to check if they were registered at the relevant time to check their enforceability.

(B) Article 102 of the TFEU and Chapter II of the Competition Act 1998 – abuse of a dominant position

The purchaser of a company which enjoys a dominant position in the market will have to consider art 102 of the TFEU (formerly art 82 and before that art 86) and Chapter II of the Competition Act 1998. The existence of a dominant position is not of itself contrary to competition laws, but dominant companies need to be careful not to act in 'abusive fashion' and mergers between companies with large market shares may be caught by EU or UK merger law (see above).

A dominant position exists where a company has the ability to act to an appreciable extent independently of its competitors and customers and is nominally inferred if a company's market share exceeds 40%, although this is not a strict threshold. Any company which has such a dominant position in the European Union (or UK as appropriate) or in part of it must not abuse that position. No exemption is available from the prohibition on abuse of a dominant position set out in art 102 or the Chapter II prohibition and art 101 and the Chapter I prohibition may also apply to the same conduct.

If the competition authorities decide that abuse of a dominant position has occurred, a company may be liable to fines of up to 10% of its worldwide group turnover.

The purchaser should therefore verify that the target has not abused its dominant position. Examples of abuse include the imposition of excessive or discriminatory prices, 'bundling' of products or services whereby the customer is obliged to accept supplementary products or services beyond those which it actually ordered, applying excessively high prices to its goods or services, predatory pricing with the aim of eliminating competitors from the market or the application of dissimilar conditions to equivalent transactions. Indiscriminate refusals to deal with the customers of the target may be regarded as abusive. If it seems likely that such behaviour may have occurred, not only will the purchaser need to ensure that a culture change is effected to stop abusive behaviour in future, but it should also consider requiring an indemnity from the vendors to cover potential losses.

10.2.10   Connected party transactions

Transactions between related parties are not always carried out on an arm's length basis because at the time of the transaction it may have suited them to load the benefit or burden of the transaction in favour of one party rather than the other. This is particularly significant as the rules relating to the ability of liquidators and administrators attacking certain transactions are weakened in the case of transactions involving 'connected' parties (see ss 249 and 435 of IA 1986 for definitions). An investigation of transactions between the target and related parties should help the purchaser establish:

- whether the financial position or trading performance of the target has been distorted. For example, if the target was a member of a group of companies it may have suited the ultimate holding company to reduce the target's cost of sales by selling its stock from another group company at cost, thereby distorting the target's gross profit and increasing its attractiveness to potential purchasers;

- the likelihood of the target being ordered to return to the original transferor assets previously transferred to it on the basis that they were acquired at an undervalue. Under IA 1986, s 238 a liquidator or administrator has power to set aside transactions and wide discretion to grant other relief prior to the onset on the transferor's insolvency (see s 240(3) of IA 1986 for the definition). For the purposes of the IA 1986, the transaction is at an under value if it constitutes a gift or if the value of the consideration received by the transferor is significantly less than the consideration provided by the transferee. The important words are 'significantly less'. At the time of the transfer it is presumed (although this can be rebutted) that the transferor was unable to pay its debts within the meaning of s 123 of IA 1986 or became unable to pay its debts as a result of the transaction;

- liquidators or administrators also have the power under s 239 of IA 1986 to seek relief where a creditor, surety or guarantor of the target company has been given a preference. A preference can include anything which has the effect of putting the recipient into a position which, in the event of liquidation, will be better than the position he would have been in if that thing had not been done. It is generally difficult to show a preference, but it is easier in respect of connected parties because a key ingredient that the person giving the preference is influenced by a 'desire' to produce the effect is presumed, although this can be rebutted. In the case of connected parties, the connected provisions apply for a period of two years (six months otherwise) from the onset of insolvency and insolvency of the target company is also presumed.

Because of the undervalue and preference provisions of IA 1986, any transfers or other relevant actions to the target company within two years prior to the date of the proposed acquisition should be investigated.

In the case of a sale and purchase of business assets, if the seller and purchaser are members of the same group of companies it is important to ensure that the assets are transferred at their market value. Following the case of *Aveling Barford v Perion Ltd* [1989] BCLC 626), if the transferor did not have sufficient distributable reserves the undervalue element of any transfer would be treated as an unauthorised return of capital. From the purchasers point of view, if it knew or had reasonable grounds for believing the transfer was at an undervalue, it would be liable to repay the distribution to the seller.

10.2.11   Effect of change of ownership

As well as trading contracts for the supply to the target of goods and services and for the sale by the target of its products or services, the target may have entered into a variety of other agreements from loan documents to collaborative agreements such as joint ventures through to contracts regulating the relationship between the target and agents and distributors of its products. Depending upon their importance, these contracts need to be investigated to ensure that they cannot be terminated unilaterally by the third party on a change of control, to ensure that they are valid and subsisting, and to understand the obligations the target has assumed by entering into these contracts.

In terms of investigating customer and supplier arrangements, given that most businesses may have a large number of such arrangements it is usual to investigate in detail only those contracts which are fundamental to the business being carried on by the target and, if necessary, for the remaining arrangements to be investigated on a random basis.

10.3   FORMS OF DUE DILIGENCE

Due diligence is usually carried out by the purchaser's own personnel and professional advisers engaged for the purpose of the acquisition (lawyers and accountants and, where appropriate, surveyors and environmental specialists). The most common forms of due diligence investigation are as follows.

10.3.1   Accountants' report

The key element of most due diligence exercises is the accountants' report on the financial aspects of the target's business. The purpose of the accountants' report is to provide the purchaser with comfort on the past trading record of the target, the current net asset and taxation position of the business, taxation implications of the acquisition and the achievability of the target's financial projections. The report will usually include an analysis of:

- historic trading results;
- current trading position and comparison to budget;
- trends as regards profitability and margins;
- forecast trading results;
- the assets and liabilities to be acquired and their relative values;
- capital investment;
- the target's accounting systems and financial controls;
- suppliers and customers;
- competitors;
- product development;
- management structure;
- the target's taxation affairs; and
- potential synergies.

It would be unnecessary for the accountants' report to cover the historic financial performance of the target if the purchaser could rely upon the audited accounts of the target, so that if the profits of the target were overstated or its liabilities understated the purchaser could pursue the target's auditors. Unfortunately, for purchasers the tortious liability of auditors to third parties has been restricted by a number of court decisions commencing with *Caparo Industries v Dickman* [1990] 2 AC 605, [1990] 1 All ER 568). In this case the then House of Lords made it clear that a company's auditors do not owe a duty of care to third parties unless the auditor knew at the time that the third party was placing reliance on the audited accounts for a particular purpose, and that the third party would act on those accounts. The exception to the principle that auditors do not owe a duty of care to third parties laid down by the House of Lords was illustrated in the case of *ADT Ltd v BDO Binder Hamlyn* ([1996] BCC 808) when the High Court held that BDO was liable to ADT when an audit partner told ADT that he stood by the accounts (which were found to be negligently audited) of a target company ADT went on to purchase. If statements instead are made by the seller which amount to a fraudulent misrepresentation then liability however may follow. In 2011 in *Erlson Precision Holdings Ltd (formerly GG 132 Ltd) v Hampson Industries plc* ([2011] EWHC 1137 (Comm)) the High Court ordered Hampson (the seller) to take back a business it had sold to Erlson Precision Holdings Ltd (called GG 132 Ltd by the time the case came to trial) as it had not informed the buyer that it had lost a key customer worth 10% of profits. Erlson had paid £2.5m for Hampson.

Notwithstanding the exception to the general principle that auditors do not owe a duty of care to third parties, because most accounts are not audited in the knowledge that a prospective purchaser is in the wings and will be placing reliance on them, it is still commonplace for accountants' reports to review historic accounts. This practice may, however, alter in the future if the government's proposed changes to the laws relating to auditors' liability becomes law. The then Department of Trade and Industry (DTI) has proposed passing legislation to reverse the *Caparo* decision in its March 2000 consultation on company law ('Modern Company Law for a Competitive Economy: Developing the Framework') and in a further consultation paper in November 2000 ('Modern Company Law for a Competitive Economy: Completing the Structure'). CA 2006 includes provisions which allow companies to agree to limit an auditor's liability arising from an audit for the financial year specified in the agreement. The agreement cannot apply to more than one year's audit. The Shareholders must authorise these terms and have rights to cancel this. Shareholders in private companies may also pass a resolution removing the need for that approval. However, any limit on liability must be limited to an amount which is 'fair and reasonable' (s 537) and there are powers in regulations for the Government to set out rules for disclosure of an agreement. Part 16 (Audit) Companies Act 2006, s 534 onwards (liability limitation agreements) came into force on 1 April 2008.

Because of the cost implications, it is unusual for a purchaser to instruct its accountants to prepare a report until the principal terms of the acquisition and the scope and timescale for the investigation have been agreed. Such agreement should also cover issues such as the accountants' access to the target and to its auditors' working papers. It should also deal with the question of confidentiality and set clear deadlines. When agreed, the purchaser should define the areas which it wishes the accountants to investigate to avoid the waste of time and expense involved in the duplication of investigations.

An accountants' report typically takes between three and six weeks to prepare and is traditionally prepared in draft and issued to various parties for comment prior to being finalised. Unless prohibited by the seller, in preparing their report the accountants will establish contact with the management to obtain an overview of the business and more detailed information regarding the specific areas to be covered by their report. The accountants will usually distribute a draft of the report to the management of the target for their comments, and to other professional advisers carrying out investigations (for example, the purchaser's solicitors), prior to release to the prospective purchaser.

In its conclusions, the report will often review the proposed price for the target in the light of the information discovered.

A copy of the accountant's report should be given to the purchaser's solicitors for drafting purposes as it is likely to contain information of relevance which will have an impact on some of the terms of the purchase agreement and the warranties/indemnities required.

Where the purchaser is a listed company and the acquisition is deemed to be a Class I acquisition within the terms of the Listing Rules published by the Financial Conduct Authority, an accountants' report on the target will need to be obtained prior to exchange of contracts or between exchange and completion because the circular to the purchaser's shareholders seeking approval to the transaction must include an accountants' report setting out the required information in accordance with the Listing Rules.

10.3.2   Legal due diligence report

In the past few years it has become increasingly common for prospective purchasers to commission their legal advisers to prepare a legal due diligence report. Although normally of secondary importance to the accountants' report on the basis that if the financial performance doesn't stack up there will be no deal for the lawyers to concern themselves about, legal due diligence reports have become an important aspect of most transactions.

To reduce exposure to unnecessary costs, and if the timescale allows, it is usually advisable to delay commencement of the legal due diligence until at least a draft accountants' report is in circulation and the prospective purchaser is comfortable that that draft doesn't raise fundamental issues which may jeopardise the transaction.

Legal due diligence reports are usually based upon the answers provided to enquiries of the target's management and the results of third party enquiries and usually include an analysis of:

- ownership of the target/target business;
- restrictions/impediments on the power to sell the target/target business;
- the target's properties;
- the employees engaged in the target business and their employment terms;
- any intellectual property rights used in the target business or necessary to carry on the target business;
- key customers/suppliers, the contractual terms entered into with customers/suppliers and disputes with them;
- any litigation the target business may be engaged in and contingent liabilities;
- health and safety issues relating to the carrying on of the target business;
- environmental and other consents necessary to carry on the target business; and
- competition issues.

(A) Enquiries of management

Enquiries are normally raised in writing in the form of a legal due diligence request. Precedent requests for a share purchase and a business transfer are set out in Part V. The due diligence request relating to the purchase of assets is similar to that relating to a purchase of shares except that it focuses more on the individual assets to be acquired and liabilities to be assumed and less on the corporate information regarding the target and its subsidiaries. The precedents should always be tailored to the particular circumstances of the transaction and the type of business being acquired. For example, the importance of employment terms is far more significant in the acquisition of a service business than a manufacturing business.

The value of such enquiries depends almost entirely upon the attitude of the seller in answering them and the relevant terms of the acquisition documentation, or the lack of them. When faced with voluminous enquiries, sellers are often slow to reply and rarely do they provide all the information requested. It is, therefore, important for the purchaser to avoid unnecessary enquiries and duplication and to set a clear and reasonable timetable for the replies to be given. Before drafting the due diligence request, the purchaser's solicitors should enquire of the purchaser the information given to it and whether or not its accountants have been instructed to prepare a report on the target and, if so, the extent of their investigation. Nothing infuriates a seller or his advisers more than duplicate requests for information.

If the purchaser places importance on the replies to the due diligence request, the replies should be the subject of a specific warranty in the sale and purchase agreement.

(B) Searches and enquiries of public registers

A common source of third party enquiries are the various public registers.

Due diligence

(i)   Companies Register

A search of the target's register at Companies House will reveal details of the company's ownership, management, historic financial position, charges and other matters relevant to the purchaser's review (for example, the memorandum and articles of association). The accuracy of a company search is not guaranteed because it is compiled by the target itself and therefore the results should be compared with the outcome of the purchaser's review of the target's statutory books (see section 10.3.2 (C)).

(ii)   Land Registry

A search at HM Land Registry against the title number to the land owned or leased by the target will reveal the registered proprietor of the land and any charges or encumbrances registered against it. Even if the title number is not known a search of the Index map at the Land Registry with a plan of the target's property will reveal whether or not the property is registered and, if so, the title number or numbers.

(iii)   Central land charges

Where title is unregistered, a central land charges search will reveal any encumbrances registered against the estate owners specified in the search in respect of its period of ownership. The purchaser can immediately search against the target, but to do so the purchaser will need to have received full details of the unregistered title to enable it to search against predecessors in title.

(iv)   Local land charges

A local land charges search of the local authority in which the property is located will reveal details of development plans, road schemes, planning decisions, resolutions made under a compulsory purchase order, breaches of planning decisions and building regulations and other matters under the control or supervision of a local authority.

(v)   Environmental registers

The following comprises a list of the main environmental registers held by the EA, water companies or Local Authorities which may currently be consulted by the public and which may provide useful information not only in relation to the terms of any relevant authorisation, licence or consent but also in respect of any past prosecutions:

- registers of authorisations relating to processes prescribed for the purposes of integrated pollution control and local authority air pollution control under those parts of Part I in force of the Environmental Protection Act 1990 and the Pollution Prevention and Control Act 1999;

- registers relating to waste under those parts of Part II in force of the Environmental Protection Act 1990;
- trade effluent register under Part VII of the Water Industry Act 1991; and
- pollution control registers under Part VIII of the Water Resources Act 1991;
- registers of remediation notices, declarations and statements under Part IIA of the Environmental Protection Act 1990;
- registers of abstraction licences under Part II of the Water Resources Act 1991; and
- registers under the Producer Responsibility Obligations (Packaging Waste) Regulations 2007 (SI 2007/871), as amended.

Defra has created a central register showing where statutory and other environmental registers can be found, as required in EU Directive 2003/4/EC, Art 3(5)(c) – see also reg 4 of the EIRs (Environmental Information Regulations 2004).

The Environment Agency hosts the register at https://www.gov.uk/access-the-public-register-for-environmental-information.

(vi)   Intellectual Property Office and Domain Names

A search of the intellectual property office in the UK (https://www.gov.uk/government/organisations/intellectual-property-office) of registered UK patents, registered designs and registered trade marks and indeed international registered intellectual property rights can be undertaken as can searches of relevant internet domain name registrations.

Statutory books

By law a company must keep registers of directors and secretaries (CA 2006, s 162) , members (CA 2006, s 113), directors' interests and charges. These registers, together with registers of share allotments and transfers and a minute book, are commonly referred to as a company's statutory books.

All inspection of the targets' statutory books should reveal the actual position in these areas rather than the 'filed' position, which is often misleading due 'to the failure by the target to register changes. In the case of members and establishing who has the right to sell the target's shares, this review is extremely important because a person does not become a shareholder until his name is registered in the register of members.

It is very common for small companies not to have completed the statutory books. Many buyers require the seller to have the books made up from scratch before the sale. A full company search should be undertaken which should produce most of the information except minutes.

(C)   Credit agency searches

Searches may be obtained from reputable credit agency companies such as Equifax and Experian to obtain information about a company's creditworthiness. This information is nearly always more up to date than that obtainable from a search at the Companies Registry.

Many different searches are available from credit agencies. A typical full search against a company will reveal the following information concerning the company, and may also provide a comparison of this information to the industry average:

- profit margin;
- current ratio;
- liquidity ratio;
- debt collection period;
- creditor payment period;
- return on shareholders' funds; and
- suggested credit limit.

10.3.3   Physical inspection

Far too many frequently carried out transactions proceed without any form of physical inspection of the business assets by either the purchaser or, more importantly, independent experts. For confidentiality reasons the seller may be reluctant to allow an inspection. However, if it takes place outside of normal working hours the seller may have no objection.

The two most common forms of physical inspection are:

- property survey;
- environmental survey.

(A)   Property survey

Physical inspection of the business premises by a professional surveyor is the most recognised and common form of inspection. It should be normal practice where the purchaser is proposing to accept an assignment of a lease under which it will be responsible for repair of the property. In such cases, the survey can provide an assessment of the cost of repairing the dilapidations.

(B)   Environmental survey

As purchasers become increasingly more aware of the potential environmental liabilities in the properties they acquire, and given the natural reluctance of sellers to give indemnities, environmental surveys are becoming commonplace when there is a risk of the purchaser inheriting contaminated land. Not only will an environmental land survey provide the purchaser with an assessment of whether the site on which the business property is located is or is likely to be contaminated, it will also provide an assessment of the likely clean-up costs. Environmental surveys will also give information on compliance with environmental and health and safety legislation.

10.3.4　Seller's disclosure letter and documents

At a much later stage in the acquisition process the purchaser is afforded another opportunity to investigate the target when the seller complies and circulates disclosures to the warranties contained in the acquisition agreement in the form of a disclosure letter. The object of the disclosure by the seller is to avoid liability under the warranties by disclosing matters which may or do contradict the warranties. If accepted by the purchaser, the seller will usually be excluded from liability for a breach of the warranties in respect of the matters disclosed. Accordingly, sellers will often seek to disclose all matters which may be relevant to the warranties, regardless of the actual terms of the warranties, and in the most general of terms.

In the first instance, the information disclosed may help the purchaser in its analysis of the target but should be checked against information obtained independently of the target and/or the seller to verify its accuracy.

Whether or not the disclosures should be accepted and, if so in what form, is discussed in Part III (see Chapter 12, section 12.2.10 (G)).

Part III

The Acquisition Agreement

Chapter 11

General principles

11.1 INTRODUCTION

11.2 PLAIN ENGLISH

11.1 INTRODUCTION

With the exception of a small number of private companies whose shares have been listed within the last 10 years or are otherwise subject to the City Code on Takeovers and Mergers, the sale and purchase of a private company or the business of a private company resident in the UK, the Channel Islands or the Isle of Man is subject to the normal principles of English law.

Given that the basic law of the sale of goods 'caveat emptor' applies and, with the exception of FSA 2012, s 89 (previously FSMA 2000, s 397), which offers a degree of protection in the case of the purchase of shares by imposing criminal liability on concealing information and making misleading statements, because of the absence of any statutory protection a purchaser will usually require the seller to enter into a legally binding agreement for three main reasons; namely to:

- protect itself against unknown or understated liabilities;
- ensure that if any of the representations made to it during the negotiation process and upon which it had placed reliance in evaluating the target and agreeing the purchase price turn out to be untrue it has a remedy against the seller; and
- protect it from the seller setting up business in competition with the target.

The overwhelming need of the purchaser to document the transaction is almost universally accepted and, for the reasons set out above, the acquisition agreement is traditionally prepared by the purchaser's solicitors. In recent times, however, with the increase in use of the tender process to sell substantial businesses it is becoming increasingly common for the seller's solicitors to prepare the acquisition agreement, which is distributed to prospective purchasers either with the information memorandum or prior to receipt of final bids.

The form of acquisition agreements (share purchase agreements and business transfer agreements) has also become standardised over the years and a typical acquisition agreement will be between 40 and 100 pages and will contain provisions setting out what is to be sold, details of the purchase price and the terms of payment, conditions to be fulfilled, completion requirements, warranties, indemnities and restrictive covenants to be given by the seller, pension arrangements (if applicable) and the terms of any ongoing relationships between the parties.

A precedent share purchase agreement and a precedent business transfer agreement are set out in Part V. Both precedents have been drafted from a purchaser's perspective although, where appropriate, additions, deletions or amendments to reflect the seller's position have been added.

The following sections contain a commentary on the precedent acquisition agreements. Many comments are applicable to both documents and are initially discussed in Chapter 12 in relation to share sales and purchases. Variations or additions to that commentary to reflect business transfers are discussed in Chapter 13.

11.2   PLAIN ENGLISH

Although the terms of the Consumer Rights Act 2015 do not apply to the sale and purchase of companies and business because of the absence of a 'consumer', the mischief which the regulations are intended to eradicate, the use of legalese, jargon and out-of-date language, is all too often found in the drafting of acquisition agreements. However there is an argument that an individual seller/shareholder/director is not a business as s 2(3) of the CRA 2015 states: '"consumer" means an individual acting for purposes that are wholly or mainly outside that individual's trade, business, craft or profession.'

The Consumer Rights Act 2015 in relevant part require that terms be in plain, intelligible language. The challenge for the draftsperson is to prepare an agreement in plain, intelligible language which can be understood by practitioners and their clients alike.

Before commencing drafting, it is important for the draftsperson to remind himself that the agreement is being prepared for the benefit of the seller and the purchaser, not for their lawyers. At the end of each provision, he should ask himself whether the seller and the purchaser will understand that provision and, if not, how it can be made clearer.

Drafting may be improved by the use of familiar rather than outdated or complex words, and short sentences. Complicated provisions should be split into several short sentences or tabulated. Sentences comprising more than 20 or so words should be reconsidered and split into a number of sentences. Most importantly of all, surplus words should be left out.

Any ambiguity is construed against the draftsperson which is reason enough to be clear.

Chapter 12

Share purchase

12.1 SHARE PURCHASE AGREEMENT OR OFFER DOCUMENT?

12.1.1 Reasons to make an offer

Although the vast majority of private company purchases are made by private treaty between the seller and purchaser through a share purchase agreement, in each of certain limited circumstances it may be necessary or desirable to effect the acquisition by way of an offer from the purchaser to each of the target's shareholders. These circumstances include:

(A) Large number of shareholders/employee shareholders

If there is a large number of unconnected sellers, it may become impractical to negotiate the sale with so many parties, let alone obtain their signatures to the agreed form share purchase agreement. Given the trend in recent years to incentivise key employees through share ownership, and depending upon whether employees own shares outright or have options to subscribe, it may be unwise to unsettle a large employee shareholder base by including them in the sale process too early, and the offer route, although less certain for the purchaser, provides a mechanism to avoid the unsettling effect until the purchaser is committed to proceed.

(B) Dissenting minority shareholders – squeeze out (CA 2006, s 979)

To avoid the potential disruption to the purchaser's post-acquisition plans for the target company and the sharing of future profits, most purchasers wish to acquire 100% of a target company. Accordingly, dissenting minority shareholders have the potential to disrupt a sale unless they can be forced to sell their shares. In the absence of effective 'drag along' rights in the target company's articles (a right of the majority to compel the minority to sell their shares to a purchaser) and provided the acquisition is switched as an 'offer', the majority sellers and the purchaser may wish to take advantage of the procedures set out in CA 2006, s 979 ff which enable a purchaser to acquire compulsorily the shares of a dissenting minority holding of less than 10% of the shares in the target. These procedures are also relevant to mop up shareholders who simply fail to respond or are absent or missing at the time of the negotiations.

In general terms, these provisions allow the purchaser to acquire compulsorily the minorities' shares for the offer price if 90% of the shares to which the offer relates are the subject of acceptances of the offer. The provisions in CA 1985 which these provisions replaced are substantially similar. In calculating whether holders representing 90% of the shares to which the offer relates have accepted, any shares which the purchaser owned at the time of making of the offer are disregarded. For example, if the purchaser held 20% of the shares at the time of making the offer it would need to obtain acceptances for a further 72% (ie 90% of the outstanding balance) before it could take advantage of these provisions.

If a purchaser wishes to take advantage of these provisions, it must take the following steps:

- within two months of reaching the 90% acceptances threshold, the purchaser must serve a statutory notice on any shareholders who have not accepted the offer; and
- within six weeks after the date of serving the notice on the shareholders, the purchaser must send a copy of the statutory notice to the target company, together with a statutory declaration signed by a director of the purchaser stating that the conditions for serving the notice have been fulfilled.

Note also the provisions of s 983 (CA 2006) which are the converse of squeeze out and are known as 'sell out'. The Explanatory Notes to the CA 2006 state:

'1256. It is clarified [by s 983] that, in addition to shares acquired by the offeror, shares subject to both conditional and unconditional contracts of acquisition are included in calculating whether the sell-out threshold has been reached. As a result of this change, there might be circumstances where the 90% threshold required for sell-out to be exercised was reached only because of shares which the offeror had conditionally contracted to acquire. However, if the conditions of such contracts were not fulfilled, the offeror could in fact find that he was being required to buy a minority shareholder's shares even though the offeror had not actually acquired 90% of the shares. So section 983 also provides that, if that is the case at the time when the minority shareholder exercises his right of sell-out, the offeror does not have to purchase the shares unless he has acquired or unconditionally contracted to acquire 90% or more of the shares by the time the period referred to in section 984(2) (the period within which shareholders can exercise sell-out rights) ends. (A corresponding change was made in section 979(6) and (7) to prevent minority shareholders in this situation who have to wait to see if they can exercise sell-out from being squeezed out in the meantime.)'

(C)   The City Code on Takeovers and Mergers

As mentioned in Part II, the City Code on Takeovers and Mergers (copies at http://www.thetakeoverpanel.org.uk/the-code/download-code) applies to acquisitions of all UK public companies (not just listed companies) and private companies if their equity has been listed on the Official List of the UK Listing Authority, if dealings in their equity share capital have been advertised in the newspaper on a regular basis for a continuous period of at least six months, their equity share capital has been traded on the Alternative Investment Market of the London Stock Exchange or Nex Exchange (previously ISDX and formerly Plus and before that OFEX), or if the company has filed a prospectus relating to the issue of equity share capital with the Registrar of Companies, all at any time during the 10 years prior to announcement of the proposed offer for them.

If the City Code on Takeovers and Mergers applies, it will be necessary for the purchaser to make an offer to the target's shareholders in accordance with the terms of the Takeover Code.

12.1.2   Form of the offer

An offer to purchase the shares of a private company is likely to constitute an 'investment advertisement'/'financial promotion'. If it does then, notwithstanding that the Takeover Code may apply, the offer must be issued or approved by an authorised person unless an appropriate exemption applies. For a more detailed consideration of investment advertisements/financial promotions please refer to Part I, Chapter 4 (section 4.5.1).

To avoid unnecessary further expense, public disclosure of the purchaser's desire to acquire the target and potential embarrassment if the offer does not succeed, it is common practice for a purchaser to seek irrevocable undertakings from the principal shareholders of the target prior to despatch of the offer document. Until FSMA 2000 came into force, there was a distinction between unsolicited calls and investment advertisements rules but that has now gone thereby making s 21 (restrictions of 'financial promotion') the principal item of legislation to be considered.

In a private company takeover, it is common to include in the irrevocable undertaking warranties and indemnities as to the target company and its business. This is because it is impractical to include the warranties and indemnities in the offer document itself as minority shareholders may find this objectionable, especially if they are unrelated to the management of the business.

The offer document will set out the terms and conditions of the offer and certain other prescribed information.

12.1.3 Terms of the offer

To take advantage of the provisions of CA 2006, s 979 (squeeze out), the offer must be on the same terms to all shareholders. It is therefore important that the only consideration given by the purchaser in any irrevocable undertaking is a promise to make the offer.

12.1.4 Summary

Unless the circumstances dictate that an offer is necessary, the conventional wisdom is to proceed by way of private treaty between the seller and the purchaser through a negotiated share purchase agreement since the professional costs involved are likely to be less, it offers greater flexibility and there are no time constraints.

12.2 SHARE PURCHASE AGREEMENT

Although there is no requirement for the share purchase agreement to follow a particular form or contain prescribed information, it is common practice for the share purchase agreement to be drafted in the first instance by the purchaser's solicitors and for the agreement to be drafted in a style, and contain provisions, which have become standard over the years. The precedent share purchase agreement set out in Part VI as Precedent F is typical, both in its content and style.

The following sections of this chapter comment on the precedent share purchase agreement in the order of the provisions contained in the precedent. To be even handed between the seller and the purchaser, these sections highlight points in the precedent which are likely to be objectionable to the seller and where amendments to it might be suggested.

12.2.1 Parties

The parties will normally be the shareholders of the target company and the purchaser. The precedent share purchase agreement has been drafted on this basis and assumes that not all shareholders will be required to give warranties and the covenant for taxation. It therefore makes provision for there to be a different category of sellers for the purpose of giving warranties and the tax covenant.

Occasionally, the parties will also include a guarantor, either to guarantee the obligations of the seller (for example, under the warranties) or the purchaser (for example, to pay deferred consideration). Where the target company is a member of a group of companies, it may be appropriate for the purchaser to seek restrictive covenants from other members of the seller's group of companies. In such cases, either the ultimate holding company should be made a party to the agreement and obliged to undertake on behalf of all members of its group of companies or the appropriate group companies are added as a party. Where the seller is a trustee, to avoid personal liability a trustee will normally seek to limit his liability to the amount held by him in trust. Accordingly, unless the purchaser can obtain restrictions from the trustee on the distribution of sale proceeds to the underlying beneficiaries, it is prudent for the purchaser to also require the beneficiaries to enter into the agreement for the purpose of giving any warranties, indemnities or other obligations on the part of the seller. Where third party guarantees are obtained and there is no consideration passing between any two relevant parties the document should be signed as a deed to ensure those third party obligations are enforceable.

12.2.2 Definitions and interpretation

To avoid the need to repeat expressions in full throughout the document, it has become customary to include as the first clause of any acquisition agreement a number of definitions which are used from time to time in the course of the agreement. It has also become customary to include provisions to clarify the interpretation of the agreement (see sub-clause 1.2 of the precedent share purchase agreement).

Both parties need to consider each definition carefully since the way in which they are drafted could easily favour one party over the other. For example, without amendment the definition of 'transaction' in sub-clause 1.1 of the precedent share purchase agreement favours the purchaser. The seller should seek deletion from the definition of the sentence starting 'and references to "any Transaction effected on or before Completion" ...'. The reason for this is that there are certain provisions in the tax legislation whereby a liability can crystallise as a result of two or more unconnected transactions happening over a period of time before and after completion – for example, where a bonus issue takes place after completion when a repayment of capital had taken place before completion. Unless resisted this extension of the definition of' transaction' effectively writes a blank cheque to the purchaser to cover it for any unusual transaction which might be entered into after completion which unwittingly has the effect of creating a tax liability, when taken in conjunction with something that happened prior to completion. Various approvals, consents and clearances may be required to authorise the seller and/or the purchaser to enter into the transaction or to give effect to the transaction. To avoid the cost and expense of finalising the agreement and, in certain cases, the embarrassment of announcing a sale or purchase which doesn't then take place because one of the conditions cannot be satisfied, it is preferable to satisfy any conditions before entering into the share purchase agreement, but this is not always possible or desirable.

Conditions are therefore used to commit each party to legally binding obligations which will be effective upon the fulfilment of certain matters, usually beyond the control of each party. To avoid confusion and misunderstandings the conditions to be fulfilled should be objective, clearly specified and the contractual provision should contain a date by which the conditions are to be satisfied and should state the alternative course of action if the conditions are not then satisfied. The precedent assumes that where any particular condition precedent is not fulfilled, the ultimate remedy is to rescind the agreement. It is not unusual to find a further provision in favour of the innocent party allowing it to recover its costs from the defaulting party as well as to rescind the agreement.

It is important to understand the effect of conditions in an acquisition agreement to ensure that they achieve the desired result. Conditions precedent (which must be satisfied before the main terms of the contract come into existence) need to be distinguished from conditions subsequent (which must be satisfied before the main terms of the contract are completed but which does not prevent a legally binding agreement arising which regulates the behaviour of the parties whilst the condition is being fulfilled). The precedent attempts to make all conditions precedent, so that the stated clauses are the only clauses which will be legally binding when the agreement is signed. This means that the beneficial ownership in the shares will not pass to the purchaser when the agreement is signed but when the last condition is fulfilled, which may be important as far as the distribution of dividends is concerned.

Approvals and consents required by the seller and/or the target which typically give rise to the need to include conditions are discussed in Part II (see Chapter 10, section 10.2.4). The purchaser may also require the consent of its shareholders and board of directors for the same reasons as the seller and, in addition to these, to authorise the issue of consideration shares. The purchaser's requirements should always be considered when preparing the conditions.

12.2.3   Conditions

Where there is a condition precedent to the effect that the transaction is subject to approval by the shareholders of either party, consideration should be given as to whether the key shareholders of the purchaser will be required to give irrevocable undertakings to the other party to vote in favour of the resolution to approve the transaction. If imposed, the obligation on any director to vote in favour of the resolution to approve the transaction will be subject to their fiduciary duties (see *Rackham v Peek Foods* [1990] BCLC 895 and *John Crowther Group plc v Catpets International* [1990] BCLC 460, on both of which doubts were expressed but not overruled in *Fulham Football Club Ltd v Cabra Estates* (1992) 65 P & CR 284, [1994] 1 BCLC 363, CA) and their codified duties under Companies Act 2006.

The implications of conditions precedent should be considered for the purposes of tax on capital gains. So far as capital gains tax is concerned, the time of disposal is the time the contract is made unless the contract is conditional, in which event it is when the condition is satisfied (TCGA 1992, s 28).

12.2.4   Conduct of business prior to completion

There will be occasions when a delay between exchange of contracts and completion is inevitable, for example, when landlord's consent is necessary to the assignment of a property lease. Where a simultaneous exchange and completion is not possible, in addition to a provision covering the conditionality of the agreement, the share purchase agreement should address the risk of adverse events occurring during the intervening period. Usually this is an issue for the purchaser and typically the purchaser may wish to consider the following issues.

(A)   Repeating the warranties at completion

By repeating the warranties at completion the purchaser is protected from events occurring during the interval between exchange and completion which give rise to a breach of the warranties and, in particular, it may allow the purchaser the opportunity to rescind the agreement on or before completion for any such breach.

(B)   Restricting the operation of the target's business between exchange and completion

Since the purchaser will bear the risk of the business during this period if the conditions are satisfied and the transaction completes, it will want to ensure that the target's business is carried on in the normal course and that no significant decisions relating to the target are made or, if they have to be made, are made without its agreement. On the other hand, the seller will be unwilling to allow the purchaser to manage the business during the interval because of the risk of the transaction not proceeding if the conditions are not then satisfied or waived. The typical approach taken to address these problems is to provide that:

- the seller remains in management control of the target between exchange and completion;
- the way in which the target carries on business between exchange and completion is subject to a number of restrictions and/or rights of veto in favour of the purchaser;
- warranties given on exchange of contracts are repeated on completion; and
- the purchaser is given a right to rescind for a material breach of warranty or, alternatively, a breach of a material warranty between exchange and completion and the seller is obliged to disclose events occurring which might give rise to a breach of warranty.

The precedent share purchase agreement contains in clause 5 a reasonably common set of restrictions on the operation of the business between exchange and completion.

12.2.5   Sale and purchase

It is essential that the share purchase agreement clearly identifies the shares being bought and sold (see clause 3 of the precedent). In this context, share purchases are less complex than business transfers as only one asset is being bought and sold.

As well as stating precisely what shares are being sold and by whom, it is traditional for the clause also to include covenants as to title of the shares being sold since, until the introduction of the Law of Property (Miscellaneous Provisions) Act 1994, there were no implied terms as to the basis on which the seller sells his shares. Practice has altered since the introduction of this Act, which implies covenants as to title where 'a disposition of property' is sold with 'full title guarantee' or with 'limited title guarantee'. While the implied covenants are most commonly used on dispositions of land, because the definition of 'property' includes' a thing in action, and any interest in real or personal property' they are regularly used in other spheres, including share purchases.

Transferring shares with 'full title guarantee' implies in the instrument effecting or purporting to effect the transfer covenants by the seller:

- that he has the right to dispose of the shares as he purports to;
- that he will at his own cost do all that he reasonably can to give the title he purports to give; and
- that he is disposing of the shares free from all charges and encumbrances (whether monetary or not) and other rights exercisable by third parties other than any charges, encumbrances or rights which he does not, and could not reasonably be expected to, know about.

Where the shares are transferred with 'limited title guarantee', the first two covenants listed above equally apply, but instead of the third the implied covenant is to the effect that the seller has not since the last disposition for value:

- charged or encumbered the shares by means of any charge or encumbrance which subsists at the time of transfer, or granted third party rights in relation to the shares which so subsist;
- suffered the shares to be so charged or encumbered and subjected to any such rights, and that he is not aware that anyone else has done so since the last disposition for value; and
- that the seller is not aware that anyone else has done so since the last disposition for value.

It is important to note that if the key words 'full title guarantee' or 'limited title guarantee' are omitted from an acquisition agreement, covenants of title will not be implied into the agreement.

The seller will not be liable under the implied covenants in respect of any matter to which the transfer is made subject or anything which at the time of transfer is within the actual knowledge, or which is a necessary consequence of facts then within the actual knowledge, of the purchaser.

A notable feature of the Law of Property (Miscellaneous Provisions) Act 1994 is that the benefit of the implied covenants is annexed and incident to, and goes with, the estate or interest of the purchaser and is capable of being enforced by every person in whom the estate or interest is (in whole or in part) for the time being vested.

As the articles of association of the target company may contain pre-emption rights on the transfer of shares, it is important for the purchaser's solicitors to check the target company's articles of association to see what restrictions (if any) are contained on the transfer of shares. If the articles contain pre-emption rights in favour of the other shareholders, it is usual to include in the share purchase agreement a provision whereby each of the sellers waives any pre-emption rights they have. Where, however, a purchaser is not acquiring all the shares in issue or, for some reason, one of the sellers is not a party to the share purchase agreement, individual waivers may need to be obtained or otherwise the pre-emption procedures must be followed.

12.2.6 Consideration

Given the number of different ways in which the consideration can be calculated and the differing forms of consideration and timing of payment, this clause can vary from being simple and straightforward (for example, in the case of a pre-determined fixed sum payable in cash on completion) to a complex series of provisions (for example, in the case of earn outs). For a detailed discussion on the methods of calculating the consideration and the forms of consideration, refer to Part II (see Chapter 9).

Whatever consideration structure is adopted, any clause dealing with the consideration payable for the shares being sold needs to address four principal issues:

- the amount payable;
- if the amount payable is not fixed, how is it to be calculated;
- when is the consideration payable; and
- in what form is it payable.

If the target company has two or more classes of shares, the consideration clause should also address the apportionment of the consideration between the different classes of shares.

The following paragraphs consider drafting issues relevant to some of the more complicated pricing structures.

(A) Completion accounts

To ascertain the value of the target on completion for the purpose of calculating the consideration or adjusting the amount payable it will be necessary to draw up accounts of the target. These are normally referred to as 'completion accounts'. In practice, they are usually drawn up shortly after completion and they can usually take a number of forms. For example, if the consideration payable is based on net assets the completion accounts may take the form of a net asset statement and, if the consideration is based on earnings, they may take the form of a profit and loss account.

The completion accounts procedure should not be seen as a way of transferring difficult decisions on to the accountants. As completion accounts form the basis for adjustments to the purchase price once the deal completes, they provide by far the best mechanism for an aggressive seller or purchaser to renegotiate the purchase price. Accordingly, it is essential that the parties, with the help of their professional advisers, agree with some precision in advance of contract first the bases on which the completion accounts are to be prepared, secondly the identity of the preparer, and thirdly what adjustments should then be made to the completion accounts to take account of special factors and so arrive at the figure which will constitute the purchase price. These accounting bases and adjustments should then be specified accurately and in detail in the agreement in order, so far as practicable, to avoid future argument. It will be the job of the draftsman to ensure that this aim is achieved.

(i) Basis of preparation

The agreement should contain a detailed set of rules governing the preparation of the completion accounts. The traditional habit of applying 'generally accepted accounting principles and statements of standard accounting practice in the United Kingdom' or 'the same accounting practices as used consistently in previous accounts business' is not sufficient, and when used together without any form of priority, can cause confusion. It is suggested that a schedule of accounting policies, principles and accounting methods to be applied should be drawn up after consultation with both the seller's accountants and purchaser's accountants and, where possible, the contentious issues should be identified and dealt with in that schedule.

(ii) Identity of the preparer

Unlike in a preparation of audited accounts where the auditors and the company are trying to reach a common view, the seller and the purchaser will be at opposite ends of the spectrum in trying to agree completion accounts. As there should be no great advantage to either side in controlling the production of the first draft, and as the seller's accountants will be more au fait with the preparation of accounts for the target, it may be cost effective for them to produce the first draft. However, to ensure that the party preparing the first draft does not have the upper hand in subsequent negotiations, it is important to provide for the reviewer to be given access to all relevant books, records and information of the target.

The share purchase agreement should impose a realistic timetable for the production of the first draft of the completion accounts, the review of them and the acceptance or rejection of them. It is usual to require the party producing the completion accounts to deliver a copy of those accounts together with a certificate giving details of the consequential purchase price or purchase price adjustment and for the recipient to state, within a given timetable, whether the completion accounts and the certificate are accepted or rejected.

It is also usual to provide a mechanism for any disputes to be resolved, which commonly involves reference of the matter in dispute to an independent accountant or firm of accountants, the independent accountant's identity to be agreed between the parties and, if the parties are unable to agree, for the independent accountant to be nominated by an independent person, typically the President for the time being of the Institute of Chartered Accountants in England and Wales. The agreement should also address whether the independent person is to act as an expert or an arbitrator and who picks up the liability for his costs. Since the mechanics of the approval process will have already given the parties an opportunity to agree the differences, it is common to appoint the independent person as an expert and not an arbitrator.

In cross-border transactions, as there is no way of enforcing an expert determination it is common to provide for any dispute to be decided by arbitration since most countries have signed up to the New York Convention on the Recognition and Enforcement of Foreign Arbitral Awards. A list of countries which have and which have not signed this is available at: http://en.wikipedia.org/wiki/Convention_on_the_Recognition_and_Enforcement_of_Foreign_Arbitral_Awards.

(iii)   Adjustment to the purchase price

As well as providing for the basis of preparation of the completion accounts and the mechanics for preparing and agreeing those accounts, the share purchase agreement it should provide for the purchase price to be adjusted to reflect the outcome of the completion accounts. This may, in the case of the consideration on the value of net assets, be a pound for pound adjustment or, in the case of a consideration based on earnings, be a multiple of the variance between the assumed earnings and the actual results. These provisions should also address the question as to whether or not interest is to be paid on the adjusted figure, the form of payment and the timing of that payment.

(B)   Deferred consideration

For the reasons stated in Part II (see Chapter 9, section 9.4.3) the parties may have structured the price to include an element of deferred consideration. The most common form of deferred consideration (known as an 'earn-out') is where the consideration payable is linked to the future performance of the business in the hands of the purchaser after completion.

As the deferred consideration will be unascertained at completion, the share purchase agreement will need to address the calculation of the deferred consideration, the form of consideration payable and the timing of the payment. Earn-outs are normally calculated on the basis of actual profits against a target over a one, two or three-year period and to ascertain the actual profits accounts need to be drawn up. These accounts are often referred to as 'earn-out accounts' and the same considerations apply to the drafting as provisions regarding them as apply to completion accounts. From the point of view of all parties, it will be necessary to agree in advance the formula for determining 'net profits' and to see that that formula is applied consistently in each of the relevant years and that the figures are certified by accountants acting for both sides. From the sellers' point of view it will be desirable to ensure that the company's existing policies and practices are maintained over the earn-out period and that no action is taken by the company or the purchaser which might adversely affect or divert profits. Clause 4.11 of the precedent is an example of the protective provisions often sought by the seller in an earn-out.

The purchaser will probably wish to ensure that, if it has warranty claims against the sellers, the amounts of the claims can be set off against the payments. The purchaser may also wish to be able to satisfy the payments wholly or partially by the issue of shares.

(C)   Seller placing

To give effect to a seller placing the share purchase agreement will need to provide that instead of paying cash at completion the purchaser may allot a number of its own shares to the seller and undertake to procure the placing of those shares to provide the seller with a sum equal to the consideration payable.

If a transaction involving a seller placing is structured traditionally (ie shares are allotted and issued to the seller either on definitive share certificates or on renounceable allotment letters and the shares are then transferred or renounced in favour of the purchaser), stamp duty or stamp duty reserve tax (SDRT) (in either case at the rate of 0.5%) is payable. SDRT now accounts for the majority of taxation collected on share transactions effected through the UK's Exchanges, ie London Stock Exchange, LIFFE etc. The majority of this taxation is collected automatically through the CREST system, although payments are also collected for transactions that are effected outside of CREST (referred to as 'Off Market Payments), or input incorrectly through CREST. An alternative is for the, shares to be allotted directly to the purchaser and for the purchaser to procure that the net placing proceeds, ie an amount which represents the bargain between the seller and the purchaser, is paid to the seller. This structure also results in the seller not needing to be a party to the placing agreement.

12.2.7   Completion

Once any conditions have been fulfilled or waived, completion can take place. The share purchase agreement should identify the business to be conducted at completion. The precedent share purchase agreement includes a typical clause where the purchaser is buying the whole issued share capital of the target company (clause 6) and is concerned with the vesting in the purchaser of effective control of the target company to the exclusion of the seller in return for payment of the price for the shares. The first sub-clause sets out the items to be physically handed over to the purchaser and the next three sub-clauses set out the matters the seller is to attend to at completion. The final sub-clause provides for payment of the purchase price.

Because there may be many documents with numerous signatories to be handed over on completion, it is helpful if the purchaser's solicitor prepares a completion agenda. This should be submitted to and agreed with the sellers' solicitor prior to completion. The agenda will set out the persons required to attend completion, the key actions required before completion can take place (for example, fulfilment of conditions precedent), the items to be produced at the completion meeting (share certificates, statutory books, cheque books and so on), all documents required to be signed at the completion meeting, with details of who is required to produce and sign them and summaries of board and/or company resolutions to be passed. If there is a risk that due to holiday or illness or otherwise any of the parties to the transaction documents may not be present at the completion meeting, it is prudent to address the issue early on in the process and to ensure that that party appoints another to sign on his behalf. Most commonly this is done by way of power of attorney, which is required to be executed as a deed to be enforceable (Powers of Attorney Act 1971, s 1(1)). In preparing a power of attorney it is important to ensure that its terms are sufficiently wide to cover the attorney's actions at the meeting. To cater for this, the precedent power of attorney (Precedent K) contains a wide, catch-all power to do anything ancillary to the contemplated transaction.

Some consideration needs to be given to the mechanics necessary to enable a purchaser to exercise control with effect from completion. CA 2006, s 112 states that the subscribers to the company's memorandum on the registration of the company are its members and every other person who agrees to become a member and whose name is entered in the company's register of members. Thus until a transferee of shares is entered in the company's register, he is not entitled vis-à-vis the company to exercise any right attaching to his shareholding, although the transferor will be bound to exercise any such rights in accordance with directions given by the transferee. Furthermore, whatever equities may exist between transferor and transferee, CA 2006, s 126 provides that no notice of any trust, express, implied or constructive, shall be entered on the register, or be receivable by the registrar in the case of companies registered in England.

The transferee of shares cannot be registered in respect of those shares until a proper instrument of transfer has been delivered to the company and the transfer approved by the directors. A proper instrument of transfer is one that has been duly stamped with the appropriate amount of stamp duty. Since stamping invariably follows completion, it will be seen that even the transferees of the whole issued share capital of the company will be unable immediately following completion to exercise control in their own right. For this reason, the usual practice is for the outgoing shareholders to agree that on completion they will pass any resolution of the company required by the purchaser, and further that they will procure the outgoing directors to pass any necessary resolutions of the board. It should be noted that the directors as such cannot bind themselves to vote since they have a fiduciary duty to the company.

The principal matters which the purchaser will require the outgoing directors to approve at the completion board meeting will be approval (subject to due stamping) of the transfer of shares to the purchaser or his nominees, the registration of the purchaser or his nominees under letters of allotment, the appointment of the purchaser's nominees as directors pursuant usually to reg 79, Table A (or Companies Act 2006 Model Articles where a company uses them) ensuring that any maximum number of directors stipulated by the articles is not exceeded, and the acceptance of the existing directors' resignations.

In accepting the existing directors' resignations, the purchaser should be aware that as a general rule a contractual provision which purports to exclude or limit the operation of any provision of the Employment Rights Act 1996 (for example, to exclude the statutory rights to compensation for unfair dismissal or redundancy) or to preclude the employee from bringing any proceedings under the Act before an employment tribunal is void (Employment Rights Act 1996, s 203(1)). However, this general rule does not apply to an agreement (known as a COT3) entered into where an ACAS conciliation officer has taken action to promote a settlement (s 203(2)(e)). Similarly (and more usually in these circumstances) the general rule is excluded where the agreement precluding the institution or continuance of proceedings in respect of such a complaint satisfies the conditions regulating 'compromise agreements' (s 203(2)(f)). The main conditions set out in s 203(3) are that the agreement must be in writing and must relate to the particular complaint; the employee must have received independent advice from a 'relevant independent adviser' as to the terms and effect of the proposed agreement and, in particular, its effect on his ability to pursue his rights before an employment tribunal; and there must be in force, when the adviser gives the advice, insurance covering the risk of a claim by the employee in respect of loss arising in consequence of the advice. 'Relevant independent advisers' not only include barristers or solicitors, but also trade union officials or workers at an advice centre, subject in both cases to the individual concerned having been certified as competent to give the advice (s 203(3A)). 'Independent', in relation to advice to the employee, means that it is given by someone who is not acting in the matter for the employer or an associated employer.

The agreement will provide for these resignations (and for those of the secretary and possibly the auditors) to be handed over at completion, together with duly executed share transfers and the relative share certificates. In addition, provision will be made for the company's books and records and documents of title to be handed to the purchaser on behalf of the company since the company will retain ownership throughout. The items which will be so handed over will include the statutory books and certificate of incorporation; the company seal; financial records; documents of title to the company's properties; cheque books and paying in books; insurance policies; counterpart service agreements and all other agreements. The agreement may also provide for alteration of a company's bank mandate by resolution of the board on completion and, in appropriate cases, for the delivery of all technical drawings and specifications of a confidential nature or the key managers entering into service agreements with the target company. In the latter case, it will be necessary to consider whether CA 2006, s 188 applies. That section requires prior approval by resolution of the company in general meeting of a term in the service agreement of a director of the company or its holding company under which his employment will continue (or may be continued otherwise than at the instance of the company) for more than two years if during that period it cannot be terminated by the company by notice or it can be so terminated but only in specified circumstances. If the appointee is a director of the company's holding company, the term must also be approved by resolution in general meeting of the holding company.

It is convenient at this point to discuss briefly directors' duties in relation to completion board resolutions. Before passing these and any other board resolutions each of the outgoing directors will need to consider his duties towards the company and its members. In summary, a director must observe the utmost good faith towards the company, may not do anything which may give rise to a conflict of interest between the director's private interests and the duties of his office and may not make use of any information or opportunity obtained in his capacity as a director of the company. In the case of the smaller unquoted company where the directors are often the major shareholders, the opportunities for breach of these provisions are legion, but any act or omission of a director which is capable of ratification is permissible. Where a director has an interest which is declared, the company's articles may or may not permit him to be counted in the quorum and vote at a directors' meeting.

12.2.8 Warranties

In agreeing to acquire the target, a purchaser will have relied upon various representations and assumptions. To compensate for the lack of statutory protection and to ensure the purchaser can recover its loss if they subsequently prove to be incorrect, the various representations and assumptions being relied on are usually included in the share purchase agreement as express representations and are known as warranties. Where, however, a specific liability has been identified an indemnity may be more appropriate. An indemnity is a contractual obligation on the part of one party to protect another from a specific liability or loss. An indemnity claim is easier to establish than a breach of warranty since there is no need to prove that the shares in the target are worth any less as a result of the matter giving rise to the indemnity claim.

(A) Purpose

Given that the principle of caveat emptor applies in all its force to the acquisition of a private company or business, warranties serve a dual purpose: they provide a mechanism for retrospective price adjustment and a means to flush out information regarding the target.

Warranties seek to readdress the balance in favour of the purchaser by allocating the risk of unknown liabilities or undisclosed obligations on the seller. In the context of a private company or business acquisition, it is generally accepted that the purchaser will seek and the seller will give warranties.

The negotiation usually revolves around the nature and extent of the warranties, the liability arising on breach and limitations on liability. Occasionally the seller will seek warranties from the purchaser. For example, if the consideration takes the form of the issue of shares in an unlisted purchaser representing a significant proportion of the purchaser's share capital, the seller would be well advised to seek contractual representations from the purchaser about its financial health and other matters of importance.

(B) Remedies

The rights and liabilities for a breach of warranty are twofold.

(i) Rescission

Rescission is one of two remedies available under the Misrepresentation Act 1967 for a false statement of fact (a misrepresentation). Rescission will only be ordered if the parties are capable of being returned to the position they were in before contracts were exchanged. For this reason, rescission is an important remedy where there is a delay between exchange of contracts and completion, but of limited benefit where a breach of warranty arises after completion. Furthermore, the remedy will be lost if, after discovery of the breach, the purchaser has taken some action affirming the agreement, for example by declaring a dividend or selling some of the acquired assets.

Because it is sometimes argued that rescission under the Misrepresentation Act 1967 is available only if the misrepresentation was made before the contract was entered into, an express right of rescission is usually included (see eg clause 10.2 of the precedent share purchase agreement).

From a seller's perspective, rescission is a particularly unattractive remedy for what could turn out to be something reasonably minor in the overall scheme of things. Accordingly, most sellers will seek expressly to exclude it.

(ii) Damages

The alternative remedy, and the remedy normally sought for breach of warranty, is damages. The measure of damages differs in contract and tort.

The contractual measure would place the purchaser in the position which it would have been in had the breach not occurred. It would result in the purchaser receiving the difference between the market value of the target as it stands and the market value of the target had the breach not occurred, ie the purchaser's loss of bargain.

The tortious measure on the other hand would compensate the purchaser for the loss suffered as a result of the tort committed by putting the purchaser in the position he would have been if the tort had not been committed.

In summary, the remedy of damages has the effect of reducing the purchase price or adjusting it retrospectively to reflect the real worth of the target.

In *T & L Sugars Ltd v Tate & Lyle Industries Ltd* [2014] EWHC 1066 the court had to decide legal proceedings for a claim under a warranty had been issued and served in time. The clause in the agreement provided that warranty claims would be deemed withdrawn if proceedings were not served within 12 months of notice of a claim. The court held 'served' meant formal legal service of legal proceedings under the Civil Procedure Rules. It is important to ensure that contracts are very clear about how notice must be given and any time limits. Then notice was served in time.

In *Ageas (UK) Ltd v Kwik-Fit (GB) Ltd* [2013] EWHC 3261 (QB) again service was held to be in time for a similar such claim, although the judge came to his conclusion for different reasons than the *T & L Sugars* case above. Here the court found that the use of the word 'serving' just meant the document had been delivered, not any special legal meaning of issuing proceedings. In practice ensure notice clauses are clear and follow the agreement to the letter in the case of claims.

In *Sycamore Bidco Ltd v Breslin* ([2012] EWHC 3443 (Ch)), the court looked at whether a claim for misrepresentation could be brought for breach of express warranties in a sale agreement. The claimant would win £16.75m damages for mispresentation but only £6m for breach of contract. The court confirming earlier law held that the warranties were not express representations so only the breach of contract claim could be brought. After the purchase mistakes were found in the arget company audited accounts from before the purchase. The company had been over valued and the buyer had paid too much. There were warranties about the accounts in the agreement but liability under the warranties was limited. The agreement had not however limited liability for misrepresentation so there was no cap on that liability and higher damages could, if mispresentation were allowed, have been claimed. Breach of a representation claim put the buyer at the position it would have been in had the contract never been entered into. Breach of warranty/contract claims put the buyer into the position it would have been in had the contract been properly performed.

The judgment was summarised by solicitors Olswang as follows (see http://www.cms-lawnow.com/ealerts/2016/08/oil--gas-ma-warranties-are-not-representations?cc_lang=en&ec_as=267CECF6991E46079320521A793085DO):

'1. There is a clear distinction between the two and that would have been understood by the draftsman of the SPA. This was apparent from the SPA itself. Representations were referred to in one clause and Warranties (with a capital "W") were referred to elsewhere.
2. The warranties were clearly and at all times described as warranties and nowhere described as representations.
3. The words of the warranting provision were words of warranty, not representation. There is a legal distinction between the two and there was no reason to extend the words beyond their natural meaning. It is not enough that the subject matter of the warranty was capable of being a representation.
4. The Disclosure Letter (referred to in the SPA) also distinguished between warranties and representations.
5. The SPA contained significant limitations on the liability under the warranties. It did not refer to representations. The clause was obviously a significant part of the overall structure of liability. If the warranties

did amount to representations, on the strict wording of the clause the limitations would not have applied to misrepresentations. The sellers would have been deprived of a large part of their protection which would have been strange and uncommercial and could hardly have been intended.

6. There was a conceptual problem in characterising provisions in the contract as being representations relied on in entering into the contract. The timing did not work. The normal case in misrepresentation involves the making of a representation and as a result the entering into of the contract. That does not work where the only representation is said to be in the contract itself.

The judge disagreed with the 2009 High Court decision in *Invertex Ltd v De Mol Holding BV and another* which concerned a similar claim in misrepresentation based on warranties in a share sale agreement. In this case the court held that the warranties did amount to representations. The judge in *Sycamore* did not try to distinguish the case but simply disagreed with the previous decision.

Practical tips and drafting tactics

Particularly in an acquisition context, in order to increase the range of remedies available to it and, as in this case, the scope of damages, the buyer may attempt expressly to provide that the warranties given by the seller are also representations. A seller will wish to resist this tactic and require that any representation wording is removed and that the agreement contains a detailed entire agreement clause which excludes claims for innocent or negligent misrepresentation based on any warranty or other statement contained in the agreement.

However, if the parties intend express warranties also to be actionable as representations, clear wording should be included to ensure they have this effect. For example, the relevant clauses should be described as warranties and representations and it may also be worth including a provision which states that the warrantor has made representations in the warranties which have induced the buyer to enter the contract.

Although there have been cases where warranties have been found to be representations, this decision confirms that this will depend on the specific wording of the contract and the facts of the case. Accordingly, this is a reminder that appropriate and accurate language should always be included when drafting warranties.'

(Dominc Dryden, Olswang).

(iii) Mitigation

In any case where a party claims damages he must take reasonable steps to mitigate the loss. This is not a particularly onerous duty. For example, if a third party claim is made against the company, reasonable steps should be taken to examine the merits of the claim and, if necessary, to contest it. Were the company to permit judgment to be entered against it in default of appearance or a defence without such an examination, a seller could reasonably complain of a failure to mitigate. In any event, in these circumstances an examination of the merits of a third party claim would be common sense, since, if the claim were unmerited, it would be unlikely to constitute a breach of warranty by the purchaser.

(C)   Multiple warrantors

Where there are multiple sellers, the purchaser may either seek warranties on a several or a joint and several basis. Joint and several liability is the basis nearly always sought because it enables the purchaser to recover against anyone of the sellers, thereby giving the purchaser maximum flexibility. Several liability, on the other hand, usually involves a ceiling on any one seller's liability (typically set at that seller's share of the sale proceeds). Accordingly, if the purchaser is unable to recover from one seller it cannot seek to recover the shortfall from another seller.

Multiple sellers are normally happy to undertake joint liability if they are all connected (for example, members of the same family) but if they are unconnected individuals they will often take exception to this suggestion. Although sellers who are forced to accept joint and several liability will have a right of contribution against the other sellers under the Civil Liability (Contribution) Act 1978 which entitles the court to determine a just and equitable basis of allocating liability between multiple covenantors, this statutory right of contribution is of no benefit if co-covenantors have spent the sale proceeds. If forced to give warranties on a joint and several basis, multiple sellers may wish to consider forming a private retention fund which is held by one or more of them as trustee so that if any claim is made under the warranties and any particular seller pays more than his fair share, there is some certainty that the money will be available with which to indemnify him. As well as the problem highlighted above, the statutory right of contribution has other limitations when not all sellers are warrantors and where different classes of shares are being sold at different values. In these cases consideration should be given to a contractual right of contribution in which these complexities can be addressed.

Sometimes a shareholder sells shares back to the company or to one of the other shareholders before the sale. The remaining shareholder then sells shares to the buyer. In such a case always consider for whom one is acting as an external solicitor and where acting for the remaining shareholder it would be wise to obtain through a separate deed a direct obligation of the departing shareholder to share liabilities with the remaining shareholder other than liability for acts or errors of the remaining shareholder. If this is not done there is a risk the departing shareholder is compensated fully for their shares whilst the remaining shareholder may face subsequent warranty claims. In a sense such an arrangement is two separate share sales although friends/relatives doing a pre-sale share transfer may not always regard it as such.

(D)   Date of warranties

Warranties are usually given on the date of signing the share purchase agreement. However, where there is a gap between signing and completing they are usually repeated on completion, with a right for the purchaser to withdraw if the seller is in breach of his warranties at that time. By this mechanism the purchaser will transfer the risk of something adverse occurring between signing and completion to the seller.

If the seller accepts repetition of the warranties at completion, then unless the seller is allowed to update the disclosure letter at completion the seller may face the prospect of a claim occurring, the purchaser completing the transaction and then subsequently suing for damages. On the other hand, the purchaser will not wish to be bound to complete the acquisition no matter what is included in any updated disclosure letter and will accordingly insist on the right of rescission and that the updated disclosure letter only includes matters arising between exchange and completion.

These provisions are usually subject to negotiation between the parties and only go to emphasise the desirability of effecting a simultaneous exchange of contracts and completion whenever possible.

(E)   Matters to be covered by warranties

The number of warranties and the matters to be covered by warranties will vary considerably depending upon the nature of the business carried on by the target company, whether shares or assets are being acquired and the identity of the warrantor. When acquiring the share capital of the target company the purchaser assumes responsibility for the company's liabilities whether or not it is aware of them. For this reason alone, the number and scope of warranties usually sought in a share purchase will far outweigh those normally sought in a business transfer.

To avoid unnecessary negotiation and in the long run, and as a result, save costs, the purchaser's lawyers should refrain from drafting warranties until they have received answers to their information request and, preferably, they have read the accountant's report. Far too often reams upon reams of warranties in standard form are introduced into the acquisition agreement without consideration of the nature of the business being acquired or the importance of the various assets of the target.

A full set of warranties is contained in Schedule 3 to the precedent share purchase agreement. The most common areas covered by warranties are:

- capacity;
- connected transactions;
- ownership of shares;
- group structure;
- insolvency;
- accuracy of information;
- accounts;
- events since last accounts date;
- banking arrangements;

- insurance;
- contracts;
- product liability;
- grants;
- licences/compliance;
- competition law;
- litigation;
- title to assets;
- intellectual property;
- employment;
- pensions;
- real property;
- environment;
- tax.

These warranties tend to relate to matters in the past or the present but would not normally relate to the future performance of the target company.

Although it is beyond the scope of this book to analyse the need for, and form of, each warranty, there follows a summary of some issues which arise in practice.

(I)   Tax warranties

It is not uncommon for practitioners to confuse the purpose of taxation warranties, on the one hand, and the covenant for taxation/deed of tax indemnity on the other. Tax warranties should be seen as a means to flush out information regarding the target and to provide a mechanism for price adjustment. However, their great value (particularly when compared with the covenant for taxation/ deed of tax indemnity) is to protect the purchaser from things that the target has done in the past which may influence the tax liability for the future. On the other hand, the covenant for taxation/deed of tax indemnity is designed to give the purchaser protection against tax liabilities of the target company in excess of those provided for in the warranted accounts or other than those liabilities arising in the normal course of business after the date of the warranted accounts and up to completion.

Tax warranties tend now to be shorter and to cover primarily aspects such as compliance issues, matters affecting the balance sheet and potential prospective charges to tax which may be influenced by the company's conduct before completion.

(ii)   General warranties

It is reasonably common for the purchaser to insert a widely worded warranty to the effect that the seller is not aware of any matter or thing which may adversely influence a purchaser of shares in the company or a variation on that theme. It should be noted that this warranty usually refers to 'a purchaser' and not to 'the purchaser', ie the seller need not take into account any special requirements or circumstances of the purchaser as regards this particular warranty. Nevertheless, great care should be taken before a seller gives such a warranty since it could cover diverse circumstances, for example a major customer about to go out of business. From the seller's point of view, any such warranty should, at the very least, limit his liability to facts of which he has become aware by virtue of his control of the company, not being facts which are of public knowledge. Usually, however, the seller insists that this type of warranty be deleted entirely since it seeks to give a purchaser protection against the ordinary commercial risks of the business.

(iii) Management buy-outs

Depending upon the degree of autonomy given to management to run the target company, a seller who has given management a free hand will be unsympathetic to a request for substantial warranties on the basis that the purchaser knows what it is buying. The difficulty arises with management financed by external bankers who know little about the target company and are unwilling to part with their money without some recourse to the seller.

(iv) Warranties by the purchaser

There will be occasions when the seller should consider seeking warranties from the purchaser. The normal example is where the purchaser issues shares as consideration for the acquisition which the seller intends to hold.

(F) Exclusion of the purchaser's knowledge

Through its due diligence investigations, the purchaser will have amassed a great deal of information and knowledge on the target. In giving warranties a seller will be concerned to ensure that the purchaser does not have knowledge of a matter which could give rise to a claim under the warranties and which has not been disclosed to the seller. For this reason, the seller may seek to include a limitation on his liability under the warranties of all matters within the purchaser's knowledge.

From the purchaser's perspective, although they are both forms of protection, warranties and due diligence investigations serve different purposes and traditionally a purchaser will insist on the warranties being qualified only on the matters disclosed in the disclosure letter and not matters within its knowledge. This is because the purchaser will be concerned that although information may have been given to it or part of its acquisition team during the due diligence process, the reviewer would not be aware that the document or information being reviewed may qualify the warranties. Also, such a qualification will in effect allow disclosure against the covenant for taxation/deed of tax indemnity, which is rarely agreed by a purchaser.

The traditional approach taken by a purchaser has been thrown into doubt by the case *of Eurocopy plc v Teesdale* [1992] BCLC 1067, where it was decided that a purchaser may not be able to rely on a clause qualifying warranties solely to matters 'disclosed in the disclosure letter' where it had actual knowledge of certain facts not disclosed in the disclosure letter. As a result of this decision, a purchaser should proceed on the basis that non-disclosure of facts in the disclosure letter of which it has knowledge will not automatically give it a course of action against the seller, and if it is relying on that matter then an indemnity should be sought. *Eurocopy* was however simple a summary application which was dismissed by the courts so has limited authority

In Infiniteland v Artisan Contracting Ltd (UK) plc [2005] EWCA Civ 758 information about a payment had been disclosed to the buyer's (Infiniteland's) reporting accountants who were doing due diligence on behalf of the buyer but they did not pass it on to the buyer as they believed the buyer's advisers had already discussed the point with the buyer. Less than six months after the sale the company purchased went into liquidation. Before the sale that company had received £1.08m from its parent company called a 'reverse management fee' which distorted the company's profits.

The share purchase agreement included a:

- warranty that the accounts gave a true and fair view of the target companies ;
- warranty that, save as set out in the disclosure letter, the warranties were true, fair and accurate;
- warranty that the contents of the disclosure letter and accompanying disclosure bundle were accurate and fully disclosed every matter to which they related; and
- provision which stated that the buyer's rights and remedies in respect of any breach of the warranties were not affected by any investigation made by it or on its behalf into the affairs of any of the target companies (save to the extent that such investigation gave the buyer actual knowledge of the relevant facts or circumstances).

In addition, the disclosure letter contained a general disclosure, stating that all the information contained in six lever arch files and related bundles were disclosed against the accounts warranty.

The Court of Appeal said the reporting accountants should have become aware of the payment and its significance and there had been adequate disclosure and no breach of warranty.

Following *Eurocopy* and *Infiniteland*, sellers would be wise to obtain a warranty that neither the buyer nor its advisers nor its agents have any actual knowledge of any breach of warranty. Buyers have the opposite view and will want it made clear knowledge of their advisers is not knowledge they have. Strong buyers will want a clause along the lines of that in *Eurocopy which allows* claims for breach of warranty to be brought by the buyer even though the buyer or advisers have knowledge of breach. They can try such a clause but it may not work given the uncertainty of the law in this area so should be told it will not necessarily be enforceable particularly if the buyer pays less because of knowledge of that element. If the buyer is very aware of an issue early on it should in practice negotiate a change in the price or an express indemnity on the issue from the seller.

In *Macquarie Internationale Investments Ltd v Glencore UK Ltd* [2010] EWCA Civ 697 the Court of Appeal held that the seller of a business was not in breach of a management accounts' warranty where those accounts did not disclose a liability which was unknown to, and not reasonably discoverable by, the seller at the relevant time. A £2.4m liability due to a computer error was not included in the audited or management accounts prepared before the sale. Later, after the sale, the buyer said the accounts did not present a fair reflection of the company's financial position.

The Court of Appeal said the accounts had been prepared in accordance with published professional standards and they did provide a true and fair view of the assets and liabilities. The liability was unknown and undiscoverable at the time of the sale.

12.2.9 Covenant for taxation

Historically, it was recognised that warranty protection was inappropriate for a purchaser where there were certain types of taxation liabilities incurred by a company arising out of actions by a shareholder, where the company had no statutory right of recovery. This occurred in two limited situations, and it became generally accepted that in these situations the sellers should indemnify the purchaser against any loss arising. Over the years, this principle has been obscured and it is now normal practice for sellers to give an indemnity in respect of taxation suffered or incurred by the target company which is referable to the period prior to completion.

It invariably used to be the case that such an indemnity would be embodied in a separate deed and the share purchase agreement would set the form of this out in full in a schedule and make it a completion requirement that the sellers should execute it. Being a deed, this particular document was always executed under seal. The original perceived advantages in having a separate deed of indemnity as opposed to dealing with the matter through warranties in the share purchase agreement were:

- in the context of an outright indemnity, there is arguably no duty to mitigate loss; and
- in the context of a contract under hand, it is generally thought that the maximum that a purchaser can recover by way of damages cannot exceed the amount which he paid for the shares. This is because shares in a company with limited liability cannot arguably have less than a nil value because the shareholders are under no liability to contribute towards any shortfall or deficiency in the company's assets.

Both these matters quickly became quite academic because:

- a well drafted deed of indemnity on the part of the sellers would always include a provision making it clear that the purchaser and/or the target company had to do what they could to mitigate their loss (although this was normally expressed in the form of a clause requiring them to do anything that the sellers might reasonably request); and

- the maximum liability in respect of all warranties, representations and indemnities (including the tax indemnity) was invariably limited to the purchase price.

Resistance to a separate deed grew following the decision in the case of *Zim Properties Ltd v Procter (Inspector of Taxes)* [1985] STC 90. This suggested that the right to damages or an indemnity was a chargeable asset for tax purposes and that receipt of any money under it constituted a disposal of that asset, with the result that the proceeds would be taxable in the recipient's hands. In the context of a share purchase agreement, relief was (and is still) afforded by TCGA 1992 (replacing the Capital Gains Taxes Act 1979, s 41), but this only applies in context of receipt of damages as a result of a claim for a breach of warranty or representation. The concept of a separate tax indemnity was considered by some to fall outside this exception and a school of thought followed that the whole aspect of tax should be dealt with through the warranties (albeit on an indemnity basis). This concern arose on the part of sellers who were invariably asked to agree to a 'grossing up' clause (see sub-clause 10.4 of the precedent share purchase agreement) in circumstances where there was a real risk that they could face significantly increased liabilities in the event of a claim.

HM Revenue and Customs (HMRC) sought to clear up the alarm through the issue of an extra statutory concession on 19 December 1988. However, this concession only applies to prevent a tax charge where the damages are paid or indemnity payment is made to the *purchaser* (and not, as was previously always the custom, to the underlying target group) and, secondly, the right to claim damages must be 'included as one of the terms of the share purchase agreement. The cautious view is that to have the tax indemnity in a separate deed will not satisfy the 'inclusion' test even though it may be a term of the agreement that the deed must be entered into as part of the completion requirements. This precedent adopts the cautious view and makes it clear that the indemnity is only in favour of the purchaser (albeit in respect of losses/liabilities of the target group). Nevertheless, you will certainly find draft documents still submitted requesting a separate deed and, when acting for the sellers, this should be amended to conform to our format. Certainly from the seller's point of view the indemnity should never be in favour of anyone other than the purchaser.

A form of covenant for taxation is included in the precedent share purchase agreement (see clause 9). The basic principle to be enshrined in any covenant/ deed of indemnity is the seller's obligation to compensate the purchaser for any tax liability of the target which exceeds the provision in the target's accounts for the period up to the accounts date and any tax liability arising after the accounts date but pre-completion to the extent that it is outside the ordinary course either of the target's business or of its trade.

It is essential to work out whether the transaction has been negotiated on historic accounts or on the basis of completion accounts. The format just explained will be used where it is based on historic accounts and the date to which the historic accounts are drawn will normally be the 'accounts date'. The position is different where completion accounts are drawn up because the purchaser is paying for the company based on its value at completion and there will be a provision for taxation in the completion accounts. Hence, in principle the seller should underwrite the tax liability without qualification all the way up to completion.

The principal components which go to make up the covenant for taxation are listed in the following paragraphs, first from the point of view of the clauses which the purchaser will wish to insert and then those which the seller will wish to see there. All references are to the covenant for taxation contained in the precedent share purchase agreement.

The purchaser will obviously wish to draft the covenant in as wide a manner as possible. The operative clause is already wide, but many advisers will go further when acting for the purchaser.

(A)   Combination of events

The definition of 'Transaction' contained in the precedent share purchase agreement which is used in the covenant is extended to bring in tax liabilities which might arise after completion, to the extent that they are somehow linked with something which occurred before completion. It is clearly very dangerous for a seller to agree to this type of clause and the first stage is to argue for its total exclusion. A standard compromise is that the events before completion must have been outside the ordinary course of business, whilst the events after completion must be within the ordinary course of business.

(B)   Tax losses

Where the target company has tax losses, the purchaser may ask the seller to warrant their continued existence. Sellers need to think carefully before agreeing to their inclusion within the covenant, especially where the purchaser is not paying for the losses.

If a relief has been taken into account in preparing the accounts, then its loss will give rise to a higher tax liability and the seller will therefore in principle be liable under the covenant. If a surplus relief ceases to be available to the target, then it seems unfair that the purchaser should have a claim for that unless the value of those reliefs have been taken into account in arriving at the price, so that the purchaser can say that it has paid for them. The covenant in the precedent makes what is normally a fair claim in respect of the loss of reliefs, in that the purchaser should only have a claim in respect of the loss of reliefs in three limited circumstances:

- where the accounts show as an asset the right to a repayment of taxation and that repayment is lost;
- where the accounts take the relief into account for some purpose other than arriving at the actual tax liability, so that the loss of relief would adversely affect some provision in the accounts, perhaps deferred taxation; and

- where a relief for a period after completion (or part of a period after completion) is used to set against profits arising before completion in respect of which there would otherwise have been a claim under the covenant. In other words, this is the case of reliefs which really belong to the purchaser being used to relieve tax which should be paid by the seller.

An alternative approach is for the purchaser to agree to pay at a specified rate for tax losses as and when allowed by the target company's tax inspector.

(C)   Conduct of tax returns

It would certainly be in the seller's interest to retain control over the tax compliance of the target company for any period for which the seller could be liable either under the warranties or under the covenant for taxation. It is clearly important to take instructions on this point from the sellers, particularly if the seller ends up paying the costs of the exercise.

(D)   Group relief arrangements

Where a group is concerned, it is important to work out precisely what the group arrangements are and to deal with (and agree) any group relief surrenders leading up to completion.

(E)   VAT

Where the target company is a member of the seller's group for VAT purposes it may be worth including a clause dealing with VAT. It is vital to understand the ramifications of this and, in particular, the fact that each member of the VAT group is jointly and severally liable for the VAT payable by the entire group (Value Added Tax Act 1994, s 43). It may be sufficient to allow the VAT accounts to be dealt with as part of the normal business arrangements as between the seller and the target company, although it is always preferable to have specific provisions included.

12.2.10   Limitations on warranty liability

As mentioned above, warranties have two purposes: to seek information regarding the target, and to impose legal liability on the warrantors in relation to undisclosed liabilities or obligations. To the extent that the warranties are given the seller accepts the liability flowing from breach of them but in doing so the seller will normally seek to restrict that liability in various ways including:

- limiting his liability on a 'several' basis;
- imposing a ceiling on liability and a threshold before claims can be made;
- limiting the time during which claims for breach of warranty may be made;

- restricting liability only to matters within the seller's knowledge;
- preventing double recovery; and by disclosure.

These limitations and others are contained in the precedent share purchase agreement at clause 11.

(A)   Share of liability

Where there is more than one seller the liability for each under the acquisition agreement will usually be expressed to be joint and several. Thus, whatever rights of contribution each seller may have against each of the others, the purchaser will be able to choose anyone (or more) of them to sue for the total liability under the contract. This may be unfortunate for the 10% shareholder who chooses to stay in the UK when the rest of his former co-shareholders emigrate to some remote jurisdiction, and joint and several liability is therefore often resisted by sellers. It is, however, precisely for this reason, ie wealthy potential defendants leaving the jurisdiction or dissipating their funds, that a purchaser should try to resist the inclusion of the provision whereby each seller is, as between himself and the purchaser, responsible only for that percentage of the loss equal to the percentage of shares sold (or price received) by him.

The sellers should, however, provide in another agreement for rights of contribution between themselves where there is not total identity between the sellers and the persons who give the warranties, ie where sellers who are minority shareholders and who have not participated in the target company's management give no warranties, or some warranties only, or all or some warranties qualified by words such as 'to the best of the sellers' knowledge, information and belief.

Another situation where a seller may wish to limit his share of liability is where a company is owned, say, 55% by individuals and 45% by trustees of a discretionary trust. On a sale of the whole issued share capital the trustees are normally unwilling to give any warranties, whatsoever other than as to title to their shares – besides being minority shareholders and having presumably taken no active part in the management of the company, they will not wish to undertake a personal liability when the benefit of the deal is for the discretionary beneficiaries. There may therefore have to be two contemporaneous agreements, the first between the individuals and the purchaser incorporating the full warranties, and the second between the trustees and the purchaser warranting title only to the shares. It is probable that in this situation, if there is a breach of warranty by the individuals, then in the absence of some limitation to the contrary, they will be liable for the whole loss suffered by the purchaser and not just 55% because the greater percentage represents the damages which may reasonably be supposed to have been in the contemplation of the parties (that is the individuals and the purchaser) at the time of the contract as the probable result of a breach of warranty.

It is sometimes suggested that trustees should give full warranties, but that their liability should be limited to an amount equal to the value of the trust capital net of tax and charges on capital for the time being held by them, and that they should agree not to distribute capital to any beneficiary without that beneficiary first giving warranties to the purchaser pro tanto. Whether trustees can agree such a provision will depend upon their powers under the trust in question and it will in any event be inappropriate where, for example, a beneficiary will become absolutely entitled during the limitation period, or where the trustees may otherwise become obliged to payout capital, albeit having a discretion as between possible beneficiaries.

(B)   Maximum liability

Although a seller may accept the principle of giving the purchaser comfort through the provision of warranties, in doing so the seller is unlikely to accept a liability in excess of the sale proceeds even though the purchaser's potential exposure may be greater because, for example, to fulfil its business objective the purchaser needs to incur capital expenditure renewing the target's production facilities. Accordingly, the seller will customarily demand a limitation on maximum liability equal to the sale proceeds. Depending upon the negotiating position of the parties and the extent and results of due diligence undertaken by the purchaser, the seller may be able to persuade the purchaser to accept a limitation fixing his maximum liability at a level substantially below the purchase price.

(C)   De minimis

To avoid being pursued for trivial matters and incurring unnecessary legal costs defending such claims, the seller should seek to agree with the purchaser a level under which it is not economical for proceedings to be commenced or action to be defended for breach of warranty. This level can either apply to individual claims or claims in aggregate. The aggregate claims limitation is generally set at between 1% and 5% of the purchase price. In some cases, the parties agree that very small individual claims are not recoverable, whether or not the threshold figure is exceeded. The principle of a de minimis restriction is generally accepted by purchasers. The contentious issue is whether, once the de minimis is exceeded, the purchaser can claim the full amount rather than the amount by which the threshold is exceeded.

(D)   Time

To avoid liability for a matter which comes to light many years after completion, the statutory limitation for an action for breach of warranties is six years from the date of breach.

Warranty claims relating to trading matters often arise as a result or consequence of the target company's audit. Accordingly, it is usual for the time limit for trading warranties to be linked to the target company's audit and purchasers often insist on a time limit allowing two full audits to be carried out.

Tax matters by their nature take longer to come to light and to deal with. HMRC's time limit for making an assessment to tax is six years from the end of the relevant financial year and 20 years where fraud or negligent conduct is involved. Therefore, the limitation on making a claim under the taxation warranties tends to be for a minimum of six years and often seven. Where seven years is chosen, however, the agreement arguably needs to be under seal because the usual limitation period for an agreement under hand is six years, and for a deed 12 years – although sometimes shorter periods are specified and in *4 Eng v Harper & Simpson* [2008] EWHC 915 an attempt to limit claims brought in two years failed where there was fraud.

(E)   To the best of the seller's knowledge

The purchaser will normally wish to ensure that all representations and warranties are given in unqualified form. In some cases, however, particularly where the warranty concerned is of a speculative nature (eg as to future profitability or future economic or market conditions) some such qualification as 'so far as the warrantors are aware' or 'to the best of the knowledge, information and belief of the warrantors' may be permitted, but even in that type of case the purchaser may seek to restrict the effect of qualification by a provision such as clause 1.2(f) of the precedent share purchase agreement.

Wholesale qualification of the warranties in this way may be appropriate in a management buy-out, particularly where the target company is a member of a group and the seller, its holding company, has in practice allowed it a great deal of autonomy. If the purchaser in such a situation is the buy-out vehicle for the continuing directors of the target company, it may well be that, through them, the purchaser knows considerably more than the seller about the day-to-day conduct of the target company's business. The seller's opening stance in such circumstances may be to decline to give any warranties either at all or unless they are qualified by reference to the extent of its knowledge. To meet the requirements of its financiers, however, the purchaser's opening stance may be to require all warranties to be in absolute form. Some compromise will be necessary if the transaction is to proceed. This may take the form of:

- the seller warranting without qualification those matters which must inevitably fall within its knowledge qua shareholder (eg as to the constitution of the target company), those matters to which it is a party (eg intra-group financing arrangements) and those which are otherwise of a group nature (eg the constitution of the group pension scheme and the rights of target company employees under it);
- the seller declining to give warranties in respect of those matters which fall within the scope of the target company's day-to-day management and on which it has no information;
- the seller giving warranties 'so far as it is aware' on all other matters but restricting its due diligence requirement in support of such matters to information available to it on its files, or known to its personnel, at head office and/or to making enquiry of certain specified employees of the target company; and

- the seller being expressly made not liable for any claim under the warranties as regards any matter of which the purchaser or the continuing directors had actual knowledge.

(F)   Double recovery

Sellers will contend that where the circumstances giving rise to the breach also provide the purchaser with the right to recover against a third party, the seller should not be liable for the breach if the purchaser has recovered the loss from the third party. It is a question of negotiation as to whether the purchaser should be able to claim against the seller without first pursuing the third party for recovery. Sellers will also contend that if they pay up and the purchaser subsequently recovers the same loss from a third party, the amount recovered less reasonable costs of recovery should be reimbursed to the seller.

(G)   Disclosure

One of the purposes of warranties is to flush out information regarding the target company prior to the purchaser entering into contractual arrangements. Having disclosed information to the purchaser to enable it to evaluate the target and decide whether to proceed with the acquisition, the seller will wish to avoid liability under the warranties for the matters disclosed. To avoid redrafting the warranties to reflect matters identified by the seller during the due diligence process, the disclosure letter is used to identify exceptions to the warranties.

Disclosure of exceptions to the warranties usually takes the form of a letter from the seller to the purchaser or from the seller's solicitors to the purchaser's solicitors and will have attached to it copies of the documentation being disclosed. It is usually divided into two parts: general disclosures followed by specific disclosures. The precedent disclosure letter (Precedent F) is prepared on this basis. The general disclosures contained in the precedent would, if accepted by a purchaser without amendment, negate the benefit of most of the warranties and as a consequence, the purchaser should not accept general disclosures unless its due diligence team has had full opportunity to review, understand and investigate those disclosures.

Copies of all documentation provided to the purchaser or its advisers during the due diligence process should be retained by the seller's lawyers to facilitate preparation of the disclosure letter and the disclosure bundles. The first draft of the disclosure letter will normally be prepared by the seller's lawyers and should include all matters previously disclosed to the purchaser or its advisers or otherwise known to the seller or its advisers which make any of the warranties untrue or inaccurate.

The seller will often try, at least in the first instance, to make its disclosure as wide as possible and to extend disclosure to the covenant for taxation. Unlike disclosure against tax warranties, sellers are rarely allowed to get away with disclosure against the covenant for taxation and there is really no justification for it.

From a contractual viewpoint, disclosure restricts the purchaser's rights under the warranties to the extent of the information disclosed, and because of this a purchaser should pay the same attention and take the same amount of care before accepting a disclosure as it would in accepting the deletion of a warranty. In any event, the purchaser will want the seller to warrant that the disclosures are true and limit disclosure to matters which are clearly identifiable and quantifiable.

The disclosure process gives the purchaser an opportunity to assess the impact of the disclosure on the target and, if necessary, to renegotiate the purchase price in the light of any matters revealed by the disclosures.

It is sometimes the case that a seller will be aware of a matter causing a breach of warranty but is reluctant to disclose it to the purchaser for fear of the purchaser's reaction and would rather complete the sale and wait for the claim. A seller considering this tactic should be reminded that under the Financial Services Act 2012, s 89 (previously FSMA 2000, s 397) it is a criminal offence to conceal information or make misleading statements in order to induce another party to enter into an investment agreement, which would include an agreement to buy shares.

12.2.11   Exclusion of non-contractual representations

It has been common practice to seek to exclude liability on the part of the seller for non-contractual representations by including in the limitations or elsewhere in the warranty section of the share purchase agreement an acknowledgement from the purchaser that 'it is not entering into the agreement other than in reliance on the warranties expressly set out in the agreement'.

The decision in the case of *Thomas Witter Ltd v TBP Industries Ltd* [1996] 2 All ER 573, has cast doubt on the enforceability of such a provision and has led to a change in practice.

In this case, the seller argued that the contractual acknowledgement, which although tucked into an 'entire agreement' provision was in terms similar to the above, given to it by the buyer protected it from any liability for pre-contractual misrepresentation. Jacob J rejected the argument on the basis that the exclusion of liability had not been made sufficiently explicit. He went on to say that even if he were wrong in construing the meaning of the clause, it would not have the effect of excluding liability because of the Misrepresentation Act 1967, s 3 (as amended by the Unfair Contract Terms Act 1977, s 8), which restricts the ability to contract out of the Misrepresentation Act 1967 unless the requirement of reasonableness is satisfied.

Jacob J found that the exclusion in this particular contract was too wide to satisfy the reasonableness test. In his opinion, since the clause before him did not distinguish between fraudulent, negligent and innocent misrepresentation, it excluded all three and it was clearly unreasonable to exclude liability for fraudulent misrepresentation. The whole clause was therefore ineffective.

Following this decision, sellers' lawyers continue to seek exclusion of liability for pre-contractual misrepresentations, but these exclusions now relate to negligent or innocent misrepresentations only and they are more explicit in the exclusion of liability.

12.2.12   Restrictive covenants

Goodwill has been defined as 'the probability that the old customers will resort to the old place' (per Lord Eldon in *Cruttwell v Lye* (1810) 1 Rose 123). Not every business has goodwill; indeed some proprietors are at pains to point out that the business is 'under new management'. To protect the goodwill being acquired, it is common to agree non-compete covenants, non-solicitation clauses and confidentiality provisions which restrict the competitive freedom of the seller in a transaction.

As a general rule, a restrictive covenant is contrary to public policy because it restrains trade and is presumed void and unenforceable unless proved to be reasonable by the parties to the restrictive covenant at the time of entering into the contract. The courts are far more willing to uphold restraints in acquisition agreements than they are in employment contracts, although even with employment contracts if the restriction is for a reasonable period and geographical area and the employee relatively senior they are enforceable. Nevertheless, the covenants should contain some sensible limitations in three respects: (i) geographical area; (ii) time; and (iii) type of business. When drafting restrictive covenants it is therefore important for the draftsperson to consider each individual covenant separately in order to try to identify what the purchaser genuinely needs in the context of legitimate protection. Where any particular provision could be diluted or otherwise scaled down without adverse prejudice to the purchaser's/target business, then the general principle is that it would be too wide and therefore unenforceable unless it is scaled down.

In addition to common law of restraint of trade above, restrictive agreements between parties fall to be assessed under the prohibitions on restrictive agreements in the Competition Act 1998 and art 101 of the Treaty on the Functioning of the European Union 1997 ('TFEU'). These provisions prohibit agreements which restrict or have the potential to restrict competition in the EC or UK or a substantial part thereof. This involves looking at the relevant market and assessing the effect on competition. The Commission has published a Notice regarding Restrictions Ancillary to Concentrations (2005, available at: http://eur-lex.europa.eu/LexUriServ/LexUriServ.do?uri=OJ:C:2005:056:0024:0031: EN:PDF). The European Commission's notice provides that such restrictions are referred to as 'ancillary restrictions' and are generally regarded as essential to a merger if a purchaser is to receive the benefit of any goodwill and/or know-how acquired, *provided that* they are properly limited. The terms of the restriction must not exceed what is necessary to attain that objective.

The EU notice indicates that a general presumption can be made that non-compete restrictions on a seller for up to three years will be acceptable if either goodwill alone or both goodwill and know-how respectively are involved. The starting point for the types of products and acceptable geographic scope of a restriction is that the restriction should be limited to those products and services and the geographical area where the seller operated before the transaction and not what the purchaser hopes it may develop into. Any legitimate extension beyond those areas is exceptional and will have to be justified by very convincing objective reasons.

The 2005 notice says:

> '20. Non-competition clauses are justified for periods of up to three years, when the transfer of the undertaking includes the transfer of customer loyalty in the form of both goodwill and know-how. When only goodwill is included, they are justified for periods of up to two years.
>
> 21. By contrast, non-competition clauses cannot be considered necessary when the transfer is in fact limited to physical assets (such as land, buildings or machinery) or to exclusive industrial and commercial property rights (the holders of which could immediately take action against infringements by the transferor of such rights).
>
> 22. The geographical scope of a non-competition clause must be limited to the area in which the vendor has offered the relevant products or services before the transfer, since the purchaser does not need to be protected against competition from the vendor in territories not previously penetrated by the vendor. That geographical scope can be extended to territories which the vendor was planning to enter at the time of the transaction, provided that he had already invested in preparing this move.
>
> 23. Similarly, non-competition clauses must remain limited to products (including improved versions or updates of products as well as successor models) and services forming the economic activity of the undertaking transferred. This can include products and services at an advanced stage of development at the time of the transaction, or products which are fully developed but not yet marketed. Protection against competition from the vendor in product or service markets in which the transferred undertaking was not active before the transfer is not considered necessary.'

The notice also looks at restrictions in licence agreements ancillary to mergers. The notice has been incorporated into the 346 document the EU issued in 2010 which contains all EU legislation relating to mergers and is at http://ec.europa.eu/competition/mergers/legislation/merger_compilation.pdf.

If a restriction cannot be considered 'ancillary' because it goes beyond the scope outlined above, and cannot be justified as necessary and directly related to the merger, it risks falling foul of the Competition Act 1998 and/or art 101 of the TFEU. To do so it must have an appreciable effect on trade. In the UK, an agreement will not usually have an appreciable effect if the combined market share of the parties (which can be a localised market, not in the UK as a whole) is less than 25%. For an agreement that will affect the EC, the figure is 10% between competitors and 15% where an agreement between non competitors (under the Commission's de minimis notice, 2014, which replaced the 2001 prior such notice) but no lower threshold if there are certain hard core restrictions such as price fixing under both UK and EU competition law. If it does so fall foul, the parties are open to the risk of being fined up to 10% of turnover, being unable to enforce the restrictions and third parties who have suffered loss can sue for damages.

The EU notice does not include restrictions on the purchaser (for the benefit of the seller) as ancillary. Any such restrictions would therefore have to be separately justified and examined under the Competition Act 1998/art 101 of the TFEU as appropriate. The EU notice is worth considering even if just UK competition law is concerned as the UK Office of Fair Trading (OFT) withdrew its earlier separate UK guidelines OFT 416 on this area, relying instead on the EU guidelines. This appears also to be the position of the Competition and Markets Authority which has adopted other OFT earlier guidelines since it took over from the OFT on 1 April 2014 but not OFT 416.

Case Example – Siemens and Areva JV (2012) EU IP/12/618 18/06/2012

In 2012 the European Commission looked at restrictions and confidentiality clauses in a joint venture between Siemens and Areva. Restrictions 7–10 years after the joint venture terminated were too long and even a negotiated reduction to 5 years after arbitration was also too long. The parties agreed to shorter periods in a settlement with the European Commission. The Commission said:

'On 16 February 2012, Siemens and Areva offered Commitments to the Commission in order to meet the Commission's competition concerns.
— The Parties commit to set aside the post-JV NCO as it was agreed in the Shareholders' Agreement and modified following the arbitral award, and replace it by the following rules.
— The Parties commit to allow Siemens to compete against Areva NP, without any restriction, as from the date at which Siemens lost joint control over Areva NP (ie on 16 October 2009), with the exception of activities directly related to the nuclear island of NPPs ("Areva NP Core Products and Core Services") which are specified in an exhaustive list.
— Competition by Siemens against Areva NP will only be prevented in relation to those Core Products and Core Services for a duration of three years following Areva's acquisition of sole control over Areva NP, and more precisely until 16 October 2012.

(22) Siemens will be prevented from using any confidential information in relation to Core Products and Core Services to which it may have had access during the lifetime of the JV until 16 October 2012. Even beyond that date, Siemens will be prevented from making available to third parties Areva NP's corporate constitution and administration documents or confidential written technical information, or use such technical information.'

Note the three year period above which is consistent with the Commission notice discussed above. In most business sales where knowhow and goodwill are sold as a rule of thumb it is best to ensure non-competition restrictions do not exceed periods of three years. If the client wants a longer period they need to be advised in writing that there is a good chance it will be void and unenforceable. Also if the ambit of the restriction is wider than that needed to protect the position of the buyer of the business and strays into unrelated business areas then specialist advice should be taken from competition solicitors.

Case Example – Cases T-208/13, Portugal Telecom SGPS, SA v Commission, and T-216/13, Telefónica, SA v Commission

Telefónica and PT (Portugal Telecom) the biggest telecoms operators in Spain and Portugal jointly controlled Vivo, one of the largest telecoms operators operating in Brazil. In September 2010, Telefónica agreed to buy out PT's stake in Vivo and the Share Purchase Agreement contained a non-competition clause. This said that to the extent permitted by law the parties would not compete against each other and refrain from competing in the Spanish and Portuguese telecoms markets. This was to last from September 2010 to December 2011. The EU began an investigation so in February 2011 the parties gave up the clause. The EU investigation continued and decided in 2013 that the clause was a market sharing agreement which aimed to restrict competition. It fined Telefónica and PT €67 million and €12 million respectively. The fines were upheld on appeal to the EU's General Court.

It was held that the clause about competition in Spain and Portugal had littled to do with a sale of shares relating to a company in Brazil and went much further than the business disposal in hand. An attempt by the parties to argue this was not a restriction of competition 'by object'. The General Court held there was no obligation on the European Commission to undertake a detailed analysis in this respect. The fact the clause existed meant it was very likely that otherwise the parties might have competed in those two countries.

Although the decision in this case is not surprising it does illustrate how important it is to take specialist competition advice before including non-competition clauses in sale and purchase of shares agreements.

See also June 2016 CJEU press release at http://curia.europa.eu/jcms/upload/docs/application/pdf/2016-06/cp160068en.pdf.

A typical set of restrictive covenants is contained in clause 13 of the precedent share acquisition agreement. The various covenants are separated into different provisions so that if the court finds one covenant unreasonable it may choose to sever this from the agreement leaving the other covenants enforceable.

12.2.13 Pensions

As previously mentioned in relation to due diligence investigations (see Chapter 10, section 10.2), given that the UK state pension scheme does not provide a generous level of benefits even after the Pensions Act 2014 abolition of SP2 and the introduction of the new single tier pension of about £150 a week for those with 35 years of NI contributions, most employers with a substantial staff of stable employees operate a pension scheme providing retirement benefits. As such, the share purchase agreement will need to address the employer's pension arrangements for the target employees.

In cases where there are issues over pensions, an acquisition clearance may be needed from the Pensions Regulator under the Pensions Act 2004 which summarises its clearance role as follows:

Pensions Regulator – clearance

Key points

Clearance is the voluntary process for obtaining a clearance statement from the regulator.

A clearance statement is not approval of a transaction such as an acquisition or merger; rather it gives assurance that we will not use our anti-avoidance powers in relation to that transaction.

Clearance is relevant for those considering corporate transactions or scheme-related events which are materially detrimental to a defined benefit pension scheme and its members (known as 'type A events').

This guidance is primarily aimed at professional advisers, who should bring it to the attention of employers involved in schemes, as well as parties who are connected and associated with employers, and trustees.

The Clearance Guidance is available at: http://www.thepensionsregulator. gov.uk/guidance/guidance-clearance.aspx (June 2009).

Clearance is used where there is a Type A event as defined in the guidance above and includes Detrimental Events. Pensions issues should be raised early on with any proposed acquisition and expert advice sought.

There are many different types of pension scheme (money purchase/defined contribution schemes, final salary/defined benefit schemes and personal pension schemes); see Chapter 10 for further details. The provisions to be included in the share purchase agreement to govern the pension arrangements will vary according to the type of scheme involved and whether that scheme relates solely to the employees of the target company or is a group scheme. In practice, however, most pension issues relate to final salary/defined benefit schemes.

(A)   Occupational money purchase/defined contribution schemes

Apart from the inclusion of warranties confirming that employer and employee contributions have been paid up to date, the amount of the contributions payable, the scheme is compliant with all legal requirements (including the requirements of the Pensions Acts) and the fact that there are no other pension obligations, there is usually no need to include any further contractual provisions as no particular level of benefits is guaranteed under a money purchase scheme.

(B)   Personal pension schemes

As these relate to the individual employee, the only contractual provision usually required is the inclusion of warranties similar to those required for money purchase schemes with the omission of any references to the Pensions Act 1995.

(C)   Final salary/defined benefit schemes

Final salary schemes are much more complicated than either money purchase or personal pension schemes and involve the consideration of a number of key issues and the subsequent inclusion in the share purchase agreement of provisions to document the outcome of negotiation on these issues. In particular, how the pension provisions will be dealt with will depend upon whether the target company's scheme is a stand-alone or a group scheme.

(i)   Stand-alone scheme

Where the target company has its own discrete scheme, the seller has little option but to allow the target to take that scheme with it to the purchaser and the purchaser little option but to accept it, irrespective of the state of its funding.

This principle insofar as it relates to a scheme in surplus follows from the case of *Re Courage Group's Pension Schemes* [1987] 1 WLR 495, where a seller's attempt to separate active members from such a discrete scheme on the sale of their employing company, with a view to retaining the scheme and its considerable surplus for the seller's own benefit, fell foul of the courts. The seller proposed to substitute itself as a new principal company for the original principal company under the scheme prior to the sale of the latter and to pay a transfer value to the purchaser in respect of all the active members while retaining most of the surplus and full liability for the pensioners. The seller had neither employed nor was going to employ the employees of the old principal company, nor had carried on the business, nor was going to carry on the business of that company. The court held that the proposed substitution was unlawful and that the members had the right not to be parted from their scheme and its surplus. Millett J commented that the members were entitled not to be irrevocably parted from the surplus as a result of the unilateral decision of a predator. In other words, the members had a right to be considered in relation to the surplus, even if they did not 'own' it. The case indicates that the court is likely to take an adverse view of any such last minute gerrymandering with pension schemes and members' pension rights on a sale of their employer.

Given the above, if such a discrete scheme is in surplus the seller should adjust the purchase price for the target company to reflect the value which will pass, to avoid handing the purchaser a potential windfall profit. Conversely, if the scheme is in deficit the purchaser should insist that the seller puts money into the scheme to eliminate the deficit prior to completion, or should insist on a reduction in the purchase price to compensate it for the additional funding which it will have to put into the scheme in due course.

However, if the purchase price is to reflect the state of funding of the pension scheme it is essential for both the seller and the purchaser to have an accurate fix on the current state of funding of the scheme. Unfortunately, such is the time-scale for preparation of actuarial valuations for final salary schemes that on any sale and purchase the last available valuation may be an historical snapshot up to three years old. It may therefore be necessary to obtain an interim valuation prior to completion of the transaction if the time constraints of the transaction permit.

In the absence of a recent or interim valuation on which the purchaser feels that it can rely, the purchaser will be driven back to relying on warranties as to the state of funding of the scheme designed to flush out all relevant information and to set up potential claims on the basis of a post-completion valuation. The seller may also look to a post completion upwards adjustment of the purchase price if the post-completion valuation reveals a surplus greater than anticipated. However, if the purchaser suspects that a deficit may exist it may be prudent to build some allowance for this into the purchase price rather than rely solely on post-completion warranty claims.

As actuarial methods of valuation vary from actuary to actuary, it is of fundamental importance to both the seller and the purchaser in providing and relying on warranties as to the level of funding of a final salary scheme for there to be agreement between them as to the actuarial basis and assumptions which will be applied in any post-completion valuation. In particular, it should be remembered that phrases in warranties such as 'the scheme is fully funded' are meaningless unless the bases on which the scheme is to be valued are agreed.

As well as warranties dealing with the state of funding, the purchaser should be seeking a number of other warranties relating to a discrete scheme. These will vary from scheme to scheme depending on the circumstances, but will normally cover the following:

- confirmation that the scheme enjoys exempt approved status for tax purposes and that the seller has not done or omitted to do anything which might prejudice HMRC approval;
- confirmation that the scheme is or is not contracted-out of State Earnings Related Pension Scheme (SERPS) and, where it is contracted-out, confirmation that a current contracting-out certificate is held by the relevant employer;
- confirmation that all contributions to the scheme, premiums, fees and other payments due up to the date of completion have been paid;
- confirmation that there is no self-investment (which includes shares issued by, and loans to, the employing company, and land and buildings leased to the employing company) or that the level of self-investment

> does not exceed the maximum permitted by legislation (5% of the current market value of the scheme's assets);
>
> - confirmation that there are no outstanding claims against the trustees other than routine claims for benefit and that no actions for breach of trust or otherwise are proceeding or pending against the trustees;
> - confirmation that the scheme complies with all relevant statutory and other legal requirements (including the Pensions Act 1995 and associated regulations); and
> - confirmation that the scheme's assets are in the trustees' possession and control.

Where appropriate, an indemnity should also be sought from the seller against potential liabilities of the purchaser under the scheme arising from any failure by the seller to comply with the requirements of art 157 (was art 141) of TFEU during any period prior to completion. This subject is discussed in more detail below.

In some cases clearance from the Pensions Regulator will be necessary as discussed in Chapter 10 and above in this chapter.

(ii) Group scheme

The situation which produces the majority of pension problems is where the target company is a participant in a centralised or group scheme comprising a number of employers, including the target company. This category of transaction includes management buy-outs.

In such circumstances, if the purchaser's aim (or the seller's requirement) is to preserve continuity of pension provision, the purchaser should be seeking a payment from the seller which is sufficient not only to fund the accrued past service benefits of the target employees but also to provide some assistance towards me future costs of providing final salary benefits linked to past pensionable service. For this purpose, the purchaser should seek a covenant from the seller to procure the making of a transfer payment by the trustees of the seller's scheme to the purchaser's nominated scheme in respect of the employees who transfer to that scheme (whether an existing scheme or a new scheme to be established for the benefit of the transferring employees). Before 6 April 1997, any member of an occupational pension scheme whose pensionable service with that scheme terminated after 1 January 1986 and more than 12 months before his normal retirement date had the right to require the trustees of the scheme to apply at the relevant date (namely when the member's pensionable service terminates, or when he makes a relevant application if later) the cash equivalent of the benefits which have accrued to him under the scheme in one or more of a number of prescribed ways, including the acquisition of transfer credits under another scheme. In broad terms, the Pensions Act 1995 extended this statutory right to a cash equivalent to include members who terminated pensionable service before 1 January 1986. It therefore follows that the seller will not be able to avoid payment of a transfer value in respect of members of its pension scheme in the employment of a subsidiary company being sold who elect to transfer their rights to an approved scheme of the purchaser – the debate between the seller and the purchaser therefore is whether transfer values should be paid on the basis determined by statute (ie the cash equivalent basis) or a more generous basis (such as on a past service reserve basis). In addition to the basis of the calculation of the transfer value, the purchaser and the seller must also decide how and when the transfer value is to be calculated and how and when it is to be paid.

Whilst the Occupational Pension Scheme (Preservation of Benefit) Regulations 1991 (SI 1991/167) allow a member's accrued rights under a scheme to be transferred to another occupational pension scheme without his consent provided certain conditions are satisfied, it is normally advisable to obtain the consent of the relevant members before transferring their accrued rights under the seller's scheme to the purchaser's scheme. This is because the member will in any event acquire the right to demand payment of a cash equivalent (as referred to earlier in this section) as there will be a termination of pensionable service, and the member can therefore choose whether he wishes the cash equivalent to be applied in acquiring rights under the purchaser's scheme or in another of the prescribed ways.

There are many ways in which a transfer payment in these circumstances can be calculated, varying from a share of fund basis (ie a share of the seller's scheme's assets proportionate to the liabilities of the scheme passing to the purchaser's scheme) at one end of the scale, to the basic statutory entitlement to the cash equivalent of accrued past service rights at the other. A calculation based on the former will give the purchaser a share of the seller's scheme's surplus (or deficit!) and a calculation based on the latter will leave the whole of any surplus (or deficit) with the seller. It is essential that the basis of calculation of the transfer value which is being proposed by the seller is identified at the earliest possible stage so that the financial and other implications of the proposal can be assessed by the purchaser and his advisers, and any counter-proposals formulated in good time. The proposals, whether the seller's or the purchaser's, are likely to be on one of the following bases.

Cash equivalent

A transfer payment calculated on this basis reflects the value of the members' accrued rights in the seller's scheme based on their salaries and pensionable service up to the agreed transfer date. No allowance is made for any future salary increases for any of the members whether on account of inflation or promotion, nor is any allowance made for discretionary pension increases above those guaranteed by the scheme. This is essentially the sum of the minimum transfer values to which the individual members would be entitled on leaving the seller's scheme.

The definition of 'transfer value' in a pensions clause intended to be a cash equivalent will normally be along the lines of 'the value of the accrued benefits of the transferring members' or 'the aggregate amount of the value of cash equivalents of the transferring members' or 'the aggregate value of the deferred pensions of the transferring members had they left service at completion'. There is, however, an argument that the pensions clauses should provide for the 'transfer value' to be calculated so that the amount for each individual transferring member is the minimum of their cash equivalent. In a money purchase scheme, the cash equivalent is normally the cash value of the member's accumulated pot.

Past service reserve

In a final salary scheme, when a member retires, his benefits in respect of every year of pensionable service are calculated on the basis of his final salary and if the scheme is to be able to pay these benefits it has to accumulate funding in advance over the members' expected pensionable service to meet the expected liabilities. The 'past service reserve' method of calculating a transfer value takes account of the fact that, if the scheme has been properly funded, provision will have been made for the funding of likely future liabilities in respect of past service, arising from anticipated future salary increases whether on account of inflation or promotion. The method differs from the cash equivalent basis in that the value of members' benefits accrued at the agreed transfer date is calculated by reference to anticipated salaries at retirement and may include some allowance for discretionary pension increases. The past service reserve is essentially what the seller's scheme should have accumulated at any particular point in time to provide benefits for the members concerned at normal retirement in respect of their past service.

The wording of a pensions clause providing for a past service reserve transfer payment will typically refer to 'the past service reserve applicable to the transferring employees at completion calculated in accordance with the Actuarial Assumptions (as defined)' or 'the value of the transferring employees' deferred pensions at completion revalued to normal retirement date with an allowance for future salary increases' or 'the value of the accrued projected liabilities of the transferring employees'.

Share of fund

The 'share of fund' basis involves the partitioning of the whole of the scheme's fund between the transferring members and the members remaining in the scheme, in proportion to the value of their respective benefits. Whilst this method of calculation is likely to produce the highest transfer payment if the seller's scheme is in surplus, if that scheme is in deficit a 'share of fund' calculation may result in a smaller transfer payment than the 'past service reserve' or cash equivalent methods. A 'share of fund' clause will include wording to the effect that the transfer payment is to be such proportion of the aggregate value of the scheme assets as the actuarial interests of the transferring members at completion bears to the actuarial interests of all members of the scheme at completion.

Before any basis of calculation can be agreed, the trust deed and rules of the seller's scheme should be examined to see what (if any) basis of calculation is laid down for transfer payments which fall to be made on the sale of a participating company or business. If the trust deed does not permit a 'share of fund' payment but the seller nonetheless wishes to pass across a portion of the scheme's surplus, the seller will have to fund the excess beyond that permitted by the trust deed out of his own resources.

In many trust deeds no basis for calculation of a transfer value is fixed but this is left to the discretion of the principal company or the trustees or the decision of the scheme actuary. In these circumstances, the basis for calculation of the transfer payment can be a matter for negotiation between the seller and the purchaser including the trustees and the actuary (as necessary) and there is no right or wrong approach. However, the comments of Walton J in *Re Imperial Foods Ltd Pension Scheme* [1986] 1 WLR 717 should be noted. In that case, following the sale of two subsidiary companies the purchaser challenged the seller's actuary's decision to calculate the transfer payment from the seller's scheme, which was in considerable surplus on a past service reserve basis, and argued that a share of fund calculation, which would have given the purchaser a share of the surplus, was the proper method. Walton J held that since the past service reserve method of calculation used by the seller's actuary was a method which might properly be adopted by any competent actuary, it could not be attacked. In any event his view, albeit obiter, was that the past service reserve method was the better method of calculation in such circumstances. He also went on to say that a surplus in a scheme to which the employer contributed on a balance of cost basis was best regarded as temporary surplus of funding by the employer, in which the members including the transferring employees had no proprietary right.

Following the *Imperial Foods* case it became common for actuaries instructed to calculate transfer payments to prescribe the past service reserve as the appropriate transfer value, although the impact of the Minimum Funding Requirement has led to a greater use of the cash equivalent basis (possibly plus one or two percentage points by way of uplift). Certainly, restricting the transfer value to a cash equivalent may be seen as parsimonious in the case of a bulk transfer of members following a disposal (although it is appropriate to individual transfers where members leave the scheme of their own accord). A share of fund transfer payment, on the other hand, may be inordinately generous except in cases where there are special overriding reasons, for example, because the seller wishes, in a management buy-out situation, to pay across a share of the surplus to enable the purchaser to minimise its pension costs in its start-up phase.

Irrespective of which basis for calculation of the transfer payment is adopted, the actuarial assumptions which are to apply for the purpose of making the calculation should be agreed between the actuaries on both sides and recorded in writing. This is frequently done by means of a letter exchanged between the two actuaries, (so-called 'actuary's letter'), attached to the pension schedule to the acquisition agreement. If clearance from the Pensions Regulator is required that should be attached too. 'Clearance' is the word used to describe the voluntary process of obtaining a clearance statement from the Pensions Regulator. This gives comfort that on the basis of the information provided, the regulator will not use its anti-avoidance powers to issue, to the applicants for clearance, either contribution notices or financial support directions in relation to a defined benefit occupational pension scheme and a particular event. Events include transactions, agreements, decisions, other acts and failures to act.

Whilst the method of calculation of the transfer payment is obviously the principal issue in a sale of a subsidiary company or business, there are a number of other important areas which need to be addressed by the seller and the purchaser. These are normally the subject of a schedule to the acquisition agreement and the following points are usually covered.

Continued temporary participation in the seller's scheme

Unless few employees are involved or the purchaser has a ready-made scheme, the purchaser will frequently want the employees of the target company or business to remain members of the seller's scheme for a period after the completion of the acquisition. HMRC are prepared to permit such continued participation for a period of up to two years. This period, often known as the interim period, is needed: (i) to allow the purchaser sufficient time to establish a new scheme for the transferring employees; or (ii) where the purchaser has an existing scheme, to allow the employees to consider whether they wish to transfer their rights under the seller's scheme to the purchaser's new scheme.

Seller shortfall provision

As the assets from which the transfer payment will be made will be under the control of the trustees of the seller's scheme, who are very unlikely to have been party to the acquisition agreement, the pensions schedule will be worded in such a way as to require the seller to procure or to use best endeavours to procure the making of the transfer payment to the purchaser's scheme by the trustees. However, the seller will not be in a position to compel the trustees to pay over the agreed transfer payment and they might refuse to do so if, for example, they considered the proposed sum to exceed the maximum permitted by the trust deed or to be inappropriate for other reasons. In these circumstances, the purchaser would have no right of action against the trustees. Accordingly, the purchaser should seek the inclusion in the pension schedule of a shortfall guarantee by the seller to the effect that it will make good any deficiency between the amount received from the trustees of the seller's scheme and the amount due under the acquisition agreement. This would extend to the whole of the transfer payment if no payment at all was forthcoming from the trustees.

On account payment

Commonly the purchaser may seek the inclusion in the pensions schedule of a provision allowing some advance payment on account of the transfer amount pending its final calculation. The calculation and verification of the transfer payment by the respective actuaries will often take a considerable time, and in the meantime if no on account payment is made the purchaser's scheme may find itself with an immediate cash flow problem. This may be a particular difficulty for new management buy-out companies.

Late payment of transfer amount

The pensions schedule should provide for a mechanism for the transfer payment to be increased between completion and actual payment (if calculated as at completion) or between the date on which the members transfer from the seller's scheme to the purchaser's scheme ('the transfer date') and actual payment (if calculated as at the transfer date). This can be, for example, by increasing the transfer payment by a specified rate of interest, or indexing the payment in line with an external index (for example the FT Actuaries Ali-Share Index), or increasing the payment by the average yield secured on the assets of the seller's scheme during the period concerned.

Equalisation indemnity

The judgment of the European Court of Justice on 17 May 1990 in the case of *Barber v Guardian Royal Exchange Assurance Group* C-262/88, [1991] 1 QB 344 established that pensions are pay for the purposes of art 157 (previously art 141 and before that art 119) of TFEU (the EC Treaty) and must therefore be equal between men and women.

A number of issues arising out of the *Barber* judgment were clarified by the European Court of Justice in subsequent judgments, including the *Ten Oever* case (*Ten Oever v Stichting Bedrijfspensioenfonds voor het Glazenwassers-en Schoonmaakbedrijf* C-109/91, [1993] ECR 1-4879) where the ECJ decided that equalisation was only required for benefits attributable to service after 17 May 1990, the date of the *Barber* judgment.

The other outstanding issues were decided by the ECJ in a series of judgments delivered on 28 September 1994, including *Coloroll Pension Trustees Ltd v Russell* [1994] ECR 1-4389. The most significant of these was that in the event of a transfer of pension rights from one occupational pension scheme to another in respect of an employee who changes jobs, including where a sale of a company or business occurs, the 'receiving' scheme is required to increase the benefits payable to the employee under that scheme to eliminate the effects of any failure by the 'transferring' scheme to equalise benefits for post-May 1990 service.

Directive 2004/113/EC prohibits all discrimination based on sex in the access to and supply of goods and services. An EU ruling in March 2011 said that 'the directive prohibits the use of gender as a factor in the calculation of insurance premiums and benefits in relation to insurance contracts entered into after 21 December 2007'. (*Test-Achats* ASBL *and others v Conseil des ministres* [2011] All ER (D) 07 (Mar)). A transitional period was allowed under the judgment. However from 21 December 2012, it has been unlawful to use sex-specific factors when determining both premiums and benefits under insurance products.

Sections 67–71 of the Equality Act 2010 and Equality Act 2010 (Sex Equality Rule) (Exceptions) Regulations 2010 provide for equal treatment in the area of pensions. They superseded an equal treatment rule provided for by ss 62–66 of the Pensions Act 1995. These contain general requirements for equal treatment in relation to pension schemes. These equal treatment requirements relate not only to the terms on which scheme members are treated, but also the terms on which employees are admitted to membership. It should be noted that these requirements are overriding so that schemes must comply with them irrespective of the actual provisions of their governing documentation. In fact, the legislation contains provisions which empower trustees of schemes with an inadequate amendment power to make whatever rule amendments necessary to ensure compliance with the equal treatment requirements. As a result of the above, unless the purchaser is completely satisfied that full equalisation has been effected under the seller's scheme for post May-1990 service and the transfer payment has been calculated on this basis, the purchaser should seek an indemnity from the seller against any additional liabilities the purchaser's scheme incurs by reason of failure to equalise post-May 1990 benefits under the seller's scheme.

One area that has attracted renewed attention recently in relation to equalisation is the issue of guaranteed minimum pensions (GMPs). Prior to 6 April 1997, if a scheme was contracted out of SERPS on a salary-related basis, the rules of the scheme had to provide for the member, and, if applicable, the member's spouse to be entitled to a pension not less than a guaranteed minimum. This guaranteed minimum, or GMP, is payable for life and must commence generally no later than the state pension age (which is now 65 for women and men but due to increase to 66, then 67 and then 68 in due course). The consensus view has been that there is a requirement for GMPs to be equalised. This issue was brought to the fore again when, in a case called *Williamson v Sedgwick Group Pension Scheme Trustee Ltd* (No 0000424, HC), the Pensions Ombudsman directed that the trustees should equalise GMPs in compliance with the equal treatment rules. Although the Pensions Ombudsman's general equalisation direction to the Trustees was set aside on appeal by Mr Justice Rimer, the main reason for doing so appears to have been largely connected with the scope of the Ombudsman's jurisdiction. It is, therefore, very unlikely that Mr Justice Rimer's decision has drawn a line under the GMP equalisation issue.

In January 2011 the Pension Protection Fund (PPF) published a second consultation on GMP. The PPF said they were legally required to equalise GMPs between men and women and the consultation paper sets out their chosen method.

See http://www.plsa.co.uk/Policy-and-Research/Defined-Benefit/GMPs.

The statement on GMP Equalisation states:

'GMPs are inherently unequal, but the way that they are paid is set in law. Therefore, equalising GMPs is an impossible task. Depending on when a member leaves service and when he or she begins to draw benefits, he or she may be better or worse off than the opposite sex. Who is better off will vary from year to year. The DWP [The Department for Work and Pensions] has suggested that schemes measure the benefits in payment each year and pay each member the better of the benefits due the member as a man or as a woman. This would be cumbersome and expensive and result in a windfall for members. NAPF is working with the Government to come up with legislation that will make it easier to convert GMPs to scheme benefits, which can then be equalised more easily.'

GMP equalisation will be applied to both PPF and Financial Assistance Scheme compensation for members in the assessment period and for members already receiving compensation. However, the PPF said its calculations were not intended to be a model for the rest of the industry. See http://www.pensionprotectionfund. org.uk/News/Pages/details.aspx?itemID=208.

'Part-time employee' indemnity

On 28 September 1994, the European Court of Justice (ECJ) held in the *Vroege* case *(Vroege v NCIV Instituut voor Volkshuisvesting BV* C-57/93 [1995] All ER (EC)) under English Law that the right to join an occupational pension scheme falls within the scope of art 157 (previously art 141 and before that art 119) of TFEU (the EC Treaty) and that the exclusion of part-time employees from a scheme may therefore amount to indirect sex discrimination if the part-time workforce comprises significantly more women than men (or vice versa) and the exclusion cannot be justified on objective grounds.

In its decision the ECJ went on to say that the limitation of the effect of the *Barber* judgment to post-May 1990 service referred to above did not apply in the case of claims made by part-time employees who rely on the principle in the *Vroege* case. The issue of how far back part-time employees can under English Law claim the right to be admitted to scheme membership following the *Vroege* decision has been the subject of a considerable amount of case law and debate in the last few years, culminating in hearings before the House of Lords and the ECJ in a series of test cases commonly referred to as *Preston v Wolverhampton Healthcare NHS Trust (No 2)* [2001] UKHL 5. The series of cases culminated in a House of Lords decision (following a referral to the ECJ) handed down in early 2001. The last House of Lords judgment considered the effectiveness of s 2(4) and (5) of the then Equal Pay Act 1970. Any claim in respect of the operation of an equality clause must, if it is not to be time barred, be brought during the course of employment or within six months following the termination of employment and there are limits in relation to retrospective claims. In the case the House of Lords held that the six-month time limit for bringing a claim as set out in s 2(4) of the Equal Pay Act 1970 (the Act in force at the time) was acceptable but that the two-year rule in regulations could not be relied on to prevent employees from retrospectively gaining membership back to 8 April 1976 (the date of the decision in the case of *Defrenne v Sabena No 2* [1981] All ER 122n) in which the ECJ ruled for the first time that art 141 had direct effect, ie it was enforceable by a private individual).

Given the above and the decision in the *Coloroll* case that the receiving scheme has to meet any shortfall in a transfer payment occasioned by the failure of the transferring scheme to comply with equalisation requirements under art 141, the purchaser will normally seek an indemnity from the seller against such claims. This will, of course, only be relevant where the transferring employees include part- timers who have been excluded from membership of the seller's scheme for any period of service where the seller's part-time workforce is comprised mainly of one sex, and the exclusion cannot be objectively justified.

Section 75 indemnity

Where the target company is a participant in a centralised or group scheme, the purchaser will often ask for what is known as a section 75 indemnity. As mentioned in Chapter 10, s 75 of the Pensions Act 1995 and the Occupational Pensions Schemes (Deficiency on Winding-Up etc) Regulations 1996 (SI 1996/3128) broadly provide that in certain circumstances (such as the winding-up of a scheme or the insolvency of an employer) employers can become liable to trustees of the scheme for a proportion of any deficit in that scheme. Also in a share purchase there may be closed or discontinued arrangements operated for the benefit of former employees under which the target company may have such a residual liability. To protect against such possibilities, the purchaser will normally seek an indemnity from the seller against any s 75 liability that the target company may have.

(D) Position of other interested parties

Where a transfer payment is to be made from a seller's scheme to a purchaser's scheme following the sale of a participating company in a seller's group pension scheme, the potentially conflicting rights and obligations of a number of other persons who are not parties to the share purchase agreement should be borne in mind when the pensions provisions of the agreement are being negotiated, to ensure that the provisions are capable of implementation in the form agreed and without argument.

The trustees of the seller's scheme will be under a duty to ensure that the terms of the trust deed are adhered to in the calculation and payment of the transfer value irrespective of the provisions of the share purchase agreement. This principle is illustrated by the case of *Stannard v Fisons Pension Trust Ltd* [1992] IRLR 27. The Fisons trustees made a transfer payment which complied with the terms of the acquisition agreement but was challenged by a number of transferring employees on the grounds that it was not in accordance with the trust deed and rules of the scheme. In particular, it was the employees' contention that the trustees should have had regard to a change in the scheme's funding position between completion of the sale and the date on which the trustees authorised the making of the transfer payment. The Court of Appeal found for the transferring employees and held that the trustees should have taken the change in circumstances into account. The significance of the case is therefore that trustees should, when determining the amount of a transfer payment, base their decision on the terms of the trust deed and any other relevant facts even if this conflicts with the acquisition agreement.

The trustees of the seller's scheme will also be under an obligation to ensure that the interests of the remaining members of the seller's scheme are not prejudiced by the amount of the transfer payments, and to be even-handed in their approach towards both categories of members.

The trustees of the purchaser's scheme (if an existing scheme) will have to satisfy themselves that the interests of the existing members of that scheme will not be harmed by the proposed transfer arrangements. For example, if the amount of the transfer payment to be made to the purchaser's scheme is insufficient to fund the benefits the purchaser has agreed to provide, the trustees will be reluctant or unwilling to accept the transfer payment and grant the benefits promised by the purchaser without the purchaser's agreement to fund the shortfall over an agreed period.

The remaining members of the seller's scheme, comprising both active members and current and deferred pensioners, will be concerned that their benefits or expectations will not suffer a reduction because of the transfer (eg because surplus which might otherwise be available for improvement of their benefits is being transferred out of the scheme).

Finally, the transferring members will want to be assured that the value of their past service benefits will be preserved in the purchaser's scheme and that the benefits to be provided under the purchaser's scheme for future service compare with the benefits which would have been provided in the seller's scheme. They will also be concerned as to the level of contributions they will be required to pay and if this is higher than under the seller's scheme, whether the benefits provided are correspondingly greater. They will invariably have particular concerns about possible redundancies following a sale and may look for a commitment from the purchaser for enhanced early leaver benefits in this situation.

12.2.14 Boilerplate provisions

In the introduction to Part III it was mentioned that the form of acquisition agreements has become standardised over the years. An integral part of this standardisation has been the role of numerous 'boilerplate' provisions at the end of the agreement. Some of the more commonplace provisions are discussed below.

(A) Alterations to the acquisition agreement

An agreement which is not required to be in writing or evidenced in writing can be varied by the oral agreement of the parties. Accordingly, to reduce the scope for future argument it has become common to insert a provision of the kind found in clause 15.3 of the precedent share purchase agreement. It is arguable that this right is overridden where this clause is included, but the effectiveness of this clause is not beyond doubt because logically it too should be capable of being orally varied.

(B)   Applicable law

In order to determine what is the governing or applicable law of a contract, an English court must apply the provisions of the Rome I Regulation 593/2008 on choice of law in contractual matters which enables them largely to choose which laws apply (as between two EU companies) by contract terms and sets out how choice of law is determined in cases where no choice of law is indicated.

It is normal practice to include in any agreement a clause stating the governing law. Two reasons for the invariable inclusion of this clause are:

- the express selection of a governing law is obviously important where the agreement has any international elements, such as where any of the parties are foreign, where the country in which the contract is negotiated or made is abroad, where the subject matter of the contract (eg goods) or the country where the contract is to be performed is abroad. However, the question of which law governs a contract may fall to be decided by a court overseas (for example, if a party moves overseas). There must be a clear direction to any court before which the contract comes that it is governed by English law; and
- in the absence of an agreed choice of governing law, the court must apply the complicated tests laid down in art 4 of the Convention. These tests can be very difficult to apply to the facts of any particular case and it is always in the interest of the parties that it should not be necessary for any court to refer to art 4. This can only be done by a clear governing law clause.

After Brexit in 2019 the position is as yet unclear as to the application of the Rome Regulation (and its accompanying recast Brussels regulation on choice of jurisdiction). It is likely a similar arrangement will be in place.

Many lawyers have given their views on this subject including this article from Brick Court Chambers, barristers, specialising in EU law – https://brexit.law/2016/07/27/contractual-proper-law-and-brexit-back-to-the-rome-convention-by-default/.

(C)   Confidentiality

An obligation to keep matters confidential is legally binding under English law. However, it may be difficult to obtain a remedy for breach of a confidentiality obligation since there may be no loss caused by the breach. In appropriate cases breach may be restrained by injunction. In addition restrictions on press releases about the deal are usually included.

(D)   Counterparts

To overcome the practical difficulties of signatories to contracts not being in the same place at the same time, a clause in the form of clause 15.8 of the precedent share purchase agreement should be included in the agreement. This enables the parties to sign separate but identical copies of the document. The counterparts should be dated with the same date, which should be the date when the last counterpart was signed or such later date as the parties agree to be the date on which the agreement is to be treated as exchanged.

Where there are two or more copies of an agreement, each executed by one or more, but not all, of the parties, they may (depending on the nature of the transaction) be read together and treated as one document. This clause confirms that rule provided that all parties sign.

(E) Entire agreement

The effectiveness of an old style 'entire agreement' clause is not free from doubt following the decision in *Thomas Witter Ltd v TBP Industries Ltd* [1996] 2 All ER 573 (see Chapter 12, section 12.2.11). However, as long as the clause is well worded it will add value to the transaction and legal protection of the parties.

(F) Further assurance

To provide a remedy against the other party who refuses to do something to fulfil the agreement and to provide a remedy against the other party when a third party refuses to do something to fulfil the agreement, the share purchase agreement will typically include a provision in the form of clause 16.8 of the precedent share purchase agreement (Part VI, Precedent F).

There is uncertainty as to the extent of this clause's ambit. Clearly it would cover specific actions on the part of any party referred to in the agreement itself. Hence, the future obligations of the parties should be referred to in the agreement as specifically as possible.

(G) Jurisdiction

The purpose of a jurisdiction clause is to provide, by agreement, for a jurisdiction where any one of the parties to the agreement may bring legal proceedings against any other party to the agreement. If any party is registered in, or centrally controlled or managed in, a European State which is party to the Brussels or Lugano Convention, the use of a jurisdiction clause will prevent that party from asserting that the courts of the agreed jurisdiction (assumed to be the English courts) will not have jurisdiction to determine any dispute and that such party cannot insist on the claim being determined in the courts of its domicile. Within the 28 EU States the EU Brussels Regulation 44/2001 also ensures a choice of jurisdiction clause will be respected when the matter is litigated in the EU. Jurisdiction clauses fall broadly into one of two categories, so far as each party is concerned:

- non-exclusive – a non-exclusive jurisdiction clause provides that the courts of the named State shall have jurisdiction but that, in addition,

      if one party can establish jurisdiction elsewhere, the courts of that other
      State also have jurisdiction; and

- exclusive – an exclusive jurisdiction clause provides that the courts of the named State are the only courts which have jurisdiction.

As stated above under (B) Applicable Law 2019 Brexit is likely to have an effect in relation to this area.

(H)   Contracts (Rights of Third Parties) Act 1999

The law in relation to contractual rights of third parties has recently been reformed to align English law with that of many European and other countries. The Contracts (Rights of Third Parties) Act 1999, which came into force on 11 November 1999, removed the doctrine of 'privity of contract' (someone who is not a party to a contract cannot bring an action under the contract).

The Act sets out the circumstances in which a third party has a right to enforce a term of the contract. For the Act to apply, the third party must be identified in the contract by name, class or description. A term of a contract can then be enforced by the third party where the contract expressly so provides, and where a term purports to confer a benefit on the third party (and on construction it appears that the parties intended him to have the right to enforce it).

Therefore, where no third party rights are intended to be in a contract, the parties should expressly state the position so as to avoid unintentionally conferring rights on them. This is the approach adopted in the precedent share purchase agreement (Part VI, Precedent F).

The remedies available to a person bringing a claim for breach of contract are now also available to third parties.

Where a third party has rights or benefits under a contract, the contracting parties may not rescind or vary the contract in a way which alters the third party's rights without his consent. This applies where the third party has relied on the term or if the parties could have reasonably foreseen that he would rely on the term. It also applies, subject to the terms of the contract, where the third party has assented to the term.

Although the Act applies to all contracts governed by English law, contracts entered into before 11 May 2000 will not be subject to the Act unless the parties elect that the provisions apply immediately.

Some sale of business agreements expressly use provisions of the Act to give greater rights to third parties to sue. Typically a very strong buying company may reserve the right not only to sue the individual director shareholders for breach of warranty but also the company (on an asset sale) and perhaps will expressly enable not only the buyer but its directors, shareholders and other group companies to sue if there is a breach. Although those various litigants cannot recover twice for any loss under the Act sellers will not want the risk of multiple litigants and should resist such provisions where possible.

12.2.15 Execution

As there is no legal requirement for an agreement relating to the sale and purchase of a company (or a business) to be in written form, never mind in the form of a deed, for the reasons mentioned above the terms of the sale and purchase are normally incorporated into an agreement which is executed as such. However, the purchaser may prefer to incorporate provisions which could comfortably sit within the acquisition agreement in a separate document (for example, tax indemnity or restrictive covenants) so as to enable the purchaser to seek enforcement of a specific seller obligation without the issue being clouded by other aspects of the sale and purchase arrangements. To avoid the question of lack of consideration for the specific obligation, a purchaser will typically incorporate the obligation in a deed which has the benefit of being enforceable in the absence of consideration.

The distinction between deeds and agreements is important since additional formalities are required for the execution of deeds. If these are not followed a deed may not be enforceable. Since the Law of Property (Miscellaneous Provisions) Act 1989, to be a deed the document must be clear on the face of it that it is intended to be a deed and it must be validly executed. The means of validly executing a deed will vary depending on whether the executing party is an individual or a company.

To be validly executed by an individual the deed must be signed either by the maker in the presence of a witness or at the maker's direction in the presence of two witnesses, and in both cases the witnesses should not be parties to the deed. In the case of a company, deeds may be executed either by affixing its common seal which will be governed by the maker's articles of association, or by two directors or a director and a secretary of the company signing the document and expressing it to be executed by the company or since parts of CA 2006 came into force one director who signs in the presence of a witness (unless the company's articles require two directors). CA 2006 removed the legal requirement that a company must have a company secretary and as many companies are one director companies and have no seal the rules on executions of deeds therefore had to be changed in consequence. The Regulatory Reform (Execution of Deeds and Documents) Order 2005 (SI 2005/1906) also made some changes in this area and in particular requires that where one individual signs on behalf of several companies of which he or she is a director he or she must sign each time separately not once for each company.

Once executed, the deed will not be effective until it has been delivered. In the sale and purchase context, under CA 2006, s 44, the deed is presumed to have been delivered on execution. Therefore a seller not wishing to create an enforceable deed upon signature should consider delivery in escrow or making it clear to the purchaser that the company does not intend the document to be treated as delivered until it is handed over by the company's agent. The statutory presumption only applies to deeds. The time an agreement is entered into by the parties is a question of fact determined by evidence.

For execution by foreign companies, see the Overseas Companies (Execution of Documents and Registration of Charges) Regulations 2009 (SI 2009/1917). Sealing is no longer required. The document may be executed by the foreign company in any manner allowed by the laws of its country of incorporation for the execution of documents (including executing under its common seal if it has one). No witness has to be present. If the document has to take effect as a deed, this must be made clear on its face. Calling the document a deed should be enough, but for good measure the words 'as a deed' should be included in the testimonium clause.

Chapter 13

Business transfer agreement

13.1   INTRODUCTION

Business transfers are substantially different from share sales and purchases, both in their form and content. This is particularly the case in business transfers involving the retention by the seller of all liabilities and the selection by the purchaser of the assets it will acquire.

A precedent business transfer agreement is set out in Part VI as Precedent H, and caters for the acquisition of a business as a going concern by a corporate purchaser from a corporate seller for a consideration to be satisfied in cash.

It is very important for a client to determine if they will buy assets or shares very early on in any proposed transaction. If a change of mind occurs then the drafting must begin from scratch with a very different form of agreement. With less sophisticated clients often some effort needs to be expended in explaining the differences between assets sale and share purchase. They also must obtain good tax advice before committing to one or the other.

13.2   BUSINESS TRANSFER AGREEMENT

There follows a discussion on the provisions found in a typical business transfer agreement. As some of these provisions are common to a share purchase agreement and have already been discussed in Chapter 12 in relation to that agreement, this section is accordingly much shorter and concentrates on those provisions which are novel to a business transfer or are otherwise a variation to the equivalent provision in a typical share purchase agreement.

13.2.1　Definitions and interpretation

The assets and liabilities to be transferred to and assumed by the purchaser should be clearly defined. To reduce the risk of a subsequent dispute as to whether a particular item was intended to be transferred, the draftsperson should consider supplementing general words in any definition with a list of the specific assets/liabilities which are to be included in that definition. For example, the definition of 'Equipment' in sub-clause 1.1 of the precedent business transfer agreement refers to 'all plant, machinery, tools … owned or used by the Seller … including those items details of which are set out in annexure A'.

In particular, the definition of 'Contracts' to be taken over by the purchaser needs careful consideration to ensure that potentially wide and unquantifiable liability is not imposed on it unless the commercial deal struck with the seller requires that to be the case.

13.2.2　Conditions

As a business transfer involves the transfer of each individual asset comprising the business to be bought and sold, the likelihood of having to obtain prior approvals and consents is significantly increased.

The approvals and consents required by the seller and/or the target which typically give rise to the need to include conditions are set out in Part II (see Chapter 10, section 10.2.4). Of these, the need to obtain landlord's consent to the assignment of leasehold property used by the target for the purposes of its business is a common problem in business transfers in view of the time it takes to obtain that approval; this is discussed in more detail below together with another condition peculiar to business transfers.

(A)　Landlord's consent

The moral is either to obtain the licence to assign prior to exchange of contracts or, if for some reason of commercial expediency this is undesirable or impossible, to allow adequate time for the licence to be obtained before the contract can be rescinded. For this reason a fixed completion date may be inappropriate, and it may be better to provide for completion, say, three business days after the licence has been obtained with an outside date of, say, three months before the contract can be rescinded.

The second point is the ease of obtaining the landlord's consent. If the lease contains a qualified covenant against assignment (ie not to assign the lease without the landlord's consent), such consent cannot be unreasonably withheld (s 19 of the Landlord and Tenant Act 1927). This means that the landlord has to show reasonable grounds for not believing that the assignee will be capable of paying the rent and performing the tenant's covenants in the lease. In addition, under the provisions of the Landlord and Tenant Act 1988, where there is a qualified covenant against assignment the landlord owes a duty to the tenant, on an application for a licence to assign, to give his decision within a reasonable time and in writing and, if the consent is conditional, to set out the conditions and if the consent is withheld, to set out the reasons. Any conditions imposed must also be reasonable. This legislation has placed an onus on the landlord to deal with licences to assign with more speed and allows tenants to be able to claim damages should the licence be unreasonably refused or delayed. With this in mind, it is sensible at the time of making the request for consent, to expressly state any timetable for assignment to put the landlord on notice of time constraints. This will assist in establishing whether or not the landlord dealt with the request in a reasonable period of time, given his knowledge of the timing that the seller and purchaser were working to. The provision of unqualified references on the assignee from a bank, current or past landlord, solicitor or accountant and a trade reference should be sufficient to persuade the landlord to grant a licence to assign, provided those references raise no doubt about the ability of the purchaser to pay the rent and any other outgoings reserved under the lease. There is no reason why all or most of these references should not be obtained in advance of, or immediately after, exchange of contracts, and in the authors' view the purchaser should be put under a positive obligation to obtain them within a stated period of exchange. The difficulty with this from the purchaser's point of view is that he cannot force his bank or anyone else to write a satisfactory reference, or any reference, within a stated time. On the other hand, if the purchaser is not under such an obligation he effectively has an option as to whether to proceed to completion, since if he fails to obtain satisfactory references he can be reasonably certain that a licence to assign will be refused. Possibly a reasonable compromise would be to oblige the purchaser to provide the seller on exchange with the names of not less than three referees, and then to oblige the seller to use his best endeavours to obtain the landlord's licence to assign and, if necessary, to provide a guarantee from a bank or directors or a rent deposit.

One of the common problems with providing satisfactory references is where the purchaser is a new or recently formed company with no accounts or references to provide enough information for the landlord to reasonably make a decision on the request for consent. In these circumstances something more than the customary references will need to be provided to persuade a landlord, and to successfully argue that consent has been unreasonably refused in the light of the information made available. The type of additional information that might be necessary will depend on the circumstances and the nature of the tenant's business. It may be necessary to provide a business plan or details of projected profit forecasts with supporting information to satisfy the landlord.

If the lease had been granted on or after 1 January 1996 and is subject to the Landlord and Tenant (Covenants) Act 1995, the lease provisions for assignment may contain an absolute prohibition against assignment in which case s 19(1) of the Landlord and Tenant Act 1927 and the Landlord and Tenant Act 1988 will not apply. More commonly, particularly for long-term leases granted on or after 1 January 1996, the lease will set out stringent conditions for a permitted assignment which the purchaser is unlikely to fulfil. The agreement should therefore set out provision for the purchaser to provide additional security, for example by guarantee, whether by a bank or an individual, a rent deposit and any other security required by the landlord. From a purchaser's point of view, the agreement should contain a provision for the seller to enter into an 'Authorised Guarantee Agreement' under s 16 of the Landlord and Tenant (Covenants) Act 1995. In addition, the parties should consider whether to enter into an underlease as an alternative to an assignment. Commonly, leases that fall within the 1995 Act will contain less stringent underletting provisions because the landlord will not in such cases lose a seller's covenant. The seller should not agree to complete an assignment without the landlord's consent as this would mean that the assignment falls outside the 1995 Act and the seller will continue to have liabilities under the lease.

Whether or not the lease is granted on or after 1 January 1996, the agreement should be drafted so as not to prejudice the condition that, if in the event the landlord's licence to assign or underlet is refused, either side may rescind the agreement in whole or, where appropriate, to the extent that it relates to the business operating from the property for which the landlord's licence is refused. A further point in connection with leases, and one which is easily overlooked, is the question of costs. It is common for a contract for the assignment of leasehold premises to provide that the assignee shall pay the tenant's legal costs, including the landlord's costs, in granting (or withholding) its consent. Many leases of commercial premises provide that the landlord's costs in dealing with any application for a licence under a lease shall be met by the tenant. It is not, however, usual for the purchaser of a business to be made responsible for the seller's costs and if it is desired that the purchaser should at least bear the costs of the application to the landlord, the agreement should so provide.

Tenants occupying premises for business purposes are entitled to security of tenure provided by the Landlord and Tenant Act 1954, Part II, unless such security has been excluded by agreement and the agreement has been approved by the court. Where the 1954 Act has not been excluded and the lease is therefore protected, the tenant has statutory rights to renew the lease on expiry. The terms on which a protected lease is renewed can either be agreed between the parties or, in the absence of agreement, determined by the court. There are a number of grounds set out in the Act on which a landlord can seek to rely to persuade a court that the tenant's lease should not be renewed, but instead should be brought to an end to allow the landlord to regain possession. In cases where the landlord does oppose renewal in this way and the court is precluded from ordering a new tenancy for certain of the statutory grounds which do not involve default by the tenant, statutory compensation for disturbance may be due to the tenant from the landlord. At present, the level of compensation is equivalent to the rateable value of the premises, unless during the 14-year period preceding termination of the tenancy the premises have been occupied by the tenant (or its predecessor in title under the lease but for the same business as that carried on by the original tenant), in which case the current level of statutory compensation is twice the rateable value. It is therefore necessary to assign the goodwill of the business as well as any lease in order to preserve the right to compensation at the higher rate.

(B) Independent valuation

If the purchaser is a public company and proposes to satisfy the consideration payable by the issue of shares in itself, the transaction will be subject to an additional condition from the purchaser's point of view that the business and assets being transferred in consideration of the allotment of shares have been independently valued pursuant to CA 2006, ss 593, 596, 1150 and 1151 and a report regarding value has been made to the purchaser by an independent person within six months preceding the allotment.

13.2.3   Sale and purchase

The principal provision of the business transfer agreement will be the clause identifying those assets and liabilities to be transferred to the purchaser (clause 4 in the precedent business transfer agreement). It has become common practice not only to identify the assets to be sold and purchased in such a clause but also to identify those assets and liabilities to be retained by the seller.

Assuming that a business is being sold as a going concern and the intention is for the purchaser to take over all of the assets used in the business and all liabilities relating to the business, the business transfer may involve the sale and purchase of the following individual assets and the assumption of the following liabilities:

Assets:	*Liabilities:*
contracts	burden of contracts
debtors	creditors
fixtures and fittings	product/service warranty claims goodwill
hire-purchase and leasing agreements	
intellectual property rights	
investments	
motor vehicles	
office furniture and equipment	
premises	
plant and machinery	
stocks of raw materials, work in progress and finished goods	

Even where the parties intend for all the assets and the liabilities of the business to be transferred to the purchaser, on closer analysis of the benefits of doing so the parties may conclude that there is no benefit in transferring any cash held by the target or the balance of the target company's bank accounts, debtors and creditors of the business and tax liabilities of the seller in relation to the business.

Some of the key assets to be transferred and liabilities to be assumed are discussed below.

(A)   Premises

Although it is not proposed to discuss questions of title, nevertheless for most businesses their premises are fundamental to their ability to be sold as a going concern. Consequently, if title cannot be deduced to the premises, or the landlord's consent to assignment cannot be obtained, the contract should make clear that the purchaser may rescind and recover any deposit so that there can be no doubt that he may not be obliged to buy the remainder of the assets. The same consideration may be true of other assets where in the particular circumstances of the case monetary compensation will not suffice.

Except where the premises are leasehold and the lease obliges the landlord to insure and further provides for abatement of rent in the case of the destruction of, or damage to, the premises, the purchaser should be reminded to insure the premises and other business assets to be acquired from the moment of exchange of contracts since the risk will, in the absence of agreement to the contrary, or an apparent different intention, pass to the purchaser on exchange of contracts and the purchaser should therefore immediately take out appropriate insurance (ss 18 and 27 of the Sale of Goods Act 1979). Even where the premises are leasehold and the landlord is obliged to insure, full abatement of rent may not cover the whole loss where the purchaser is paying a premium for leasehold premises to reflect an actual rent below current market value. In this case, additional cover should be arranged on exchange of contracts. In any event the purchaser should try to have its interest noted on the landlord's policy.

(B)   Plant and machinery

The transfer of plant and machinery typically involves consideration of three principal issues.

(i)   Identification

As mentioned in section 13.2.1, to reduce the risk of a subsequent dispute as to whether a particular item of plant and machinery was intended to be transferred it is important that a detailed list of all known items of plant and machinery to be transferred is drawn up, agreed by the seller and the purchaser and included as part of the definition of plant and machinery.

(ii)   Exclusion of implied covenants of title

The Sale of Goods Act 1979 applies to every contract for the sale of goods and implies conditions into the sale contract. For the 1979 Act purposes, 'goods' are defined as all personal chattels, other than things in action and money, but excluding things attached to or forming part of the land unless agreed to be severed before the sale or under the acquisition agreement. Accordingly, the 1979 Act may apply to the assets to be transferred as part of the business transfer.

The implied conditions likely to be relevant to a business transfer include the implied undertaking as to title (Sale of Goods Act 1979, s 12), the implied condition that goods sold by description (which would, for example, include an inventory of plant and machinery) correspond to that inventory (s 13) and the implied condition of fitness for purpose (s 14).

Sellers often seek to exclude liability under the 1979 Act insofar as they may have any and insofar as they may be permitted to do so by virtue of the Unfair Contract Terms Act 1977. On the other hand, purchasers usually seek to supplement the implied covenants by seeking contractual warranties regarding title, fitness for purpose and condition of plant and machinery to be transferred to it. The Consumer Rights Act 2015 applies where liability as against consumers (who may be individual sellers on an asset sale) is excluded.

(iii) Third party rights

Most businesses have certain plant and machinery subject to hire-purchase or leasing agreements. Unless the contract otherwise provides, and unless the owner of the goods agrees, the liabilities under such an agreement will remain with the seller who may have no further use for the equipment in question. Assuming therefore that the purchaser wishes to take over the agreement and that the owner of the goods consents to the agreement being assigned, the business transfer agreement should provide that the seller has complied with all obligations under the agreement up to completion, and that the purchaser will so comply following completion. Suitable cross indemnities between seller and purchaser should be incorporated. The purchaser should also require a warranty that the disclosed terms of any such agreement are true and complete.

(C) Stocks of raw materials, work in progress and finished goods

Stock is normally simply described as such and purchased at a valuation made on, or shortly before or after, completion. If stock is to be valued after completion the business transfer agreement will normally provide for an estimated value to be paid on completion with the balance to be settled once the valuation has been agreed or determined. The same mechanism is sometimes used in respect of creditors and debtors, if the provisions relating to them (for example, the provision for bad and doubtful debts) have not been valued by completion. The business transfer agreement can be used to provide a means for the valuation of stocks and for their valuation being agreed by the parties or determined by an independent third party. Whether these provisions or others are used it is important for them to contain specific details of the basis on which stocks are to be valued, how they are to be counted and who, by and how the valuation is to be agreed or determined. The comments made in Chapter 12 (section 12.2.6) with regard to completion accounts are equally applicable here).

Save for the implied conditions as to title, it is unlikely that any of the other conditions implied by the Sale of Goods Act 1979 will apply. Section 13 will only apply if the goods are sold by description. Section 14(2) and (3) may, however, apply to stock, even where it is sold with the fixed assets of the business, where the stock is sold at its ordinary market value (*Buchanan-Jardine v Hamilink* [1983] SLT 149). Frequently, specified professional valuers are agreed between the parties and named in the contract. Whether or not named, valuers need guidance in the contract as to the criterion for valuation; ie open market value, cost to the seller and cost plus or minus a certain percentage depending upon, for example, whether the stock is classed as growth claret or daily newspapers.

There are two dangers to a purchaser in agreeing to purchase stock at valuation without qualification. First, there is the danger that between contract and completion the stock will be run down, and second, there is the opposite danger, namely that for some reason the seller will make large purchases of stock just before completion. It may at first sight seem improbable that the seller would wish to do this, but the situation may be that he is selling one of a number of similar businesses and that he can obtain a substantial discount on the stock purchased for his other businesses by buying in quantity and off-loading surplus stock onto the business being sold. Both dangers may be avoided to some extent by providing elsewhere in the contract that pending completion the seller will carry on the business in the same way and to the same extent as before, but it would be advisable to reinforce such a provision with specified minimum and maximum amounts of stock.

(D) Debtors and creditors

It often happens that trade debtors and creditors are not taken over by the purchaser. One of the reasons for this used to be that stamp duty of up to 4% was payable by the purchaser on the consideration paid for the transfer of the debtors but now the only stamp duty would be on land and buildings.

Stamp duty on the acquisition of assets (with the exception of shares and marketable securities) was abolished by the Finance Act 2003. Stamp duty land tax (SDLT) is levied on land and buildings. On an acquisition of shares, the buyer will pay 0.5% stamp duty. See Chapter 9.6.3 (E) and Chapter 16.

The other major reason why debtors and creditors are not taken over by the purchaser is because of the difficulty in agreeing a price for them. Sellers will obviously seek to obtain their book value whereas a purchaser will be concerned that some of those debts will prove to be bad or doubtful. Even if they do not prove to be bad or doubtful, there will obviously be a cashflow disadvantage to the purchaser. It is therefore more common to find that the debtors and creditors remain with the seller and, if this is to happen, the purchaser should take steps to protect its customer base. In other words, the purchaser should negotiate to include in the business transfer agreement an undertaking from the seller not to be heavy handed in the collection of debts and to pay creditors as and when they fall due. The position regarding debtors is usually dealt with by the seller undertaking, for a specified period, not to issue proceedings for non-payment by debtors who continue to be customers of the business and, at the end of the specified period, to give the purchaser the option to purchase the debts at their book value. If the purchaser wishes to ensure that creditors of the business are promptly paid, one solution would be for part of the purchase price to be lodged in the joint account of the seller's and purchaser's respective solicitors for this purpose. The basis for release of this money should be set out in the contract. The purchaser will thus know that bills will be met when presented, and the seller will be assured that his liability to the creditors will be satisfied.

If an assignment of debts is required, then to make such assignment fully effective as against the debtors, and enforceable by the purchaser in his own name, the purchaser will have to give notice in writing to each of them, a possibly time consuming and costly exercise. A schedule of debtors and the amounts owed by each of them would also have to be annexed to the business transfer agreement. As regards creditors, the seller should undertake to indemnify the purchaser in respect of all obligations and liabilities incurred up to completion, and this would include trade and other creditors.

Some arrangements provide that the purchaser will discharge the seller's debts out of the proceeds of book debts collected by the purchaser as agent for the seller. This used to mean no stamp duty was payable when otherwise it might Since the Finance Act 2003, there is no stamp duty in any event but this method is often found attractive to both parties and, in particular, to the seller if the entire business (including all employees) is being transferred therefore leaving the seller with no facilities or manpower to administer the collection process. Where the obligation to account is likely to be onerous, the purchaser may stipulate for a fee based either on the value or the number of the seller's book debts collected.

(E)   Intellectual property rights

Although most businesses will use some intellectual property, the importance of intellectual property to the business being bought and sold will vary considerably. Depending on the importance of the intellectual property rights for the particular business, the purchaser will usually require the business transfer agreement to protect it, in the form of warranties, against not acquiring or having the valid rights to use sufficient intellectual property to enable it to conduct the business in a manner in which it is currently conducted and to transfer the intellectual property rights to the purchaser.

Registered patents, registered design rights and registered trademarks will need to be transferred into the name of the buyer unlike on a transfer of shares and licensees will need to be notified that their licensor has changed. Contracts must be checked however in case they give the licensee who is paying large royalties to a licensor to terminate the licence which could affect the value of the business acquired unless the licensee can be 'got on side' early on and persuaded not to object.

(F)   Contracts

The burden (as opposed to the benefit) of a contract cannot be transferred to the purchaser without the consent of the other contracting party. As a result, the seller will seek either to novate or subcontract its obligations to the purchaser or require the purchaser to assume its obligations as agent.

Novation involves the replacement, with the consent of the customer, of the existing contract between the seller or the customer by a new one between the purchaser and the customer. Depending upon the attitude of the customer, in the novation it may be possible to assume and be liable for the obligations of the seller from the time of transfer rather than the date of the original contract. Where novation is not possible, either because the customer consent is not or would not be forthcoming or because of time constraints, the purchaser will normally assume the seller's obligations under the existing contract as subcontractor or agent. Under these arrangements, the seller will remain responsible directly to the customer and therefore the acquisition agreement will need to allow the seller to recover against the purchaser for any loss it may suffer as a result of claims by the customer.

Transferring the benefit of the contract can be dealt with by novation, but more typically by way of assignment. Assignment involves the transfer of the right in relation to a contract. Provided the assignment is absolute, in writing, and written notice has been given to the customer, the purchaser will be able to enforce the benefit of the contract directly against the customer (Law of Property Act 1925, s 136). Where it is not possible to effect a statutory assignment because, for example, the parties do not wish to give written notice to a customer, the assignment will be effective as between the parties but will not give the purchaser the right to enforce the assignment directly against the customer.

Whether the benefit of the contract can be assigned at all will depend upon whether the contract itself contains a bar or restriction against assignment. Where consent is needed, the normal practice is for the business transfer agreement to provide that the seller will hold the benefit of such a contract on trust for the purchaser until the consent is obtained and pay any sums which the seller receives after completion to the purchaser immediately upon receipt (for example, see sub-clause 9. 3 of the precedent business transfer agreement). This avoids any argument on the part of the customer that the contract may have been breached.

Where certain contracts are fundamental to the business being acquired, for example agency or licensing agreements, provision should be made for these to be either novated or assigned to the purchaser with the agreement of the third party and for completion to be conditional on such novation or assignment. The contract will provide that, pending completion, the seller will not vary or release its rights without the purchaser's prior consent. Assignments usually transfer pre-completion liabilities under the contract so it is preferable from this point of view for the business transfer agreement to provide for cancellation of the original contract and for an entirely new agreement to be entered into.

In some deals unassignable material contracts where the other contracting party indicates they would not consent to assignment or novation can sometimes stop the deal proceeding at all. Material contracts therefore need to be considered very early on in any transaction.

(G)   Liabilities

On a business transfer there can also be the assumption of liabilities as well as the acquisition of assets. As a business transfer offers the purchaser an opportunity to select the assets it wishes to acquire and the liabilities it will assume, in most cases the liabilities assumed will be those the purchaser has chosen to accept. The principal exception to this is liabilities in relation to employees (see section 13.2.8), environmental liabilities (see Chapter 10, section 10.2.5) and liabilities under contracts transferred to the purchaser (see section 13.2.3 (F)). The business transfer agreement should state specifically the liabilities the purchaser has agreed to assume and those to be retained by the seller, and include indemnities in favour of the other to underwrite those obligations.

(H)   Product/service warranty claims

Questions always crop up in negotiations as to the extent of the purchaser's liability to take on service and repair obligations or other warranty obligations relating to goods or services supplied prior to completion or such other transfer date. If the seller accepts this liability then the question of how, in practice, the seller can assume such responsibility needs to be addressed as the seller is likely to have no facilities available to it once the business is sold. The precedent business transfer agreement assumes that the seller will accept liability but that the purchaser shall carry out the physical act of remedying defects in products and will be paid at the actual cost of doing so together with an agreed margin.

13.2.4   Consideration

In addition to the comments made in Chapter 12 (see section 12.2.6) relating to the drafting of the consideration provisions of a share purchase agreement, two additional issues arise in connection with business transfers.

(A)   Effective date

The parties sometimes agree that the business should be transferred with effect from a date earlier than the date of execution of the business transfer agreement. As it is not possible to backdate the agreement or by agreement to:

- pass title to assets with effect from a date earlier than the date of execution;
- deem the business to have been carried on by the seller as agent for the purchaser from such earlier date (a retrospective appointment of an agent is not effective); or
- deem the business to have been carried on by the seller on trust for the purchaser from such earlier date (a trust cannot be constituted retrospectively);

and because of the complications mentioned in section 13.2.4 (A), the preferred method of achieving that objective is to adjust the consideration so as to reflect the benefit or burden of trading since the earlier date. For example, this can be done by adjusting the consideration by reference to debtors arising and liabilities incurred between the relevant earlier date and completion. The complications referred to above include tax (HM Revenue and Customs (HMRC) will treat the income arising between the effective date and completion as belonging to the seller whatever the contract terms) and VAT (the seller will have charged and paid VAT during the interim period as principal).

(B)   Apportionment of purchase price

There is normally a conflict when apportioning the purchase price between the various assets. A business is a collection of assets, and where the parties have agreed a global figure for the whole concern it is usual to apportion the price between the constituent assets. An apportionment will have opposing tax consequences for both the seller and the purchaser because of the differing tax treatment of the assets being transferred. Each case will depend upon its own facts, so one can only point to a few general principles.

Generally, the purchaser will be seeking to maximise the apportionment of consideration to those assets which attract capital allowances whereas the seller would like to minimise the amounts apportioned to avoid balancing charges. Equally, as trading stock is a deductible business expense, the purchaser will seek to maximise the apportionment of price to trading stock; however from the seller's point of view the consideration allocated to trading stock will be treated as income and for that reason may not be acceptable. Following changes in the Finance Act 1995, where the parties are connected transfers of stock will be deemed to occur at a price which would have been agreed by independent parties dealing at arm's length.

Equally, one of the parties may wish to claim or utilise roll-over relief, which may influence the amount which they would wish to see attributed to capital assets (see https://www.gov.uk/capital-gains-tax-businesses#2) and see Chapter 9 at 9.6.2 (E). Alternatively, the seller may have losses and therefore not care either way.

13.2.5   VAT

Probably the most important tax point relating to the business transfer agreement is to get the VAT treatment right. A person registered for VAT must, in principle, charge VAT on anything which is sold unless it is an exempt or zero-rated supply. VAT is not solely chargeable on the sale of stock; it is also chargeable on the sale of capital assets, be it the sale of a surplus typewriter or the goodwill of a business. However, relief is available where a business is sold as a going concern, which will often be the case, but it is important to distinguish this from cases where the seller is merely selling a collection of assets, and it is important to be sure that it is being sold as a going concern.

Article 5 of the VAT (Special Provisions) Order 1995 (SI 1995/1268) treats the supply of a business, or part of a business, as neither a supply of goods nor a supply of services provided that the necessary conditions are satisfied. The overriding condition is that the supply must consist of a transfer of a business (or part) as a going concern, but there are also special conditions in relation to land.

Article 5 is mandatory, so if an error is made in its application either the seller or purchaser can be at a severe financial disadvantage. For example, if a seller sells his business to a purchaser and charges VAT where it should not have been charged, HMRC may refuse to allow the purchaser to reclaim the VAT, ie they would disallow any input tax credit to the purchaser. Alternatively, if the seller sells business assets in a transaction which does not attract the relief and fails to charge VAT to the purchaser, HMRC will demand output tax from the seller which he may, depending on how the contract was worded, be in no position to recover from the purchaser, the presumption being that if the contract is silent on the point, the purchase price is VAT inclusive.

The conditions contained in art 5 involve determining questions of fact which may not be all that clear. In deciding whether a transaction amounts to a taxable supply, regard must be had to its substance rather than its form, and consideration must be given to all of the circumstances, weighing the factors which point in one direction against those which point in another. The points listed should be adopted as standard tests:

- the effect of the transfer must be to put the purchaser in possession of a business which can be operated as such: a sale of capital assets alone is not in itself enough;
- the assets transferred must be intended for use by the new owner in carrying on the same kind of business;
- there must be no significant break in the normal trading pattern before or immediately after the transfer;
- if only a part is being transferred that part must be capable of operating alone; and
- the purchaser must be registered for VAT or, at the time of the transfer, become liable to be registered.

The overriding consideration is, of course, that the business must be a going concern at the time of the transfer and not a mere collection of assets.

There is a restriction on the operation of art 5 where land is concerned. The first point is to work out whether VAT will be charged on the sale of the land without art 5. This would be the case either if the seller had made an election to charge VAT over the land (Value Added Tax Act 1994, Sch 10, para 2) or because it is the sale of the freehold of a new commercial building or civil engineering works (Value Added Tax Act 1994, Sch 9, item 1, Group 1). In these cases, the sale of the land will only be within art 5 if the purchaser, normally before the date of the contract, both makes an election to charge VAT in respect of the land and has given written notification to HMRC. There are also anti-avoidance provisions in relation to elections over land and these need to be borne in mind as well.

The factors listed below are worth considering to determine whether the transaction is a transfer as a going concern. No one factor is conclusive, for example, the absence of the assignment of premises and outstanding contracts is not conclusive. Nevertheless, some factors will carry particular weight. Particular emphasis should be placed on the transfer of goodwill, the right to use the business name and the preservation of some continuity in the activities of the business.

What is stated in the written sale agreement?

- Is goodwill, intellectual property or know-how expressly or de facto transferred?
- Is the right to use the business name or the product names transferred and used?
- Is the equipment, outstanding contracts, specialists tools or trading stock taken over?
- Are customer lists transferred, and does the purchaser have the right to approach customers of the seller?
- Are existing staff employed by the purchaser? (This is more relevant in the case of expert staff but not so relevant in the case of unskilled or semi-skilled staff.)
- Is the business to be conducted by the purchaser in the same way as by the seller?
- Can the activities be carried on without interruption? (A short closure by the purchaser may not be enough to preclude a going concern.)
- What was stated in any advertising, and what is said or implied in any announcements to actual or potential customers?

These factors are listed in no order of priority. It is not necessary for them all to exist for art 5 to apply, but they should allow the seller to build up the necessary overall picture. In cases of doubt a ruling should be obtained from HMRC prior to exchange of contracts.

All contracts for the transfer of a business should be carefully worded. Where acting for the seller, it is important that it is expressly stated that the price is VAT-exclusive (see clause 5.1 of the precedent business transfer agreement). The seller should reserve the right subsequently to charge VAT, and if possible this should cover both the charge to VAT and any penalty and interest which may be raised by HMRC (see clause 6 of the precedent business transfer agreement).

Where a business is transferred as a going concern the seller must notify HMRC in writing within 30 days that it has ceased to make or have any intention of making taxable supplies. This procedure should also be followed where part of a business is transferred as a going concern. Additionally, where a transfer of the whole business occurs, it is possible for the purchaser to take over the seller's old VAT registration number provided an appropriate application is made on behalf of both parties. The purchaser then assumes responsibility for submitting any tax returns due at the date of the transfer and accounting for any continuing tax liability. Both parties should give careful thought to these conditions and their inherent dangers. In practice, transferring registration in this way would be most relevant to transfers between related or friendly parties (eg in the context of family businesses or a group reorganisation). A purchaser would be ill advised to agree to it in a transaction at arm's length, because it would also be taking over the seller's VAT liabilities.

As regards business records, these must be kept for six years unless HMRC have agreed a shorter period. The seller must transfer any VAT records he was obliged to keep to the purchaser unless, exceptionally, he applies to the local VAT office for permission to retain them. Permission may be forthcoming where only part of the business is sold and it would be impracticable to split the records. Either way, the seller would normally wish to reserve a right to access over any records that are taken over by the purchaser.

Detailed HMRC guidance states:

'1.2 What is a Transfer of a business as a going concern (TOGC) for VAT purposes?

Normally the sale of the assets of a VAT registered or VAT registerable business will be subject to VAT at the appropriate rate. A transfer of a business as a going concern for VAT purposes (TOGC) however is the sale of a business including assets which must be treated as a matter of law, as "neither a supply of goods nor a supply of services" by virtue of meeting certain conditions. Where the sale meets the conditions then the supply is outside the scope of VAT and therefore VAT is not chargeable.

It is important to be aware that the TOGC rules are mandatory and not optional. So it is important to establish from the outset whether the sale is or is not a TOGC.

The main UK law concerning TOGCs is The VAT (Special Provisions) Order 1995 (SI 1995/1268 Art 5). The UK law is derived from Articles 19 and 29 of the Principal VAT Directive (Directive 2006/112/EC). But there are several other legal provisions relating to TOGC. These are Sections 44, 49, 94(6) and Para 8 Schedule 4 VAT Act 1994. Extracts of UK VAT law are shown at section 10.

We see the main conditions as being:

- the assets must be sold as part of the transfer of a "business" as a "going concern"
- the assets are to be used by the purchaser with the intention of carrying on the same kind of "business" as the seller (but not necessarily identical)
- where the seller is a taxable person, the purchaser must be a taxable person already or become one as the result of the transfer

- in respect of land which would be standard rated if it were supplied, the purchaser must notify HMRC that he has opted to tax the land by the relevant date, and must notify the seller that their option has not been disapplied by the same date
- where only part of the "business" is sold it must be capable of operating separately
- there must not be a series of immediately consecutive transfers of "business"

Our view of what these mean in practice as well as other rules and effects of TOGC treatment are dealt with in this Notice and in our Internal Guidance.

Note: For the purposes of this paragraph the word "business" has the meaning set out in section 94 VAT Act 1994 and "going concern" has the meaning that at the point in time to which the description applies, the business is "live or operating" and "has all parts and features necessary to keep it in operation, as distinct from its being only an inert aggregation of assets". (However also see sub-paragraph 2.3.1).

1.3 What is not a TOGC?

Examples of situations that do not fall under the TOGC provisions include;

- There is no transfer of a business as a going concern through changes in the constitution of a partnership.
- If there has been no transfer of assets there is nothing to which the TOGC provisions can apply.
- When there is a transfer of shares in a limited company from one person to another, the assets still belong to the limited company. Thus there is no change in the ownership of the assets so no supplies to which the TOGC provisions could apply.
- Where a VAT registered farmer transfers his business as a "going concern" to a farmer who is certified under the Agricultural Flat Rate Scheme there can be no TOGC for VAT since the purchaser is not registered or registerable for VAT (see notice 700/46).

If you are registered for VAT but you have not yet made taxable supplies, the transfer of your business might not be the transfer of a "going concern". However, where sufficient preparatory work has been undertaken prior to making taxable supplies there may be a business capable of being transferred as a going concern. Section 6 gives examples of transfers of property, some of which are transfers of businesses as a going concern.

1.4 Business assets

For there to be a transfer capable of being treated as a TOGC it must include the transfer of business assets. Business assets can include stock in trade, machinery, goodwill, premises and fixtures and fittings. Where the assets are transferred from one person to another the transfer may, subject to the meeting of the conditions, be covered by the TOGC provisions. For TOGC provisions to apply it is important that the assets, whatever they are and however many are to be transferred, put the purchaser in possession of a business, rather than simply assets. The assets of a business may be transferred in a number of situations. Below are examples of common transfers, but the list is not exhaustive:

- the assets may be bought by another person and the existing business may cease to trade
- the existing owner may die or retire and the business assets be taken over by another person
- part of an existing business may be sold to another person and
- the assets may be transferred to a new legal entity, for example, a sole proprietor may take on a partner, or form a limited company'.

The guidance continues in more detail at https://www.gov.uk/government/publications/vat-notice-7009-transfer-of-business-as-a-going-concern/vat-notice-7009-transfer-of-business-as-a-going-concern.

13.2.6   Completion

The business transfer agreement should identify the business to be conducted at completion (see clause 7 of the precedent business transfer agreement). Unlike a share purchase, this clause is concerned with the vesting in the purchaser of the individual assets comprising the business to be acquired.

In the case of certain assets, although the business transfer agreement will operate to transfer beneficial title a further transfer document will need to be executed to transfer legal title. In such cases, the business transfer agreement will need to provide for separate transfer documents to be executed.

Typically separate transfer documents will be required to transfer legal title to the following assets.

(A)   Contracts

To novate or statutorily assign a contract (see section 13.2.3 (F)) to the purchaser a new contract/deed of novation/form of assignment will be required and the business transfer agreement should provide for these documents to be executed and delivered on completion.

(B)   Intellectual property

In the case of registered intellectual property rights (patents, trademarks, service marks and registered designs) a separate transfer document is usually executed to present at the appropriate registry and indeed also a domain name assignment agreement too. Patents, applications for patents and rights into patents, for example, are transferable under the Patents Act 1977, s 30. However, to be effective against third parties, the assignments must be in writing signed by both the seller and the purchaser and registered with the patent office in the UK and, where appropriate, with patent offices in other countries. No stamp duty is due on intellectual property assignments although older precedents still make reference to it and must be altered.

(C)   Real property

The transfer of legal title to freehold and leasehold property registered at HM Land Registry can only be effected by the execution by the seller and the purchaser of a transfer document in a prescribed form, the stamping of that document and the registration of that document, duly stamped, together with payment of the appropriate fee, at one of the Land Registries.

13.2.7   Apportionments

Almost invariably, business transfers need to address the question of whether sums paid in advance prior to completion and payable in arrears after completion should be apportioned between the seller and the purchaser or otherwise taken into account in calculating the consideration. If they are to be taken into account, the business transfer agreement will need to address this. Clause 6 of the precedent business transfer agreement (Part VI, Precedent H) contains a typical provision and apportions the liabilities on a time basis with completion being the date to or from which the liabilities are apportioned.

13.2.8   Employees

The employment issues which arise whenever a target's business is acquired are potentially more complex than where the target itself is acquired by means of a share sale. In the case of a share sale, the sale of the target's shares from seller to purchaser will have no direct impact on the employment relationship between the target and its employees.

The sale and purchase of a business is quite different. It is governed by TUPE 2006 (SI 2006/246). As a result, materially different principles exist concerning employee liabilities on the acquisition of a business compared with the acquisition of a company.

TUPE 2006 has no application whatsoever to the acquisition of a company. However, one note of caution. Following the acquisition of the target, there may be a reorganisation so that the target's business is the subject of an inter-group transfer. In these circumstances an inter-group transfer of a business (or part of it) will be subject to TUPE 2006 *(Allen v Amalgamated Construction Co Ltd* [2000] IRLR 119, ECJ). Similar considerations would apply to the presale re-organisation of businesses by the seller.

(A)   TUPE 2006 – introduction

TUPE 2006 and its predecessor TUPE 1981 were introduced in order to implement the European Community's Acquired Rights Directive (Nos 77/187) in the UK. TUPE 1981 became fully operative on 1 May 1982, since when there has been an increasing volume of case law concerning the effect and application of TUPE on the transfer of a business. TUPE does not mirror the Directive. However, where there is divergence between TUPE and the Directive, or where questions of TUPE 's effect have been raised, the courts have become increasingly prone to construe TUPE in such a way which is consistent with the Directive and a manner best calculated to preserve the rights of the employee on transfer. The provisions of the Directive may also be relied upon directly by an individual against a public body.

TUPE applies to the 'transfer from one person to another of an undertaking situated immediately before the transfer in the United Kingdom or a part of one which is so situated'.

An undertaking is defined to include 'any trade or business'. If TUPE applies then a 'relevant transfer' is deemed to have occurred. The question of whether there has been a 'relevant transfer' has been the subject of many cases, both in the domestic courts and also in the European Court of Justice, whose decisions have influenced the approach taken by the domestic courts to determine whether TUPE will apply. An overview rather than a detailed analysis of what is or is not a relevant transfer follows.

(B)   Application of TUPE to business transfers

Most cases dealt with by the courts in considering the application of TUPE have been concerned with situations where there is the contracting-out of services. Where there is the sale of the target's business, then TUPE will almost certainly apply – although not necessarily. TUPE 2006 brought even more service contracting out within the scope of TUPE. There may be certain exceptional circumstances where the current application of the appropriate test leads to a conclusion that TUPE does not apply on certain business sales.

However, the basic test in all cases is to establish whether there has been 'the transfer of an economic entity'. Regulation 3(2) of TUPE 2006 provides – 'in this regulation "economic entity" means an organised grouping of resources which has the objective of pursuing an economic activity, whether or not that activity is central or ancillary'. In answering that question two issues should be considered:

- to identify the economic entity which is the subject of the transfer;
- to establish whether that economic entity retains its identity after the 'transfer'.

This test was established in one of the earliest 'headline cases' dealt with by the European Court of Justice (ECJ) concerning the application of the Acquired Rights Directive: *Spijkers v Gebroeders Benedik Abbatoir CV* [1986] 2 CMLR 296. Despite the varying analysis and tests applied in various cases dealing with TUPE and the Directive, the '*Spijkers* test' continues to be the fundamental and accepted test.

In *Spijkers* the ECJ held that the 'decisive' criterion was whether the undertaking retained its identity following the transfer. The relevant factual circumstances, none of which alone is decisive, include:

- the type of undertaking;
- whether tangible assets have been transferred;
- the value of any intangible assets transferred;
- whether the majority of employees are transferred;
- whether customers and work in progress are transferred;
- the degree of similarity between the activities carried on before and after the transfer.

In applying this test it has been held that the transfer of assets alone is unlikely to amount to the transfer of an undertaking. The transfer of goodwill has traditionally been regarded as necessary for there to be a transfer of an undertaking, but less emphasis has been placed upon this in recent years. The fact that goodwill or existing contracts are not transferred may not preclude TUPE's application.

Such a scenario occurred in *Spijkers*. An abattoir had ceased trading. After several months of inactivity a new operator began operating from the same building, carrying on the same activity using the old equipment but without having taken over existing business contracts or having acquired goodwill. However, these factors were held not to preclude the application of the Directive.

Ultimately, whether there is a 'relevant transfer' will be a question of fact to be determined by the court by looking at all the circumstances surrounding the transaction.

In determining whether there is a transfer, the courts look at the substance of the transaction and not the transfer document. So if there is a transfer of a business effected in a document entitled 'Asset Sale Agreement' then TUPE will still apply. A transfer may be effected without the need for any formal documentation. A de facto, and even temporary, transfer will suffice. The seller and purchaser may give effect to the transfer of a business without realising that they have done so. If the business is sold in a series of separate transactions by transferring various items at different times, TUPE will still apply. The fact that an employee is unaware of the fact of a transfer or the buyer's identity (*Secretary of State for Trade & Industry v Cook* [1997] IRLR 150) or the fact that the buyer is unaware that an individual was employed in the business (*TC Cleaning Contractors v Joy* EAT 134/96) does not prevent TUPE from applying to the individuals concerned.

As provided for in the definition of a 'relevant transfer' (reg 3(1)), TUPE applies not only to the transfer of a business but also to the transfer of a part of a business (and also a 'service provision change'). This is so long as the 'part' is sufficiently identifiable as a business in its own right and can be severed from the remainder of the business; but the 'part' need neither be separate nor self-contained and may even be integrated to a degree with the remainder of the business prior to transfer. Again, the fundamental test is *Spijkers* – to identify the economic entity and determine whether it retains its identity post transfer.

Although exactly the same considerations will apply as where the whole business is transferred, additional issues need to be considered. This can be best demonstrated by use of an example.

The purchaser intends to acquire the sales outlets, but not the manufacturing division, of the target. The business being transferred will therefore be the sales division of the target. All the staff employed in the sales division will, per se, be automatically transferred to the purchaser. All employed in the manufacturing division will not.

However what if there are head office staff, say in personnel, finance, administration, who are not obviously employed in either division? Whether the head office staff will be transferred to the purchaser or remain with the seller is likely to depend on whether they are employed in the part transferred. Those that have duties solely in relation to the sales operation are likely to form part of that business and will go across. Other employees who do not work in relation to the sales operation at all will not.

Particular difficulty arises with staff who spend time working in connection with both the sales and manufacturing divisions of the business. The authorities dealing with this point are not entirely clear. The leading case of *Botzen v Rotterdamsche Droogdok Maatschappi BV* [1986] 2 CMLR 50 considered the criteria that should be used to determine whether an individual was assigned to the transferring business. The ECJ held that it is necessary to consider whether an employee is 'wholly' engaged and 'assigned' to the part of the business that is transferring. If this is the case, the Directive will apply.

Employees engaged in activities for the whole undertaking, such as employees in accounts or administrative positions, will often not be 'wholly' employed in the part of the business that is transferring. Therefore, the Directive will not usually apply, even if such employees carry out certain duties for the benefit of the part of the business that has transferred. Two domestic authorities show the contrasting approach taken where an individual may not be obviously employed in the business being sold:

- an executive director employed by the parent company was held not to be employed in the undertaking being sold *(Michael Peters Ltd v Farnfield* [1995] IRLR 190);
- an executive director again not employed by the particular company which owned the transferring business and who worked in a number of the group businesses was transferred to the purchaser when the business he spent most of his time working in was sold *(Sunley Turriff Holdings Ltd v Thomson* [1995] IRLR 184).

In the case of such 'hybrid' employees, it is again important for the seller and the purchaser to agree their intentions with regard to them and to document this in the business transfer agreement. As has been said before, nothing in the business transfer agreement can override the operation of TUPE. Defining an employee as working in the transferring business does not mean they will transfer, if application of TUPE determines they will not (unless of course the individual agrees). However, by agreeing beforehand which employees are considered to be part of the business being transferred, both parties will know where they stand and can apportion liability for any employee claims in the employment indemnities.

(C)   Implications of TUPE

There are three main legal principles associated with TUPE:

- The automatic transfer principle
  This means that the employees employed in the business automatically transfer from the employment of the seller to the purchaser from the moment of transfer so that their contracts of employment take effect as if they had originally been made between the employee and the purchaser.
- Special protection against dismissal
  Any dismissal connected with a business transfer is automatically unfair unless it is for an 'economic, technical or organisational reason entailing changes in the workforce'.
- Informing and consulting with recognised trade unions/employee representatives
  Both the seller and the purchaser have to inform recognised unions or employee representatives of certain specified information associated with the business transfer and, in certain situations, this can give rise to an obligation to consult with them.

These principles are discussed in more detail below.

(i)   Automatic transfer principle

TUPE usurps the common law position. Whereas an employee's contract with the seller would otherwise be terminated on the sale of the business (essentially by reason of redundancy), there is effectively a statutory novation of that contract. The purchaser stands in the seller's shoes taking over the employee, his contract and (with some exceptions) all rights, duties, powers and liabilities associated with the contract. It is not possible to contract out of TUPE.

Regulation 4 of TUPE 2006 provides that a relevant transfer shall not operate to terminate the contract of employment of any person employed by the seller in the undertaking or part transferred, but such contracts of employment shall 'have effect after the transfer as if originally made between the [employee] and the [purchaser]'. By reg 4(3), someone is deemed to be employed in the undertaking if they are employed in it 'immediately before the transfer'.

Frequently the transfer is effected by exchange of contracts followed sometime later by completion. It is now accepted that the transfer is deemed to occur on the moment of completion.

The interpretation of the words 'immediately before' was resolved by the Court of Appeal in *Secretary of State for Employment v Spence* [1987] QB 179. Employees who were dismissed only a few hours before the moment of completion were not employed 'immediately before' the transfer. The contract of employment must therefore exist between the employee and the seller at the moment of transfer if it is to be caught by reg 4.

This gave rise to situations where employees were often dismissed shortly before the completion, re-employed by the purchaser, but not subject to TUPE as they were not employed in the business at the moment of transfer.

The principle established in the *Spence* case is subject to one important caveat, which arose in one of the most significant cases concerning the application of TUPE. In their landmark decision in *Lister v Forth Dry Dock & Engineering Co Ltd (In Receivership)* [1989] IRLR 161, the House of Lords considered the position of employees who had been dismissed by the seller so that they were not employed in the business 'immediately before' the transfer of that business to the purchaser, for a reason connected with the transfer which, according to the then reg 8(1), is deemed to be automatically unfair. They ruled that a purchaser would not only be required to take on employees of the business employed at the moment of transfer, but also inherit liability for those employees of the seller who would have been employed at the moment of transfer had they not been automatically unfairly dismissed beforehand.

Therefore, although the seller had dismissed the employees, the purchaser inherited liability for their unfair dismissal claims.

This had a significant effect on the principle of automatic transfer, which cannot be avoided by the seller dismissing employees prior to completion. The position can be summarised as follows.

- the purchaser takes on all employees of the seller working in the business immediately before the transfer (as defined in *Spence)*;
- if employees have been dismissed solely for a reason connected with the transfer then the purchaser inherits liability for the pre-transfer dismissal of all such employees;
- if the seller had dismissed employees prior to the transfer not just for a reason connected with the transfer, but also for an economic, technical or organisational reason entailing a change in the workforce (due to provisions of TUPE 2006 which remove the principle of automatic unfairness) then any liability arising out of the employees' dismissal will remain with the seller;
- even if such a dismissal is nevertheless deemed to be unfair because it was not implemented fairly (eg because of a lack of consultation), liability remains that of the seller; and
- liability for any claims made by employees dismissed prior to the transfer for any reason that is not connected with it (eg misconduct) also remains that of the seller.

Not all employees employed in the business will, however, transfer. TUPE contains express provisions allowing the employee to 'opt out' and, in certain cases, they may claim unfair and wrongful dismissal.

Regulation 4(7) of TUPE 2006 precludes the automatic transfer provisions of reg 4(1) where the employee informs either seller or purchaser that he objects to becoming employed by the purchaser. However, this is a somewhat hollow right, as the employee is deemed to have resigned (TUPE 2006, reg 4(8)). This is unless they can demonstrate a 'substantial change in ... working conditions to their detriment' or where the change of identity of their employer arising out of the transfer is 'a significant change and to their detriment' (TUPE 2006, reg 4(9)) and in which case the employee can claim damages for wrongful and/ or unfair dismissal.

There is now some uncertainty as to whether that liability will be of the seller or the purchaser.

Despite these changes in the law, it is nevertheless wise to identify with some certainty which employees are working in the business and who the seller and purchaser consider will transfer in accordance with TUPE. This is usually done by preparing a list of such employees. If the purchaser inherits employees who were not on the list, his position can be protected by appropriate warranties and/ or indemnities in the business transfer agreement.

TUPE does not automatically transfer self-employed persons (eg consultants).

The purchaser will assume virtually all statutory and contractual rights under or in connection with the contracts of employment of the employees who are automatically transferred to it (TUPE 2006, reg 4(2)). The few exceptions to this include criminal liabilities, the retirement element of an occupational pension scheme (although any obligation in the contract of employment to pay contributions into a pension scheme which is part of the employee's remuneration will be transferred), and PAYE liabilities. Share options and rights under profit sharing schemes may not go across if they do not form part of the employment contract and are a separate collateral contract (eg with the holding company). Restrictive covenants may cease to be binding on the employee after the transfer and the purchaser should consider rewriting these to protect its position.

Because, with limited exceptions, the purchaser is taking on all liabilities of the seller in respect of transferred employees, and the liability of employees automatically unfairly dismissed by the seller prior to completion, it is all the more important for the purchaser to institute a very thorough due diligence exercise. Details of all aspects of employment and all matters which could give rise to a claim in an employment context should be requested. Lack of prior knowledge on the purchaser's part will not prohibit him from assuming liability.

(ii)   Special protection against dismissal

Regulation 7 of TUPE 2006 must be considered whenever dismissals associated with the transfer of a business are proposed.

Regulation 7(1) provides that any person dismissed before or after the transfer (whether by the seller or the purchaser) for a reason connected with it, shall be treated as having been unfairly dismissed, if the transfer or a reason connected with it is the reason or principal reason for the dismissal.

However, reg 7(2) provides that where the reason for dismissal is connected with the transfer but is also for an 'economic, technical or organisational reason entailing changes in the workforce of either the transferor or the transferee before or after a relevant transfer' then reg 7(1) will not apply.

The following should be noted by way of general comment on reg 7(2):

- 'economic reasons' must relate to the running of the business concerned. Thus changes motivated by a desire to facilitate the sale of the business to achieve a higher price may fall outside reg 7(2);
- a genuine redundancy situation would be an acceptable 'economic or organisational' reason;
- 'entailing a change in the workforce' is an integral and fundamental part of the test. It is not a question of whether something is desirable in the commercial interests of the business. There must also be changes to the numbers of employees or the functions they undertake;
- importantly reg 7(2) will not apply to transfer related dismissals resulting from attempts to standardise terms and conditions. TUPE 2006 did make a change to permit changes to contract terms but it is very limited in scope. Variations to contracts of employment are void, unless the main reason for the change is an economic, technical or organisational reason entailing changes in the workforce; or, the transferor is insolvent, and either the transferor or transferee agrees the variations with the appropriate representatives of the employees (ie a trade union or elected employee representatives).

(iii)   Information and consultation

Regulation 13 of TUPE 2006 provides that both seller and purchaser must disclose information to employee representatives, at a time sufficiently early before the transfer to enable any necessary consultation to take place between them and the representatives. The information is as follows:

(a)   the fact that the transfer is to take place, the date or proposed date of the transfer and the reasons for it;

(b)   the legal, economic and social implications of the transfer for any affected employees;

(c)   the measures which he envisages he will, in connection with the transfer, take in relation to any affected employees or, if he envisages that no measures will be so taken, that fact; and

(d)   if the employer is the transferor, the measures, in connection with the transfer, which he envisages the transferee will take in relation to any affected employees who will become employees of the transferee after the transfer by virtue of reg 4 or, if he envisages that no measures will be so taken, that fact.

This obligation arises not only in respect of the employees who will transfer from the seller to the purchaser but also any others (of either seller or purchaser) who may be affected by the business sale.

The seller would have to consult concerning changes it envisages making to its workforce, and the purchaser should do likewise in relation to its employees.

If there are no measures to be taken about employees, then strictly speaking there is no requirement to do anything other than inform the representatives of the matters listed above. However, from an industrial relations perspective, the seller and the purchaser may consider it prudent to engage in consultation. Similarly, the strict wording of TUPE 2006 may excuse the purchaser from initiating consultation with the transferring workforce about future changes until after the sale has completed, but early discussions may be advisable.

When there is consultation with representatives then this must be with a view to reaching agreement with them. This means that the employer should engage in meaningful consultation and discussion rather than engaging in lip service discussion. The employer is required to consider representations and reply to them and (if appropriate) explain why they are rejected. However, there is no obligation to agree with the representations.

Originally these obligations would only arise in situations where either the seller or the purchaser recognised trade unions, who would be 'the representatives' to be notified of matters and consulted (if appropriate). However, regulations now provide for the notification and consultation requirements to apply not only to a business where there are recognised trade unions, but with elected employee representatives where there are not.

This introduced a significant new issue for sellers and purchasers to address when there is a sale and purchase of a business. With the increasing decline of recognised unions in the workplace TUPE 1981's (as it then was) consultation and notification requirements were not an issue of frequent concern to either party. The requirement to consult with recognised trade unions or elected employee representatives imposed an added requirement on every sale and purchase of a business.

There is one get-out clause available to employers (TUPE 2006, reg 13(9). If they can show that there were special circumstances rendering it not reasonably practical either to notify and/or consult with representatives then they can be excused those obligations. The need to maintain commercial confidentiality about a transaction may be accepted by an employment tribunal as a special circumstance so long as the employer can demonstrate the need to maintain total confidentiality about the transaction and that it did all it could in the circumstances.

Failure to comply with these obligations of notification and consultation could result in a claim for up to 13 weeks' pay per employee.

However, the employment tribunal will not automatically impose this level of financial penalty simply because of a failure to comply with the notification and consultation obligations. They will consider the element of default and the consequences for the employees before deciding on the appropriate amount of financial penalty.

Under TUPE 2006 'employee liability information' must be provided at least a fortnight before the transfer. This includes information about:

(a)   the identity and age of employees;

(b)   their statement of terms and conditions of employment;

(c)   any disciplinary proceedings or grievance issued in the last two years;

(d)   any court or tribunal cases brought by the employees in the last two years, or any court or tribunal cases which the transferor has reasonable grounds to believe that an employee might bring;

(e)   any collective agreement which will have effect after the transfer.

If this is not done then a claim can be brought in an employment tribunal for such compensation as is just and equitable having regard to any loss suffered. There is a minimum award of £500 per employee, unless the tribunal considers it just and equitable to award a lesser sum. See also Data Protection and the Information Commissioner's guidelines, Chapter 4, para 4.4.1. For pension issues on a TUPE transfer see 10.2.5 (D) (ii).

13.2.9   Pensions

The pension provisions on a business transfer will invariably differ from those on a share purchase since a business transfer will involve the actual transfer of the pension arrangements to the purchaser whereas, save for group schemes, a share purchase involves no transfer.

Broadly, the comments made in Chapter 12 (see section 12.2.3) in relation to the share purchase agreement also apply to business transfers and, in particular, the comments made in relation to group final salary schemes will be of relevance if the business transfer involves a transfer payment from the seller's pension scheme to the purchaser's pension scheme. However, there are certain additional issues which need to be borne in mind in the case of a business transfer.

First, the purchaser may wish for the target employees to stay in the seller's scheme for an interim period. In such circumstances, the purchaser will normally be required to execute a deed of adherence to the seller's scheme, covenanting to comply with the provisions of the seller's scheme during the interim period. Should the purchaser require an interim period the purchaser will normally require a section 7 indemnity (see section 12.2.13) to be included in the pensions clauses. The purchaser will also need to consider what steps need to be taken to regularise the contracting-out position of its new employees under the seller's scheme.

Second, the trust deed and rules of the seller's scheme should be reviewed to see if there are any special provisions applying on the sale of a business. It may sometimes be the case that different terms will apply and that the transfer payment will fall to be calculated on some other basis than that which applies on the sale of a participating company.

Whilst warranties are not quite as significant here as in the case of a sale of a company with its own discrete pension scheme, the purchaser should still seek the inclusion in the business transfer agreement of such warranties as it considers necessary for its protection in the light of the particular transaction.

As a general rule, more warranties relating to the seller's scheme should be sought if the purchaser is to participate in the seller's scheme for an interim period.

The principal additional pension complication that needs to be addressed in business transfers is the effect of TUPE 2006 in relation to pensions. As explained above in section 13.2.8, the effect of TUPE is to novate the contracts of employment of the target employees so that their contracts take effect as if they had originally been made between the employee and the purchaser.

However, reg 10 of TUPE 2006 specifically excludes from the statutory novation the rights of employees in respect of 'occupational pension schemes'.

The wording of this regulation under the previous TUPE 1981 was intended to reflect the provisions of art 3(3) of EC Directive 77/187 which allows an exclusion covering employees' 'rights to old-age, invalidity or survivors' benefits under supplementary company or inter-company pension schemes outside the statutory Social Security Schemes in Member States'. The article also states that 'Member States shall adopt the measures necessary to protect the interests of employees and of persons no longer employed in the transferor's business at the time of the transfer ... in respect of rights conferring on them immediate or prospective entitlement to old-age benefits including survivors' benefits under (such) supplementary schemes'.

There have been a number of industrial tribunal decisions concerning challenges as to whether reg 7 properly implements the terms of art 3(3).

In *Warrener v Walden Engineering Co Ltd* Case No 22672/92, the tribunal held that a scheme which is contracted out of the State Earnings Related Pension Scheme was not a 'supplementary company pension scheme' as referred to in art 3(3) because such a scheme provides benefits in substitution for the State benefits rather than benefits which are supplementary to these benefits. However, the Employment Appeal Tribunal hearing the appeal in *Walden Engineering Co Ltd v Warrener* [1993] 3 CMLR 179, [1993] ICR 967 reversed this decision and held that both contracted out and contracted in schemes were 'supplementary pension schemes'.

More significantly, in *Perry v Intec Colleges Ltd* [1993] IRLR 56 the industrial tribunal held that art 3(3) is to be interpreted as meaning that, whilst an automatic transfer of pension rights is not possible because this would necessitate the employee remaining in the transferor's scheme, the transferee is still required to provide comparable pension benefits under its own pension scheme. As the transferee did not offer Mr Perry membership of any pension scheme or arrangement, the tribunal decided that it should compensate him accordingly.

Whilst the tribunal's decision in *Perry* is not binding on any court or other industrial tribunal and was in fact criticised by the Employment Appeal Tribunal in the *Warrener* case, the possibility remains that *Perry* might be upheld by a UK court or the European Court of Justice although, with the passage of time, this likelihood has diminished. A purchaser who wishes to avoid any possibility of a claim for compensation based on the *Perry* decision should therefore ensure that it offers transferring employees' membership of a scheme under which comparable benefits are provided for both past and future service.

If, on the other hand, the *Perry* decision is wrong and employees are precluded from bringing a claim against the purchaser because of the terms of reg 7, the only redress available to employees who do not enjoy continuity of pension provisions would be to sue the seller for breach of its contractual obligations. Therefore, the seller should, until such time as the validity or otherwise of reg 7 has been finally established beyond all doubt, seek to ensure that under the business transfer agreement the purchaser is required to grant comparable pension benefits to the transferring employees or, perhaps more practically, seek an indemnity from the purchaser to cover the eventuality of such claims arising.

There are a couple of additional points concerning TUPE 1981 that are also worthy of a mention. First, it should be noted that the exclusion only applies to occupational pension schemes within the meaning of the Pension Schemes Act 1993. Consequently, any obligation of the seller to pay contributions to a personal pension plan (or to a group personal pension plan) of an employee of the target business, will automatically transfer to the purchaser under TUPE 2001. It is, therefore, important for the buyer to establish the nature of the pension arrangements that benefit employees of the target business.

Notwithstanding that TUPE 2006 excludes the transfer of occupational pension scheme rights, since 6 April 2005, the transferee has been obliged to provide some form of pension protection in relation to transferring employees with occupational pension rights relating to their employment with the transferor (sections 257 and 258 of the Pensions Act 2004). See further on this point at 10.2.5 (D) (ii).

13.2.10   Warranties

Broadly the comments made in Chapter 12 (section 12.2.8) in relation to a share purchase agreement equally apply to a business transfer. The main difference is in the matters to be covered by the warranties.

The number and scope of warranties necessary to provide the purchaser with reasonable protection in a business transfer will vary enormously depending upon whether the purchaser agrees to assume some or all of the seller's obligations or liabilities in relation to the target business. If all liabilities and obligations are retained by the seller the function of the warranties is reduced considerably. On the other hand, if the purchaser is to assume all liabilities and obligations the warranties will need to be more detailed and comprehensive and, with a few exceptions (share capital, tax etc), will mirror those required on a share purchase.

(A)   Sale of a division

If the seller company operates other businesses, care must be taken to phrase the warranties to catch only the target business. For example, the accounts warranty (see warranty 6.1 of the precedent business transfer agreement) should be amended so that the seller warrants the accounts only insofar as they relate to the target business.

(B)   Tax

There is no real need for tax warranties or a covenant for taxation in the case of business transfer. There are two cases, however, where a warranty may be useful and these are contained in the warranty schedule of the precedent business transfer agreement at warranty 33 (Value Added Tax) and warranty 20 (PAYE). They are both aimed at obtaining information as to whether there are any unusual aspects of the seller's business which the purchaser should know about. This may include specific concessions which have been agreed with HMRC.

(C)   Administration/Receivership sales

Almost without exception receivers refuse to offer any warranty protection to a purchaser of a business from him for fear of personal liability. For this reason, administration and receivership sales are usually structured as a business transfer so that, with the exception of employee liabilities as a result of the operation of TUPE 2006 (see section 15.1), the purchaser is protected from unknown liabilities.

Given the lack of warranty protection, a purchaser from a receiver must rely on its due diligence investigations for protection and seek protection in the price negotiation for the target business. This can be done in a number of ways. First, the purchaser may discount the price it is prepared to pay to reflect the lack of protection. Second, the purchaser could structure the consideration so that a proportion is held in escrow/retained to reimburse the purchaser should any substantiated claims arise during a specified period, for example, third party claims as to title to any of the assets sold.

Part IV
Post-completion

Chapter 14

Announcements and notifications

14.1 NOTIFICATION OF AQUISITIONS FALLING WITHIN THE EC
      MERGER RULES TO THE EC COMMISSION

14.2 NOTIFICATIONS
     14.2.1   Customers and suppliers
     14.2.2   Debtors and creditors
     14.2.3   Employees
     14.2.4   Regulatory Information Service and shareholders

14.3 CONSUMER CREDIT LICENCE APPROVAL – FSMA 2000, S 178
      NOTICES AND THE FCA

14.1 NOTIFICATION OF AQUISITIONS FALLING WITHIN THE EC MERGER RULES TO THE EC COMMISSION

If the transaction is a concentration with a Community Dimension for the purposes of the EC Merger Rules it will need to be notified to the EU Commission within one week of the earlier of the announcement of a public bid, the conclusion of a binding agreement or the acquisition of a controlling interest. For more detail on whether a transaction falls within the EC Merger Rules, see Chapter 10 (section 10.2.4 (G)(i)).

14.2 NOTIFICATIONS

14.2.1 Customers and suppliers

Depending upon the particular circumstances of the sale and purchase, the purchaser may wish to publicise the change of ownership to the customers and suppliers of the target business and potential customers and suppliers of the target business.

In addition to the commercial need to notify customers and suppliers of the change of ownership, there may be a legal need to do so to obtain their consent to the assignment of contracts, engagements and orders relating to the business from the seller to the purchaser or to novate a particular contract or order. As the purchaser is likely to insist on obtaining novation or consent to the assignment of key contracts prior to completion, post-completion notifications are likely to be less critical to the ongoing business, but important all the same.

The acquisition agreement may contain provisions regarding the notification of customers and suppliers (for example, that it should be a joint notification from both parties) and should be checked prior to either party taking any action.

14.2.2   Debtors and creditors

In the case of business transfers involving the sale of debtors to the purchaser and the assumption of liabilities by it, all debtors and creditors of the target business should be notified of the change of circumstances. As with customers and suppliers, the form of this notification may be governed by the terms of the business transfer agreement.

14.2.3   Employees

Consideration should be given to the announcement of the acquisition to the employees of the target company and to the target's own workforce. Notwithstanding the automatic novation of employment contracts pursuant to TUPE 2006, the change in the identity of the employer will need to be notified to employees within one month.

14.2.4   Regulatory Information Service (RIS) and shareholders

If either the seller or the purchaser is a listed company and the sale/purchase constitutes a Class 1, Class 2, Class 3 (if the acquisition includes the issue of shares for which listing will be sought), reverse takeover or related party transaction, the relevant party will need to notify the Companies Announcement Office in the terms required by the Listing Rules. A summary of some of the rules on such notifications for listed companies is at http://www.slaughterandmay. com/media/39320/a-guide-to-takeovers-in-the-united-kingdom.pdf. See also the Takeover Panel's list of Regulatory Information Services at http://www. thetakeoverpanel.org.uk/disclosure/regulatory-information-services-riss.

14.3   CONSUMER CREDIT LICENCE APPROVAL – FSMA 2000, S 178 NOTICES AND THE FCA

As discussed in Chapter 10.2.4 (E) where the target entity has consumer credit licences prior clearance is necessary in many cases and must be obtained from the Financial Conduct Authority. Such clearance may be a condition for completion. For further details of s 178 see p 167.

Chapter 15

Implementing changes to the workforce

15.1 GENERAL CONSIDERATIONS

15.2 REDUNDANCY

15.3 CHANGES TO TERMS AND CONDITIONS OF EMPLOYMENT

15.4 THE IMPLICATIONS OF TUPE 2006

15.5 CONSULTATION

15.6 CHANGES TO THE TARGET'S BOARD OF DIRECTORS OR
SENIOR MANAGEMENT
  15.6.1   2018–19 changes

Having acquired the target, the purchaser may then wish to make changes to the
target employees (or even to its existing workforce).

The considerations which will need to be taken into account will vary depending
upon whether the purchase took the form of a share purchase or a business
transfer and how soon after the purchase the changes are to be implemented.

15.1   GENERAL CONSIDERATIONS

When implementing changes to the workforce, an employer will be concerned
to minimise the financial consequences, especially where the changes result in
the termination of employees' employment. These financial consequences will
primarily be:

- notice pay or other contractual payments due to the employees;
- where appropriate, a redundancy payment;
- the risk of unfair dismissal claims; and
- the possibility of discrimination claims.

The maximum compensatory award for unfair dismissal claims of £80,541 from
6 April 2017 (or 52 weeks' pay if lower) is a risk for employers of implementing
change.

This will also reinforce the need for caution where the employer may contemplate
dismissals because of the individual's conduct or poor performance, especially
where the performance expectations and standards of the purchaser are somewhat
different to those of the target.

In order to avoid a contractual claim for wrongful dismissal the requisite notice of termination must be given, unless payment in lieu is made. The amount of notice to be given will be contained in the employee's contract (if no written contract exists, the courts will imply a reasonable notice period). However, this is subject to the minimum period of notice provided for in the Employment Rights Act 1996, s 86(1). Failure to give the requisite notice will entitle the employee to bring a wrongful dismissal claim for the value of net salary and all other emoluments the employee would have received had he worked out his notice period.

In the case of an employee with two or more years' service, a dismissal must be for one of five 'potentially fair' reasons set out in the Employment Rights Act 1996, s 98, and the decision to dismiss must be fair and reasonable to avoid a successful unfair dismissal claim.

15.2   REDUNDANCY

Redundancy, as defined in the Employment Rights Act 1996, s 139, is one of the five reasons available to defeat a claim for unfair dismissal, but carries with it the requirement to make a redundancy payment to the employee (provided that the employee has two years' service). The redundancy payment is calculated by reference to the employee's age, length of service (capped at 20 years) and gross weekly salary (currently capped at £489 – 2017). The minimum redundancy pay will be one week's salary (up to £489), the maximum £14,67020. The DirectGov redundancy online calculator is available at: https://www.gov.uk/calculate-your-redundancy-pay. Note that these figures apply to employees whose employers base redundancy payments on the statutory scheme and does not apply to employers who offer redundancy payments over the statutory maximum. However employers should be aware of the Equality Act 2010 which prohibits age discrimination. A redundancy situation will exist where either the employer has closed a site or discontinued an operation (so that the position of all employees in that part of the business are redundant) or no longer requires so many employees to carry out a particular type of work (so there is a downsizing situation).

When implementing a redundancy programme, the purchaser must do so fairly. The issues which the employer must address are:

- to ensure adequate consultation and discussion with trade unions/ employee representatives (see below) and individual employees;
- to invite volunteers for redundancy;
- to determine from which group employees are to be selected for redundancy;
- to apply appropriate criteria (objective not negative) to undertake a fair selection; and
- to consider what alternative employment could be offered to an employee selected for redundancy.

Failure to do so could result in a dismissed employee bringing a successful unfair dismissal claim to an employment tribunal. The employee could recover a 'compensatory award' to compensate him for losses arising out of the dismissal.

15.3 CHANGES TO TERMS AND CONDITIONS OF EMPLOYMENT

If the employer implements contractual changes, this can prompt a number of alternative scenarios:

- if the contractual change amounts to a fundamental breach of the employee's contract, the employee may resign and bring claims for wrongful and (if appropriate) unfair dismissal, as if they had been dismissed. This concept is known as constructive dismissal;
- the employee may alternatively carry on working having expressed their objection to the change and claim for any loss resulting from it;
- if the employer dismisses the employee for refusing to accept such changes they are likely to be on the receiving end of wrongful, and possibly unfair, dismissal claims.

A dismissal of an employee for refusing to change terms and conditions is capable of being deemed by an employment tribunal to be a fair dismissal, 'for some other substantial reason' if there are good commercial reasons for implementing the change. Employment tribunals are becoming more amenable to steps taken by an employer to change the terms of the employee contract. The employer does not have to demonstrate that the change is vital for the survival of the business. However, there will be greater difficulty persuading the Tribunal of the necessity of a change if its purpose is to increase the profitability of an already profitable business, particularly if the change is at significant cost to the employee. Even if the tribunal accepts the necessity for change it will also need to be satisfied that the employer has acted fairly, with adequate warning of the change, consultation with employees/unions/representatives, and consideration of alternative strategies.

An employee who succeeds with an unfair dismissal claim in these circumstances will recover a basic and compensatory award.

Notwithstanding potential employee claims, the purchaser may wish to implement changes to the employees' contractual terms of employment for the commercial good of the target company. If the employees are unwilling to accept such changes, then rather than unilaterally imposing them (which may give rise to constructive dismissal claims) or dismissing the employees, the purchaser should consider offering incentives (such as a one off bonus payment or increase in salary) to encourage the employees to agree to the changes.

15.4 THE IMPLICATIONS OF TUPE 2006

Where the purchase of a business brings with it the application of TUPE 2006, then it is still possible for the employer to make redundancies. This will be an economic, technical or organisational (ETO) reason so that TUPE will give the employer a defence to any claim of automatic unfair dismissal, even if the redundancy dismissal is connected to the transfer. However, the usual principles of fairness summarised in section 15.3 will apply.

Certain particular considerations will nevertheless apply:

- whether the seller can carry out redundancies on behalf of the purchaser prior to completion. From an industrial relations perspective, there may be advantages in this. However, taking this approach may exclude the protection of TUPE;
- the other consideration concerns the 'pool for selection'. A process of selecting employees for redundancy only from either the seller's or the purchaser's workforce alone is likely to give rise to successful unfair dismissal claims.

Changing terms and conditions is even much more difficult for the purchaser in the case of a business transfer. The provisions of TUPE 2006 preserve terms and conditions of employment and make it difficult to vary them in connection with the transfer. The position is quite complicated, but can be summarised as follows:

- in order to implement a change, even if the employees agree, the employer must terminate the old contract and re-engage the employees on a new one;
- however, the act of terminating a contract amounts to a 'dismissal' for the purposes of an unfair dismissal claim, even if the employee continues working under the new contract;
- this dismissal will be automatically unfair;
- therefore, if the employee is worse off under the terms of the new contract they will be able to successfully claim compensation;
- changing the contract in any other way will be ineffective – even if the employee agrees!

It was held by the Court of Appeal in *Regent Security Services Limited v Power* [2007] EWCA Civ 1188 that an employee can agree to an additional beneficial right in his/her contract of employment, as long as the employee is not deprived of any rights that transfer, and such changes would not be void under TUPE. Therefore, only detrimental changes to the employee's terms and conditions would be void if they are due to the transfer itself or a reason connected with the transfer which is not an economic, technical or organisational reason. For pensions changes and TUPE see Chapter 10, section 10.2.5 (D) (ii).

15.5   CONSULTATION

There have been long-standing statutory requirements that an employer must engage in collective consultation with recognised trade unions where redundancies are proposed. This obligation will also apply to scenarios where there are proposed changes to the terms and conditions of employment (as these might result in dismissals). The obligation was also extended so as to apply whether or not there are recognised trade unions, in which case the employer must consult with elected employee representatives.

The employer's obligation is to consult as soon as reasonably practicable with the representatives with a view to reaching agreement concerning the proposed redundancy exercise or change to terms and conditions.

There are also set minimum periods for consultation which the Government summarises as follows at https://www.gov.uk/redundant-your-rights/ consultation:

'Collective redundancies

If your employer is making 20 or more employees redundant at the same time, the consultation should take place between your employer and a representative (rep).

This will either be:

- a trade union rep (if you are represented by a trade union)
- an elected employee rep (if you are not represented by a trade union, or if your employer does not recognise your trade union)

Collective consultations must cover:

- ways to avoid redundancies
- the reasons for redundancies
- how to keep the number of dismissals to a minimum
- how to limit the effects for employees involved, for example by offering retraining

Your employer must also meet certain legal requirements for collective consultations.

Length of consultation

There is no time limit for how long the period of consultation should be, but the minimum is:

- 20 to 99 redundancies – the consultation must start at least 30 days before any dismissals take effect
- 100 or more redundancies – the consultation must start at least 45 days before any dismissals take effect'.

Employers have sought to avoid this obligation where their operation is spread over a number of locations, so even if there are more than 20 redundancies, there may only be a few at each 'establishment'. However, in *The Bakers Union v Clarks of Hove Ltd* [1977] IRLR 167 the courts determined that a number of different sites could constitute one establishment. This is now overturned by the CJEU decision – see below.

The extension of the consultation regulations imposed much wider consultation obligations for employers. Whereas in the past such obligations would only exist where there was a recognised trade union in the workplace, the situation was changed so that the employer must always consult. Where there is a recognised union the employer now no longer has the option of consulting with them or with elected employee representatives. Where there is a union the employer must consult with it.

Fines can be imposed for failure to consumer – see https://www.gov.uk/staff-redundant/redundancy-consultations.

It should also be noted that where a protective award is made, the employer cannot mitigate the cost of paying such an award by offsetting it against any salary or notice pay which the employee will have received during what is deemed to have been the appropriate consultation period.

The Woolworths decision (*USDAW v Ethel Austin Ltd (in administration)* [2014] EWCA Civ 142) originally held that where a business makes redundancies over various branches then, under the legislation, it must count all the redundancies, not just those at individual branches. In January 2014 the Court of Appeal referred to the Court of Justice of the EU questions on how to interpret the relevant EU law and in 2015 the CJEU ruled for the employer in Case C-80/14 holding that the place of establishment was just that particular location where the employees worked, not several added together in ascertaining the number of workers for these purposes. See http://ohrh.law.ox.ac.uk/usdaw-v-ethel-austin-in-the-ecj/.

15.6   CHANGES TO THE TARGET'S BOARD OF DIRECTORS OR SENIOR MANAGEMENT

In the case of share purchases, the purchaser may also wish to make changes to the board of directors of the target following its acquisition. There may be executive and non-executive directors on the board. Executive directors (ie those employed by the target) will have the same rights as all other employees on the termination of their employment.

If they have long notice periods in their contracts, or have a fixed term contract with a lengthy unexpired period, their claim for wrongful dismissal may be substantial. The dismissed director would be entitled to receive a sum by way of compensation equal to the net value (in other words, after deduction of tax) of his salary and other benefits (car, BUPA, pension, etc) which he would have received had he worked out his notice period. This sum will be subject to an appropriate deduction to take into account accelerated receipt.

Often the first £30,000 of the compensation payment received by the executive will be free of tax, and any balance over £30,000 will be taxable (Income Tax (Earnings and Pensions) Act 2003, ss 403 and 404). Therefore to enable the executive to receive a payment equivalent to the net value of his salary and benefits in kind this sum must be 'grossed up' by the employer to take account of the tax consequences of the payment. For example, if net value of the employee's salary and benefits in kind is £60,000 then it would be necessary to gross up the excess over £30,000 – so assuming the employee will be taxed on the excess at 40%, the compensation sum will need to be grossed up to £80,000 with the employer remitting £20,000 to HM Revenue and Customs (HMRC) under the PAYE system and the employee receiving the balance of £60,000.

HMRC is forever chipping away at the £30,000 exemption, so it should not be assumed without careful analysis. Indeed the Finance (No 2) Act 2017 made further changes to foreign service payments and these payments and more are to come in 2018/19. The executive will be under an obligation to attempt to mitigate his loss, and reliance on this principle may result in the payment of compensation for less than the full value of the whole period or outstanding balance of the fixed-term contract.

However, there may be no duty to mitigate (or account for mitigated earnings) where there is a clause in the contract of employment providing that the employer will make a payment in lieu of notice. In *Abrahams v Performing Right Society* [1995] IRLR 486, the Court of Appeal determined that in these circumstances the employee's claim is for debt for the full value of notice pay. In those circumstances the £30,000 tax-free exemption does not apply. The effect of *Abrahams* has been limited following the judgment in *Cerberus Software Ltd v Rowley* [2001] IRLR 160 where a 'pay in lieu of notice' ('PILON') provision giving a discretion to pay in lieu of notice retained the duty to mitigate. However note that from April 2018 the easier treatment where a payment is PILON will be abolished.

The purchaser should also consider the position if the dismissed executive has restrictive covenants in his contract. In the absence of a PILON, dismissing the employee with immediate effect and paying him in lieu of notice will be a breach of contract. Even if the employer pays the employee the full value of his notice pay, then although the employee will have suffered no financial loss, this will not remedy the breach of contract and all other provisions of the contract (including the restrictive covenants) will fall. In such cases, when negotiating the compensation package, the purchaser should consider the need (if any) to obtain fresh restrictive covenants from the dismissed executive. This may in itself further prejudice the £30,000 exemption referred to above, which underlines the need for careful analysis.

Whenever there is a termination of a senior executive's employment then the usual practice will be to record the severance terms in a compromise agreement.

As mentioned in Chapter 3, from 6 April 2011 the rules in this area altered. An 0T tax code is applied to the sum in excess of the tax free £30,000. So if someone were paid £40,000, £30,000 remains tax free (where it meets the conditions of the law for tax free payments and that can depend what is stated in the employment contract) but the £10,000 excess is deemed to be a monthly payment and inflates the individual's earnings. Even though the £30,000 is tax free it is still added to income to work out upper tax bracket so a total redundancy payment of £42,500 may bring the individual into the £150k plus 50% tax bracket and all earnings for the rest of the year may be taxed at the highest rate. Refunds may be possible when a new job is begun, a pension is taken or if someone chooses not to work but claims no taxable social security benefits, but only if an application is made for this.

HMRC states:

> **'How are the different components of a redundancy package dealt with for tax and NIC purposes?**
>
> * Unpaid salary and holiday pay are earnings for tax and NICs.
> * Redundancy payments are tax-free up to £30,000 (see EIM13750) and not liable for NICs (see NIM02580). Note that in some situations the £30,000 is reduced (see EIM13530).
> * For payments in lieu of notice the position can be complex: see EIM12975-9. The NICs position follows that for tax.
> * Payments for restrictive covenants are earnings for tax and NICs purposes (see EIM03600 and NIM02320).
> * Damages payments are dealt with in the same way as redundancy payments (see EIM13070).'.

15.6.1   2018–19 changes

It is likely that from April 2018 all payments in lieu of notice, whatever the employment contract may or may not provide, will be taxable whereas damages up to £30,000 will continue to be tax free. This is a major change.

From 2019 employer's national insurance contributions will be payable on payments over £30,000. The current employer NI rate is 13.8%.

See https://www.clydeco.com/blog/the-hive/article/tax-treatment-of-termination-payments?utm_source=Mondaq&utm_medium=syndication&utm_campaign=View-Original and https://www.lexology.com/library/detail.aspx?g=78730b22-7e8d-44c1-b993-09d8695300d6.

Chapter 16

Stamp duty

16.1 GENERAL PRINCIPLES

The stamp duty legislation is still largely contained in the Stamp Act 1891 (with further provisions contained in a multitude of subsequent Finance Acts), but the Finance Act 1999 now contains many of the charging provisions. The law on stamp duty reserve tax is set out in Part IV of the Finance Act 1986. The first UK stamp duty was brought in during 1694 as a tax on paper transactions to fund the war against France. The duty ranged between 1 penny to several shillings on a number of different legal documents including insurance policies, documents used as evidence in courts, grants of honour, grants of probate and letters of administration. It was brought in as a temporary measure but has continued.

Although there are no actual legal requirements for a document to be stamped, a document which is subject to duty which is either executed in the UK or relates to property situated in the UK cannot be produced as evidence before a UK court unless it is properly stamped (Stamp Act 1891, s 14(4)). Further, in the context of share transfers, it is unlawful to enter a transfer on the target company's register unless the transfers have been properly stamped (CA 2006, s 770) and, in any case, share transfers are subject to stamp duty reserve tax which must be paid. For readers in Scotland and Wales reference should be made to Chapter 9.6.3 (E) for details of the different regime in Scotland and Wales and its land and buildings transaction tax which applies in place of stamp duty land tax (SDLT). From 1 April 2018 buyers of property in Wales are subject to a Welsh 'Land Transaction Tax' instead of SDLT.

16.2 SHARE PURCHASES

Ad valorem stamp duty at the rate of 0.5% is currently payable on a sale of shares because the transfer is a 'conveyance on sale' for stamp duty purposes. Stamp duty reserve tax at the same rate is payable in respect of an agreement to sell shares for a consideration, whether or not it is in writing. The stamp duty reserve tax will be repaid if within six years the agreement is completed and ad valorem stamp duty is paid on the transfer.

There are a number of important reliefs from stamp duty, but two have a particular importance in the context of a share purchase.

16.2.1 Relief for intra-group transfers

The Finance Act 1930, s 42 applies to relieve stamp duty on certain intra-group transfers. The relevant grouping test is based upon 75% of the ordinary share capital (following changes in recent Finance Acts) and it does not matter whether the link is held through overseas companies or if it is held indirectly.

The relief is subject to the anti-avoidance provisions contained in the Finance Act 1967, s 27 and, following the Finance Act 2000, the ownership rules for the stated 75% of the ordinary share capital follow the grouping rules for corporation tax so the group must, essentially, be a proper economic group.

If shares are transferred between companies in a group within three years of the sale of the recipient company the stamp duty which had previously been exempt from charge may be brought within charge when the company leaves the group. Tax advice should be sought to ensure stamp duty exempt previously under the Finance Act 1930, s 42 is not clawed back.

16.2.2 Finance Act 1986, s 77

This provision allows relief essentially where a new holding company is put on top of an existing company. Its application is in fact somewhat wider, but the conditions which must be satisfied are onerous. A wider example of its use is that it could be used where a shareholder owns 100% of the share capital of two trading companies and wishes to amalgamate them underneath a common holding company of which he will be the sole owner.

In addition to the reliefs, the purchaser may wish to avail itself of a stamp duty saving scheme to mitigate the effect of stamp duty on a share transaction. However, given the relative complexity of the relevant schemes and the costs likely to be incurred to put a scheme into effect, it will only be appropriate where the stamp duty payable is significant and there is sufficient time to implement the planning.

The schemes include buying a company for a low consideration (so reducing the stamp duty and stamp duty reserve tax payable) but where the company owes debt to the seller. The purchaser can arrange for the debt to be repaid after acquisition. Alternatively, it may be possible to use bearer shares on the sale of a company to reduce the stamp duty and stamp duty reserve tax payable.

HMRC simple summary says as follows (see https://www.gov.uk/guidance/stamp-duty-on-shares#share-transfers-for-more-than-1000):

'**Stamp Duty on share transfers for more than £1,000**

If you buy stocks and shares for more than £1,000 you have to pay Stamp Duty. This means you have to send HMRC the stock transfer form for stamping, along with your payment.

Calculating how much Stamp Duty is payable

The amount of Stamp Duty you pay is based on the 'consideration' you give for the stocks or shares. The consideration can be:

- cash;
- other stocks and shares;
- debt, which is usually related to the loan stock.

You pay Stamp Duty at the rate of 0.5 per cent of the value of the consideration, rounded up to the nearest £5, on each document to be stamped.

Example

Ben Harris buys shares using a stock transfer form. He pays £1,995.

The Stamp Duty rate is 0.5 per cent. So £1,995 × 0.5 per cent = £9.97. This is rounded up to the nearest £5, which means Ben pays £10 Stamp Duty.

You can use the HMRC Stamp Duty calculator to work out how much you have to pay.'

16.3 BUSINESS TRANSFERS

Stamp duty is chargeable only on land when the assets of the business are transferred to the purchaser.

Stamp duty land tax is the tax payable. It was introduced in the Finance Act 2003 as a charge on transactions and replaced the then current stamp duty on land and buildings. The tax was effective from 1 December 2003.

Stamp duty is over 300 years old. It is a charge on documents that transfer property and when duty is paid stamps are impressed physically on the document. Unlike modern taxes there is no provision for the tax to be collected directly from taxpayers by assessment. In contrast, stamp duty land tax is a modern transaction tax on land transactions involving any estate, interest, right or power in or over land in the UK.

Documents evidencing land transactions effected on or after 1 December 2003 and chargeable to stamp duty land tax are no longer physically stamped.

Documents evidencing an acquisition of land or an interest in land not chargeable to stamp duty land tax remain chargeable to stamp duty.

Prior to 2003 in the case of a deed of transfer incorporating a certificate for value, there was a nil rate of stamp duty where the consideration did not exceed £60,000. Transfers of shares did not, however, enjoy this exemption.

Thus, on the sale of a business any instrument vesting an interest in land in the purchaser was taxable if the consideration exceeded £60,000.

The general rate has increased over the past few years so that assets sold for more than £500,000 are subject to up to 5% duty (with different rates for residential property, different rates for first time buyers, additional properties and different rates/tax in Scotland and different rates for residential properties worth over £500,000 owned by companies as well as the annual tax on such properties – ATED below), (except in the case of stock and marketable securities which is 0.5%). Chapter 9.6.3 (E) gives further details of rates. Where the agreement involves the sale of other assets as well as land an apportionment must be made between dutiable and non-dutiable assets. The apportionment must be made bona fide and may have other tax consequences (see section 13.2.4 (B)). The apportionment should be made on a form SDLT1. A guide to completing that form is online at https://www.gov.uk/government/publications/sdlt-guide-for-completing-paper-sdlt1-return/guide-for-completing-paper-sdlt1-returns. HMRC's guidance looks at the following non-dutiable assets starting with stock which is excluded as it is not 'land'.

'Stock

For example, stock in a manufacturing environment could be all of:

- raw materials
- work in progress
- finished items

Goodwill

See SDLTM04005. [HMRC document]

A payment for goodwill that is part of the land is part of the chargeable consideration for Stamp Duty Land Tax purposes. The price paid for this goodwill should be included in the figure shown at question 10 of the SDLT1 where code **A**, **F** or **O** has been entered at question 2.

Chattels and moveables

See SDLTM04010. [HMRC document]

"Fixtures and fittings" may include assets that are in law part of the land (the strict meaning of "fixtures"). A payment for fixtures is part of the chargeable consideration for Stamp Duty Land Tax purposes and should be included in the figure shown at question 10 of the SDLT1 where code **A**, **F** or **O** has been entered at question 2.

Other

Anything which is part of the deal that is not an interest in land and which falls outside the other three categories'.

From https://www.gov.uk/hmrc-internal-manuals/stamp-duty-land-tax-manual/sdltm62780.

16.3.1 Non-residential land or property rates and thresholds

Purchase price/lease premium or transfer value (non-residential or mixed use) (Not Scotland)	SDLT rate
Up to £150,000	Zero
The next £100,000 (the portion from £150,001 to £250,000)	2%
The remaining amount (the portion above £250,000)	5%

There are some different rates for disadvantaged areas and also for residential property (mentioned above) which is less likely to be relevant to sales of a business and also for leasehold. See http://www.hmrc.gov.uk/sdlt/intro/rates thresholds.htm.

16.3.2 Higher rate for corporate bodies – residential property only

From 20 March 2014 SDLT is charged at 15% on interests in residential dwellings costing more than £500,000 purchased by certain non-natural persons. 'Non-natural persons' include companies, partnerships including a company and collective investment schemes. There are exclusions for trustees of a settlement, property rental businesses, property developers and traders, properties made available to the public, financial institutions acquiring dwellings in the course of lending, dwellings occupied by employees and farmhouses.

For residential properties held by companies where the residential property is worth more than £500,000 the Annual Tax on Enveloped Dwellings (ATED) applies. ATED unlike SDLT applies equally in Scotland and England. However it is very unlikely to apply on business sales which rarely includes residential property although some companies do own properties lived in by staff. HMRC summarise this as set out below (see https://www.gov.uk/guidance/annual-tax-on-enveloped-dwellings-the-basics#2):

Annual chargeable amounts – ATED – residential property

The annual chargeable amounts for ATED are increased each year in line with the Consumer Prices Index (CPI).

Chargeable amounts for 1 April 2017 to 31 March 2018	
Property value	**Annual charge**
More than £500,000 but not more than £1 million	£3,500
More than £1 million but not more than £2 million	£7,050
More than £2 million but not more than £5 million	£23,550
More than £5 million but not more than £10 million	£54,950
More than £10 million but not more than £20 million	£110,100
More than £20 million	£220,350

Stamp duty

HMRC SDLT calculators are online at https://www.gov.uk/stamp-duty-land-tax.

All HMRC l Guidance in the area of stamp duty is online at https://www.gov.uk/topic/business-tax/stamp-taxes.

Reference should also be made to Chapter 9.6.3 (E).

Part V

Special Situations

Chapter 17

Buy-outs

17.1   INTRODUCTION

'Management buy-outs' or 'buy-outs' are generic terms used to describe the majority of business or company purchases which equity houses and acquisition financiers seek to finance.

The traditional form of buy-out was one initiated by the management, often without financial support, and once heads of terms have been agreed with the seller, management would seek finance to support the deal. With the management familiar with the business to be acquired, in the traditional management buy-out little due diligence was done prior to making a formal offer to the seller. As a result the equity and debt financiers often found themselves in a difficult position where they were morally and commercially bound by a term sheet not negotiated by them or, if they were involved, not having had the benefit of due diligence before the key commercial terms were negotiated.

Partly because of the above, the fact that the venture capitalists found themselves being one of many being asked to quote to finance the buy-out and consequently they found themselves wasting a lot of time and effort and, more particularly, due to the move of sellers more actively to initiate the sales process and to opt for the sale by auction in more instances than was previously the case, a large majority of the buy-outs in recent times have arisen as a result of a seller-initiated sale process conducted by way of auction and where the parties contacted include financial institutions. In these instances, the financial institutions (usually venture capitalists) would generally line up a management team (a new team or the existing team) in support of its offer. This latter form of buy-out is often referred to as an 'IBO' (institutional buy-out) and these transactions dominate the current market. In 1998, IBOs and management buy-ins accounted for 64% of the buy-out market. Management buy-ins and IBOs rather than management buy-outs (MBOs) have continued to make up the majority of total market value since 1996, with a then record MBI/IBO value of £35.5 billion and a record MBO value of £10.6 billion being achieved in 2007. The MBI figures then fell significantly due to the recession since 2007 when 264 deals were completed. 198 MBIs with a total value of £15 billion were recorded in 2008 and only 52 MBIs with a total value of £2.9 billion were recorded in the first six months of 2009. MBO figures also fell in the same period. However, figures from the Centre for Management Buy-out and Private Equity Research (CMBOR), sponsored by Equistone Partners Europe and Investec, show that deal values climbed from £1.4bn in Q4 of 2017 to £5.3bn in Q1. This represents the largest value recorded since Q1 2015 and more than the whole of H2 2016's £4.6bn.

The large majority of the issues to consider in buy-outs are, in relation to the sale and purchase of the target or its business and assets, the same or substantially similar to those in relation to a trade sale and purchase. There are, however, certain issues that arise (or assume greater importance) in a buy-out context, and they are highlighted in the following sections of this chapter.

17.2   CONFLICT OF INTERESTS

If management are contemplating a buy-out or are allowed to bid in an auction process or, which is now more common, financial bidders are allowed to team with management, great care should be taken from both the seller's and purchaser's perspective to ensure that the obvious conflicts of interest do not hamper the process and impede on the proper performance of management's duties as an employee and, if they are also directors of the target, as a director.

In these situations, management's natural desire to minimise the price to be paid for the target places them in direct conflict with their duties as directors to act in the best interest of the company, its shareholders and employees. Less obviously, if a management buy-out (MBO) is contemplated a conflict may arise in relation to any Board decisions which involves consideration of investment for longer-term benefits against short term profitability.

In a traditional MBO scenario, as soon as a director decides to initiate an MBO he should approach the Board to declare his interest and to seek consent to proceed. Failure to do so may place the manager in breach of his director's duties and/or employment contract since the MBO process inevitably leads to the disclosure of confidential information in soliciting financial support for the buy-out and conversations with colleagues to join the management team. These breaches could lead to the manager's dismissal as an employee and a potential action against the proposed financial backers to the MBO if they induced the executives to breach their employment contracts. It is vital that solicitors acting for the parties are very clear as to who is their client and to whom they owe their duties.

17.3   DUE DILIGENCE

Although the equity and acquisition financiers will have the benefit of teaming with management, in a well run auction process the seller will have controlled their access to management, often only allowing meaningful access after they have submitted a final offer or entered into heads of agreement. Accordingly, in their appraisal of the business being marketed for sale, equity and acquisition financiers rely heavily on accounting, tax, commercial, exit, legal, market, pensions and other due diligence carried out by professional advisers.

As professional advisers will seek to limit their liability for due diligence, one of the more tedious aspects of the transaction from the perspective of management and the equity and debt financiers tends to be the negotiation of the professional adviser's engagement letters. The engagement letters commonly cover the scope, duration of work and responsibilities of the adviser in addition to their fees and details of any limitations on liability. Many of the professional advisers seek to limit their liability in a number of ways, such as including caps on liability (which is discussed below) and proportionality clauses. Proportionality clauses have been developed to ensure that the adviser's liability is proportionate to its contribution to the fault.

Engagement letters may also contain a 'make whole' approach. This basically applies where management/equity and debt financiers agree an exclusion or limitation of liability with another adviser, which prevents one adviser being able to claim a contribution from the other person. Consequently, the liability of the adviser will be reduced by the amount of any contribution which he has been unable to claim.

The move to impose limitations on liability was driven by the 'Big Five' accountancy firms in a common approach in the mid-1990s. These firms dominate the market for the principal due diligence – the accountants report. Early in 1997, the British Venture Capital Association (BVCA) asked the then Office of Fair Trading (OFT) to look into the arrangements between the (then) Big Six firms (which they had submitted for registration) on grounds of being contrary to restrictive trade practices law. Chiefly as a result of this, in February 1998 the Big Five entered into a Memorandum of Understanding with the BVCA containing a set of guidelines, which the UK private equity/venture capital and acquisition finance markets have generally adopted in respect of liability for due diligence reporting. As a result, the Big Five withdrew their application for registration of their arrangements which under the then competition law had to be registered under the Restrictive Trade Practices Act 1976 (which was later replaced by the Competition Act 1998).

Under the guidelines, there are three separate sets of rules. In summary:

- for small transactions (under £10m) – liability may be capped at the deal size;
- for mid-market transactions (£l0m–£55m deal size) – liability may be capped at £10m plus one-third of the amount by which the deal size exceeds £l0m (up to a maximum of £25m); and
- for large transactions (above £55m deal size) – liability will generally be capped at £25m, but if there are unusually high or low risks involved (unrelated to the size of the transaction) this may be altered.

ICAEW guidance is at http://www.icaew.com/en/members/regulations-standards-and-guidance/practice-management/managing-professional-liability.

In 2007 solicitors' firms engaged in due diligence work were reported to be including caps on liability as indeed many of their insurers have recommended for some years. See http://www.thelawyer.com/cc-risks-banks-wrath-with-due-diligence-liability-cap/125322.article.

In 2013 the then Competition Commission investigated the audit market and decided:

- audit appointments in respect of FTSE 350 companies should be subject to mandatory re-tendering every ten years. This is a significant change from their provisional remedy of mandatory re-tendering every five years;
- the Audit Quality Review (AQR) team should review every audit in the FTSE 350 every five years, with the findings and grade to be reported to shareholders;
- there should be increased accountability of the auditor to the Audit Committee;
- there should be a shareholder advisory vote on the annual Audit Committee Report;
- the Financial Reporting Council (FRC) should be given a secondary objective to have due regard to competition; and
- so-called 'Big 4' clauses in loan agreements should be prohibited.

The Competition and Markets Authority keeps all these matters under review. The CMA 2013 report is at https://assets.publishing.service.gov.uk/media/5329 db35ed915d0e5d00001f/131016_final_report.pdf.

To ensure that the relevant parties can rely on the various due diligence reports, appropriate reliance wording should be included in them and they should be clearly addressed to the relevant parties.

17.4   SHAREHOLDER CONSENT

CA 2006 requires shareholders' consent to the sale of 10% or more of a company's net tangible assets, or assets valued at £100,000 or more, to a director of the company or its holding company or anyone connected with him (which may include the MBO vehicle).

17.5 FINANCIAL ASSISTANCE

In a typical buy-out the purchasing vehicle will require debt funding to finance the acquisition. Given that the purchasing vehicle will normally be newly formed and have little or no assets to secure the loan, the debt financiers will commonly require the acquisition finance to be guaranteed by the target company and/or secured on the target's assets.

In the case of a share purchase, any security or guarantee given by the target company to the purchaser's lender will constitute 'financial assistance' for the acquisition of its shares, which is prohibited by CA 2006 (s 677), in force from 1 October 2009, but only for public companies. Under s 151 of CA 1985, until that date, it was prohibited even for private companies unless the so-called 'whitewash' procedure contained in the then s 155 of the old Act was followed (for further detail refer to Chapter 9, section 9.5).

17.6 TAX CONSIDERATIONS

17.6.1 Avoiding an income tax charge on investment

Management will be anxious to avoid an income tax charge arising when they make their investment. This can happen if they are deemed, by reason of their employment with the target company, to have acquired or subscribed for shares on terms which differ from those on which shares are available to other investors.

If it appears that they have received their shares at an undervalue, this could be treated as taxable income and an employment income tax (formerly Schedule E) may arise, even though they have not, as yet, realised any gain.

Investments in MBOs are therefore typically structured through new companies formed specifically to acquire the target company or business. The share structures of these are designed so that management pay the same price as the equity providers for shares which, at least initially, have identical rights. It is only later, at exit, that management may acquire additional rights, and then this is generally done by reducing the rights of the institutional shares rather than increasing those of the management shares in order to reduce or defer the risk of a tax charge.

17.6.2 Capital gains treatment

Management will generally want their gains to be taxed under capital gains tax rules. Each individual now has a £10m lifetime capital gains tax (CGT) allowance up to which gains are taxed only at 10% rather than the upper rate of

20% which will often apply (other than for residential property – which is up to 28% – and carried interest). Each person has one £10m lifetime allowance for entrepreneur's relief where their gain qualified and therefore there may be scope for several family members such as two parents and three adult children investing and on sale having £50m taxed at 10% rather than one investing and being taxed principally at 20% on any gains. The capital gains treatment also permits them to mitigate their liabilities in various ways, such as giving the shares to their children before they accrue any significant value, or transferring some shares to their spouses, so that they can shelter the gains with their own tax rates and reliefs. They might even plan to leave the UK to take their gains in a lower tax environment, although it should be noted that HM Revenue and Customs (HMRC) has recently tightened the rules governing exemption from taxation when going non-resident. Details on the new rules in this field described in Chapter 3, section 3.3.1 I (tightening of the law on tax residence in the UK).

Finally, there are alternative methods of mitigating tax liabilities which do not require them to give their shares away or to emigrate.

17.6.3 Income tax relief on investment

In a buy-out, management are normally invited to subscribe shares for cash rather than being granted options, to ensure that they are additionally incentivised by the prospect of a downside risk. They will want to minimise the cost of their investment with tax reliefs.

HMRC and the UK government have, over the past few years, introduced various schemes (for example, Enterprise Investment Relief and Enterprise Management Incentive options considered in Chapter 3) to provide tax incentives for such investment. The importance of these reliefs has increased as their benefits have improved in the last couple of years but, unfortunately, they are sometimes incompatible with significant investments by institutions.

Individual investors can, however, obtain income tax relief for interest paid on loans taken out to finance their investments, subject to various conditions. In particular, the company must be 'close' at the time that they make their investment, and it must exist for the purpose of carrying on a trade, or owning trading companies. The introduction of a financial institution as investor is likely to render any company non-close, so management must normally subscribe their shares, before the institutions come on board.

17.7 WARRANTIES/DISCLOSURE

17.7.1 Traditional MBO

(A) Scope of warranties

In the traditional MBO situation, sellers often successfully argue that they should not be providing warranties to the management team since they run the business on a day-to-day basis and are the most likely to know whether problems exist or not. In practice, whether or not sellers give warranties often depends upon whether they are a private individual or a corporate vendor, whether the seller was involved in the management of the target and whether the seller has a stronger negotiating position. Usually a compromise is reached whereby the seller will warrant ownership of the target's shares/assets to be sold, that it has power to sell them and they were not charged, and in respect of elements of the target's business which are run either exclusively by the seller or for which the seller had responsibility. For example, if the target is a subsidiary of a large group it is common for the group head office to be responsible for the accounts, payroll, tax, insurance and pensions of the subsidiaries comprised in the group and for the seller to warrant these arrears.

(B) 'Knowledge' limitations of liability

In addition to the scope of the warranties, in a traditional MBO sellers also seek to restrict their liability for breaches of warranty of which they have 'actual knowledge' so that they avoid liability for any intentional or unintentional disclosure to them by management.

17.7.2 Institutional buy-outs

(A) Scope of warranties

The purchaser (at the behest of the equity and debt financiers) will typically prefer to have fuller warranties from the seller (even if this results in wider seller protections) than to have limited warranties, even though the gaps in the warranty cover would normally be the subject of management team warranties in favour of the equity financier pursuant to the equity documents and buy-out vehicle warranties in favour of the debt financier pursuant to the banking documents. This is because recourse to the seller (assuming a claim can be made) will generally be more fruitful, and less controversial, than against the individual members of the management team.

(B) 'Knowledge' limitation of liability

In a trade purchase, the purchaser would rarely accept a qualification that the seller is only liable for breach of warranty in respect of matters of which it is actually aware of, or should have been aware of. The purpose of warranties is to allocate risk between the seller and the purchaser for matters which come to light rather than merely identifying the extent of the seller's knowledge. On this basis, the equity and debt financiers will argue that it is a third party buyer (as with a trade purchaser) and should (through its acquisition vehicle) receive full unqualified warranties irrespective of what its management team is aware of.

A compromise position may be reached where matters for which the seller can be expected to take responsibility (such as head office functions including accounting, tax, insurance and pensions) will not be subject to knowledge qualifications whilst others will.

(C)   Waiver of claims against management

In many acquisition situations, sellers rely heavily on management to supply information for disclosure against the warranties. Accordingly, most sellers would feel aggrieved if a claim for breach of warranties or an indemnity arose in circumstances where they felt that management had knowledge of the information giving rise to the claim or ought to have known about the matter. If management clearly knew of a matter which should have been disclosed and they failed to make the disclosure, any members of management who are also directors of the target could be at risk for an action for breach of his fiduciary duties. To avoid the risk of management disruption if any such claim were made, and to restrict sellers from 'reversing' any warranty claim onto management, the equity and debt financiers usually insist on the seller waiving all rights against the management team save for fraud (or any lesser standard that may be negotiated).

17.8   ASSIGNABILITY OF WARRANTY/INDEMNITY CLAIMS

The question of assignability of the contractual rights of the purchaser under the sale and purchase documentation becomes more critical in the case of a buy-out where the buy-out vehicle is dependent upon acquisition finance to fund the purchase. As mentioned in section 17.4, given that the buy-out vehicle will be newly formed and have little or no assets to secure the loan, the debt financiers will commonly require the acquisition finance to be guaranteed by the target company and/or secured on the target's assets as well as on the assets of the buy-out vehicle itself. The key asset of the buy-out vehicle will usually be the rights it has against the seller under the sale and purchase documentation, principally under the warranties and indemnities. These rights will commonly form part of the debt financier's security package. Given this, the debt financiers are keen to ensure that benefit of any seller warranties and indemnities are capable of being assigned to them without restriction so they may make a direct claim against the seller if the buy-out vehicle is not in a position to repay the acquisition finance.

Chapter 18

Buying and selling technology businesses

18.1 INTRODUCTION

18.2 DISTINGUISHING FEATURES OF THE SALE AND PURCHASE
OF A TECHNOLOGY BUSINESS
    18.2.1   Relationship with seller
    18.2.2   The nature of technology assets
    18.2.3   Skilled staff

18.3 DUE DILIGENCE
    18.3.1   Seller's perspective
    18.3.2   Purchaser's perspective

18.4 EMPLOYEES

18.1 INTRODUCTION

The process of buying and selling technology businesses is not unlike that of any other business, save that the value of technology businesses is tied up in assets represented by people and intellectual property rather than bricks and mortar. For the purposes of this chapter, reference to 'technology businesses' are to businesses which are heavily dependent on intellectual property that they have developed or that they use.

The purpose of this chapter is not to provide an in-depth guide to the mechanics of the sale and purchase process, which is covered elsewhere in this book, but to provide an insight into some of the key issues when considering sale or purchase of a technology business.

18.2 DISTINGUISHING FEATURES OF THE SALE AND PURCHASE OF A TECHNOLOGY BUSINESS

There are three main issues which may distinguish the sale or purchase of a technology business from other company or business sale and purchase transactions: the relationship of the target company with the seller, the nature of technology assets and the importance of the highly skilled staff.

18.2.1 Relationship with seller

The target company is often the former IT division of a group of companies which has outgrown its purely in-house function and is being sold to a buyer who can better integrate this kind of business into its existing one (for example, another technology company). In these circumstances, there will frequently be an ongoing relationship between the buyer and seller since the target and/or the buyer will continue to provide services to the selling group. In practice, this means that the efforts of the buyer will be more focused on its own enquiries rather than relying on warranties and indemnities, as it will be reluctant to resort to these post-completion for fear of affecting the continuing service relationship.

18.2.2   The nature of technology assets

Where a company is a manufacturer, for example, it is relatively easy to see what it does and what its assets are as they are predominantly tangible and have a value. A technology business, on the other hand, is far more dependent on intangible rights and, in particular, intellectual property rights (IPRs). These will usually comprise the bulk of the valuable assets, and it is on these that the due diligence process is concentrated.

There are three central types of intellectual property which are particularly relevant for present purposes: (a) patents for inventions; (b) copyright for 'literary works', loosely defined, including computer programs; and (c) trademarks and names for the goodwill attaching to marketing symbols. In addition there are registered designs and design right and more obscure rights such as plant variety rights but these are not covered here.

(A)   Patents

Patents can be granted in respect of technical improvements of any kind, provided that they are new, inventive, and capable of industrial application. They are issued by the British, or by the European Patent Office or UK Intellectual Property Office, and last for a maximum of 20 years from the date of application. Once issued, they 'prevent all others – not just imitators, but even independent devisers of the same idea – from using the invention for the duration of the patent'.

Although the most important intellectual property right in relation to software is copyright, software is, in limited circumstances, patentable. The grant of such patents in the UK is governed by s 1(2) of the Patents Act 1977, and in Europe by a corresponding provision, art 52 of the European Patent Convention 1973. In IBM's Application, the European Patent Office Technical Board of Appeal decided that computer programs were prima facie excluded from patent protection. However, art 52 excluded computer programs 'as such', so it was clearly intended that there could be exceptions to this exclusion. A computer program might be patentable where it had 'technical character': ie where the program controlled an industrial process or a piece of machinery, or where it had a technical effect beyond the normal physical interaction of computer and program.

Important cases on the subject in 2007 led to a new Intellectual Property Office note on the subject. If a program is developed which offers some substantial 'technical improvement', it may be worth undertaking the costly business of patent application in order to obtain the superior protection which a successful application will confer.

In January 2008, the UK examined a case brought by five small UK businesses and held that the Intellectual Property Office (IPO) was wrongly applying the law by automatically throwing out patent applications for computer programs. *Astron Clinica Ltd v Comptroller General of Patents, Designs and Trade* [2008] EWHC 85 (Pat) appealed in cases where all the products were distributed on computer disks or made available by download over the internet. The IPO had held that in November 2006, following a landmark case, *Aerotel/Macrossan* [2006] EWCA Civ 1371, CA, that computer program inventions were usually not patentable. This was wrong. If it can be shown that programs running on a computer bring about a further technical effect, then patent claims should be considered.

The UK IPO in their guidance – Patenting computer-implemented inventions (software patents) at http://webarchive.nationalarchives.gov.uk/20140610084455/http://www.ipo.gov.uk/p-policy-computer.htm – states:

> 'the law on what is patentable is the same across Europe, so if something is unpatentable under UK law, it will generally also be unpatentable elsewhere in Europe, although individual countries may has slightly varying interpretations of the law. The same does not apply to countries outside Europe. In the US and Japan, the laws allow a wider range of computer-implemented inventions to be patented'.

Readers should note that in 2017/18 progress was made towards an EU-wide Community or unitary patent although at the date of writing a German constitutional law challenge to the new rules has been put before the CJEU and the UK's position after 2019 Brexit is unclear. This is different from a 'European patent' which is simply a bundle of a few national patents rather than one IP right covering the whole of the EU member states.

(B) Copyright

Copyright gives rights to the creators of original literary, dramatic, musical and artistic works, including computer programs. These rights arise automatically through the creation of the 'work' and, in the case of computer programs, last for the lifetime of the author plus 70 years. Copyright operates to prevent unauthorised copying of the work in question, protecting 'the particular expression making up a work … rather than the idea behind it'. This regime can lead to considerable problems when it is extended to something essentially practical such as computer programs. It remains, however, the most important intellectual property right where such programs are concerned.

In terms of software, copyright is by far the most important type of intellectual property. The position in the UK is governed by the Copyright, Designs and Patents Act 1988, which was amended by Statutory Instrument in 1992 in an effort to bring the UK into line with the rest of Europe following the EC's Software Directive of 1991 (consolidated into the software directive 2009/24/EC) and again later to implement the EU database directive and EU legislation on copyright exceptions and fair dealing and other copyright directives. For copyright to arise in a computer program, its creation must have required the exercise of 'sufficient labour, skill and judgment to satisfy the requirement that there is an "original literary work"'. Whether this test is satisfied will require detailed analysis of the circumstances of each case, but in general most programs, provided that they are not extremely simple or substantially copied, will satisfy the test.

The key question for those involved in the creation of software is 'who will own any intellectual property rights which do arise?' The key point to remember (which applies both to software and content, see section 18.2.2 (B)) is that the copyright in any materials will be owned by the person who develops those materials – not the person who pays that person to develop them unless otherwise agreed in writing. The only general exception to this rule is where the materials in question are developed by an employee in the ordinary course of his/her employment, in which case the copyright will be owned by the employer. A person who has developed materials can assign the copyright in them to the person who pays for the development. However, in order to be effective such an assignment needs to be in writing and signed by the copyright owner. If on an assets or indeed share sale it is found that the target company does not own the rights of any kind which it believed that it did then in many cases as long as the original inventor/software programmer has not fallen out with the company a retrospective assignment signed as a deed can correct the position. IP warranties from the seller should not solely be relied upon. In addition, the written agreements under which the copyright or other IP rights was developed should be asked to be seen, as so many companies assume they own the IP rights but later it is found that a self employed consultant never assigned the rights or the rights remain in the ownership of a director /shareholder or a different group company.

(C)   Trademarks

Trademarks are signs which distinguish the goods and services of one trader from those of others, protecting the goodwill and reputation of a firm. They do not need to be registered, and can be enforced at common law by showing that the owner has an established reputation in the mark, and that the use of a similar mark by another would be likely to confuse the public. Registration does, however, make it easier to police and prevent infringement, removing the need to prove the above elements of reputation and confusion. If there is no registration either as a UK trade mark or an EU-wide 'Community' or other foreign trade mark then in the UK rights to prevent others copying the name or trading style are limited – an action for 'passing off' would have to be brought.

If the seller of a business does not own registered trademarks it may be wise to require them to put in applications for registration before the sale proceeds. A similar issue arises with internet domain names – sometimes it is found that the target company does not own its own domains which can be its most valuable asset for online businesses. Plenty of director/shareholders hold companies or their buyers to ransom when it is found later that the domain registrations were kept in the name of a director or a group company.

It should not be assumed that ownership of a domain name or of a limited company equals ownership of a registered trade mark. Many clients wrongly assume this is the case.

(D) Design right and other miscellaneous intellectual property rights

Other intellectual property rights include unregistered design rights, which are monopoly rights for the outward appearance of an article which is three dimensional. These arise automatically and can run alongside copyright and last for 15 years in the UK (although in their last five years there is a right for third parties to use under a 'licence of right' regime). There are also EU unregistered design rights which last for three years.

In addition, it is possible to register designs either EU-wide as community designs or just in the UK as UK registered designs and such registered protection is better and broader and longer than relying simply on unregistered rights. It is also available for two dimensional designs, not just three dimensional, in contrast to unregistered design right. It is possible to register visual elements on screen and fonts as registered designs. Plenty of tablet computers are protected by registered design rights (as well as copyright protecting the software source code within the item). This 'miscellaneous' category also includes database rights: these cover any database, whether in computerised form, or in the form of a store of information in a filing cabinet. The legal position is governed by Community Directive 96/9/EC, implemented in the UK by the Copyright Rights in Databases Regulations 1997 (SI 1997/3032). This legislation accords full copyright protection to newly created databases where the selection and arrangement of the contents constitutes the author's own intellectual creation. If a database does not satisfy this test it might still qualify for the lesser sui generis database right which lasts 15 years although the period is extended every time new data is added to the database. These rights can co-exist in the same database. Databases which were created before 27 March 1996 and enjoyed copyright protection at that time continue to enjoy full copyright protection. In contrast to copyright the default ownership for designs and registered designs is that the person paying for the work – the commissioner – will own the rights unless agreed otherwise. For copyright the position is reversed.

There are also separate intellectual property rights protecting plant variety rights and semi-conductor topographies.

(E) Data Protection Law

In addition, in an era of 'Big Data' and the 'internet of things', it is essential to take good legal advice on data protection law and privacy risks applicable to the company concerned including advice as to complaint with the General Data Protection Regulation in force across the EU from March 2018.

(F)   Competition/Anti-Trust Law

Also take competition law advice, given the attention of the US and EU anti-trust authorities in the technology sector.

18.2.3   Skilled staff

A key asset of any technology company is 'know-how', another intangible which resides solely in the highly skilled staff. Investigating the 'sites' of this know-how and conducting due diligence in a manner that does not alienate staff is at the core of a successful acquisition. Good staff are able to move easily to other employment if they are unsettled. Aligned to this is the obvious ease of communication in an electronic environment which means that any news regarding the proposed transaction is likely to spread quickly. This can put considerable time pressure on the parties to complete quickly.

18.3   DUE DILIGENCE

18.3.1   Seller's perspective

As with any sale, it will be critical to ensure that each of the potential buyers has entered into a suitable confidentiality undertaking before information is disclosed. In addition, in the case of a sale of a technology business in particular the seller should consider the following areas:

(A)   Non-solicitation

Where the business is dependent on key people or key customer relations, a prospective buyer can achieve many of the objectives of the acquisition by recruiting these staff or customers. The seller should consider including in any confidentiality agreement non-solicitation of staff and non-solicitation of customer covenants.

No matter how well these covenants are drafted, they may be difficult to enforce in practice. For example, it is not easy to prove that an employee was solicited rather than simply responding to an advertisement or that the customer did not voluntarily choose to change suppliers. As a result it is extremely important to manage the information flow (see (B) below).

(B) Managing the information flow

The due diligence information flow should be carefully controlled to ensure that material which discloses the value elements of the business is held back until a relatively late stage of the sale process when it is clear that a purchase is committed. Even then, there is always the risk that the sale will not proceed and that damage will be done to the business through the earlier disclosures. These risks can be minimised to a certain extent. In any event a strong non-disclosure agreement is needed and must be signed.

(C) Product functionality/technical review

In addition to the legal aspects of due diligence, the buyer will often want to carry out a technical analysis of the product or systems used by the target. Allowing access to review how the product works is not a difficult issue for many businesses. However, since a large part of the value of technology assets lies in their confidentiality, allowing them to be analysed can be disastrous if the transaction does not proceed.

Sellers should consider having the analysis carried out by an independent expert who may disclose conclusions (but not content) and who is bound by confidentiality restrictions in favour of the seller. Alternatively, this issue can be dealt with in a similar way to access to customers and employees (as a final stage of the process or as a post-exchange condition to completion).

(D) Access to suppliers/customers

This can also cause significant damage to the business if not handled properly. One approach is to allow one preferred buyer access to customers and suppliers, and then under supervision. In practice, once the identities of the important customers are disclosed, policing contact will be difficult. Sellers should consider making access a condition to completion.

18.3.2 Purchaser's perspective

The ultimate objective of due diligence is to gain a greater understanding of the target's business and assets and to identify issues of risk which may influence the purchaser's decision to acquire the business or the price it may pay for the business.

In the context of the acquisition of a technology business, it is extremely important to identify and investigate:

- what the target business receives from third parties;
- what it owns; and
- what it provides to third parties (see diagram, below);

and in this context what IPRs are key to the target business. The IPRs of a technology business normally fall within one or more of the following categories:

In the acquistion of a technology business, it is important to identify and investigate what the target business:

receives

- **IPR licences – VAR**
- **Supplier contracts**
- **Hardware leases**
- **ASP/FM agreements**

owns

- **IPR created internally**
- **Owned assets**

provides to third parties

- **Customer contracts**
- **Goods**
- **IPR**

VAR = Value Added Reseller
ASP = Application Service Provider
FM = Facilities Management

- IPRs which are owned by the business outright, either because they have been developed internally or developed by third parties and ownership has been transferred;
- IPRs which are owned by third parties and their use is licensed to the target;
- IPRs which the target has shared ownership of, either because they have been jointly developed with a third party through a joint venture or development agreement or otherwise.

It is common to find that the development of a product and the identities of the parties responsible for development have become blurred with the passage of time. In the early stages of development, for example, there may have been outside consultants or other third parties involved who may have been instrumental in developing either the whole or one of the 'building blocks' of the product. Similarly, the founders may have developed certain aspects of the target's products prior to the setting up of the company.

It is important to ensure that the 'development trail' of the IPRs which the target believes it owns outright can be traced. In the UK, if someone develops or invents something within the course of their employment then the rights to these inventions are generally owned by their employer (unless their contract of employment states otherwise), but this is not the case in several other jurisdictions. In addition, in the UK, where a consultant develops technology for a company the consultant will own the IPRs in the developed work unless the IPRs are transferred to the company or their contract for services states otherwise. This is often overlooked by technology companies, in particular during the start-up stages.

If there is any doubt as to ownership, this should be resolved by retrospective assignments of these rights as early as possible, although the value and tax implications of such assignments will need to be considered.

Similarly, the terms on which any third party has licensed any technology to the target need to be checked in detail. In particular, the right of the target to modify or adapt those IPRs or the right of the third party to terminate the licence on a 'change of control' of the target may have a serious effect on the future use and exploitation of the target's own IPRs or its general ability to operate its business.

Alternatively, the third party IPRs used in the process may be available from alternative sources at little further expense, in which case the third party IPRs may not prove to be crucial.

Alternatively, where the target being sold is part of a larger group, it may be the case that the IPRs proposed to be sold may be required by other parts of the group and/or licensed by another group company. Again, any failure to secure the outright ownership of these IPRs can be covered by the group granting a licence.

Finally as regards legal due diligence on IPRs, it is important to form a view as to whether or not the target's technology could be open to challenge in the future

– for example, that the technology for which protection is sought in a patent application is not, in fact, 'novel' and hence is an invalid application. As regards commercial due diligence, any technology which has not yet been converted into saleable products clearly has to be commercially evaluated.

18.4   EMPLOYEES

The retention and incentivisation of key employees is one of the most difficult matters to achieve within the technology industry. Apart from the founders, key employees such as engineers provide great value to the current and future business of a company. Indeed, it has become increasingly common for the valuation of certain companies to be directly related to the number of skilled engineers they employ.

It has also become common to incentivise key employees in a technology business by granting them options over the shares in the employer company. In most cases, the option scheme rules allow for early exercise of options on a sale or flotation of the company, which often provides a quandary for the buyer and seller in that both parties will want to reward the employees for past efforts, but the buyer will want to ensure that the reward is not so great that there is little incentivisation for the employees to continue working for the company after the sale.

Depending on the rules of the option scheme, the choices available to the buyer in dealing with these options are as follows:

- 'cashing out' the options by paying a cash sum to the option holders to relinquish and cancel their options;
- allowing the option holders to exercise the options and participate with the shareholders in the sale; and
- 'rolling over' the existing options into options in the share capital of the buyer.

The way that the buyer deals with the option holders may encompass one or more of the above alternatives. Ideally, the buyer and seller will want to provide some reward to the existing employees for past performance, for example by allowing them to exercise a certain number of the options or giving them a small cash sum.

But they will also want to ensure that the employees are suitably incentivised for the future and will remain with the company by 'rolling over' some or all of the existing options or granting them new options.

Whichever way the option holders are dealt with, it will pay to try and agree a way forward between the parties before the option holders are approached. Some consultation with the option holders themselves will be required, although in order to preserve confidentiality surrounding the purchase, this may not be until a late stage in the sale process.

Part VI
Precedents

Precedent A – Confidentiality letter

The form of confidentiality letter set out in this annexure is suitable for use by a corporate seller at the outset of the sale process.

The confidentiality letter is an indicative draft only and has been drafted from the seller's perspective. This precedent should be treated as being little more than a collection of useful clauses.

Warning:

All precedents can be dangerous. There are major risks in using this precedent without competent legal advice. It is unlikely that any precedent will be able to be used in any transaction without considerable modification.

[*To be retyped onto seller's headed notepaper*]

Private and confidential

The Directors

.... Limited

[*insert address*]

Dated 20....

For the attention of [*name of recipient*]

Dear Sirs,

1. THE PROPOSED TRANSACTION

We refer to the current discussions concerning the proposed sale and purchase of [the entire issued, share capital of] [the business and assets of] .... Limited ('the Proposed Transaction').

We understand that .... Limited ('B') is interested in receiving certain information about .... Limited ('A') for the purposes of evaluating the Proposed Transaction.

In consideration of being supplied with Confidential Information, B is willing to give the undertakings contained in this letter.

2. DEFINITIONS

For the purposes of this letter:

'Advisors'	means professional advisors advising any party in relation to the Proposed Transaction, including (unless the context otherwise requires) partners in and directors and employees of such advisors and other persons;
'Confidential Information'	means confidential commercial, financial, marketing, technical or other information of whatever nature [(including, without limitation, information in or relating to ....)], know-how, trade secrets and other information concerning the [project/transaction/ arrangement or the results of recipient party's valuation of such information] in any form or medium whether disclosed orally or in writing before or after the date of this letter, together with any reproductions of such information in any form or medium or any part(s) of such information (and 'confidential' means that the information, either in its entirety or in the precise configuration or assembly of its components, is not publicly available);
'Representatives'	means the directors, officers, employees and consultants of, and individuals seconded to work for, any party.

3. UNDERTAKINGS

B shall, and shall procure that its Representatives and Advisors shall, save to the extent that the other party has given its prior written consent:

(a) *use for authorised purposes*
   use the Confidential Information relating to the other party only for the purpose of considering, advising in relation to or furthering the Proposed Transaction and not for any other purpose whatsoever, and not permit the Confidential Information to go out of its possession or custody or control other than as provided in this letter;

(b) *treatment of Confidential Information*
   keep the Proposed Transaction confidential at all times and treat the Confidential Information relating to the other party as private and confidential and safeguard it accordingly;

(c) *storage of Confidential Information*
   store the documents recording the Confidential Information at ....;

(d) *non-disclosure*
   not disclose the Confidential Information to anyone other than those individuals who are both:
   (i) Advisors or Representatives of the party whose names have previously been notified in writing to the other party; and
   (ii) who need to know such information for the purposes of considering, advising in relation to or furthering the Proposed Transaction and

who are aware of the obligations of confidentiality and agree to keep the Proposed Transaction and such Confidential Information confidential and to be subject to the same restrictions as those to which the party is subject pursuant to this paragraph 3;

(e) *notification*

notify its Advisors or Representatives having access to the Confidential Information of the confidential nature of the information and the recipient's obligations under this Agreement, and upon the discloser's request, to ensure that they each enter into a direct undertaking with the discloser to keep the information confidential; and the recipient will take such steps as may be necessary to enforce such obligations;

(f) *enforced disclosure*

if a party (or its Representatives or Advisors) is obliged to disclose Confidential Information relating to the other party to any third party, it shall disclose to that third party only the minimum amount of information consistent with the satisfaction of the obligation to make such disclosure; give the other party prior written notice of the information proposed to be disclosed containing a confirmation that the party's Advisor's opinion is that such disclosure is required; and obtain appropriate confidentiality undertakings from the third party;

(g) *storage of Confidential Information*

not use, copy, transfer or store any of the Confidential Information in an externally accessible computer or electronic information retrieval system, nor transmit it over any such system;

(h) *copying of Confidential Information*

not make more copies of the Confidential Information relating to the other party than are strictly necessary for the purpose of furthering the Proposed Transaction, place the discloser's proprietary notices on any copies which the recipient is permitted to make; and keep separate, as far as practicable, the Confidential Information relating to the other party and any copies, reproductions or summaries of the Confidential Information relating to the other party from all other documents and records held by it (or its Representatives or Advisors);

(i) *announcements*

not announce or disclose the existence of negotiations relating to, or any of the terms of, the Proposed Transaction without the prior written consent of the other party unless such announcement or disclosure is required by any applicable law or by any supervisory or regulatory body to whose rules a party (or its Representatives or Advisors) is subject or with whose rules it is necessary for a party (or its Representatives or Advisors) to comply, and in such circumstances announce or disclose only the minimum amount of information consistent with the obligation to make such disclosure;

(j) *notification of proceedings*

notify the other party in writing as soon as reasonably practicable if any proceedings are commenced or action taken which could result in it (or its Representatives or Advisors) becoming compelled to disclose any of the Confidential Information relating to the other party and take all reasonable steps at its expense to resist or avoid such proceedings or action, including all steps that the other party may reasonably request and to keep such party fully and promptly informed of all matters and developments relating to it;

(k) *return of Confidential Information*

upon written demand from the other party:

(i) return to the other party all Confidential Information relating to the other party (and any copies of it or of any part of it);

(ii) expunge all Confidential Information relating to the other party from any computer, word processor or other similar device into which it was entered or programmed;

(iii) destroy all notes, analyses or memoranda containing Confidential Information relating to the other party;

(iv) furnish the other party with a certificate signed by a director of the first party confirming that the provisions of paragraphs (i)–(iii) above have been complied with;

(l) *protection of goodwill*

not, during the period of .... months commencing on the date of this letter, without the other party's prior written consent, directly or indirectly:

(i) initiate, accept or engage in any discussions or contacts of any kind with an employee or agent of the other party;

(ii) solicit any person who is employed by the other party at the date of this letter to terminate such employment; or

(iii) [solicit the custom or business of any customer of the other party in respect of products or services similar to those manufactured or supplied by the other party;]

(iv) [without the prior consent in writing of the other party, be involved in acquiring or seeking to acquire any interest (as defined in Companies Act 2006, s 820) in the share capital or any material part of the assets and undertaking of the other party]; or

(v) use the Confidential Information in any other way which is likely to be or may be directly or indirectly detrimental to the discloser or its business;

(vi) nor enable a third party to do any of the above.

4. GENERAL MATTERS

B acknowledges and agrees:

(a) *notice*

to give notice to the other immediately that it becomes aware that the Confidential Information has been disclosed to an unauthorised third party;

(b) *injunctive relief*

that damages would not normally be an adequate remedy for a breach of the terms of this letter, and B agrees to waive any rights it may have to oppose the granting of equitable or injunctive relief sought by the other party in relation to any breach or suspected breach of the undertakings contained in this letter;

(c) *remedies for breach of this letter*

to indemnify and hold the other harmless from and against all actions, claims, costs, proceedings, expenses, loss or damage (including, without limitation, legal costs) which may arise directly or indirectly from the unauthorised disclosure or use of the Confidential Information or from any other breach of the terms of this letter;

(d) *exclusion from further negotiations*

that A may exclude from participating further in negotiations with any Representative or Advisor of the other party who it reasonably believes has breached the terms of this letter in a material respect and B hereby undertakes to comply forthwith with any such direction from the other party;

(e) *no offer, contract or representation*

that the furnishing of Confidential Information will not constitute an offer by A, nor the basis of any contract nor a representation which may be relied upon by B;

(f) *no grant of IP rights*

that there is no grant of any intellectual property rights in the Confidential Information which is disclosed;

(g) *right to terminate*

that each party reserves the right in its sole and absolute discretion to reject all or any proposals, and to terminate discussions and negotiations involving the Proposed Transaction at any time;

(h) *no warranty*

(i) that A, its Representatives and Advisors has not made nor will make any representation or warranty as to the accuracy, completeness or otherwise of the Confidential Information supplied by it (save as otherwise provided in any agreement entered into to effect the Proposed Transaction);

(ii) that (save as otherwise provided in any agreement entered into to effect the Proposed Transaction) B has not relied on or been induced to enter into any such agreement by any representation or warranty save for any representation or warranty expressly set out in such agreement and subject to such limitations and restrictions as may be specified by it;

(iii) in particular, but without limiting the provisions of sub-paragraphs (i) and (ii) above, that any projected results for future periods or management accounts which may be contained in the Confidential Information are for indicative purposes only and, while they will represent the current estimates of the board(s) of A, will not warrant, or in any way accept liability for, their accuracy. B must make its own independent assessment of the other party and rely on its own judgment in reaching any conclusion;

(i) *no waiver*

(i) that no single or partial exercise of, or failure or delay by A in exercising any right, power or privilege to which it is entitled shall operate as a waiver of, or impair or preclude any other or further exercise;

351

      (ii)   that the terms of this letter and each party's obligations and acknowledgements under it may only be:

         (A)   waived by the other party in writing; and

         (B)   varied in writing signed by both parties;

(j)   *invalidity*

that if any term or provision in this letter shall be held to be illegal or unenforceable, in whole or in part, under any enactment or rule of law, such term or provision or part shall to that extent be deemed not to form part of this Agreement but the enforceability of the remainder of this letter shall not be affected;

(k)   *law and jurisdiction*

that the terms of this letter and each party's obligations and undertakings under it shall be governed by and construed in accordance with English law and the English courts shall have exclusive jurisdiction for all matters arising under it, whether in contract, tort or otherwise;

(l)   *requests and enquiries*

that unless we agree otherwise from time to time, requests for Confidential Information and all enquiries relating to the Proposed Transaction will be made as follows and to no other person or fax number:

      (i)   of A on fax number ....; or

      (ii)   of B on fax number ....;

(m) *notices*

that notices under this letter shall be given in writing to the relevant party at the address stated above (or such other address as it shall previously have notified to the other party) and any notice sent by fax shall be deemed received when sent, any notice sent by hand shall be deemed received when delivered and any notice sent by first-class post shall be deemed received two working days after posting;

(n) *nature of this letter*

that this letter is in substitution for and supersedes all previous agreements entered into between the parties with respect to the Confidential Information. This letter and the terms hereof will terminate and be of no further effect on the signing of an agreement to effect the Proposed Transaction;

(o) *expenses*

that should, for whatever reason, the Proposed Transaction not proceed or not be successfully completed, each of A and B will pay their own Adviser's fees and disbursements together with any Value Added Tax.

If you are in agreement with the provisions of this letter please indicate your agreement by signing and returning to us the enclosed copy of this letter.

Yours faithfully

Director

For and on behalf of

.... Limited

.... Limited agrees, undertakes and acknowledges in the terms set out in the above letter.

Director

For and on behalf of

.... Limited

Precedent B – Data room rules

The form of data room rules set out in this annexure are suitable for use by the seller's professional advisors or other hosts of the data room set up for use by prospective purchasers in an auction process.

The data room rules are an indicative draft only and they have been prepared from the seller's perspective. This precedent should be treated as being little more than a collection of useful clauses.

Warning:

All precedents can be dangerous. There are major risks in using this precedent without competent legal advice. It is unlikely that any precedent will be able to be used in any transaction without considerable modification.

These rules regulate access to and use of the facilities made available at the data room located at the offices of .... at ....

The visitor (or the person he or she is representing) must confirm by signing a copy of these rules, that they have read the rules and fully understand the obligations contained in them and agree to be bound by and comply with them and that they are authorised to sign for and on behalf of the person/company who they are representing.

Visitors will only be admitted to the data room after they have signed a copy of these rules.

THE RULES

In consideration of being granted access to the data room and to the confidential information contained in it, you [and your professional advisors both] on your own [and their] behalf and on behalf of any of your [and their] employees who visit the data room acknowledge and agree to the following terms and conditions of access.

1.   **Confidential Information**

1.1   The information and documentation in the data room and any other information or opinion subsequently supplied or given to you ('the Confidential Information') by .... Limited ('the Company'), [*insert name of lawyers*] or [*the accountants*] is strictly confidential and is made available subject to and on the terms contained in these Rules.

1.2 The Confidential Information is being made available to you [and/or your professional advisors] for the sole purpose of assisting you to decide whether you wish to make a final offer for the [business and assets of the] Company.

1.3 The Confidential Information will not constitute or form part of any offer, nor will any such information form the basis of any contract in respect of it. You must rely on the terms and conditions contained in such a contract subject to such limitation and restriction as may be specified in it.

1.4 Subject to paragraph 1.5 you will keep the confidential information in strict confidence and will not, without the prior written consent of the Company, [*the lawyers*] or [*the accountants*] or except as required by law, publish, reproduce, copy or disclose any of the information to any person other than to your professional advisors, officers and senior employees ('the Advisors') who need to know it for the purpose of deciding whether you wish to make a final offer for the [business and assets of the] Company.

1.5 You will ensure that each of the Advisors to whom any of the Confidential Information is disclosed in accordance with paragraph 1.4:

(a) is, before disclosure, made aware that the Confidential Information is confidential and subject to these Rules; and that they may not use it for any other purpose; and

(b) adheres to these Rules as if he or she were a party to them.

1.6 You shall indemnify the Company, [*the lawyers*] or [*the accountants*] and hold them harmless against any actions, claims, costs, proceedings, expenses, losses or damage (including legal costs) which any of them incur, however they accrue, in the event of any unauthorised disclosure of any Confidential Information by you, your Advisors or any person to whom you or they have disclosed Confidential Information.

1.7 You will, on request and in any event no later than two months from the date of these Rules if no offer is made within that period:

(a) return or procure the return of the Confidential Information from any professional adviser without retaining any copies in whatever form; and

(b) destroy any notes, analysis or memoranda or other stored information of any kind prepared by you or on your behalf to the extent that they contain or are based on the Confidential Information.

1.8 The Confidential Information:

(a) does not purport to be all inclusive or necessarily to contain all the information that you may desire for the purpose of the proposed acquisition of the [business and assets of the] Company and may

356

be subject to updating, revision or amendments. You should carry out your own investigations and analysis of the [business and assets of the] Company and of the Confidential Information and should consult your own Advisors before proceeding with any offer; and

(b)   has been provided by the Company and has not been independently verified as to its accuracy. No representation or warranty, expressed or implied, is given by the Company, [*the lawyers*] or [*the accountants*] or any of their respective directors, partners, officers, affiliates, employees, advisors or agents as to the accuracy or completeness of the contents of the Confidential Information or any other document or information supplied, or which may be supplied at any time or any opinion or projections expressed in them or in these Rules. [In particular for reasons of commercial sensitivity, some information on certain matters has not been included at this stage, although such information may be made available at a later date.]

1.9   The part of the Confidential Information which contains projected financial information is based on judgmental estimates and assumptions made by the management of the Company, about circumstances and events that have not yet taken place. Accordingly, there can be no assurance that the projected results will be attained, and no representation or warranty whatsoever is given in relation to the reasonableness or achievability of the projects or in relation to the basis and assumption underlying these projections. You must satisfy yourself in relation to the reasonableness, achieve ability and accuracy of them.

1.10   No responsibility or liability is accepted and any and all responsibility and liability is expressly disclaimed by the Company, [*the lawyers*] and [*the accountants*] and any of their respective directors, partners, officers, affiliates, employees, advisors or agents for any misstatements, misrepresentations in or omissions from the Confidential Information or any other documents or information, however communicated to you or your advisors in the course of your evaluation of the [business and assets of the] Company.

1.11   Any person who breaches the terms of this letter in any material respect may be excluded from participating further in negotiations and you undertake to comply with any such direction from us.

2.   Access to documents

2.1   No documents in the data room may be removed. Reasonable requests for copies of documents will be considered. Photocopying will be carried out by a representative of [*insert name of host*], [and will be available for collection after 1 pm on the business day following the request for photocopying].

2.2   Documents or records may be removed from any file or folder in which they are located for viewing or examination but must be replaced in the same place in which they were found. Documents which are bound or contained in a ring binder in a particular sequence must not be removed from the binder in which they are held.

2.3   No document may be marked, altered, modified, varied (including altering its sequence), damaged or destroyed in any way.

3.   Conditions of entry

3.1   The data room will be available between the hours of 9 am and 6 pm.

3.2   Access will only be granted to those persons who have requested access in writing no later than .... pm on the business day prior to access being sought to the data room. Unauthorised persons will be refused access to the data room.

3.3   Authorisation to visit the data room may be withdrawn by [*insert name of host*] at any time (prior to or during a visit) in respect of any person without prior notice and without the need to provide any explanation.

3.4   Visitors must at all times comply immediately with any requests by a representative of [*insert name of host*] concerning the use of the data room, including a request to leave the data room and the building.

3.5   Visitors must submit to all reasonable security regulations and procedures required by [*insert name of host*]. No access should be requested nor will any be granted to any other areas of the building.

3.6   Hand-held dictating equipment and personal computers may be used in the data room. However, no coats or briefcases may be taken into the data room. Suitable cloakroom facilities will be provided.

4.   General

4.1   [*Insert name of host*]'s representative in attendance at the data room is instructed only to supervise the operation of the data room. Visitors are not permitted to ask any questions of such representative as to documents other than to ask where a certain document may be found. Any questions arising in connection with the information, the data room or otherwise must be submitted in writing to [*insert name of host*] with a copy to the Company and [*the accountants*].

4.2   A telephone will be situated in the data room, and an external line can be obtained by dialling 9. Coffee and tea will be provided at reasonable intervals and can be requested by dialling 0. Lunch will not be provided.

4.3   Visitors must sign in at reception upon entering the offices of [*insert name of host*] and sign out at reception upon leaving the offices.

4.4   [*Insert name of host*] reserve the right to change the procedure governing the data room at any time.

5. Governing law and jurisdiction

5.1   These Rules are governed by and construed in accordance with English law.

5.2   Each of the parties irrevocably submits for all purposes in connection with this Agreement to the exclusive jurisdiction of the courts of England.

We confirm that we have read these Rules, fully understand the obligations contained in them and agree to be bound by and to comply with the terms and regulations set out above.

Signed: ....

(Print Name): ....

For and on behalf of: ....

Dated: ....

Precedent C – Offer letter: share purchase

The offer letter set out in this annexure is suitable for use by a purchaser in the context of a share purchase and is an indicative draft only. The precedent should be tailored to suit the particular circumstances of the proposed transaction.

Warning:

All precedents can be dangerous. There are major risks in using this precedent without competent legal advice. It is unlikely that any precedent will be able to be used in any transaction without considerable modification.

[Name and address of the Vendors]

[Date]

Dear Sir(s)

Proposed acquisition of the .... **of** .... **Limited ('the Company')**

Further to our recent discussions, we are writing to set the principal terms and conditions on and subject to which .... Limited ('the Purchaser') is willing, in principle, to purchase from .... ('the Sellers') the whole of the issued share capital of .... ('the Company'), subject to the agreement and execution of legally binding documentation.

The principal terms and conditions are as follows:

1. THE OFFER

The Purchaser proposes to acquire the full legal and beneficial interest in the issued share capital of the Company, free from all encumbrances, for a consideration of £........... [payable in full on completion] [payable as follows:

(a) £........... payable in cash on completion;
(b) £........... to be satisfied by the allotment of [........... unsecured loan notes of the Purchaser] [£.................. ordinary shares of .... each of the Purchaser having a market value equal to this amount];
(c) a sum equal to the excess of the [net tangible] assets of the Company [and its subsidiaries] as at .... [consolidated] [trading] profit of the Company [and its subsidiaries] before tax for the period ending on .... over £............... If the net [[tangible] assets] [profits] are

361

less than £..............., the Sellers will pay an amount equal to the deficit to the Purchaser;] [and]

(d) the sum of £.............. payable on the date .... days after publication of the audited accounts of the Company for the year ending .... ('the Accounts'). If, however, the trading profit before tax of the Company (as shown in the Accounts) is less than £..............., the price will be reduced by an amount equal to the shortfall multiplied by a factor of ....]

[The Purchaser may elect to satisfy any part of the cash price by carrying out a [vendor] placing of its [ordinary] shares.]

[For the purposes of (c) above, the [net [tangible]] assets of the Company [and its subsidiaries] as at .... [[consolidated] [trading]] profit of the Company [and its subsidiaries] before tax for the period ending on .... will be ascertained from a [consolidated] balance sheet prepared as at .... [consolidated] profit and loss account prepared for the period ending on .... ('the Completion Accounts').]

[[The Completion Accounts] [For the purposes of (d) above, the Accounts] will be prepared in accordance with UK generally accepted accounting principles and practices and, subject to those principles and practices, the Company's last audited [consolidated] accounts. The [Completion Accounts] will be subject to review by the Purchaser's accountants and any matter which cannot be agreed between the Sellers and the Purchaser will be referred to an independent accountant who will act as an expert and whose decision will be final.]

The price for the Shares has been calculated [on the basis of the information contained in the Information Memorandum dated .... which was provided to the Purchaser and] on the following assumptions:

[(i) that the [consolidated] [trading] profit before tax of the Company [and its subsidiaries] (as shown in the [Completion] Accounts) will be not less than £.................;]

[(ii) that the [consolidated] net [tangible] assets of the Company [and its subsidiaries] (as shown in the [Completion] Accounts) will be not less than £.................;]

[(iii) that the Company [and its subsidiaries] will at Completion have no indebtedness to any [Seller] [member of the Seller's group] or to any third party (other than normal trading debts).]

2. CONDITIONS

This sale and purchase will be conditional upon:

(a) the carrying out of a satisfactory financial, legal and commercial, due diligence exercise in relation to the Company and its business, assets and liabilities. [Specifically, particular attention will be paid to: [*set out specific areas of concern*];

(b) there being no material adverse change in the financial or trading position or prospects of the Company (and its subsidiaries] between the date of this offer and completion;

(c) that no dividends or other distributions are paid, made or declared by the Company between the date of this offer and completion;

(d) the net assets of the [Company] at Completion being not less than those shown in the management accounts as at .... 20......;

[(e) approval of the purchase by the board of [the Purchaser] [Purchaser's parent]] [and] (the passing of a resolution of the Purchaser's shareholders approving the purchase [and related matters]];

[(f) the admission to Listing of the Purchaser's shares issued as part of the price or for the purposes of a [vendor] placing to satisfy the cash price;]

[(g) the purchase not being referred to the Monopolies and Mergers Commission or being subject to proceedings brought by the European Commission;]

[(h) the obtaining, in a form reasonably satisfactory to the Purchaser, of all statutory and regulatory approvals and consents which are necessary or desirable in relation to the proposed acquisition of the Shares;]

[(i) .... entering into a service agreement with the Purchaser and the Company for .... years and otherwise on the terms and at the salary set out in [his] existing service agreement with the Company (a copy of which has been provided to the Purchaser);]

(j) others.

3. SALE AND PURCHASE DOCUMENTATION

In the sale and purchase agreement, the Sellers will give full warranties as to the accuracy of statements relating to the Company's [and its subsidiaries'] financial, commercial and taxation position and [its] [their] accounts, properties and employees, subject only to such matters as are fairly disclosed to the Purchaser prior to signing.

The Sellers will indemnify the Purchaser in respect of taxation liabilities [and any other presently undisclosed liabilities, including potential environmental liabilities, which emerge in the course of the Purchaser's due diligence investigation in respect of which the Purchaser requires protection over and above the warranties].

[After signing of the sale and purchase agreement and pending Completion, the Sellers will obtain the Purchaser's consent prior to taking certain material actions in relation to the Company [and its subsidiaries] and the conduct of [its] [their respective] business[es].]

On completion, the Sellers will procure the settlement of all indebtedness due from the Sellers and any connected persons to the Company [and its subsidiaries] and the release of the Company [and its subsidiaries] from all guarantees and indemnities.

The Sellers will enter into non-compete, non-solicitation and confidentiality covenants in forms acceptable to the Purchaser, which shall subsist for [such periods as the Purchaser may reasonably require to protect its business interests] [not less than .... years respectively after completion].

The Purchaser will have the exclusive right to use all trade names currently used by the Company [and its subsidiaries].

The Purchaser will require certain key executives, to be notified by the Purchaser to the Seller[s] to enter into new service agreements with the Company on completion.

The Purchaser will require [a transfer payment to be made from the Seller's pension scheme which is not less than the share of the fund attributable to, and is at least sufficient to fund the prospective benefits of, the employees of the Company [and its subsidiaries]. If the fund is in surplus the Purchaser will require the transfer payment to include the proportionate share of that surplus. The transfer payment will be determined in accordance with fair and reasonable actuarial assumptions (including future salary increases) to be agreed between the Sellers' actuary and the Purchaser's actuary].

4. TIMING

It is the Purchaser's intention to proceed as quickly as possible with the proposed transaction and aims to complete on [or before] .... (or as soon as reasonably practicable thereafter).

5. DUE DILIGENCE

The Sellers will procure that the Purchaser and its professional advisors have full access to the books and records of the Company to enable the due diligence process to proceed.

6. EXCLUSIVITY AND CONFIDENTIALITY

In consideration of the mutual agreement of the parties to work towards the proposed acquisition and the Purchaser incurring the expense of instructing various professional advisors to commence their due diligence investigations, by countersigning and returning the enclosed copy of this letter the Sellers jointly and severally agree:

  (a) that until .... 20.......... no Seller will sell, contract, negotiate or offer to sell any of his shares in the Company [and its subsidiaries] to any other person, nor provide any information to any other person with a view to the acquisition by that person of any shares in the Company [and its subsidiaries] nor act in its capacity as shareholder or director of the Company [and its subsidiaries] to sell the business or assets of the Company [and its subsidiaries]. Any existing negotiations and discussions with other parties will be determined upon signing this letter;

(b) that none of them nor their respective directors, officers, employees or professional advisors will disclose the contents of this letter or any discussions with the Purchaser to any third party apart from their own professional advisors and bankers who will be under the same obligation to keep all aspects of the proposed transaction confidential.

7. COSTS

Either:

each party shall bear its own costs incurred in relation to this proposed transaction, whether or not it proceeds;

or:

in the event of the proposed acquisition not proceeding, either because the Sellers withdraw from the transaction or the Purchaser withdraws because of some material item coming to light of which it was not previously aware, the Sellers will reimburse the Purchaser for all reasonable costs incurred with advisors from this date forward.

8. GENERAL

This letter is a statement of intention and is not (other than paragraphs 5, 6, 7 and 10 which will be legally binding on the parties) intended to create a legally binding relationship between any party.

The Purchaser very much looks forward to progressing negotiations with you as quickly as possible, and would be grateful if you would kindly sign and return the enclosed copy of this letter to us to indicate your agreement with its terms.

Yours faithfully

....

for and on behalf of ....

Agreed:

....

[for and on behalf of] [by] the Sellers

.... 20...........

Precedent D – Offer letter: business transfer

The offer letter set out in this annexure is suitable for use by a purchaser in the context of a business transfer and is an indicative draft only. The precedent should be tailored to suit the particular circumstances of the proposed transaction.

Warning:

All precedents can be dangerous. There are major risks in using this precedent without competent legal advice. It is unlikely that any precedent will be able to be used in any transaction without considerable modification. It is 'subject to the agreement and execution of legally binding documentation' and is not therefore intended to be legally binding except for clauses 11/12/13 as stated in the document. It is crucial the parties are aware of this issue in relation to any document of this type.

[*Name and address of Seller company*]

[Date]

Dear Sir(s)

Proposed acquisition of the business and assets of [the ....
.. division of] .... Limited
('the Business')

Further to our recent discussions, we ('the Purchaser') are writing to set the principal terms and conditions on which we (or such subsidiary nominated by us) would agree to purchase from .... Limited ('the Seller') the Business as a going concern, subject to the agreement and execution of legally binding documentation.

The principal terms and conditions are as follows:

1. THE OFFER

We propose to acquire the following assets free from encumbrances [and certain specific liabilities [as shown in the balance sheet as at ....]] of .... Limited for the consideration set out in paragraph 3 of this letter:

    (a)   the goodwill and know-how of the Business together with all intellectual property including patents and trademarks, designs, design rights and information and records relating to the Business;

   (b)   all computer hardware, software and networks owned or used by the Business including all arrangements relating to the provision of maintenance and support, security, disaster recovery, facilities management, bureau and online services to the Business;

   (c)   all plant, machinery and equipment, including spare parts used in the Business at the date of completion;

   (d)   all stocks of raw materials, work in progress, finished goods and consumables held for the purposes of the Business at completion;

   (e)   the benefit (subject to the burden) of the contracts of the Business including all trading contracts, leasing agreements, intellectual property licences, contracts of employment including all undischarged contracts, pending contracts at the date of completion;

[(f)   the [freehold/leasehold] properties at ....;]

[(g)   all debts due to the Seller at completion]; [and]

[(h)   all other assets used in the Business not specifically excluded below.]

2.   EXCLUDED ASSETS AND LIABILITIES

The following assets and liabilities will be excluded from the acquisition:

   (a)   all cash in hand at bank at completion;

   (b)   all amounts (including any bank overdraft and tax liabilities) owing by the Seller to its creditors in respect of the period up to completion;

   (c)   all debts due to the Seller in respect of the period up to and including completion;

[(d)   all amounts due to or from any number of the Seller's group]; [and]

   (e)   any assets or liabilities of the Seller not relating to the Business; [and all other liabilities of the Business not specifically assumed].

3.   PRICE

The consideration for the acquisition of the Business and assets [and liabilities] set out in paragraph 1 above shall be £.................. [payable in cash in full on completion] [payable as follows:

   (a)   £................. payable in cash on completion;

   (b)   £................. to be satisfied by the allotment of [unsecured loan notes of the Purchaser] [ordinary shares of .... each of the Purchaser having a market value equal to this amount];

   (c)   a sum equal to the excess of the [net] [tangible] assets of the Business as at .... over £.................. [and a sum equal to the trading profit of the Business before tax for the period ending on .... over £..................]. If the [[net] [tangible] assets] [profits] are less than £.................., the Seller will pay an amount equal to the deficit to the Purchaser; [and]

[(d)   the sum of £.................. payable on the date .... days after publication of the audited accounts of the Business for the year ending .... ('the Accounts'). If, however, the trading profit before tax of the Business (as shown in the Accounts) is less than £.................., the price will be reduced by an amount equal to the shortfall multiplied by a factor of ....]

[The Purchaser may elect to satisfy any part of the cash price by carrying out a [vendor] placing of its [ordinary] shares.]

[For the purposes of (c) above, the [net] [tangible] assets of the Business as at .... [and the [trading] profit of the Company before tax for the period ending on ....] will be ascertained from a balance sheet prepared as at .... [and the] profit and loss account prepared for the period ending on .... ('the Completion Accounts').]

[[The Completion Accounts] [For the purposes of (d) above, the Accounts] will be prepared in accordance with UK generally accepted accounting principles and practices and, subject to those principles and practices, the Business' last audited accounts. The [Completion] Accounts will be subject to review by the Purchaser's accountants and any matter which cannot be agreed between the Sellers and the Purchaser will be referred to an independent accountant who will act as an expert and whose decision will be final.]

The price for the Business has been calculated on the following assumptions:

[(i) that the [trading] profit before tax of the Business (as shown in the [Completion] Accounts) will be not less than £................;]
[(ii) that the net [tangible] assets of the Business (as shown in the [Completion] Accounts) will be not less than £................;]
[(iii) that the Business will at completion have no indebtedness to any [Seller] [member of the Seller's group] or to any third party (other than normal trading debts).]

4. CONTRACTS, LIABILITIES AND APPORTIONMENTS

The Purchaser will agree to perform the trading and other contracts to be assumed by it in respect of the period from completion. All contracts will be assigned to the Purchaser so far as possible. Where an assignment is not possible, the Seller will make arrangements to enable the full benefit of the contracts to be made available to the Purchaser.

All items of receipt and expenditure, pre-payments and accruals (except those relating to an asset or liability excluded from the sale and purchase) will be apportioned and, except to the extent they are reflected in the Completion Accounts, will be paid by or to the Seller within .... days of completion.

5. CONDITIONS

The sale and purchase of the Business will be conditional upon:

(a) the carrying out of a satisfactory financial, legal and commercial, due diligence exercise in relation to the Business, its assets and liabilities.

[Specifically, particular attention will be paid to: [*set out specific areas of concern*]];

(b) there being no material adverse change in the financial or trading position or prospects of the Business between the date of this offer and completion;

(c) the net assets of the Business at completion being not less than those shown in the management accounts as at .... 20.........;

[(d) approval of the purchase by the board of [the Purchaser] [Purchaser's parent] [and] [the passing of a resolution of the Purchaser's shareholders approving the purchase [and related matters]];]

[(e) the admission to listing of the Purchaser's shares issued as part of the price or for the purposes of a [seller] placing to satisfy the cash price;]

[(f) the Transfer not being referred to the Competition and Markets Authority or being subject to proceedings brought by the European Commission;]

[(g) the obtaining of all necessary tax clearances;]

[(h) satisfactory consultations with all trade unions recognised by the Seller for collective bargaining purposes;

[(i) lessors' consents]

[(j) the obtaining of consents of key customers/suppliers;]

[(k) others].

6. EMPLOYEES

The Purchaser will assume responsibility for all employees of the Business from completion. The Purchaser will require [certain key executives] to enter into new service agreements with the Purchaser on completion.

7. PENSIONS

[The Seller will permit the employees of the Business to remain in the Seller's group pension scheme for a period of up to 12 months following completion. As soon as practicable a transfer will be made from the Seller's pension scheme which is not less than the share of the fund attributable to, and is at least sufficient to fund the prospective benefits of, the employees of the Business. If the fund is in surplus the transfer payment will include the proportionate share of that surplus. The transfer payment will be determined in accordance with fair and reasonable actuarial assumptions (including future salary increases) to be agreed between the Seller's actuary and the Purchaser's actuary.]

8. SHARED FACILITIES

The Seller will procure that shared facilities currently supplied by the Seller [Seller's group] [*identify*] to the Business will continue to be supplied to the Purchaser for .... [at cost] [free of charge].

9. BUSINESS TRANSFER AGREEMENT

In the business transfer agreement, the Seller will give full warranties as to the accuracy of statements relating to the Business, the assets used in the Business and the financial and commercial position of the Business, subject only to such matters as are fairly disclosed to the Purchaser prior to signing.

[After the signing of the business transfer agreement and pending completion, the Seller will obtain the Purchaser's consent prior to taking certain material actions in relation to the conduct of the Business.]

The Seller will enter into non-compete, non-solicitation and confidentiality covenants in forms acceptable to us, which shall subsist for [such periods as we may reasonably require to protect its business interests] [not less than .... years respectively after completion].

We will have the exclusive right to use all trade names currently used by the Business.

10. TIMING

It is our intention to proceed as quickly as possible with the proposed transaction and aims to complete on or before .... (or as soon as reasonably practicable thereafter).

11. DUE DILIGENCE

The Sellers will procure that we and our professional advisors have full access to the books and records of the Business to enable the due diligence process to proceed.

12. EXCLUSIVITY AND CONFIDENTIALITY

In consideration of the mutual agreement of the parties to work towards the proposed acquisition and the Purchaser incurring the expense of instructing various professional advisors to commence their due diligence investigations, by countersigning and returning the enclosed copy of this letter the Seller agrees:

    (a)   that until .... 20......... the Seller will not sell, contract, negotiate or offer to sell any of the Business to any other person, nor provide any information to any other person with a view to the acquisition by that person of any of the Business or assets comprised in the Business. Any existing negotiations and discussions with other parties will be determined upon signing this letter;

    (b)   that neither the seller or its directors, officers, employees or professional advisors will disclose the contents of this letter or any discussions with the Purchaser to any third party apart from their own professional advisors and bankers who will be under the same obligation to keep all aspects of the proposed transaction confidential.

371

13. COSTS

Either:

Each party shall bear its own costs incurred in relation to this proposed transaction, whether or not it proceeds;

or:

In the event of the proposed acquisition not proceeding, either because the Seller withdraws from the transaction or the Purchaser withdraws because of some material item coming to light of which it was not previously aware, the Seller will reimburse the Purchaser for all reasonable costs incurred with advisors from this date forward.

14. GENERAL

This letter is a statement of intention only and is not (other than paragraphs 11, 12 and 13 which will be legally binding on the parties) intended to create a legally binding relationship between any party.

The Purchaser very much looks forward to progressing negotiations with you as quickly as possible, and would be grateful if you would kindly sign and return the enclosed copy of this letter to us to indicate your agreement with its terms.

Yours faithfully

……………………………………………………………..

for and on behalf of ……………………………………………………………

Agreed:

……………………………………………………………..

[for and on behalf of] [by] the Seller

……………………………… 20………

Precedent E – Due diligence request

The form of due diligence request set out in this annexure is suitable for use by a purchaser in connection with its legal due diligence and is applicable (with modification) for both share purchases and business transfers.

The due diligence request is an indicative draft only and has been drafted from the purchaser's perspective. The precedent should be tailored to suit the particular circumstances of the target company/business and to avoid duplication with any other due diligence requests made by the purchaser and/or its other advisors.

Warning:

All precedents can be dangerous. There are major risks in using this precedent without competent legal advice. It is unlikely that any precedent will be able to be used in any transaction without considerable modification.

REQUEST FOR INFORMATION

Proposed acquisition of the [entire issued share capital] [business and assets of] .... Limited ('the Company').

This request for information is being made as part of the purchaser's evaluation of the Company and the business carried on by it ('the Business'). We have tried to ensure that this request does not duplicate similar requests made by the purchaser or its other advisors.

[References in this request to 'the Company' are to the Company and each of its subsidiary undertakings.]

This request for information is not exhaustive and supplemental requests for information may be made. We suggest that you retain photocopies of any documents sent to us, so that in due course they can be incorporated, where applicable, in the formal disclosure letter.

Please supply the following copy documents and information in relation to the Company and the Business and identify replies by using the same numerical reference system. Where a full understanding of the position cannot be obtained from the copy documents alone please also provide an explanation. We suggest that you supply responses as and when the information is available rather than waiting until all the information has been collected.

1.   [Constitution[1]

1.1   Certificate of Incorporation and any Certificate of Incorporation on Change of Name.

1.2   Memorandum and articles of association, together with relevant resolutions and agreements.

1.3   Written confirmation of:

(a)   authorised share capital (including classes and denominations);

(b)   issued and paid up share capital (including classes and denominations);

(c)   changes in the issued share capital in the last six years;

(d)   name and address of each shareholder together with the number and class of shares held by each of them. Where shares are held on trust, please give the name and address of the beneficial owner and supply a copy of the declaration of trust;

(e)   names and addresses of the directors and secretary;

(f)   accounting reference date; and

(g)   where and when the statutory and minute books may be inspected.

1.4   Shareholders' or similar agreements which would require third party consent or otherwise affect the proposed acquisition.

1.5   Agreements granting options over or the right to call for the issue of any share or loan capital of the Company.

1.6   Details of all other corporate bodies in which the Company holds or owns any shares or other securities or loan stock or other forms of debentures or where the Company has entered into any agreement relating to the same. Please supply copies of all documentation which relate to any such bodies corporate to which the Company is party.

1.7   Details of when dormant subsidiaries last traded.]

1   Delete if this Due Diligence Request is to be issued in connection with a proposed business transfer.

2.   Business

2.1   Description of the business carried on by the Company or, if it is dormant, details of when (if at all) it last traded.

2.2   Details of any change in the nature of the Business within the last two years.

2.3   Copies of any corporate brochures, trade pamphlets and any other marketing or promotional literature produced by the Company.

2.4   Details of any contract at risk as a result of negotiations leading to the change in ownership of the Company.

2.5   Details of all business opportunities open to the Company including negotiations in relation to them.

3. **[The Seller and connected persons**[2]

3.1 In relation to each company which carries on the Business or owns assets employed in the Business ('the Seller'):

    (a) details of:
        (i) the name and address of each shareholder together with the number and class of shares held by each of them; and
        (ii) the names and addresses of the directors and secretary; and
    (b) a copy of:
        (i) its memorandum and articles of association; and
        (ii) any shareholders or similar agreements which would require third party consent to, or otherwise affect, the proposed acquisition.

3.2 Where the assets employed in the Business are owned by more than one company:

    (a) a legal structure chart of the companies in the group which carry on the Business or own assets employed in the Business; and
    (b) an organisational chart showing activities carried on, location, facilities, management, structure and reporting responsibilities, naming key individuals and summarising their roles.

3.3 Details of any contracts or arrangements relating to the [Company] [Business] in which any of the shareholders or directors of the Seller(s) or persons related to or otherwise connected with them are or have been interested, whether directly or indirectly.

3.4 Details of all business activities or interests of each Seller and their shareholders and directors (any persons related to or otherwise connected with them) where these compete with or are material to the Business.]

2 Delete if this Due Diligence Request is to be issued in connection with a proposed share purchase.

4. **Accounts**

4.1 Audited accounts [of each Seller[3]] for the last three years.

4.2 Management accounts [of each Seller[3]] since the last audited accounts.

4.3 The current business plans [of each Seller[3]] and to the extent they are not contained in the current business plan, current budgets and forecasts and the underlying assumptions.

3 Delete if this Due Diligence Request is to be issued in connection with a proposed share purchase.

5. **[Finance**[4]

Details of:

    (a) the Company's bank accounts (including name and address of bank branch) and copies of all facility and loan arrangements with the Company's bankers or other financiers;

(b)   all debenture stocks, loan stocks, loan notes or other debt instruments issued by the Company and copies of all relevant documents;

(c)   debt factoring and similar arrangements and copies of all relevant documents;

(d)   customer deposits;

(e)   consultants' commissions;

(f)   any mortgages, charges or debentures over the Company's undertaking, assets or share capital and supply copies of the charging documents;

(g)   any guarantees, indemnities, or counter-indemnities given by the Company and supply copies of the relevant documents;

(h)   all grants and allowances made to the Company during the past six years;

(i)   any current, proposed or projected capital commitments;

(j)   any hire-purchase, lease, rental, conditional sale or other similar credit agreements;

(k)   any contingent liabilities;

(l)   any debts owed to or from any group company;

(m)   an aged list of debtors showing debts considered bad or doubtful; and

(n)   any credit arrangements in favour of a customer giving unusually long or otherwise beneficial terms for payment.]

4   Delete if this Due Diligence Request is to be issued with a proposed business transfer.

6.   [Taxation[5]

6.1   Details of the status of tax computations and assessments for all completed accounting periods, including details of matters unresolved with HMRC or other taxation authorities.

6.2   Details of all VAT arrangements, including details of any VAT group of which the Company is a member.

6.3   Details of tax losses.

6.4   Details of PAYE/NI returns and of any potential liabilities.]

5   Delete if this Due Diligence Request is to be issued in connection with a proposed share purchase.

7.   Premises

7.1   A list of all premises owned, leased, occupied or [in which any other interest is held by the Company] [used in connection with the Business] and in relation to all such premises:

(a)   the full postal address, a full description of its use and the tenure held;

(b)   a plan;

(c)   office copy entries or an abstract of title in relation to any freehold or long leasehold titles forming part of the proposed acquisition;

(d)   copies of all leases and sub-leases, tenancies and licences under which the premises are held or sub-let to third parties;

(e)   copies of all licences to assign, sub-let, for alterations, change of user, assignments, side letters, deeds of variation, rent review memorandum, guarantees or warrantees relating to any of the documents revealed in (d) above;

(f)   a list of all the occupiers of the premises;

(g)   copies of all planning permissions, building regulations approvals and fire certificates relating to the premises;

(h)   copies of any valuations of the premises which have been made within the last three years;

(i)   full details of any development carried out by the [Company] [Sellers] together with copies of all planning permissions obtained;

(j)   full details of any notices served by any local or other authority in respect of the premises;

(k)   full details of any disputes concerning such premises or their use;

(l)   particulars of all rents, service charges and other outgoings accrued due but not yet paid or received; and

(m)   full details of any covenants, restrictions, licences, easements, agreements or encumbrances to which such premises are subject insofar as not covered above.

7.2   [List of any properties previously leased, occupied or used by the Company and/ or in respect of which the Company is or may be liable[6].]

6   Delete if this Due Diligence Request is to be issued in connection with a proposed business transfer.

8.   Fixed assets

8.1   List of all fixed assets owned or used [by the Company in carrying on its] [in the] Business, giving acquisition costs, written down value and estimated realisable value.

8.2   Details of:

(a)   all fixed assets used by the Company in carrying on its Business owned by third parties;

(b)   all fixed assets used by the Company in carrying on its Business shared with third parties;

(c)   major items of capital equipment purchased in the last two years or contracted for or otherwise proposed to be purchased; and

(d)   significant repairs required for plant and equipment in the last two years.

9.   Patents and registered designs

9.1   List all UK and foreign patents and registered designs which are [owned by the Company or] used in the Business together with all pending patent applications.

9.2   Describe the significance of the patents and registered designs [owned by the Company or] used in the Business and state whether additional patents or registered designs are necessary or desirable.

9.3   In relation to the patents and patent applications [owned by the Company] [used in the Business]:

   (a)   what was the date on which the relevant inventions in their first form were made?

   (b)   in each case, who is the true and first inventor?

   (c)   is the Company aware of any claim or basis for claiming that the inventions (or any of them) may not be patentable or the subject of valid patents? If so provide details not limiting the answer to matters arising in the UK;

   (d)   has the Company or its predecessor in title or any of them disclosed information on the inventions whether in confidence or otherwise to any person? If so, provide details with names and addresses of the recipients.]

9.4   In relation to any registered designs or applications for registered designs [owned by the Company] [used in the Business], is the [Company] [Seller] aware of any claim or basis for claiming that the relevant designs (or any of them) may not be registerable or the subject of valid registrations? If so provide details not limiting the answer to matters arising in the UK.

10.   Trade marks and brands

10.1   List all UK and foreign registered trade marks, together with all pending trade mark applications [owned by the Company] [used in the Business].

10.2   List all business/trading names and proprietary brands used [by the Company] [in the Business].

10.3   List all licences to and from third parties in relation to trade marks and proprietary brands.

10.4   List all internet domain names owned by or used in the operation of the Business.

10.5   In relation to any registered trade marks [owned by the Company] [used in the Business], is the [Company] [Seller] aware of any claim or basis for claiming that the relevant registrations (or any of them) may be invalid or susceptible to revocation? If so provide details not limiting the answer to matters arising in the UK.

11.   Know-How and Confidential Information

11.1   Provide details of any secret technical information or other know-how ('Know-How') which forms part of or supplements the [Company's] intellectual property rights [used in the Business].

11.2   In relation to the Know-How please provide:

    (a)   details of the key personnel responsible for or in possession of the relevant information or skills including their full name and address, country of residence and job title;

    (b)   a copy of their current employment contract.

11.3   Supply details of any Know-How used under licence from third parties, providing copies of any written licence agreements.

11.4   Describe the significance of Know-How [used by the Company] [in the Business].

11.5   Describe and supply details of arrangements for the disclosure of confidential information either by or to the business.

12.   Copyright and unregistered design right

12.1   List all copyright works or unregistered design rights which record or embody intellectual property rights ('IPR') [owned by the Company] [used in the Business], together with their dates of creation and names of creators.

12.2   List all licences to and from third parties in relation to such works.

12.3   Please provide a copy of the standard copyright assignment used [by the Company] [in the Business].

13.   Information technology

13.1   Hardware

    (a)   specify all elements of hardware used [by the Company] [in the Business] together with their location;

    (b)   (except low value peripherals) is the [Company] [Seller] the absolute owner of the hardware? Where it is not, please supply details of the leases, hire-purchase, credit or other arrangements relating to such hardware.

13.2   Communications

Confirm whether or not all cabling is owned by the [Company] [Seller]. If not, give details.

13.3   Services

    (a)   Is a disaster recovery service used in connection of the Business? If so, please provide a copy of the relevant agreement.

    (b)   Is part or all of the management and operational responsibility for the computer system used in connection of the Business delegated to an external supplier either under a facilities management agreement or other arrangement? If so, please provide a copy of the relevant agreement.

    (c)   Does the [Company] [Business] have the benefit of maintenance services for the hardware? If so, give details.

13.4   Software

    (a)   Please list the software used [by the Company] [in the Business] and indicate that software owned by the [Company] [Seller], that jointly owned, that developed using consultants and that licensed to the [Company] [Seller].

    (b)   In relation to any software developed in whole or in part by third party consultants, please confirm whether such consultants have assigned their rights in the work to the [Company] [Seller] together with copies of the agreement between the [Company] [Seller] and the consultants.

14.   Euro compliance

14.1   Details of any investigation by the [Company] [Business] into the effect of the introduction of a single European currency on its services, products, suppliers, customers and insurance policies and copies of all reports resulting from such investigations.

14.2   Details of any problems with software that may be due to matters related to the introduction of a single European currency.

15.   Data protection

15.1   Has the [Company] [Business] begun any processing, as defined by the Data Protection Act 1998, since 24 October 1998, and if so has it registered such processing with the Information Commissioner?

15.2   Does the [Company] [Business] hold any personal data for marketing purposes, and does the company conform with the Data Protection Act 1998?

15.3   Does the [Company] [Business] transfer personal data to countries outside the European Union?

16.   Trading matters

16.1   Details of, together with copies of all related documentation:

    (a)   any long term, unusual, non-routine, onerous or other material contracts or commitments and any current tender which, if accepted, would create such a contract or commitment;

    (b)   all licences, permissions, authorisations and consents necessary or which will be necessary for the carrying on of the Business;

    (c)   all standard terms and conditions of business;

    (d)   contracts made with major customers (ie those accounting for more than 5% of turnover) and value of sales attributable to them in each of the last three financial years;

    (e)   any major customer lost in the last three financial years, together with the reasons for such loss;

    (f)   contracts made with major suppliers (ie those accounting for more than 5% of goods or services supplied) and value of purchases from them in each of the last three years;

(g)   contracts made with any third parties with whom the Company contracts concerning the supply of its products or services to customers;

(h)   contracts made with any third parties concerning the research and development of the [Company's] products or services [of the Business] ;

(i)   complaints by or disputes with (either current or in the past years) any major supplier or customer;

(j)   any major competitor;

(k)   any intra-group trading;

(l)   any sales agency, distributorship, licence, franchise and other similar agreements or arrangements to which it is party;

(m)   any partnership, joint venture, profit sharing or other similar form of agreement or arrangement to which it is party;

(n)   current insurance cover, specifying the nature and amount of cover, annual premiums and next renewal date together with details of significant claims made during the last 12 months;

(o)   any obsolete stock; and

(p)   any agreements or arrangements with competitors, whether written or oral and regardless of their legal enforceability, which relate to the prices or conditions of sale under which any products, goods or services of the Company are to be sold, supplied or acquired.

(q)   Details of agreements or arrangements [to which the Company is a party] [relating to the Business] which may be terminated, varied or otherwise affected as a result of a change of [control of the relevant Company] [ownership of the Business].

17.   Litigation

17.1   Details (including pleadings) of any significant litigation.

17.2   Details of any arbitration, expert reference or other quasi-judicial or non-judicial dispute resolution procedure in which the Company is involved and which may have a material effect on the Company [the Business].

17.3   Details of any argument, dispute, claim or other facts or circumstances which might give rise to any significant litigation or other dispute resolution procedures which may have a material effect on the [Company] [the Business].

17.4   Details of any notices or communications received by the Company which indicates any material liability or potential material liability on the part of the Company or any obligation or restriction being placed on the Company which may have a materially adverse effect on its business.

17.5   Details of any investigation, finding or decision of any competent court or regulatory authority or body in relation to the Company.

18.   Employees

18.1   An up-to-date list of all persons currently employed [by the Company] [in the Business] ('the Employees') showing:

(a)   name;

(b)   date of birth;

(c)   date of commencement of employment;

(d)   job title;

(e)   normal working hours;

(f)   current annual salary (including date of last review and details of any proposed review or increase);

(g)   commission and bonus arrangements;

(h)   benefits;

(i)   notice period;

(j)   grade of employee;

(k)   disciplinary action taken during the last three years; and

(l)   job status temporary, permanent, (full time or part time).

18.2   Copies of:

(a)   all service agreements, contracts for services and consultancy agreements with directors and senior employees;

(b)   all standard terms of employment;

(c)   all terms and conditions of employment where they differ from the standard terms;

(d)   all staff handbooks;

(e)   disciplinary rules and procedures;

(f)   equal opportunities policies;

(g)   harassment (sex and race) policies;

(h)   all relevant agreements; and

(i)   all documentation confirming compliance with the Working Time Regulations 1998.

18.3   Details of:

(a)   any share option or profit sharing schemes or other employee incentive schemes;

(b)   all agreements or arrangements with trade unions or other such bodies;

(c)   any redundancy/rationalisation (whether or not notified to those concerned);

(d)   all disputes, negotiations or claims in respect of any past or present director, officer or employee [of the Company] [engaged in the Business] or any trade union or other similar body;

(e)   any consultation with trade unions and/ or Employees or their representatives relating to the potential sale;

(f)   any complaint or grievance about discrimination raised by any past or present employee within the last six months;

(g)   any complaint or grievance relating to the Working Time Regulations 1998;

(h)   any suspension of any Employee and an outline of the surrounding circumstances;

(i)   any enhanced redundancy entitlement under the terms and conditions of employment or under collective agreements or other incorporated documents;

(j)   the maternity/paternity policy relating to Employees;

(k)   any Employees or consultants seconded or transferred temporarily to the Company;

(l)   personal commitments given to (or agreements reached with) individual Employees which depart from or vary standard terms of employment;

(m)   all persons entitled or required to occupy a company flat and details of any service occupancy; and

(n)   any Equality and Human Rights Commission formal investigations in the last three years and copies of any non-discrimination notices issued by either body.

18.4   Details of all pension or retirement benefit schemes or similar arrangements [to which the Company is a party or in which the Company participates or is otherwise involved] [operated in relation to employees engaged in the Business], whether such scheme is legally enforceable or ex gratia and what auto-enrolment pension arrangements the company operates and/or when the company's 'staging date' will bring it within the auto-enrolment scheme (and stakeholder pensions it has operated, if any).

18.5   In relation to each such scheme, the names and address of:

(a)   the trustees;

(b)   the actuary;

(c)   members;

(d)   deferred pensioners; and

(e)   pensioners.

18.6   Whether the scheme:

(a)   is established on interim or definitive documentation;

(b)   is exempt, approved or awaiting such approval or unapproved;

(c)   is funded or unfunded;

(d)   was contracted-in or contracted-out of SERPS and if contracted-out whether it was contracted-out on a GMP basis or on a protected rights basis;

(e)   is a final salary scheme or money purchase scheme or a group personal pension plan;

(f)   is an insured or self-administered scheme;

(g)   is a small self administered scheme;

(h)   is contributory or non-contributory;

(i)   is a single employer scheme or a group scheme. If the latter please give the name of the principal employer if it is not the Company;

(j)   provides fully equalised benefits in accordance with the principles established in *Barber v GRE*; and

(k)   provides separately insured death benefits.

18.7   In relation to each such scheme, copies of:

(a)   all interim and definitive trust deeds and rules, any relevant board or trustee resolutions, all supplementary deeds of adherence, appointment, retirement, amendment or otherwise and all relevant announcements to members and scheme booklets;

(b)   any relevant HMRC letter of approval;

(c)   any relevant contracting-out certificate;

(d)   the most recent actuarial report;

(e)   the most recent scheme accounts;

(f)   a schedule of all members giving names, ages, sex, current salaries, and details of all employees, and employers, contributions;

(g)   all relevant insurance policies; and

(h)   confirmation that all employers' contributions and all contributions accrued due from each member have been duly paid.

19.   Environmental matters

19.1   Details of any:

(a)   trade effluent or waste substances discharged or disposed of;

(b)   hazardous substances handled or kept; and

(c)   pollution discharged into the atmosphere, water or land [by the Company] [arising as a result of carrying on the Business].

19.2   Copies of:

(a)   all consents, approvals or licences obtained in connection with water abstraction, waste disposal, hazardous substances, electrical equipment subject to WEEE regulations or any other environmental matters relating to the Business; and

(b)   any notices or correspondence received from a local authority or government department threatening any environmental enquiry, investigation or enforcement against [the Company] [in connection with the Business].

19.3   Details of:

(a)   any complaint from members of the public, adjoining landowners or pressure groups or organisations concerning environmental matters;

(b)   any claim or prosecution concerning environmental matters or product liability;

(c)   claims under any policy of insurance for any product liability or environmental matter;

(d)   internal environmental audit procedures and any environmental audits, surveys, reports or investigations;

(e)   capital expenditure or increased operating expenditure known or likely to be required over the next three years in relation or anticipated to environmental matters;

(f) any known, notified or suspected contamination in, on or under any of the properties owned, leased, occupied or used by the [Company] [Business];

(g) previous uses of any of the properties owned, leased, occupied or used by the [Company] [Business]; and

(h) any properties disposed of by the [Company] [Business] which were known, notified or suspected of being contaminated, with details of that contamination.

20. Health and safety

20.1 Copies of:

(a) the written statement of health and safety policy applied by the [Company] [Business];

(b) the organisation and arrangements for carrying out the said policy including but not limited to all documented arrangements, practices or procedures relating to:

(i) the health and safety management structure of the [Company] [Business];

(ii) individual responsibilities including all job descriptions which include health and safety duties;

(iii) safety committees, trade union safety representatives and representatives of employee safety;

(iv) health and safety rules;

(v) reporting, recording and investigating accidents and incidents;

(vi) risk assessments;

(vii) manual handling operations;

(viii) personal protective equipment;

(ix) noise;

(x) electricity supply and use;

(xi) gas supply and use;

(xii) hazardous substances/preparations supply and use;

(xiii) provision of information and training to both employees and non-employees (such as but not limited to lawful visitors, self-employed people, cleaners, contractors, etc);

(xiv) first aid;

(xv) fire and other serious and imminent dangers;

(xvi) monitoring and auditing health and safety arrangements;

(xvii) operations for which the [Company] [Business] has adopted a 'permit to work' system;

(xviii) health surveillance; and

(xix) insurance of employers' and public liability risks.

20.2 Copies of:

(a) the Company's Accident Book entries for the last three years; and

      (b)   any forms, notices or correspondence sent to or received from a local authority, government department or the Health and Safety Executive concerning health and safety matters arising as a result of carrying on the Business.

20.3   Details of:

      (a)   any claim or prosecution relating to the [Company] [Business] concerning health and safety matters;

      (b)   any complaint from any person, group or body (not being or representing any employee of the [Company] [Business]) threatening any health and safety enquiry, investigation or enforcement in connection with the [Company] [Business];

      (c)   claims under any policy of insurance for health and safety matters;

      (d)   any health and safety audits, surveys, reports or investigations; and

      (e)   agreements or arrangements with trade unions or other bodies relevant to health and safety matters.

20.4   Details of any of the following hazardous substances/hazards (not already disclosed under the above requests) handled, kept or present at the Company's premises:

      (a)   asbestos;

      (b)   lead;

      (c)   ionising radiation;

      (d)   highly flammable liquids and liquified petroleum gases;

      (e)   biological agents; or

      (f)   micro-organisms.

20.5   Details of any 'construction work', as defined by reg 2 of the Construction (Design and Management) Regulations 2007 and the predecessor regulations of 1994, undertaken after 31 March 1995.

Precedent F – Share purchase agreement

The form of share purchase agreement set out in this annexure is suitable for use by a purchaser in the conditional acquisition of a company with subsidiaries from a number of individual sellers for a pre-determined consideration payable in cash at completion. The share purchase agreement is an indicative draft only and has been drafted from the purchaser's perspective. This precedent should be treated as being little more than a collection of useful clauses.

Warning:

All precedents can be dangerous. There are major risks in using this precedent without competent legal advice. It is unlikely that any precedent will be able to be used in any transaction without considerable modification.

This Agreement is made the .... day of .... 20.........

Between:

    (1)   The persons whose names and addresses are set out in Schedule 1 ('the Sellers'); and

    (2)   .... Limited (company number: ....
.....................) whose registered office is at ....
.... ('the Purchaser').

Background:

The Sellers have agreed to sell and the Purchaser has agreed to purchase the Shares (as defined) on the terms of this Agreement.

It is agreed as follows:

1.   Definitions and interpretation

1.1   In this Agreement, unless the context otherwise requires, the following words have the following meanings:

'the Accounts'	the audited balance sheet as at the Accounts Date and the audited profit and loss account for the year ended on the Accounts Date of each Group Company, including all documents required by law to be annexed to them and, in the case of the Company, the audited consolidated balance sheet as at that date and the audited consolidated profit and loss account for that year;
'the Accounts Date'	.... 20.................;

'this Agreement'	this Agreement (including any schedule or annexure to it);
'the Board'	in relation to each Group Company, its board of directors;
'Business Day'	a day (other than a Saturday or a Sunday) on which clearing banks are open for business in the City of London;
'the Circular'	the circular to be sent by the Purchaser to its shareholders to obtain their consent to the purchase of the Shares;
'Claim'	a claim by the Purchaser against the Warrantors under the Covenant for Taxation or under the Warranties and 'Non-Tax Claim' means any claim which is not a Tax Claim;
'Claim for Taxation'	any notice, demand, assessment, letter or other document issued or action taken by any Tax Authority or any person (including any Group Company) indicating that any person is or may be placed or sought to be placed under either a Liability to Taxation or a claim for Taxation to which paragraph 10 may apply;
'the Company'	.... Limited, details of which are set out in Schedule 2; 'Completion' the completion of the sale and purchase of the Shares under this Agreement;
'Conditions'	those matters listed in sub-clause 2.1;
'the Consideration'	the consideration payable by the Purchaser to the Sellers for the Shares under sub-clause 4.1;
'the Covenant Taxation'	the covenant given by the Warrantors under for paragraph 4 of Schedule ....;
'Dangerous Substance'	any natural or artificial substance (whether in the form of a solid, liquid, gas or vapour), the generation, transportation, storage, treatment, use or disposal of which (whether alone or in combination with any other substance) gives rise to a risk of causing harm to any other living organism or causing damage to the Environment;
'Disclosed'	matters contained in the Disclosure Letter which are disclosed with sufficient particularity to enable the Purchaser to assess the impact on the Company of the matter disclosed;
'the Disclosure Letter'	the letter of the same date as this Agreement in the agreed form from the Sellers to the Purchaser, together with any attachments, disclosing matters that are exceptions to the Warranties;
'the Environment'	the environment as defined in section 1(2) of the Environmental Protection Act 1990;
'Environmental Consent'	any permit, exemption, filing requirement, licence or registration from time to time necessary or desirable under Environmental Law;
'Environmental Law'	any directive, treaty, code of practice, circular, law guidance note and the like, in each case of any jurisdiction, in force or enacted relating or pertaining to the Environment, any Dangerous Substance, human health, comfort, safety or the welfare of any other living organism;

'the Group Companies'   the Holding Company of the Company and any Subsidiary of any such Holding Company and 'Group Company' means any of them;

'Guarantee'   any guarantee, suretyship, indemnity, bonding liability or similar contingent liability given or undertaken by a person to secure or support the obligations of any third party;

'Holding Company'   any holding company within the meaning of section 1159 of the Companies Act 2006 and any parent undertaking within the meaning of section 1162 of the Companies Act 2006 from time to time, details of which are set out in Schedule 3;

'ICTA'   the Income and Corporation Taxes Act 1988;

'Intellectual Property'   patents, trade marks or names whether or not registered or capable of registration, registered designs, design rights, copyrights, database rights, the right to apply for and applications for any of the preceding items, together with the rights in inventions, processes, software, know-how, trade or business secrets, confidential information, internet domain names or any other similar right or asset capable of protection enjoyed, owned, used or licensed by any Group Company;

'the Leases'   any leases (including underleases) under which the Properties are held, particulars of which are set out in Schedule 5 and 'Lease' means any of them;

'Liability to'   (a) any liability to make a payment of or in respect of Taxation regardless of whether such Taxation is chargeable or attributable directly or primarily to a Group Company or to any other person; (b) the loss of any Relief which would (were it not for the loss) have been available to any Group Company and which has been treated as an asset in preparing the Accounts or taken into account in computing (and so reducing) or obviating any provision for deferred taxation which appears in the Accounts (or which, but for the availability or presumed availability of such Relief prior to its loss, would have appeared in the Accounts); (c) the setting off against any liability to Taxation or against Profits earned, accrued or received on or before the Accounts Date of any Relief which belongs to the Purchaser or which arises in respect of any period after the Accounts Date or in respect of any Transaction effected on or after the Accounts Date in circumstances where, but for the setting off, any Group Company would have had a liability to Taxation in respect of which the Purchaser (ignoring any limitations on liability contained herein) would have been able to make a claim against the Warrantors under the Covenant for Taxation; and (d) any liability to make a payment by way of indemnity or damages, or any other payment pursuant to a contract or arrangement, in each case arising out of or in connection with Taxation; and references to a Liability to Taxation shall include the settlement of a Claim for Taxation;

'Management Accounts'   the unaudited management accounts of each Group Company for the period from Accounts Date to ....
20............... and, in the case of the Company, the consolidated management accounts for that period;

'Non-Tax Warranties'   the representations referred to in clause 9 and set out in Schedule 4;

'Notice'   includes any notice, demand, consent or other communication;

'the Pension Scheme'   the Company's pension scheme [governed by a Definitive Trust Deed dated .... 20................];

'Planning Acts'   the Town and Country Planning Act 1990, the Planning (Listed Buildings and Conservation Areas) Act 1990, the Planning (Hazardous Substances) Act 1990, the Planning (Consequential Provisions) Act 1990, the Planning and Compensation Act 1991, Planning and Compulsory Purchase Act 2004, The Town and Country Planning (Control of Advertisements) (England) Regulations 2007, Planning and Compulsory Purchase Act 2004 and Planning Act 2008 and all other statutes containing provisions relating to town and country planning;

'the Policies'   all insurance policies maintained by the Company on the date of this Agreement and 'Policy' means any of them;

'Profits'   income, profits and gains, the value of any supply and any other consideration, value or receipt used or charged for Taxation purposes and references to 'Profits earned, accrued or received' include Profits deemed to have been earned, accrued or received for Taxation purposes;

'the Properties'   the freehold and leasehold properties, particulars of which are set out in Schedule 5 and 'the Property' means any of them;

'Purchaser's Relief'   a Relief falling within the definition of Liability to Taxation;

'Relevant Claim or Surrender'   any claim or surrender to or by any Group Company of group relief, group refund or group payment arrangement under Chapter 4, Corporation Tax Act 2010;

'Relief'   any relief, loss, allowance, exemption, set-off, deduction or credit in computing or against Profits or Taxation or any right to repayment of Taxation and references to the 'loss of any Relief' include the loss, reduction, counteraction, disallowance, setting-off against Profits, crediting against a liability to make an actual payment of Taxation or failure to obtain a Relief and 'lose' and 'lost' shall be construed accordingly;

'Seller Associate'   any Seller or any Group Company and any other person with whom any Seller or any Group Company is either associated (within the meaning of ss 448 and 449 of CTA 2010) or connected (within the meaning of section 1176 of CTA 2010).

'the Shares'	all the issued shares of the Company at Completion, as set out in Schedule 2;
'Subsidiaries'	any subsidiaries of the Company within the meaning of sections 1159 Companies Act 2006 and any subsidiary undertakings within the meaning of section 1162 of the Companies Act 2006 from time to time, details of which are set out in Schedule 3, and 'Subsidiary' means any of them;
'Taxation'	all forms of taxation and statutory, governmental, supra governmental, state, provincial, local governmental or municipal impositions, duties, contributions and levies (including withholdings and deductions), whether of the United Kingdom or elsewhere in the world, whenever imposed and however arising and all penalties, fines, charges, costs and interest, together with the cost of removing any charge or other encumbrance, relating thereto and 'Tax' shall be construed accordingly;
'Tax Authority'	any taxing or other authority, body or official competent to administer, impose or collect any Taxation;
'Tax Claim'	a claim by the Purchaser against the Warrantors under the Covenant for Taxation or that any of the Taxation Warranties is untrue or inaccurate in any respect or is misleading or, as the case may be, a claim by the Warrantors against the Purchaser under the covenant in paragraph 5;
'Tax Warranties'	the representations set out in paragraph 2 of Schedule .... (Tax Schedule) and each of them;
'TCGA'	the Taxation of Chargeable Gains Act 1992;
'the Tenancies'	any tenancies or other occupational arrangements under which the Properties are held by third parties, particulars of which are set out in Schedule 5;
'TMA'	the Taxes Management Act 1970;
'Transaction'	any transaction, deed, act, event, omission, payment or receipt of whatever nature and whether actual or deemed for Tax purposes and references to 'any Transaction effected on or before Completion' include the combined result of two or more Transactions, the first or anyone of which shall have taken place or commenced (or be deemed to have taken place or commenced) on or before Completion;
'VATA'	the Value Added Tax Act 1994; and
'Warranties'	the Non-Tax Warranties and the Tax Warranties, and 'Warranty' means anyone of them;
'Warrantors'	[the Sellers] [the following Sellers:];
'Working Time'	the Working Time Regulations 1998 (SI 1998/1833).

1.2   In this Agreement, unless the context otherwise requires:

(a)   words in the singular include the plural and vice versa and words in one gender include any other gender;

(b) a reference to a statute or statutory provision includes:

    (i) any subordinate legislation (as defined in section 21(1) of the Interpretation Act 1978) made under it;

    (ii) any repealed statute or statutory provision which it re-enacts (with or without modification); and

    (iii) any statute or statutory provision which modifies, consolidates, re-enacts or supersedes it except to the extent that it would create or increase the liability of the Sellers under clause 9;

(c) a reference to a jurisdiction shall include any union, country, state, province, district or division of whatever nature which imposes or raises Taxation;

(d) references to specific parts of the law of the United Kingdom shall be taken to include a reference to the law of any other jurisdiction so far as the same may apply to [the Company] [any Group Company] and may be similar to or have a similar purpose to the law of the United Kingdom to which reference is made; and

(e) references to the VATA shall include all law relating to Value Added Tax in the United Kingdom and any value added, turnover, sales, purchase or similar tax of any other jurisdiction and references to Value Added Tax shall be construed accordingly;

(f) a reference to:

    (i) any party includes its successors in title and permitted assigns;

    (ii) a 'person' includes any individual, firm, body corporate, association or partnership, government or state (whether or not having a separate legal personality);

    (iii) clauses and schedules are to clauses and schedules of this Agreement and references to sub-clauses and paragraphs are references to sub-clauses and paragraphs of the clause or schedule in which they appear;

    (iv) any provision of this Agreement is to that provision as amended in accordance with the terms of this Agreement;

    (v) any document being 'in the agreed form' means in a form which has been agreed by the parties on or before the date of this Agreement and for identification purposes signed by them or on their behalf by their solicitors;

    (vi) 'indemnify' and 'indemnifying' any person against any circumstance include indemnifying and keeping him harmless from all actions, claims and proceedings from time to time made against him and all loss or damage and all payments, costs or expenses made or incurred by that person as a consequence of or which would not have arisen but for that circumstance;

(g) except as set out in sub-clauses 1.1 and 1.2, terms defined in the Companies Act 2006 have the meanings attributed to them by that Act;

(h) 'sterling' and the sign '£' mean pounds sterling in the official currency of the United Kingdom save that if, following the introduction of the Euro, pounds sterling ceases to exist as the currency of the United Kingdom, then all references in this Agreement to pounds sterling shall be construed as references to the Euro at the conversion rate applicable at the close of business on the day on which sterling ceased to exist;

(i) the table of contents and headings are for convenience only and shall not affect the interpretation of this Agreement;

(j) general words shall not be given a restrictive meaning:

    (i) if they are introduced by the word 'other' by reason of the fact that they are preceded by words indicating a particular class of act, matter or thing; or

    (ii) by reason of the fact that they are followed by particular examples intended to be embraced by those general words;

(k) where any liability or obligation is undertaken by two or more persons, the liability of each of them shall be joint and several; and

(l) where any statement is qualified by the expression 'so far as the Sellers are aware' or 'to the best of the Sellers' knowledge and belief' or any similar expression it shall be deemed to include an additional statement that it has been made after reasonable enquiry of each of the Sellers and the directors, officers and senior management of each Group Company.

2. Conditions precedent

2.1 Except for the obligations set out in this clause, clause 5 (Pre-completion obligations) and sub-clause 16.11 (Termination), the obligations of the parties under this Agreement are in all respects conditional upon:

(a) [a resolution being passed at a general meeting of the Purchaser approving the purchase of the Shares;

(b) *any other conditions.*]

2.2 Each of the parties shall (so far as it lies within their powers) use all reasonable endeavours to procure that the Conditions are satisfied as soon as possible and, in any event, not later than .... (or such later date as the parties may agree). [In respect of the Condition specified in sub-clause 2.1 (a), the obligations of the Purchaser under this clause shall be satisfied by it sending the Circular to the Purchaser's shareholders on or before .... containing a recommendation by the directors of the Purchaser to vote in favour of the resolution to approve the purchase of the Shares).]

2.3 If any of the Conditions is not satisfied in full by the date specified in sub-clause 2.2 then [(in the case of the Condition[s] specified in sub-clause[s] 2.1 (.....)] the Purchaser [and (in the case of the Condition[s] specified in sub-clause[s] 2.1(.....) the Sellers] shall be entitled at its [or (as the case may be) their] option either:

(a)   to waive the unsatisfied Condition;

(b)   extend the period for satisfying the unsatisfied Condition to a date not less than seven nor more than 28 days after that date (in which case the provisions of this sub-clause shall also apply as if the revised date were the date specified in sub-clause 2.2); or

(c)   to rescind this Agreement by notice in writing.

3.   Sale and purchase

3.1   Subject to the terms of this Agreement, the Sellers shall sell and the Purchaser shall purchase, with effect from Completion, the Shares with:

(a)   full title guarantee (but free from all charges and encumbrances (whether monetary or not) and all other rights exercisable by third parties which the Sellers do not, and could not reasonably be expected to, know about); and

(b)   all rights attaching to or accruing to them at Completion (including all dividends and distributions declared, paid or made on or after that date).

3.2   Each of the Sellers waives all rights of pre-emption over any of the Shares conferred on him by the articles of association of the Company or in any other way and undertakes to take all steps necessary to waive any rights of pre-emption over any of the Shares.

3.3   The Purchaser shall not be obliged to complete the purchase unless the sale and purchase of all the Shares is completed simultaneously.

4.   Consideration

4.1   The Consideration is the payment by the Purchaser to the Sellers of the sum of £.............. which shall be payable in cash at Completion in accordance with clause 6.

4.2   The Consideration shall be apportioned between the Sellers in accordance with Schedule 1.

5.   Pre-completion obligations

The Sellers shall procure that, between the date of this Agreement and Completion, each Group Company shall carry on business in the normal course and shall not without the consent of the Purchaser do anything which is not of a routine or unimportant nature. In particular, the Sellers will procure that (save with the prior written consent of the Purchaser):

(a)   reasonable advance notice is given to the Purchaser of meetings of the Board of Directors of each Group Company (together with an agenda of the business to be transacted at such meetings and all supporting documents) and that a duly authorised representative of the Purchaser is permitted to attend and to participate fully in the discussions at all those meetings;

(b)   the officers, employees and agents of each Group Company shall, upon the request of the Purchaser, supply to the Purchaser such information concerning the business of each Group Company as the Purchaser may reasonably require, [and allow representatives of the Purchaser access to each Group Company's premises, employees and agents for the purpose of obtaining an intimate knowledge of the day to day activities of all aspects of each Group Company's business];

(c)   each Group Company conducts its affairs in a manner which enables it during the period from the date of this Agreement until Completion to achieve the profits of which it is fairly and reasonably capable without unreasonably prejudicing its long-term future and shall refrain from any act or omission which would result in it not achieving the profits of which it is fairly and reasonably capable during that period;

(d)   no Group Company shall, save in the normal course of business:

    (i)   lend any money;

    (ii)   lend any money to any shareholder, director or employee;

    (iii)   borrow any money except in relation to the operation of bank overdrafts within existing limits as required in the ordinary course of business;

    (iv)   give or allow to exist any further debenture, mortgage, charge or other encumbrance over any of its assets or undertaking;

    (v)   enter into capital expenditure commitments, hire-purchase, leasing, rental or conditional sale agreements or arrangements;

    (vi)   enter into any agreement which is outside the ordinary course of its business or which is onerous or long term;

    (vii)   declare, make or pay any dividend or other distribution or allot, issue, grant any options over, redeem, purchase, consolidate, convert, subdivide or reduce any share or loan capital or issue any share warrants or securities convertible into shares;

    (viii)   sell, transfer or otherwise dispose of the whole or any part of its business, undertakings or assets otherwise than in the ordinary course of its business;

    (ix)   give any financial or other guarantees, securities or indemnities for any purpose;

    (x)   commence any litigation or compromise or settle any claim, dispute or other matter in which it is involved;

    (xi)   attempt to do any of the matters set out in sub-clause (d)(i)–(x);

(e)   no additional directors shall be appointed to the Board of any Group Company;

(f)   no resolution is passed by the shareholders of any Group Company;

(g)   there shall be no change in the terms and conditions of employment of any employee of any Group Company;

(h)   no act is performed or omission allowed, either by themselves or by any Group Company, which would result in any of the Warranties being breached or becoming misleading at any time up to and including Completion;

(i)   each Group Company maintains its existing insurance cover;

(j)   each Group Company pays its creditors in the ordinary course of its business or within the normal terms of payment of such creditors; and

(k)   each Group Company maintains its usual level of stock and raw materials.

6.   Completion

6.1   Completion shall take place at the offices of ....
at .... am/pm on the business day following satisfaction and/or waiver of the Conditions (or on such other date, time and place as the parties may agree] but, in any event, no later than ....)].

6.2   On Completion:

   (a)   the Sellers shall deliver to the Purchaser:

      (i)   stock transfer forms, duly completed and executed by the registered holders, in favour of the Purchaser (or as it may direct) in respect of the Shares together with the relevant share certificates;

      (ii)   stock transfer forms, duly completed and executed by the registered holders, in favour of the Company (or as the Purchaser may direct) of all the shares of the Subsidiaries which are not registered in the name of a Group Company together with the relevant share certificates;

      (iii)   letters of non-crystallisation dated not earlier than the second business day immediately preceding Completion from the holders of all outstanding floating charges given by any Group Company;

      (iv)   the certificate of incorporation, any certificates of incorporation on change of name or re-registration, the statutory books written up to date, share certificate books, minute books, all unused cheque books and the common seal of each Group Company;

      (v)   [duly executed transfer[s] and conveyances together with] all title deeds relating to the Properties including all documents relating to the Tenancies and, where the Properties are charged, Forms DS1 or receipted Legal Charges as appropriate;

      (vi)   all credit and charge cards held for the account of each Group Company;

      (vii)   all other papers and documents relating to each Group Company which are in the possession of or under the control of any of the Sellers;

      (viii) letters of resignation in the agreed form from [each of the directors of each Group Company] and [the company secretary of each Group Company];

      (ix)   letters of resignation from the auditors of each Group Company containing the statement specified in section 519 of the Companies Act 2006;

(x)   a statement of all overdraft and credit balances from each Group Company's bankers and other lenders as at the close of business on the day preceding Completion; and

(xi)   the Disclosure Letter.

(b)   The Sellers shall repay all money then owing by them to any Group Company whether due and payable or not.

(c)   The Sellers shall [use all reasonable endeavours to] procure that .... and .... enter into service agreements with the Company in the agreed form.

(d)   The Sellers shall procure that a board meeting of each Group Company is held at which:

(i)   the stock transfer forms referred to in sub-clauses (a)(i) and (ii) are approved and (subject to them being appropriately stamped) registered in the relevant Group Company's books;

(ii)   the persons nominated by the Purchaser are appointed as directors [and secretary] of each Group Company;

(iii) [each director and the secretary] of [each Group Company] ceases to be an officer of that Group Company with immediate effect;

(iv) the accounting reference date of each Group Company is changed to ....;

(v)   .... resign from their office as auditors to each Group Company and. are appointed in their place;

(vi) the registered office of each Group Company is changed to ....;

(vii) the mandates given by each Group Company to its bankers are revoked or revised as the Purchaser may require; and

(viii) the execution and completion of the other documents to be entered into by each Group Company under this Agreement is approved.

(e)   When the Sellers have complied with the provisions of sub-clauses (a)–(d) inclusive, the Purchaser shall:

(i)   [deliver to the Sellers a certified copy of the shareholder resolution approving the purchase of the Shares; and]

(ii)   pay the Consideration to the Sellers in the proportions set out in Schedule 1 by telegraphic transfer to the client account of the Sellers' solicitors at .... Bank plc, account number ...., sort code ....

6.3   If any of the requirements of sub-clause 6.2 are not complied with on the date set for Completion under sub-clause 6.1, the Purchaser (in the case of the requirements of sub-clauses 6.2(a)–(d) inclusive) or the Sellers (in the case of the requirements of sub-clause 6.2(e)) may:

(a)   defer Completion with respect to some or all of the Shares to a date not less than seven nor more than 28 days after that date (in which case the provisions of this sub-clause shall also apply to Completion as so deferred); or

(b)   proceed to Completion so far as practicable (including, at the Purchaser's or, as the case may be, the Sellers' option, completion of the purchase of some only of the Shares) but without prejudice to any other rights which it or they may have under this Agreement; or

(c)   rescind this Agreement by notice in writing.

6.4   The Sellers undertake to indemnify the Purchaser against any loss, expense or damage which it may suffer as a result of any document delivered to it under this clause being unauthorised, invalid or for any other reason ineffective.

6.5   The Sellers undertake to indemnify the Group Companies concerned against any and all claims which may be made against them by any person who resigns at Completion as a director under sub-clause 6.2(a)(viii) whose claim arises out of his resignation or the termination of his employment and against all costs, charges and expenses incurred by the Group Companies concerned which are incidental to any such claim.

7.   Release of guarantees

7.1   The Purchaser shall use all reasonable endeavours (short of actual payment of any money or the substitution of the guarantee of any person other than the Purchaser, any company within its group or any Group Company) to procure the release of the Sellers from any Guarantee forthwith upon being notified of its existence or otherwise becoming aware of it and shall indemnify the Sellers against all liability arising after Completion in respect of it.

7.2   The Sellers shall on Completion procure the release of the Company from any Guarantee given by the Company in respect of any obligations of any Seller or Seller Associate and shall indemnify the Purchaser against all liability arising after Completion in respect of it.

8.   Post-completion matters

8.1   The Sellers declare that for as long as they remain the registered holders of the shares after Completion they will:

(a)   hold the shares and the dividends and any other money paid or distributed in respect of them after Completion and all rights arising out of or in connection with them in trust for the Purchaser;

(b)   deal with the shares and all such dividends, distributions and rights as the Purchaser may direct for the period between Completion and the day on which the Purchaser or its nominee is entered in the register of members of the Company as the holder of the shares.

8.2   The Sellers irrevocably appoint the Purchaser as their attorney for the purpose of exercising any rights, privileges or duties attaching to the shares including receiving notices of and attending and voting at all meetings of the members of the Company from Completion to the day on which the Purchaser or its nominee is entered in the register of members of the Company as the holder of the Shares.

8.3   For the purpose of clause 8.2, the Sellers authorise:

(a)   the Company to send any notices in respect of their share holdings to the Purchaser;

(b)   the Purchaser to complete and return proxy cards, consents to short notice and any other document required to be signed by the Sellers as a member.

9.   Warranties

9.1   The Warrantors jointly and severally warrant and represent to the Purchaser that each of the Warranties is true and accurate in all respects and not misleading at the date of this Agreement and will continue to be true and accurate in all respects and not misleading up to and including Completion.

9.2   The Warrantors acknowledge that they give the Warranties with the intention of inducing the Purchaser to enter into this Agreement and that the Purchaser does so in reliance on the Warranties.

9.3   Each of the Warranties is a separate and independent Warranty and shall not be limited by reference to any other Warranty or anything in this Agreement.

10.   Covenant for taxation

10.1   The Warrantors jointly and severally shall pay to the Purchaser an amount equal to any Liability to Taxation of any Group Company:

(a)   arising directly or indirectly from any Transaction effected on or before Completion;

(b)   in respect of, or by reference to, any Profits earned, accrued or received on or before Completion;

(c)   which would not have arisen but for the failure by any person who is or has been a Seller Associate to discharge a Liability to Taxation which falls upon such Seller Associate:

(i)   arising directly or indirectly from any Transaction effected or deemed to have been effected at any time by such Seller Associate; or

(ii)   in respect of any Profits earned, accrued or received at any time by such Seller Associate;

(d)   which arises on or with respect to any income or emoluments paid, benefits given or loans or advances made (or which are deemed for tax purposes to be made) to the Sellers or any Seller Associate;

    (e)   in respect of the liability of any Group Company:

        (i)   to repay in whole or part any payment for any Relevant Claim or Surrender in respect of any period commencing prior to Completion; or

        (ii)   to make a payment for any Relevant Claim or Surrender to any Seller Associate in respect of any period commencing prior to Completion;

    (f)   arising in respect of the failure of any Group Company to receive any payment for any Relevant Claim or Surrender (other than from any other Group Company) shown as an asset in the Accounts; or

    (g)   *[Specific matters arising from the Sellers' pre-sale planning/ due diligence]* together with all costs and expenses reasonably and properly incurred by the Purchaser or any Group Company in connection with any such Liability to Taxation or Claim for Taxation or in bringing any claim or defending any action under the provisions of this clause.

10.2   Where the Warrantors become liable to make any payment under the Covenant for Taxation, the due date for the making of that payment shall be:

    (a)   in a case that involves an actual payment of Taxation by any Group Company, the date that is the last date on which the relevant Group Company is liable to pay to the appropriate Tax Authority the Taxation in question in order to avoid incurring a liability to interest or penalties or, if later, five days following a written demand from the Purchaser;

    (b)   in the case of the loss of any Relief, the date falling five days following the date when the Warrantors have been notified by the Purchaser that the auditors for the time being of the relevant Group Company have certified, at the request of the Purchaser, that the Warrantors have a liability for a determinable amount in respect of the loss of such Relief under the Covenant for Taxation; or

    (c)   in any other case, the date falling five days following the date on which the Warrantors receive a written demand for such amount from the Purchaser.

10.3   In a case of a loss of any Relief, the amount that is to be treated under the Covenant for Taxation as a Liability to Taxation shall:

    (a)   be the amount of that Relief, if the Relief that was the subject of the loss was either a deduction from or offset against Taxation or a right to a repayment of Taxation;

    (b)   be the amount of Taxation which has been saved in consequence of the setting off where the Relief that was the subject of the loss was a deduction from or offset against gross Profits, and the Relief was the subject of a setting off; and

    (c)   in any other case where the Relief that was the subject of the loss was a deduction from or offset against gross Profits, be the amount of Taxation which would, on the basis of the rates of Taxation current at the date of the loss, have been saved but for the loss.

10.4 If, in respect of or in connection with any Claim, or otherwise in connection with any payment made hereunder, any amount payable to the Purchaser by the Warrantors is subject to Taxation, the amount to be paid to the Purchaser by the Warrantors shall be such amount as will ensure that the net amount received by the Purchaser after such Taxation has been taken into account is equal to the full amount which would be payable to the Purchaser had the amount not been subject to Taxation.

11. Purchaser's remedies

11.1 Each of the Warrantors undertake to disclose in writing to the Purchaser anything which is or may constitute a Claim or be inconsistent with the contents of the Disclosure Letter directly as it comes to the notice of any of them either before, at the time of, or after Completion.

11.2 If, between the date of this Agreement and Completion, the Purchaser becomes aware that there has been any material breach of the Warranties or any other term of this Agreement the Purchaser shall be entitled to rescind this Agreement by notice in writing to the Sellers.

11.3 The rights and remedies of the Purchaser in respect of any breach of the Warranties or the Covenant for Taxation shall not be affected by Completion or by any investigation made, or which could have been made, by it or on its behalf into the affairs of any Group Company.

11.4 If any Claim is made, no Warrantor shall make any claim against any Group Company or any director or employee of any Group Company on whom he may have relied before agreeing to any terms of this Agreement or authorising any statement in the Disclosure Letter. This sub-clause shall not preclude any Warrantor from claiming against any other Warrantor under any right of contribution or indemnity to which he may be entitled.

11.5 In the event of a Claim under the Warranties, without prejudice to the right of the Purchaser to claim damages on any basis available to it or to any other right or remedy available to it, the Warrantors agree to pay on demand in cash to the Purchaser a sum by way of damages as agreed between the Warrantors and the Purchaser or, in default of such agreement, as determined by order of a court of competent jurisdiction which is the higher of:

(a) an amount sufficient to put the Company into the position which would have existed if the Warranties had been true and accurate or not misleading when given or repeated;

(b) an amount equal to the resulting diminution in value of the Shares;

(c)   the amount by which the assets of the Company are less, or less valuable, or its liabilities greater, than the values at which the same were included in the Accounts or (if the Purchaser so elects) than they would have been if the Warranty concerned had been true and accurate and not misleading; and

(d)   the amount by which the profitability of the Company is less, or its losses greater, than would have been the case if the Warranty concerned had been true and accurate and not misleading, calculated on the same basis as if such reduction in profitability or increase in losses were suffered as the result of an actionable wrong done to the Company.

11.6   The Warrantors shall indemnify the Purchaser against all costs (including legal costs on an indemnity basis as defined in rule 44.4(3) of the Civil Procedure Rules 1998), expenses or other liabilities which the Purchaser may reasonably incur either before or after the commencement of any action in connection with:

(a)   the settlement of any Non-Tax Claim;

(b)   any legal proceedings in respect of any Non-Tax Claim in which judgment is given for the Purchaser; or

(c)   the enforcement of any such settlement or judgment.

11.7   Any amount paid by the Warrantors to the Purchaser in respect of any of the provisions of this Agreement shall be treated as paid to the Purchaser by way of pro rata reduction in the Consideration.

12.   Limitations on liability

12.1   The liability of the Warrantors under the Covenant for Taxation shall be reduced if and to the extent that the loss shall have been recovered under the Warranties (and vice versa).

12.2   In the absence of fraud or dishonesty or wilful non-disclosure on the part of any of the Warrantors, their agents or advisors:

(a)   the Purchaser shall not have any claim under the Warranties in respect of any matter if, and to the extent that, it is Disclosed provided that:

(i)   [only the disclosures in section .... of the Disclosure Letter shall be treated as having been Disclosed against the Tax Warranties;]

(ii)   [nothing in the Disclosure Letter shall limit the Warrantors' liability under the Tax Covenant or the Tax Warranties;]

(iii)   only the disclosures in section .... of the Disclosure Letter shall be treated as having been Disclosed against the Warranties in clause 32.1 (Pensions) of Schedule 4, only the disclosures in section .... of the Disclosure Letter (to the extent Disclosed) shall be treated as having been Disclosed against the Warranties in clauses 41.1 and 42.2 (Contamination and Environment) of Schedule 4; and

(b)   the Warrantors shall not be liable for any Claim unless:

    (i)   they have received written notice from the Purchaser giving reasonable details of the Claim and, if practicable, the Purchaser's estimate of the amount involved on or before the expiration of three years from Completion or, in the case of any claim relating to Taxation, not later than seven years from Completion or in the case of any claim relating to environmental liabilities not later than .... years from Completion;

    (ii)   the amount of the Claim, when aggregated with all other Claims made on the same occasion or previously, is equal to or exceeds £.................... (in which case the Warrantors shall be liable for the whole amount and not simply the excess);

(c)   the aggregate liability of the Warrantors in respect of the Warranties [and the Covenant for Taxation] shall not exceed £..................;

(d)   the Warrantors shall not be liable for any Non-Tax Claim if and to the extent that a liability arises or is increased as a result of:

    (i)   any voluntary act or omission of the Purchaser (or, any persons deriving title from it) or any Group Company after Completion done or suffered outside the ordinary course of business and other than:

        (A)   pursuant to a legally binding obligation entered into by the Group Company concerned before Completion; or

        (B)   in order to comply with any law; or

        (C)   at the request of or with the consent of the Warrantors; or

    (ii)   [other Non-Tax exclusions.]

12.3   If the Warrantors make any payment to the Purchaser or any Group Company in relation to any Non-Tax Claim and the Purchaser or any Group Company subsequently receives from a third party any amount referable to, or any benefit which would not have been received but for the circumstances giving rise to, the subject matter of that Claim, the Purchaser shall, once it or any Group Company has received such amount or benefit, immediately repay or procure the repayment to the Warrantors of either:

(a)   the amount of such receipt (after deducting an amount equal to the reasonable costs of the Purchaser or any Group Company incurred in recovering such receipt and any Taxation payable on it); or if lesser

(b)   the amount paid by the Warrantors

together with any interest or repayment supplement paid to the Purchaser or the Group Company in respect of it.

13.   Conduct of non-tax claims

13.1   The Purchaser shall notify the Warrantors in writing of:

(a)   any claim made against it by a third party which may give rise to a Non-Tax Claim; and

(b)   any claim any Group Company is entitled to bring against a third party which claim is based on circumstances which may give rise to a Non-Tax Claim.

13.2   The Purchaser shall procure that the conduct, negotiation, settlement or litigation of the claim by or against such third party is, so far as is reasonably practicable, carried out in accordance with the wishes of the Warrantors and at their cost subject to their giving timely instructions to the Purchaser and providing reasonable security for any costs and expenses which might be incurred by the Purchaser or a Group Company.

13.3   The Purchaser shall not be liable for any delay in giving any notice under sub-clause 13.1 and shall not by reason of such delay be precluded from bringing any such Non-Tax Claim against the Warrantors.

13.4   The Purchaser shall provide and shall procure that each Group Company provides to the Warrantors and their Warrantors' professional advisors reasonable access to premises and personnel and to any relevant assets, documents and records within their power, possession or control for the purpose of investigating any Non-Tax Claim and enabling the Warrantors to take the action referred to in sub-clause 13.2 and shall allow the Warrantors and their advisors to take copies of any relevant documents or records at their expense.

14.   Non-competition covenants

14.1   In order to assure to the Purchaser the full benefit of the business and goodwill of the Group Companies, [the] [each] Seller undertakes that he shall not, either alone or in conjunction with or on behalf of any other person, do any of the following things:

(a)   within .... years after Completion carry on or be engaged, concerned or interested in (except as the holder of shares in a listed company which confer not more than 1% of the votes which could normally be cast at a general meeting of that company) any business within a .... mile radius of any of the [depots] of any Group Company which competes with any part of the business of any Group Company;

(b)   except in the circumstances referred to in sub-clause 16.12(b) (Confidentiality), disclose to any other person any information which is secret or confidential to the business or affairs of any Group Company or use any such information to the detriment of the business of any Group Company for so long as that information remains secret or confidential;

(c)   in relation to a business which is competitive or likely to be competitive with the business of any Group Company as carried on at Completion, use any trade or business name or distinctive mark, style or logo used by or in the business of any of the Group Companies at any time during the .... years before Completion or anything intended or likely to be confused with it;

(d)   neither before nor within .... years after Completion solicit or accept orders or otherwise seek custom from any person to whom any Group Company has sold its goods or services in the .... years before Completion in respect of similar goods or services; or

(e)   neither before nor within .... years after Completion solicit or seek to entice away any employee from the employment of any Group Company engaged in a senior managerial, supervisory, technical, sales or marketing capacity.

14.2   Each undertaking contained in sub-clause 14.1 shall be construed as a separate and independent undertaking.

15.   Pensions

The provisions of Schedule 6 shall apply from Completion.

16.   General

16.1   Entire agreement and conflicts

(a)   This Agreement sets out the entire agreement and understanding between the parties in respect of the subject matter of this Agreement;

(b)   This Agreement supersedes .... dated .... except for any of its provisions which this Agreement specifically preserves;

(c)   To the extent that the provisions of this Agreement conflict with the provisions of ...., this Agreement shall prevail.

16.2   Contracts (Rights of Third Parties) Act 1999

Unless expressly provided in this Agreement, no term of this Agreement is enforceable pursuant to the Contracts (Rights of Third Parties) Act 1999 by any person who is not a party to it.

16.3   Assignment

(a)   This Agreement shall be binding upon and ensure for the benefit of the successors in title of the parties but, except as set out in sub-clause (b), shall not be assignable by any party without the prior written consent of the other.

(b)   The Purchaser may assign the benefit of this Agreement (including, without limitation, the Warranties) to any successor in title or any subsequent Purchaser of the shares.

16.4   Variation

No purported variation of this Agreement shall be effective unless it is in writing and signed by or on behalf of each of the parties.

16.5   Effect of completion

Except to the extent already performed, all the provisions of this Agreement shall, so far as they are capable of being performed or observed, continue in full force and effect notwithstanding Completion.

16.6   Invalidity

To the extent that any provision of this Agreement is found by any court or competent authority to be invalid, unlawful or unenforceable in any jurisdiction, that provision shall be deemed not to be a part of this Agreement, it shall not affect the enforceability of the remainder of this Agreement nor shall it affect the validity, lawfulness or enforceability of that provision in any other jurisdiction.

16.7   Releases and waivers

(a)   The rights, powers and remedies conferred on the Purchaser by this Agreement and remedies available to it are cumulative and are additional to any right, power or remedy which it may have under general law or otherwise.

(b)   The Purchaser may, in whole or in part, release, compound, compromise, waive or postpone, in its absolute discretion, any liability owed to it or right granted to it in this Agreement by any other party or parties without in any way prejudicing or affecting its rights in respect of that or any other liability or right not so released, compounded, compromised, waived or postponed.

(c)   No single or partial exercise, or failure or delay in exercising any right, power or remedy by the Purchaser shall constitute a waiver by it of, or impair or preclude any further exercise of, that or any right, power or remedy arising under this Agreement or otherwise.

16.8   Further assurance

After Completion, each party shall execute such documents and take such steps as the other party may reasonably require to fulfil the provisions of and to give to each party the full benefit of this Agreement.

16.9   Counterparts

(a)   This Agreement may be executed in any number of counterparts and by the patties on separate counterparts, but shall not be effective until each party has executed at least one counterpart.

(b)   Each counterpart, when executed, shall be an original of this Agreement and all counterparts shall together constitute one instrument.

16.10   Time of the essence

Except as otherwise expressly provided, time is of the essence as regards every obligation of any party under this Agreement.

16.11   Termination

Without prejudice to any remedy available to any party arising out of any outstanding breach of this Agreement on the part of any other party, if this Agreement is terminated in accordance with its terms, the following shall occur:

(a)   the Sellers shall jointly and severally indemnify the Purchaser for all costs, charges and expenses incurred by it in connection with the negotiation, preparations and determination or rescission of this Agreement and all matters which this Agreement contemplates;

(b)   the restrictions contained in sub-clause 16.12 (Confidentiality) and clause 17 (Announcements) shall continue to apply; and

(c)   except as referred to in sub-clause (b), all obligations of the Purchaser under this Agreement shall cease.

16.12   Confidentiality

(a)   Except as referred to in sub-clause (b), each party shall treat as strictly confidential all information received or obtained as a result of entering into or performing this Agreement which relates to the provisions or subject matter of this Agreement, to any other party or the negotiations relating to this Agreement.

(b)   Any party may disclose information which would otherwise be confidential if and to the extent:

(i)   it is required to do so by law or any securities exchange or regulatory or governmental body to which it is subject wherever situated;

(ii)   it considers it necessary to disclose the information to its professional advisors, auditors and bankers provided that it does so on a confidential basis;

(iii)   the information has come into the public domain through no fault of that party; or

(iv)   each party to whom it relates has given its consent in writing.

16.13   Default interest

If any party defaults in the payment when due of any sum payable under this Agreement (whether payable by agreement or by an order of a court or otherwise), the liability of that party shall be increased to include interest on that sum from the date when such payment was due until the date of actual payment at a rate per annum of 4% above the base rate from time to time of National Westminster Bank plc. Such interest shall accrue from day to day and shall be compounded annually.

16.14   Set-off

The Purchaser shall be entitled to set off the amount of any Claim against any sum due from it to the Sellers under this Agreement.

17. Announcements

17.1 Except as referred to in sub-clause 17.2, no announcement concerning the terms of this Agreement shall be made by or on behalf of any of the parties without the prior written consent of the others, such consent not to be unreasonably withheld or delayed.

17.2 Any announcement or circular required to be made or issued by any party by law or under the regulations of the UK Listing Authority or the City Code on Takeovers and Mergers issued by the Panel on Takeovers and Mergers may be made or issued by that party without consent if it has first sought consent and given the other parties a reasonable opportunity to comment on the subject matter and form of the announcement or circular (given the time scale within which it is required to be released or despatched).

18. Costs and expenses

18.1 Except as set out in sub-clauses 18.2 and 16.11 (Termination) each party shall bear its own costs and expenses incurred in the preparation, execution and implementation of this Agreement.

18.2 The Purchaser shall pay all stamp and other transfer duties and registration fees applicable to any document to which it is a party and which arise as a result of or in consequence of this Agreement.

19. Notices

19.1 Any notice to a party under this Agreement shall be in writing signed by or on behalf of the party giving it and shall, unless delivered to a party personally, be left at, or sent by prepaid first class post, prepaid special delivery to the address of the party as set out [on page 1 of] [in Schedule ....] of this Agreement or as otherwise notified in writing from time to time.

19.2 Except as referred to in sub-clauses 19.3 and 19.4, a notice shall be deemed to have been served:

(a) at the time of delivery if delivered personally 48 hours after posting in the case of an address in the United Kingdom and 96 hours after posting for any other address.

19.3 If the deemed time of service is not during normal business hours in the country of receipt, the notice shall be deemed served at or, in the case of faxes, two hours after the opening of business on the next business day of that country.

19.4 The deemed service provisions set out in sub-clause 19.2 do not apply to a notice served by post, if there is a national or local suspension, curtailment or disruption of postal services which affects the collection of the notice or is such that the notice cannot reasonably be expected to be delivered within 48 hours or 96 hours (as appropriate) after posting.

19.5   In proving service it will be sufficient to prove:

     (a)   in the case of personal service, that it was handed to the party or delivered to or left in an appropriate place for receipt of letters at its address;

     (b)   in the case of a letter sent by post, that the letter was properly addressed, stamped and posted.

19.6   A party shall not attempt to prevent or delay the service on it of a notice connected with this Agreement.

20.   Governing law and jurisdiction

20.1   This Agreement shall be governed by and construed in accordance with English law.

20.2   Each of the parties irrevocably submits for all purposes in connection with this Agreement both in contract and in tort to the exclusive jurisdiction of the courts of England.

This Agreement has been signed on the date appearing at the head of page 1.

SCHEDULE 1

(The Sellers)

Name:

Address:

No of Shares:

Consideration (£................)

Total ....

SCHEDULE 2
(INFORMATION CONCERNING THE COMPANY)

Registered number:

Address of registered office:

Class of company:

Authorised share capital: £………….. divided into:

………….. [ordinary] shares of £………….. each

Issued share capital: £………….. divided into:

………….. [ordinary] shares of £………….. each

Directors:

Full name

Usual residential address

Nationality

Secretary:

Accounting reference date:

Tax residence:

SCHEDULE 3
(INFORMATION CONCERNING THE HOLDING
COMPANY AND THE SUBSIDIARIES)

………………………. Limited

Registered number:

Address of registered office:

Class of company:

Authorised share capital: £………….. divided into:

………….. [ordinary] shares of £………….. each

Issued share capital: £………….. divided into:

………….. [ordinary] shares of £………….. each

Members:

Full name

Registered address

Number of shares held

Directors:

Full name

Usual residential address

Nationality

Secretary:

Tax Residence:

………….. Limited

Registered number:

Address of registered office:

Class of company:

Authorised share capital: £………….. divided into:

………….. [ordinary] shares of £………….. each

Issued share capital: £………….. divided into:

………….. [ordinary] shares of £………….. each

Members:

Full names

Registered address

Number of shares held

Directors:

Full name

Usual residential address

Nationality

Secretary:

Accounting reference date:

Tax residence:

SCHEDULE 4
(NON-TAX WARRANTIES)

The Sellers

1.   Capacity

1.1   Each Seller has the requisite power and authority to enter into and perform this Agreement.

1.2   No Seller is bankrupt, has proposed a voluntary arrangement or has made or proposed any arrangement or composition with his creditors or any class of his creditors.

1.3   This Agreement constitutes and imposes valid legal and binding obligations on each Seller fully enforceable in accordance with its terms.

2.   Arrangements between Group Companies and Seller Associates

There are no contracts, arrangements or liabilities, actual or contingent, outstanding or remaining in whole or in part to be performed between any Group Company and any Seller Associate.

3.   Other interests of any Seller Associate

No Seller has or intends to acquire any interest, direct or indirect, in any business which has a close trading relationship with or which competes or is likely to compete with any business now carried on by any Group Company and, so far as the Sellers are aware, no Seller Associate has or intends to do so.

Share capital

4.   Company

4.1   The Shares constitute the entire issued and allotted share capital of the Company and are fully paid or credited as fully paid.

4.2   Apart from this Agreement, there is no agreement, arrangement or commitment outstanding which calls for the allotment, issue or transfer of, or accords to any person the right to call for the allotment, issue or transfer of, any share or loan capital of the Company.

4.3   None of the Shares was, or represents assets which were, the subject of a transfer at an undervalue, within the meaning of sections 238 or 339 of the Insolvency Act 1986, within the past five years.

4.4   The Company has not at any time:

(a)   reduced its share capital;
(b)   redeemed any share capital;
(c)   purchased any of its shares; or
(d)   forfeited any of its shares.

5.   Subsidiaries

5.1   Schedule 3 lists all the Subsidiaries of the Company, each of which are wholly owned by the Company.

5.2   The Company does not have, and has never had, a participating interest (as defined in section 421A of the Financial Services and Markets Act 2000 and/or in regulations made under Part 15 of the Companies Act 2006) in any undertaking which is not a Subsidiary, nor has it agreed to acquire such an interest.

5.3   No Group Company holds or is liable on any share or relevant security which is not fully paid up or which carries any liability.

5.4   Apart from this Agreement, there is no agreement, arrangement or commitment outstanding which calls for the allotment, issue or transfer of, or accords to any person the right to call for the allotment, issue or transfer of, any share or loan capital of any Subsidiary.

5.5   None of the shares in the capital of any Subsidiary was, or represents assets which were, the subject of a transfer at an undervalue, within the meaning of sections 238 or 339 of the Insolvency Act 1986 within the past five years.

Corporate matters

6.   Insolvency of the Group

6.1   No order has been made, no resolution has been passed, no petition presented, no meeting convened for the winding up of any Group Company or for a provisional liquidator to be appointed in respect of any Group Company and no Group Company has been a party to any transaction which could be avoided in a winding up.

6.2   No administration order has been made and no petition for one has been presented in respect of any Group Company.

6.3   No receiver or administrative receiver has been appointed in respect of any Group Company or any of its assets.

6.4   No Group Company is insolvent, has failed or is unable to pay, or has no reasonable prospect of being unable to pay, any of its debts as they fall due, as those expressions are defined in section 123 of the Insolvency Act 1986.

6.5   No voluntary arrangement has been proposed under section 1 of the Insolvency Act 1986 in respect of any Group Company and no Group Company has made or proposed any arrangement or composition with its creditors or any class of them.

6.6   No distress, execution or other process has been levied on any Group Company's assets or action taken to repossess goods in the possession of any Group Company.

6.7   No unsatisfied judgment is outstanding against any Group Company and no demand has been served on any Group Company under section 123(1)(a) of the Insolvency Act 1986.

6.8   No event analogous to any referred to in sub-paragraphs 6.1–6.7 has occurred anywhere in the world.

7.   Statutory books and documents filed

7.1   The statutory books, including all registers and minute books, of each Group Company have been properly kept and contain an accurate and complete record of the matters with which those books should deal.

7.2   All documents which should have been delivered by any Group Company to the Registrar of Companies are complete and accurate and have been properly so delivered.

7.3   The copy of the memorandum and articles of association of each Group Company contained in the Disclosure Letter has embodied in it or annexed to it a copy of each resolution as referred to in section 853 of the Companies Act 2006, and is accurate and complete in all respects.

7.4   Since the Accounts Date the members of any Group Company in general meeting, or of any class of them, have not passed any resolution other than resolutions relating to the ordinary business of annual general meetings.

Information

8.   Accuracy and adequacy of information

8.1   The information contained in Schedules [......... to ....] to this Agreement is accurate and complete.

8.2   The information contained in the Disclosure Letter and all written information supplied to the Purchaser or its advisors by or on behalf of the Sellers or any of their advisors or by any Group Company is complete and accurate and is not misleading because of any omission or ambiguity or for any other reason and where the information is expressed as an opinion, it is truly and honestly held and not given casually, recklessly or without due regard for its accuracy.

8.3   So far as the Sellers are aware, there is no fact or circumstance relating to the business and affairs of any Group Company which, if Disclosed to the Purchaser or any of its advisors, might reasonably be expected to influence the decision of the Purchaser to purchase the Shares on the terms contained in this Agreement and which has not been so Disclosed.

Accounts

9.   Preparation and contents of the Accounts

9.1   The Accounts were prepared in accordance with the requirements of all relevant statutes and generally accepted United Kingdom accounting practices including, without limitation, all applicable Financial Reporting Standards issued by the Accounting Standards Board, Statements of Standard Accounting Practice issued by the Institute of Chartered Accountants of England and Wales and Statements from the Urgent Issues Task Force current at the Accounts Date and, where the accounting practice used to prepare the Accounts differs from those applicable in previous financial periods, the effect of any such difference is Disclosed in the Disclosure Letter.

9.2   Without prejudice to the generality of sub-paragraph 9.1:

    (a)   the Accounts:

        (i)   give a true and fair view of the state of affairs of each Group Company at the Accounts Date and the profits or losses of each Group Company for the financial period ending on that date;

        (ii)   contain full provision or reserve for all liabilities and for all capital and revenue commitments of each Group Company as at the Accounts Date;

        (iii)   disclose all the assets of each Group Company as at the Accounts Date and none of the values placed in the Accounts on any of those assets was in excess of its market value at the Accounts Date;

        (iv)   make full provision for bad and doubtful debts;

        (v)   do not include any figure which is referable to the value of an intangible asset; and

        (vi)   make full provision for depreciation of the fixed assets of each Group Company having regard to their original cost and life;

    (b)   in the Accounts:

        (i)   in valuing work-in-progress no value was attributed in respect of eventual profits and adequate provision was made for such losses as were at the time of signature of the Accounts by directors of each Group Company reasonably foreseeable as arising or likely to arise; and

        (ii)   slow-moving stock was written down appropriately, redundant, obsolete, obsolescent or defective stock was wholly written off and the value attributed to any other stock did not exceed the lower of cost (on a first in first out basis) and net realisable value (or replacement value) at the Accounts Date.

9.3   The profits and losses of each Group Company shown in the Accounts were not, save as disclosed in the Accounts or in any note accompanying them, to any material extent affected by any extraordinary, exceptional, unusual or non-recurring income, capital gain or expenditure or by any other factor known to the Sellers rendering any such profit or loss for such period exceptionally high or low.

9.4 The audited profit and loss accounts and audited balance sheets of each Group Company contained in the Accounts were prepared on a consistent basis with each other.

10. Accounting records

10.1 The accounting records of each Group Company comply with the requirements of sections 386 and 388 of the Companies Act 2006, do not contain or reflect any material inaccuracy or discrepancy and present and reflect in accordance with generally accepted accounting principles and standards the financial position of and all transactions entered into by the relevant Group Company or to which it has been a party.

10.2 All relevant financial books and records of each Group Company are in its possession or otherwise under its direct control.

10.3 Where any of the records of any Group Company are kept on computer, that Group Company:

(a) is the owner of all hardware and all software necessary to enable it to use the records as they have been used in its business to the date of this Agreement and to Completion;

(b) does not share any hardware or software relating to the records with any person; and

(c) maintains adequate back-up records and support in the event of any fault or failure of such computer hardware and software.

11. Management Accounts

The Management Accounts have been carefully prepared on a basis consistent with the Accounts, fairly reflect the trading position of each Group Company as at their date and for the period to which they relate and are not affected by any extraordinary, exceptional, unusual or non-recurring income, capital gain or expenditure or by any other factor known by the Sellers rendering profits or losses for the period covered exceptionally high or low.

12. Events since the Accounts Date

12.1 Since the Accounts Date there has been no material change in:

(a) the financial or trading position or prospects of any Group Company;

(b) the value or state of assets or amount or nature of liabilities as compared with the position disclosed in the Accounts; or

(c) in the turnover, direct or indirect expenses or the margin of profitability of any Group Company as compared with the position disclosed for the equivalent period of the last financial year.

12.2   Each Group Company has since the Accounts Date carried on its business in the ordinary course and without interruption, so as to maintain it as a going concern and paid its creditors in the ordinary course and within the credit periods agreed with such creditors.

12.3   Since the Accounts Date no supplier of any Group Company has ceased or restricted supplies or threatened so to do, there has been no loss or material curtailment of the business transacted by any Group Company with any customer which at any time in the preceding financial year represented .... % or more of the turnover of that Group Company and the Sellers are not aware of any circumstances likely to give rise to any of the above.

12.4   Since the Accounts Date no Group Company has:

(a)   incurred or committed to incur:
  (i)   material capital expenditure; or
  (ii)   any liability whether actual or contingent except for full value or in the ordinary course of business;

(b)   acquired or agreed to acquire:
  (i)   any asset for a consideration higher than its market value at the time of acquisition or otherwise than in the ordinary course of business; or
  (ii)   any business or substantial part of it or any share or shares in a body corporate;

(c)   disposed of or agreed to dispose of, any of the assets of any Group Company, except in the ordinary course of business and for full value;

(d)   repaid wholly or in part any loan except upon the due date or dates for repayment;

(e)   issued or allotted share or loan capital, increased its authorised share capital, purchased or redeemed any shares, reduced or reorganised its share capital or agreed to do so; or

(f)   declared or paid any distribution of profit.

12.5   None of the debts included in the Accounts or any of the debts subsequently arising have been the subject of factoring by any Group Company and the Sellers are not aware of any circumstances which could result in any presently outstanding debt in excess of .... not being paid in full.

Financial

13.   Financial commitments and borrowings

13.1   Complete and accurate details of all overdraft, loan and other financial facilities available to the Group Companies and the amounts outstanding under them at the close of business on the day preceding the date of this Agreement are set out in the Disclosure Letter and none of the Sellers or any Group Company has done anything, or omitted to do anything, as a result of which the continuance of any of those facilities might be affected or prejudiced.

13.2   No Group Company is a party to, or has agreed to enter into, any lending, or purported lending, agreement or arrangement (other than agreements to give credit in the ordinary course of its business).

13.3   No Group Company is exceeding any borrowing limit imposed upon it by its bankers, other lenders, its articles of association or otherwise nor has any Group Company entered into any commitment or arrangement which might lead it so to do.

13.4   No overdraft or other financial facilities available to any Group Company are dependent upon the guarantee of or security provided by any other person.

13.5   No event has occurred or been alleged which is or, with the passing of any time or the giving of any notice, certificate, declaration or demand, would become an event of default under, or breach of, any of the terms of any loan capital, borrowing, debenture or financial facility of any Group Company or which would entitle any person to call for repayment prior to normal maturity.

13.6   No Group Company is, or has agreed to become, bound by any guarantee, indemnity, surety or similar commitment.

13.7   No Group Company has any credit cards in issue in its own name or that of any officer or employee of any Group Company or any person connected with any officer or employee.

13.8   No Group Company has received any grants, allowances, loans or financial aid of any kind from any government department or other board, body, agency or authority which may become liable to be refunded or repaid in whole or in part.

13.9   No Group Company has engaged in financing of a type which is not required, or has not been, shown or reflected in the Accounts.

14.   Working capital

Having regard to existing bank and other facilities available to it, each Group Company has sufficient working capital for the purposes of continuing to carry on its business, in its present form and at its present level of turnover, for the period of 12 months after Completion.

15.   Insurances

15.1   Each Group Company maintains, and at all material times has maintained, adequate insurance cover against all risks normally insured against by companies carrying on a similar business, for the full replacement or reinstatement value of its business and assets, and in particular has maintained product liability, professional indemnity insurance and all insurance required by statute and insured against loss of profits for a period of not less than six months and for loss of rent for a period of not less than three years.

15.2 The Policies are valid and enforceable and all premiums due have been paid. There are no outstanding claims or circumstances likely to give rise to a claim under the Policies or which would be required to be notified to the insurers and nothing has been done or omitted to be done which has made or could make any Policy void or voidable or as a result of which the renewal of any Policy might be refused or the premiums due in respect of them may be liable to be increased.

15.3 There are no claims outstanding or threatened, or so far as the Sellers are aware, pending, against any Group Company which are not fully covered by insurance.

Trading and contracts

16. Contracts and commitments

16.1 All contracts, agreements, transactions, obligations, commitments, understandings or arrangements requiring in relation to its discharge any payment in excess of .... to which the Group Companies are a party are Disclosed.

16.2 No Group Company is a party to any agreement, arrangement or commitment which:

(a) has or is expected to have material consequences in terms of expenditure or revenue;

(b) relates to matters outside the ordinary business of that Group Company or was not entered into on arms' length terms;

(c) constitutes a commercial transaction or arrangement which deviates from the usual pattern for that Group Company;

(d) can be terminated in the event of any change in the underlying ownership or control of that Group Company or would be materially affected by such change;

(e) cannot readily be fulfilled or performed by it on time; or

(f) cannot be terminated, without giving rise to any liabilities on any Group Company, by that Group Company giving three months' notice or less.

16.3 No Group Company:

(a) has outstanding any bid, tender, sale or service proposal which is material in relation to its business or which, if accepted, would be likely to result in a loss;

(b) or Seller is aware of any actual, potential or alleged breach, invalidity, grounds for termination, grounds for rescission, grounds for avoidance or grounds for repudiation of any contract to which any Group Company is a party; or

      (c)   has granted any power of attorney or other such authority (whether express or implied) which is still outstanding.

17. Terms of trade

No Group Company has given any guarantee or warranty (other than any implied by law) or made any representation in respect of any product or services sold or supplied by it nor has it accepted any liability to service, maintain, repair or otherwise do or refrain from doing anything in relation to such goods or services after they have been sold or supplied by it except for those contained in its standard conditions of trading, complete and accurate copies of which are contained in the Disclosure Letter.

18. Product liability

No Group Company has manufactured, sold or provided any product or service which does not in every respect comply with all applicable laws, regulations or standards or which is defective or dangerous or not in accordance with any representation or warranty, express or implied, given in respect of it.

19. Licences and consents

19.1   Complete and accurate details of all licences, consents, permissions, authorisations and approvals required by each Group Company for the carrying on of its business are contained in the Disclosure Letter and all of them have been obtained by that Group Company and are in full force and effect.

19.2   All reports, returns and information required by law or as a condition of any licence, consent, permission, authorisation or approval to be made or given to any person or authority in connection with the business of any Group Company have been made or given to the appropriate person or authority and there are no circumstances which indicate that any licence, consent, permission, authorisation or approval might not be renewed in whole or in part or is likely to be revoked, suspended or cancelled or which may confer a right of revocation, suspension or cancellation.

20. Trading partners

20.1   No Group Company acts or carries on business in partnership with any other person or is a member of any corporate or unincorporated body, undertaking or association.

20.2   No Group Company is a party to any joint venture agreement or arrangement or any agreement or arrangement under which, it is to participate with any other person in any business.

20.3   No Group Company is a party to any agency, distributorship, licence or management agreement or is a party to any contract or arrangement which restricts its freedom to carry on its business in such manner as it may think fit in any part of the world.

20.4   No Group Company has any branch, agency, place of business or establishment outside the United Kingdom.

21.   Competition and trade regulation law

21.1   No Group Company is or has been a party to, or is or has been concerned in any agreement or arrangement, or is conducting or has conducted itself, whether by omission or otherwise, in a manner which:

(a)   contravenes Chapters 1 or II of the Competition Act 1998 or the competition provisions of the Enterprise Act 2002 or any secondary legislation made under it;

(b)   infringes articles 101 or 102 of TFEU (the EC Treaty) or any regulation or directive made under it or any other anti-trust or similar legislation in any jurisdiction in which any Group Company has assets or carries on or intends to carry on business or where its activities may have any effect; or

(c)   contravenes the provisions of the Consumer Protection from Unfair Trading Regulations 2008 and Business Protection from Misleading Marketing Regulations 2008.

21.2   No Group Company has:

(a)   given an undertaking to, or is subject to, any order of or investigation by, or has received any request for information or statement of objections or damages claim or threat relating to competition matters from;

(b)   received, nor so far as the Sellers are aware, is it likely to receive any process, notice or communication, formal or informal by or on behalf of;

(c)   been or is a party to, or is or has been concerned in, any agreement or arrangement in respect of which an application for negative clearance and/or exemption when such clearances and exemptions were available;

(d)   made a leniency application in relation to competition law to the Competition and Markets Authority (and before they were abolished the Office of Fair Trading and the Competition Commission), the European Commission or any other governmental or other authority, department, board, body or agency of any country having jurisdiction in anti-trust or similar matters in relation to its business or third party private litigant.

21.3   The Company has not received any aid from any European Community member state or through any state resources in breach of articles 107 and 108 (previously 87 and 88) of the TFEU.

21.4   No employee or director of the Company or a Group Company has been the subject of a fine, jail sentence, extradition, plea bargain or prosecution or investigation under EU or UK or other competition law.

22. Compliance with law

22.1 No Group Company has committed or is liable for, and no claim has been or, so far as the Sellers are aware, will be made that any Group Company has committed or is liable for any criminal, illegal, unlawful or unauthorised act or breach of any obligation or duty whether imposed by or pursuant to statute, contract or otherwise.

22.2 No Group Company has received notification that any investigation or inquiry is being, or has been, conducted by, or received any request for information from any governmental or other authority, department, board, body or agency in respect of the affairs of any Group Company and, so far as the Sellers are aware, there are no circumstances which would give rise to such investigation, inquiry or request.

22.3 None of the activities, contracts or rights of any Group Company is ultra vires, unauthorised, invalid or unenforceable or in breach of any contract or covenant and all documents in the enforcement of which any Group Company may be interested are valid.

23. Litigation and disputes

23.1 Except for actions to recover any debt incurred in the ordinary course of the business owed to any Group Company where each individual debt and its costs outstanding amounts to less than ....:

(a) no Group Company nor any person for whose acts a Group Company may be liable is engaged in any litigation, arbitration, administrative or criminal proceedings, whether as claimant (plaintiff), defendant or otherwise;

(b) no litigation, arbitration, administrative or criminal proceedings by or against any Group Company or any person for whose acts a Group Company may be liable are threatened or expected and, as far as the Sellers are aware, none are pending;

(c) there are no facts or circumstances likely to give rise to any litigation, arbitration, administrative or criminal proceedings against any Group Company or any person for whose acts a Group Company may be liable.

23.2 No Group Company is subject to any order or judgment given by any court or governmental or other authority, department, board, body or agency or has not been a party to any undertaking or assurance given to any court or governmental or other authority, department, board, body or agency which is still in force, nor are there any facts or circumstances likely to give rise to any Group Company becoming subject to such an order or judgment or to be a party to any such undertaking or assurance.

Assets

24.   Ownership and condition of assets

24.1   Each of the assets included in the Accounts or acquired by any Group Company since the Accounts Date (other than the Properties and current assets subsequently disposed of or realised in the ordinary course of business) is owned both legally and beneficially by a Group Company free from any third party rights and, if capable of possession, is in the possession of that Group Company.

24.2   Each item of plant and machinery, vehicle and office equipment used by each Group Company is:

(a)   in good repair and condition, regularly maintained and certified safe and without risk to health when used;

(b)   capable and will remain capable of doing the work for which it was designed or purchased until the time when (on the basis of depreciation adopted in the Accounts) it will have been written down to a nil value;

(c)   not surplus to requirements; and

(d)   not expected to require replacement or additions within six months of Completion.

24.3   No Group Company has acquired, or agreed to acquire, any asset on terms that title to that asset does not pass until full payment is made or all indebtedness incurred in connection with the acquisition is discharged.

24.4   The assets owned by each Group Company, together with all assets held under hire-purchase, lease or rental agreements which are contained in the Disclosure Letter, comprise all assets necessary for the continuation of the business of each Group Company as it is currently carried on.

25.   Stock

No part of the stocks of materials of any Group Company is redundant, obsolete, obsolescent or defective.

26.   Charges and encumbrances over assets

26.1   No option, right to acquire, mortgage, charge, pledge, lien (other than a lien arising by operation of law in the ordinary course of trading) or oilier form of security or encumbrance or equity on, over or affecting the shares or the whole or any part of the undertaking or assets of any Group Company, including any investment in any other Group Company, is outstanding and, apart from this Agreement, there is no agreement or commitment to give or create any of them and no claim has been made by any person to be entitled to any of them.

26.2   No floating charge created by a Group Company has crystallised and there are no circumstances likely to cause such a floating charge to crystallise.

26.3   No Group Company has received notice from any person intimating that it will enforce any security which it may hold over the assets of any Group Company, and there are no circumstances likely to give rise to such a notice.

26.4   All charges in favour of a Group Company have, if required, been registered in accordance with the provisions of the Companies Act 2006.

27.   Intellectual Property

27.1   Complete and accurate details of all Intellectual Property and copies of all licences and other agreements relating to it are contained in the Disclosure Letter.

27.2   All Intellectual Property is either:

(a)   in the sole legal and beneficial ownership of the Group Company which uses it, free from all licences, charges or other encumbrances; or

(b)   the subject of binding and enforceable licences from third parties in favour of the Group Company which uses it:

(i)   of which no notice to terminate has been received;

(ii)   all parties to which have fully complied with all obligations in those licences; and

(iii)   in relation to which no disputes have arisen or are foreseeable;

and in either case nothing has been done or omitted to be done whether by any Group Company or as far as the Sellers are aware by any person which would jeopardise the validity, enforceability or subsistence of any Intellectual Property or any such licences.

27.3   Any Intellectual Property which is capable of registration has been registered or is the subject of an application for registration, and is or will when duly registered be valid, binding and enforceable and:

(a)   in the case of registrations, all renewal fees have been paid and renewals made by their due date and all such action necessary to preserve and maintain the registration has been taken;

(b)   in the case of registrations contained in the Disclosure Letter each is presently used by the Seller and is in full force and effect and has not been abandoned;

(c)   in the case of pending applications, the Sellers are aware of no reason why any such applications should not proceed to grant;

(d)   (in the case of a patent application) the invention which is the subject matter of such application has not been used or published except experimentally prior to the date of the UK patent application and the true and first inventors thereof have no outstanding rights to compensation pursuant to the Patents Act 1977; and

(e)   none of the Intellectual Property is subject to any use, claim, application or attack by any other person.

27.4   No licences, registered user or other rights have been granted or agreed to be granted by any Group Company to any person in respect of any Intellectual Property.

27.5   No Group Company uses any Intellectual Property in respect of which any third party has any right, title or interest.

27.6   Each Group Company owns or has the right to use all Intellectual Property rights required in connection with the conduct of its business as presently carried on or expected to be carried on in the future.

27.7   So far as the Sellers are aware, at no time during the past six years has there been any unauthorised use or infringement by any person of any Intellectual Property.

27.8   None of the processes employed, or products or services dealt in, by any Group Company infringes any rights of any third party relating to Intellectual Property nor makes any Group Company liable to pay a fee or royalty and no claims have been made, threatened or so far as the Sellers are aware are pending, in relation to any Intellectual Property against any Group Company.

27.9   Except in the ordinary course of business and on a confidential basis, no disclosure has been made of any of the confidential information, know-how, technical processes, financial or trade secrets or customer or supplier lists of any Group Company.

27.10   Any names used by any Group Company other than its corporate name are contained in the Disclosure Letter and do not infringe the rights of any person.

28.   Data Protection Act

28.1   The Company has complied in all respects with the provisions of the Data Protection Act 1998 ('DPA') and the principles contained in the DPA.

28.2   Except as notified under the DPA, the Company has either not held or processed any personal data or is exempt from notifying under the DPA under one of the exemptions contained in the DPA.

28.3   Insofar as personal data are subject to registration or notification:

(a)   the Company has at all times maintained full and accurate notification under the DPA and has operated wholly within the terms of such notification;

(b)   no disclosure has taken place outside the terms of the Company's notification.

28.4   The Company has not been served with a notice under sections 10, 11 or 12 of the DPA.

28.5   The Company has not been served with any information or enforcement notice under the DPA, nor are there any circumstances which might give rise to the Company being served with such a notice in the future.

28.6   To the extent the Company has personal data processed by third parties written agreements relating to such processing have been signed and where personal data is exported from the EEA compliance with the DPA has been achieved in relation to such exports.

29.   Euro compliance

29.1   The products, systems and services are 'Euro Compliant' and are capable of satisfying the legal requirements applicable to the common currency adopted or to be adopted by the relevant participating member states of the European Union and known as the 'Euro' as set out in the European Commission Regulation number 1103.97 ('the Regulation'). For the purposes of this warranty 'Euro Compliant' shall mean the ability of the systems to perform using the Euro and to allow any currency recognised by the systems, including but not limited to the Euro and all other currencies belonging to and adopted by full member states of the European Union, to be converted to other currencies, and in particular (but without limitation) to:

(a)   perform all monetary functions in Euros;

(b)   process multiple currencies and in particular the dual currencies during the transition phase set out in the Regulation of countries adopting the Euro;

(c)   recognise the industry standard keyboard configurations or key-strokes and screen layouts for the Euro symbol;

(d)   correctly implement the conversion and rounding requirements (including the triangulation rule) set out in the Regulation; and

(e)   interface with other Euro Compliant products.

29.2   None of the Group Companies nor the Sellers have any knowledge that the introduction of the Euro will or may cause any agreement, arrangement or obligation to which the Company is a party to terminate or to be capable of termination or will or may alter the terms of or excuse or discharge performance of such an agreement.

Employment

30.   Directors and employees

30.1   Complete and accurate details of the terms and conditions of employment of all employees of each Group Company, including the date of commencement of their continuous period of employment and any arrangements or assurances (whether or not legally binding) in relation to their employment, are contained in the Disclosure Letter.

30.2 Each Group Company has maintained up-to-date, adequate and suitable records regarding the service and terms and conditions of employment of each of its employees.

30.3 Each Group Company has maintained up-to-date adequate and suitable records for the purposes of the Working Time Regulations and has complied with all other obligations to its workers (as 'workers' is defined in regulation 2 of the Working Time Regulations) and there are no claims capable of arising or pending or threatened by any officer or employee or former officer or employee or the Health and Safety Executive or local authority Environmental Health Department or any trade union or employee representative related to the Working Time Regulations.

30.4 No Group Company is a party to any consultancy agreement any agreement for management services or any contract services [with any director].

30.5 Since the Accounts Date there has been:

(a) no material alteration in the terms of employment or material change in the number of employees employed by any Group Company; or

(b) no material increase in any fees, remuneration or benefits paid or payable to any officer or employee of any Group Company, nor are any negotiations for any such increase current or likely to take place in the next six months.

30.6 No officer or employee of any Group Company is remunerated on a profit-sharing, bonus or commission basis.

30.7 Other than salary for the current month and accrued holiday pay, no amount is owing to any present or former officer or employee of any Group Company.

30.8 There is no share option or share incentive scheme in operation by or in relation to any Group Company for any of its office or employees, nor has the introduction of such a scheme been proposed.

30.9 Each Group Company has at all relevant times complied with all its obligations under statute and otherwise concerning the health and safety at work of its employees and there are no claims capable of arising or pending or threatened by any employee or third party in respect of any accident or injury which are not fully covered by insurance.

30.10 Save as provided for or taken into account in the Accounts:

(a) no claim or liability to make any payment of any kind to any person who is or has been an officer or employee has been received or incurred by any Group Company whether under the Employment Rights Act 1996, Equality Act 2010 and any and all sexual, race, disability, age, religious and sexual orientation discrimination legislation or otherwise; and

(b)   no gratuitous payment of a material amount has been made or promised by any Group Company in connection with the actual or proposed termination or suspension of employment or variation of any contract of employment of any present or former officer or employee.

30.11   No officer or employee of any Group Company has given notice or is under notice of dismissal, nor are there any service contracts between any Group Company and its officers or employees which cannot be terminated by the relevant Group Company by 12 weeks' notice or less without giving rise to a claim for damages or compensation (other than a statutory redundancy payment).

30.12   No Group Company has, in contravention of the Companies Act 2006:

(a)   entered into any arrangement involving the acquisition of non-cash assets from or disposal to;

(b)   granted any loan or quasi-loan to, or entered into any guarantee or credit transaction with; or

(c)   provided any security in connection with any loan, quasi-loan or credit transaction to or with any director or person connected with a director within the meaning of the Companies Act 2006.

31.   Industrial relations

31.1   No Group Company is a party to any contract, agreement or arrangement with any trade union or other body or organisation representing any of its employees.

31.2   Each Group Company has in relation to its officers and employees and former officers and employees complied with all conditions of service, customs and practices and, where relevant, all collective agreements, recognition agreements workforce agreements and relevant agreements for the time being.

31.3   Within the last 12 months, no Group Company has:

(a)   given notice of any redundancies to the Secretary of State, started consultations with any appropriate representatives or failed to comply with any obligation under the provisions of Chapter II of the Trade Union and Labour Relations (Consolidation) Act 1992; or

(b)   been a party to any relevant transfer as defined in the Transfer of Undertakings (Protection of Employment) Regulations 2006, or has failed to comply with any duty to inform and consult any appropriate representative under the Regulations.

31.4   No dispute has arisen between any Group Company and a material number or category of its employees, nor are there any present circumstances known to the Sellers which are likely to give rise to any such dispute.

31.5 No training schemes, arrangements or proposals exist, nor have there been any such schemes, arrangements or proposals in the past in respect of which a levy may become payable by any Group Company under the Industrial Training Act 1982.

32. Pensions

32.1 Save as Disclosed in the Disclosure Letter, no Group Company has any plans, schemes or arrangements in relation to death, disability or retirement of any of its current or past directors or employees.

32.2 In relation to each plan, scheme or arrangement Disclosed under paragraph 32.1 in the Disclosure Letter:

(a) complete and accurate details:
  (i) of it (including, where appropriate, copies of all trust deeds and rules together with copies of all amending deeds and resolutions and the latest actuarial reports); and
  (ii) of the basis on which the relevant Group Company makes, or is liable to make, contributions to it are contained in the Disclosure Letter;

(b) all contributions which are payable by any Group Company in respect of it and all contributions due from the employees of the relevant Group Company as members of it have been duly made and the relevant Group Company has fulfilled all its obligations under it including with limitation all legal obligations in relation to auto-enrolment which are applicable;

(c) it has been administered in accordance with all requirements of the Pension Schemes Act 1993, the Pension Act 1995, the contracting-out requirements of Part III of the Pension Schemes Act 1993 and Pensions Act 2004 and Pensions Act 2014 and in accordance with the trusts, powers and provisions of such plans, schemes or arrangements and all other applicable laws, regulations and requirements of any competent governmental body or regulatory authority;

(d) every person who has had a right to join, or applies to join, it has been properly advised of that right and no employee has been excluded from membership of it or from any of the benefits under it in contravention of article 157 (previously article 141) of the TFEU or section 62 of the Pensions Act 1995;

(e) no undertakings or assurances have been given to any employee of any Group Company as to the continuance, introduction, increase or improvement of any pension rights or entitlements which any Group Company and/or the Purchaser would be required to implement in accordance with good industrial relations practice and whether or not there is any legal obligation so to do;

(f) no power to augment benefits has been exercised;

(g) no discretion has been exercised to admit to membership a present or former director or employee who would not otherwise be eligible for admission to membership;

    (h)   no discretion has been exercised to provide in respect of a member a benefit which would not otherwise be provided;

    (i)   all benefits (other than a refund of contributions with interest where appropriate) payable on the death of a member while in service, or during a period of sickness or disability of a member, are fully insured under a policy effected with an insurance company to which section 659B of the ICTA applies and the Sellers are not aware of any circumstances in which such insurance would be invalidated;

    (j)   all liabilities or benefits accrued in respect of service completed at Completion are secured on an ongoing basis taking account of future increases in salary to normal retirement date and increases in pensions on the basis of realistic actuarial and financial assumptions and the obligations imposed on it as a result of *Barber v Guardian Royal Exchange*;

    (k)   it is an exempt approved scheme and/or retirement annuity approved, or capable of being approved, under the Taxes Act and the Sellers are not aware of any reasons why any such approval could be withdrawn;

    (l)   all consultancy, legal or other expenses have been paid and no such services have been provided for which an account has not been rendered;

    (m)   no claim has been threatened or made or litigation commenced against the trustees or administrator or against the Company or any other person whom the Company is or may be liable to indemnify or compensate in respect of any matter arising out of or in connection with the plan, scheme or arrangement and so far as the Sellers are aware, there are no circumstances which may give rise to any such claim or litigation;

    (n)   no application for clearance has been made to the Pensions Regulator.

32.3   No death, disability or retirement gratuity is currently being paid or has been promised nor will pending Completion be paid or promised by any Group Company to or in respect of any officer or employee of any Group Company.

Properties

33.   Title

33.1   The Properties comprise all the properties presently owned, occupied, held, controlled or otherwise used by any Group Company and a Group Company is in actual and exclusive occupation and is the legal and beneficial owner of each Property.

33.2   The relevant Group Company's title to each of the Properties is good and marketable.

33.3   Each Property is occupied or otherwise used by a Group Company by right of ownership or under the Leases, the terms of which permit its occupation or use as tenant and not under any provision allowing the parting of or sharing of possession with Group or Associated Companies and there are no outstanding circumstances which would restrict the continued possession and enjoyment of any Property or any part of it.

33.4   All deeds and documents necessary to prove title to each Property are in the possession and control of the Group Companies and consist of original deeds and documents or properly examined abstracts.

33.5   No person is in adverse possession of any Property or has acquired or is acquiring any rights or overriding interests (as defined by section 70 of the Land Registration Act 1925) adversely affecting any Property.

33.6   No Group Company has had occasion to make any claim or complaint in relation to any neighbouring property or its use or occupation and there are no disputes, claims, actions, demands or complaints in respect of any Property which are ongoing nor are any disputes, claims, actions, demands or complaints anticipated and no notices materially affecting any Property have been given or received and not complied with.

34.   Encumbrances

34.1   No Property is subject to any outgoings other than business rates, water rates and insurance premiums and, in the case of leasehold properties, rent, insurance rent and service charges.

34.2   No Property is subject to any restrictive covenant, reservation, stipulation, easement, profits à prendre, wayleave, licence, grant, restriction, overriding interest, agreement for sale, estate contract, option, right of pre-emption or other similar agreement or right vested in third parties.

34.3   No matter exists which is registered or is properly capable of registration against any Property as a Land Charge, Local Land Charge, caution, inhibition, notice or restriction.

34.4   Where sub-paragraphs 34.1–34.3 inclusive have been Disclosed against in the Disclosure Letter, the obligations and liabilities imposed and arising under the Disclosed matter have been fully observed and performed and any payments in respect of it which are due and payable have been duly paid.

35.   Planning matters

35.1   The use of each Property is a lawful and permitted use for the purposes of the Planning Acts.

35.2   Planning permission has been obtained, or is deemed to have been granted for the purposes of the Planning Acts for each Property; no permission is the subject of a temporary or personal consent or has been modified or revoked; no application for planning permission is awaiting decision; no planning permission has been granted within the last three months and the validity of no planning permission is currently or may be challenged.

35.3   Building regulation consents have been obtained with respect to all development, alterations and improvements to the Properties.

35.4   In respect of each Property, the Group Companies have complied, and are continuing to comply, in all respects with:

(i)   planning permissions, orders and regulations issued under the Planning Acts, the London Building Acts and building regulation consents and by-laws for the time being in force;

(ii)   all agreements under section 52 of the Town and Country Planning Act 1971 and planning obligations under section 106 of the Town and Country Planning Act 1990; and

(iii) all agreements made under sections 38 and 278 of the Highways Act 1980, section 33 of the Local Government (Miscellaneous Provisions) Act 1982, section 18 of the Public Health Act 1936 and section 104 of the Water Industry Act 1991.

35.5   No Property is listed as being of special historic or architectural importance or located in a conservation or other area, or subject to an order, designation or affected by a planning proposal which may regulate or affect its use in the future.

35.6   All claims and liabilities under the Planning Acts or any other legislation have been discharged and no claim or liability, actual or contingent, is outstanding.

36.   Statutory obligations

36.1   Each Group Company has complied with and is continuing to comply with all applicable statutory and by-law requirements with respect to the Properties, and in particular with the requirements as to fire precautions under the Regulatory Reform (Fire Safety) Order 2005and under the Public Health Acts, the Offices, Shops and Railway Premises Act 1963, the Health and Safety at Work etc Act 1974, the Factories Act 1961.

36.2   No licences are required in relation to any of the Properties under the Licensing Act 1988 or Licensing Act 2003 or Gambling Act 2005.

37.   Adverse orders

37.1   There are no compulsory purchase notices, orders or resolutions affecting any of the Properties and there are no circumstances likely to lead to any being made.

37.2   There are no closing, demolition or clearance orders, enforcement notices or stop notices affecting the Properties and there are no circumstances likely to lead to any being made.

38.   Condition of the properties

38.1   The buildings and other structures on each Property are in good and substantial repair and fit for the purposes for which they are used and no building or other structure on any Property has been affected by structural damage, electrical defects, timber infestation or disease.

38.2   The principal means of access to each Property is over roads which have been adopted by the local or other highway authority and which are maintainable at the public expense and no means of access to any of the Properties is shared with any other person nor subject to rights of determination by any other person.

38.3   Each Property enjoys the mains services of water, drainage, electricity and gas.

38.4   No Property is located in an area or subject to circumstances which makes it susceptible to subsidence or flooding.

39.   Leasehold properties

39.1   Each Lease is valid and in full force and there are no circumstances which would entitle any landlord or other person to exercise any power of entry or take possession of the Properties.

39.2   Each Group Company has paid the rent and observed and performed the covenants on the part of the tenant and the conditions contained in any Lease to which it is a party, and the last demands (or receipts for rent if issued) were unqualified.

39.3   All licences, consents and approvals required from the landlords and any superior landlords for the grant of the Leases and during the continuance of the Leases have been obtained and any covenants on the part of the tenant contained in those licences, consents and approvals have been duly performed and observed.

39.4   There are no rent reviews outstanding or in progress under any Lease.

39.5   Any alteration or improvement carried out on any Property is to be disregarded for rent review purposes.

39.6   There is no obligation to reinstate any Property by removing or dismantling any alteration made to it by any Group Company or any of its predecessors in title and no Group Company has incurred or is likely to incur any liability for dilapidation.

39.7   In the case of a lease granted for more than 21 years, the lease is registered at HM Land Registry with absolute title.

39.8   No Group Company has in the past been the tenant of or guarantor of any leasehold premises not listed in Schedule 5 in respect of which any obligations or liabilities could still accrue to that Group Company.

39.9   The sale of the Shares will not constitute an assignment or other dealing in respect of any Property under the terms of the Leases.

40.   Tenancies

40.1   The Properties are not held subject to, and with the benefit of, any tenancy other than the Tenancies.

40.2   Complete and accurate details of:

(a)   the rent and any rent reviews and, with respect to rent reviews, the date for giving notice of exercise of the reviews and the operative review date;

(b)   the term and any rights to break or renew the term;

(c)   the obligations of the landlord and tenant in respect of outgoings, repairs, user, insurance services and service charge;

(d)   any options, pre-emption or first refusal rights;

(e)   the user required or permitted under the terms of the Tenancies;

(f)   any entitlement of a tenant of the whole or any part of the Properties to compensation on quitting the premises let to him in respect of disturbance and improvements or otherwise; and

(g)   any unusual provisions in relation to each Tenancy are contained in the Disclosure Letter.

40.3   The Sellers are not aware of any material or persistent breaches of covenant or agreement by a tenant of any of the Properties.

41.   Contamination

No Property is likely to be entered in any register introduced under the Environment Act 1995 or otherwise as land which may be contaminated or which may have been put to a contaminative use.

There is not on, in or under any of the Properties or any adjoining property any substance which could give rise to harm to human health or safety or damage to the Environment.

Each property formerly owned or occupied by any Group Company was free of such substances at the time it ceased to be owned or occupied by the relevant Group Company.

Environment

42.   Environmental matters

42.1   In relation to its business, each Group Company holds and has since [its incorporation] always held all Environmental Consents.

42.2   Complete and accurate details of all Environmental Consents held by each Group Company are contained in the Disclosure Letter and are valid and subsisting.

42.3   No Group Company has received any notification that any Environmental Consent it holds is or is likely to be modified, restricted or withdrawn and no works or other upgrading or investment are or will be necessary to secure compliance with or to maintain any such Environmental Consent.

42.4   No Group Company has breached the terms, conditions or provisions of any Environmental Consent.

42.5   No Group Company has received any notification or informal indication that further Environmental Consents will be required under Environmental Law in order for it to continue its present business.

42.6   Each Group Company (and each of its officers, employees and agents in the course of its business) has complied with all applicable Environmental Laws and has never received any notification under Environmental Law requiring it to take or omit to take any action.

42.7   No Group Company has been threatened with any investigation or enquiry by any organisation, or received any complaint, in connection with the Environment.

Taxation Warranties
Events since the Accounts Date

43.   **Since the Accounts Date:**

(a)   no transaction has occurred, either in circumstances where the consideration actually received or receivable (if any) was less than the consideration which could be deemed to have been received for Tax purposes or which will give rise to a Liability to Taxation on any Group Company calculated by reference to deemed as opposed to actual Profits;

(b)   no transaction has occurred which will result in any Group Company becoming liable to pay or bear a Liability to Taxation directly or primarily chargeable against or attributable to another person other than another Group Company;

(c)   no disposal has taken place or other event occurred which will, or may have, the effect of crystallising a Liability to Taxation which would have been included in the provision for deferred taxation contained in the Accounts if such disposal or other event had been planned or predicted at the Accounts Date;

(d)   no Group Company has been a party to any transaction for which any Tax clearance provided for by statute has been, or could have been, obtained; and

(e)   no accounting period or period of account by reference to which Taxation is measured of any Group Company has ended within the meaning of section 12 of the ICTA (basis of, and periods for, assessment).

44.   **Records and compliance**

44.1   Each Group Company has duly complied with all requirements imposed on it by law, and in particular:

(a) each Group Company has paid all Taxation for which it is liable and made all withholdings and deductions in respect, or on account, of any Taxation from any payments made by it which it is obliged or entitled to make and has paid to the appropriate Tax Authority all amounts so withheld or deducted;

(b) each Group Company will not be liable to pay any Tax the due date for payment of which will arise in the 30 days following Completion;

(c) each Group Company has properly prepared and punctually submitted all notices, returns and applications for clearances or consents required for Tax purposes and provided complete and accurate information to any Tax Authority, and all such notices, returns, applications and information remain complete and accurate and in compiling the same no Group Company has taken the benefit of any doubt, such that the relevant Tax Authority may discover information of which it was not reasonably aware and thereby make an enquiry into or dispute the Tax affairs of any Group Company;

(d) each Group Company has kept and maintained complete and accurate records, invoices and other documents and information of whatever nature appropriate or requisite for Tax purposes and has sufficient such records, invoices and other documents and information relating to past events to calculate its liability to Taxation or the relief from Taxation which would arise on any disposal or on the realisation of any assets owned at Completion;

(e) there are no disputes, unsettled or outstanding assessments or appeals in respect of Taxation and no Group Company has within the last six years been subject to any enquiry, investigation or other dispute with any Tax Authority, and there are no circumstances which may give rise to such an enquiry or dispute;

(f) no Group Company has within the last six years been liable or will in respect of any Transaction occurring on or before Completion become liable to pay any interest, penalty, fine or sum of a similar nature in respect of Taxation nor, in relation to Value Added Tax, has received any penalty liability notice, surcharge liability notice or other written notice or warning under the VATA; and

(g) each Group Company has duly submitted all claims and elections which have been assumed to have been made for the purposes of the Accounts.

44.2 Each Group Company has at all times been resident for Tax purposes in [....................] and no Group Company has during the past six years paid and is not liable to pay Tax in any other jurisdiction.

44.3 No Group Company has within the last six years received any audit, visit or inspection from any Tax Authority and no such audit, visit or inspection will take place on or after Completion has been arranged or requested.

44.4   The amount of Tax chargeable on each Group Company or subject to withholding or deduction by the relevant Group Company during any accounting period ending on or within the last six years has not to any material extent depended on any concession, agreement, dispensation or other formal or informal arrangement with any Tax Authority.

45.   Employee shares

No shares or securities have been issued by any Group Company, and no options have been granted or issued in respect of such shares or securities, such that any Group Company will or may be liable to account for income tax under the PAYE system or to collect or pay any national insurance contributions.

46.   VAT

46.1   Each Group Company:

(a)   is registered for the purpose of, and has complied in all respects with, the VATA and is not subject to any conditions imposed or agreed with any Tax Authority; and

(b)   is not, and has not within the last three years been a member of a group for value added tax purposes under section 43 of the VATA (groups of companies).

46.2   All supplies made by each Group Company are taxable supplies, and all input tax for which any Group Company has claimed credit has been paid by that Group Company, in respect of supplies made to it relating to goods or services used or to be used for the purpose of the business of that Group Company.

46.3   No Group Company has made, nor will prior to Completion make, any election to waive exemption under paragraph 2, Schedule 10 of the VATA (election to waive exemption).

46.4   The Disclosure Letter contains full details of all assets owned by each Group Company to which the provisions of Part XV of the Value Added Tax Regulations 1995 (the Capital Goods Scheme) may apply, including the date of acquisition, the cost of the asset, the amount of the input tax for which credit has been claimed and the adjustment period relating to that asset.

47.   Customs duties

Each Group Company has made all necessary returns in relation to the collection and payment of customs duties, excise duties and other Taxes having an equivalent effect and has provided to any relevant Tax Authority all necessary information, returns and documentation and paid all amounts due in relation to the same and within the prescribed time limits.

48.   Balance sheet values

48.1   No Liability to Taxation will arise or be incurred on a disposal by any Group Company of any of its assets for:

(a)   in the case of each asset owned at the Accounts Date, a consideration equal to the value attributed to that asset in preparing the Accounts; and

(b)   in the case of each asset acquired since the Accounts Date, a consideration equal to the consideration given for the acquisition.

48.2   No Group Company has at any time in respect of any asset owned at the date hereof made, nor will prior to Completion make, any claim under sections 152 to 158 (inclusive) of the TCGA (replacement of business assets) and there is no proposal or plan to make any such claim either in the claims and elections assumed to have been made for the purposes of the Accounts or otherwise.

49.   Close company

49.1   No Group Company is, nor has it at any time within the last six years been, either a close company within the meaning of section 414 of the ICTA (close companies) or a close investment holding company for the purposes of section 34(1) and (2) of the CTA 2010 (close investment-holding companies).

49.2   No Group Company has at any time made any loan or advance or payment or given any consideration or effected any transaction falling within s 344 of CTA 2010, as amended by Finance Act 2013, Sch 30 (loans to participators etc).

50.   Group transactions

50.1   Within the last six years no Group Company has:

(a)   been a member of a group of companies within the meaning of section 170 (as amended) of the TCGA (groups of companies), other than one of which the Group Companies were the only members;

(b)   acquired any asset from any other company which was at the time of acquisition a member of the same group of companies as that of which the relevant Group Company was also a member; or

(c)   entered into any group payment arrangements in respect of corporation tax pursuant to Chapter 4 of the CTA 2010 (arrangements with respect to the payment of corporation tax).

50.2   No Liability to Taxation will be suffered by any Group Company in consequence of Completion or otherwise by virtue either of this Agreement or of the relevant Group Company ceasing to be a member of a group of companies with any other company.

51.   Deductible expenses

51.1   No Group Company has since the Accounts Date made or provided nor is under any obligation currently or for the future to make any payment of an income or revenue nature which, or to provide a benefit the cost of which, will be prevented from being deductible for Tax purposes, whether as a deduction in computing the profits of a trade or as an expense of management or as a charge on income.

51.2   The accounting treatment adopted by each Group Company in its accounts in relation to any loan relationship as defined in Part 5, Ch 4 of CTA 2009 (meaning of 'loans relationships', etc) will be treated as an authorised accounting method for the purposes of ss 335–347 of CTA 2009 (authorised accounting methods).

51.3   All debits and credits in respect of the Company's loan relationships or derivative contracts are brought into account by the Company as debits or credits for the purposes of Part 5 CTA 2009 (Loan Relationships) (formerly Chapter II Part IV Finance Act 2002) (as the case may be) at the time and to the extent that such debits and credits are recognised in the statutory accounts of the Company. The carrying value of any loan relationship or derivative contract in statutory accounts of the Company is equal to the face value of the debt or the amount or value of the consideration given for the acquisition of the rights under that loan relationship or contract.

52.   Dividends and distributions

No Group Company has at any time purchased, repaid or redeemed or agreed to purchase, repay or redeem its share capital, or capitalised or agreed to capitalise in the form of redeemable shares or debentures any profits or reserves, or otherwise issued any share capital or other security as paid up otherwise than by the receipt of new consideration within the meaning of ss 441–446 of the CTA 2009.

SCHEDULE 5
(PARTICULARS OF THE PROPERTIES)

1. Freehold properties

Address:

Description including Title Number/Root of Title:

2. Leasehold properties

Address of Lease:

Date and parties:

Term:

Authorised user:

Current rental:

Rent reviews:

3. Particulars of the Tenancies

Address of Lease:

Date and parties:

Term:

Authorised user:

Current rental:

Rent reviews:

SCHEDULE 6
(THE PENSION SCHEME[S])

Executed as a Deed by

....

in the presence of:

....

Signature of witness:

Name:

Address:

Occupation:

[The Common Seal of .... Limited/plc was affixed to this Deed (which is not delivered until the date appearing at the head of page 1)

in the presence of:

....

Director

Director/Secretary]

[Executed as a Deed (but not delivered until the date appearing at the head of page 1) by .... Limited/plc

acting by:

....

Director

Director/Secretary]

Precedent G – Limitations on warranty liability

The precedent share purchase agreement (Precedent F) is drafted from a purchaser's perspective and, as such, it contains a full set of warranties and a covenant for taxation but limited limitations on liability.

This precedent contains a full list of limitations on warranty and covenant for taxation liability, which are designed to fit with the precedent share purchase agreement and would replace sub-clause 12.2. In practice, these limitations will need to be modified to fit into the purchaser's draft agreement. It is very rare that all of them would be included – the drafts person should carefully consider which are relevant or appropriate given the particular facts of the transaction. The general limitations are then followed by further limitations/controls to the tax covenant which could be added as a separate schedule and referred to in clause 10 of the precedent share purchase agreement (Precedent F).

Warning:

All precedents can be dangerous. There are major risks in using this precedent without competent legal advice. It is unlikely that any precedent will be able to be used in any transaction without considerable modification.

12.2.1   The Warrantors shall not be liable for any Claim if and to the extent that:

    (a)   it exceeds the Consideration;

    (b)   in respect of a Claim other than a Claim under the Covenant for Taxation, the Purchaser has actual knowledge of any matter which could give rise to a Claim on or before Completion;

    (c)   an allowance, provision or reserve in respect of any liability the subject of the Claim was made or taken into account, or payment or discharge of which was taken into account, in or in preparing the Accounts;

    (d)   any provision for Taxation in the Accounts is an over provision or the subject matter of the Claim gives rise to a corresponding benefit of any kind;

    (e)   any liability included in the Accounts has been discharged or satisfied below the amount attributed to it or included in respect of it in the Accounts;

    (f)   it arises directly or indirectly in respect of, or as a consequence of, any event in the ordinary course of the business of the Group Company concerned after the Accounts Date;

    (g)   it would not have arisen or would have been reduced or eliminated but for:

        (i)   a failure or omission on the part of any Group Company after Completion to make, or an adjustment or revision

> to, any claim, election, surrender or disclaimer or the failure or omission after Completion to give any notice or consent to do any other thing the making, giving or doing of which in each case was taken into account in computing the provision or reserve for Tax in the Accounts or was expressly referred to in the Disclosure Letter; or

(ii) any claim, election, surrender or disclaimer made or notice or consent given or any other thing done after Completion by any Group Company or the Purchaser or any person connected with them;

(h) any Relief of any Group Company arising in respect of a period ended on or before Completion is available to relieve or mitigate such Claim or Liability for Taxation;

(i) the Sellers have surrendered or procured the surrender of surplus advance corporation tax' or group relief for no consideration which has offset such Taxation at no cost to the Purchaser, or could have done so but for a failure by any Group Company after Completion having received notice in writing from the Sellers to claim such surrender; or

(j) to the extent that the income, profits or gains in respect of which it arises were actual income, profits or gains earned, accrued or received by any Group Company but were not reflected in the Accounts;

(k) it is attributable to or arises as a result of:

(i) any voluntary act or omission of the Purchaser (or any persons deriving title from it) or any Group Company after Completion done or suffered outside the ordinary course of business;

(ii) a change in the law (whether retrospectively or not);

(iii) any change after Completion in the bases upon which the accounts of any Group Company are prepared or any change in accounting or taxation practice, policies or principles; or

(iv) any change after Completion in the date to which any Group Company makes up its Accounts;

(l) other than in respect of a Claim under the Covenant for Taxation, the Purchaser is indemnified against any loss or damage suffered by it under the terms of any insurance policy for the time being in force, or would have been so indemnified had the insurance policies held by the Group Companies immediately prior to Completion remained in full force and effect;

(m) other than in respect of a Claim under the Covenant for Taxation, the liabilities under it is contingent, future or unascertainable in which case the Warrantors shall not be liable to recompense the Purchaser until such time as the Purchaser shall actually have suffered the loss or incurred the liability in question;

(n) it arises or is increased by a failure of the Purchaser or any Group Company to comply with their respective obligations under this Agreement;

(o) other than in respect of a Claim under the Covenant for Taxation, it is disclosed in this Agreement or in the Disclosure Letter or done as a condition precedent to Completion or arises in or as a consequence of the execution or performance of this Agreement;

(p) any diminution in the value of any Group Company arises or is increased as a result of or in or connection with any delay or failure to deal with any matter in a proper and efficient manner at the time when such facts became known or ought to have become known to the Purchaser or any of its officers;

(q) other than in respect of a Claim under the Covenant for Taxation, in relation to the tangible assets of any Group Company, the matter or thing giving rise to the Claim would have been revealed by any inspection or survey actually carried out (or which would be carried out by a prudent purchaser) on behalf of the Purchaser prior to Completion;

(r) it relates to any expression of opinion or future intention or any forecasts, projections, speculation, assessment or budget;

(s) such Claim arises as a result of a combination of two or more Transactions, any of which were carried out, effected or completed after Completion;

(t) other than in respect of a Claim under the Covenant for Taxation, it relates to the fact that any Group Company has lost goodwill or possible business;

(u) it would not have arisen or would have been reduced but for a cessation of a trade or a change in the nature or conduct of a trade carried on by any Group Company in either case occurring after Completion.

TAX LIMITATIONS TO CLAUSE 10 OF PRECEDENT F (IN ADDITION TO THOSE ABOVE)

[...] Limitations on liability

The liability of the Warrantors under the Covenant for Taxation shall be reduced if and to the extent that the Liability to Taxation shall have been recovered under the Warranties or under any other part of the Covenant for Taxation (and vice versa).

[...] Repayment

If the Warrantors shall make any payment to the Purchaser in relation to any Tax Claim and the Purchaser or any Group Company subsequently receives from any Tax Authority or any person (other than another Group Company) any amount referable to the subject matter of that Tax Claim, the Purchaser shall, once it or any Group Company has received such amount, repay (after deducting the costs and expenses of the Purchaser or any Group Company incurred in recovering such amount and any Taxation payable on it or on any interest) to the Warrantors either:

(a) a sum equal to such amount; or

(b) if lesser a sum equal to the Tax Claim paid by the Warrantors to the Purchaser,

together with any interest paid to the Purchaser or that Group Company in respect of such sum.

[...] Claims procedure

[...].1 Upon the Purchaser or any Group Company becoming aware of a Claim for Taxation which may result in a Tax Claim, the Purchaser shall:

(a) as soon as reasonably practicable (but not as a condition precedent to the making of a Tax Claim) give written notice of that Claim for Taxation to the Warrantors or, as the case may be, shall procure that the Group Company forthwith give written notice of that Claim for Taxation to the Warrantors;

(b) subject always to the terms of this paragraph [...] and the Warrantors agreeing to indemnify and secure the Purchaser and/ or the relevant Group Company to its reasonable satisfaction against all losses, costs, damages and expenses, including interest on overdue Tax, which may be incurred, further procure that the Group Company take such action and give such information and assistance in connection with the affairs of the relevant Group Company as the Warrantors may reasonably and promptly by written notice request to avoid, resist, appeal or compromise the Claim for Taxation.

[...].2 The Purchaser shall not be obliged to procure that the Group Company appeals against any tax assessment if, the Warrantors having been given written notice of the receipt of that Claim for Taxation in accordance with paragraph [...].1 above, the Group Company has not within 21 days (or, if there is a statutory time limit of not more than 30 days, within 14 days) thereafter received instructions in writing from the Warrantors, in accordance with the preceding provisions of this paragraph [...], to make that appeal.

[...].3 The Purchaser shall not be obliged to procure that any Group Company take any action under paragraph [...].1 above which involves contesting any matter with any Tax Authority (excluding the authority or body demanding the Tax in question) or any court or tribunal unless the Warrantors furnish the Group Company with the written opinion of leading tax counsel to the effect that the appeal in question will, on the balance of probabilities, succeed. Such tax counsel shall be instructed by the Warrantors at the Warrantors' expense, but the Warrantors shall promptly provide the Purchaser with a copy of such instructions and give the Purchaser or its representative a reasonable opportunity to attend any conference with Counsel.

[...].4 The Purchaser shall not be required to take any action or procure that any Group Company take any action under this paragraph [...] if it reasonably determines that such action would have an adverse effect on the amount of tax payable by the Purchaser or any Group Company in respect of a period after Completion.

[...]   Tax returns

[...].1   The Warrantors or their duly authorised agent shall at the Warrantors' sole expense prepare the corporation tax returns of each Group Company for the accounting period ended on the Accounts Date to the extent that they have not been prepared prior to Completion.

[...].2   The Purchaser shall procure that each Group Company shall cause the tax returns mentioned in paragraph [...].1 above to be authorised, signed and submitted to the relevant Tax Authority without amendment or with such amendments as the Warrantors shall reasonably agree provided that the Purchaser shall not be obliged to procure that any Group Company takes any such action as is mentioned in this paragraph [...] in relation to any tax return that is not true and accurate in all material respects.

[...].3   The Warrantors or their duly authorised agent shall at the Warrantors 'sole expense prepare all documentation and deal with all matters (including correspondence) relating to the tax returns of each Group Company for all accounting periods ended on or prior to the Accounts Date, and the Warrantors shall provide the Purchaser with copies of any correspondence relating to such tax returns prior to their submission and copies of any correspondence from HM Revenue and Customs. The Warrantors shall give the Purchaser a reasonable opportunity to comment on such correspondence Prior to submission and shall take account of the Purchaser's reasonable comments. The Purchaser shall, upon reasonable notice (having regard to the circumstances) being given by the Warrantors, procure that the relevant Group Company shall afford such access to its books, accounts and records and personnel as is necessary and reasonable to enable the Warrantors or their duly authorised agent to prepare those tax returns and conduct matters relating thereto in accordance with the Warrantors' rights under this paragraph [...].

[...].4   The provisions of paragraph [...].3 shall be without prejudice to the rights of the relevant Group Company in relation to any audit or any enquiry resulting therefrom, and if the Purchaser shall at any time become aware of a Claim for Taxation which may result in a Tax Claim, the Purchaser may at any time thereafter by notice in writing to the Warrantors require that the provisions of paragraph [...].3 shall lapse, in which case the provisions of paragraph [...] (Claim procedure) shall come into operation in accordance with its terms.

Precedent H – Business transfer agreement

The form of business transfer agreement set out in this annexure is suitable for use in the unconditional sale and purchase:

- of a business as a going concern operating from one site and the assets used in connection with the business;
- from a corporate seller;
- by a corporate purchaser;
- for a consideration payable on completion in cash; and
- with the business liabilities remaining with the seller.

The business transfer agreement is an indicative draft only and must be modified as appropriate for the transaction in which it is being used. As business transfers vary greatly, this precedent should be treated as being little more than a collection of useful clauses. It has been generally drafted from the point of view of a purchaser, although certain provisions for the protection of the seller have been added. If being used in connection with a conditional acquisition, the provisions relating to 'conditionality' in Annexure A (Share Purchase Agreement) can be used with modification.

A commentary on the provisions contained in the precedent business transfer agreement is set out in Chapter 13.

Warning:

All precedents are dangerous. There are major risks in using this precedent without competent legal advice. It is unlikely that any precedent will be able to be used in any transaction without considerable modification.

This Agreement is made the .... day of .... 20......

Between:

    (1) .... Limited (company number: ....)
        whose registered office is at ....
        ('the Seller'); and

    (2) .... Limited (company number: ....)
        whose registered office is at ....
        ('the Purchaser'); and

    [(3) .... of ....
        ('...') ('the Guarantors')].

Background:

    (A) The Seller has agreed to sell, and the Purchaser has agreed to purchase, the Assets (as defined below) with a view to carrying on the Business (as defined below) as a going concern in succession to the Seller on the terms of this Agreement.

(B) [The Guarantors, as shareholder(s) of the Seller and in consideration, inter alia, of the Purchaser acquiring the business of the Seller, have agreed to guarantee jointly and severally the obligations of the Seller under this Agreement and to join with the Seller in giving warranties and indemnities on a joint and several basis under the terms of this Agreement.]

It is agreed as follows:

1. Definitions and interpretation

1.1 In this Agreement, unless the context otherwise requires, the following words have the following meanings:

'the Accounts'	the Seller's audited balance sheet as at, and its audited profit and loss account for the year ended on, the Accounts Date, including all documents required by law to be annexed to them;
'the Accounts Date'	.... 20...............;
'this Agreement'	this Agreement (including any Schedule or Annexure to it and any document referred to in it or in agreed form);
'Assets'	the assets to be sold pursuant to sub-clause 2.2;
'Business'	the business of .... now carried on by the Seller;
'Business Day'	a day (other than a Saturday or a Sunday) on which clearing banks are open for business in the City of London;
'Business Information'	all information, know-how and techniques (whether or not confidential and in whatever form held) which in any way relates to: (a) all or any part of the Business and Assets; (b) any products manufactured and/or sold or services rendered by the Business; (c) any formulas, designs, specifications, drawings, data, manuals or instructions; (d) the operations, management and administration of financial affairs of the Business including any business plans or forecasts, information relating to future business development or planning, information relating to litigation or legal advice; and (e) the sale or marketing of any of the products manufactured and/or sold or services rendered by the Business, including, but not limited to, all customer names and lists, sales and marketing information (including but not limited to targets, sales and market share statistics, market surveys and reports on research);
'CAA 2001'	the Capital Allowances Act 2001 as amended;
'Capital Goods Scheme'	the mechanism set out in Part XV of the Value Added Tax Regulations 1995 ('adjustments to the deduction of input tax on capital items'), as amended by The Companies Act 2006 (Consequential Amendments) (Taxes and National Insurance)

	Order 2008 and all terms and expressions used in this Agreement in relation to that Scheme shall, unless the contrary intention appears, have the meanings ascribed to them in those regulations;
'Cash'	cash in hand of the Seller or in the Seller's bank accounts on the Transfer Date and all cheques and securities representing it;
'Claims'	all rights and claims of the Seller against third parties relating to any of the Assets or otherwise arising (whether before or after Completion) out of or in connection with the Business under any warranties, conditions, guarantees, indemnities or insurance policies or otherwise;
'Completion'	the performance by the parties of the obligations set out in clause 5 (Completion);
'Computer System'	all computer hardware, software and networks owned or used by the Business, including all arrangements relating to the provision of maintenance and support, security, disaster recovery, facilities management, bureau and online services to the Business;
'Consideration'	the purchase price for the Business and Assets referred to in sub-clause 3.1;
'Contracts'	(a) the Leasing Agreements; (b) the Intellectual Property Licences; and (c) save for the [Excluded Contracts and] contracts of employment, all undischarged contracts, pending contracts, commitments and orders entered into by or on behalf of the Seller relating to the Business, and where such contract has a value greater than £................ in aggregate, that contract has been listed in Annexure ....;
'Dangerous Substance'	any substance (whether in the form of a solid, liquid, gas or vapour) the generation, transportation, storage, treatment, use or disposal of which (whether alone or in combination with any other substance) gives rise to a risk of causing harm to human health, comfort or safety or harm to any other living organism, or causing damage to the Environment, or any waste (as defined in the Environmental Protection Act 1990);
'Debts'	all amounts owing to the Seller on the Transfer Date (whether or not then due and payable) in relation to the Business;
'Disclosure Letter'	the letter of the same date as this Agreement in the agreed form from the Seller's solicitors to the Purchaser's solicitors together with any attachments, disclosing exceptions to the Warranties;
'Employees'	all the employees of the Seller engaged in the Business at the date of this Agreement whose names are set out in Annexure ...., and 'Employee' means any of them;
'Environment'	the Environment as defined in section 1(2) of the Environmental Protection Act 1990;

'Environmental Consent'	any consent, approval, authorisation, permit, exemption, filing requirement, licence or registration from time to time required by the Business under Environmental Law;
'Environmental Law'	any common or statutory law, regulation, directive, treaty, code of practice, circular, guidance note and the like, in each case of any jurisdiction, in force or enacted relating to the Environment, any Dangerous Substance, human health, comfort, safety or the welfare of any other living organism;
'Excluded Assets'	(a) cash in hand or at a bank and all cheques and other securities representing them; (b) all policies of insurance relating to the Business together with the benefit of any claims under them; (c) the Excluded Contracts; and (d) the Debts;
'Excluded Contracts'	those contracts relating to the Business listed in Annexure ....;
'Excluded Liabilities'	[*list those liabilities that the Purchaser is to acquire*];
'the Expert'	an independent chartered accountant to be nominated by the Seller and the Purchaser and in default of agreement between them within five Business Days of the obligation to appoint arising, on the request of either party by the President for the time being of the Institute of Chartered Accountants in England and Wales;
'Financial Records'	the originals of all accounting, financial and taxation records relating to the Business for the six years ending on the accounting reference date of the Seller next following Completion;
'Fixed Assets'	all fixtures and fittings, plant, machinery, equipment and other tangible assets physically attached to the Property and owned or used by the Seller in relation to the Business at the Transfer Date including those listed in Annexure ....;
'Goodwill'	the goodwill and other know-how of the Business and the exclusive right for the Purchaser to represent itself as carrying on the Business in succession to the Seller and to use all trade names associated with the Business;
'Holding Company'	any Holding Company within the meaning of section 1159 of the Companies Act 2006, and any parent undertaking within the meaning of section 1162 of the Companies Act 2006 from time to time;
'ICTA 1988'	the Income and Corporation Taxes Act 1988 as amended/ replaced by Income Tax (Earnings and Pensions) Act 2003, the Income Tax (Trading and Other Income) Act 2005 and the Income Tax Act 2007;
'Intellectual Property'	patents, plant varieties rights, trademarks or names and service marks (whether or not registered or capable of registration), registered designs, design rights, copyrights, database rights, the right to apply for and applications for any of the preceding items, together with the rights in inventions, processes, software, know-how, trade or business secrets, confidential

information, internet domain names, or any process or other similar right or asset capable of protection enjoyed, owned, used or licensed in relation to the Business; the licences and other agreements granted by third parties to the Seller for the use of the Licence's Intellectual Property including those listed in Part 2 of Annexure ....;

'the Leases'
any lease (including underleases) under which the Property is held, particulars of which are set out in Schedule 1;

'Leasing Agreements'
any leasing, conditional sale, credit sale, hire-purchase and like agreements to which the Seller is a party, under which title to assets used by the Seller in or in relation to the Business does not pass or has not passed to the Seller, including those listed in Annexure ....;

'Liabilities'
all claims, liabilities, obligations and debts of the Seller on the Transfer Date relating to the Business whether matured or not, fixed or contingent including, but not limited to, any and all liabilities in respect of bank loans, overdrafts and other loans owing by the Seller other than the Excluded Liabilities;

'Motor Vehicles'
the motor vehicles owned or used by the Seller in relation to the Business as listed in Annexure ....;

'Moveable Assets'
all plant, machinery, equipment, tools, furniture and other tangible assets not physically attached to the Property and owned or used by the Seller in relation to the Business at the Transfer Date, including those listed in Annexure ....;

'the Name'
.... or any representation or application of it, whether in terms of packaging, get-up or otherwise, as used in the Business on or before the Transfer Date, and any other name which is similar to it or capable of being confused with it;

'Notice'
includes any notice, demand, consent or other communication;

'Pension Scheme'
the Company's pension scheme governed by a Definitive Trust Deed dated ....;

'Planning Acts'
the Town and Country Planning Act 1990, the Planning (Listed Buildings and Conservation Areas) Act 1990, the Planning (Hazardous Substances) Act 1990, the Planning (Consequential Provisions) Act 1990, the Planning and Compensation Act 1991 and the Planning and Compulsory Purchase Act 2004 and the Town and Country Planning (Control of Advertisements) (England) Regulations 2007, Planning Act 2008, Localism Act 2011, and all other statutes containing provisions relating to town and country planning;

'Product Warranty Liabilities'
liabilities of the Seller (whether actual or contingent) in respect of products manufactured, assembled, sold or supplied or services provided on or before Completion by the Seller in relation to the Business including, for the avoidance of doubt, any after sales or maintenance liabilities;

'the Property'
details of which are set out in Part 1 of Schedule 1;

'Records'	the originals of the Financial Records, sales literature, price lists, advertising and publicity material, customer and supplier lists, stock records, lists of outstanding and unfulfilled orders and contracts, and other files, books, correspondence and other records relating to the Business and the Employees, held on whatever medium, excluding any which the Seller is required by law to retain and copies of those retained;
'Relief'	any relief, loss, allowance, exemption, set-off, deduction or credit in computing or against income, profits or gains or Taxation, including any right to repayment of Taxation;
'Statement of Apportionments'	the statement of apportionments, agreed between the parties in accordance with the terms of clause 6;
'Stock'	all stock-in-trade, raw materials, components, finished and unfinished goods, bought-in goods, consumables, stores, packaging materials, packages and work in progress relating to the Business as at the Transfer Date;
'Subsidiaries'	any subsidiaries within the meaning of section 1159 of the Companies Act 2006 and any subsidiary undertakings within the meaning of section 1162 of the Companies Act 2006 from time to time, details of which are set out in Schedule 3, and 'Subsidiary' means any of them;
'Tax Authority'	any taxing or other authority, body or official competent to administer, impose or collect any Taxation;
'Taxation'	all forms of taxation and statutory governmental, supra-governmental, state, provincial, local governmental or municipal impositions, duties, contributions, and levies (including withholdings and deductions) whether of the United Kingdom or elsewhere in the world, whenever imposed and however arising, and all penalties, fines charges costs and interest, together with the cost of removing any charge or other encumbrance relating thereto, and 'Tax' shall be construed accordingly;
'Transfer Date'	the date on which Completion occurs;
'TUPE 2006'	the Transfer of Undertakings (Protection of Employment) Regulations 2006;
'VAT'	Value Added Tax;
'VATA 1994'	the Value Added Tax Act 1994 and all other statutes, statutory instruments, regulations and notices containing provisions relating to VAT;
'Seller's Group'	the Seller, the Seller's Holding Company and any Subsidiaries of any such Holding Company;
'the Warranties'	the representations and warranties referred to in clause 13 (Warranties) and set out in Schedule 2 and 'Warranty' means any of them;
'Warranty Claim'	a claim by the Purchaser against the Seller that any Warranty is untrue or inaccurate in any respect or is misleading;

'Working Time   the Working Time Regulations 1998.
Regulations'

1.2   In this Agreement, unless the context otherwise requires:
         (a)   words in the singular include the plural and vice versa, and words
               in one gender include any other gender;
         (b)   a reference to a statute or statutory provision includes:
               (i)   any subordinate legislation (as defined in section 21(1) of
                      the Interpretation Act 1978) made under it;
               (ii)   any repealed statute or statutory provision which it re-
                      enacts (with or without modification); and
               (iii) any statute or statutory provision which modifies,
                      consolidates, re-enacts or supersedes it [except to the
                      extent that it would create or increase the liability of the
                      Seller under clause 13 (Warranties)];
         (c)   a reference to:
               (i)   any party includes its successors in title and permitted
                      assigns;
               (ii)   a 'person' includes any individual, firm, body corporate,
                      association or partnership, government or state (whether or
                      not having a separate legal personality);
               (iii) clauses and schedules are to clauses and schedules of this
                      Agreement, and references to sub-clauses and paragraphs
                      are references to sub-clauses and paragraphs of the clause
                      or schedule in which they appear;
               (iv)   any provision of this Agreement is to that provision as
                      amended in accordance with the terms of this Agreement;
               (v)   any document being 'in the agreed form' means in a form
                      which has been agreed by the parties on or before the date
                      of this Agreement and for identification purposes signed by
                      them or on their behalf by their solicitors; and
               (vi)   'indemnify' and 'indemnifying' any person against any
                      circumstance include indemnifying and keeping him
                      harmless from all actions, claims and proceedings from
                      time to time made against him and all loss or damage and
                      all payments, costs or expenses made or incurred by that
                      person as a consequence of or which would not have arisen
                      but for that circumstance;
         (d)   except as set out in sub-clause 1.1, terms defined in the Companies
               Act 2006 have the meanings attributed to them by that Act;
         (e)   'sterling' and the sign '£' mean pounds sterling in the currency
               of the United Kingdom save that if, following the introduction
               of the Euro, pounds sterling ceases to exist as the currency of
               the United Kingdom, then all references in this Agreement to
               'pounds sterling' and '£' shall be construed as references to the
               Euro at the conversion rate applicable at the close of the business
               day before that on which the pound sterling ceased to exist;

(f) the table of contents and headings are for convenience only and shall not affect the interpretation of this Agreement;

(g) general words shall not be given a restrictive meaning:

(i) if they are introduced by the word 'other' by reason of the fact that they are preceded by words indicating a particular class of act, matter or thing; or

(ii) by reason of the fact that they are followed by particular examples intended to be embraced by those general words;

(h) where any liability or obligation is undertaken by two or more persons, the liability of each of them shall be joint and several; and

(i) where any statement is qualified by the expression 'so far as the Seller is aware' or 'to the best of the Seller's knowledge and belief', or any similar expression, the Seller shall be deemed to have knowledge of anything of which it would have known about had it made due and careful enquiry of its executive directors, company secretary, financial controller and general managers of the Business and the professional advisors who act, or at the relevant time acted, for it or in relation to the Business.

2.   Sale of the business and the assets

2.1   The Seller with full title guarantee shall sell to the Purchaser and the Purchaser shall purchase as at Completion the Business and:

(a) the Fixed Assets;

(b) the Moveable Assets;

(c) the Motor Vehicles;

(d) the Stock;

(e) the Computer System;

(f) the Business Information;

(g) the Goodwill;

(h) the Intellectual Property;

(i) the benefit (so far as they can lawfully be assigned, transferred to or held in trust for the Purchaser) of the Claims;

(j) the benefit (subject to the burden) of the Contracts;

(k) the Records; and

(l) all other property, rights and assets employed, exercised or enjoyed in or in connection with the Business other than the Excluded Assets.

2.2   The Property is sold in accordance with the terms set out in Part 2 of Schedule 1.

2.3   The Business and Assets are sold free from all charges and encumbrances (whether monetary or not) and all other rights exercisable by third parties (including those which the Seller does not, and could not reasonably be expected to, know about) and the covenant implied by section 3(1) of the Law of Property Act 1994 shall be extended accordingly.

2.4   Title in, and risk of loss or damage to, the Assets shall pass to the Purchaser on Completion. From Completion the Seller shall hold the Assets on trust for the Purchaser absolutely until they shall have been delivered, formally transferred or assigned to the Purchaser, and shall act in accordance with the Purchaser's instructions in respect of any Asset which it so holds as trustee.

3.   Consideration

3.1   The Consideration is the payment by the Purchaser to the Seller of the sum of £............... (exclusive of VAT), which is payable in cash at Completion in accordance with clause 5 (Completion).

3.2   The Consideration shall be apportioned between the Assets as set out in Schedule 3.

3.3   In addition, the Purchaser shall:

(a)   assume the burden of the Contracts and any liabilities associated with them in accordance with this Agreement; and

(b)   indemnify the Seller in respect of the Liabilities.

4.   Value Added Tax

4.1   Where one party ('the supplier') makes or is deemed to make a supply to another party ('the recipient') for the purposes of VAT, whether the supply is for a monetary consideration or otherwise, the recipient shall pay to the supplier an amount equal to the VAT and any penalty or interest chargeable to the extent that it is attributable to any delay by the recipient in addition to the consideration provided in this Agreement. The recipient shall account to the supplier for any amount so payable upon presentation of a valid VAT invoice from the supplier.

4.2   If any amount paid by the recipient to the supplier in respect of VAT is subsequently found to have been paid in error, the supplier shall repay such amount to the recipient and the supplier shall at the same time present to the recipient a valid VAT credit note where by law it is required so to do.

4.3   The supplier shall be entitled to demand any amount payable under sub-clause 4.1 at any time on or after the time of the supply and the recipient shall be entitled to demand any amount repayable under sub-clause 4.2 at any time after the error is discovered, and any such amounts shall be paid or repaid within five Business Days following the date of the demand, but such amounts shall not be payable or repayable unless and to the extent that the supplier has issued to the recipient an invoice pursuant to sub-clause 4.1, or the error referred to in sub-clause 4.2 is discovered, within the period of three years referred to in section 77(1)(a) of the VATA 1994 (Assessments: time limits).

4.4   The Seller and the Purchaser agree that the sale of the Assets is for VAT purposes the transfer of the business of the Seller as a going concern

457

for the purposes of both section 49 of the VATA 1994 and article 5 of the Value Added Tax (Special Provisions) Order 1995 ('article 5'). The Seller and the Purchaser shall use their reasonable endeavours to secure that, pursuant to such provisions, the sale of the Assets is treated as neither a supply of goods nor a supply of services for the purposes of VAT.

4.5   The Purchaser warrants that:

(a)   it is, or shall be at Completion, a taxable person and duly registered for the purposes of VAT; and

(b)   with effect from Completion it intends to use the Assets in carrying on the same kind of business as previously carried on by the Seller.

4.6   The Seller shall ask HMRC (**'Customs'**) for permission to retain such of the financial records as relate to VAT and shall retain them if Customs so determine. In this event, the Seller shall:

(a)   preserve such records in the United Kingdom for such period as may be required by law; and

(b)   allow the Purchaser and its agents (at the Purchaser's sole expense) on giving reasonable notice and at all reasonable times to have access to such records.

If Customs do not grant permission for the Seller to retain such records, the Seller shall promptly notify the Purchaser of this and shall forthwith deliver such records to the Purchaser, and (a) and (b) above shall apply as if references to the Seller were references to the Purchaser and vice versa.

4.7   The Seller warrants that neither it nor a relevant associate has made an election, nor will prior to Completion make an election, to waive exemption from VAT pursuant to paragraph 2, Schedule 10 of the VATA 1994 in relation to the Property ('an election') and that the sale of Property will not fall to be treated as a supply subject to VAT at the standard rate by virtue of it falling within item 1 (a) of Group 1 of Schedule 9 of the VATA 1994. Accordingly:

(a)   the Purchaser need not elect to waive exemption pursuant to Article 5; and

(b)   notwithstanding the provisions of sub-clause 4.1 above, the Purchaser shall not be liable to pay any V AT in respect of the Property and the consideration provided in this Agreement for the Property shall be deemed to be inclusive of VAT.

4.8   The Seller warrants that the Capital Goods Scheme will not apply to the Property at Completion.

5.   Completion

5.1   Completion shall take place at the offices of .... on .... 20................. at .... [am] [pm].

5.2   On Completion:

(a)   the Seller shall permit the Purchaser to enter into and take possession of the Business and shall deliver or cause to be delivered to the Purchaser:

(i)   vacant possession of the Property;

(ii)   if required by the Purchaser, duly executed agreements in agreed form for the assignment or novation of the benefit of the Contracts to the Purchaser, or as the Purchaser shall direct, and all the requisite consents and licences for such assignments;

(iii)   a duly executed assignment in agreed form to vest the Goodwill in the Purchaser;

(iv)   if required by the Purchaser, duly executed assignments and licences in agreed form of the Intellectual Property (including, without limitation, any required assignments of trademarks);

(v)   at the Property, the Assets which are capable of transfer by delivery;

(vi)   any instruments of transfer which the Purchaser may reasonably require to vest title in the Assets (including, without limitation, transfers, conveyances and assignments) together with all deeds and documents of title relating to the Assets;

(vii)   those Records which are not stored at the Property;

(viii) releases from the holders of all outstanding charges over the Business and/or any of the Assets;

(ix)   a special resolution passed by the shareholders of the Seller, changing its name to a name which is in no way similar to the Name, together with a cheque for the relevant fee made payable to Companies House; and

(x)   a change of registered office form, duly signed by the secretary or director of the Seller, changing its registered office; and

(b)   when the Seller has complied with the provisions of sub-clause (a) the Purchaser shall pay the Consideration to the Seller by telegraphic transfer to the client account of the Seller's Solicitors at .... Bank plc, account number ...., sort code ....

5.3   If any of the requirements of sub-clause 5.2 are not complied with on the date set for Completion under sub-clause 5.1, the Purchaser (in the case of the requirements of sub-clause 5.2(a)) or the Seller (in the case of the requirement of sub-clause 5.2(b)) may:

(a)   defer Completion to a date not less than seven nor more than 28 days after that date (in which case the provisions of this sub-clause shall also apply to Completion as so deferred); or

(b)   proceed to Completion so far as practicable (including, at the Purchaser's or, as the case may be, the Seller's option,

459

> completion of the purchase of some only of the Assets) but without prejudice to any other rights which it or they may have under this Agreement; or
>
> (c) rescind this Agreement by notice in writing.

5.4 The Seller undertakes to indemnify the Purchaser against any loss, expense or damage which the Purchaser may suffer as a result of any document delivered to it under this clause being unauthorised, invalid or for any other reason ineffective.

6. Apportionments

6.1 All charges and outgoings relating to and payable in respect of the Business or any of the Assets which relate to a period commencing before or on and ending after the Transfer Date shall be apportioned on a time basis (save all charges and outgoings specifically referable to the extent of such use) so that such part of each charges and outgoings as is attributable to the period ending on the Transfer Date shall be borne by the Seller and each part of such charges and outgoings as is attributable to the period commencing on the day immediately after the Transfer Date shall be borne by the Purchaser.

6.2 For the purposes of sub-clause 6.1, charges and outgoings shall exclude the amounts due to creditors under the liabilities, but shall include, without limitation, rents, rates, water and other periodic outgoings, gas, electricity and telephone charges, licences, royalties, road tax licences and insurance premiums and obligations, and liabilities in respect of salaries, wages, bonuses, accrued holiday pay and other remuneration, national insurance, pension and other statutory contributions, income tax deductible under PAYE for which the Seller is accountable, contributions to retirement benefit schemes and all other payments to or in respect of the Employees.

6.3 Such part of all royalties, discounts, rebates and other sums receivable in respect of the Business or any of the Assets which relates to a period commencing before and ending on the Transfer Date shall be for the benefit of the Seller, and such part of the royalties, discounts, rebates and other sums receivable in respect of the Business or any of the Assets which relates to a period commencing on the day immediately after the Transfer Date shall be for the benefit of the Purchaser save that this sub-clause shall not apply to the Debts.

6.4 The Seller shall cause a Statement of Apportionments relating to the Business and the Assets to be prepared and delivered to the Purchaser within 14 Business Days from and including the Transfer Date, and the Purchaser will give to the Seller all assistance necessary to enable the Seller to do this.

6.5 The Seller and Purchaser shall use all reasonable endeavours to agree, within ten Business Days of the date it was delivered to the Purchaser, the Statement of Apportionments and the net amount (if any) payable under it.

6.6   If the Statement of Apportionments and/or all the items set out in it are not agreed within the time stated in sub-clause 6.5, the following provisions shall apply:

(a)   either the Seller or the Purchaser may require any item which is not agreed to be referred to the decision of an Expert. The Expert shall act as an expert and not as an arbitrator and his decision shall, in the absence of manifest error, be final and binding on the parties;

(b)   all the costs of the Expert shall be shared equally by the Seller and the Purchaser unless the Expert decides otherwise;

(c)   the Seller and the Purchaser shall each procure that the Expert is afforded all facilities and access to personnel, premises, papers, accounts, records and such other documents as may reasonably be required by him in order to reach his decision;

(d)   the Seller and the Purchaser (or their professional advisors on their behalf) shall each be entitled to make one submission (or more at the request or with the agreement of the Expert) (whether written or oral or a combination of both) to the Expert in relation to any item or question referred to him;

(e)   the Seller and the Purchaser shall each use all reasonable endeavours to procure that the Expert issues his determination within 30 Business Days of the initial reference to him under sub-clause (a) and shall accordingly co-operate with the Expert and with each other in agreeing, and complying with, any procedural requirements and any timetable suggested by the Expert or the other party; and

(f)   the items decided by the Expert shall be amalgamated with the items (if any) which had previously been agreed by the parties to ascertain a balance of money due by the Purchaser to the Seller or vice versa.

6.7   As soon as the Statement of Apportionments has been agreed in accordance with sub-clause 6.5, or determined in accordance with sub-clause 6.6, then the party shown by this Statement of Apportionments to owe the balance of money to the other shall pay that amount to the other party within two Business Days after agreement is reached or determination is made, by way of electronic funds transfer for same day value to the credit of such account as the other may notify it for the purpose of this sub-clause.

7.   Post-Completion

7.1   Immediately after Completion:

(a)   the Seller shall wholly discontinue carrying on the Business;

(b)   the parties shall, at the expense of the Purchaser, send to the suppliers and customers of the Business letters in a form agreed between them; and

(c)   the Purchaser shall file the special resolution and Companies House form referred to in sub-clause 5.2 at Companies House and shall forward the Certificate of Incorporation on Change of Name to the Seller forthwith upon receipt.

7.2   For a period of six months after the Completion Date, the Seller shall, forthwith upon receipt, forward to the Purchaser any notices, correspondence, information or enquiries which relate to the Business.

7.3   The Seller shall preserve or procure the preservation of all books, documents and records relating to the Business in respect of the period prior to Completion which it retains following Completion for a period of seven years, and shall allow, upon being given reasonable notice and during business hours, the Purchaser and/or its agents, accountants or other representatives access to, and at its own expense to take copies of, them.

7.4   The Purchaser shall preserve or procure the preservation of Financial Records of the Business for a period of seven years and shall permit and allow, upon giving reasonable notice and during business hours, the Seller and/or its agents, accountants or other representatives access to, and at its own expense to take copies of, them.

7.5   If one party receives any money after Completion which belongs to the other party, the recipient shall (subject to any provisions to the contrary contained in this Agreement) hold them on trust for, and account to that other party for them, within five Business Days of receipt.

8.   Liabilities

8.1   Save as expressly provided in this Agreement, the Seller shall be solely responsible for the liabilities, shall duly and punctually pay and discharge the Liabilities and shall indemnify the Purchaser fully at all times from and against them.

8.2   The Purchaser shall not be responsible for any liability in respect of the Business or Assets which is not expressly assumed by it under this Agreement, and the Seller shall indemnify the Purchaser accordingly.

8.3   The Purchaser shall, at the request and on behalf of the Seller, meet and discharge all claims in respect of the Product Warranty Liabilities, and the Seller shall indemnify the Purchaser (at cost) for all costs, charges and expenses incurred by the Purchaser in so doing except to the extent that the costs, charges or expenses are recovered by the Purchaser from a third party.

9.   Contracts

9.1   With effect from Completion, the Purchaser shall assume the obligations, and become entitled to the benefits, of the Seller under the Contracts.

9.2   The Seller undertakes with effect from Completion to assign to the Purchaser or to procure the assignment of all of the Contracts which are capable of assignment without the consent of other contractual parties.

9.3 If any Contract cannot be assigned by the Seller to the Purchaser except by an agreement of novation or with a consent to assignment or without the assignment constituting an event of default or termination, no assignment takes place by virtue of this Agreement until legally able to do so, but:

    (a) the Seller and the Purchaser shall (at the request of the Purchaser) together take all reasonable steps to procure that the Contract be novated or to obtain the consent or waiver to the event of default or to the termination;

    (b) unless or until the Contract has been novated or assigned or the provision waived, the Seller shall hold it on trust for the Purchaser;

    (c) the Purchaser shall, at its own cost and for its own benefit, perform the Seller's obligations under the Contract arising after the Transfer Date and shall carry out and complete it (or shall procure that it is carried out and completed), to the extent that it has not previously been carried out or completed, in the ordinary course in a proper and workmanlike manner and in accordance with its respective terms; and

    (d) unless the Purchaser is prevented by the other party to the contract from performing it, the Purchaser shall indemnify the Seller against the defective or negligent performance or non-performance of the Contract.

9.4 If, prior to the Transfer Date, the Seller has subcontracted the performance of any Contract to any person, the Purchaser shall, on behalf of the relevant customer, seek or accept delivery from such person of the goods or other products or services in respect of which that Contract was made and shall make it available to, or for collection by, such customer.

10. Debts

10.1 The Purchaser shall do all it reasonably can to collect, on behalf of the Seller, the Debts substantially in accordance with the debt collection practices and procedures adopted by the Seller immediately prior to Completion and shall, subject to its rights of deduction under sub-clause (d), hold the amount so collected in a special bank account on trust for the Seller.

10.2 The Purchaser shall not, without the prior written consent of the Seller, effect a settlement, compromise or release in respect of any Debts nor institute, take any part in, defend, compromise, abandon or submit to judgment in, any legal proceedings or arbitration in connection with such Debts.

10.3 The Purchaser shall report and account to the Seller at weekly intervals for all sums received by it, and the report shall be accompanied by a cheque for the amount held for the Seller as shown in the account (less any commission to which the Purchaser may be entitled under sub-clause (d)) and such evidence of the receipts as the Seller may reasonably require.

[10.4   As payment for its services under the provisions of this clause, the Purchaser shall be entitled to deduct a commission (exclusive of any VAT) equal to .... % of the amounts collected.]

10.4   Unless otherwise agreed in writing, the provisions of this clause shall terminate on .... 20............., and the Purchaser shall account to the Seller for any balance then held for the Seller who shall thereafter itself be responsible for collection of any outstanding Debts.

10.5   The Purchaser shall be under no obligation to institute any legal proceedings or join in any such proceedings, or take or refrain from taking any action which it reasonably considers to be contrary to its own commercial interests.

11.   Employees

11.1   The parties acknowledge and agree that, pursuant to TUPE 2006, the contracts of employment between the Seller and each of the Employees will (subject to the provisions of sub-clause 11.5) have effect from the Transfer Date as if originally made between the Purchaser and each Employee.

11.2   The Seller acknowledges and warrants that it has complied with regulation 13 of TUPE 2006.

11.3   The Seller shall indemnify and keep the Purchaser indemnified against all costs, claims, losses, liabilities and expenses which the Purchaser may incur in relation to any Employee or any other person employed in the Business prior to the Transfer Date:

(a)   arising out of or in connection with any claim made by or on behalf of any person which relates to his employment by the Seller prior to the Transfer Date;

(b)   arising out of or in connection with a dismissal by the Seller of any employee and which the Purchaser may incur pursuant to TUPE 2006;

(c)   incurred by the Purchaser in dismissing any person (other than an Employee) whose employment transfers to the Purchaser as a consequence of TUPE 2006; and

(d)   arising out of the Seller's failure to discharge its duty to consult with its Employees in accordance with regulation 12 of TUPE 2006.

11.4   The Seller shall indemnify and keep the Purchaser indemnified against all costs, claims, losses, liabilities and expenses which the Purchaser may incur in relation to any claim made by any representative of a trade union recognised by the Seller, or by any candidate for election or representative of the Seller's employees who is elected by the Seller's employees either for the purposes of any Workforce Agreement (as that term is defined in the Working Time Regulations) or for any other purpose for which representatives of the Seller's employees are elected arising out of or in connection with any act or omission by the Seller, or any other event, matter or circumstance occurring prior to the Transfer Date.

11.5 The Purchaser shall indemnify and keep the Seller indemnified against all costs, claims, losses, liabilities and expenses whatsoever arising out of or in connection with:

(a) any claim made at any time against the Seller by or on behalf of an Employee arising from any substantial change to the Employee's terms and conditions and/or working relationship to the detriment of the Employee where such change has been proposed by or is causally linked to the Purchaser or any of its agents or employees and which is to take effect after the Transfer Date;

(b) any claim made by or on behalf of any Employee which relates to his employment by the Purchaser on or after the Transfer Date;

(c) the employment or termination of employment of any Employee on or after the Transfer Date;

(d) any change in the working conditions of any Employee on or after the Transfer Date; or

(e) the Purchaser succeeding the Seller as employer of the Employees pursuant to TUPE 2006

11.6 As soon as reasonably practicable after Completion the parties shall together deliver to the Employees a letter, in the agreed form, between them notifying the Employees of the transfer of their employment to the Purchaser.

11.7 The provisions set out in Schedule 4 shall apply in relation to the pension rights of the Employees.

12. Restrictive covenants

12.1 In order to assure to the Purchaser the full benefit of the Business and the Goodwill and the Intellectual Property, the Seller, for itself and on behalf of the other members of the Seller's Group, undertakes with the Purchaser that without the prior written consent of the Purchaser (which is not to be unreasonably withheld or delayed) no member of the Seller's Group shall, either alone or in conjunction with or on behalf of any other person, do any of the following things:

(a) within .... years after Completion carry on or be engaged, concerned or interested in (except as a holder of shares in a listed company which confer not more than 1% of the votes which could normally be cast at a general meeting of that company) any business [within a .... mile radius of any of the (depots) of the Business] which competes with any material part of the Business as now carried on;

(b) except in the circumstances referred to in sub-clause 20.12(b) (Confidentiality), disclose to any other person any information which is secret or confidential to the business or affairs of the Business or use any such information to the detriment of the Business for so long as that information remains secret or confidential;

(c)   in relation to a business which is competitive or likely to be competitive with the Business as carried on at Completion, use any trade or business name or distinctive mark, style or logo used by or in the Business at any time during the .... years before Completion, or anything intended or likely to be confused with it;

(d)   neither before nor within .... years after Completion solicit or seek to entice away any Employee whether or not such person would commit a breach of his contract of employment by reason of leaving the service of the Purchaser; or

(e)   neither before nor within .... years after Completion accept orders from any person to whom the Business has sold its goods or services in the .... years before Completion in respect of similar goods or services.

12.2   Each undertaking contained in sub-clause 12.1 shall be construed as a separate and independent undertaking. If any of those undertakings is determined to be unenforceable in whole or in part, its unenforceability shall not affect the enforceability of the remaining restrictions or (in the case of restrictions enforceable in part) the remainder of that restriction.

13.   Warranties

13.1   The Seller represents to the Purchaser that each of the Warranties is true and accurate in all respects and not misleading at the date of this Agreement, and will continue to be true and accurate in all respects and not misleading up to and including Completion.

13.2   The Seller acknowledges that it gives the Warranties with the intention of inducing the Purchaser to enter into this Agreement and that the Purchaser does so in reliance on the Warranties.

13.3   Each of the Warranties is a separate and independent Warranty and shall not be limited by reference to any other Warranty or anything in this Agreement.

14.   Claims

14.1   The Seller undertakes to disclose in writing to the Purchaser anything which is or may constitute a Warranty Claim or may be inconsistent with the contents of the Disclosure Letter as soon as it comes to its notice at any time either before, at the time of, or after Completion.

14.2   If, in respect of or in connection with any Warranty Claim, any amount payable to the Purchaser by the Seller is subject to Taxation, the amount to be paid to the Purchaser by the Seller shall be such so as to ensure that the net amount retained by the Purchaser after such Taxation has been taken into account is equal to the full amount which would be payable to the Purchaser had the amount not been subject to Taxation.

14.3 If any Warranty Claim is made, the Seller shall not make any claim against any employee of the Business on whom it may have relied before agreeing to any terms of this Agreement or authorising any statement in the Disclosure Letter.

14.4 Any amount paid by the Seller to the Purchaser in respect of any of the provisions of this Agreement shall be treated as paid to the Purchaser by way of pro rata reduction in the consideration payable for the purchase of the Business and the Assets.

15. Limitations on Seller's liability

15.1 In the absence of fraud or dishonesty on the part of the Seller, its agents or advisors:

(a) the Purchaser shall not have any claim under the Warranties in respect of any matter if, and to the extent that, it is fully and fairly disclosed in the Disclosure Letter;

(b) the Seller shall not be liable for any Warranty Claim unless it has received written notice from the Purchaser giving reasonable details of the Warranty Claim and, if practicable, the Purchaser's estimate of the amount involved on or before the expiration of three years from Completion or, in the case of any Warranty Claim relating to Taxation, not later than seven years from Completion;

(c) the aggregate liability of the Seller in respect of the Warranties shall not exceed £.............;

(d) except as provided in sub-clause 15.1(e), the Seller shall be under no liability in respect of breaches of the Warranties unless:

(i) the amount of the Warranty Claim exceeds £.............; and

(ii) the amount of the Warranty Claim, when aggregated with all other Warranty Claims made on the same occasion or previously, is equal to or exceeds £............. [*this figure is usually 1% of the total consideration*] (in which case the Seller shall be liable for the whole amount up to the figure stated in sub-clause 15.1(c) and not simply the excess);

(e) sub-clause 15.1 (d) shall not apply where the individual claims arise from the same event or series of events or out of the same subject matter or source of claim;

(f) the Seller shall not be liable for any Claim if and to the extent that a liability arises or is increased as a result of:

(i) any voluntary act or omission of the Purchaser (or any persons deriving title from it) after Completion done or suffered outside the ordinary course of business and other than pursuant to a legally binding obligation entered into by the Seller before Completion; or

(ii)   the retrospective imposition of taxation or by a change in the law (whether retrospectively or not) occurring after Completion or the withdrawal after Completion of any published concession or general practice of a Taxation Authority.

15.2   If the Seller makes any payment to the Purchaser in relation to any Warranty Claim and the Purchaser subsequently receives from a third party any amount referable to, or any benefit which would not have been received but for the circumstances giving rise to, the subject matter of that Warranty Claim, the Purchaser shall, once it has received such amount or benefit, immediately repay or procure the repayment to the Seller of the lesser of either:

(a)   the amount of such receipt (after deducting an amount equal to the reasonable costs of the Purchaser incurred in recovering it and any Taxation payable on it); and

(b)   the amount paid by the Seller.

16.   Conduct of Warranty Claims

16.1   The Purchaser shall notify the Seller in writing of:

(a)   any claim made against it by a third party which may give rise to a Warranty Claim; and

(b)   any claim the Purchaser is entitled to bring against a third party which claim is based on circumstances which may give rise to a Warranty Claim.

16.2   The Purchaser shall not be liable for any delay in giving any notice under sub-clause 16.1 and shall not by reason of such delay be precluded from bringing any such claim against the Seller.

16.3   The Purchaser shall procure that the conduct, negotiation, settlement or litigation of the claim by or against such third party is, so far as is reasonably practicable, carried out in accordance with the wishes of the Seller and at its cost subject to it giving timely instructions to the Purchaser and providing reasonable security for any costs and expenses which might be incurred by the Purchaser.

16.4   The Purchaser shall provide to the Seller and the Seller's advisors reasonable access to premises and personnel and to 'any relevant assets, documents and records within their power, possession or control for the purpose of investigating any Warranty Claim, and enabling the Seller to take the action referred to in sub-clause 16.3, and shall allow the Seller and its advisors to take copies of any relevant documents or records at their expense.

17.   Purchaser's remedies

17.1   If, between the date of this Agreement and Completion, the Purchaser becomes aware that there has been any breach of the Warranties or any other term of this Agreement, the Purchaser shall be entitled to rescind this Agreement by notice in writing to the Seller.

17.2   The rights and remedies of the Purchaser in respect of any breach of the Warranties shall not be affected by Completion or by any investigation made, or which could have been made, by it or on its behalf into the affairs of the Business.

17.3   In the event of a Warranty Claim, without prejudice to the right of the Purchaser to claim damages on any basis available to it or to any other right or remedy available to it, the Seller agrees to pay on demand in cash to the Purchaser a sum by way of damages as agreed between the Seller and the Purchaser or, in default of such agreement, as determined by order of a court of competent jurisdiction which is the higher of:

(a)   an amount sufficient to put the Purchaser into the position which would have existed if the Warranties had been true and accurate or not misleading when given or repeated;

(b)   an amount equal to the resulting diminution in value of the Business and the Assets;

(c)   the amount by which the Assets are less, or less valuable, or its liabilities greater, than the values at which the same were included in the Accounts or (if the Purchaser so elects) than they would have been if the Warranty concerned had been true and accurate and not misleading; and

(d)   the amount by which the profitability of the Business is less, or its losses greater, than would have been the case if the Warranty concerned had been true and accurate and not misleading, calculated on the same basis as if such reduction in profitability or increase in losses were suffered as the result of an actionable wrong done to the Business.

17.4   This clause applies if at any time the Purchaser makes any Claim against the Seller in circumstances where no disclosure has been made in the Disclosure Letter and (notwithstanding the express provisions of this Agreement) the Seller avoids or limits liability as a result of a court of competent jurisdiction holding that the Claim (or any part of it) should fail or the quantum recoverable should be reduced because the Purchaser has or is deemed to have knowledge of the matters which give rise to the breach of Warranty. The Seller covenants to pay to the Purchaser on demand an amount equal to the amount which the Purchaser would have been entitled to recover from the Seller but for the Purchaser having or being deemed to have knowledge of the matters giving rise to the breach of Warranty.

17.5   The Seller shall indemnify the Purchaser against all costs (including legal costs on an indemnity basis as defined in rule 44.4(3) of the Civil Procedure Rules 1998), expenses or other liabilities which the Purchaser may reasonably incur either before or after the commencement of any action in connection with:

(a)   the settlement of any Warranty Claim;

(b) any legal proceedings in respect of any Warranty Claim in which judgment is given for the Purchaser; or

(c) the enforcement of any such settlement or judgment.

[18. Guarantee

18.1 In consideration of the Purchaser agreeing to buy the Business and Assets on the terms of this Agreement, the Guarantors jointly and severally unconditionally and irrevocably guarantee:

(a) the due, punctual and full performance by the Seller of all its obligations under this Agreement; and

(b) the payment by the Seller when due of any amount payable under this Agreement, as if the Guarantors were the principal obligors under this Agreement and not merely a surety.

18.2 As an independent and primary obligation, without prejudice to sub-clause 21.1 the Guarantors hereby unconditionally and irrevocably agree to indemnify and keep indemnified the Purchaser against all and any losses, costs, claims, liabilities, damages, demands and expenses suffered or incurred by the Purchaser arising from failure of the Seller to comply with any of its obligations or discharge any of its liabilities under this Agreement or arising from the termination of this Agreement, or by reason of the Seller not being at any time, or ceasing to be, liable in respect of the obligations and liabilities purported to be assumed by it in accordance with the express terms of this Agreement.

18.3 The guarantee and indemnity set out in this clause is a continuing guarantee and indemnity and shall remain in full force and effect until all the obligations of the Seller guaranteed or indemnified by this clause have been discharged in full. It is in addition to, and shall not prejudice nor be prejudiced by, any other guarantee, indemnity or other security or right against any third party which the Purchaser may have for the due performance of these obligations.

18.4 The Guarantors acknowledge that their liability under this clause shall not be discharged or affected in any way by time or any other indulgence or concession being granted to the Seller or by any other act, omission, dealing, matter or thing whatsoever (including without limitation any change in the memorandum or articles of association of the Seller, any amendment to this Agreement, or the liquidation, dissolution, reconstruction or amalgamation of the Seller or their illegality or enforceability of this Agreement) which but for this provision might operate to release the Guarantors from their obligations under this clause.]

19. Certificate of value

It is certified that the transaction effected under this Agreement does not form part of a larger transaction or a series of transactions in respect of which the amount or value of the aggregate amount or value exceeds £.............

20. General

20.1 Entire agreement

    (a) This Agreement sets out the entire agreement and understanding between the parties and supersedes all prior agreements, understandings or arrangements (oral or written) in respect of the subject matter of this Agreement.

    (b) This Agreement supersedes the heads of terms dated .... 20............. except for any of its provisions which this Agreement specifically preserves.

20.2 Contracts (Rights of Third Parties) Act 1999

Unless expressly provided in this Agreement, no term of this Agreement is enforceable pursuant to the Contracts (Rights of Third Parties) Act 1999 by any person who is not a party to it.

20.3 Assignment

    (a) This Agreement shall be binding upon and enure for the benefit of the successors of the parties but, except as set out in sub-clause (b), shall not be assignable by any party without the prior written consent of the other.

    (b) The Purchaser may assign the benefit of this Agreement (including, without limitation, the Warranties) to any successor in title or any subsequent purchaser of the Business.

20.4 Variation

No purported variation of this Agreement shall be effective unless it is in writing and signed by or on behalf of each of the parties.

20.5 Effect of Completion

Except to the extent already performed, all the provisions of this Agreement shall, so far as they are capable of being performed or observed, continue in full force and effect notwithstanding Completion.

20.6 Invalidity

If any provision of this Agreement is found by any court or competent authority to be invalid, unlawful or unenforceable in any jurisdiction, that provision shall be deemed not to be a part of this Agreement, but it shall not affect the enforceability of the remainder of this Agreement, nor shall it affect the validity, lawfulness or enforceability of that provision in any other jurisdiction.

20.7 Releases and waivers

    (a) The rights, powers and remedies conferred on any party by this Agreement and remedies available to any party are cumulative and are additional to any right, power or remedy which it may have under general law or otherwise.

    (b) Any party may, in whole or in part, release, compound, compromise, waive or postpone, in its absolute discretion, any liability owed to it or right granted to it in this Agreement by any other party or parties without in any way prejudicing or affecting its rights in respect of that or any other liability or right not so released, compounded, compromised, waived or postponed.

(c) No single or partial exercise, or failure or delay in exercising any right, power or remedy by any party shall constitute a waiver by that party of, or impair or preclude any further exercise of, that or any right, power or remedy arising under this Agreement or otherwise.

20.8 Further assurance

After Completion, the Sellers shall execute such documents and take such steps as the Purchaser may reasonably require to vest the full title to the Business and Assets in the Purchaser and to give the Purchaser the full benefit of this Agreement.

20.9 Counterparts

(a) This Agreement may be executed in any number of counterparts and by the parties on separate counterparts, but shall not be effective until each party has executed at least one counterpart.

(b) Each counterpart, when executed, shall be an original of this Agreement and all counterparts shall together constitute one instrument.

20.10 Time of the essence

Except as otherwise expressly provided, time is of the essence as regards every obligation of any party under this Agreement.

20.11 Termination

Without prejudice to any remedy available to any party arising out of any outstanding breach of this Agreement on the part of any other party, if this Agreement is terminated in accordance with its terms, the following shall occur:

(a) the Seller shall indemnify the Purchaser for all costs, charges and expenses incurred by it in connection with the negotiations, preparations and determination or rescission of this Agreement and all matters which this Agreement contemplates;

(b) the restrictions contained in sub-clause 20.12 (Confidentiality) and clause 21 (Announcements) shall continue to apply; and

(c) except as referred to in sub-clause (b), all obligations of the Purchaser under this Agreement shall cease.

20.12 Confidentiality

(a) Except as referred to in sub-clause (b), each party shall treat as strictly confidential all information received or obtained as a result of entering into or performing this Agreement which relates to the provisions or subject matter of this Agreement, to any other party to this Agreement or the negotiations relating to this Agreement.

(b) Any party may disclose information which would otherwise be confidential if and to the extent that:

    (i) it is required to do so by law or any securities exchange or regulatory or governmental body to which it is subject wherever situated;

    (ii) it considers it necessary to disclose the information to its professional advisors, auditors and bankers provided that it does so on a confidential basis;

    (iii) the information has come into the public domain through no fault of that party; or

    (iv) each party to whom it relates has given its consent in writing.

20.13 Default interest

If any party defaults in the payment when due of any sum payable under this Agreement (whether payable by agreement or by an order of a court or otherwise), the liability of that party shall be increased to include interest on that sum from the date when such payment was due until the date of actual payment at a rate per annum of 4% above the base rate from time to time of National Westminster Bank plc. Such interest shall accrue from day to day and shall be compounded annually.

20.14 Set-off

The Purchaser shall be entitled to set off the amount of any Warranty Claim against any sum due from it to the Seller [under this Agreement].

21. Announcements

21.1 Subject to sub-clause 21.2, no announcement concerning the terms of this Agreement shall be made by or on behalf of any of the parties without the prior written consent of the others, such consent not to be unreasonably withheld or delayed.

21.2 Any announcement or circular required to be made or issued by any party by law or under the regulations of the London Stock Exchange plc or the City Code on Takeovers and Mergers issued by the Panel on Takeovers and Mergers may be made or issued by that party without consent if it has first sought consent and given the other parties a reasonable opportunity to comment on the subject matter and form of the announcement or circular (given the time scale within which it is required to be released or despatched).

22. Costs and expenses

22.1 Except as referred to in sub-clause 22.2 and in sub-clause 20.11 (Termination), each party shall bear its own costs and expenses incurred in the preparation, execution and implementation of this Agreement.

22.2 The Purchaser shall pay all stamp and other transfer duties and registration fees applicable to any document to which it is a party and which arise as a result of or in consequence of this Agreement.

23.   Notices

23.1   Any notice to a party under this Agreement shall be in writing signed by or on behalf of the party giving it and shall, unless delivered to a party personally, be left at, or sent by prepaid first-class post, prepaid special delivery to the address of the party as set out on page 1 of this Agreement, or as otherwise notified in writing from time to time.

23.2   Except as referred to in sub-clause 23.3, a notice shall be deemed to have been served:

   (a)   at the time of delivery if delivered personally; or

   (b)   48 hours after posting in the case of an address in the United Kingdom and 96 hours after posting for any other address.

   If the deemed time of service is not during normal business hours in the country of receipt, the notice shall be deemed served at or, in the case of faxes, two hours after, the opening of business on the next Business Day of that country.

23.3   The deemed service provisions set out in sub-clause 23.2 do not apply to:

   (a)   a notice served by post, if there is a national or local suspension, curtailment or disruption of postal services which affects the collection of the notice or is such that the notice cannot reasonably be expected to be delivered within 48 hours or 96 hours (as appropriate) after posting; and

   (b)   a notice served by facsimile, if, before the time at which the notice would otherwise be deemed to have been served, the receiving party informs the sending party that the notice has been received in a form which is unclear in any material respect, and, if it informs the sending party by telephone, it also despatches a confirmatory facsimile within two hours.

23.4   In proving service it will be sufficient to prove:

   (a)   in the case of personal service, that it was handed to the party or delivered to or left in an appropriate place for receipt of letters at its address;

   (b)   in the case of a letter sent by post, that the letter was properly addressed, stamped and posted;

   (c)   in the case of facsimile, that it was properly addressed and despatched to the number of the party.

23.5   A party shall not attempt to prevent or delay the service on it of a notice connected with this Agreement.

24.   Governing law and jurisdiction

24.1   This Agreement shall be governed by and construed in accordance with English Law.

24.2   Each of the parties irrevocably submits for all purposes in connection with this Agreement to the exclusive jurisdiction of the courts of England whether in relation to contract, tort or otherwise.

This Agreement is made on the date appearing at the head of page 1.

SCHEDULE 1

Part 1
(Description of the Property)

Part 2
(Provisions relating to the Property)

Part 3
(The Lease)

SCHEDULE 2
(THE WARRANTIES)

The Sellers

1.   Capacity

1.1   The Seller has the requisite power and authority to enter into and perform this Agreement.

1.2   The Seller is not bankrupt, has not proposed a voluntary arrangement and has not made or proposed any arrangement or composition with his creditors or any class of his creditors.

1.3   This Agreement constitutes and imposes valid legal and binding obligations on the Seller fully enforceable in accordance with its terms.

2.   Arrangements between the Business and the Seller's Group

There are no contracts, arrangements, engagements, orders or liabilities, actual or contingent, outstanding or remaining in whole or in part, to be performed affecting the Business between the Seller and any member of the Seller's Group or any person connected (within the meaning of section 839 of the ICTA 1988) with a shareholder of any member of the Seller's Group.

3.   Other interests of the Seller's Group

No member of the Seller's Group has or intends to acquire any interest, direct or indirect, in any business which has a close trading relationship with, or which competes or is likely to compete with, the Business.

Information

4. Accuracy and adequacy of information

4.1 The information contained in Schedules .... and .... to this Agreement is accurate and complete.

4.2 There are fully and accurately disclosed in the Disclosure Letter all matters, information and documents which are, or could on reasonable enquiry be known, to the Seller and which are necessary to qualify the paragraphs of this Schedule in order for such statements when so qualified to be fair, accurate and not misleading.

4.3 The information contained in the Disclosure Letter and all written information supplied to the Purchaser or its advisors by or on behalf of any member of the Seller's Group or their advisors is complete and accurate and is not misleading because of any omission or ambiguity or for any other reason, and where the information is expressed as an opinion, it is truly and honestly held and not given casually, recklessly or without due regard for its accuracy.

Financial matters

5. Insolvency

5.1 No distress, execution or other process has been levied against the Seller in relation to the Business or the Assets, nor any action taken to repossess any goods of the Business in the Seller's possession.

5.2 No Receiver (including an Administrative Receiver), Trustee or Administrator has been appointed of the whole or any part of the assets or undertaking of the Seller which relates to or would or might affect the Business or the Assets, and the Seller is not aware of any circumstances likely to give rise to the appointment of any such Receiver, Trustee or Administrator.

5.3 The Seller has not been a party to any transaction with any third party or parties which relates to or would or might affect the Business or any of the Assets and which would, if any such third party went into liquidation or had a bankruptcy or administration order made in relation to it, constitute (in whole or in part) a transaction at an undervalue, preference or invalid floating charge, or otherwise would or might constitute any other transaction or transfer at an undervalue or involving an unauthorised reduction of capital.

6. Preparation and contents of the Accounts

6.1 To the extent that the Accounts relate to the Business they were prepared in accordance with the requirements of all relevant statutes and generally accepted United Kingdom accounting practices including, without limitation, all applicable Financial Reporting Standards issued by the Accounting Standards Board, Statements of Standard Accounting Practice issued by the Institute of Chartered Accountants of England and Wales and Statements from the accounting practice used to prepare the Accounts differs from those applicable in previous financial periods, the effect of any such difference is disclosed in the Disclosure Letter.

6.2   Without prejudice to the generality of sub-paragraph 6.1:

(a)   the Accounts:

    (i)   give a true and fair view of the state of affairs of the Business at the Accounts Date and the profits or losses of the Business for the financial period ending on that date;

    (ii)   contain full provision or reserve for all liabilities and for all capital and revenue commitments of the Business as at the Accounts Date;

    (iii)   disclose all the assets of the Business as at the Accounts Date and none of the values placed in the Accounts on any of those assets was in excess of its market value at the Accounts Date;

    (iv)   make full provision for bad and doubtful debts;

    (v)   do not include any figure which is referable to the value of an intangible asset; and

    (vi)   make full provision for depreciation of the fixed assets of the Business having regard to their original cost and life.

(b)   in the Accounts:

    (i)   in valuing work-in-progress no value was attributed in respect of eventual profits, and adequate provision was made for such losses as were (at the time of signature of the Accounts by directors of the Seller) reasonably foreseeable as arising or likely to arise; and

    (ii)   slow-moving stock was written down appropriately, redundant, obsolete, obsolescent or defective stock was wholly written off and the value attributed to any other stock did not exceed the lower of cost (on a first in first out basis) and net realisable value (or replacement value) at the Accounts Date.

6.3   The profits and losses of the Business shown in the Accounts were not, save as disclosed in the Accounts or in any note accompanying them, to any material extent affected by any extraordinary, exceptional, unusual or non-recurring income, capital gain or expenditure, or by any other factor known to the Seller rendering any such profit or loss for such period exceptionally high or low.

7.   Accounting records

7.1   The accounting records of the Seller comply with the requirements of sections 386 and 388 of the Companies Act 2006, do not contain or reflect any material inaccuracy or discrepancy and present and reflect in accordance with generally accepted accounting principles and standards the financial position of, and all transactions entered into by, the Seller or to which it has been a party.

7.2   All relevant financial books and records of the Business are in the possession of the Seller or otherwise under its direct control.

7.3   Where any of the records of the Business are kept on computer, the Seller:

(a)   is the owner of all hardware and all software necessary to enable it to use the records as they have been used in the Business to the date of this Agreement and to Completion;

(b)   does not share any hardware or software relating to the records with any person; and

(c)   maintains adequate back up records and support in the event of any fault or failure of such computer hardware and software.

8.   Euro compliance

8.1   The computer systems are 'Euro Compliant' and are capable of satisfying the legal requirements applicable to the common currency adopted or to be adopted by the relevant participating Member States of the European Union and known as the 'Euro, as set out in the European Commission Regulation No 110397 ('the Regulation'). For the purposes of this warranty, 'Euro Compliant' shall mean the ability of the systems to perform using the Euro and to allow any currency recognised by the systems, including but not limited to the Euro, and all other currencies belonging to and adopted by full Member States of the European Union, to be converted to other currencies, and in particular (but without limitation) to:

(a)   perform all monetary functions in Euros;

(b)   process multiple currencies and, in particular, the dual currencies during the transition phase set out in the regulation of countries adopting the Euro;

(c)   recognise the industry standard keyboard configurations or key-strokes and screen layouts for the Euro symbol;

(d)   correctly implement the conversion and rounding requirements (including the triangulation rule) set out in the regulation; and

(e)   interface with other Euro-Compliant products.

8.2   So far as the Sellers are aware, the introduction of the Euro will not cause any Contract to terminate or to be capable of termination nor alter the terms of or excuse or discharge performance of any Contract.

9.   Management accounts

The management accounts of the Seller relating to the Business for the period from .... 20............ to .... 20............... have been prepared on a basis consistent with the Accounts, fairly reflect the trading position of the Business as at their date and, for the period to which they relate, are not affected by any extraordinary, exceptional, unusual or non-recurring income, capital gain or expenditure or by any other factor known by the Seller rendering profits or losses for the period covered exceptionally high or low.

10.   Events since the Accounts Date

10.1   Since the Accounts Date there has been no material change in:

(a)   the financial or trading position or prospects of the Business;

(b)   the value or state of assets or amount or nature of liabilities as compared with the position disclosed in the Accounts; or

(c)   in the turnover, direct or indirect expenses or the margin of profitability of the Business as compared with the position disclosed for the equivalent period of the last financial year.

10.2   The Seller has, since the Accounts Date, carried on the Business in the ordinary course and without interruption so as to maintain it as a going concern, and paid its creditors in the ordinary course and within the credit periods agreed with such creditors.

10.3   Since the Accounts Date no supplier of the Business has ceased or restricted supplies or threatened so to do, there has been no loss or material curtailment of the business transacted with any customer which at any time in the preceding financial year represented 1% or more of the turnover of the Business, and the Seller is not aware of any circumstances likely to give rise to any of the above.

10.4   Since the Accounts Date, in relation to the Business the Seller has not:

(a)   incurred or committed to incur:
(i)   material capital expenditure; or
(ii)   any liability, whether actual or contingent, except for full value or in the ordinary course of business;

(b)   acquired or agreed to acquire:
(i)   any asset for a consideration higher than its market value at the time of acquisition or otherwise than in the ordinary course of business; or
(ii)   any business or substantial part of it or any share or shares in a body corporate; or

(c)   disposed of, or agreed to dispose of, any of its assets except in the ordinary course of business and for full value.

Trading and Contracts

11.   Contracts and commitments

11.1   True and complete copies of the Contracts have been given to the Purchaser.

11.2   None of the Contracts:

(a)   is expected to have material adverse consequences in terms of expenditure or revenue;

(b)   relate to matters outside the ordinary course of the Business or were entered into other than on arms'-length terms;

(c)   can be terminated in the event of any change in the underlying ownership or control of the Business or would be materially affected by such change; or

(d)   cannot readily be fulfilled or performed by it on time.

11.3   In relation to the Business there are no outstanding bids, tenders, sales or service proposals which are material or which, if accepted, would be likely to result in a loss.

11.4   The Seller is not aware of any actual, potential or alleged breach, invalidity, grounds for termination, grounds for rescission, grounds for avoidance or grounds for repudiation of any Contract.

12.   Terms of trade

The Seller has not given any guarantee or warranty (other than any implied by law) or made any representation in respect of any product or services sold or supplied by the Business, nor has it accepted any liability to service, maintain, repair or otherwise do or refrain from doing anything in relation to such goods or services after they have been sold or supplied by it except for those contained in its standard conditions of trading, complete and accurate copies of which are contained in the Disclosure Letter.

13.   Product liability

In relation to the Business, the Seller has not manufactured, sold or provided any product or service which does not in every respect comply with all applicable laws, regulations or standards or which is defective or dangerous or not in accordance with any representation or warranty, express or implied, given in respect of it.

14.   Licences and consents

14.1   Complete and accurate details of all licences, consents, permissions, authorisations and approvals required for the carrying on of the Business have been disclosed to the Purchaser and all of them have been obtained by the Business and are in full force and effect.

14.2   All reports, returns and information required by law or as a condition of any such licence, consent, permission, authorisation or approval to be made or given to any person or authority in connection with the Business have been made or given to the appropriate person or authority, and there are no circumstances which indicate that any licence, consent, permission, authorisation or approval might not be renewed in whole or in part or is likely to be revoked, suspended or cancelled, or which may confer a right of revocation, suspension or cancellation.

15.   Competition and trade regulation law

15.1   In relation to the Business, the Seller is not, nor has it been a party to, or is or has been concerned in any agreement or arrangement, or is conducting or has conducted itself, whether by omission or otherwise, in a manner which:

(a)   contravenes Chapters I or II of the Competition Act 1998 or the competition provisions of the Enterprise Act 2002 or any secondary legislation made under it;

(b)   infringes articles 101 or 102 of TFEU or any regulation or directive made under it or any other anti-trust or similar legislation in any jurisdiction in which any Group Company has assets or carries on or intends to carry on business or where its activities may have any effect; or

(c)   contravenes the provisions of the Consumer Protection from Unfair Trading Regulations 2008 and Business Protection from Misleading Marketing Regulations 2008.

15.2   In relation to the Business, the Seller has not:

(a)   given an undertaking to, or is subject to, any order of or investigation by, or has received any request for information from or statement of objections or damages claim or threat relating to competition matters;

(b)   received, nor so far as the Seller is aware, is likely to receive any process, notice or communication, formal or informal, by or on behalf of; or

(c)   been or is a party to, or is or has been concerned in, any agreement or arrangement in respect of which an application for negative clearance and/or exemption has been made to;

(d)   the Competition and Markets Authority (or where relevant the Office of Fair Trading or the Competition Commission), the Secretary of State, the European Commission or any other governmental or other authority, department, board, body or agency of any country having jurisdiction in anti-trust or similar matters in relation to the Business or third party private litigant.

16.   Compliance with law

16.1   The Seller has not in relation to the Business committed, nor is it liable for, and no claim has been or, so far as the Seller is aware, will be made, that it has committed or is liable for any criminal, illegal, unlawful or unauthorised act or breach of any obligation or duty whether imposed by or pursuant to statute, contract or otherwise.

16.2   The Seller has not in relation to the Business received notification that any investigation or inquiry is being, or has been, conducted by, or received any request for information from any governmental or other authority, department, board, body or agency in respect to its affairs and, so far as the Seller is aware, there are no circumstances which would give rise to such investigation, inquiry or request.

16.3 None of the activities, contracts or rights of the Business is ultra vires, unauthorised, invalid or unenforceable or in breach of any contract or covenant, and all documents in the enforcement of which it may be interested are valid.

17. Litigation and disputes

17.1 Except for actions to recover any debt incurred in the ordinary course of the Business owed to the Seller where each individual debt and its costs outstanding amounts to less than £1,000:

    (a) neither the Seller nor any person for whose acts the Seller may be liable is in relation to the Business engaged in any litigation, arbitration, administrative or criminal proceedings, whether as claimant, defendant or otherwise;

    (b) no litigation, arbitration, administrative or criminal proceedings by or against the Seller or any person for whose acts it may be liable relating to the Business are threatened or expected and, as far as the Sellers are aware, none are pending; and

    (c) there are no facts or circumstances likely to give rise to any litigation, arbitration, administrative or criminal proceedings against the Seller or any person for whose acts it may be liable in relation to the Business.

17.2 The Seller is not, in relation to the Business, subject to any order or judgment given by any court or governmental or other authority, department, board, body or agency, or has not been a party to any undertaking or assurance given to any court or governmental or other authority, department, board, body or agency which is still in force, nor are there any facts or circumstances likely to give rise to it becoming subject to such an order or judgment or to be a party to any such undertaking or assurance.

18. Ownership and condition of the Assets

18.1 Each of the Assets is owned both legally and beneficially by the Seller free from any third party rights and, if capable of possession, is in its possession.

18.2 Each item of Equipment is:

    (a) in good repair and condition, regularly maintained and certified safe and without risk to health when used;

    (b) capable and will remain capable of doing the work for which it was designed or purchased until the time when (on the basis of depreciation adopted in the Accounts) it will have been written down to a nil value;

    (c) not surplus to requirements; and

    (d) not expected to require replacement or additions within six months of Completion.

18.3   The Assets comprise all assets necessary for the continuation of the Business as it is currently carried on, and no Asset is shared by the Business with any other person.

18.4   The Business does not depend upon any assets, facilities or services owned or supplied by the Seller or any member of the Seller's Group.

19.   Stock

No part of the Stock is redundant, obsolete, obsolescent, defective, or otherwise unsaleable.

20.   Charges and encumbrances over the Assets

20.1   No option, right to acquire, mortgage, charge, pledge, lien (other than a lien arising by operation of law in the ordinary course of trading) or other form of security or encumbrance or equity on, over or affecting the Assets is outstanding and, apart from this Agreement, there is no agreement or commitment to give or create any of them, and no claim has been made by any person to be entitled to any of them.

20.2   No floating charge created by the Seller has crystallised, and there are no circumstances likely to cause such a floating charge to crystallise.

20.3   The Seller has not received notice from any person intimating that it will enforce any security which it may hold over any of the Assets, and there are no circumstances likely to give rise to such a notice.

21.   Intellectual Property and Data Protection

21.1   Complete and accurate details of all Intellectual Property and copies of all licences and other agreements relating to it are contained in the Disclosure Letter.

21.2   All Intellectual Property is either:

(a)   in the sole legal and beneficial ownership of the Seller free from all licences, charges or other encumbrances; or

(b)   the subject of binding and enforceable licences from third parties in favour of the Seller:

(i)   of which no notice to terminate has been received;

(ii)   all parties to which have fully complied with all obligations in those licences; and

(iii)   in relation to which no disputes have arisen or are foreseeable;

and in either case nothing has been done or omitted to be done which would jeopardise the validity, enforceability or subsistence of any Intellectual Property or any such licences.

21.3   Any Intellectual Property which is capable of registration has been registered or is the subject of an application for registration, and is or will when duly registered be valid, binding and enforceable and:

(a)   in the case of registrations, all renewal fees have been paid and renewals made by their due date and all such action necessary to preserve and maintain the registration has been taken;

(b)   in the case of registrations contained in the Disclosure Letter, each is presently used by the Seller and is in full force and effect and has not been abandoned;

(c)   in the case of pending applications, the Seller is aware of no reason why any such applications should not proceed to grant; and

(d)   none of the Intellectual Property is subject to any use, claim application or attack by any other person.

21.4   No licences, registered user or other rights have been granted or agreed to be granted by the Seller to any person in respect of any Intellectual Property.

21.5   The Seller does not use any Intellectual Property in respect of which any third party has any right, title or interest.

21.6   The Seller owns or has the right to use all Intellectual Property rights required in connection with the conduct of its business as presently carried on or expected to be carried on in the future.

21.7   So far as the Seller is aware, at no time during the past six years has there been any unauthorised use or infringement by any person of any Intellectual Property.

21.8   None of the processes employed, or products or services dealt in, by the Business infringes any rights of any third party relating to Intellectual Property nor makes the Seller liable to pay a fee or royalty, and no claims have been made, threatened or, so far as the Seller is aware, are pending, in relation to any such Intellectual Property against it.

21.9   Except in the ordinary course of business and on a confidential basis, no disclosure has been made of any of the confidential information, know-how, technical processes, financial or trade secrets or customer or supplier lists of the Business.

21.10   Any names used by the Business other than the corporate name of the Seller are contained in the Disclosure Letter and do not infringe the rights of any person.

Data Protection

21.11   The Company has complied in all respects with the provisions of the Data Protection Act 1998 ('DPA') and the principles contained in the DPA.

21.12   Except as notified under the DPA, the Company has either not held or processed any personal data or is exempt from notifying under the DPA under one of the exemptions contained in the DPA.

21.13   Insofar as personal data are subject to registration or notification:

(a) the Company has at all times maintained full and accurate notification under the DPA and has operated wholly within the terms of such notification;

(b) no disclosure has taken place outside the terms of the Company's notification.

21.14   The Company has not been served with a notice under sections 10, 11 or 12 of the DPA.

21.15   The Company has not been served with any information or enforcement notice under the DPA, nor are there any circumstances which might give rise to the Company being served with such a notice in the future.

21.16   To the extent the Company has personal data processed by third parties written agreements relating to such processing have been signed and where personal data is exported from the EEA compliance with the DPA has been achieved in relation to such exports.

Employment

22.   Directors and Employees

22.1   Complete and accurate details of the terms and conditions of employment of all the Employees, including their dates of birth and commencement of employment, their remuneration (including bonus, commission, profit sharing, share options, permanent health insurance, medical expenses insurance, life assurance and pension benefits), notice periods and any arrangements or assurances (whether or not legally binding) for the payment of compensation on termination of employment are contained in the Disclosure Letter.

22.2   The Seller has maintained up-to-date, adequate and suitable records regarding the service and terms and conditions of employment of each of the Employees.

22.3   The Seller has maintained up-to-date adequate and suitable records for the purposes of the Working Time Regulations and has complied with all other obligations to its workers (as 'workers' is defined in regulation 2 of the Working Time Regulations), and there are no claims capable of arising or pending or threatened by any officer or employee or former officer or employee, or the Health and Safety Executive or any local authority Environmental Health Department, or any trade union or employee representative, related to the Working Time Regulations.

22.4   True and complete copies of all contracts of employment and other documents relating to the employment of the Employees are contained in the Disclosure Letter.

22.5   Since the Accounts Date there has been no material alteration in the terms of employment or any material change in the number of employees employed in the Business.

22.6 Other than salary for the current month and accrued holiday pay, no amount is owing to any Employee.

22.7 No Employee has given notice or is under notice of dismissal, nor are there any service contracts between the Seller and any of the Employees which cannot be terminated by the Seller by 12 weeks' notice or less without giving rise to a claim for damages or compensation (other than a statutory redundancy payment).

22.8 No claim or liability to make any payment of any kind to any person who is or has been an officer or employee has been received or incurred by any Group Company whether under the Employment Rights Act 1996, the Equality Act 2010 and any and all sexual, race, disability, age, religious and sexual orientation discrimination legislation or otherwise; and no gratuitous payment of a material amount has been made or promised by any Group Company in connection with the actual or proposed termination or suspension of employment or variation of any contract of employment of any present or former officer or employee.

23. Industrial relations

23.1 In relation to the Business, the Seller is not a party to any contract, agreement or arrangement with any trade union or other body or organisation representing any of the Employees.

23.2 In relation to its officers, the Employees and former employees, the Seller has complied with all relevant legislation (including, without limitations, TUPE 2006 and the Working Time Regulations 1998), conditions of service, customs and practices and, where relevant, all collective agreements and recognition agreements, workforce agreements and relevant agreements for the time being.

23.3 No dispute has arisen between the Seller and a material number or category of the Employees, nor are there any present circumstances known to the Seller which are likely to give rise to any such dispute.

24. Pensions

24.1 Save as disclosed in the Disclosure Letter, the Seller has no plans, schemes or arrangements in relation to death, disability or retirement of any of the Employees.

24.2 In relation to each plan, scheme or arrangement disclosed in the Disclosure Letter:

    (a) complete and accurate details:

        (i) of it (including, where appropriate, copies of all trust deeds and rules together with copies of all amending deeds and resolutions and the latest actuarial reports); and

(ii)   of the basis on which the Seller makes, or is liable to make, contributions to it; are contained in the Disclosure Letter.

(b)   all contributions which are payable by the Seller in respect of it, and all contributions due from the Employees as members of it, have been duly made and the Seller has fulfilled all its obligations under it including in relation to auto enrolment pensions;

(c)   is registered under the Finance Act 2004 and has been administered in accordance with all relevant pensions legislation including the Pensions Acts 2004 and 2014, and in accordance with its trusts and rules for the relevant pension scheme;

(d)   no undertakings or assurances have been given to any Employee as to the continuance, introduction, increase or improvement of any pension rights or entitlements which the Seller and/or the Purchaser would be required to implement in accordance with good industrial relations' practice and whether or not there is any legal obligation so to do;

(e)   no power to augment benefits has been exercised;

(f)   no discretion has been exercised to admit to membership a present or former director or employee who would not otherwise be eligible for admission to membership;

(g)   no discretion has been exercised to provide in respect of a member a benefit which would not otherwise be provided;

(h)   all benefits (other than a refund of contributions with interest where appropriate) payable on the death of a member while in service to which it relates, or during a period of sickness or disability of a member, are fully insured under a policy effected with an appropriate insurance company, and the Seller is not aware of any circumstances in which such insurance would be invalidated;

(i)   all liabilities or benefits accrued in respect of service completed at Completion are secured on an ongoing basis taking account of future increases in salary to normal retirement date and increases in pensions on the basis of realistic actuarial and financial assumptions and the obligations imposed on it as a result of *Barber v Guardian Royal Exchange;* and

(j)   it is a registered scheme under FA 2004, s 153 as amended and the Seller is not aware of any reasons why such registration could be removed; and

(k)   no application for clearance has been made to the Pensions Regulator.

24.3   No death, disability or retirement gratuity is currently being paid or has been promised, nor will pending Completion be paid or promised by the Seller to or in respect of any Employee.

Properties

25. Title

25.1 The Properties comprise all the properties presently owned, occupied, held, controlled or otherwise used by the Seller in relation to the Business, and the Seller is in actual and exclusive occupation and is the legal and beneficial owner of the Property.

25.2 The Seller's title to the Property is good and marketable.

25.3 None of the contracts relating to the Property entered into on or after 11 November 1999 and before 11 May 2000 expressly provides that the Contracts (Rights of Third Parties) Act 1999 is to apply to it.

25.4 None of the contracts relating to the Property entered into on or after 11 May 2000 expressly gives any third party the right to enforce it or purports to confer a benefit on any third party.

25.5 The Property is occupied or otherwise used by the Seller by right of ownership or under a lease, the terms of which permit its occupation or use as tenant and not under any provision allowing the parting or sharing of possession with group or associated companies, and there are no outstanding circumstances which would restrict the continued possession and enjoyment of the Property or any part of it.

25.6 All deeds and documents necessary to prove title to the Property are in the possession and control of the Seller and consist of original deeds and documents or properly examined abstracts.

25.7 No person is in adverse possession of the Property or has acquired or is acquiring any rights or overriding interests as under the Land Registration Act 2002 or otherwise adversely affecting the Property.

25.8 The Seller has not had occasion to make any claim or complaint in relation to any neighbouring property or its use or occupation and there are no disputes, claims, actions, demands or complaints in respect of the Property which are ongoing, nor are any disputes, claims, actions, demands or complaints anticipated, and no notices materially affecting the Property have been given or received and not complied with.

26. Encumbrances

26.1 The Property is not subject to any outgoings other than business rates, water rates and insurance premiums and, in the case of leasehold properties, rent, insurance rent and service charges.

26.2 The Property is not subject to any restrictive covenant, reservation, stipulation, easement, profits à prendre, wayleave, licence, grant, restriction, overriding interest, agreement for sale, estate contract, option, right of pre-emption or other similar agreement or right vested in third parties.

26.3   No matter exists which is registered or is properly capable of registration against the Property as a Land Charge, Local Land Charge, caution, inhibition, notice or restriction.

26.4   Where sub-paragraphs 25.1–25.3 inclusive have been disclosed against in the Disclosure Letter, the obligations and liabilities imposed and arising under the disclosed matter have been fully observed and performed and any payments in respect of it which are due and payable have been duly paid.

27.   Planning matters

27.1   The use of the Property is a lawful and permitted use for the purposes of the Town and Country Planning Act 1990.

27.2   Planning permission has been obtained, or is deemed to have been granted for the purposes of the Planning Acts, for the Property; no permission is the subject of a temporary or personal consent, or has been modified or revoked; no application for planning permission is awaiting decision; no planning permission has been granted within the last three months and the validity of no planning permission is currently or may be challenged.

27.3   Building regulation consents have been obtained with respect to all development, alterations and improvements to the Property.

27.4   In respect of the Property, the Seller has complied, and is continuing to comply, in all respects with:

(a)   planning permissions, orders and regulations issued under the Planning Acts, the London Building Acts and building regulation consents and by-laws for the time being in force;

(b)   all agreements under section 52 of the Town and Country Planning Act 1971 and planning obligations under section 106 of the Town and Country Planning Act 1990;

(c)   all agreements made under sections 38 and 278 of the Highways Act 1980, section 33 of the Local Government (Miscellaneous Provisions) Act 1982, and section 104 of the Water Industry Act 1991, as amended by the Water Act 2014.

27.5   The Property is not listed as being of special historic or architectural importance or located in a conservation or other area, or subject to an order, designation or affected by a planning proposal which may regulate or affect its use in the future.

27.6   All claims and liabilities under the Planning Acts or any other legislation have been discharged and no claim or liability, actual or contingent, is outstanding.

28.   Statutory obligations

28.1   The Seller has complied with and is continuing to comply with all applicable statutory and by-law requirements with respect to the Property, and in particular with the requirements as to fire precautions under the Regulatory Reform (Fire Safety) Order 2005 and under the Public Health Acts, the Offices, Shops and Railway Premises Act 1963, the Health and Safety at Work etc Act 1974, the Factories Act 1961.

28.2   No licences are required in relation to the Property under the Licensing Act 2003 or Gambling Act 2005.

29.   Adverse orders

29.1   There are no compulsory purchase notices, orders or resolutions affecting the Property and there are no circumstances likely to lead to any being made.

29.2   There are no closing, demolition or clearance orders, enforcement notices or stop notices affecting the Property, and there are no circumstances likely to lead to any being made.

30.   Condition of the Property

30.1   The buildings and other structures on the Property are in good and substantial repair and fit for the purposes for which they are used, and no building or other structure on the Property has been affected by structural damage, electrical defects, timber infestation or disease.

30.2   The principal means of access to the Property is over roads which have been adopted by the local or other highway authority and which are maintainable at the public expense, and no means of access to the Property is shared with any other person nor subject to rights of determination by any other person.

30.3   The Property enjoys the mains services of water, drainage, electricity and gas.

30.4   The Property is not located in an area or subject to circumstances which makes it susceptible to subsidence or flooding.

31.   Leasehold properties

31.1   Each Lease is valid and in full force and there are no circumstances which would entitle any landlord or other person to exercise any power of entry or take possession of the Property.

31.2   The Seller has paid the rent and observed and performed the covenants on the part of the tenant and the conditions contained in any Lease to which it is a party, and the last demands (or receipts for rent if issued) were unqualified.

31.3   All licences, consents and approvals required from the landlord and any superior landlords for the grant of each Lease, and during the continuance of each Lease, have been obtained, and any covenants on the part of the tenant contained in those licences, consents and approvals have been duly performed and observed.

31.4   There are no rent reviews outstanding or in progress under any Lease.

31.5   Any alteration or improvement carried out on the Property is to be disregarded for rent review purposes.

31.6   There is no obligation to reinstate the Property by removing or dismantling any alteration made to it by the Seller or any of its predecessors in title, and the Seller has not incurred or is likely to incur any liability for dilapidation

31.7   In the case of a lease granted for more than 21 years, the lease is registered at HM Land Registry with absolute title.

31.8   The Seller has not in the past been the tenant of or guarantor of any leasehold premises not listed in Schedule 1 in respect of which any obligations or liabilities could still accrue to the Seller.

32.   Tenancies

32.1   The Property is not held subject to, and with the benefit of, any tenancy, other than those set out in the Disclosure Letter.

32.2   Where sub-paragraph 32.1 has been disclosed against in the Disclosure Letter, in relation to each tenancy disclosed the Disclosure Letter contains complete and accurate details of:

(a)   the rent and any rent reviews and, with respect to rent reviews, the date for giving notice of exercise of the reviews and the operative review date;

(b)   the term and any rights to break or renew the term;

(c)   the obligations of the landlord and tenant in respect of outgoings, repairs, user, insurance services and service charge;

(d)   any options, pre-emption or first refusal rights;

(e)   the user required or permitted under the terms of the tenancy;

(f)   any entitlement of a tenant of the whole or any part of the Property to compensation on quitting the premises let to him in respect of disturbance and improvements or otherwise; and

(g)   any unusual provisions.

32.3   The Seller is not aware of any material or persistent breaches of covenant or agreement by a tenant of the Property.

33.   Contamination

33.1   The Property is unlikely to be entered in any register introduced under the Environment Act 1995 or otherwise as land which may be contaminated or which may have been put to a contaminative use.

33.2   There is not on, in or under the Property or any adjoining property any substance which could give rise to harm to human health or safety or damage to the Environment.

Environment

34.   Environmental matters

34.1   The Seller holds and has always held all Environmental Consents.

34.2   Complete and accurate details of all Environmental Consents held by the Seller are contained in the Disclosure Letter and are valid and subsisting.

34.3   The Seller has not received any notification that any Environmental Consent it holds is or is likely to be modified, restricted or withdrawn, and no works or other upgrading or investment are or will be necessary to secure compliance with or to maintain any such Environmental Consent.

34.4   The Seller has not breached the terms, conditions or provisions of any Environmental Consent.

34.5   The Seller has not received any notification or informal indication that further Environmental Consents will be required under Environmental Law in order for it to continue its present business.

34.6   In relation to the Business, the Seller (and each of its officers, employees and agents in the course of its business) has complied with all applicable Environmental Laws and has never received any notification under Environmental Law requiring it to take or omit to take any action.

34.7   In relation to the Business, the Seller has not been threatened with any investigation or enquiry by any organisation or received any complaint in connection with the Environment.

Taxation

35.   Stamp duty land tax

Stamp duty land tax/stamp duty has been paid whenever it is due relating to the business and where relevant all documents relating to the Business or the Assets have been duly and properly stamped, and no such document has been executed and retained outside the United Kingdom in circumstances in which a liability to stamp duty would arise if such document were to be brought into the United Kingdom.

36.   Capital allowances

36.1   None of the Assets is a long life asset for the purposes of Chapter 10, Part 2 of the CAA 2001.

36.2   None of the Assets is a fixture for the purposes of Chapter 6, Part 2 of the CAA 2001.

36.3   The provisions of Chapter 17, Part 2 (Anti-Avoidance) of CAA 2001 do not apply to any of the Assets or to the lease of any asset entered into in respect of the Business.

36.4   All tax legislative provisions in relation to leasing arrangements do not apply to any of the Assets or to the lease of any asset entered into in respect of the Business.

37.   Disputes, records, etc

37.1   The treatment of the Business or Assets for Taxation purposes has not to any material extent depended on any concession, agreement, dispensation or other formal or informal arrangement with any Tax Authority.

37.2   The Seller has sufficient records relating to past events concerning the Business and the Assets to enable the Purchaser to calculate any relief available in respect of any Assets or any liability to Taxation arising on the disposal or realisation of any Asset, and such records remain complete and accurate.

37.3   The Seller has kept and maintained complete and accurate accounting records, invoices and other documents appropriate or requisite and all proper returns and payments for Taxation purposes have been duly and punctually made, including for the avoidance of doubt all payments in respect of VAT, PAYE and National Insurance Contributions.

37.4   In the six years prior to the date of this agreement there have been no disputes or disagreements with any Tax Authority, and there are no unsettled or outstanding assessments or appeals, in either such case in respect of Taxation or the availability of any Relief relating to the Business or the Assets, and there are no circumstances which may give rise to such a dispute or disagreement after Completion.

37.5   None of the Assets the subject of any charge or other encumbrance in respect of Taxation and no circumstances exist under which a power of sale could be exercised by any person in respect of any Asset.

[37.6   *Matters arising from due diligence.*]

SCHEDULE 3
(APPORTIONMENT OF CONSIDERATION)

£

Property

Fixed Assets

Moveable Assets

Motor Vehicles

Stock

Computer System

Business Information

Goodwill

Intellectual Property

The benefit of the Claims

The benefit of the Contracts

Records

SCHEDULE 4
(PROVISIONS RELATING TO THE PENSION SCHEME)

Signed by ....

for and on behalf of ....

....Limited

in the presence of: ....

Signature of witness:

Name:

Address:

Occupation:

Signed by ....

for and on behalf of

.... Limited

in the presence of: ....

Schedule 4   (provisions relating to the pension scheme)

Signature of witness:

Name:

Address:

Occupation:

Signed by .... [*Guarantors*]

in the presence of: ....

Signature of witness:

Name:

Address:

Occupation:

Precedent I – Disclosure letter

The form of disclosure letter set out in this annexure is suitable for use by the seller(s).

The disclosure letter is our indicative draft only and has been drafted from the perspective of the seller(s). This precedent should be treated as being little more than a collection of useful clauses.

Warning:

All precedents can be dangerous. There are major risks in using this precedent without competent legal advice. It is unlikely that any precedent will be able to be used in any transaction without considerable modification.

Private and confidential

The Directors

.... Limited

[*insert address*]

Dated .... 20.......................

Dear Sirs,

Sale of [the business and assets of] .... **Limited ('the Company')**

1.   **Introduction**

1.1   This is the disclosure letter defined in the agreement entered into immediately prior to the delivery of this disclosure letter between yourselves and ourselves for the sale and purchase of [the whole of the issued share capital] [the business and assets] of the Company ('the Agreement').

1.2   Words and expressions defined in the Agreement, unless the context otherwise requires, have the same meaning in this Disclosure Letter.

1.3   The purpose of this disclosure letter is to limit the scope of the Warranties [and the Covenant for Taxation] by disclosing matters which are exceptions to the Warranties [and the Covenant for Taxation].

497

1.4   The headings and numbering used in this disclosure letter are for convenience only and shall not affect its interpretation.

1.5   Annexure A to this disclosure letter is an index of copy and original documents which have been supplied to the Purchaser or its solicitors ('the Disclosure Bundle'). In this disclosure letter, references to numbered documents are to those so referenced in the Disclosure Bundle.

1.6   Where brief particulars of a matter are set out in this disclosure letter or in the Disclosure Bundle, full particulars of it are deemed to be disclosed and it is assumed that the Purchaser does not require any further details.

1.7   [If there is any conflict between the contents of any document appearing in the Disclosure Bundle and the contents of this disclosure letter, this disclosure letter shall prevail.]

2.   General disclosures

This disclosure letter shall be deemed to disclose:

(a)   any matter apparent from:
  (i)   the Agreement [and all documents in agreed form];
  (ii)   all documents contained in the Disclosure Bundle, and where a document is referred to in, but not attached to, the Disclosure Bundle the full content of that document is deemed to be disclosed;
  (iii)   all correspondence between the Seller(s) or its advisors and the Purchaser or its advisors together with all enclosures attached to it [as listed in Document ....];

(b)   any matter:
  (i)   appearing on the file of each Group Company at Companies House on ....;
  (ii)   which would be revealed by a search made at the Central Registry of Winding-up Petitions in England and Wales on ....;
  (iii)   which would be available from a search of [any other public registry] [the Office of Fair Trading, the Consumer Credit registry or any public registry of intellectual property rights in England];

(c)   any matter apparent from the minutes and other statutory books of each Group Company, [which have been made available to the Purchaser];

(d)   any matter:
  (i)   apparent from the deeds of the [property] [properties] [which have been made available to the Purchaser]; or
  (ii)   which would be disclosed by or as a result of searches in registers held by the relevant local authorities, HM Land Charges Registry searches, HM Land Registry searches, Commons Register and/ or Register of Village Green searches, index map searches and searches at the Environment Agency;
  (iii)   apparent from all planning consents and building or bye- law approvals; or

(iv)   revealed in replies to formal enquiries between ourselves or the Seller and the Purchaser in each case in relation to the [Property] [Properties] at the date of this disclosure letter; or

(v)   which would be apparent from an inspection of the [property] [properties];

(e)   any matter, fact or event in respect of each Group Company which is attributable to or appeared in the period preceding the date on which the Company and each Group Company was acquired, directly or indirectly by the Seller;

(f)   all matters disclosed in the [report produced by the Purchaser's accountants as to the business and affairs of the [Company] dated ....];

(g)   [any matter disclosed, provided for, noted or referred to in the Accounts [or in the audited [consolidated] accounts of the Group Companies for the [three] financial years ended on ....;]

(h)   any matter which is in the public domain [and any matter of] which the Purchaser ought reasonably to be aware as affecting a business similar to the business carried on by the Company and each Group Company; and

(i)   any matter which is in the actual knowledge of the Purchaser.

3.   Specific disclosures

For convenience only, each of the following specific disclosures is numbered to correspond to the paragraph number of the Warranty to which it is considered most likely to relate. However, each matter disclosed is a disclosure in respect of all Warranties to which it is or may be appropriate and shall not be limited to the specific paragraphs referred to below:

[Set out detailed disclosures, in respect of each paragraph of Schedule ....]

4.   Receipt

Please confirm your receipt and acceptance of this letter by countersigning and returning the enclosed duplicate.

Yours faithfully

[On duplicate]

We confirm receipt of your letter dated .... of which the above is a true copy and confirm our acceptance of its terms.

ANNEXURE A

Index to the Disclosure Bundle

Precedent J – Completion agenda

The completion agenda is an indicative draft only. The precedent should be tailored to suit the particular circumstances of the proposed transaction and, in particular, whether it is a share sale and purchase or a business transfer.

Warning:

All precedents can be dangerous. There are major risks in using this precedent without competent legal advice. It is unlikely that any precedent will be able to be used in any transaction without considerable modification.

Sale and purchase of
[the business and assets of]
[the issued share capital of]
[Target] Limited
Completion Documents and Agenda

Parties:

'Seller[s]' ....

'Purchaser' ....

'Target' ....

'Managers' ....

'Seller['s][s'] lawyers' ....

'Purchaser's lawyers' ....

Action		Responsibility	Current position
1.	Acquisition agreement	Purchaser's lawyers	....
2.	Deed of tax indemnity	....	....
3.	Seller['s] [s']	Seller['s] [s'] lawyers disclosure letter	....
4.	Seller board minutes approving the sale	....	....
5.	Stock transfer form and share certificate	....	....
6.	[Target] board minutes	Purchaser's lawyers	....

7.	Directors' letters of resignation	....	....
8.	Form AP01	....	....
9.	Actuaries letter	....	....
10.	Completed statutory books of [Target]	Seller	....
11.	Management accounts to	Seller	....
12.	[Release of [Target] from .... cross-guarantee in favour of the Bank]	Seller	....
13.	[Target] bank balances at close of business on	Seller	....
14.	Press release	Seller/Purchaser	....
15.	Communication to employees, customers and suppliers	Seller/Purchaser	....

Precedent K – Target board minutes

The form of board minutes set out in this annexure is suitable for use by the target company to approve the transfer of ownership to the purchaser and other matters relating to the change of ownership.

The board minutes are an indicative draft only and have been drafted to cover the matters required to be approved to satisfy the completion requirements set out in the precedent share purchase agreement (Precedent F). This precedent should be treated as being little more than a collection of useful clauses.

Warning:

All precedents can be dangerous. There are major risks in using this precedent without competent legal advice. It is unlikely that any precedent will be able to be used in any transaction without considerable modification.

.... Limited

Minutes of a meeting of the board of directors of the company held at .... on .... at ...... pm

Present: .... (in the chair)

In attendance: ....

1. Preliminary

1.1 The chairman reported that a quorum was present in accordance with the company's articles of association and declared the meeting open.

1.2 [Each of the directors] [.................................. ....] declared his interest in the matters under discussion at the meeting, being a director and shareholder of the company.

2. Purpose

The chairman reported that the purpose of the meeting was to consider and, if thought fit, to approve various matters relating to the acquisition by .... ('the Purchaser') of the issued share capital of the company from .... ('the Vendor[s]').

3. Share transfer

3.1 [There was produced to the meeting a duly stamped share transfer form by which the Vendor transferred .... [ordinary]

shares in the company to the Purchaser]. [There was produced to the meeting share transfer forms transferring the following shares in the company to the Purchaser:

Vendor's name   Number and class of shares

shares of £1 each

shares of £1 each]

3.2   It was resolved that:

(a)   the share transfer form[s] be and [it is] [they are] approved and accepted for registration;

(b)   the Purchaser be entered in the register of members of the company as the holder of [that] [those] share[s]; and

(c)   a share certificate in [his] [her] [its] favour be prepared and sealed and issued accordingly.

4.   Resignation of secretary

There was produced to the meeting the resignation of .... as secretary of the company. It was resolved that this resignation be accepted and that .... be appointed secretary of the company, both with immediate effect.

5.   Resignation of directors

There were produced to the meeting the resignations of .... and .... as directors of the company. It was resolved that these resignations be accepted with immediate effect.

6.   Appointment of directors

It was resolved that .... and .... be appointed directors of the company with immediate effect.

7.   Service Agreement

7.1   There was produced to the meeting a draft Service Agreement to be entered into by the company (1) and .... (2) ('the Service Agreement').

7.2   After due and careful consideration, it being in the best interests of the company, it was resolved (.. abstaining from the vote) that the Service Agreement be approved and that any director of the company be authorised to sign it on behalf of the company.

7.3   After due and careful consideration, it being in the best interests of the company, it was resolved (...

abstaining from the vote) that the Service Agreement be approved and that the common seal of the company be and is affixed to it in the presence of [any two directors of the company] [any director and the secretary of the company] [.. and ....].

8. Auditors

8.1   There was produced to the meeting a letter of resignation from ...., the company's auditors, containing the statement required by section 519(1) of the Companies Act 2006.

8.2   It was resolved that their resignation be and it is accepted with immediate effect.

8.3   It was further resolved that .... be appointed as auditors of the company with immediate effect, to hold office until the next annual general meeting of the company.

9. Bank mandates

9.1   It was resolved that the existing bank mandate given to Bank plc be revoked and that a mandate in the form produced to the meeting and attached to these minutes be approved.

9.2   The secretary was instructed to forward this new bank mandate to the Bank as soon as possible.

10. Accounting reference date

It was resolved that the accounting reference date of the company be changed to .... in each year.

11. Registered office

It was resolved that the registered office of the company be changed to ....

12. Filing

It was resolved that the secretary be and it is instructed to file the appropriate returns and forms with the Registrar of Companies in connection with the above matters.

13. Close

There being no further business the meeting was then closed.
....

Chairman

Precedent L – Power of attorney

The form of power of attorney set out in this annexure is suitable for use in the context of a share sale and purchase by a seller who is scheduled to be absent at the proposed date of signing of the sale documents. From the seller's perspective, there is no substitute for entering into the sale documentation personally, but if absence at the proposed signing date is unavoidable, considerable care should be taken to:

- select the most appropriate attorney (commonly a fellow shareholder or a director of the target);
- understand the key provisions in the documents to be entered into by the attorney; and
- limit the attorney's powers, where appropriate. For example, if the seller is not expecting to give warranties the seller may wish to limit the scope of the attorney's powers accordingly.

The power of attorney is an indicative draft only and has been drafted from a purchaser's perspective.

Warning:

All precedents can be dangerous. There are major risks in using this precedent without competent legal advice. It is unlikely that any precedent will be able to be used in any transaction without considerable modification.

This Power of Attorney is given by me, ...
of .... and witnesses as follows:

1.   Recital

I am the holder of .... [ordinary] shares of .... each ('the Shares') in the capital of .. .. Limited (no ....) ('the Company').

2.   Appointment

In connection with the proposed sale of the entire issued share capital of the Company ('the Sale') to .... ('the Purchaser'), I appoint .... of ....
.... or failing him ....
.... of .... to be my true and lawful attorney in my name and on my behalf generally to agree the form of and amendments to, and execute all such instruments, agreements and deeds in such form, and do all such acts and things, in each case as my attorney shall think fit and have approved, [whether] in my capacity as a shareholder [or as a director

507

or as an employee] of the Company or otherwise for the purposes of and in connection with effecting completion of the Sale including, without limitation:

(a) to agree the form of and execute a share purchase agreement ('the Share Purchase Agreement') containing [warranties, undertakings, covenants and other obligations given by me and] which records the terms of the Sale, together with the agreed form documents referred to therein;

(b) to execute a stock transfer form transferring the Shares to the Purchaser;

(c) to receive notice of, sign any forms of consent, including consent to short notice, or forms of proxy, relating to, and to attend on my behalf, all general meetings of the Company and any class meetings of the Company to be convened for the purposes of considering any resolutions proposed, and to sign any written resolutions in connection with the Sale, or any reconstruction, variation of class rights, increase or issue of the share capital of the Company proposed to take place, as a pre-condition to, or prior to, or after completion of the Sale and all matters incidental to the Sale; and

(d) to exercise at any such general or class meeting any and all rights and powers of and incidental to the holding or ownership of the Shares;

and I hereby agree to ratify and confirm whatsoever my attorney shall do or purport to do in good faith by virtue of this Power and I shall indemnify him and his estate against all actions, claims, expenses and liabilities which may arise from the exercise, or the purported exercise, of any power conferred by this Power.

3.   Duration

I declare that this Power of Attorney shall be irrevocable until .... and shall be conclusively binding on myself and my personal representatives in favour of third parties who have not received notice of revocation.

4.   Jurisdiction

This Power shall be governed by and construed in accordance with English law and is subject to the exclusive jurisdiction of the English Courts.

The parties intend this document to be delivered as a deed.

In witness whereof this Power of Attorney has been executed as a deed and delivered this .... day of .... 20......

Signed and delivered as a Deed

By ....

in the presence of: ....

Witness' signature:

Witness' name and address:

Witness' occupation:

Precedent M – Deed of contribution

The deed of contribution is an indicative draft only and has been drafted from the perspective of the contributor. It is suitable where those sellers giving warrantors and/or a covenant for taxation in favour of the purchaser wish to apportion liability between themselves. The precedent should be tailored to suit the particular circumstances of the proposed transaction.

Warning:

All precedents can be dangerous. There are major risks in using this precedent without competent legal advice. It is unlikely that any precedent will be able to be used in any transaction without considerable modification.

This Deed is made the .... day of ....
20............

Between:

(1) .... of   ('Mr A');

(2) .... of   ('Mr B'); and

(3) .... of   ('Mr C')

(together 'the Contributors').

Background:

(A) The Contributors have entered into the Acquisition Agreement under which they have accepted joint and several liability for any claim under the Warranties or the Covenant for Taxation.

(B) The Contributors are entering into this Deed to regulate their liabilities under and arising out of their joint and several liability under the Acquisition Agreement.

This Deed witnesses as follows:

1. Definitions and interpretation

1.1   In this Deed, unless the context otherwise requires, the following words have the following meanings:

'the Acquisition Agreement'   a sale and purchase agreement of the same date as this deed and made between the Contributors (1) and .... (2), relating to the sale by the Contributors of the entire issued share capital of .... Limited;

'Claim'   a claim made by the Purchaser under [clauses ....
                        (Warranties) and .... (Covenant for Taxation) of] the
                        Acquisition Agreement;

'this Deed'   this Deed (including any schedule or annexure to it and any
                        document in agreed form);

'the Defaulter'   as defined in clause 5 (Inability to contribute);

'Due Proportion'   the percentage set opposite each Contributor's name in the
                        schedule; and

'Payment'   (a) the amount which is decided to be paid in respect of any Claim in
                        accordance with sub-clause 4.1; or (b) the amount (including costs,
                        interests and penalties) which a court of competent jurisdiction
                        orders should be paid in satisfaction of any Claim; and (c) the costs
                        associated with a Claim (including any fees, costs or disbursements
                        in connection with the settling or contesting of any Claim).

1.2   In this Deed, unless the context otherwise requires:

(a)   words in the singular include the plural and vice versa and words
        in one gender include any other gender;

(b)   a reference to:

(i)   any Contributor includes its successors in title and
        permitted assigns;

(ii)   a 'person' includes any individual, firm, body corporate,
        association or partnership, government or state (whether or
        not having a separate legal personality);

(iii)   clauses and schedules are to clauses and schedules of this
        Deed and references to sub-clauses and paragraphs are
        references to sub-clauses and paragraphs of the clause or
        schedule in which they appear;

(c)   except as set out in sub-clause 1.1, terms defined in the Acquisition
        Agreement have the meanings attributed to them by it; and

(d)   the table of contents and headings are for convenience only and
        shall not affect the interpretation of this Deed.

2.   Contribution to claim

2.1   The Contributors agree that each of them shall be liable for his Due
        Proportion of each Payment.

2.2   Other than as set out in clause 5 (inability to contribute), no Contributor
        shall be liable to pay more than his Due Proportion of any Payment.

2.3   If any Contributor pays more than his Due Proportion of any Payment,
        the other Contributors shall immediately upon demand pay such
        amount to him as may be necessary to ensure that each Contributor
        bears only his Due Proportion of that Payment.

3.   Warranties between Contributors

3.1   Each of the Contributors severally warrants to the others that the
        information contained in the Disclosure Letter is, to the best of his

knowledge and belief, in accordance with the facts and that there has been no omission from the Disclosure Letter which he knows is likely to affect the import of such information and further that, to the best of his knowledge and belief, save for as disclosed in the Disclosure Letter, there are no matters which he knows could at the date of entering into the Acquisition Agreement result in a Claim.

3.2 In the event that there is any breach of the warranties contained in this clause 3, each of the Contributors severally agrees to indemnify the others against any Claim and any costs arising out of such a breach up to the proportion of the Consideration received by him or her.

4.   Agreeing the payment and meetings of Contributors

4.1 If any Claim is made against any Contributor, that Contributor shall within seven days notify the other Contributors of the Claim, giving such details of the Claim as have been notified to him. The Contributors shall meet as soon as possible after that to consider the Claim and to decide on what action (if any) should be taken in respect of it.

4.2 Save in the event of the bankruptcy or death of a Contributor or where a material conflict of interest exists between the Contributors, no Claim shall be settled, nor other action taken, without the prior written consent of [the Contributors whose Due Proportions exceed 75%] [a majority in numbers of the Contributors].

4.3 Each Contributor shall be entitled to summon meetings of the Contributors on not less than 21 days' notice. [Two] Contributors present in person or by proxy shall constitute a quorum. Other than set out in this clause, the Contributors shall regulate their meetings as they see fit.

5.   Inability to contribute

5.1 [If any Contributor is unable to satisfy his Due Proportion of any Payment due to bankruptcy] ('the Defaulter') then his Due Proportion shall be borne by the other Contributors in the same proportions as their Due Proportions bear to each other (excluding for these purposes the Defaulter's Due Proportion), and each Contributor's Due Proportion shall, from that date, be so adjusted.]

OR:

5.2 [If any Contributor is unable to contribute pursuant to the terms of this Deed ('the Defaulter') he shall at the written request of the other Contributors assign such number of Loan Notes (as defined in the Acquisition Agreement) as he may hold or subsequently receive to the other Contributors (in such proportions as they shall direct the Defaulter) in order to satisfy any additional liability ('the Liability') incurred by the other Contributors arising as a result of the default of the Defaulter.

5.3 To the extent that the Liability has not been satisfied in full in accordance with the provisions of sub-clause 5.1, the Defaulter shall at the written request of the Contributors procure that any payments due to him pursuant to the Acquisition Agreement shall be made directly to the other Contributors in such proportions as they shall direct the Defaulter until the Liability has been extinguished.

5.4 The Defaulter undertakes to execute such documents and take such steps as the other Contributors may require in order to give full effect to the provisions of this clause.

5.5 Each Contributor irrevocably appoints each of the other Contributors as his attorney to execute on his behalf all such documents as may be necessary to give effect to the provisions of this clause.]

6. Costs

All costs, expenses and other charges [reasonably and properly] incurred by the Contributors [with the consent of the Contributors whose Due Proportions exceed 75%] in implementing this Deed and in challenging any Claim shall be borne by them in their Due Proportions.

7. General

7.1 Entire agreement

This Deed sets out the entire agreement and understanding between the parties in respect of the subject matter of this Deed.

7.2 Variation

No purported variation of this Deed shall be effective unless it is in writing and signed by or on behalf of each of the parties.

7.3 Counterparts

(a) This Deed may be executed in any number of counterparts and by the parties on separate counterparts, but shall not be effective until each Contributor has executed at least one counterpart.

(b) Each counterpart, when executed, shall be an original of this Deed and all counterparts shall together constitute one instrument.

7.4 Default interest

Other than in respect of a default due to bankruptcy [or insolvency, as the case may be], if any Contributor defaults in the payment when due of any sum payable under this Deed the liability of that Contributor shall be increased to include interest on that sum from the date when such payment was due until the date of actual payment at a rate per annum of 4% above the base rate from time to time of National Westminster Bank plc. This interest shall accrue from day to day and shall be compounded annually.

8.   Notices

8.1   Any notice to a Contributor under this Deed shall be in writing signed by or on behalf of the Contributor giving it and shall, unless delivered to a Contributor personally, be left at, or sent by prepaid first class post or prepaid special delivery to the address of the Contributor as set out on page 1 of this Deed or as otherwise notified in writing from time to time.

8.2   Except as referred to in sub-clause 8.3, a notice shall be deemed to have been served:

(a)   at the time of delivery if delivered personally; or

(b)   48 hours after posting in the case of an address in the United Kingdom and 96 hours after posting for any other address.

If the deemed time of service is not during normal business hours in the country of receipt, the notice shall be deemed served on the next business day of that country.

8.3   The deemed service provisions set out in sub-clause 8.2 do not apply to a notice served by post, if there is a national or local suspension, curtailment or disruption of postal services which affects the collection of the notice or is such that the notice cannot reasonably be expected to be delivered within 48 hours or 96 hours (as appropriate) after posting.

8.4   In proving service it will be sufficient to prove:

(a)   in the case of personal service, that it was handed to the Contributor or delivered to or left in an appropriate place for receipt of letters at its address; or

(b)   in the case of a letter sent by post, that the letter was properly addressed, stamped and posted.

8.5   A Contributor shall not attempt to prevent or delay the service on it of a notice connected with this Deed.

9.   Assignment

No party to this Deed may assign his rights or obligations in whole or in part pursuant to this Deed without the prior written consent of the other parties to this Deed.

10.   Governing law and jurisdiction

10.1   This Deed shall be governed by and construed in accordance with English law.

10.2   Each of the parties irrevocably submits for all purposes in connection with this Deed to the exclusive jurisdiction of the courts of England in connection with any claims in contract, tort or otherwise arising herefrom.

The parties intend this document to be delivered as a deed.

This Deed has been signed on the date appearing at the head of page 1.

SCHEDULE
(DUE PROPORTION)

Contributor	Percentage (%)
A	………..
B	………..
C	………..

Executed as a Deed by ……………………………………………………………

in the presence of: …………………………………………………………

Signature of witness:

Name:

Address:

Occupation:

Executed as a Deed by …………………………………………………………

in the presence of: …………………………………………………………

Signature of witness:

Name:

Address:

Occupation:

Executed as a Deed by …………………………………………………………

in the presence of: …………………………………………………………

Signature of witness:

Name:

Address:

Occupation:

Index

[References are to paragraph number and Precedents]